A SHORT HISTORY OF CULTURE
FROM PREHISTORY TO THE RENASCENCE

A SHORT HISTORY

A SHORT HISTORY OF CULTURE

OF CULTURE

From Prehistory To the Renascence

Jack Lindsay

Studio Books · London

TO A. VECHT
of Amsterdam

First published in 1962 by Studio Books, Longacre Press Limited, 161 Fleet Street, London, EC4. Printed in England by Hunt Barnard and Co. Ltd., The Sign of The Dolphin, Aylesbury, Bucks.

Contents

Preface

In 1939, just before the war, I published a book with a title similar to the title here; the present book is, however, entirely new. Certain main ideas are the same as before; but the earlier book did not systematically work them out. It was rather a rash sketch. Here I have tried to fill the gaps in and work out a satisfying correlation and sequence of cultural phases. Since a reaction against the scholastic methods of the great compilers like Frazer or the oversimplified conceptions of the Victorian evolutionists has made integrative approaches unfashionable, the attempt here carried out goes against all contemporary preconceptions and prejudices. It does not seem to me therefore any the less worth doing; on the contrary.

The word culture is a large one. It is used anthropologically for anything that makes up a society's way of life; the *Concise Oxford Dictionary*, after mentioning tillage, production, bacteria, adds 'improvement by (mental or physical) training; intellectual development'. Which is not very helpful. I have been concerned mainly with the various forms of self-expression in the arts, literature, science and philosophy; but, especially in the earlier sections, the anthropological interpretation cannot but intrude, since one is largely dealing with ritual-forms. And at least a rough framework of history is needed throughout to make the cultural changes intelligible. Science is the field with which I have dealt most cursorily. While in the arts a certain amount of particular analysis is necessary, my aim has been to show the emergence or development of the deep-lying patterns, archetypes, or what one likes to call them, which give significance and coherence to the various works and forms. And this aim continues, even when I deal with highly complex expressions like those of Dante or Shakespeare. What is there attempted is not anything like a complete discussion. Essential points are disentangled, to bring out where the person under consideration relates to the general stream of cultural process; the angles from which he strikes off. More is not possible in such a wide-reaching study, or desirable. I have given much space to origins, since, unless they are clarified, one is attempting to progress by a hit-or-miss method in a mist.

In many ways I have been working at this book, on paper or in my head, ever since 1919 when I first read Jane Harrison's writings and incompetently discussed some of the issues with V. Gordon Childe on Mount Tambourine in Queensland. Only after I had finished the book did I strike W. R. Lethaby's brief and suggestive *Architecture, Nature and Magic*, posthumous papers collected in 1956, in which I was happy to find that my views on architecture were in all essentials anticipated. There is no writer on the subject whom I should be more pleased to find myself echoing.

JACK LINDSAY

1 : The First Stages

Men of the Old Stone Age.   We need not here glance at the evolutionary process whereby an ape-like creature developed slowly into the ancestor of our human species. For our purposes we can begin with the artefacts of the earliest known stages of the Old Stone Age: the crudely chipped pebbles of Africa's Lower Pleistocene, which grew into rough hand-axes. Born in Central Africa, the hand-axe culture appears to have spread over most of the continent as well as into Western Europe and probably South Asia. The tools seem used for cutting and scraping, with a pointed variety for piercing the hide before skinning; and though waste flakes were at times also taken up as tools, the axe remained the essential type for some hundreds of thousands of years. The uniformity of style in its production over a vast area is remarkable—with gradual refinements in the stage called Acheulian and with innovations such as ovate shapes and cleavers. The Acheulians lived in fairly open country, along lake or river, and liked rock-shelters.

However, to the north and east of the handaxe-wielders were groups who mainly used the flake and chopper tool. In the Choukoutien cave near Pekin the first stone-industry was one of chopper-like cores and many flakes, some with secondary workings. Such industries are found through the Pleistocene in South-East Asia. It is not easy to make out the relations between the hand-axe and the flake cultures; but hunters from Central Africa may have made a rapid migration into Eastern Asia and flake-workers from the east may have moved west with such a culture as the Clactonian, camping in areas where the handaxe-users had retreated before the second glaciation. Later the Clactonians were in part supplanted by Acheulian handaxe-makers, and locally the two cultures merged. The earliest known use of fire in Africa occurs in the last Acheulian phase, in a Transvaal cave; but Pekin man also built fires.

We need not follow in detail the interlocking phases and changing forms of the stone-tools. But we may note that Clactonian seems to grow into Mousterian, associated with Neanderthal man as exemplified in Kents Cavern, Devon. The Neanderthal cavedweller with his gorilla-ridge of bone over the eye, his low cranial vault and lack of chin, was a cannibal with a liking for the brain as food. But we find his fellows burying their dead within a stone circle (in the cave on Monte Circeo) or in a small rock-shelter with flint tools and portions of a bison (at La Chapelle-aux-Saints). They hunted with flint-tipped thrusting-spears, heavy missiles and probably simple traps, and knew how to make fire. They are considered distinct from our race, *homo sapiens*, but there may have been interbreeding, as there certainly seems an inheritance by the latter of Neanderthal equipment and techniques.

The Upper Paleolithic gave way to the Lower some 35,000 years ago in many parts of Europe. There seem new groups coming from Southwest Asia

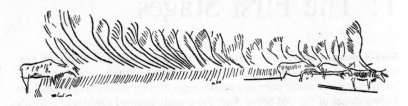

Line of reindeer: engraving on eagle's bone, from Teyjat, Dordogne.

and East Europe with a widening range of tools and weapons. They decorated their bodies and gave the dead a ritual burial. Their instruments show an overall likeness, consisting of narrow parallel-sided flakes (blades) made by a punch-technique and including burins for engraving or working soft stone, wood, antler, bone. After the Chatelperronean phase came the Crômagnon or Aurignacian, which had probably emerged in East Europe and spread west. Now we meet a highly developed art. Animals were painted or engraved in outline, and human figures were carved in relief. The Aurignacians knew how to fish rivers and wore skin-clothes. They made polished pins or awls and points with the base cleft for insertion in spears; they had a rudimentary woodworker's kit and knew how to haft; they worked antlers by splitting, sawing and rubbing down to the needed form. Their blades were more efficient, produced by a more economical process; and we may guess at an increase in both food-supply and population.

In the west the Gravettian culture took the place of the Aurignacian, apparently growing out of the earlier Chatelperronean or arriving from the Eurasian steppes. The new men made shelters dug in the loess a couple of feet and then roofed with hides over a frame of tusks or saplings. In the east they harried the herds retreating along the steppes; in South Russia and Bohemia they trapped mammoth; in East France they hunted wild horses. The piles of bones at their open camps suggest that they hunted in large groups. They used red ochre, doubtless on their bodies, wore headgear and necklaces of shells, fossils, animal teeth, cut bracelets with geometrical patterns and carved women-figures in the round, at times making them of clay mixed with powdered bone. In these figures the sex was stressed, but only two of some 60 examples show facial features. We seem certainly to meet here the ancestors of the mother-figures of the later peasantry. But the Gravettians also modelled mammoths and other game, as the peasants were to shape bulls and cows.

About this time appear forms called Solutrean: pressure-flakes resulting in fine willowleaf or laurel-leaf points for missiles. Bows and arrows also occur, possibly coming from Africa. During the well-organised hunts of the bison and reindeer herds, as the ice-sheets moved north, we find the Magdalenians centred on Southwest France, one of the local cultures of the last paleolithic period in Europe. They exploited the salmon runs and carried on the Late Aurignacian tradition of cave-painting. In the Dorgogne they could hunt reindeer all the year and in these conditions of unusual plenty their great cave-art flowered. Bone-needles show that they could sew. (Two carbon-dates help to fix these phases. The Gravettians of Lascaux cave seem to have lived about 13,560 B.C., with a margin either way of 900 years; and the Magdalenian level at La Garonne is given as 11,030, with a margin of 560 years. Clactonian is conjectured to have flourished about half a million years ago.)

Wandering hunters, apparently of African origin, left late paleolithic rock-paintings in Southeast Spain, establishing a tradition that carries on there into neolithic times. The affinities are North African; the animated style suggests Bushman rather than Magdalenian art. The paintings occur mainly on open faces, not in deep recesses.

Paleolithic life broke down with the ending of the climatic conditions that had filled Europe and the steppes with great herds of mammoth, reindeer and the like. Now stone industries became increasingly microlithic, using smaller and smaller flints—in Africa and Asia as well as in Europe. (In Australia such microliths appear as the teeth of saw-knives or the side-blades of spears.) We are on the verge of the Mesolithic period, the transition from foodgathering and hunting to settled agriculture.

Tool and Speech. Tool-making, it is generally agreed, was what constituted the difference of men from other creatures. Not the mere use of tools, but their purposive making. The hives of bees and the nests of ants are striking examples of group-organisation constructively directed. Some ants of the Amazon valley, who build in trees, carry up with crumbs of soil the seeds of special plants whose leaves are needed to protect the nests from rain and sun. Bird-nests show a mastery of weaving and twining. Rooks at times take acorns and break them against stones, as thrushes do with snails; other birds thrust small bits of stick between the open valves of sea-shells. Apes throw stick or stone, or use sticks to knock things down.

The crucial turn in human origins must have come when the co-ordination of hand and brain in the making and use of tools had reached a certain point —above all when this co-ordination brought about the first rudiments of speech. A stable relation of cause and effect could then be grasped, and our ancestors could begin to lay hold of past and future as well as present. The activity of work (the making and use of the tool) produced a point of conscious contact between man and the world. Otherwise reasoning could never have grown beyond the elementary basis seen in apes, or the elaborated but rigidly limited basis seen in insects. Now creatures were evolving who could draw themselves up out of the overwhelming succession of sensations and grasp the connections of themselves and the world. The power of objectification arose from the active contact with the object in work-process. The contact of man with nature through the focusing point of the purposive tool created the root-quality of human life.

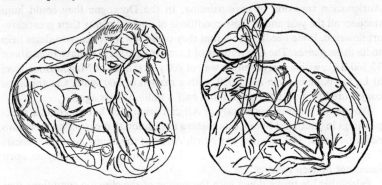

Magdalenian engravings on stone, showing figures imposed on figures: presumably artists' trial sketches.

This contact implied three simultaneous developments: the growth of skill and freedom in the hand, the increasing co-ordination of the brain and the mobile hand, the increasing complexity of the brain itself, with the ratification of the new objectifying or reasoning process in speech.

The process was at every point inner as well as outer. To grasp the workings of cause and effect in nature was also to discover analogous relationships or connections within oneself. The fusion of inner and outer in tool-activity brought about in turn a stable sense of the separate existence of inner and outer. So men grew aware of themselves as no other animal had ever done. They gradually became separated out from Nature by the process that was powerfully merging them with Nature and giving them power over it.

The concentration on the tool, on its making and its use, gave men the capacity to canalise attention: to create a universe of discourse, an isolate, without which reasoning could never stably and freely arise and develop. Thus was born speech. And every step in the extension of speech intensified the power to reason, to see relationships, to make and use tools, to bind together the family or the work-group. The animal cry or signal, the emotional interjection, found a coherent point of meaning from which a secure construction could grow, a continually-enhanced power of communication. An infinitely involved set of relationships between hand and brain, work-process and speech, man and nature, individual and group, was thus slowly but with gathering momentum brought about. The word became the emblem of men's power to arrest and examine the flux of the world, since it made possible a conscious union in work as well as a purposive and active relationship to nature.

This aspect of the situation was already stated in 1877 by Noiré: 'It was joint activity, directed towards a common end; it was the primordial labour of our ancestors, which gave birth to language and to reasoning.' And Boucher extended the thesis: 'Work, music and poetry were in their primitive stage a united whole, but the basic element in the trinity was work.'

Forms of communication exist among other animals. Cries of warning, exclamations of all sorts, even signals connected with food-getting. But this method of ejaculation can never by itself rise to speech. The new quality given to vocal expression by men proceeded from the new power of objectification and union based in the tool.

From the cohering We was born the intensified I. (At the phases we are considering men do not think of nature as moved or motivated in ways different from themselves. The process of union and separation initiated by the tool involves equally man and nature, individual and group, subject and object; each element of the situation shares in the dynamic process which both unites and cuts apart.) In primitive languages the basic element is a unity of impressions, with subject and object merged in an active situation or field, which is slowly brought under the control of analysis.

The facts of language show that the plural and all other forms of number in grammar arise not by multiplication of an original I, but by selection and gradual exclusion from an original collective We. This We represents the aggregate personality of the food-group, and therefore includes the undifferentiated I of the speaker of the time being. The procedure is from synthesis to analysis, from the group to the individual. (CRAWLEY)

The collective We also includes Nature, since the group includes its ancestors, who are merged with the forces of Nature, and the aim of rite and magic is to clarify the situation, to harmonise human desires and those forces.

We see in plain form at these early stages the process by which humanity differentiates itself from the rest of the animal world. But because thereafter the process grows ever more complex, the original basis is not discarded. In essence it persists at all phases, even when the division of labour seems to sever mental from manual activity and the relationships of parts within the whole is often hard to distinguish. The sense of union or unity, involving individual and group in their contacts with Nature, and based in the tool, in production, is the creative leaven. It continually breaks through accumulated details or facts of perception, moulding and transforming, seeking for the image or definition which will provide a comprehensive meaning, a single focus. Thus alone do men make the creative leap into new understandings or discoveries about Nature and themselves. We may put the matter, following Durkheim, by saying that logical classification arises from social. Categories of thought or definitive images are modes of collective rather than of individual thinking— though the process which breeds them involves a rich interplay of individual and collective.

Playform and Artform. We cannot however explain the growth of human consciousness, the full scope of our activity, by labour-process alone. Theorists who try, for instance, to give a primary place to the work-song in the development of art have omitted several essential links; the work-song to which they point is comparatively late in origin and could not play a momentous part in forming men and their art. The necessary complement of labour-process is to be found in the play-impulse born of overbrimming energies when the more pressing appetites have been satisfied.

A naturalist describes a water-turkey sitting at leisure on the bough of a swamp-cedar, then plucking off twigs, tossing them up and catching them in her beak.

It might be said, of course, that the catching of twigs is a practise for beak and eye, and helps the bird in training for the serious business of catching fish. This is no doubt true; but, as regards the evolution of the habit, I incline strongly to the belief that it must be quite secondary—that the bird, desirous of occupying its restless self in a satisfying way, fell back upon a modification of its everyday activities, just as these are drawn upon in other birds to provide much of the raw material of courtship. (JULIAN HUXLEY)

The key-terms here are 'in a satisfying way' and 'modification of everyday activities'. In catching the twig the bird repeats in fantasy an act which in everyday life has a central importance for her survival. She is not simply or deliberately training herself. The fantasy-act has its own satisfaction. But it is not devised abstractly; it has a strong link with the food-activity that it mimes. The emotional satisfaction is bound up with memories of successful hunts and hunger-appeasements, but is not a mere ghost or reflection of them. Its own particular pleasure derives also from the skill in tossing and catching, the feeling of enhanced mastery, which is both related to and separated from the direct hunting act.

Three archers, apparently dancing, painted in black: Cueva del Civil, Valltorta Gorge, Castallon.

Primitive men do exactly the same as the turkey. They mime their everyday activities in a satisfying way. And because of the new purposive sense that has pervaded those activities through the tool, they feel that the fantasy-act too must have its own special purpose and value. Thus is born the idea and practice of magic, of ritual. Once men see the fantasy-act as magical, they lift it from the mere impulsive and random level of the bird tossing and catching twigs. The fantasy-act becomes as real and significant a thing as the food-getting that it mimes. It develops its own systems and traditions.

In the fantasy-mime most of the difficulties and problems of the everyday activity no longer exist. The bird can tear off any number of twigs, whereas for a fish it has to wait an indefinite time, and the conditions of twig-catching are much easier than those of fishing. Hence the increased satisfaction and sense of unerring skill, of power.

The fantasy-mime is expressed above all in the dance, where the most compellingly rhythmic or concentrated expression of action is made. Early men were stirred to develop in new and complex ways the dance-forms of moving in file or circle which we find among many gregarious animals or birds. They evolved dance-forms, dance-images, closely connected with their productive needs and acts. The new co-ordinations of body and mind, hand and brain, which the tool had brought about, and which were themselves a form of rhythm, were lifted on to a new level of liberated activity and became art.

For instance, in dancing a hunt the hunter repeats the kind of movements made when actually hunting, but he co-ordinates and simplifies them in a new way; and he is sure to catch the spirit-animal, the image of his desire. If he introduces difficulties and dangers, it is only because they provide tensions and excitements, making the final triumph all the more satisfying and potent. They prove and reveal his magical power. He is no longer thwarted by material problems that may deflect or defeat an actual hunt: a mistake in tracking, a failure to avoid treading on a twig, a bad spear-throw, a fall. He dances the hunt in his mind and expresses it through the free rhythm of his body. Body and mind are keyed together in new, adventurous and interfused ways.

That does not mean that there are no technical problems to be met and overcome. There are many such problems, but they are those of the dance, which has its own system or method of transposing reality into an imaginative form. The material of life remains, but the form with its disciplines and techniques changes. If the dance-image is successfully developed, if the dance-hunter consistently keeps within the form which is based in the dance-circle and its absorbing rhythmic spell, then the conviction of triumphant dance-power, hunt-power, is held in dancer and spectator. The participant goes forth a more assured hunter, in a joyous harmony with his prey and with Nature as a whole. The energy liberated by production into art returns into production, into everday life.

Comes the deer to my singing, comes the deer to my song,
       comes the deer to my singing.
He the blackbird, he am I, bird beloved of the wild deer,
       comes the deer to my singing.
From the Mountain Black, from the summit, down the trail, coming,
       coming now, comes the deer to my singing.
Through the flower dewdrops, coming, coming now,
       comes the deer to my singing.
Through the pollen, flower pollen, coming, coming now,
       comes the deer to my singing.
Starting with the left forefoot, stamping turns the frightened deer,
       comes the deer to my singing.
Quarry mine, blessed am I in the luck of the chase,
       comes the deer to my singing.
Comes the deer to my singing, comes the deer to my song,
       comes the deer to my singing.

Even in translation that song of the Navaho of North America holds a rhythmically compulsive force and suggests the hypnotic dance-pattern in which the
mime of gaining power over the deer may be expressed.

The dance-hunt is thus the 'more perfect' hunt. Not an abstracted hunt, but
the living hunt on a level of comparatively liberated functioning, where the
hunter is so confident in the purposive co-ordinations of his movements that
his triumph is concretely certain. It is the essential hunt—the hunt freed from
accidents and defined in terms of concentrated rhythms. The release of the
danceforms swings men from a world of entangled and confusedly-impinging
circumstances into a world of pure potentiality. Momently desire and act are
one. Because the group is united in its productive needs and hopes, there is no
split between the actual world of work and the emotionally-captured world of
potentiality, of enhanced freedom and delight. One level flows into the other
and back again. Actuality provides theme and material; the artform shapes
the material to a more free pattern of movement; and the art-experience of
rhythmic freedom yields an ecstatic emotion which convinces that the actual
can become the potential—the everyday hunt can be made to approximate
more and more to the delighted ease and freedom of the danceform.

We may then tentatively define art as consisting of forms and images
generated out of the productive sphere, the life-process, and developed
through surplus-energy in rhythmical fantasy, with the result of deepening
men's grasp on reality. Art seizes on the most deeply felt or significant images
born of the life-process and gives them a free field of expansion in rhythmic
fantasy.

These definitions are oriented towards tribal art; but as we shall see they
maintain their relevance even when a gap widens between economic and
spiritual production in more complicated societies. At all periods we cannot
over-emphasise the importance of rhythm, which is at once the most individual
thing, a quality of one's own body and spirit, and the great uniting factor. It
shouts aloud the secret processes of the body (as Caudwell says) and at the

same time is the signature of a mass-element. It is the form by which we see and feel and hear and know many persons acting as one person, and yet it impacts immediately on our pulse, our central nervous organisation, our body as a whole. Its sharpest effect is in sound, which is materially measurable, but it is equally important in pictorial or plastic art, in poetry or in prose—though the ways in which it operates are different.

Dance-round. We see then why the dance develops as the fundamental form of the fantasy-mime. In it men feel most bodily-free, most released in action; in it is a maximum co-ordination of bodily and spiritual purpose through rhythm. Rhythm we may here define as movement functionally using the utmost economy of effort in the maximum attainment of an aim, so that energy may be conserved and released for further movement. In the dance (as in labour-process) it exists in a tension between the whole body and the specific gesture; and the resolution of this tension in terms of the successful movement becomes the moment of grace and beauty, giving a feeling of enhanced life to exponent and observer.

Rhythm is not something added to movement. It is of the essence of movement itself. For men it is the body in the fullest flowering of energy and is inherent in the body's structure. Out of the harmoniously adapted movements of the body are spiritual patterns evolved at moments of high tension and release. The growth of conceptual systems implies a long growth of patterns from dance and labour-process.

The patterns do not arise in a void. Rhythm involves as well as the tension inside the individual, a tension of organism and environment. And for man environment always involves a social group as well as Nature. The social relationships here are centred on labour-process and on sexual life—both of which in turn have their deep correspondences in the secret life of the body with its rhythms of decay and renewal, of exhaustion and energy, of sleeping and waking, of metabolic change. The result is a complex series of relations and tensions from which is born (through labour-process and dance) the heightened consciousness flowing into art and science. The formations of mind come about by the same laws as the formations of matter, but, taking place on a new level, there are new causal factors in their precipitation.

Consider the infinitely subtle ways in which matter responds rhythmically to the tensions of environment: the proliferating rings and chains of carbon atoms which compose organic matter, the inexhaustible kaleidescope of snow-crystals. Take the radiolarians, microscopically small one-celled protozoans. They are all much alike in build and lead the same sort of swimming life under the same general conditions. There seems an extremely limited scope for variation; yet in every radiolarian of the 5,000 kinds the small flinty shellfloat is distinct in the rhythmical ordering of its pattern.

Man in devising artforms works on the same system as Nature in her compacting of rhythmical patterns out of the tensions between the organism and its environment. Many forms which men have laboriously hammered out of their minds as art-structures can be found already defined in the hidden world of the radiolarians or in vegetable designs revealed by the microscope. Gothic art is rich in organic forms that were invisible to the artists who made it. Men differ from radiolarian or snow-crystal in their environment as well as in their complex organic inheritance; in the activities that help to create their environ-

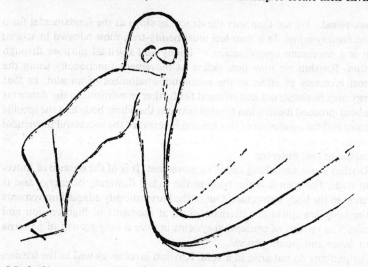

Masked man with arms imitating tusks, wall engraving: Les Combarelles Dordogne.

ment. The forces driving them to devise art-patterns or conceptual systems are social forces. Men do not passively inherit a shellfloat that is part of their body with its patterns. They project form-concepts mentally and in externalised structures. There are thus entirely new factors of mobility and freedom. But both radiolarian and man obey the law that rhythm is the expression of a tension between organism and environment.

The realising rhythm of the dance begets more than art. It makes science also possible—though for long art and science alike are united in the complex of magical ideas concentrated in dance-ritual. What are the problems of mathematics and physics but questions as to the rhythmical spacing, ordering, and balancing of material or abstracted relationships? The underlying issues are the same whether we are considering wave-mechanics or the division of the cell. The primitive dance with its dramatisation of rhythmical tensions opened the way to both art and science in their later detached forms.

The dance expressed the highest intensity of social and individual consciousness, basing itself on the world of food-getting and generation. Through it men grasped the new active unity between their lives and natural process. Take this dance of the New Hebrides:

A beautiful dance symbolises the coming of a first canoe, the chorus moving forward
with feathered and painted paddles, to the nut-rattled rhythm from the bangles tied
on their ankles, all the upper body moving in muscle as their feet strike forward like
waves over the earth, while at the back the two steersmen work their big paddles
as if in a storm. (T. HARRISON)

Man with pointed beard, from same cave as previous drawing.

The dancers, merging with the natural forces they both represent and control,
are working out methods for the definition of those forces. Art and science are
in a state of solution, brought purposively together in work, in technique, and
richly colouring the dance-fantasy. At long last, with the accumulation of
technical devices which the dance helps to bring about, they break off into
separate lines of creative inquiry and expression.

No doubt the heart-beat played an important part in developing the consciousness of rhythmic intervals and repetitions, of measure in time and space,
and in bringing about a rudimentary musical expression through hand-claps
or the knocking and rattling of objects. And perhaps the localisation of the
heart on one side of the body aided the dance in its tendency to swing in a
circular direction. Apes lurch vaguely in a repetitive rhythm as they dance in
a circle; a spinning dance by a pair has been observed, as well as a time-
keeping movement of a group round a post. Birds at mating time (for example,
partridges) may move in a round-dance.

The circular movement is for men also early linked with the sensation or idea of birth and rebirth. The Latin *vulva* (womb) has a root-meaning of revolving movement; and in the Roman ceremony of freeing a slave, the master gripped the man, touched him with a rod, and turned him right round. The man was then free. When a child of the Omaha Indians assumed a tribe-name (that is, was 'born' into a new sphere of relationships), the priest carried him from stone to stone set at the four points of the sky, or the winds, put him on each stone and turned him round singing:

Turned by the wind goes the one I send yonder,
yonder he goes who is whirled by the wind,
goes where the four hills of life and the four winds are standing,
there in the midst of the winds do I send him,
Into the midst of the winds, standing there.

Here the birth-turn is seen as one with the sky-circle given whirl-power by the winds.*

The circling of the ritual dance, with its ecstatic climax, thus itself becomes a birth-movement, a whirl of renewal and transformation.

Magic. By devising the tool men have matched themselves against Nature. They no longer seek merely to adapt themselves to a given environment; rather they seek to adapt the environment to their needs. Each gradual step in mastery has the effect of cutting them yet further off, because it makes them more aware of external reality with its basis in cause and effect: something that stands over against them with threat and challenge. On the one side the small area of secure control; on the other, the enormous complex of forces that remain unknown. Paradoxically then, the more men advance, the more they grow aware of the odds against them and see death as a definite though incalculable enemy. At the same time the group-bond, the sense of We, gains in strength and is projected on to Nature. Men feel it necessary to imagine themselves as one with the vast forces they combat and from which they are imperfectly detached—forces momently friendly but liable to turn hostile without warning between one heartbeat and the next. A complicated relationship of fear and hope, confidence and terror, is developed out of the process of union and separation.

Men's growing sense of cause and effect, of their own needs and motivations, is for long accompanied with a very vague ability to distinguish

---

* As further turn-rites we may take the *amphidromia* at Athens when the newborn babe was carried at a run round the hearth; the Roman marriage by *confarreatio* when the pair went round the altar left to right. (Similar marriage-customs among Buddhist peoples and S. Germany.) Pyre-circling, well-circuiting, etc. are very widespread. The left-to-right movement, following the sun, dominates; indeed it becomes a basis of moral conceptions: the image of choosing between two roads and taking the turn to the 'right'. Here orientation becomes morality.

between the subjective and the objective. They see their own life reflected everywhere in surrounding Nature; and efforts to rationalise and stabilise their situation are made in terms of this assumption that natural process and their psychic life are identical in kind. To say that they attribute their own impulses and ideas to Nature is to speak in words which make the process seem more willed and intellectual than it in fact is. Men simply do not conceive the possibility that the life and movement they see around them is in any way different from the life they feel within. There is no definite division of animate and inanimate. A tree-root that can trip you or a bough that waves in the wind is as alive as a man, actuated by emotions of friendliness or malice. There is no distinction of material and spiritual; all things or forces are simultaneously both.

Men thus, in part, escape from the crushing sense of alienation from Nature by their thought-processes, which make even the most hostile aspects of things and forces akin, even if still frightening, and by their inability to conceive death as an end. The dead still exist, though in some changed form. For they still affect the living, in dreams, memories, and the like. They have merely gone

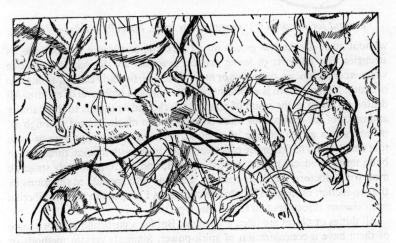

Man guising as animal with bow, reindeer and (?) young bison: wall engraving,
Les Trois Frères.

off into the unknown, which is thus further humanised, even brought within the group-boundaries. If one keeps on good terms with the ancestors, one has gone far to banish the terrible from the surrounding world.

Perhaps then the first great generalisation made by men is that which seeks to apprehend the unity of the life-process in terms which apply the concept of cause and effect, but fail to distinguish the subjective from the objective. *Mana*, the Polynesian word, or *orenda*, the Iroquis, are the best known terms for the omnipresent energy or willpower which the primitive feels to be the fundamental stuff of life. The endless practices of magic, by which men seek to influence Nature or their fellows, show the effort to canalise or control *mana*. In the ritual dance is to be found the highest point of magical activity collectively developed to maintain the food supply and the survival of the group;

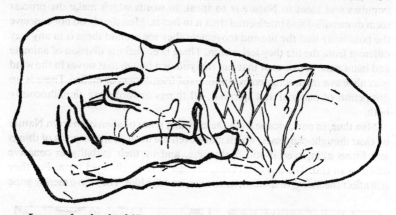

Lament for the dead (?): engraving on stone, Limeuil, Dordogne.

without such dances the group would lack the confidence to continue its struggles. But all sorts of lesser magical practices are devised to deal with various contingencies, collective or individual—particularly the disturbing fact of death. Natural death is a concept possible only at a high level of culture. All deaths are taken as the result of magical attack; and as threats to the stability and unity of the group, they must be answered in magical terms. Though all members of a group partake of its *mana*, some have special powers or lores that enable them to deal more effectively than others with magical threats or to build up the magical resources of the group; and so from an early stage we meet witch doctors, medicine-men, or shamans with specialised functions in the production of magic. (To obviate confusion I propose to use the Siberian term *shaman* throughout to define this type.)

All things or places are filled with *mana*. But for a particular purpose some of them have a concentration of spirit-power. Similarly certain methods or procedures have a superior power to canalise *mana* and direct it along desired lines. In magical practice men seek to conjure up a phenomenon by *Imitation*; and as cause and effect are equated, it is enough to imitate the effect to produce the cause. Thus, a roaring noise is an aspect of the *mana* of thunder; it makes manifest the thunder-spirit. And so to produce a roaring noise is to create and control thunder, the mightiest noise or power of all, connected with sky-crashing and rain. In ancient Greece as among the Australian aborigines, in initiation-ritual, thunder was conjured up by the bull-roarer, a cone or piece of notched wood whirled round at the end of a string. The bull-roarer gave the ritual an intensified power and sanctified the passage from one level of life to another. (In ritual myth it was connected with the monster supposed to threaten the initiate, sometimes swallowing and vomiting him up, as the whale did with Jonah.) In *Contagious* or *Sympathetic Magic* an object is thought to keep the *mana* of another object with which it has been in contact. Since spirit-power is undifferentiated, a part is the same as the whole (just as a symbol is identified with the object symbolised). Hence the belief that by getting somebody's hair or nail-trimming, one could gain power over him by a magical act such as making an image in which the hair or nail-trimming was imbedded, then burning or stabbing it. Francis Bacon in the seventeenth century still discussed seriously if a sword had curative powers of sympathetic magic for the wound it had caused.

Magic is not simply irrational or prelogical. In both its strengths and weaknesses it corresponds to the social situation from which it springs. It is based on an intuitive sense of the unity of the life-process and the indissolubility of cause and effect. If it errs in its applications of the idea of cause and effect, it represents a profound effort of thought without which our ancestors could never have gained the courage to carry on with the hardy adventure of becoming human. Indeed we cannot merely isolate its 'irrationalities' and ignore the fact that it represented the first grand attempt at a comprehensive understanding of life and of man's place in the universe, without which all later developments in culture are unthinkable.

Upper Paleolithic groups had clearly arrived at advanced magical ideas. We have noted the ritual aspect of Neanderthal burials. Dead Grimaldians and Crô-Magnons interred their dead with even more elaborate ceremonies. The graves were supplied with ornaments, implements, food, and bones were sprinkled with red ochre. Presumably the ochre was meant to impart the *mana* of blood to the pallid corpse. The Mousterians buried articles and bison-meat with their dead. There was some idea of spirit-survival and therefore also of living ancestors. Until the growth of a sophisticated religion with a creed or personal immortality in an otherworldly location, we must not however oppose the actual world and the spirit-world as separate entities. For the primitive the spirit-world is a part of Nature, in some ways its most vital part, the core of its fertility-power. In the intense moment of ritual there is no distinction at all between the two worlds; the living group and the ancestral spirits are one; they are also triumphantly part of all natural process, which they control through the dance, the ritual decorations, the masks.

The Crucial Evolutionary Phase. If we have been right in considering that a considerable amount of surplus-energy, expressing itself in play-mimes which ultimately become dance-ritual, was necessary for the creation of tool and speech, then we may look for the transformation of an ape-like creature into the proto-anthropoid in some sanctuary of special fertility during the Eocene period early in the Tertiary geological epoch. It seems that then fruits and nuts were specially plentiful.

Perhaps very abundant food obtainable without effort determined a special high tide of rhythmic creative activity, about the same way that Hugo de Vries considered such crises in nutrition to be the cause that released marked variations generally. In any event, rhythmical over-production could go the playful limit, particularly at the expense of utility, only in a state of excellent production. (w. BÖLSCHE)

And recently it has been suggested that the crucial change occurred when the creatures who were to become men had returned to the seashore—after their ancestors had long past left the water and developed in an ape-direction, living in trees. On the shore they spent much time in water, catching fish or prising up shells from the rocks. Hair was thus reduced on the body, save on the head, where it did not cause any resistance during swimming. (Hair in water no longer acts as an overcoat preventing the loss of heat.) The thick layer of fat under the human skin is an aquatic characteristic. Standing in water, which served as a partial support, the proto-anthopoids would tend to become upright, while their fingers would have developed their fineness in exploring the seafloor, digging in sand and opening shellfish. (The only other mammal using a tool is a sea-creature, the Californian sea-otter, which holds sea-urchins against its chest while cracking them with a stone.)

It is also perhaps significant that the great advance of the Aurignacians and Magdalenians came about during a period 'with game so abundant as to ensure security and even leisure', as Childe says.

Paleolithic Art. There is a fundamental likeness throughout the art of the Old Stone Age despite the variety and differences in method, which range from rough finger-tracings in clay, slight or deep engravings, carvings in low relief or in the round, modellings in clay, paintings on outline or in flat wash, with one or more colours. At Limeuil we seem to meet a studio; for slabs incised with animal forms show varying degrees of skill and some lines appear corrected. The approach throughout is realistic, with stress on organic simplification and characteristic attitude. The works represent horses, wild oxen, ibex bison, mammoth, lion, bear, rhinoceros—animals which the hunters would want to kill because they supplied food or were dangerous. Vegetation is almost wholly lacking and human beings are not common. Some forms depict hybrids with beast-heads, who have been interpreted as ancestors or as masked dancers. Generally the humans lack the vitality of the animals—except in the case of the fertility-figurines, which belong to a different art-tradition.

At times the artists used the natural contours of the rock. Indeed at the outset their inspiration may have come primarily from natural forms that suggested animals. At Altamira they used the bumpy ceiling, turning each lump into a beast; at Lascaux they used a ledge to suggest the ruffled stream where the deer swim. Stylisations were controlled by the strong sense of organic form. We meet horses with small heads and flattened nostrils, even with a sort of duckbill; Pech-Merle shows schematic bisons and spotted horses; and there are a few fantastic creatures. But the overall effect is of subtle observation and a rich feeling for the essentials of form. Beasts are shown grazing, leaping, running; but everywhere the vital simplifications make us feel the living creature in a dynamic relation to the artist. The essence of the art is rhythmic movement organically conceived.

Incisions were made by a flint graver and the thick, or liquid, paint was spread by fingers, brush, or pad. At times a blow-tube or reed seems used. Ochre provided the reds, yellows, browns; oxide of manganese, the blacks and dark browns. As among the Australian aborigines, hands were stencilled on

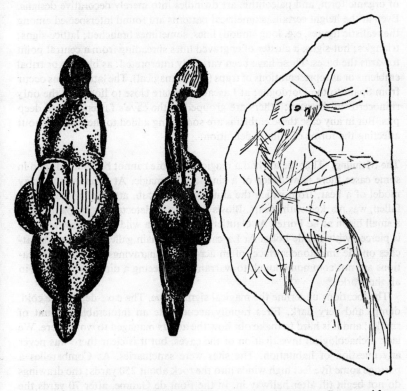

Aurignacian ivory figurine: the 'Venus' of Lespugue, Haute-Garonne (front and side). Sorcerer engraved on slate slab, Espélugues, near Lourdes.

the walls. Certain phases of development can be made out. The artists trace winding lines with finger or toothed implement; what seems an aimless meandering turns into a suggestive silhouette. Then come engraved or painted contours of animals, in which we see only the legs on the near sides; lines grow less stiff and the thickness of strokes is varied. The silhouette encloses a form of fine breadth. The twisted-perspective, which brings in details that would not actually be visible, yields to a realistic perspective in Magdalenian art. Mass and depth replace sharp outlines, while spots and disconnected strokes suggest modelling. Thus, at La Grèze the contours of a bison grow supple and flow; at Lascaux the beast is realised as a whole; at Altamira a subtlety of colour and movement of surface is added. A sense of volume goes hand in hand with a strong feeling for anatomical structure, and the wash of black or red gives way to a polychrome richness. (The Magdalenians also perfected the art of engraving.)

Then the powerful impulse flags. Stylisations grow stronger than the sense of organic form, and paleolithic art dwindles into merely decorative designs. Even at the height certain geometrical patterns are found interspersed among the realistic figures, e.g. long sinuous lines, sometimes branched; lattice-signs; triangles; hut-signs, a cluster of engraved lines spreading from a central point towards the bases. These have been variously interpreted: as blazons or tribal emblems or as representations of traps (real or magical). The lattice-signs occur from Spain to the Dordogne; at Lascaux they are close to lions and the only rhinoceros in the cave; others are grouped at the cave's far end above deep pits. But in any case these emblems are something added to the walls without affecting the forms of animal definition.

The Meaning. That the art had a magical purpose cannot be doubted; and in some cases there is evidence of a simple hunt-magic. At Montespan a clay model of a bear, from which the skull of a bear-cub, attached as head, had fallen, was marked with spears. Blows can also be detected on the painting of a small bison at Le Portel. At Gautier-Montespan a wild horse drawn in clay is pierced with missile-holes. At Lascaux, in the main gallery, there are scratches on the limestone surface, often across the engravings. But such indications are not common enough to warrant us in seeing a direct hunt-magic in all the works.*

The locations underline the magical significance. The cave-depths are cold, damp, and very dark. Fires rapidly accumulate an intolerable amount of smoke; and it is hard to make out how the artists managed to work there. We lack archaeological investigation of the caves, but it is clear there was never any question of habitation. The sites were sanctuaries. At Combarelles a passage some five feet high winds into the rock about 250 yards; the drawings do not begin till after halfway in. In the Font de Gaume, after 70 yards the walls close in and the intruder must squeeze through sideways to reach the art. At Lascaux engravings in the Chamber of Felines are high up on walls of a

---

* Representations of darts and other missiles are found. e.g. at Lascaux darts are painted or engraved across the bodies of various animals or around them. Some are feathered, and sharp points are shown by one or two small strokes. A few harpoons are engraved in the Chamber of Engravings. Strokes from nostrils are generally taken as blood from a wound, though they may represent the breath of life—as patches of lines on a flank may mean a wound or rage-flushes. A bison in the Shaft is however certainly wounded, as also the dart-pierced deer in the Chamber of Engravings. There are also animals that seem falling back, and the emblems that may be traps.

narrow steep tunnel, hard to view. At Niaux the paintings start over 800 feet from the entry. At Arcy-sur-Cure the engravings can be seen only after a painful climb over slippery clay and sharp rock-edges, and so on.

That there were congregations is shown by the way in which some cave-walls are worn by friction. At Lascaux a stone at the mouth of the Shaft-of-the-Dead-Man is polished black by the passage of bodies. (Limestone however is easily rubbed smooth.) Fertility-magic is suggested by many representations of pregnant animals; and near the two bisons at Tuc d'Audoubert were a number of phallic forms modelled in clay. The floor revealed the imprint of lads' feet, covered by calcareous crustations; and we may assume an initiation-rite.

In the Trois Frères cave is a small chamber with engraved walls, dominated by a sort of pulpit, rising some 12 feet and reached from behind. To the left is depicted a stag-man, with a kind of window in front. His head is full-face with round owl-eyes but with human nose; the ears are like a wolf's and above the brow are two stag-antlers; there are lion-claws and the tail of horse or wolf. The forearms are raised, horizontally joined and ending in two hands. The pose suggests a dance-movement and the creature seems certainly a shaman.

Support of this interpretation is given by a second figure in the same cave: a bison-headed and tailed player on a musical bow; his arms end in hooves, but his back, penis and legs are human. Before him goes an animal with bison's head and hind's body, and a reindeer whose forelegs seem to end in webbed feet. A bearded and horse-tailed figure again turns up on a schist slab from Espéligues near Lourdes; similar designs are found at Altamira and Hornos de la Peña, Santander; and three odd little horned dancers appear on a perforated staff of reindeer antler from Teyjat, Dordogne, with deer, horses, swans, while other figures with beast-heads occur at Marsoulas, Haute-Garonne.

At Lascaux we meet a bird-headed man in black outline, his body a mere rectangle, with phallus, arms, legs; at his side is a hooked stick, perhaps a

Dead man, bird, and wounded bison (rhinoceros on left by different artist): Lascaux.

spear-thrower; in front, a schematised bird with a head like a man's, perched on a pole. The man seems falling back from the bison before him, which thrashes the air with its tail while entrails hang from its body—a long spear lying across the wound. At Mas d'Azil a bone spear-thrower was decorated with a carved black cock; and at Cougnac and Pech-Merle are little creatures with heads somewhat like birds, their bodies pierced with darts. It is possible that the spear-thrower, an invention increasing the accuracy and range of the spear's flight, was magically linked with bird-power. Indeed it has been suggested that the Lascaux bird-man is a shaman in a trance, the bird on the post representing his flyaway soul as it watches the kill. Such a shamanist procedure has been enacted into our own days among Siberian tribes before a hunt begins, with a bird as emblem of trance-flight. The Lascaux shaman would then seem the ecstatic magician whose spiritpower prophesies and compels the hunt-success.

However, we shall return to the significance of ancient cave-art after we have looked at the Australian tribes, the main bearers of a paleolithic culture into our own times. But first we must note that line of paleolithic art which is concerned with figurines of women.

Mother-figures. These belong to a wider sequence than the cave-art we have been considering, and seem to date from the Gravettian period onwards. They cover an area from Lake Baikal to the Pyrenees and show that by Gravettian days a fertility-cult of the Mother was well-established, though we must beware of thinking of her as a goddess. The face is rarely portrayed but the female characteristics are heavily stressed. Take for instance the figure from Willendorf, Austria, a station of late Aurignacian mammoth-hunters. We see a woman with hair braided in a sort of beehive shape, with vast hanging breasts and broad hips; on her bosom rest her thin arms. She wears, as well as her head-dress, a scalloped bracelet, and the limestone shows traces of having been painted red. Despite the exaggerated corpulence the work has a strong realistic note and oddly a kind of assured balance and control of proportions. (In the same level was a less gross figure in mammoth ivory.)

The Willendorf type, with the same hairstyle, appears in two examples from Gagarino, Ukraine; and in less exuberant form is widely spread, e.g. two specimens from Menton, Riviera, a torso of some grace from Brassempouy, Landes, a fragment from Mayence in Germany, and yet another example from Malta; near Lake Baikal, Siberia, there have also been found some slender statuettes with features, a few even with clothing. A less ponderous variant occurs also at Vestonice, Moravia, and on two Ukraine sites.

An interesting example is the ivory statuette from Lespugue in South France where the monstrous proportions are again managed with realism and with masterly balance:

The axial structure is uncommonly limpid. The longitudinal axis, the median lines separating the breasts and the legs, divides the body into two perfectly similar halves; the same is true of the horizontal arrangement in which the upper parts correspond rhythmically to the lower ones—the shoulders to the powerful thighs and the head to the rounded calves. The contour is enclosed in a continuous line, the upper arms merging in the shoulders and the forearms resting on the bosom, as in the woman of Willendorf. Another motif that comes strongly to the fore is the emphasis laid on the central region of the female anatomy, in contrast to which the other parts appear to be consciously neglected and the proportions consciously altered. (MARINGER)

The same capacity for an harmonious ordering of forms appears in the serpentine statuette from Savignano near Modena, Italy. This figure is steatopygous, like others from the Grimaldi caves on the Riviera or from Sireuil, Dordogne; but its lengthened-out form has a strong axial construction and a tall hood or coiffure corresponds to the tapering legs. A slim Magdalenian figure at Laugerie-Basse is intermediate between the gross and slim types.

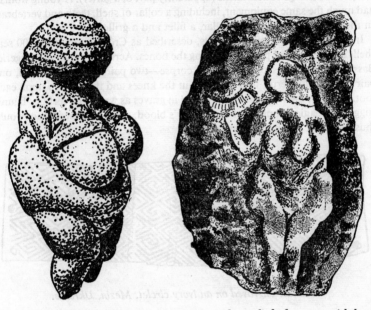

The 'Venus' of Willendorf, Austria. Carving in low relief of woman with horn, Laussel, Dordogne.

Only at Pech-Merle, Lot, do we find the female figures linked with the underground sanctuary. Here they are thought to be the oldest work in the cave, traced with fingers on the clay of the main chamber's ceiling. They consist of silhouettes with prominent breasts and are closely connected with mammoths. In 1949 the gallery of Le Combel was discovered, probably part the Pech-Merle system; and here in a small room, reached through a narrow cleft, were paintings of imaginary animals with heavy bodies and slight heads. The vaulted ceiling was cut across by a row of short semi-circular stalactites with pointed ends like female breasts; the paleolithic artists noticed them and smeared them with black.

Shells as life-giving amulets are common in Upper Paleolithic graves, e.g. in

Grimaldi burials in the Grotte des Enfants four rows of pierced shells were set round the head of a young man whose skeleton was red with peroxide of iron. A woman with him had shell-bracelets on her tightly-flexed arms. Between the skulls lay two pebbles of serpentine, with a third close to the woman's jaw. Nearby in the Grotte du Cavillon were 7,868 seashells, 875 of them pierced, possibly for necklaces; 200 were near the head. On the skull was a fillet of seashells, with 22 perforated canine deer-teeth near the frontal bone. In the fifth cave in the series a boy's skeleton lay in a grave lined with red ochre; here too were seashells and canine teeth, all perforated, with ivory pendants, necklace, and two large cowrie-shells (apparently part of a garter). A young woman had much the same equipment, including a collar of shell, teeth and vertebrae. In the sixth cave was a shell-collar, a fillet and a grille.

In the rock-shelter of Les Eyzies, described as Crômagnon, were 300 seashells and perforated pendants among the bones. Across the river at Laugerie-Basse cowries were set in pairs on a corpse—two pairs on the forehead, one pair near the humerus, four pairs about the knees and thighs, two upon each foot. Further, the widespread use of red in graves as well as on fertility-figures suggests a magical concept of the mother's blood. The reddened bones would thus represent a definite rebirth-rite.

Meander engraved on an ivory circlet, Mezin, Ukraine.

Dancers seem represented, as we would expect, from other cave-arts, the Australian, Bushmen, Spanish. The heelmarks of the Tuc d'Audobert have been taken as made by young men who danced before the clay bison, round the small hillock in the centre of the chamber. And we have noted the shamanist or beast-masking figures, who at times suggest dancers. Further examples occur in the tunnel-like Les Combarelles where as well as many animals there is a series of anthropoid figures on a recess-wall, who may be skin-clad and tailed dancers in masks. In one outline the shape of a mammoth head is suggested, with the man's arms used for the tusks. Here indeed we seem to have a mammoth-man.

In the rock-shelter near Cogul in Catalonia we meet nine narrow-waisted women with long pendant breasts, caps and bell-shaped skirts reaching their knees. They lack facial features and at a glance seem associated with a small naked figure, whose phallus is not erect; but the black woman-group seems earlier than the dark brown male, and probably represents dancers.

With the weakening of cave-art in the Magdalenian epoch we find the mother-figures becoming abstract, e.g. the small carvings in lignite from the station of Petersfels, Baden, perforated for use as pendants. Similar images in ivory have been found in Moravia, the Pekarna cave, and in the Ukraine, at

Meander pattern painted in red, Hinna, Norway.

Mezin. One from Mezin is engraved with nose, arms, and genital triangle; the geometrical designs about head and hips have been described as tattooing.*

The later paleolithic groups in Europe and the steppes then seem to have had a fertility mother-cult as well as magical practices connected with animals. Different art-traditions gathered round mothers and animals, though their rituals were clearly complementary and could be brought together as at Pech-Merle.

---

* Scandinavian paleolithic art shows, in the first glacial period, the same general sequence: realistically represented animals of the hunt, a transitional period of conventionalised forms, thirdly schematic animals and stylised humans. The sequence is proved by superimpositions.

2: The Totemic Tribe

Australia. The Australian aboriginals lived, and in some parts still live, in an economy analagous to that of the Old Stone Age. How far can we use their customs to illuminate the customs and organisation of the Aurignacians and Magdalenians? The question cannot be decisively answered. Clearly the men of the later Old Stone Age in richly-stocked Europe some 20,000 years ago cannot be equated with a people who have stood still, economically, and have been far from the main highway of human evolution. The complex systems of the Australians cannot be shifted back to the earlier scene; but that does not mean there is nothing we can learn from the Australian about certain essential characteristics of paleolithic life.

We do not know for sure when the Australians reached their continent, though it is likely they arrived as far back as the close of the Ice Age. Skulls from Tangai, South Queensland, and Keilor, Victoria, are dated from that period. The archaeological strata from Pejark Marsh has been set by the test of radioactive carbon at about B.C. 11,500 The oldest known tools have been excavated near the mouth of the Murray River and on Kangaroo Island off the southern coast. They are pebbles roughly shaped on one side and stone chips something like horse-hooves; forerunners of the scrapers used right down to our own day. At Tartanga on the lower reaches of the Murray River and on Devon Downs a chronological sequence has been sketched out, beginning with very primitive implements and ending with ground-edged axes and other well-made articles. So far 12 prehistoric cultures have been traced; but the work is still in its infancy. Much will yet be filled in, but it seems safe to say that the oldest forms look to Indonesia, Malaya, and Tonkin. The origins of Australian culture lie in Southeast Asia; and thence, with New Guinea as the stepping-stone, almost all the later currents have flowed in. The microliths suggest the transitional period between Old and New Stone Ages, while axes made by pecking, or to some extent polished, suggest the New Stone Age. But neo-lithic argiculture, practised in New Guinea has never entered Australia—though certain customs and tools do seem to have carried across Torres Straits; the multi-pronged fish-spear and the fish-hook, probably platform-burial and mummification of bodies as well as the spiral design so important in the art of Kimberley and Central Australia. This spiral may ultimately derive from the Bronze Ages of China and Indonesia. As the natives of North

Queensland can hardly have been unaware of New Guinea's agriculture, they may have been inhibited from taking it over by the rigidity into which the social system had settled and which made them incapable of the large-scale adaptation needed for such a change.

The Australians, then, cannot in any simple way be equated with the Aurignacians. Yet they have the interest of tribes persisting in a paleolithic way of life over large tracts of country, whatever modifications in their original systems may have filtered in or however ossified the systems may have grown. If one is correct in seeing the Australians as on the whole having carried on the paleolithic way-of-life with which they entered the continent, then we would expect that over the millenia they would extend and elaborate the rudimentary forms of social organisation with which they began. And this considerable elaboration would strengthen the resistances to any fundamental change. There is in general a remarkable uniformity of culture all over the continent, though there were about 500 tribes when Australia was discovered and a study of their material products has led to their classification in eleven districts. The wide uniformity of natural conditions over large areas has

Kangaroo hunt: bark drawing, Kakadu tribe, Northern Territory, Australia.

certainly helped to maintain the similarity of living conditions and outlook among the tribes. The ethnic stock too is generally uniform, though with suggestions of a strain corresponding to the extinct negroid aborigines of Tasmania (about whom we know very little). The dialects too, despite their divergences, fit in with the general picture of an underlying unity.

Social System. Each tribe has its own territory, and so have the sub-divisions. Tribes do not try to encroach or gain new land; and this pacific attitude is aided by the *alcheringa*-myths which tell how the ancestors traversed and still inhabit the tribal area. For the friendly spirit-power would be absent outside the boundaries. Only on ceremonial occasions does the whole tribe gather. There are strict rules as to the division of game and all natural products among the family or camp; but a man has his own chattels, weapons, tools and sacred objects such as the *churinga* (which however is kept in a collective store). At times of plenty, the circle of sharers is much enlarged: when a whale is driven ashore or when the mimosa-gum appears on the Swan River. At the ripening of the bunya-cones, the Kabi tribe sends messengers round to invite other tribes to a feast that may last a month. On ceremonial occasions—the settlement of a bloodfeud or the great initiation-rites—inter-tribal markets or fairs are held, at which bartering takes place, and no one is molested along the immemorial trade-routes, which mostly follow water-courses. At times an individual sets out on his own or his friends' account and walks round for months, even a year. A message-stick, carved with signs, may be used—as also when summoning guests to one of the big festivals—and the person of a 'herald' is sacred, even when the business is war. Long journeys are made for special materials, red ochre, stones suitable for axe-heads or other tools, and (most important) the leaves and shoots of the pitjuri bush, which, fried and eaten with ash, is a drug-stimulant. Men of the Dieri tribe go 700 miles to Northeast Queensland for pitjuri; and deputations from the Adelaide district travel to the land east of Lake Torrens for the red ochre used in mourning.*

Custom is law. Some customs are sacred, others are derived from the local group and can be changed by the old men at tribal gatherings—e.g. matters of descent reckoning. The unit for justice, as indeed for nearly all purposes outside ritual, is the local group. Thus, in North Queensland each camp has an elders' council which runs things; in some parts women share in deliberations. Members of a strange tribe are feared and are liable to be killed if encountered —though there are often friendly relations with surrounding tribes and women may be carried off rather than killed. Intercourse is governed by ceremonies. The messenger with the carved token approaches and may make a small fire; an elder comes up with a firestick and is given the token with its signs. As many as 20 tribes may assemble at the meetings in West Victoria, and big hunts are carried out by tribes in association. At the great *bora* (initiation) rites men of neighbouring tribes are invited and 'universal brotherhood prevails'. In some areas tribes meet at short intervals all the year round for a tournament, *prun*, to settle disputes. Fighting goes on under strict rules till dark; then friendly relations are established and corroborees performed. The *prun* thus settles disputes and promotes social intercourse. Quarrels are mainly concerned with women, suspicions of murder by magic, and trespass. The normal procedure is for the accused, or others of his group, to undergo an expiatory punishment; or a regulated combat takes place. Death is not sought in any duel, which stops as soon as blood is drawn. Indeed, to kill a man in a *prun* ranks as murder.

In general there is right of assembly for all men, free speech, and delegation of specific powers to elected representatives whose authority can be rescinded. A missionary describes the *tendi*, the clan-judgment, among the Narrinyeri. The judges numbered 46 and acted as in a trial-by-jury; there was much discussion, often very excited; in the end no decision was reached.

The marriage-system is strictly enforced under pain of death. Mostly the

---

* We may compare the evidence for barter in paleolithic Europe: Mediterranean shells in the Dordogne as well as the bones of sea-fish. Flints at Gagarino on the Don seem brought from more than 70 miles downstream.

tribes are divided into two exogamous halves, but these moieties may be divided into further sections and sub-sections. The moieties are important for rites like youth-initiation and burial as well as marriage-regulation.

Totem. Social organisation is throughout based on the totem—a North American term which has come into general use to express a complex set of ideas and practices. The totem is usually a beast or plant, with which a kindred group has a close ritual-relation: with which indeed it is identified. (All animals are thought of as once being men.) Members of the same totemic group are of the same flesh and cannot intermarry. Hence the exogamous moieties or clans. It is possible that the earliest system involved the need to marry one's cousin and that from this basis there developed the schemes of intermarriage between groups who stood in a cross-cousin relationship. What concerns us here, however, is the essence of the taboo underlying the systems which evolve from the need to find a wife outside the group with the same totem. Instead of a prohibition saying that anyone outside the group is available, a symmetrical system is devised—two intermarrying moieties. The incest-horror which forbids marriage with mother or sister extends to all women in a mother or a sister relationship, that is, all women who share the same totemic object. There is often a secondary taboo-series, e.g. a brother may not directly address his sister, or a man finds his relationship to his mother-in-law governed by strict taboos.

Where a tribe has more than two inner divisions, the criss-crossing of the marriage-rules can be highly complex, but the ruling idea is always the same. Myths describe the exogamous system, which keeps marriage within the tribe while forbidding it among the totemic divisions, as devised to end conflict and confusion. Thus, the Murray natives say that beings called Nooralle, shaped as crows or eaglehawks, created the world. The two groups went on fighting till they decided that the black-fellows should be divided into the Eaglehawks and the Crows. A song declares, 'Strike the crow at the knee, I will pierce his father'.

There are also sex-totems, concerned with ceremonial occasions like wedding preparations; and individual totems, important for witchdoctors or shamans who usually have a lizard or snake as familiars. These creatures, gained in a dream, act as assistants. But the lesser totemic forms are clearly derivations from the main group-totem.

No member of a group may eat his totem, except sometimes at special ritual feasts held once a year. The group however has the duty of multiplying the totem by magic rites and incantations. The fertilising ritual is called *intichiuma* by the Arunta of Central Australia, and we may use this as the generic term. Among the Arunta the men of the kangaroo totem do their multiplying rites on a rocky ledge considered full of kangaroo spirits ready to inhabit bodies. A short way up the hillside are two stone blocks which represent male and female kangaroos: these are rubbed with a stone by two men. Then the ledge is decorated with alternate stripes of red and white to represent the red fur and white bones of the kangaroo. Young men sit on the ledge, open their veins and let blood sprinkle over the rock-edge, driving the kangaroo-spirits in all directions. Other men below sing songs about the increase of kangaroos.

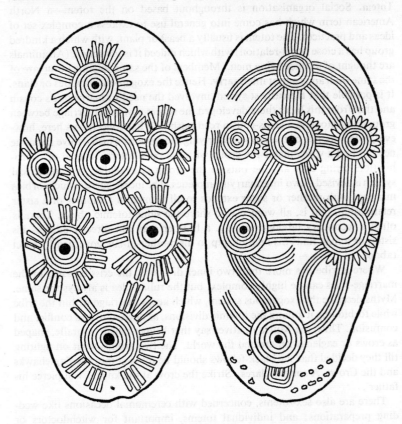

Churinga, Unmatjera tribe: a red-ochred slate slab, black and red, decorated both sides. The black dots are holes. It is a Spirit-child Stone-churinga, which a woman owned. (Liebler's note: 'They point to the side where the concentric circles are connected with stripes as the ovary of the mother with embryos.' Reverse: with seven children: strokes round head are hairs.

The *alcheringa* or dreamtime is a paradisiac state or place which expresses both the ancient time when the ancestors roamed the earth and the spirit-place where they still live. The ancestors are so closely linked with the beasts or plants whose name they bear that an *alcheringa*-man of the kangaroo-totem may be called a man-kangaroo or a kangaroo-man. *Alcheringa*-ancestor and totem are ultimately the same. A typical myth is that of the Warramunga tribes, among whom each totemic group has one great ancestor who rose in some particular spot and walked across the tribal area, making various natural features as he went, and leaving behind him the spirit-individuals who have since been incarnated. *Intichiuma* consists of tracking out the ancestral paths and repeating one after the other the rites connected with the *mungai* spots (*oknanikilla* in Arunta), totem-centres where the spirits were deposited. *Mungai* spots are represented by abstract drawings, concentric circles painted on the ritual ground or the body of a performer.

Every Arunta is a reincarnation of an ancestor. Spirits of the various totems gather by their *churinga nanja*, the tree or stone assigned to them, and any woman passing is liable to be entered. The child she bears belongs to the totem of the locality where it was thus conceived. After its birth the woman's husband hunts for the *churinga ilkinia* of the child, a long stick or stone showing the totem-marks, which is put in the *ernatulunga* with the other *churingas* of the group. No woman may look on the *churingas*; a man may see them only after initiation. Coitus is not considered the primary cause of conception; it merely opens the way to a spirit.* The *ernatulunga* is a cave where dwell the spirit-ancestors and babes awaiting birth. The *iruntoarinia*, spirit-doubles of the tribesmen, live in underground caves; the totemic ancestors inhabit with red bodies the spots where they went down into the earth.

The individual has many doubles. The *churinga* is his main external soul or soul-object, closely connected with the totemic ancestors and itself loosing spirit-children as its emanation. But there are other halves or soul-objects. In one myth an old opossum-man meets another called *Illinja* (his double, shadow) and she prevails on him to lay aside some of the gum-tree seed he was about to eat; in the middle of the night they rise and perform *intichiuma*. The man sees beside *Illinja* another man come up from the seed. 'That man is the same as you and me. Why did he come up?' In the Yaraikanna tribe if an old man dreams of something, it is the *ari* of the person he first meets in the morning. A lad's *ari* is discovered through a shape detected in the blood-clot after his tooth is knocked out in the initiation-rite.

The duality of the individual is closely linked with the symmetrical or dual system inside the tribe, and finds expression in myths of dual heroes, e.g. an *alcheringa* pair of kangaroo-hunters who institute circumcision. When they have finished skinning the kangaroo, they fasten the edges of the skin to the ground and raise it in the middle, forming the sky-vault. 'Now from this time people can walk upright and need not hide themselves for fear of the sky

---

* Typical ideas are these among natives of the Tully river. A woman is got with child if she sits over a fire on which she has roasted a piece of fish that her husband gave her; if, hunting, she catches a certain kind of bullfrog; if some man tells her to have a child, or if she dreams a child has got inside her. In Melanesia, if an unmarried girl gets with child, she blames the food she has eaten. Among the Trobrianders a child is begotten on a woman by a Baloma or ghost; the natives admit a loose girl may have a better chance of impregnation than a chaste one, but any girl would prefer to stop bathing at high water than give up coitus as a precaution against pregnancy.

falling'. Here is the myth of the separation of sky and earth which we find among the Greeks, Sumerians, Polynesians and many others: the imagery often being that of a child who thrusts apart the coitus-locked parents. The Australian myth is the same in kind, for its association is with the circumcision-rite, in which a physical cutting-apart expresses the discarding of an old life-phase and the achievement of a new union, a new social level.

Cutting off the foreskin is exactly equivalent to pulling out a tooth (in Australia, etc.), to cutting off a little finger above the last joint (in South Africa), to cutting off the ear lobe or perforating the ear lobe or the septum, to tattooing, scarifying, or cutting the hair in a particular fashion. The mutilated individual is removed from the common mass of humanity by a rite of separation (this is the idea behind cutting, piercing, etc.) which automatically incorporates him in a defined group; since the operation leaves ineradicable traces, the incorporation is permanent. The Jewish circumcision is in no way extraordinary: it clearly marks a 'sign of union' with a particular deity and a mark of membership in a single community of the faithful. (VAN GENNEP)

We may add that the cutting rite is also a birth-mime, releasing a new body by the piercing or slashing of the old.

The *alcheringa* dual heroes are also fertility-figures connected with the bull-roarer. Their camp can be recognised by the luxuriant growth of the *moku*, which is tabooed as their special food. They save the initiates from circumcision by firestick. Rising from the earth, they show a stone-knife or teach its use. 'Fire is death and the stone is life'. They demonstrate how to make fire by twirling a stick. When travelling through the great snake's stomach, they give rise to the totem-centres. Among the Kaitish, their stone-knife has been thrown down from heaven and streams derive from the subincision wound. Among the Baninga, they were circumcised at Akuralla, then

they went to an old woman and asked her for food. She said, 'I have no food for you'. So, being angry, they tear off their pubic tassels, throw them at her and run away. After going a little way they make a fire, carrying a firestick with them, at Narulunka they make a waterhole. They go and kill a female kangaroo, make a hole in the ground to cook the body and thus give rise to another pool of water. The snake Bobbi-bobbi hears the noise they make with their stones and sends flying-foxes to find out what they are doing. They kill the flying-foxes, but when they open the earth-oven in which the foxes are being cooked, the foxes jump out and fly away screeching. The snake who is watching underground takes out one of his ribs, transforms it into a boomerang, and throws it up on the plain. They kill more flying-foxes. At last the snake drags them underground by means of the boomerang.

Intichiuma. When the *intichiuma* of the honey-ant totem is to be performed, the *churingas* are brought out of the honey-ant cave, which lies in a depression of a rocky range well above the surrounding plains. All around, blocks of stone stand on end and lean in all directions; each one is related to an *alcheringa* honey-ant-man. On the east side of the pit is a mulgy tree, abode of the spirit-guardian of the sacred ground. In the pit-centre a stone projects some 18 inches: it is the *nanja* of the *alcheringa* man who originated here and performed *intuchiuma*. The rite of the kangaroo totem is carried out at the *nanja* stone of a great *alcheringa* kangaroo. The head man in charge of the *ernatu-*

lunga or holy cavern orders a place to be swept nearby and greased with fat and red ochre.

The symbolism of the pit is brought out by a Watchandie rite enacted at the height of the season of plenty (yams, eggs, and so on). Women and children retire on the festival-eve and the men may not look on the women till the end. They rub their bodies with charcoal and wallaby-fat, then dig a large hole and rest. Early next morning they assemble, decorate themselves with ochre and emu-fat, and pit shavings and garlands in their hair. They dance round the pit, singing and shouting, a few of them whistling (which is unusual for a corroberee). With brief rests and gorgings, the dance goes on all night. The pit has been adorned with bushes to represent the vagina and the dancers carry spears for penises; all their gestures have a direct coitional reference. A song runs: *Bool-lie, neera, bool-lie neera, bool-lie neera, wadaga* (female pubic hair, none, female genitals). Finally they copulate with the women and set up sticks in the ground to mark the spot which is henceforth taboo; to look at it now means death.

The quivering shaking movement in the *intichiuma* dances is thought to

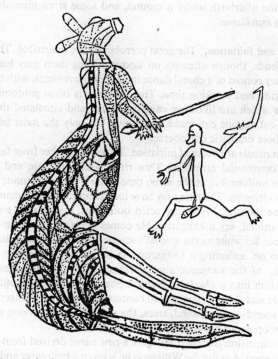

Bark drawing, Kakadu: native spearing Black Rock Kangaroo. X-ray method showing spine, ribs, organs of beast. Spearman holds throwing-stick, with dillybag hanging from neck.

throw off spirit-children (represented by the white down that does in fact fly off). The greasing and rubbing of the stones is also thought to let out spirit-children. The smeared *churinga* again emits such spirits. But we must not think of the rites as simply representations of coition and orgasm. The aborigine makes no distinction between one kind of fertility and another: the production of children and the increase of kangaroos or witchetty-grubs. The down flying from the dancers at times represents clouds in a rain-charm; and the *churinga* among the Worgaia is a magical object fertilising yams with the aid of songs.

The shape of the totem-centre is significant, as we shall see later—a circular hollow with a central stone or a mound. The characteristic feature of the Bunan Bora and Dora initiation-rites in the south-east is the rounded mound, which is often said to represent a human or an animal, especially the high beings (Baiamai, Duramulun), in a reclining position. The serpent ancestor of the Wollunqua totem is represented by an earth-mound, and an attack is made on the mound to compel the ancestor to the will of the living group. Grave-mounds are also known, especially in Western Australia. Some are circular; some are crescentine, made of earth and stones at the gravehead. There are rites of putting the afterbirth under a mound, and some stone-mounds are connected with *intichiuma*.

Corroberee and Initiation. The great corroberees are intertribal. They put an end to all feuds, though attempts on women during them may lead to fresh trouble. They consist of a choral dance in various movements, with the women merely singing and marking time. The character is often pantomimic. New corroberees which are liked are eagerly learned and circulated through the tribes. Almost anyone can make up a song, but only the most talented can invent a whole dramatic corroberee.

The main rituals are those of initiation. Tribesmen gather from far and wide under the ceremonial armistice. Thus ritual ideas circulate and there is a tendency to uniformity; at the same time there is an opportunity for introducing new elements. The rites may have long connected performances lasting two to three months. Myths are acted out. Thus, a man may represent an *alcheringa* animal, say a kangaroo. He comes hopping out, a fur-string ball hanging from his waist as the animal's scrotum; he leaps about, lies down to rest, and so on, imitating a kangaroo. As he performs, the men round the novices sing of the kangaroo's wanderings in the *alcheringa* and his final transformation into a *churinga*. Natural phenomena like rain and storm are also mimed; and the aborigines hold concerts in which each singer imitates a particular sound—waves, wind, trees, the sacred beasts. Among the Kurnai we meet an opossum game and a kangaroo-hunt.

After circumcision the Dieri boy gets a new name derived from the legend of his *mura-mura*. Among the Willyaroo he is given a bullroarer and instructed to whirl it when hunting so that the tribe may get a good harvest of reptiles and other creatures. Myths tell of a giant animal chased in the *alcheringa*. The

Narrinyerri have a hero Wyungare who, before ascending to heaven, took a giant kangaroo, tore it to bits, and scattered it through the shrub where the kangaroos now live. Oundjik found a single kangaroo, emu, and so on, caught and cut them up; from every shred came a new animal. In the same way mankind was dispersed over the earth. The Kupirri of Port Lincoln have a giant kangaroo who, when finally killed, releases from his belly the comrades of his hunters, whom he has swallowed and who are now restored to life.

Such monsters derive from initiation-experience. In the rite of the Black Palm shown to novices on the McIvor River, men cover the lad's eyes while a large palmleaf is brought in and stuck in the ground. The novices are allowed to look and the old men say that they have made the leaf grow. The leaf is then shaken and torn to shreds. The uninitiated are informed that a being named Thuremlin takes each youth off, kills and at times cuts him up, then restores him to life and knocks a tooth out. Among the Wiradthuri Daramulun declares to Baiamai that he has killed the boys, cut them up and burned them to ashes, then formed the ashes into human beings and given them life, each minus a tooth. The Loritja say that a bullroarer spirit knocks the boy's head off as he stares up at the sky, then runs after the head and puts it back; the boy at once gives the spirit a deadly wound with a spear. Among the Bibinja on the Gulf of Carpentaria the bullroarer is made by a spirit named Katajalina, who comes out of an ant-hill, eats up the boy, then restores him to life. Nearby the Anula say the spirit is Gnabaia who swallows the lads and disgorges them. In some tales wild dogs tear the initiates to shreds.*

The ordeals, the fastings, the moments of ecstatic excitement, make it difficult in the end for the initiate to distinguish myth from ritual experience. Among the Kurnai the rites last up to two or three weeks. One evening, after a couple of days' preparation, the novices lie in an enclosure of bushes while all night long the men and women dance round them, mimicking the cry of the emu-wren, their ancestor and sex-totem. The novices may not speak, but may make a twitter like the birds into whom they are about to be changed. The dancing and the cries induce a trance-condition out of which the boys

---

* Women may not see the bullroarer. The Ualaroi of the Upper Darling say the novice meets a ghost, who kills him and restores him as a young man. On the Lower Lachlan and the Murray, Thrumalun kills and revives; the Unmatjera of Central Australia have a spirit Twanyirika who thus acts. In New Guinea the initiation-monster appears as a long hut modelled in its shape, with head on high and a tapering end, with goggle-eyes and gaping jaws. The bullroarer sounds from its belly, and the act of deglutition is variously performed. All the tribes use the same word for monster as for bullroarer; three languages also use it for spirits-of-the-dead; the fourth, for grandfather. Among the Tugeri the bullroarer is a stone giant. In parts of Viti Levu, Fiji, the initiates are shown men who lie bloody with protruding entrails in the sacred enclosure; at the priest's cry the 'dead men' (covered with pigs' guts) leap up and run to the river, then march back cleansed and garlanded, 'resurrected'. On Rook, between New Guinea and New Britain, masked men dance through the village and take the boys off to Marsaba, from whose belly the villagers ransom them, and so on. In ancient Greece the *rhombos*, bullroarer, was associated with Dionysiac initiation and was used by the Bacchanals in their rites as well as in magic practices.

awake into their new character. At daybreak the women go and the men rest. At nightfall the spirit-emu-wren reappears, heralded by the low-pitched hum of the bullroarers. It comes closer and closer, while the lads wait with covered heads. Then the veil is tweaked off and the leader stands before them with uplifted spear, crying thrice, 'Look up!' The men point their spears at the lads and threaten death for any disclosure of the mysteries. The headman solemnly recites the myth of their descent from the emu-wren and shows the bullroarer in which the ancestral voices are hidden. Finally rules of behaviour are inculcated. But before the initiate may rejoin the tribe, he must spend a month at least in isolation in the bush.

Resurrection Drama. The ritual among the Coast Murring tribe of N.S.W. is worth a detailed account. The setting is the bottom of a deep valley with a sluggish stream flowing through tall sharp-edged sedge. The morning sun is just showing over the mountains and the valley is still dank with shadow. The novices, who have each had a tooth knocked out, warm themselves by a fire, while the men prepare decorations of stringy bark and dig a grave, discussing what shape to give it. The man to be buried settles things by saying that he wants to be laid on his back, full length. (He is a man of the eaglehawk totem, named Yihai.) While two men dig, he superintends the costumes. Six men are clad from head to foot in barksheets beaten into fibrous fleeces, so that their faces are quite concealed. Four are tied by a cord; the other two walk free, nobbling and bent in the role of very old and powerful medicine-men. When the grave is ready, Yibai lies down on a bed of leaves as if dead. His hands, crossed on his chest, hold a young tree that has been pulled up by its roots and planted above him, so that its top rises several feet above ground.

The novices are led to the grave by their sisters' husbands and sit in a row, while a singer on the trunk of a fallen tree at the grave's head croons a sad song, the song of Yibai. To the slow plaintive beat the actors come forward,

Australian music: Yina, Initiation into tribal laws.

winding among the trees, logs, rocks, swaying and clashing bark-clappers at every step. The two old men keep a little aloof in their tottering dignity. The group represents a party of medicine-men, led by two especially old, who have come on a pilgrimage to the grave of a brother magician, chanting an invocation to Duramulun. They draw up to the grave on the side opposite the novices, with the two aged leaders to the rear of the dancers. Dance and song continue till the grave-tree begins to quiver. 'Look there', cry the sisters' husbands. The tree shakes more and more, till, violently agitated, it falls to the ground, and, amid the exulting song and dance the dead man throws off the leaves and sticks, springs to his feet, and dances his dance of resurrection in the grave itself, showing in his mouth the life-substance received from Daramulun in person.

Among the Aranda the rites are much protracted, starting when the boy is ten or twelve, when he is repeatedly tossed in the air. Later he undergoes circumcision, and some weeks afterwards, subincision or scrotum-piercing. Finally he is ritually purified (and reborn) by lying on a fire covered with leaves. Here is a fire-passage. In the Melville Islands the novice is passed through a water-hole.

Shaman. The shaman or medicine-man may be defined as someone who feels himself specially open to spirit-communication, so that he lives all the while at the point of tension which others feel only during their initiation. We have an account of the trance-journeying of Wiradjuri of the kangaroo totem who became a medicine-man.

My father is a Lizard-man. When I was a small boy, he took me into the bush to train me to be a doctor. He placed two large quartz-crystals against my breast, and they vanished into me. I do not know how they went, but I felt them going through me like warmth. This was to make me clever, and able to bring things up. He also gave me some things like quartz-crystals in water. They looked like ice, and the water tasted sweet. After that, I used to see things my mother could not see. When out with her I would say, 'What is that out there like men walking?' She used to say, 'Child, there is nothing'. These were the ghosts which I began to see.

[He goes on to say that at puberty he went through the regular initiation rites. He saw the doctors bringing up crystals and shooting their virtue into them to make them 'good'. Then he retired into the bush in the usual way to fast and meditate.] While I was there in the bush, my old father came out to me. He said, 'Come here to me', and then he showed me a piece of quartz-crystal in his hand. When I looked at it, he went down into the ground; and I saw him come up all covered with red dust. It made me very frightened. Then my father said, 'Try and bring up a crystal'. I did try, and brought up one. He then said, 'Come with me to this place'. I saw him standing by a hole in the ground, leading to a grave. I went inside and saw a dead man, who rubbed me all over to make me clever, and gave me some crystals.

When we came out, my father pointed to a tiger-snake, saying, 'That is your familiar. It is mine also'. There was a string extending from the tail of the snake to us. My father took hold of the string, and said, 'Let us follow the snake'. The snake went through several tree trunks, and led us through them. At last we reached a tree with a great swelling round its roots. It is in such places that Daramulun lives. The snake went down into the ground, and came up inside the tree, which was hollow. We followed him. There I saw a lot of little Daramuluns, the sons of Baiame. Afterwards the snake took us into a great hole, in which were a number of snakes. These rubbed themselves against me, and did not hurt me, being my familiars. They did this to make me a clever man and a doctor.

Then my father said 'We will go up to Baiame's Camp'. He got astride a thread, and put me on another, and we held by each other's arms. At the end of the thread was Wombu, the bird of Baiame. We went up through the clouds, and on the other side was the sky. We went through the place where the doctors go through, and it kept opening and shutting very quickly. My father said that, if it touched a doctor when he was going through, it would hurt his spirit, and when he retuned home, he would sicken and die. On the other side we saw Baiame sitting in his camp. He was a very great old man with a long beard. He sat with his legs under him, and from his shoulders extended two great quartz-crystals to the sky above him. There were also numbers of the boys of Baiame, and of his people who are birds and beasts. [The totems]

After this time, and while I was in the bush, I began to bring up crystals; but I became very ill, and cannot do anything since.

Howitt, recording the statement, says, 'I feel very strongly assured that the man believed the events which he related were real, and that he actually experienced them'. We need not doubt the narrator's good faith. His words are so closely in key with initiation-experience that they convince as an account of what he felt at moments of heightened and dissociated consciousness. Incidentally they illuminate such myth-motives as the Clashing Rocks or Ariadne's Thread—as well as the witch-thread or cable in Gaelic tales and the Gaelic use of magical crystals. And they show the underearth-passage and the sky-ascent in their primitive form.

An Euahlayi lad of the iguana totem, wishing to be a medicine-man, first sees his totem. The iguana crawls over him, but he feels no fear. Next however comes a snake, the hereditary foe of his totem. Then a huge figure drives a yamstick into the lad's head, pulls it out through the back, and sets in the hole a *gubberah* or sacred stone, by means of which the lad will be later able to work magic. Among the Arunta a man wishing to be initiated as a medicine-man leaves the camp alone and goes to a cave-mouth. At daybreak one of the *iruntarinia*, spirit-doubles of alcheringa ancestors, comes to the mouth, finds the man asleep, and pierces his neck from behind with an invisible lance. The man, falling dead, is taken in to the depths where the *iruntarinia* live. They remove his internal organs and supply a new set, also implanting a supply of the *atnongara* stones, which he will be able to project into a patient's body. The Awakabal medicine-men get a bone called murrokun by sleeping three together in the grave of a recently-dead man. The latter inserts the bone which can be used to kill others.*

---

* For the Kabi and Wakka a magician is a man full of magic stones. With crystal-filled body he lies by the edge of the waterhole of Dkakkan (Rainbow), is taken down into Daramulun's abode, where he gives crystals for rope; awakening by the water-hole, he is 'full of life'. The N.W. tribes use a 'live-stone', *millia gurlee*, in rainmaking *intichiuma*. The Granjie for rain-magic use crystals, *bi-oka*, sent at request by a great rain-man in the north; They pulverise the stones and compel rain by throwing them in all directions. In W. Australia the *boglia* has quartz crystal in his stomach, which, on his death, passes into the stomach of his son. In S. Australia the *mundie*, a crystal considered spirit excrement, is used in initiations.

The shaman's work largely consists of counter-magic against those believed to have committed murder. He points a stick with charms or merely throws the magic crystals; or he creeps on the sleeping murderer, removes his kidney-fat without disturbing him, and leaves him to die. The pointing-bone is attached to a string that passes through it and through a small hollow receptacle of bone or wood; the end through which it passes is closed. Held in one hand, it is pointed at the victim, who may be miles off, and draws some of his blood in. It is then sealed. If it is burned, he dies; if warmed, he falls ill; if rinsed out, he recovers. A lump of resin, with two teeth and a long string, is sung or charmed, catching the heat of the sun. It it is set in the victim's tracks, the heat enters into him and kills him. A dead man's hair also provides much power.

The shaman also cures sickness by removing its cause. He rubs the suffering body and sucks out the afflicting stone or bone. If the man dies, he finds the murderer by special signs.

The shaman is thought to be able to commune with spirits, fly in the night-sky, visit hostile camps and insert sticks or bones in the enemy. Some use ropes to climb to the sky or descend from it. (In the myths shape-shifting is common.) The narcotic *pitjuri*, chewed or smoked, begets voluptuous dreams; and the leaves of a stinging-tree are chewed at corroborees, inducing a state of frenzy.

The shaman may also play a part in normal rites. Thus, a distinguished medicine-man may be asked to take the lead even in other tribes' totemic ceremonies.

Art. All artistic expression is closely related to the totemic system and its rituals. Art functions primarily in the decorations of bodies and in the designs used in rites, but it also appears in paintings and engravings in caves. How far the cave-art goes back it is impossible to say, though old paintings have certainly been worked over and over. Again there is widespread uniformity, even at distances of 1,500 miles, though some designs may have a limited range, e.g. a key-pattern used by the Karadjeri of the northwest, who alone know the chant that gives it meaning and animates it. The paintings include outline drawings, silhouettes with or without borders, and polychrome works (four colours). There are also stencilled hands.

The decorative designs are abstract, though the natives attach definite traditional meanings to them. Rules are hard to formulate, as the same lines, curves, circles, have different meanings according to context. Concentric circles can signify wild yams, emu meat, and so on. A Yirrkale native explained a sacred design as follows: the black cross-hatched bands were branches and tree-roots, the white dots above were bees, the white and yellow dots their droppings, a string of white and yellow dots the hard wax, and panels across the middle were 'sugarbags'. (The first find of honey made by a boy has magical significances for his future.) On cricket churingas of the western Aranda, large concentric circles seem to represent the tree where the crickets sit; small ones, the chrysalis stage from which they fly up; wavy lines, footprints in the sand; dots, the body-decorations of grub ancestors. The commonest and perhaps oldest systems consist of parallel fluting, V-figures, and zigzag lines; later, though still ancient, are diamond patterns (perhaps from New Guinea). Concentric circles and U-figures are spread in north and central areas (perhaps again from New Guinea) as also the totemic paintings.

The latter show a clear effort at realism; and dancers are depicted with the vital grasp of movement found in African cave-art. More stylised methods appear when the artists deal with ancestral or mythical figures like the Lightning Brothers, dual heroes, at the centre of the lightning totem near Delaware. We find the larger brother depicted twelve feet high, including headgear, with red and yellow stripes for his body-painting. Natives say the works are produced by ancestral spirits returning to the totem-centre in the rainy season.

Generally there is an affinity with paleolithic cave-art; but the artistic impulse seems arrested, capable within its limits (especially on the decorative side), but lacking expansive energies as compared with the great festivals, their myth-rituals and songs.

Mothers. There is nothing analagous to the mother-figures of paleolithic art. Yet there are many signs that at some distant time the Australians had mother-cults. We find women among the ancestors, with the usual myths of wandering. Thus, in West Australia the Wadamun tell of the old woman Dodaduriman who came up from the salt water to travel the Valley of the Daly River. She made the river-valley and all its natural features; before going down where a spring still bubbles, she gave the natives their marriage-system and class-names. The Kakadu tell of a similar mother, Ungulla Robumbun, who carried her children around, leaving them at various points to start off the different languages. She threw away her genitals and breasts, with a woman's fighting-stick, for the lubras, and gave a flat spear-thrower and a reedspear to the men; then created mosquitoes and went into a waterhole. The Kakadu also tells of an ancester Imberombera, who came from the sea with a belly full of children. From bamboo-rings round her head hung dilly-bags packed with yams. She encountered Wuraku coming from the west with his monstrous penis, which weighed him down. He rested and turned into a rock, but she travelled on, planting yams and spirit-children, the mother of ten tribes. She gave them all instructions as to the food supply and totems.

Some myths make women the inventors of the bull-roarer; and at times an old woman takes the place of the dual heroes in introducing the stone knife for circumcision, e.g. among the southern Arunta. The women of the Bandicoot totem at Alkniara performed down-ceremonies and made introcision on one another; a great gully arose on the spot with a large stone in the middle to mark the spot where they went down into the earth. The Kariera let women take part in totemic rites. And some anthropologists interpret the *churinga* as the mother or as part of her undying body.

In east Arnhem Land we meet the Djanggawul, two sisters and a brother.

The sisters are the important figures, the dual heroes. They come across the sea, stopping at the island-of-the-dead of the moiety concerned with their ritual. They are closely linked with the sun. A name for the noon-sun is *dagu*, meaning their vaginas. They bring emblems that express their procreative and productive powers; they urinate streams or pools; and throughout, the natives make the sexual implications explicit. The act of the Djanggawul's striking-out water from the earth is compared to coitus; trees are penises; certain forms of plant-life are divided into male and female; children are 'semen'. But the term for coitus is to 'work a woman'; children are the 'result of work'. The sexual imagery is thus in fact at all points fused with the productive.

The Two Sisters are Original Mothers of the various *dua* moiety clansfolk, as well as of the *jiritja*. They are Mother Goddesses in the true sense of the term, for although they were allegedly instrumental in populating the greater part of eastern Arnhem Land, they are responsible also for all subsequent fertility. Aborigines call the Sisters 'Our Mothers'. When men cut the fringes of the sacred dilly-bags, or perform ritual, they are the 'Sons of the Djanggawul', when they enter the sacred ground, marked out in a special way, they are entering their Mothers' uteri; when they enter the sacred hut on the ritual ground, they are also returning to their Mothers' uteri (or uterus, when one hut is used, referring to the elder). The same theme is expressed symbolically in a variety of ways. The whole concept of the return to the Mother on ritual occasions is particularly interesting. (BERNDT)*

The Kunapipi Mother again is said 'to let postulants out from her womb during ceremonial times'.

Arnhem land used to be visited by Indonesians down to the last century. There is a story, derived from songs, of the fishermen who taught the natives to make pottery for them. But the natives never made it for themselves.* (It would be of little value in their nomadic life.) But it would be hard to believe that the Djanggawul are simply an Indonesian intrusion, especially when we relate their ritual myth to the other indications of ancestresses of high importance; and after all, the totemic system hinges on the mother-taboo and the kinship-systems based on it.

Much of the Djanggawul rites are taken up with totemic dancing; and the ceremony, *dua nara*, is essentially revelatory. The dance-drama represents the arrival at a sacred spot and the journey of the Djanggawul, with invocations. The natural species of each visited spot are depicted. At one point the women

---

* The *dua* moiety carries on the Sisters' rites; the opposing moiety, the *jiritja*, is concerned with the ancestor Laintjung and his son Banaiyja. Other important ancestral figures, the Wanwaluk, are daughters of the Djanggawul.

† At least as late as the 16th-19th centuries pearl and trepang fishers from the Celebes visited Arnhem Land; there may well be influences from their rites in the Djanggawul complex. Certainly we cannot present that complex as in any way a primordial element of Australian rites and myths. At the most we can say that it shows how aspects of the outlook were able to accommodate themselves to procedures which look towards a developed mother cult.

gather round a tree or forked stick in the camp. The rite-leader climbs the tree and to the accompaniment of clapping stakes make invocations. The women, painted, dance round the tree. Pairs of dancers enact totemic creatures. Twice the women and children are covered with mats while the men dance round with spears, womeras, sticks, while invocations refer to the sites where the Sisters gave birth to the people. The men call out the sacred names for child-birth, coitus, and so on; and the women and children emerge. Near the end of the rites the novices are painted as dead men, so that their spirits may enter the timespace where the Djanggawul preside, with the dead and the living, and when the totems and ancestors and *wongar* dreaming-spirits are all one. Finally comes a sacramental bath of men, women and children, led by men representing geese or diving-duck; dances of totemic fish and then the higher totem dances and the manifestation of the *rangga* emblems to the neophytes in various stages of initiation. The older men meditate or enter into 'theo-logical' arguments; and there is a sacramental meal of the cycad-palm nut-bread, which has been made by the women and sung over on the ritual ground. The bread symbolises the food-resources as a whole and has been given a sacredness that approximates it to a *rangga* emblem.* By eating it, the novices become 'more *rangga*', more a vital part of the Djanggawul life and world.

We may note that as the Djanggawul go about they leave Dreamings, sacred drawings and emblems. Songs towards the conclusion of the rite-cycle stress the sacredness of women, and the myth recounts the men's taking-over of the rituals which they originally devised. The rite-pattern in its entirety expresses the development of the individual and the group from childhood to initiation, from birth to death, defining the movement in terms of the seasonal rhythm of the earth.

Here is an example of the songs of the dance-mime, the song of the mangrove-bird:

> O, what is this? A small mangrove bird, *waridj*.
> Yes, it is a mangrove bird. I thought I heard a strange sound,
>   as it cried among the mangroves.
> Yes, it saw the daylight coming, the stars fading.
> This is the mangrove bird: it heard the water rising and roaring,
>   with foam splashing:
> Crying at the water swirling within the well at Wagulwagul,
>   splashing against the mat, the fish-traps.
> So the bird looked back, and saw the daylight spreading from Bralgu,
>   driving away the night:
> saw the daylight coming, the darkness clearing away.

---

* *Rangga* are sacred poles. There are several types: tree *rangga* from which trees arose when the Djanggawul plunged them into the earth; *rangga* connected with the creation of springs. They represent vulva, penis or testicles; stone ones are derived from the stone out of the younger Sister's vagina. Or they are symbols of Djanggawul. Many *rangga* emblems have been developed, poles or objects of totemic origin. All are decorated with clan patterns, and most have feathered string attached.

Looking back, it saw the Morning Star sinking.
  Its longdrawn cry echoed up to the clouds—to the woman clouds,
    to the large spreading pregnant clouds.
  Sound drifting upward into the message clouds, clouds massing together.
  Its long cry comes from the *djuda* tree, the poles of the fish-trap:
    scratching the trunk as it sits clasping the tree.
  Tired, it cries as the water comes rising up :
    the longdrawn cry merges with the roar of the water.
  The longdrawn cry, as the water rises, tossing:
    it grows tired from the splashing spray, the rising wellwater.
  With a long cry it clasps the *djuda*, watching the water at Wagulwagul,
    rising against the mat.

Totem and Taboo. We have now glanced at Australian culture enough to
bring out something of its richness and complexity. The problem of sorting out
its ingredients and levels has hardly been scratched. How then are we to distinguish any essential paleolithic aspects from later intrusive elements and
from the elaborations built up over the more or less static millenia under
various strains and stresses (including the external contacts and intrusions) ?
It has been argued for instance that the fourfold or eightfold segmentation
inside the tribe is of fairly recent growth and originated in the Kimberley area.

Generally, as we would expect, the cultures seem richer in the north than in
the south. Cape York Peninsula seems the main point of entry for new
influences, and the principal trade-routes suggest the lines on which they would
operate—down the east coast, through the grassland to round Lake Eyre and
on to the south coast; or via Arnhem Land and Kimberley to the centre and
southwest. In the southeast, from Victoria to South Queensland, we find the
rather vague skyfather or supreme being. Most tribes trace descent through
the mother—in almost all Queensland and N.S.W., most South Australia and
southern West Australia—but in the west and north and a small part of
Victoria they are patrilineal.

In the taboos concerning Totem and Mother we can however safely claim
to touch a deep element which must go far back. Here lies the obscure yet
pervasive element which alone makes a unity of Australian culture and differentiates it from other cultures where these taboos may be present but do not
show themselves with such simple force, such irreducible purity. In every way
the taboos appear as the natural expressions of a hunting and foodgathering
society in the throes of separating itself out from nature. Though they persist
in early agricultural communities, they could not arise from them. Here then
we touch the core of Australian stone-age society.

First, let us note the strong element in initiation-rites, which, as well as
expressing separation-and-union, also aims at making the male ritually a
female. We see this aspect most clearly among the Aranda (who show little or
no revulsion from menstruation). These people declare that men can bear
children as well as women; by the painful operation of subincision they carve

the female genitals on the male making a wound in the urethra which they call a vagina. At certain rituals they make this *aralta* hole bleed.*

A little consideration will bring out that the two taboos central in Australian life are in fact identical. Both totem and mother are sources of life, of food. The prohibition against eating the totem is only a different aspect of the taboo against mating with the mother. Eating and coitus are not clearly differentiated; food is indeed thought one of the main sources of impregnation. Among the Kurhai if a young man meets a girl and says, '*Djeetgun*', and she replied, '*Yeering*, what does the *yeering* eat?' the result will be a marriage. Among the Dieri Mundoo the term 'taste' is also used for 'family'.

In the *alcheringa* both taboos did not exist. There was no prohibition of incest or of eating the totem. *Alcheringa* ends in some act of violence, conflict, guilt, which brings about the taboos. Thus, the dual heroes who introduce circumcision operate on their father and kill him. The Loritja say that the Tukutitia came out of the earth in various places in human form; but an evil being, a huge dog striped white and black, came out of the west and attacked them. They took animal shapes to escape; the dual heroes appeared and drove the demon back to his western cave; the totem-ancestors then regained human form but kept their power of animal shape-shifting. The Dieri myth declares that totemism was introduced to stop incestuous marriages.

The way in which the taboos arose is not hard to imagine. We have noted how human evolution involved a deep conflict between a sense of union and a sense of separation. As men develop the first stages of their specific consciousness, they feel their oneness with all life, all nature. In killing animals, even in snatching a berry or digging up a root, they are killing or maiming their own flesh. At the same time they feel in the woman a mysterious power to renew life, to replace the killed or broken thing. They devise their imagery of relationship to nature out of birth and coitus. (Coitus is not realised for what it is, but it is felt as resulting from a strange and deep compulsion to enter the very cavern of the mysterious life-power, a dangerous act.) Woman and earth are vaguely but potently linked; and the flowings of menstrual blood are related to the life-giving streams and rain-showers. Coitus and killing are equally frightening, yet men cannot live without them.

The first clear relationship which is consciously established must be to the mother; and the awareness of this relationship involves the differentiation of her from other women. At the same time the problem of the relationship to the animals on whom men depend for food continues to trouble. The life-cavern from which a man came cannot but have a special power for him. To return into it by coitus begins to seem a reversal of the life-process, perilously

---

* Among the Wiko of New Guinea, the first woman who passes over the spot where the novice's blood spilt at circumcision is buried will fall ill of a constant bleeding of the menses. 'The blood is definitely identified with menstrual blood' (GLUCKMAN). Altars in the villages are made of sticks stuck in the ground. 'The lodge altar is a stick (man), thrust into a ring of leaves (woman), which is buried below the ground.'

confounding life and death. And how is he to protect himself against the revenge of the killed animal? The creature must survive, the hunter feels, in some form; indeed he knows that it has actually gone inside himself—to be evacuated in a different shape. (There are many Australian myths of spirit-creation by evacuation.)

Apes and monkeys, who, like men and unlike most other mammals, do not have a limited season of rut, but enjoy a continuous sexual life, are capable of inflicting self-mutilation. We hear of a rhesus monkey who, separated from his mate, bit himself violently in the legs; caged monkeys often mutilate themselves out of what seems thwarted rage; orang-utangs in a natural state commonly lack a nail or a joint of the big toe—apparently as the result of their own action, though one observer has suggested that the mother intentionally mutilates her offspring. This capacity to turn back on oneself an emotion of rage, frustration, fear, could easily beget the first scarifications and mutilations among the earliest men as the result of a sense of guilt—the procedures in time being systematised as custom at crucial moments in the life-process, moments when the accumulated fears were purged by a collective act. (From the stencillings it seems that the paleolithic men mutilated their fingers.)

Here we must recollect the ideas and forms of magic which primitive men developed. There, the part is identical with the whole. On this basis have been built up the many forms of vicarious sacrifices and redemptions, which carry on into the full light of history. One man dies for the many; a pig dies for a man; a valuable belonging is thrown overboard to save a seafarer in a storm. If men renounce the dangerous mother, they may safely embrace another woman; if they concentrate on some particular beast or plant the guilt that they feel at all killing and rending, then they can safely kill or rend the others. Thus the two taboos develop together, intertwined; and by forswearing mother (or sister, who has had contact with the same womb), and totem, a man controls his sense of guilt, his deep anxiety, and regains a secure place in the universe.

However, to phrase the process like this is to falsify it. For the essence of the matter is social. It is the collective agreement, the ritual, which provides the conviction of safety; and to bring this conviction about, the group develops the dance-mime of death and rebirth, in which the danger is dramatised and overcome.

Primitive hunting groups often show clearly the guilt they feel in the hunt. To compensate the killed animals, the Eskimos, who think that their souls have take refuge in the bladders, hold a Bladder Festival. They preserve the bladders, blown-up and hung in the Men's Houses; at the end of the rites they take them to a hole in the ice, open them, and thrust them under; the spirits swim out to sea and enter into an unborn animal of their own kind. Thus a supply of game is assured and the hunter feels that the animals will let him approach and kill them. Mask-dances are aimed at influencing and propitiating the spirit-in-the-mask, which has the power of multiplying the species it represents.

At the Inviting-in-Feast the spirits of the animals are called in to participate and enjoy the songs, dances, offerings in their honour.

Masked dance, Bushmen: some with antelope heads. Women and other men clap hands: rock shelter near Orange Springs.

Among bear-hunters from the Lapps to the Aino of the Japanese islands we find similar propitiary rites.* Among the Aino we see the beast becoming sacred and almost a sort of deity. A woman suckles a cub, thus making it a member of the group. When it is full grown, it is baited, gagged and strangled. The invitation to the feast runs on these lines: 'I am about to sacrifice the dear little divine thing who resides among the mountains. My friends and masters, come to the feast. We will then unite in the great pleasure of sending the god away'. The killing is accompanied with many apologies and with promises that it will be sent with all due ceremony to its ancestors. 'O you divine one, you were sent into the world for us to hunt. O you precious little divinity, we worship you, pray hear our prayer. We have nourished and brought you up with a great deal of pains and trouble, all because we love you so. Now, as you have grown big, we are about to send you to your father and mother. When you come to them, please speak well of us and tell them how kind we have been; please come to us again and we will sacrifice you.'*

---

* Among the Lapps the man who has found the lair leads the hunt with a brass ringed staff (brass being magical). The killed bear is stuck with twigs and part of a praise hymn is sung. (For a year no woman may ride behind the reindeer who draws the body home.) The hunters sing all the way back. The women, in their best clothes, stand in the tents with backs to the entries, holding brass rings (to keep the bear out). The men creep in under the covers at the back. The women greet them with songs, peer at them through the brass rings, and sprinkle them with juices of chewed alder-bark (neutralising the spirit-power emanating from them). The meat has to be eaten all in one day with various rites. All sing antiphonally and smear themselves and the tent poles with blood. The bones must not on any account be broken; they are buried with the snout and tail to the sound of incantations, with a bark vessel of alder juice set before the snout. The skin is stretched between two trees and the women shoot arrows at it; the husband of the woman who hits will kill the next bear. Not for three days and nights must the men touch their wives. Then they run round the fire three times while the women throw ashes on them and sing the end of the bear song. The men return to normal life at last.

Among the Australians the totemic rites salve the guilt at killing the animals, who are thought once to have been human. But the fear and sense of guilt bursts out at the death of a fellow-tribesman—as it does also at any infringement of the totemic taboo. Not all the magical apparatus of detection and reprisal avails. Thus, as a man of the Warramunga of Central Australia lay dying, groups of men and women flung themselves on to him in a wild scrum. Then the women cut into their scalps with digging-sticks till blood poured down their faces. Male relatives gashed themselves deeply across the thighs with stone knives till they could not stand. When a few hours later the man died, the scene was repeated more violently, the women battering one another over the heads with war-clubs. Next morning men were lying about with slashed thighs, but the women were still lacerating their scalps and the dead man's widows were searing their own wounds with burning sticks. The natives said that these actions placated the dead man.

The sense of guilt, centred on the fear of death and of spirit-reprisals, at higher levels of social organisation can lead to collective ordeals, e.g., by poison, which for instance in Africa have at times almost wiped groups out; or it can beget waves of self-mutilation and flaggellation as in medieval Europe at moments of crisis. The emotions gathering in such actions are more socially complex than at the Australian level; but there is an affinity at the core.*

Any acquaintance with the intensity of emotion concentrated in the taboos under consideration makes ridiculous the theory that men agreed not to eat their totems so as to build up a system of self-denying ordinances whereby one group helped the others by fertilising its particular choice.

The Dual Systems. Still, the exogamous system derived from the incest-taboo and the 'mutual aid' implied by the totem-taboo are clearly entangled; and we have yet to ask why such symmetrical and deftly interwoven systems evolve. The answer seems to lie in the fact that as men manage to build up fair-sized groups they feel a deepening kinship within their group, which does not apply to groups outside it. The tribe is 'the people', just as later the Egyptians, for example, looked on themselves as 'men', but did not allow the title to non-

---

* No native of Madagascar believed in natural death; with the exception of centenarians, all were thought to die of magic. The usual form of condolence was, 'Cursed be the magician who killed him'. The Papuan Kais took all deaths as magical and the kin pursued the 'murderer' with blood vengeance. 'Nearly all wars between villages and tribes are caused by such punitive expeditions'. Unavenged, the dead send bad luck in the hunt, wild boars ravaging the fields, etc. An epidemic shows the wrath of the spirits, which can be appeased only by the death of the magic-worker. On the Ivory Coast each normal death used to cause four or five more deaths through ordeals used to find the guilty. The Madagascar poison-ordeal was computed to kill one in five. In the last century a tenth of the population had undergone it, with some 40 to 50,000 deaths in a generation. Some tribes, such as the Uwet of the Calabar river in W. Africa, almost wiped themselves out with collective ordeals. 'Direct survivals of the ordeal appear in all the earliest known legal codes of civilised peoples; and after Roman law had wiped the ordeal out in Western Europe, the barbarians re-introduced it and the Catholic Church organised it for criminal trials'.

Egyptians. If a man may not find his bride in the family, he must still find her inside the group. The woman who is safe and who yet owns the strongest woman-*mana* is the daughter of the mother's brother. Thus it seems that from cross-cousin marriage arose the large scale system of marriage with anyone who belonged to a group equivalent to that of cousins. Indeed such an evolution would be inevitable among people who think collectively.

It is only by realising the fact that the group, and not the individual, lies at the basis of tribal organisation, that this organisation, as well as their habits, customs, and beliefs, can be understood. For example, in the Pitta Pitta tribe (Queensland) a woman calls her actual mother *Umma*, but applies the same name to each member of the group of women any of whom her father might lawfully have married; a man calls his actual wife or wives *Nupa*, but applies the same term to each member of the group any of whom he might lawfully have married; and so on right through the whole series of terms. (B. SPENCER)

There is however more to the matter than that. The principle of rhythmic economy and balance applies here as in the dance. The dual system not only provides a method of safe marriage and of interlinking totems, it also offers an organisation which is stable in its equipoise and helps men to feel at home in the universe. The equation of the living tribe and the spirit-ancestors (who are also the forces of nature) finds its inner reflection in the equation of one moiety with another. That is, a dual system is felt to embody an harmonious balance which in itself helps to provide a sense of safety.

We may validly point to the various phenomena of nature which reveal the principle of unity based on fused opposites or of development brought about by the halving of an original unity: electricity with its dual aspects, mitosis or cell-halving, the bilateral symmetry of so many organisms, and so on.

The growth of segmentary structures is a constant feature of social development, and it seems that certain forms of structure can only reach stability and permanence by that means. (RADCLIFFE-BROWN)

This segmentation can express itself by an expanding complexity of inner balances or by a rupture which discards an inadequate system for a new set of balances and fused opposites.

That the dual system of totemic society was no accidental growth is proved by the way in which it is not discarded by the following phases of social development. What we see in history is the continual re-assertion of dual systems according to the general law suggested above.

Cave-art Reconsidered. We can now glance back at paleolithic art and ask how much our investigation of the totemic tribes helps us to understand it. At once we can say that there seems no system such as we see in the Australian cave-art. There is no question of moieties or clans, each depicting its own beast or plant. Wild oxen, bisons, equids mingle; and the signs do not vary from cave to cave.

Still, there can be no doubt that what is represented is the paleolithic spirit-world, a version of *alcheringa*; and so in a rudimentary way the beasts may have elements of the totemic ancestor. The Australian Dreamtime, like the holy store-cave of the *churingas*, lies underground; the ancestors come out of the earth and go down into it.:

The souls of the totem-gods went into the earth and they are called *iwopata*, i.e. the inner hidden ones, the invisible ones. The eastern Arunta called them *eriutarinja*. These souls of the totem-gods have a red body and live in great subterranean caves, and therefore they are called *rella ngantja* (hidden men). At night they emerge from the caves to visit their *tjurunga*-sticks and stones, which are regarded as their former bodies. (STREHLOW)

The *alcheringa* heroes sleeping in their caves are the lineal ancestors of the Arthurs and Barbarossas sleeping in caves till awakened by some magical sign to return and redeem their people.

The imagery of ancestral beings who live in caves or underground spaces remains central in creation-myths such as those of pre-Columban America. It persists in the imagery of a life after death in the underworld, which in time becomes hell; and it plays an important part in shamanist ritual of the spirit-journey as well as in epic poetry and the religious motive of hell-harrowing. The paleolithic artists, shamans, and initiates made their daring and difficult journey into the bowels of the earth under some deep compulsion. They must have been terrified, yet upheld by a conviction of penetrating into the very heart of the mystery of birth, death, and rebirth.

Only at Pech-Merle however do the mother-cults and the cults of animal-fertility come together. Among the paleolithic folk, as among the Australian, some sort of divorce had come about between the two cults; but here the mother as well as the beast-to-be-killed receives her full due.

The cave-art then seeks to fill *alcheringa* with its spirit-denizens, to ensure the fertility-multiplication. On this interpretation there is no conflict between the animal-representations, the fantasies, the masked dancers or shamans. Sometimes the art-image was connected with direct hunt-magic, but the main impulse seems rather that of peopling the spirit-world. Though we need not look for compositions in our sense of the term, it is probable that the caves, besides showing random juxtapositions and superimpositions, often embody a definite system of images. They may even express various paleolithic myths. There is an association of equine and bovid forms that seems to have a magical significance in paintings and engravings. On some small objects and in sculptures of Southwest France we find the mother-figure linked with the bison. Thus, in the Laussel relief the mother holds a bison horn in a way that suggests the later horn-of-plenty. Coloured with red pigment, she is perhaps pregnant, and turns her egg-shaped featureless face to the horn. On the ground were four similar reliefs and a figure that seems to represent childbirth. A male figure may be shooting a bow.

The apparent division between the cults of the animal and the mother may represent a sex-division in the persons looking after the cults, the men dealing with the animals and the women with the mother; or it may merely mean that separate fraternities have arisen for each cult. In the ancient world we find the

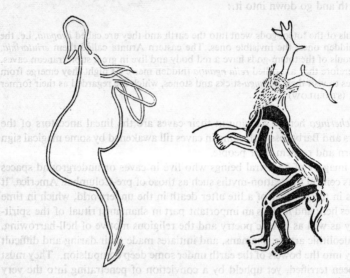

Female figure, finger-drawn, Pech-Merle, Lot: ? masked sorcerer from Les Trois Frères, Ariège, painting in black.

Great Mother with purely female rites on some occasions and with womanised (eunuch) priests. Rites like the Eleusinian Mysteries are dominated by the Mother, and the Dionysiac cult has at its heart the female *thiasoi*. In West Africa we find mysteries restricted to women (among the Ibibio, in the Ekoi cult of Nimm, and in the Bundu of Sierra Leone). Among the Ibibio of Southern Nigeria the important Egbo Society of the Efik and Ekoi men has the tradition of having been originally a women's society, of which the men learned the secrets and which they then forcibly took over. The most dreaded of all the secret societies, the Ekkpo Njawhaw (Ghosts, the Destroyers) with its terrible Mother, is also declared to have once belonged to the women. Even in the Great Warriors Club, the Ekong (War), at the yam harvest a man dresses as a woman and sings from a tree-arbour as the Mother of Ekong; and without this mime there would be no blessing on the next year. (The Fuegian rite, Kina, was said to express the rising of the males against the women 'who had formerly held the authority and possessed the secrets of sorcery'.)

There is no reason why already in Aurignacian days there may not have been female cults which at least in part were the sole preserve of the women. But what of the totem? We have seen how totem, incest-taboo and dual organisation are organic sections of a single whole, which plays a crucial part in human history; they represent a phase which has a necessary role in human development. (This does not mean that every group has to pass through it. In history we find groups skipping whole phases through contacts with other groups that have already passed through them, and so on.) Various hypotheses, all unproveable, can be advanced to explain why the totem seems absent from paleolithic art. The groups may have passed through a totemic phase before cave-art arises, so that by the Aurignacian period they carry on a social system with a large number of plants and creatures as totems, but apply general ideas and rites drawn from that system to deal with the great herds or the feared beasts-of-prey—just as the Plains Indians of America did not seek to incorporate strictly in their totemic systems the bison-herds on which they had come to depend. Alternatively we may see the paleolithic groups as in a proto-totemic phase, in which the sharp systematisation of the Australians has not yet grown up, and in which perhaps even an *alcheringa* phase without incest-taboo exists. The totemic system, with its two sets of taboos, would then arise in the period of decline, when fear, frustration and guilt would plausibly accompany the crisis in development, the need for large scale re-adaptations. Without some such hypothesis as either of the above it is hard, indeed impossible, to explain the social and cultural forms we find emerging into the light of history in neolithic days.

A Final Glance at the Totem.   Much argument has gone on as to whether we can call the totemic system religious. Certainly the totem does not demand worship and abase the worshipper; but we err if we draw any sharp line between religion and totemism. Nor can we call the totemic phase simply one of magic. The totemic rites are sacramental, just like the main rites of elaborated religion (which in turn are permeated with magical concepts). Further we cannot see the primitive as functioning in a prelogical condition. There are limitations to his thinking, as there are to the thought-forms of any cultural phase, but he does his best to grapple with cause and effect, and to build a comprehensive world-picture.

True, the tribesman, though unable to do without his totem, feels it a fellow rather than a deity set up over against him. He is therefore ready to demand fertility-aid rather than pray for it. The Kakadu hold out the sacred sticks and stones in a dance round a central figure, crying '*Brau brau*' (give give). Society has to be broken by inequalities and oppressions before the totem or ancestral spirit loses its close bond of fellowship with the group and stands above it as a god demanding prayer and submission. The old totemic attitude however continues in what is often called a legalist or formal attitude to the gods: the belief that if one faithfully carries out one's ritual duties, one has the right to demand co-operation from the spirit-world. Though such an attitude does take legalistic tinges in a world of property rights and dues, at root it treats the deity as an equal in a contractual relation, not as a lord whose ways cannot be questioned or controlled.

The dual system has its aspect as a vital balance between men and Nature, but also it seeks a point of arrest. The deadening and abstracting side appears above all in the external soul or *churinga*, where we see the tendency to reverse the notion of all things as alive (as spirit) and see them as dead (as things). The way in which the primitive carves and cuts himself up, or at least tattoos and paints himself, for ritual reasons, is linked with his idea of his real-self as a stone or piece of wood which can be carved without loss of character—indeed with a valuable addition to its being. His abstract art is the extreme expression of the self as a dead thing that can be hacked about and reconstructed to its advantage. In this way his artistic expression wavers between a vital fusion of organic rhythms and a dead geometrical abstraction, between a powerful sense of the unity of all natural forces and a reduction of the life-process to static and abstract forms, a thingification of man and Nature.

In describing the formation of the dual system an important aspect has so far been neglected: the division of the sexes, made all the more mysteriously significant by the relation of maternity to the spirit-world, and the division of labour that further cuts the sexes apart. At the totemic level the sole specialised profession is that of the shaman. Otherwise division of labour appears only in the allocation of different tasks to men and women. From the rich set of opposites—tribe and nature, individual and group, man and *churinga*, *alcheringa* and the present, male and female (with male and female work)— there derives the idea of life as, in all respects, a fusion of opposites. We shall see how this idea develops.

Meanwhile we may note how the totemic system with its symmetrical elaborations builds a complete world picture, with man and nature both separate and united. Everything is fitted in. Thus a Kimberley group, fighting to maintain its dual organisation of the cosmos despite intrusions of the modern world, allotted aeroplanes to one world-half and lorries to the other. The tribe thus reflects the order of the universe, a unity composed of a pair of opposites.

3: Transition to Civilisation

Mesolithic. With the ice-age ending, mammoths extinct, herds replaced by more solitary game, and forest-trees moving into the steppes, men had to find new equipment and methods. Hunting was still the main source of food, but more stress was now laid on fishing, and the dog had come in as an aid. Bands of archers ranged over the coasts and woodlands. Boats were used for short journeys—timber being the main barrier to movement. (Techniques to deal with it may have come in time from the descendants of the paleolithic folk who followed the reindeer north.) With pine and birch filling the tundras, groups from the Pennines to the Urals adapted themselves to the new conditions. At Star Carr in Yorkshire fish-spears mingle with heavy adze-blades for chopping wood. The fens and lakes gathered specialised hunter-fishers. These men mounted flint-axes in a way that suggests the modern axe or adze; they had sledges and canoes with paddles. Though making seasonal movements, they were beginning to settle on the coasts. (Towards 4000 B.C. the North Sea and the Baltic appeared.) The climate grew moister. There were signs of differences in social status beginning, and of warfare, e.g., a man killed by an arrow in the lung in the settlement at Téviec in Brittany.

Drawings and pictographs: first four lines from Spanish rock paintings, with pebbles from Mas d'Azil, S. France; fifth line, all pebbles: sixth, paintings, Sierra Morena and La Pileta, Spain—the last two on right, and all seventh line, early Egyptian designs and marks.

Art-forms are meagre, abstract. Tentative scrawls seem to be attempting clumsy generalisations of structure and movement; perhaps there is no conscious aim and men surrender their hands to a blind impulse. However at times definite geometrisations are achieved, e.g., the meander at Mezin. We may compare the key-pattern of the Karadjeri tribe of N.W. Australia; meandering forms seem to represent the wanderings of totemic ancestors.

The collapse of the art-faculty had its positive aspect. Paleolithic art had been fundamentally intuitive; the artist's eye was unable 'to isolate those simple geometrical shapes we know so well'. When the special conditions of plenty—and probably of group harmony—are ended, the pressures of fear and the need to grapple with new problems break down the intuitive comprehension of wholes, and the artist lacks analytic powers to re-adapt his art. Men have to start all over again, from bedrock, this time applying the analytic faculty in a slow and painful rediscovery of the nature of form.

Agriculture. The neolithic revolution creating agriculture took place in southwest Asia. Wheats and barleys were developed, and about the same time sheep and goats domesticated. Early farming villages began by 7000 B.C. as we know from Jericho, founded about the time when the mesolithic group at Star Carr was flourishing. A perennial spring made Jericho an oasis in the bare Rift valley, its inhabitants growing till they occupied some six acres guarded by a rockcut ditch, 27 feet wide and 8 feet deep, and an inner stone rampart. At least one tower existed, 25 feet high. After several reconstructions the site was left. Then new folk came in, building a new wall and houses of stone and mud-brick before B.C. 6000. They did not grind stone or make pots.

By the 5th millenium farming villages or townships were growing up in the wide area called the Fertile Crescent, which reached from Egypt through Mesopotamia to North India and included three great river-systems, those of the Nile, the Tigris-Euphrates, the Indus. The folk made pots built up out of clay and had well-adapted tools. Female figures are common and show the importance of the mother-cult, with perhaps a strong economic and social position of women as hoe-cultivators and potters. (Fingerprints on a Russian neolithic pot have been diagnosed as female; and rings, usually worn by women, were used to decorate Iron Age pots in Germany.)

The farming method seems dry cultivation which involves soil-exhaustion and a certain amount of moving about. By B.C. 4000 farmers had reached the Middle Elbe. In the main centres, however, ways of ending nomadism were developed. There may have been a certain alternation of tillage and pasturage; along the Nile and in lower Mesopotamia the farmers could rely on the river-waters. Slowly agricultural methods travelled west into Europe and east into Asia. Rice appears in China about B.C. 2000, probably earlier in India. Cultivated gourds, lima beans and squashes, found in a cave near Ocampo, Mexico, are dated about 6500; maize was grown in the southwest of the U.S.A. by 3600.

The grasp of cause and effect had been momentously extended. Men (or women) had realised that many plants grew from seeds and that their growth could thus be controlled. From this discovery grew the idea that the man planted a seed inside the woman, and the process of impregnation was rationalised, exalting the male as the seed-bearer. At the same time a new scheme evolved for explaining the survival of the spirits of the dead and their return: the dead rotted and germinated and brought forth new life. Under the shock of such ideas the systems of descent from the mother, which we may assume to have ruled (since we find so many survivals of them everywhere), began to break up. Their tenacity however was considerable, and we meet a confused series of transitional kindred forms.

Dual Organisation. The sets of symmetrical balance also came in for severe strain. One aspect of the dual organisation, however, long survived intact: the games played by two opposing sides and the antiphonal or dual structure of much ritual and dance-mime. The Australians practised ball-games with a fertility-significance. In Victoria the game was played with strips of opossum-pelt rolled up and sewn with sinews, or the grass-stuffed scrotum of a kangaroo. Here there was no inequality; simply the best side won. In Australia, Fiji and North America, the teams were the opposing moieties. This sort of ball-game has persisted into our day in such sports as football or cricket, derived directly from ritual practices, e.g., the Celtic game of hurling, played by two adjoining parishes, or the Indian game of lacrosse, taken over by the settlers in Canada.

On the other hand the ritual use of opposing voices or dance-groups also persisted both in religious services and in art-forms, though shedding much of its direct significance. Here are examples of it from groups in our own day still holding fast to the primitive dance-mime. First, the comparatively sophisticated Balinese:

For the greater part of the ritual the crowd moves absolutely as one man, now one arm describing a curve, now all the hands high in the air, and the thousand figures moving rhythmically like the sea churned by breezes, now all falling back with the arms at the sides, palms upwards, overlaying one another to form a huge rose, each petal a naked torso.

As the ritual reaches its climax, the crowd divides into two halves, each side rising in turn, those nearest the middle crouching, and each rank rising higher till the outermost are on tiptoe, accompanying their guttural noises with violent and dramatic gestures. This interplay between the two halves continues faster and faster, the human force now in another dimension, agitated more and more violently; until one is possessed and rushes to the centre between the two contending groups; as he speaks, the circles are reformed. (GORER)

There we have beautifully expressed the unity born of two opposing halves, with the emergence of the shaman, the possessed individual, at the point of crisis and resolution: the man who takes unto himself the whole movement and seeks no project it on a new level.

A more dramatic form appears among the Tukanos of Central Brazil, a people driven down from better conditions by the advent of the Spaniards. Here the balance is broken.

One of the dances was a vivid characterisation of the triumph of death, given by people to whom no death could be natural but always the result of dark magic and of the anger of demons. In the last three months three of the tribesmen had gone to join the shades of their fathers, and their death was now ceremonially to be bewailed.

Most of the masked dancers went outside of the *moloka*, sang a low mournful song, and danced in an endless circle. Two of the performers remained behind in the communal house, but they, too, were destined to play an important role. For when the other dancers attempted to return to the *moloka*, the two who remained behind, barred the entrance, and a ceremonial but very realistic fight broke out between the two groups. The dancers outside were the dark angry demons who were attempting to storm the *moloka* and bring death and disease in its midst. The two dancers inside were friendly spirits who were determined to prevent the advent of all evil.

During the struggle several of the womenfolk, the relatives of the dead men, raised up a long wailing croon. For a long time, in spite of inferior numbers, the defenders put up a successful fight, but in the end the spirits of evil broke through and obtained possession of the *moloka*. The wailings of the women changed into a chant of despair and ended with bitter sobs.

I had witnessed the Indian equivalent of a mystery play, but whereas most mystery plays represent the eventual triumph of good over evil, this Indian ritual showed with bitter realism the overwhelming victory of death. (McGOVERN)

However it was followed by a phallic dance in which seed was scattered from cones; and there were animal-miming dances. At the end the masks, which had been 'the temporary homes of the demons', were all burned. The medicine-men and others who had taken a drug *kaapi* swore that they had witnessed the spirits incarnating themselves in the masks during the dance; but the fire-passage carried them away and prevented harm to the Tukanos. The dancers were all lesser tribesmen; the chief and his relatives merely watched. 'Some of the most important roles were played by two insignificant members of the community. This, it seemed, was done purposely'.

The ball-game appears in myth, to express the dual element in the universe. In Persian religion the good and evil principles, Ormuzd and Ahriman, played at it. In Mexico, where the game is *tlachtli*, played in an enclosed court with a rubber ball, it was associated with Xolotl (the twin, the double, the shadow, especially the night-shadow accompanying the sun). 'Old Xolotl plays ball, plays ball, in the magic playing ground', says a hymn cited by Sahagun. Bright and dark colours for the balls and the courts show the light-darkness symbolism. Manuscripts depict Xolotl playing ball with gods like the Moon. In one myth the sungod comes down on a spiders-web from the sky and engages in a ballgame at Tollan with the culture-hero Quetzalcoatl; in mid-game he changes to a jaguar and pursues his opponent off to Tlapallan, whence the people hope for his return. In these myths we see how a moral and social conflict has entered into the heart of the ball game.

The once equally-opposed moieties in fact are now rent by hatreds and inequalities. In Fiji the folk are divided into camps according to social status;

the villages are split into land-owning nobles and commoners (teeth-of-the-land). Sometimes the two halves of a tribe turn on one another as in the Pelews. Sometimes the conflict is merely between two sides of a village, two sides of a street, two parts of an island. In India, Micronesia and North America we meet the battling groups, generally organised round leading families.

A geometric sherd from Boiotia showing the goddess flanked by two lions, a waterbird above each arm, a fish on her skirt showing her as a goddess of river and lake.

Sometimes, especially in North America where the totemic elements are still strong, efforts are made to redefine the dual organisation on lines that maintain equipoise. Thus the Omaha have one great spirit, Wakonda, which reveals itself in two great principles, sky and earth. The tribe is divided into sky-people and earth-people, each with five sub-divisions. The former are concerned with the creative and directing forces of social and individual life, the latter with the rites and duties of physical welfare. The two groups take part in a ballgame; they hold the sacred pipes together; the sky-people camp to the north, the earth-people to the south. The Winnegabo are divided into two exagomous halves: Those Above and Those Below. The clan-totems of Those Above are birds; the clan-totems of Those Below are land and sea animals. The leading clan of the former is the Thunderbird, the clan of peace; that of the latter, the Bear, the clan of war.

On Tikopia in the Solomon Islands, the folk are divided into two main geographical groups, who are rivals in flying-fish netting, dancing, dart-hurling, and other matters. The competition is expressed also in boasting and slandering. Clan and kindred divisions survive, but the district-feud is perpetuated in clan-jealousies. (Here the clans have chiefs, elected from the chiefly houses, who are thought to own much lore and so to be influential with the feared clan-gods.)

The Masai of East Africa maintain a warrior organisation embracing all men between the years of 17 and 30. They are divided into a settled agricultural group and a nomadic pastoral group. The conflicts of the two halves resulted in the victory of the nomads. There are two groups of deities: the friendly black and the malevolent red, who are in ceaseless struggle.

In such examples we see the uneasy carrying-on of the dual form, which now often involves the superiority of one side. Homer had a clear memory of the phase we are describing. His utopian Isle of Ortygia contains Two Countries which divide the whole place between them; and on the Shield of Achilles we find Two Cities, one of peace and one of war. The peace-group spend their time in mating, in songs and round-dances, while the war-group is treacherous and violent, with gold as their emblem. We may compare dual chieftainship where one chief is often of war, as in Polynesia and in parts of New Guinea, or where at times the higher chief of the two is of peace, with feast-functions, opposed to the war-side and even with magical powers to stop war. In ancient Scandinavia the kings at Upsala seem temple-kings, differentiated from the war-kings of Vendel.

The causes for the violence are often much the same as those we found causing trouble between tribes in Australia; but now the feuds and furies occur between moieties as well. Thus, on San Cristoval in the Solomons, the villages and districts are divided into two moieties, and fighting goes on at the boundaries. In the Arosi district it comes about through women, magical deaths, unfair distribution of land among relatives at a man's death, grabbing of disputed land, breaking of a chief's taboo, desire on the part of a chief to own some famed weapon or ornament, a woman's stepping over a leaning tree under which man walks and so is degraded.

The Dual Heroes. The dual heroes of the myths now tend to quarrel and oppose one another. A euhemerised example is the legend of Romulus and Remus, the founders of Rome; Remus is killed by Romulus. (Rome, like Sparta, had dual magistracies.) The Biblical tale of Abel and Cain shows the conflict of the agricultural and pastoral brothers, with the land-settler blamed for the advent of murder and conflict. The mythological basis behind the tale is brought out by the Sumerian poem, *The Wooing of Inanna*, where the goddess has to choose between farmer and pastoralist in debate. Another example of the break is the allocation of immortality to one twin, mortality to other, as with the Greek Dioscures or with Herakles and Iphikles.*(This development is in turn linked with a worldwide series of customs and rites concerning twins, one of whom is often connected with sky-power. The advent of twins is usually

---

* An example of the yet-harmonious pair: a song of the Yimsungr clan of the Ao Nagas in Africa: 'A huge spreading rubber tree were the two brothers, and under its shade the village dwelt in peace. From the ripe berries that fell from the tree, sprang a race splendid as cock-hornbills.' Here they are compared to the mother-tree. Romulus and Remus had the fig tree of their original harmony. Compare the twin ancestors of the Baikari of Central Brazil, whom the Mother bears.

terrifying; for it seems as if the two halves of the individual have manifested themselves, the actual and the spiritual. Hence one twin is often killed or exposed.)

The Mother herself often appears in dual form. We have seen the Djanggawul Sisters in Australia. In Egypt there is the pair Isis and Nephthys; and in Sumeria Inanna owns a shadowy double. The Minoan Mother seems to have a younger self, foreshadowing Demeter and Kore of ancient Greece; and we find the same sort of doubling in the Irish and Gaelic folklore of the ancient earthmother. Further, the Mother, especially in archaic forms, maintains a sort of totemic symmetry in the designs where she stands between two animals or birds. In America we find the dual heroines, e.g., in the star-husband cycle of tales where two girls are rapt into the sky, one bearing the culture-hero who destroys monsters. Among the Navahoes there is a sungod, but the most revered figure is Estsanatlehi (the Woman who Transforms or Regenerates Herself), who is closely associated with a younger sister, White Shellwoman. There are dual war-gods or heroes, but of lesser importance.

More on Twins. As the part played by twins in myth and custom brings out so strongly the points made about the dual organisation and all that is connected with it, it is worthwhile to linger a little on the theme. The material about the twin-heroes in the phase of tribal breakdown has been thus summarised:

They have similar names, they are hostile, they are connected with different colours, they are elder and younger, superior and inferior. . . . They occur as Sunda and Upusandu and the numerous pairs of brothers with linked names in Indian Epic; as the founders of Tha-thun and Pegu in Burma, Titha Kumma and Dzaya Kumma, Thama and Wimala; as Khunlun and Khunlai, prince elder and prince younger, who come out of the sky to found the Ahom kingdom of Assam; the great ruins of Nanmatel in Ponape of the Carolines are connected with Olo-sipa and Ola-sopa. . . . The Kolta of British New Guinea claim descent from two brothers, Kirimai-kulu and Kirimaika; on Manu'a of Samoa, Fue, the son of Tangaloa, that came down from heaven, had two names, Fue-tan-gata and Fue-sa; he peopled two flat lands; one account of the early rulers of Tau in Manu'a makes the rulers of the two sides of the island. . . . the younger Alia and the elder Alia; in the story of the foundation of Samata in Savai'i the two boys are named Mata-i-uta and Mata-i-tai, Eyes-to-inland and Eyes-to-sea; in Tahiti Honoura called himself Maui-behind and Maui-in-front, a dual name for a single person; the ancestors of the race were Tiimaaraauta and Tiu Maarati; in America dual names of twins occur; the Kiche twins were Hun-came and Cucub-came, Hunbatz and Unchouen. Throughout the region, therefore, culture-heroes and other traditional beings have dual names.

They are also hostile and different in disposition; the story of Sunda and Upusandu centres round their ultimate quarrel over a girl; in Melanesia To Kumbinana and To Kovuvuru of the Gwelle Peninsula have different qualities, being clever and full of guile on the one hand, stupid and ignorant on the other; one is light and the other dark. In the Banks Islands and the New Hebrides, the two culture-heroes are hostile and possess different qualities: they play the ball game; one is light and the other dark among the Iroquis; the Huron twins are distinct, one being good and the other bad. The twins are connected, by the Zuni, with the right and the left hands.

Culture-heroes and other traditional beings differ in their characteristics from place to place, but correspond in their association to the ruling groups of the particular community with which they are connected. Where the community as a whole is connected with the underworld, no apparent distinction exists between the culture-heroes. (PERRY)

The Dioskouroi or Sky-youths of the Greeks seem the same in origin as the Aryan Asvins, who are connected with rain and the water-supply, and with horses. In Italy, as well as the founding twins, Romulus (Romus) and Remus, we meet Picumnus and Pilumnus; and the Greek cult fused with native ones. 'Throughout Italy we meet temples of these gods. . . Nothing is more common or more varied than the figured representations of Castor and Pollux'. In Greece they are commonly shown in the symmetrical design, flanking the Mother. Timaios tells us that the Dioscuric type of cult was the most striking fact of Celtic religion; and Tacitus records the Germanic twin-cult.*

Two Peruvian dual symmetrical designs.

The Dioscuric characteristics are roughly as follows. The twins have healing and fertilising powers, they cure blindness in particular; they are guardians of

---

* In Sumeria Tammuz has a vague second-self, Ningishzida: the pair seem identified with the constellation Twins. In Greece, Akrisios and Proitos are twins who quarrel even in the womb. Twins gather in the Argo (at root on a spirit-journey after the otherworld plunder of the Golden Fleece): Castor and Pollux, Idas and Lynceus, Herakles and Iphikles, Amphion and Zethos (with traces of the family of Aktor). One tradition says that Danae went to Italy with twin-sons, Argos and Argeus, and settled where Rome was later built. Apollo and Artemis were twins and Artemis had the Hyperporean pairs associated with her on Delos. Note Disocuric connection with Kabeiroi. We hear of a Welsh farmer afraid of a cow that bore twin-calves, and wanting to get rid of her. The fear is said to have spread in S. Wales and Cardiganshire; in La Vendée as in S. Africa—or, with regard to llamas, in Peru.

the Truth (e.g. in their relation to Mithras); in their later form they are horse-riders who appear in mid-battle (e.g. at Lake Regillus or Delphi) to help the faithful; they are associated with crafts, especially city-building; they uphold the rights of hospitality—visiting people in disguise and blessing those who are kindly, bring misfortune on the inhospitable. The *Book of Maccabees* records Dioscuric apparitions in support of the Jewish patriots against Seleucid oppression; and after the triumph of the Christian church large numbers of Dioscuric saints were provided as city-wardens. In the Syrian area and elsewhere even Jesus was looked on as a twin and coupled with St. Thomas; the Acts of Thomas make the pair do typical Dioscuric deeds. There was also a Gnostic tradition that looked on the Holy Ghost or Paraclete as Jesus's twin.

We have noted the reason for the fear of twins, but may further stress the way in which they upset the balance of the universe. The primitive believes in a cyclic series of births, so that normally a child is the returning grandfather. Custom decides how it will receive the appropriate Great or Umbilical Name, as it is often called. In East Greenland the name is a second soul and the child is named after the last person who has died in the group and whose spirit becomes one of the child's souls. Among the Lango in Africa the mother, when first offering her breast, speaks the names of the generation of the child's grandparents; the child is called by the name uttered at the moment he suckles. Among the Yoruba the parents ask a priest to tell. Further there is a strong belief that the caul or placenta is a spirit-double, and there is a wide series of customs connected with these magical objects. Natives of Queensland bury the caul under a twig-cone in a circle; the Bataks of Sumatra bury it under the house; others hang it in a tree or treat it with some sympathetic magic to control the child's future. Such beliefs ranged from the peasants of modern Europe to the folk of ancient Peru.

The Karo Bataks even affirm that of a man's two souls it is the true soul that lives with the placenta under the house; that is the soul, they say, which begets children. The Baganda believe that every person is born with a double, and this double they identify with the afterbirth, which they regard as a second child. The mother buries the afterbirth at the root of a plaintain tree, which then becomes sacred until the fruit has ripened, when it is plucked to furnish a sacred feast for the family (FRAZER). The navel-string and the placenta are called in South Celebes the 'brother' and 'sister' of the child. (CRAWLEY)

Twins upset all these elaborate schemes and introduce a startling disequilibrium into the family and the group. Among the Indians of British Guiana one of the twins was considered the child of a *kenaima*—which was both an external soul (such as all things, animate or inanimate, were thought to possess) and 'a man, who, having devoted himself to the slaying of some other man, has the power of separating the spiritual from the bodily substance'. Only the best efforts of the *pui* man (shaman) could avert the dangers inherent in such a situation.

When the twins were boy and girl, things were worse, as the cohabitation of the same womb amounted to a form of incest and made it necessary to kill them. The Ibibio of Southern Nigeria explained the impossibility of a twin-girl ever marrying:

Since the girl is not as other women, but part offspring of a demon, so the souls of children born to her go, sooner or later, to join their kindred, the evil spirits. When the husband dies also and comes to the ghost town, he finds the spirits of his accursed brood waiting to claim him as their father and shame him in the sight of all the shades.

Hence we find two diametrically opposed attitudes to twins. On the one hand is fear and horror, an impulse to kill or expose one or both of the twins at once; and on the other hand is a great awe amounting to a sort of worship, since here is revealed the full dual balance of life. Both fear and worship stem from the same ideas of the nature of twins.

Thus in the Niger Delta:

It is the standing law of the priests that no time is to be lost in removing the unfortu-ate infants. This is generally done by throwing them into the Bush, to be devoured be wild animals, or the equally ferocious driver ants, or sometimes, as is done by thy Ibibio, Ijo, and other coast tribes, by setting them adrift on creeks in roughly made baskets of reeds and bulrushes, when they are soon drowned or swallowed by sharks or crocodiles. (LEONARD)

(In Java the afterbirth is bedded on a little bamboo float, with flowers and fruit and burning candles, then set adrift in the stream.) The Ibibio used to throw the twins out to die, and the mother was sent to a sanctuary town for women in her condition, where she spent a year before she was considered purified. During that time she had to hide in the bush if she saw anyone. When the missionaries saved the children, the women were terrified. 'The wretched mother shook with fear whenever her glance fell on them. It is difficult indeed to persuade such women to nourish their unfortunate babes'.

Yet among other African tribes the twins were regarded as blessings, as potential bringers of plenty, even if rituals were needed to control the *mana* of such power-charged creatures. In America, both among the Peruvians and the northern tribes, twins were imagined as having control of the weather, especi-ally rain and thunder-and-lightning, and spirits or deities who manage sky-phenomena are either twins or are represented in a dual way, e.g. Haokah, the Sioux thundergod has his face divided into halves and the Chinook's culture-gods are two sons of the thundergod's daughter. The Baronga of South Africa call twins the Children of the Sky, a title corresponding to the Greek *dioskouroi* or the Lithuanian *dewa deli*, who ride in a chariot and free the sun's daughter from a tower. The water-relation of twins also appears in the way they are regarded at times as salmon and as fishing-controllers.

In Sicily, near Etna, was Palikeine, a town with a twin-cult and tradition of being founded, like Rome, as a sanctuary for runaway slaves. It is possible that such towns were brought into being as sanctuary-towns for mothers and their twin-children. The Paliki were twins born by a nymph whom Zeus ravished on a riverbank and who prayed, in fear of Hera, that the earth would open and take her in. In due time the earth opened again to let the twins out. (The name was thus thought to be derived from *palin ikesthai*, to come again: an impossible piece of etymology, but showing perhaps a memory of initiation ritual.) The Paliki gave oracular responses, connected with 'bottomless' springs that jetted boiling water and were called the Brothers of the Paliki. An oath-ordeal was enacted before these springs: the oath, written on a tablet, was thrown in—if it floated, all was well; if it sank, the penalty was said to be blindness or death.

Among the Igarras of the upper Niger, a yearly festival in honour of all twins in the community is held, and twins are held to be incapable of being poisoned as well as to own foresight about children yet to be born—i.e. are in special contact with the spiritworld in the matter of birth. On the Slave Coast the folk make a two-faced single block if both twins die. The block is set up in the house and given offerings for the granting of favours, especially for revelations of the future. In Liberia, the twins have an interesting relation to the bushgoat:

Twins have in effect the singular privilege of learning many things by dreams. Perhaps it is because they see the spirits of the dead, whose life in the other world is a replica of earthly life... However it is, the twins have the privilege of learning things by means of dreams... And why then may not twins eat the bushgoat? Twins, long ago, the old men informed us, have seen, it appears, in their dreams that the spirits of the dead take the bodies of bushgoats. They have seen bushgoats which were not animals but man. If you see a bushgoat saving itself in a certain way, it is not an animal, it is a spirit. So, twins knowing, on account of seeing it in a dream, that certain bushgoats are men, they know them to be men, cannot eat them: that would be wrong, and besides if they should eat them, they would lose their privileges. *They cannot get good head again, and they no fit see again the things they fit see otherwise.*

(This is from the French of a missionary: the italics are English in the original)

In Minoan Crete and early Anatolia we find a shield of dual form and the double-headed axe with sky-connections, especially related to the fertility-cult of the spring-rains and the lightning-thunder marriage of sky and earth. On a gold ring from Mycenai the double-shield, roughly anthropomorphised, descends from a sky where sun and moon (and perhaps milky way) are shown; below the Mother, holding three poppies, sits under her tree, approached by three women with offerings under sun and moon is the double-axe. On a vase from the banks of the Ilissos (about 800-700 B.C.) a man makes rain-magic with gourd-rattles before a cone and double-shield. The Kwakiutl think twins can control weather and disease by swinging a large wooden rattle. In Incan Peru one of a pair of twins was held to be the Child of the Lightning, and a severe penance was exacted as for a great sin; in *Mark* the brothers James and John are considered Sons of Thunder.

Gold ring from Mycenai; the goddess with poppy under sacred tree, three women offer flowers, double-axe in sky, double-shield figure coming from the sky, sun, moon and (?) milky way. Horns of consecration and double-axes from a Mycenean vase.

Taboo. A general disruption of all the totemic sanctions and balances appears with settled existence.* In pre-Columban America totems existed, but had lost their great uniting force; in Africa we find many signs of them, but the disintegration has gone even further. And in South America:

> The totem is generally looked upon as the ally of the ancestor of the clan and generally called his blood-brother. . . The ancestor generally took the name of his ally, but was not confused with it. Hence the Indians spoke of themselves as children of the Totem, referring to their real human ancestor. Real cases where they believed they were descended from the totem were rare. . . In all these languages, the term used to express totem was brother. (PERRY)

That is, a kinship-system derived from totemic bases is present, but the dynamic force making an organic unity of the taboos and the dual system has broken down. In Africa definite totemic systems are sporadic except in the region of the great lakes. The Baganda are divided into some forty patrilinear exogamous clans; each has a main and a secondary totem, generally plant or animal, which cannot be eaten—indeed, members of, say, the leopard clan

---

* In Melanesia and Polynesia we find every degree of totemism. Throughout most of North America we find the system in more or less typical forms; and totemic groups are commonly divided into moieties. But the taboo-force has waned and the totem is often killed by its members. In fact it is little more than a clan badge. The marrilinear Iroquis have tribes divided into exogamous clans, with animal totems and with moieties. But descent is rarely claimed from the totem. Among the Siouian tribes, e.g. the Ponkas we find complex exogamous totemic divisions. On the N.W. coast totemism is much merged with the cult of guardian spirits which are individually acquired through fasting, etc. in a dream. They usually have an animal form. Sometimes they seem species rather than individual and are parcelled out among the clans or social groups of the tribe. In India there are many traces of totemism, but mainly in its social aspects. The Santals of Bengal are divided into exogamous totemic patrilinear clans and sub-clans, with some sort of avoidance of the totem; totemism also occurs in Assam, Central India and Madras, etc.

cannot eat meat that has been even scratched by a leopard. But they do not claim descent from the totem. Among the West Bantu, 'Whenever a woman bears a child, she is delivered at the same time of a leopard, for that is the name, *ngo*, by which the afterbirth, *The Brother Born at the same time*, goes'. Here the totem has disintegrated, leaving a mixture of *churinga*-self and animal familiar.*

What happens to the all-important taboos in this situation?

The incest-taboo continues, but is progressively robbed of its set of rules derived from the dual organisation and exogamy. The totem-taboo is broken up into a complicated set of taboos, sometimes connected with food, but no longer integrally determining the position of a person in tribal structure and holding that structure together. All sorts of things become dangerous and involve taboos of varying terror.

Social relations are describable in terms of danger: through contagion there is social participation in danger. And we find expressed in the same terms, those of taboo, two quite separate functions: (1) the classification and identification of transgressions (which is associated with, though it can be studied apart from, processes of social learning), and (2) the institutional localisation of danger, both by specification of the dangerous and by the protection of society from endangered and hence dangerous, persons. (STERNER)

That is true. But to understand the origins and workings of taboos we must see that both their classification and their localisation are determined by certain deep fears (of the maternal womb and its blood, of the shedding of blood and the destruction of life), and that the magical notion of a part for a whole operates. The individual felt himself free for coitus with women in general by tabooing the mother, or for killing animals and eating them by tabooing the totem. This is the principle which is now applied in a wide series of relations.

The equalitarian totemic unity of the tribe is breaking down.

Within primitive societies, the economic system subordinates property relations to human relations, to human welfare. Between tribes, however, commercial relations obtain.

The economic system of primitive peoples is identified largely with the kinship system and is therefore characterised by co-operation, mutual aid, and sharing. The widespread custom of exchanging goods promotes solidarity. But it is also the means of sharing food and other goods in times of scarcity; it is a system of social security.

Private and personal property are institutions of primitive society as they are of our own, but use is emphasised rather than ownership in the sense in which the latter term is used in our culture. But the private ownership of natural resources or of means of production is never extensive enough in primitive society to exclude any class or any individual from the resources of nature: it is a fundamental fact of primitive society that everyone has free access to the resources of nature. This is the basis of the freedom and equality of tribal societies. (WHITE)

But with the increase of settled life this basis is sapped and finally overthrown. And so the totemic taboo, which in the last resort guarded and systematised that basis, is disintegrated and shared out by the individuals who are cornering property and power. The resulting taboo-forms are endless and often very

odd, but the essential thing is the seizure by the dominant individuals of fragments of the totemic power, which they manipulate for their own ends. They
use them above all to give sanctity and security to their prestige, their power-
positions, and their property.

This sort of extension of the taboo is to be seen most clearly in Polynesia
(whence the word itself comes). There the political hierarchy was based on
various powers of veto, which were exercised in terms of taboo. The sphere of
anyone's power was delimited by the kind of taboos he could impose; and
taboo provided the means of relating a person to his inferiors and superiors.
A chief could claim any object by a sort of anatomical taboo, *tapu tabu*, which
merely involved his statement that the object was his head. Personal property
was secured by imposing a taboo on it. Thus, a man might stop thieves from
taking his breadfruit by plaiting coconut leaves in the form of seapikes and
hanging them from the trees. The thief then feared that if he touched the trees
he would be attacked by fish of this kind when entering the sea and mortally
wounded. An ulcer-taboo was created by burying bits of clam-shell and setting
up three or four reeds tied at the top like a man's head; a death-taboo by
burying a calabash with oil in it and by marking the spot with a little mound
of white sand.

We see here how the taboo tends to merge with the curse-spell. The development of property-seals in early Sumeria seems to have at root the taboo-
principle. And the dual power often noted in holy objects (e.g. the Hebrew ark)
of blessing and blasting leads back to the taboo. The totem concentrated the
mana of food in a tabooed form, making other articles of food safe for con-
sumption. A specially holy place or object similarly concentrates *mana*, which,
if incorrectly handled, can destroy instead of blessing. This dual aspect appears
in the Hebrew *quadosh* as in the Latin *sacer*.

The Fiji chief, we saw, maintained his power by his superiority as a taboo-
imposer. But there were disadvantages in thus becoming a centre of *mana*; it
meant that one, oneself, was beset by all sorts of restrictions and prohibitions—
not temporarily, as was, for example, a menstruating woman, but at every moment of one's existence. Hence the weight of taboos borne by the divine kings
at a further stage along the road we are mapping. Thus, the king of the Jukun
tribe of Nigeria was strangled every seven years; he was so charged with *mana*
that his feet might not touch the ground for fear of damaging the crops; and
his brain, heart and kidneys were eaten by his successors. (Jukun masks are
highly abstract.) The Egyptian Pharaoh was surrounded by a network of such
vexatious taboos, though we know little about them. They were the penalty
he paid for carrying right into the highly-developed State the taboos bristling
round the prehistoric divine kingship.

Fraternity or Secret Society. The ordered system of fertility-rites and initiations which we found in the totemic tribe are broken down like the taboo-
system. The old forms of obligation get more and more out of hand, and the

men in superior positions use them for their own aggrandisement. Supplanting the tribal rituals, or growing beside them at their expense, there emerge all sorts of closed fraternities or secret societies, modelled on the old initiation-forms, but existing largely to enhance prestige and make a corner in magic. The old kinship-rites, open to all of the requisite age-class, are disrupted. Thus, the Melanesian *sukwe* have individual admission dependent on a fee, with hierarchical grades and their own house-centres. In America, among the Winnebago, beside the clan-groupings, we meet societies made up of those who have won the blessings of a special spirit, medicine-groups with their own initiations, and semi-permanent organisations such as that of the outstanding warriors, who perform certain rites. Among the Kwakiutl the tribal systems are displaced in wartime or during the winter-dances by societies of a different order, whose bond is a 'common spiritual experience'. At times a shamanist individual founds new societies, e.g. the tobacco society among the Crow.

We find an even greater medley of fraternities in Africa. Here an important object is the fetish, which we might describe as the *churinga* detached from its place in the totemic unity. The fetish is an object of spirit-power which one can appropriate. Among the Dahomeans, cult-groups were composed of the *voduno* who possessed the fetish, the *hunso* who carried it, the *vodunsi* vowed to its service, and the *legbans* incarnating the *vodu's* power. The fetish is not a god because of its limited range; like the *churinga* it is the link between an individual and the spirit-world and can be used to liberate spirit-force; but whereas the *churinga* merely played its part in the tribal ritual, linking the individual to the collective and to the *alcheringa*, the fetish is made a channel of particular magical purposes and the object of a special cult.

In America, too, the fetish-form is found; and an interesting attempt was made to correct the egocentric elements by holding a council of fetishes just before or after the new year. The fetishes were put together, with chants and dances and cries to the fetish-beasts; the prayer ended with a grand invocation. The fetish-form here is much closer to the totemic level than in Africa, where it is moving towards the god. The sacred bundles of the tribe contained 'medicine'—a feather or other part of the bird or beast that had appeared to the bundle's owner. The latter was expected to know the songs and rites connected with its use. But among the Blackfoot, for example, the bundles with their magic power were the subject of an active trade, so that almost all of them had belonged at some time or other to leading men of the tribe. The Mandan even held that trading increased the bundle's power. Participation in a war-expedition used up much of the enclosed magic, so that after four expeditions most of it had evaporated and the owner then lived in peace. The Pawnee bundles all held an ear of maize and were the centre of fertility-rites carried on from the first spring-thunder to the end of autumn, with the human sacrifice at the summer solstice. (The soul-bundles of the Hebrews were analogous objects.)

One important development of the fraternities is into a sort of actors' guild, as the collective rituals break off into mystery-plays which become the guild's own property, though attached to a personal deity. In the Pacific we meet the Areoi of the Society Islands, who had eight grades distinguished by tattoo and dress, and who developed into actors resembling the Dionysiac guilds of Greece.

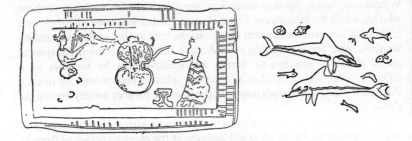

Two female worshippers in symmetrical relation to a double-shield figure: Mycenai. Dolphins: Knossos.

In the fraternities, in general, secrecy is strictly enforced and the full lore is imparted only after a period of privation and a death-rebirth rite. A new name may be given and a secret language divulged; normally at least a code of doctrine, ritual, and organisation. Myths explain the acts of worship, the instruments used, the sacred places and the words used, the qualifications and duties of functionaries. Ecstatic states of possession play a central part. Prayer, sacrifice, lustration are supplemented by dramatic performances, especially masked dances. Centres of education and instruction, the fraternities can play a key-part in the political and economic life of the group. The tendency is towards complexity and hierarchy of organisation. An important part is played by

outstanding, powerful individuals, primitive prophets. Inspired by their visions, they believe themselves divine instruments. Possessing particular training and special propensities, these leaders develop unusual faculties of insight and enjoy tremendous prestige among the people. The prophet or seer may remain an isolated figure or lead a group of followers; his activity may be sporadic, or continuous and professional. Hardship, and even suffering, may be his daily bread. (WACH)

All early craft-associations are forms of the secret society; and as well as the actors' guilds there are born the mystery-groups in whom traditional rites take on some special character. Among the Greeks, the *thiasoi* were connected with the clan, but there were also *orgones*, local associations of persons devoted to a particular god, e.g. Asklepiadai, worshippers of the healing saviour Asklepios. Important forms grew out of the clan-cults, e.g. at Eleusis, Olympia and so on. The Eleusinian Mysteries were in origin mysteries of the earthmother in relation to agriculture, but they developed into a religious centre of individual initiation and redemption; at Olympia arose the famous Games. The Orphic and Dionysiac cults, and those of the Great Mother, again had deep roots in tribal fraternity-forms. The Isiac and Mithraic Mysteries followed in the Graeco-Roman world.

The mystery-group is the form in which these cults with direct continuity from tribal days persist inside large scale political units such as the Roman Empire or China (where they mostly show Buddhist or Taoist influences). The Karmatians among the Muslims were originally an ethnic group which grew into a mystery-society with ritual, initiation-grades and theology of its own. The rite of rebirth is always essential, though it has lost its reference to the stages of the individual's growth in an ordered tribal system and has become abstracted into a yearning for release and regeneration from a corrupted and callous world.

The Plains Indians provide good examples of the use of the fraternity to concentrate political power in the hands of a privileged group. Each had its leader and kept a united front to the world. They could thus sway the council, and the chief often gave them the job of carrying out the resolutions. Usually one of them policed the camp or the hunt. The shamanist aspect varied. Sometimes a fraternity was connected with the sacred bundles; but among the Hidatsa, Mandan, Arapho, Atsina and Blackfoot, the character was predominantly military, with age-groups. Admission to the higher groups took place through a block-purchase by the lower grade from the higher, but each buyer had to find his own seller, preferably of his father's clan. The buyer had to hand over his wife to the seller, or, if unmarried, had to borrow someone else's wife.

The mask-guisings had totemic elements, but without the deep totemic meaning. The Hidatsa Dogs owned a myth connecting them with dogs; but their dance-decorations were a confused mixture—headgear of owl and magpie feathers, bird-bone rattles round the neck, hoof-rattles as well as bows and arrow in the hands. Before the dance they howled like dogs and their chief was the Real Dog. He had to be addressed with the opposite of what was meant, i.e. 'Come' meant 'go'. The group was noted for battle-courage. The warriors of the Bull fraternity had horned headgear and feathered shields and lances; their two dance-leaders wore bison-masks, and a woman in an antelope-skin offered them drinking water. The Hidatsa and Mandan had women's fraternities, whose functions included the calling of the bison herds and the fostering of the maize-growth.

Cannibal Spirit and Potlach. Our few examples of the adaptation of totemic forms in the period of tribal disintegration show that something of the old equilibrium was maintained where the growth of property-power and prestige had not fatally undermined the system.* But there was a ceaseless pressure of change, in which the desperate efforts to rearrange and reconstruct the old forms were continually disrupted. The competition for power deepened. In North America the cannibal spirit appeared as supreme patron of the fraternity. Among the Kwakiutl, this spirit,

hamatsa, stood at the pinnacle of the hierarchy, superior to all the rest and owning the most exalted masks, chants, dances and rites. Possession of the spirit could be obtained only through a series of initiations lasting over at least eight years. (DAVY)

In the South Seas the final aim of rising in the grades was at times to gain the right of human sacrifice. Thus, in the New Hebrides, pig-sacrifices made the pig-owner a 'new man' with a new name and the hope of reaching human sacrifice as the seal on an admired career. Cannibal imagery is strong in myths expressing this stage. Polynesian mythology tells of violent combats between the sons of heaven and earth (recall the way in which moieties may be opposed as Sky-people and Earth-people). A fighter triumphs over all his brethren save one, whom he fails to transmute into food.

The king of Buganda in Africa, on his accession, was described as 'eating the country'. In West Africa, in Benin, the Oba built up his aristocracy from men who had committed from seven to fourteen murders and brought him the dried genitals or breasts of the victims. And the climax of the cannibal imagery of power appeared in the Egyptian Pyramid Texts of the Old Kingdom, where was inscribed the pharoah's frenzied efforts to achieve the sole and supreme power of immortality:

He has broken up the backbones and the spinal marrow, he has taken away the hearts of the gods. He has eaten the Red Crown, he has swallowed the Green One. He feeds on the lungs of the Wise Ones, he is satisfied with living on hearts and their magic. . . He flourishes and their magic is in his belly. . .

The increasing instability of the tribal forms finds its expression in potlach, with its extravagant prestige-display, and in the rise of the war-chief. Thus, the totem-poles of the northwest Americans show the totem-animals reduced to power-emblems on the same lines as taboo became an expression of property-power in Polynesia. Some poles illustrated myths as well as clan-affiliations, but the designs were on the way to heraldic devices. (We may compare the way in which the Mother between her dual animals represented a fixation of the totemic concept; but in this case the basis remained communal.) Much time and labour was put into the poles. We hear of most of the male inhabitants of a village spending a whole year on carving one. Some poles stood 80 to 90 feet

---

* Some typical tale-types of the phase: British Columbia, the poor man achieving high position, two chiefs struggling for prestige. Blackfoot: the acquisition of ceremonies. Chuckchu of Siberia: the villagers' struggle against a tyrannous athletic hunter or warrior—here (as with the Eskimos) the saviour of the community is generally a weak despised lad.

high in front of houses holding several hundred persons. In the 19th century individuals accumulated them by war, violence, purchase, marriage. The more totem-poles a man had, the greater his prestige. In the designs, the totem is itself often disintegrated to a set of symbolic representations, e.g. a beaver is intended if the form has a short fat nose, large incisor teeth, or a broad tail with cross-hatch markings, or if it holds a stick.

The potlach of these groups derives from the tribal cycle of rites and customs, but has wrenched itself loose into uncontrolled competition. The prestations or customary dues are transformed by the introduction into their heart of the principle of reckless rivalry and challenge; they are now used to beget and stress inequality, not to maintain equilibrium. The potlach is a feast given in expectation of a return. In origin a rite of communion uniting the living and the dead, it consists of a solemn distribution of food and presents. The giver thus gains the right to be the recipient of similar distributions and to annex part of the names, crests and privileges of rivals he has beaten in munificence and exposed publicly as unable to meet his challenge. The collective aspect is swallowed up in the conflict of chiefs.

Shield, New Ireland. Kwakiutl design for housefront: Raven.

The potlach-giver also wants to corner spirit-possession. Among the Haida he can be inspired by a fresh spirit at each potlach as long as it is not owned by a chief of the opposing clan. The maddened destruction of food and property is remarkable; the articles may even be hurled into the sea. At the same time there is a close link with trade. The potlach-folk were great traders, avid for gain, eager to engage in a scramble for blankets, their currency; and the potlach-wastes were made possible only by individuals' accumulation of wealth through trade.

In modified forms the potlach system persists into barbarian societies and plays its part in the medieval ethic:

In the course of these distributions it is just the quality of the morsels distributed that determines the rank of each participant in the hieratic distribution. For instance, in the Kwakiutl legend of Omaxtalale the place allotted at the banquet determines a whole hierarchy of vassals, of retainers, as our own Middle Age would call it. These will henceforth enjoy the right of participating in the distribution of victuals and commodities at the potlach. At the same time, they will undertake the duty of assisting the chief to amass the reserves of wealth necessary to swell the abundance of these feasts with which the chief's power and the clan's honour are alike bound up. (DAVY)

Money and the Quest for Life. Trade, property-accumulation, and religious prestige are thus inextricably entangled. Monetary systems develop with magical values far ahead of the cruder barter-systems used for utilitarian commodities. We have hints of a far flung trade-system in magical shells among the paleolithic groups. With the breakdown of the totemic system which kept the stone-or-stick *churinga* in the communal cave, the spirit-stone is liable to become the property of the fraternity. Thus, among the natives of the Gazelle Peninsula, New Britain, each initiate gets a stone in the shape of human being or animal and henceforth his soul is identified with the stone; if the stone breaks, they say that thunder has struck it and the man must soon die. The sacred monetary systems are in a sense a quest for the lost self, the external-soul which is no longer stored socially away. In Polynesia:

Sometimes the voyages were in search of the sacred *kura*, whose red feathers were emblems of the highest chiefliness, symbol of the great gods widely over many lands of this sea. It was in quest of the *kura*, too, that many impacts came back westward. (HARRISON)

The *kura* was in part an ancestor, and was seen incarnated especially in the frigate-bird with scarlet throat-pouch—'killer of the seas, bird of the great esoteric god Io, source of finest artforms such as the spiral carving of south-east Papua, the kites and canoe-prows of Malekula, the Matanavat dances of Na-leng, the bird-cult figures of Easter Island'.

> O Frigate-bird of lustrous black, bathing in the far land of Ahatea,
>   boundless expanse of the skies,
> O behold—ascending !
> The sacred *kura* mounts on high.
> O Frigate-bird of shimmering black,
>   bathing in the remote ceiling of the sky.

We hear of wars for *kura*; and the great culture-hero Maui puts red *kura* feathers on his hook when fishing up islands.

In the Homeric world the relationship between the *aristoi*, the nobles, was expressed in the idea and practise of guest-friendship, with its concomitant prestige-wealth: gifts of precious metal never put into purchasing circulation but exchanged according to strict formulas of hospitality. Here we see a controlled carrying-on of tribal prestations by the chiefs who have cornered power and wealth, without the potlach-frenzy.

There are also genuine money-systems, such as the small *nassa immersa* shells used on the Gazelle Peninsula; but at this phase the magical value is apt to predominate, even with commodities of high use-value. Thus, in East Africa, 'cattle serve as fines, sacrifices and gifts', but 'the social and religious importance is greater than the economic use'.

The idea of a special life-force in such objects as stones or shells goes back into paleolithic times. The Australians had their quartzes associated with shamanist practice; but it is now, with the collapse of the group-store for the soul-objects, that the promiscuous quest for the lost self in some object or material of spirit-concentration begins. *Kura*, gold, precious stones or metals: the list is large, but the idea is the same in them all. All jewellery and such decorations originate in the quest for life-enhancing things; and a characteristic myth-form deals with the quest for the life-source, a plant or a spring of water, or seeks to explain how the gift of life was lost, how death came into the world, with loss of Eden and our subsequent woe.

War and Sacrifice. The growth of war, as distinct from the tournaments of totemic society, results from the increasing competition and the demands of power and prestige. At the same time the systems of murder-prestige are entangled with fertility-rites, so that head-hunting may go on both to aggrandise the individual and to aid the rice-crops. A good example of the general process is given in the creation-myth of the Zuni of New Mexico, which preserves a clear memory of the change from a generally peaceful basis to one of war. Twin heroes led the tribe out of the underworld in a quest of the mother-navel, the lost homeland. 'At times they met people who had gone before them, learning much of the ways of war' (probably the Aztecs, who had organised mining in the Pueblo area). The quest for the lost mother-centre now turned into a war-wandering. 'For in the fierceness that had entered into their hearts with fear, they did not deem it well, neither liked they to look on strangers peacefully'. Driven by the fear, 'they sought more than ever to war with all strangers, whereby they became still more changed in spirit'. So they founded a fraternity, the Society of the Knife, the Stout Warriors of the Twins, and sang:

> Of blood we have tasted the hunger.
> Henceforth by the power of war
> and the hazards of omen and dance
> shall we open the ways of our people
> and guide them in search of the Twain

> who hold the high places of earth.
> come forth, ye warmen of the knife,
> our chosen the priests of the bow. . .
> you shall be changed forever,
> the foot-rests of eagles
> and signs of our order.

Changed for ever. Now 'twain full of magic and terror were they'. The new magic and terror was the sort of outlook that brought about practices like those of the Pawnees, who, as late as 1838, roasted a young girl every spring over a slow fire, then shot her to death with arrows, tore out her heart and devoured it, and squeezed her blood over the crops.

Fraternity-forms and wars both played their part in bringing about deep social divisions issuing in distinct classes. Thus, among the Omaha we find chiefs, priests, medicine-men, and fraternity-members opposed to the commoners or non-privileged. Among the Tanala of Madagascar there used to be the free *hova*, with gentilic affiliation, and the descendants of war-captives.

Religion in its developed form is appearing with the advent of priests and the failure of tribal equality. Even in pre-historic Jericho a large building seems a shrine; in Halafian settlements there are sanctuaries that grow steadily into the great temples of historical times. Sacrifice has been born; and it is this practice which above all else points to the difference between the totemic relation to the spirit-world and the fully-fledged religious one. The guilt-sense which totemism controlled by the taboo on eating the beast-brother breaks loose in exacerbated form, especially after animals are domesticated and killed. For the tamed animal is a part of the group as no wild animal ever was. The slaughter of such an animal must be hedged round by a whole series of safeguarding rituals. Totemism had had its sacraments in which we meet a yearly eating of the tabooed animal; but such a system will not work in the new situation. The god (whose roots are in the totem and the totemic ancestor) is needed to relieve the guilt of those who murder a bull or a sheep.* Finding a new application of the principle that the part equals the whole, they offer up a part of the animal to the god, who thus assumes the responsibility for the murder and saves the people from spirit-attack. The rest of the flesh can then be eaten by the worshippers. (In estimating the Christian reaction against the pagan temples, we must see those temples as reeking slaughter-houses; yet so deeply rooted was the idea of beast-sacrifice, then even those who rejected it had to conceive their communion as the eating of the god and the washing in the blood of the lamb. The rejection of meat went deep in early Christian attitudes, e.g., Jerome says, 'The eating of flesh is the seed-plot of lust', and Augustine concurred. Prudentius sets out the accepted ideal and practice:

> Far from us that filthy greed,
> the gluttony that loves to feed
> on slain oxen's bloodstained flesh.

---

* In the Bouphonia (Ox murder) at Athens, the sacrificiants were given a formal murder-trial, and the knife, found guilty, was cast into the sea.

He builds a picture of the true Christian life as one of pastoral innocence, in the garden that regains paradise. But the Church after establishment could not maintain such positions, which were taken over by hermits and monks, and which reappear later in the great mass-heresies right into late medieval days.)

An entanglement of totemic emotions indeed appears in the way in which the god is in a sense himself the beast that is sacrificed to him. This image is particularly strong among the masses, and so is liable to irrupt in the mystery-religions; Dionysos is one with the beast torn to pieces by his possessed women-worshippers. For it is in the sacrificed beast and the torn god that the people recognise the image of their own life as well as that of nature's death-life. In scape-goat rituals a man or an animal, made the emblem of the whole group, is killed or driven away, taking the group's sins with him and enabling them to make a new start. In Babylonia we find anguished ritual-songs in which the identification of the sacrificed beast and the sacrificing people is made:

> The lamb is the substitute for humanity.
> He has given up a lamb for the life.
> He has given up the lamb's head for the man's head.
> He has given up the lamb's neck for the man's neck.
> He has given up the lamb's stomach for the man's stomach.

While on the other hand the practices elaborated for inspecting the entrails or liver of the sacrificed animal for omens shows the belief that at the murder-moment the creature somehow becomes divine, commensurate with the universe (the liver-markings being related to sky-divisions).

We thus find a contradictory set of ideas and emotions born round the sacrifice, which is simultaneously the rejected and lost self, the god himself, and the whole of ransomed humanity. The sacrifice is thrown away, cut off from life, and yet is a channel between men and the spirit-world, a point of lightning-contact.

The identification of the sacrificed beast with men as well as with the god was aided by the fact that human beings had in fact become sacrifices. Apart from the prestige-murders of the fraternities, agricultural processes also claimed their victims; for if the greatest act of power lay in the murder of a man in the safeguarded ritual form, then the crops as well as the chiefs needed the fertilisation of human blood. Hence such rites as those of the Pawnees or of the Khonds in India. But the core of the demand for human sacrifice lay in the chiefly ethic. Thus in Borneo such sacrifices were made at the funeral rites of a great chief, the building of new houses, and the return of a successful war-expedition. In the Norse world there was a close connection between human sacrifice to Othin and the offering of the battle-dead to him. (His Valhöll was 'a glorified copy of a military king's court', and he was affiliated with king and nobles, as Thor was with the farmers and peasants.) The rise of war and sacrifice indeed seems connected with the turning from the earthmother to a skyfather. In Babylonia we find 'a close connection between the astral and martial types'.*

The ingredients of any mature religion are highly complex and many elements combine to form a god; but from our survey it would seem that the cult of ancestors plays a key part—a cult that cannot be reduced to the simple cult-of-the-dead—as well as the *churinga* broken loose into fetish. Thus the collective and the individual elements in totemic ritual, each wrenched away from its old basis and moving along its own lines of change, come together again in a new conception of the spiritworld and its controlling forms or forces.

Pre-Columbian America. In ancient America we find neolithic communities who fail to break through into cultures based on metallurgy. Metal-working was known, especially in the Incan area, but it remained at the magical level, used for cult-objects and decorations; it did not radically affect production. It began apparently in Ecuador and Peru; the techniques moved on to the

Xipetopec, Flayed Lord, god of spring and jewellery; his priest wore the skin of a flayed slave (to help the earth into a new skin of life). Xockiquetzal, goddess of beauty, love, courtesans, patroness of home-labours.

---

* Othin welcomes aloft the Kingly or Warrior dead, while the rest of the people are consigned to a dim underworld. The Aztec battle-dead gained the solar paradise; the others went to the Mother's ancestral under-earth. In Polynesian Mangaia the warriors went to a heaven above, while the commoners who died a normal death had no hopeful future.

Panama and Costa Rica, reaching Mexico by the 11th century A.D., mainly applied to gold-work. We can then, in effect, call the great civilisations of Central and South America neolithic. We see in them what happens to the neolithic bases carried to their extreme, just as we saw in the Australians what happened to the paleolithic bases when isolated over a long period of time. The ultimate sources of the American cultures seems to lie in South-east Asia; but in any event they developed on their own momentum. They show all the expected traces of tribal systems breaking down and reconstructed to fit into large scale State-forms. Oppressive tribute-exactions were devised, but much of the tribal patterns persisted. Above all we see the war-ethic, expressed in the Zuni myth, dominating the situation, especially under the Aztecs.

The latter people show clearly the way in which tribal groups pass into a settled condition under State-control. More than 1500 years before they arrived in Central America there had been civilisations like that of the Olmecs, on the east coast of Mexico, that of the Maya to the south, or that centred in Teotihuacan in the highlands. About the 10th century A.D. there was a period of collapse and confusion. The Toltecs from the north moved in over large areas. After some three centuries they in turn were torn by inner troubles and broken by the attack of more tribes from the north, mainly hunters and food-gatherers with a smaller section of farmers, among whom were the Aztecs.

At first the Aztec social organisation seems that of a kinship-society with much tribal democracy. The people are divided into four *calpullis*, certainly kin-groups, though it is not clear how the marriage system worked. The *calpulli* owned the land. The members owned what they harvested, and could pass land on to their heirs, but had no right to lease or sell. Excess land was distributed among poor or landless members. The headman was elected by the whole group, but from a given family. The main decisions were taken by a council of representatives from the *calpullis*. (Legend spoke of a priest as originally having been head of the tribe, followed by the chiefs.)

Land was burned off and ash-fertilised. After one to three years it was left fallow for eight to ten. But in the high valley of Mexico the lakes were filled with islands built on rafts; seed-beds and transplantings were known. With the resulting two or three harvests a year, a large population could be fed. The concentration was helpful in view of the lack of any draught-animal, wheel or cart; and the area was strategically protected—while its inhabitants could swoop down, harry and loot the lowlands of cotton and cocoa. Mexico City seems to have had some 300,000 inhabitants.

By the 14th century one tribe subjugated the others. Among its mercenaries were the Aztecs, keen for war and scorning 'to sit at home and work like women'. The warriors had their insignia, honours and privileges. An aristocracy of war, they pushed the old headmen out of tribal leadership and at least some warriors seem fed at the ruler's court. The assemblies still controlled the most important matters; but side by side with the rise of the war-nobility the chieftainship too grew in power—though limited by council, assembly, and a double or proxy-ruler called Snakewoman—an odd example of the dual form in decay. Elected, the ruler came from a particular family.

In 1427-30 the Aztecs with two tribal allies seized power and expanded their rule by war, exacting ever more tribute. The war-nobles clashed with the assembly and took power; they demanded their own land and held most of the conquered territories, gaining hereditary control through a fiction of renewed grants and acting as tribute-collectors, judges, administrators, as the system extended. The ruler meanwhile was growing ever closer to absolute power, with the tribal forms losing all vitality. In this last phase, merchants and slaves appear. Slavery was weakly developed, as war-prisoners were sought for sacrifice; slaves were recruited from criminals and debtors, and used as servants and porters, rarely in agriculture. Construction-works were carried out by forced levies.

Characteristic of the earlier cultures had been the growth of priestly groups concerned with astronomical calculations, number-systems and elaborate calendars; and a large proportion of surplus productive energy went into large-scale building. The result seems to have been a break between the upper or priestly levels and the lower level of tribute-paying farmers, so that, despite the remarkable astronomical computations, there were no new developments of technique. Neither metallurgy in its economic bearings, nor the complex of new techniques that evolve with the wheel, ever showed up. Agriculture became entangled with bloody forms of human sacrifice, and the societies lacked any power of inner renewal or advance after the neolithic period of intense creativeness. We find rollers attached to clay animals, with wooden axles socketed to holes in the legs, apparently for some ritual use; but society lacked the inner drive to apply the magical idea.

The lack of metallurgy meant that households tended to be self-sufficient. But trade was growing, e.g. one village might have a good bed of clay for pots, another a surplus of peppers. Obsidian and flint were sought for magical reasons as well as practical, and jade or stones like it were much valued. Shells from the Caribbean reached as far as what is now the middle of the United States, and gold ornaments from Panama were used as offerings in a holy well of Yucatan. Each town held a market at specified intervals.

The world-picture was one of cyclic destruction and creation. The Aztecs held that the world had passed through five ages or suns. Thus, according to the Calendar Stone of Tenochtitlan, the first era, Four Ocelot, had Tezcatlipoca as presiding god; in the end he turned himself into the sun while jaguars ate up the men and giants populated the earth. Quetzalcoatl ruled the second era, Four Wind, which ended in hurricanes and the transformation of men to monkeys. Next, Four Rain, under Taloc, broke up in fiery rain; and Four Water, under a water-goddess. Our Lady of the Turquoise Skirt, ended in a flood with men as fishes. The present age, Four Earthquake, is under the sun-god and will end in earth-cataclysm.

Time-computations varied, but the start of any new period involved important ceremonies. The cycles concerned could be so complex as to involve epochs of 102 years. A rich collection of gods grew up; and much time was taken in ritual. The modern Navahoes spend a third of their time in ceremony; and the Aztecs had much more wealth and leisure. We meet many mother goddesses but they have often had their fertility-aspect contaminated with the ethic of human sacrifice. In the cult of the earthmother Tlazolteotl (Filth-eater), Mother of the Gods, who, by eating refuse, ate up the sins of men, a rite of confession developed. What outstands however is the insensate blood-lust, especially round the sun-cult, in the competition to offer up hearts torn from the living breasts of men. The idea of battle and blood-sacrifice entered into the whole of Aztec life and gave its particular colour to the imagery born of the dual system:

The great gods of the sky play an important part in the duality of the Aztec world in which an eternal war was fought symbolically between light and darkness, heat and cold, north and south, rising and setting sun. Even the stars were grouped into armies of the east and west. Gladiatorial combats, often to the death, expressed this idea in ritual; and the great warrior orders, the Eagle Knights of Huitzilopochtli and the Ocelot Knights of Tezcatlipoca, likewise reflected the conflict between night and day. The Sacred War permeated the ritual and philosophy of Aztec religion. (VAILLANT)

The Knights were fraternities like that of the Knife among the Zunis. As examples of the war-contamination of the mothers, we may take two hymns. The first is to Ciuacoatl, in whose cult appear aspects of an antelope, a maize-deity, a deity of war and of rain. The hymn depicts her as a victory-warrior:

> Morning has dawned.
> The order to the warriors has gone forth.
> Drag the captives hence [to sacrifice.]
> [Or] the whole land will be destroyed.
> The deer from Colhuaçan,
> She is covered with feathers.
> Those who fight bravely in war
> are painted with eagle-feathers.

The second hymn is to Itzpapalotl, a figure with butterfly-wings edged with stone-knives, jaguar-claws, and woman's face:

> O she has become the goddess of the melon-cactus,
> Our Mother Itzpapalotl, the Obsidian Butterfly;
> her food is on the Nine Plains,
> she was nurtured on the hearts of deer,
> Our Mother, the Earthgoddess.

The art of the high cultures of America tends to overlay its figures with an accumulation of attributes and decorations drawn from ritual and expressing such symbolism as the Obsidian Butterfly. The forms are often extremely powerful in their broad grasp, but developed with a heavy strees on terror and cruelty. The human shape is merged with that of ruthless felines and plastered with skulls, tusks, claws, necklaces of hearts and hands. The skill of the people in weaving may have contributed to the strong sense of complex but ordered design in the reliefs. Like the Egyptians the artists used passive attitudes for the gods, who are generally seated; the feeling of the cubic block of stone persists, sometimes begetting a massive simplicity of planes. But too often the ritualistic elaborations and incrustations, born of the terrors of sacrifice, weaken and weigh down the total effect; and the designs pullulate like tropical vegetation got out of hand.

Popul Vuh. We have the text in Latin characters of a sacred book of the Quiché Maya; any original would have been in pictographic form, resembling the Mexican codices. Probably the transmission had been oral. The work consists of a series of legends and traditions. It opens with a cosmogonic vision (as for example does the Finnish *Kalevala*). The first men are carved mannikins, drowned in a flood. The beasts and utensils rebel: thus, the millstones say, 'Very much were we tormented by you, and daily daily night and day it was squeak screech screech for your sake. Now you shall feel our strength and we will grind your flesh and make meal of your bodies'. Cups and dishes, dogs and hens, combine in the attack on the mannikins. (We may compare the Norse poem of *Frothi's Quern*. There as in the *Popul Vuh* the imagery expresses the productive processes turning on men who have misused them.) Only the giants survive, under Vukub-Cakix. Twin-heroes are sent to chasten Vukuk; he is wounded and they persuade him to submit to an operation; but they substitute mortal elements such as maize grains for his organs of emerald and the like, and he dies. The twins then kill the two giant sons.

We now learn of the twins' birth. Two brothers playing ball, had approached the underworld, Xibalba. The dual rulers there sent messengers in owl-guise with a challenge. Led by the owls, the heroes crossed a river of blood, and mistook two wooden effigies for the kings. Their seat of honour turned out to be a red-hot stone, to Xibalban merriment. Thrust into the House of Gloom, they were sacrificed and buried. The head of one was hung on a tree among the gourds; the tree's fruit was forbidden to all Xibalbans. A virgin princess disobeyed the taboo. The Head spat into her palm and she conceived. Her father bade the owl-messengers kill her and fetch her heart in a vase. She bribed the owls with promises and they substituted clotted bloodwort sap for her heart. Going to the mother of the hero whose gourd-head spat on her, she proved her story by gathering maize where no maize grew. She then bore twins, the heroes who destroyed the giant.

Chased out by their grandmother, they become hunters. Ill-treated by their uncle, they change to apes. As culture-heroes, they clear a maize-plantation with magical tools and so on. The underworld-kings challenge them to a ball-game. The twins send on an animal, Xan, to prick the Xibalbans with a hair from one of their legs, to find which are wooden and what names they address each other with. Forewarned, they evade the ordeals and win the ball-game. The kings set a new ordeal-task, to get four flower-bouquets, and shut the twins in the House of Lances. Ants get the flowers and the twins bribe the lancers, escaping death. They continue to win in the ordeals (in the House of Tigers and the House of Fire). In the House of Bats, one of them has his head cut off, but a tortoise is substituted for the head and the twin revives. More wonders are performed. The twins go through a resurrection-rite, arranging things beforehand with two sorcerers. Their bones are ground to powder and thrown into the river; they do much shape-shifting, being men-fishes on the fifth day after death, old ragged men on the sixth, killing and restoring each other to life. They burn down the palace and restore it, kill and restore the kings' dog, cut a man to pieces and resurrect him. The kings, curious about the experience of death, ask to have the process repeated on themselves. The brothers kill them but leave out the restoring rite. They call the underworld princes, deprive them of the right to the ballgame, and restrict their power to

Aztec game of patolli, symbolising the 52-year cycle, with beans or cut reeds as counters, and with dice; the men make invocations as they play.

the realm of the forest-beasts. The underworld-lords wane into owl-spirits. The original twin pair are translated to the skies and become sun and moon.

Another creation-myth intrudes. Four men are made, but they are too perfect and know too much. 'Let us contract their sight', say the gods, 'so that they be able to see only a portion of the earth and be content.' So four women are made, the ancestors of the Quichés. After them come the ancestors of other folks. But no sun rises. A god gives the Quichés fire, but rain quenches it. The god renews the fire, but the people still suffer from cold and famine. They wander on through many hardships, climb mountains, and pass through the miraculously-opened sea. (This magical trick occurs in an Egyptian tale before reaching the Hebrew Testament.) At last they rest on a promised mountain where they see the sun rise. Town-foundations follow, and the narrative drifts into tribal history mixed with legend. The four great ancestors die singing the song, 'We see', which they chanted as the light came up.

Here in shamanist form we have the ordeals and death-rebirths of initiation-ritual; and much light is thrown on many folktale types and motives.

The Incas. In Peru also there developed an imperial State, based on tribute, which had perhaps reached its highest point when the Spaniards came in about 1523. There had been a rapid expansion, in some thirty years, into a vast empire, which was carrying out resettlement and colonisation. Two degrees of nobles were supported by the State and had land-grants as well as llamas, though they could not dispose of the land. (Some domestication of llama and alpaca for wool and carrying was achieved.) As in Central America we find a large series of deities, of sky, earth and water; the earthmother-cult seems the oldest and was the most popular. The Incas themselves were sun-worshippers and claimed the sun, Inti, as begetter of their dynasty. On festivals, celebrants drank *chicha* beer and were expected to become dead drunk; tobacco-snuff and ground datura-seeds were also used in ritual and in shamanist practices. Everyone had a personal fetish considered his twin brother or *huauqui*; and confession of sin played a prominent part in religion. Human sacrifice was rarer than in Central America, but was used in moments of crisis at great popular festivals. Intellectual life was absorbed in astronomy and the calendar, and shamanist healers gained their power by dream or vision.

The idea of the spirit-centre was specially strong, expressed by the term *huaca*, *waca*, which came to be applied to a wide range of sites—especially to springs, cairns and stones, mountains and hills, but also to caves, roots, quarries, bridges, temples, tombs, mythological or historical locations. A sacred stone near the capital Cuzco (Navel) represented the brother of the emperor Manco Capac and protected the dynasty. The *huacas* of this region were thought of as lying on lines radiating from the Temple of the Sun.

4: Arts and Crafts

Shaman. In all the phases we have glanced at the shaman shows an increase in importance, which wanes with the secure establishment of the kingship—though he has contributed much to the ideas and practices making possible the divine king. He always claims direct inspiration; and his method of spirit-contact is that used to induce a state of trance or possession generally in ritual dancing and initiation-experience. As we have noted, he seeks that state and lives in it all the while, not on special occasions; he stakes everything on a ceaseless experience of ordeal, exaltation, self-renewal, spirit-communication. He represents in actual life what the culture-hero does in myth, perpetually seeking to succour the community and avert its dangers attempting to wrest from the spirit-world the secrets which ensure health, security and prosperity to his fellows. The call normally comes in youth: from illness or a vision or dream of an ancestor or of a beast or plant encountered during the crisis.*

Though he often carries on rites to ensure good hunting or good crops, his independent viewpoint prevents him from settling down into a priestly position. As the main bridge between the magics of totemism and those that follow, he helps to make priesthoods possible, though they also derive from the hierarchical fraternities and the arrogated powers of the chief. Opposed as he is to set forms, in fact in his procedures, songs, dances, and ideas, he is deeply traditional; and so in the transitional phases after the breakdown of the totemic system there is no conflict on the whole between shamanist freedom and institutional forms.

The shaman's main procedure consists of enacting the spirit-journey, either aloft or underground, for the purpose of gaining some benefit or prophetic knowledge from the spirit-world, of convoying a dead man, or of rescuing the

---

* To become a *peai* among the Caribs the novice lives with an 'elder', sometimes ten years, and for 25-30 years after he subjects himself to tests, fasts, and so on. The old *peais* whip the novice and make him dance in a secluded hut till he faints; he is 'bled' by black ants and made to 'go mad' by drinking tobacco-juice; then undergoes a three-years fast, which slowly grows less harsh; from time to time he drinks tobacco juice. Among the Barundi of Tanganyika one becomes *kiranga* by inheriting a sacred spear from father or mother, by being thunder-struck, or by feeling a sudden call. During one of the Ceremonies of the Spear, a boy or girl abruptly rises and stands opposite the officiating *kiranga*, stares at him till he (or she) trembles and faints. After a sleep of three or four days he (or she) is a priest or priestess-spouse of the god.

soul of someone lying ill. He carries out his journey in a state of possession. In Central Asia he rides a goose or horse as his spirit-steed, and ascends heaven after heaven. A tree is also associated with his ascent, and a drum is important for catching spirits and inducing ecstasy. The shaman is further the narrator of the tribal legends and a repository of tribal lore. In Tibet shamanist figures visibly wrestle with death in their struggle to save someone from dying. Though

Egyptian: men, baboons and women weaving net-spells.

the shaman is in many ways a one-man performer, shamanist groups do exist, and forms of initiation or inheritance from one shaman to another. Female shamans occur, and indeed the shaman himself is often sexually abnormal, taking on a feminised character. There are sometimes penalties for failure: the Eskimo *angekok*, who holds spirit-seances and is expected to make the hunts successful, is punished if he does not obtain results.

The war-leader, in the stages we are considering, is largely a berserk or possessed character, who is thus a modification of the shaman. The shaman proper in fact is not averse from warfare, like the Irish druid who follows in his steps; but he has his own methods of fighting, e.g. the *noaidde* of the Lapps, who in a drum-induced trance roams with his spirit-helpers the *saivo* land (the underearth, a replica of the world above); there he uses magic reindeer to fight a foe or obstruct hostilities. But his main functions are of peace, where he enacts the parts of priest, poet, dancer, historian, and even (in terms of the cultural level) scientist. His concentration of functions breaks up at the end of the transitional period; but he still survives as the protesting prophet and the founder of religions and heresies. The careers of the Buddha, Vardhamana, Zarathustra, John the Baptist, Jesus, Mohammed, Mani—and we may add Orpheus and Pythagoras—all show strong shamanist characteristics.

The shaman feels strongly his rôle as mediator between men and the spirit-world. One replied to a questioner:

God has appointed that I must wander both beneath and upon the earth, and has bestowed on me such power that I can comfort and cheer the afflicted, and on the other hand I can cast down those that are too happy. . . I am a shaman who knows the future, the past and everything that is taking place in the present, both above and below the earth. (CASTREN)

The shaman is grave and reserved, cut apart from ordinary folk:

People who are about to become shamans have fits of wild paroxysms, alternating with a condition of complete exhaustion. They will lie motionless for two or three days without partaking of food or drink. Finally they retire to the wilderness, where they spend their time enduring hunger and cold in order to prepare for their calling. . . . The process of gathering inspiration during the first stages is so severe that a bloody sweat often issues from on the forehead and temples. Every preparation of a shaman for a performance is considered a sort of repetition of the initiatory process. (KOHN)

In shamanist myth, shape-shifting plays a prominent part. Conflicts go on at great distances, with spirit-missiles hurled at one another. Descents to the underworld and ascents to the heavens are common. Spirit-flights, hunts and and pursuits are connected with shape-shifting, and there are tales of the soul-object located inside some object like an egg inside a bird inside something else on an island in the middle of the sea. The gaining of a spirit-bride (especially by stealing her feather-garb when she bathes with her sisters, so that she cannot fly off) and the quest for the life-source are also central. The wandering theme of the culture-hero, single or dual, takes on a new fullness, such as we saw in the Zuni myth or the *Popul Vuh*.

Tatar Shaman. The Yakut shaman is linked with three kinds of spirits: the *amagyat*, through which he communicates with the underworld; the *yekua*, an external-soul, which is always carefully secreted; the *kaliany*, a possessive demon. The *yekua* is normally an animal familiar; the word means animal mother. 'My *yekua* will not be found by anyone', said one shaman. 'It lies hidden far away on the mountains of Edjigan'.

Among the Yakuts the young shaman is consecrated on a mountain top or in a forest-clearing. He is dressed in ritual clothes, given a ritual rattle, and set with nine chaste youths one side and nine chaste maids the other. He repeats certain words. He is told that he must renounce all worldly things and is instructed as to the sites of the spirits to whom he is about to dedicate his life. He is sprinkled with the blood of an animal victim. There are eight further grades, with increasingly involved ceremonies of initiation.

The great moment for the Shaman of the Altai and Lebed Tatars is the yearly tribal horse-sacrifice to Bai Ulgen, at which he officiates.* Here is an account from about 1840. On the first evening the *kam* (shaman) set up a new yurt in a birch-thicket and put a pen-fence round. Inside the yurt stood a birchtree, with nine notches cut in its truck for footholds. A light-coloured horse, acceptable to the sky-god, was chosen, with a man to act as groom— the Footholder, whose soul is thought to accompany the horse's spirit into the upperworld. The *kam* entered the yurt and sat by the fire kindled beside the birch, letting the smoke envelop his tambourine. He summoned the spirits one by one in songs, and as each was caught in the tambourine he replied in a hollow voice, 'Hail, *kam*, here I am'. The *kam* then went to a goose of hay-stuffed cloth, sat on it, and flapped his arms like wings, chanting as he flew.

* He is a solo performer here as in all other rites, though there may be mute extras at the large public shows, e.g. the Lebed shaman has nine men stationed round the victim-horse. Different parts of the song-dance-mime are rendered by voice-throwing, mimicry, change of voice. The way in which shamans conserve and consecrate the group's culture may be gauged by the fact that they have some 12,000 words at their disposal, in comparison with 4,000 in common use. In North America the shaman exerted a similar linguistic function.

'Below the white heaven, above the white clouds, below the blue heaven, above the blue clouds, rise up to heaven O bird'. He replies for the goose, '*Ungai gak gak, ungai gak, kaigai gak gak, kaigai gak*'. A long dialogue of man and bird went on. The aim of the hunt was to catch the soul of the *pura* (sacrificial horse), which neighed, '*Myjak myjak myjak*'. At last it was snared and tied to a pen. The *kam* neighed, kicked, plunged, till the horse was quieted and fumigated with juniper, ready for sacrifice. He then dismissed the goose, 'Take food from Sürö-Berg, take drink from the White Milk Sea, Mother Goose you my Cackler, Mother Bird Kurgai Khan, Mother Bird Engkai Khan, press close upon the people, call upon them crying Jä Jä'. He sacrificed the horse and ended the first part.

Next day he mimed the roles in pilgrimage with the pura to Bai Ulgen. As the fire burned up, he chanted a blessing to the *bash-tukhan*, his assistant, then offered food and drink to the spirits, the Lords of the Tambourine, on behalf of the assembled household, chanting addresses. He also offered rich clothing to Ulgen on behalf of the household's master. The Lord of the Fire was the personified power of the yurt family providing the sacrifice. 'Take it O Kaira Khan [originator of all things], Three-headed Fire-Mother, Four-headed Maiden Mother, when I call *chok*, take it. When I call *Mä*, receive it'. (*Chok* is the libation; *mä* means, 'there, take'.) He then fumigated the drum, at last assumed his full shaman-regalia (generally representing a bird, less often some animal). There were special boots, hat and coat decorated with feathers, or made to look like them; often too little iron pendants or coloured handkerchiefs that swung in the dance. The *kam* stayed by the fire, enveloped in smoke, then beat the drum with measured strokes, summoning many spirits with invocations (including Bai Ulgen and his family). Near the end he invoked Merkyut, the Bird of Heaven, 'Come to me singing, come sporting to my right eye, settle on my right shoulder'. Finally, after various ritual acts he reached his climax, the ascent. This was done slowly, stage by described stage, with recitative and pantomime, and with episodes varied for effect. He treated the *kara-kush* or black bird in his service to a pipe of tobacco; he watered the *pura*, imitating the horse as it drank; he sent his servant to course a hare; he interviewed the great *jajuchi*, who foretold the future in the fifth heaven. In the sixth he did honour to the moon, in the seventh to the sun. He went up through the eighth and ninth with enacted scenes: prayers, prophesies, narrations, blessings. (The greater power a shaman has, the more heavens he climbs, some getting as far as the sixteenth.) At last he called on Bai Ulgen, lowered the drum, humbly bowed, and offered up a prayer; learned if the sacrifice had been accepted, and heard prophecies about weather and crops with injunctions as to sacrifice. Finally the ecstasy broke, the *kam* sank exhausted while the *bash-tushkan* gently withdrew his drum and stick. There was silence in the yurt. The *kam* awoke, rubbed his eyes, smoothed his hair, and spread out his hands, wrung the sweat from his shirt and greeted those around as if after a long journey.

The Yakut say that once the shaman really soared up and they saw sacrificial animals float on clouds while the drum sped after them, followed by the shaman in his prophet's coat. The Ostyak shaman sings that he climbs a rope let down from aloft, brushing aside the stars; he sails the sky in a boat, then comes down so fast that the winds blow through him; next he goes on the underworld journey, aided by winged devils. At other times he comes down a river from the sky. The Buryat shaman has a large tree planted in yurt-middle with its top through the smoke-hole; silk ribbons are strung for the rainbow. Strings are carried to a tree called the Pillar a short way off, and tied to the highest branch. Some shamans go to the treetop and make offerings from there. In the old times, it is said, they walked the silk-strings, an operation called *Walking the Rainbow*. At a shaman's investiture, the yurt-tree is the janitor god allowing him to enter heaven; the red and blue ribbons stretched from its top to the birches outside is the path to the spiritworld. The shaman climbs the yurt-tree and at least some of those outside; at times he leaps from crest to crest along the whole row—from one heaven to the next.

Another great ritual-mime is the convoying of dead souls to the underworld. The shaman describes his journey. He goes across steppes and up a mountain along the track of men's bones. 'The mountains are piebald with the bones of horses'. In through a hole, the earthjaws. then across a sea by a hair-bridge—pointing to more bones at the sea-bottom, bones of men with less spirit-prowess than he. He enters the abode of Erlik Khan, which resembles a Buddhist monastery-settlement, passes a great dog not averse from presents, wins over the great khan with wine and gifts, adding comic relief by a mime of the drunken god who at last gives his blessing and bestows knowledge of the future. The joyous *kam* returns on a goose, not a horse, and walks about the yurt on tiptoe, cackling.

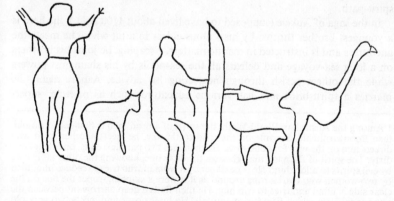

Rock-engraving, Tiout, Sahara Atlas, N. Africa. Man on ostrich-hunt with dog: note his wife seems dancing at home with magic force-line connecting their genitals.

In the Tibetan border areas we meet the *bon*, who fights a death-demon on behalf of the dead man.

He travels; the way is long and hard, full of obstacles. This the sorcerer indicates by his contortions... The Bon has accomplished his task: now he has seized the 'spirit' and prepares to take him away. The demon has received the ransom demanded, but he usually breaks faith and tries to hold on to his slave. The sorcerer fights him, one can see him struggling and panting, one can hear his screams. The family and friends of the dead man follow the phases of the drama with the greatest anxiety. They are overjoyed when the sorcerer declares that he has been successful, and has led the spirit to an agreeable place. (DAVID-NEEL)

We see there the raw material of the myth of Herakles wrestling with Death to save Alkestis; and for his presentation in Euripides' play on that theme, we may recall the *kam's* mime of the drunken god.

Polynesian Myth. We find the shamanist type of myth especially well set out in Polynesia (as also in Siberia and Central Asia). Take the hero Tawhaki. He has married a spirit-wife. After the first child is born, he insults her one day with a casual remark, she flies up to the rooftree and chants farewell, then flies skywards with the child. Tawhaki tries to follow her with his younger brother Kariki. They first visit an old blind ancestress in the underworld and cure her of blindness (a common Polynesian motive*). She directs them to heaven. They climb up vineroots that have reached down into the underworld. Kariki fails and goes home. Tawhaki reaches heaven and is ultimately reunited with wife and child. (There are ten to twelve sky-levels in the Polynesian universe.) In variants he ascends by a tall coconut-palm, a rope, a spiders-thread, or a kite. In a Maori version the kite fails him and he gets on to a hawk; and chants depict him as battling with the winds in kite-fashion. In Tahiti he climbs a high mountain and catches up with his wife on the spirit-path.

In the saga of Aukele (supposed to have lived about 1100 A.D.), the hero is a youngest brother thrown by his jealous elders in a pit where he meets the ancestress and is instructed in mantic matters. Escaping, he joins his brothers on a long sea-voyage and defeats all the sea-perils by his shamanist powers while the others perish through neglecting his advice. Ashore again, he marries a spirit-bride and has various adventures such as meeting super-

---

* Among the Australian Wathi-Wathi the spirit of a dead man is first called Bo-oki, then Boongarnitchie. Starting on the road to the sky, he meets another spirit who directs him on the way for good men. He then sees two parallel roads, one clean, one dirty. The spirit of the good man chooses the dirty one, knowing the other is cleaned by evil spirits to allure him. He is next met by a woman who tries to seduce him, then by two women who twirl a rope around as if it were a skipping-rope; the one on the clear side is blind and tries to trip him. He then finds a deep narrow pit between the two roads, from which flames rise and fall. He jumps over and meets two very old women, who take care of him. Finally he is tested by Thatha-pulli, and has to throw a nulla-nulla in an emu-drive and knock one down. (A shooting-star is the trial throw by a new spirit.)

natural birds and travelling the underworld to steal the Waters of Kane and resurrect the dead. In his first adventure he has a guardian spirit, the god Lono, in a box; in his second he follows the counsel of his wife who knows the ways of the skyworld and the underworld. He is also helped by ancestors whom he encounters.

Ngaru in Mangaia is instructed underground by an ancestress and tackles monsters on earth, then journeys through the underworld and the heavens. His fate is controlled by the Four Daughters of Miru, who bind and truss him as Mangaians truss corpses for burial. They take him to the oven of Miru, the blind underworld ogress, but he escapes by catching at a plant below, reaches the land Taumareva 'where fruits and flowers grow profusely and the inhabitants excel in flute playing', and returns to earth. Finally he is raised to heaven in a sky-demon's basket and his grandfather sends up little lizards to help him kill the demon.

Pit or cave represent the place of initiation ordeal and seclusion. The hero Ono-Kura, a youngest son, is put in a cave where he grows up and gains mantic powers that enable him, with a familiar's aid, to direct an expedition, kill monsters, and cure illness. The myth-motives have their counterpart in many practices. The youthful heir to the rule on Gambier Island was cave-secluded, and the last high priest of Mangaia recounted how he was 'kept in a cave by his mother apart from all others and from his infancy was taught these . . . precious truths'. (In Tibet the novice seeking mantic powers must sit three years secluded in a pit, then jump up, crosslegged, so that his head come through the hole of the cupola over him.)

Samoa abounds in tales of heaven-visits, with the hero returning loaded with fruits and vegetables. Once nine men go aloft and are challenged by the gods must pay forfeits. As among the Tatars, the heroes win by wit. At the gods in a series or ordeals from which they emerge victorious, so that times a bride is brought down. Two Tongoloans or sky-gods steal birds of the chief Lu, who chases them through nine heavens. In the tenth, Tongaloa appears and says they are now in the great sanctuary where no strife is allowed. He hears Lu's complaints and gives him his daughter in marriage and Lu returns peaceably home. In the Marquesas the hero makes the journey after the soul of a dead wife. Kena goes twice and brings his wife back in a basket.

The tales of Maui and Hina his wife or sister are known widely over the Pacific. Maui is small, prematurely born on the seashore. (Polynesian heroes' births are often abnormal.) He is educated by sea-deities, then by an ancestor, rejoins his mother and brothers, and sleeps by his mother. Finding that she slips off every morning into a hole, he changes to a wood-pigeon, follows her, and comes on both his parents. His father purifies him over a running stream and performs the naming rite. (Similar rites took place in the Whare Wananga of New Zealand, done by the *tohuna* on his pupils.) But the chant omits one name, so Maui gets into the wrong relationship with the gods and ultimately dies through it. But meanwhile he returns to earth, teaches his brothers agriculture, and has many marvellous adventures. Thus, he snares the sun in a noose. (In a pass in the Peruvian Andes, iron rings on ruined towers were said to have been once used to stretch a net from hill to hill for catching the sun.) Maui steals fire from underworld-spirits and invents the calabash for navigation. A cycle deals with his fishing exploits; he improves ell-spears and fishes islands up, and so on. As his greatest deed he goes down into the earth to defeat death itself. He tries to enter the body of the great ancestress Hine-nui-to-Io from the nether end and creep up, emerging through the mouth. By thus reversing the normal process of things he hopes to find a permanent rebirth for himself and mankind. But he fails through the name-flaw.*

Maui is a thoroughly popular hero, who never ascends the sky. The tradition distinguishes carefully between him and Tawhaki. He is placed much earlier in the pedigrees. The Maori sage called his saga mere 'ovenside tales'.

Tatar Poems. Tatar culture is even richer than Polynesian in shamanist heroes. The poem *Kogutei* of the Altai Tatars tells of a beaver's adoption by a childless old couple. The beaver grows up and is married, but his wife's family despise him. He does all the work on the hunt, but his brothers-in-law claim the credit. However, he insists of getting their little toes and fingers for his aid. Finally colts, carried off by the Bird Khan Kerede, have to be rescued. The hero leaves his beaver-coat with his wife and rides off on a splendid raven-black steed. Killing a snake that threatens the Bird's fledglings, he wins the Bird's gratitude and is given the colts. The cowardly brothers-in-law dig a deep pit, decoy him into it, and take the colts. The Bird rescues the hero, who returns home and exposes the villains by producing their fingers and toes. He lays a death-curse on the *aul* and goes back to his adoptive father.†

There are a large number of variants, as well as similar tales that involve journeys underground and aloft. In a Kachin poem *Kara Tygan* the opening scene is a wedding. The hero is told by his wife and brother-in-law that when drunk he bragged of his power to resurrect a couple of corpses. The latter turn to swallows and their horses to swans; they fly to a tree on the Altai. On the summit is the white life-herb with raven nestlings lying over it, guarded by two ravens. The men-birds gain the herb and the vow is redeemed. The rest of the poem deals with the theft of the soul of the hero's horse and a skill contest.

---

* The rites that seek to imitate birth-process are endless—from the stripping of sick children in Cornwall and their passage by a woman nine times under a donkey's belly, to the crawling of Balinese adults on all fours under a wooden cow, from between the hind legs out through the front ones. In Travancore the rulers, descending by the female line, were taken at night, before they ascended the throne, to a special temple where they entered the effigy of a large gold cow and emerged blessed and accepted as Brahmans: they were of the Kshatriya caste before. Then came immersion in a closed tank in the temple.

† The Bear's Son cycle of folktales to which this tale belongs is one of the main ingredients underlying *Beowulf*. In a poem of the Kysyl Tatars the hero who is put in the pit wears a bear-skin; he is drawn out by the long hair of a woman. L. R. Carpenter, in *Folk Tale Fiction* and *Saga in the Homeric Epic* detects the Bear's-son type in the Odyssey.

The opponent steals the hero's eyes without his noticing it; next night the hero steals the other's tongue, and wins. In a poem from the Sayan Steppe, the hero is hurt hunting a fox (a daughter of Erlik in fox-guise). A nine-headed Jelbagan rides up on a forty-horned ox, cuts off the hero's head, and takes it below. The hero's sister, Kubai Ko, follows the tracks through the hole. In the underworld she sees people in troops being tortured in ways appropriate to their sins, and comes on a riverbank where stands Erlik's gabled house, nine larches growing from a single root in front.* She ties her horses to the larches, like Erlik's horses, enters the house and is tormented by unseen hands, which tear her clothes. She follows Erlik, who ignores her, into a room where the eight princes of death are seated, Erlik in their midst. She is told that she may have her brother's head if she pulls up a goat buried to its horns. Led through nine rooms full of heads, she pulls the goat up, gets her brother's head from among the others, while the death-princes expound the meaning of all she has seen. Returned to earth, she sticks the head back on the body, but can do no more. She weeps. Kudai pities her and sends the waters of life, which she sprinkles thrice on the dead lips. Her brother revives.

The Kazak *Erkäm Aidar* tells of a brother's quest of the herb of healing for his sister, who is pretending illness to get him out of the way. Succeeding with the aid of the Three Wise Maids, he is slain by his sister's lover. His horse bears him to the Maids, who revive him with the medicines they have taken from his bag at each stage of the journey home. Finally he kills his sister and her lover, and marries the Three. In *Kadysh Märgän* the hero slays three Jelbägän and takes their wives for himself and his brothers. The latter treacherously wound him, but he is healed by a root which he saw mice use as balsam. Then he and two halfmen are restored to youth and health by an old giantess, and he takes revenge on his brothers.

In a Sagai poem, *Altyn Pyrkan*, the hero is pursued through air, earth and underground. He is saved by being sucked up a young foal's nostril. His foe is aided by two royal eagles and two hounds, Kasar and Pasar, a seven-headed monster, the Swanwoman and the great carp from the sea-bottom. In the end the foal calls on the aid of the heroine, who comes as a golden cuckoo, sprinkles the life-water on the dead hero and lays a yellow herb on his mouth. He then has such strength that when he cracks his whip even the *jaj*, tutelary

---

* Erlik Khan rules the underworld, an old black-bearded man, sometimes a wholly black man. His retainers may act as familiars of the Earth-hero, who borrows them to hunt human quarry. Among other underworld-spirits are the Swanwoman Chekchäkäi with leaden eyes, hempen plaits, yellow nailed hands, and Altyn Sibaldi the Golden Witch, leaden-eyed and coppernosed, mother of nine sons, the Jelbägän with seven or nine heads whose house is guarded by flame-breathing dogs. (Jelmogus, singular of Jelbägän, seems a sort of dragon-hero.) The superimposed planes of heaven are ruled by Khaira Khan (Bai Ulgen, Kydyr, Kudai the Strong One) who has under him the nine Jajan or Creators and the Wise Maidens, generally a triad, who guard the herbs of healing and the waters of life. The hero often meets the Jajan first, and they guide him to the Maids and instruct him as to behaviour. There is a world-tree connected with the heaven-ascent.

spirit, in heaven cannot remain seated. He slays his foe and the familiars, overcomes two brothers but lets them go after purifying their souls, then ascends to heaven to woo the heroine. The Jajan discourage him in the first heaven, but in the second he gets a better reception because he has purified and spared the two brothers. (Mercy and gentleness are often the supreme virtues inculcated in the poems.) The heroine has sworn to wed only the man who can beat her in wrestling and archery. She and the hero wrestle and their match takes on a cosmic aspect; the Jajan cannot hold the disintegrating earth together. At last the hero wins, puts the girl in his pocket, and rides home with her to his yurt, where he makes her his wife.

In these tales and poems, the division between the sky-world and the under-earth, seen in the Polynesian differences of Tawhaki and Maui, is systematised; the sky-world has become the superior place, the source of aid for the good hero. The two spirit-peoples do not, themselves, meet; they act through their effect on the hero, who is often opposed by the Black or Earth Hero. The soul is throughout regarded as an object, though it sometimes is a bird instead of an inanimate thing. Victory is by wit (magic) and the contriver of it is normally 'a woman or a horse or a supernatural being'. The lost soul is often a severed head.*

Craft Associations. We have been omitting one fraternity-form of the utmost importance, that of the craft-workers. This form arises with the specialisation or division of labour, and is particularly significant when we reach metal-working. However, it has a general continuity from the early days of tribal disintegration.

In ancient Egypt professional groups were set under various deities, the artisans for example under Ptah; the handicraftsmen were well organised. Babylonia and Assyria had merchant guilds. The Graeco-Roman world was thick with fraternities of crafts and trades, collegia; and through the Byzantine area the antique form played its part in building the medieval guilds of the west, merging with forms developed direct from the clan; and the guilds in turn lead on to the trade unions, directly in France with its campagnonnage, indirectly in England through the breaking-up yeomanry of the guilds. The early trade-unions kept up ordeals and initiations for the entrant. In Anatolia there was a steady development of the collegia into Moslem times. Africa was specially full of craft-fraternities; in the advanced states they were organised

---

* A form of the double that is halfway between the ordinary spirit-twin and the familiar is the sex-double, which is found strongly among the Hausa. These people consider everyone has a *bori* of the opposite sex, who may be lost at marriage but may cling on. Men and women copulate with their *bori*; the *bori* is generally jealous, and so has to be ritually circumvented at marriage. A remnant of this belief seems widespread in the motive of the False Bride. We find also conflicts in legends between actual wife and spirit-bride (*Er Toshtuk* of the Kara-Kirghi, or the Irish Cuchulainn saga).

from above, e.g. the sultan of the smiths in Haussa and Mana Wadi had court-privileges, needed to be read in the Koran, and collected taxes.*

These historical forms of the craft-fraternity inherited much from the early days we are considering. The first professionals—carpenters, smiths, physicians, bards, and seers (shamans) are known to Homer—slowly emerge as there is sufficient surplus to maintain specialised workers, and are organised with initiation-ritual and the like derived from tribal society. What is of particular importance, however, is the way they apply the imagery and lore of the death-rebirth rite. In the mysteries, these elements are used to meet the needs of the suffering masses for a formula of escape from the wheel of necessity; in the craft-fraternities, they are used to develop ideas of the transformation of matter and of the active relation of man to nature. In this way the craft-fraternities, like the shamans and the mysteries, vitally carried on certain aspects of tribal thinking, which would otherwise have been lost.

The craftsmen employed the only thought-processes available, which were magical; and partly to conserve their monopoly and partly because magical powers must by their nature be kept from the profane, the uninitiated, they built up a considerable store of spells and charms. of rituals considered as techniques and techniques considered as rituals. Without this equipment their work could not have been carried on; and the folklore of the smith shows how consistently an aura of dread and strangeness accompanied his activities.

Torres Straits, with its immigrant population, does not possess the canoe, nor any substitute for it that will carry passengers farther than to the next island of that closely-placed group; the Banks Islands, the larger group of which the Torres Straits form a part, are in little better case; Mangarava, which used to have a large and tolerably seaworthy raft, applied to them a name properly meaning the outrigger of a canoe. And this degeneracy is quite readily accounted for; the canoe-makers have died out; now as no one else knows the correct magic, it follows that no one can make canoes. Only in a few populations like that of Lakon, in the island of Sta. Maria, who are apparently daring freethinkers, has the lost art been recovered, possibly there by the immigration of some native missionary who initiated them into the precious gospel of canoe-making once more. (ROSE)

In ancient Greece a number of semi-mythical groups, the Telchines, Daktyls (Fingers), Cyclops, and others, represent the early craft-fraternities with their mysterious lores.

Such associations played their part in fostering the growth of gods. The natives of the Society Islands worshipped gods of farming, carpentry, canoe-making, forestry, acting, singing, hairdressing, combing and other forms of

---

* Among the Moslem corporations we may note from 10-12th centuries the influence of Sufism, with ascetic and monastic motives. Under the Abassids they were connected with the court and took on chivalric colours, with a prevalence of military and sporting activities; then after the Mongol conquests trade-interests reasserted themselves. Another professional group were the Ghazi, fighters for the faith, who begot the Janissary corps. India, China, Korea, Japan, in historical times show everywhere the professional or craft fraternities.

work. Craft-groups among the Zuni worshipped special deities and maintained priesthoods, rites and places of worship, for them. Among the Yoruba we find the *orisha* or god, Ogun, patron of blacksmiths, hunters, warriors, and snake-charmers; among his symbols is a piece of iron; and he is worshipped by all handicraftsmen, who thus form a special group. (The adherents of each *orisha* follow exogamic rules.)

Transformations. In the neolithic era trade was going on, especially in magic objects such as bright pebbles from the deserts, shells from the sea. Small articles, made of (probably native) copper, appear. By the 'Ubaid phase in Mesopotamia and the Gerzean in Egypt, men had found out the clue to extracting copper from ores by the chemical process of reduction—smelting. Potters kilns, derived from bread-ovens, perhaps gave the needed heat. Soon glazing was discovered and faience made. It is highly likely that these first steps in the use of heat for transformation were made in the quest for magical or life-giving substances. The processes of chemical change were interpreted as a form of ritual death-birth and were guarded by the fraternities which took them over.

Let us glance at the discoveries of applied science that men had so far made. A stick in the hand increases the radius of muscular activity; a club accumulates that activity in kinetic form. The bow-and-arrow turns muscular energy into the form and action of the drawn bow, from which it is released instantaneously and with great intensity. (In the later crossbow the energy can be stored up.) Sword and spear unite the increased length of the arm-radius with the concentrated effectiveness of edge and point. Such concentrations, by diminishing resistance, exert a much greater intensity of pressure. (The same principle leads on to levers, wheels, ball-bearings and the like.)

Fire had been early discovered. Perhaps sparks were struck from flints, especially iron pyrites, a mineral with superior spark-emitting qualities, which is found in glittering nodules and crystals. The feeling of a magical power in stones might draw attention to such a mineral, and the emission of the sparks would increase the conviction of magic. With fire, men could cook. Cooked food eased the digestion and released blood to feed the stimulated brain. Thus the first processes of transformation were carried on.

The decisive moment came with the firing of pots. The expulsion of the water-of-constitution from clay by heat changes a plastic lump into a solid one, into a 'stone'. Probably the women found the secret out by noting that clay, plastered on fibre-baskets, hardened in a strong fire. The next step was metallurgy, which may have resulted accidentally through fires being lighted on an ore-bearing outcrop or which may well have been achieved experimentally in the handling of life-giving materials and objects. Directed into stone moulds, the molten metal hardened to required forms.

Here was the moment when men realised that they could do more than utilise natural objects, trimming or shaping them for greater efficiency. They could actually change things, change what seemed their essential being.

Khnum making human beings on the potters' wheel while the frog-goddess offers the ankh (*life*).

All the practical science of the ancient smiths and miners was certainly embedded in an unpractical matrix of magic ritual. Assyrian texts, even in the First Millenium B.C., contain hints of what such rituals may have involved—foetuses and virgins' blood. So do the remains of a bronze-workers' encampment on Heather Burn Cave (Co. Durham) in England. (CHILDE)

But we do not do justice to the situation in simply seeing a core of fact confused by a mass of irrational magic. The ideas pervading the magic were what enabled men to get at grips with the problem at all, enabled them to generalise the facts and to develop hypotheses which linked the processes with human life. To deplore the magic is to deplore the ways in which men have become human and to substitute an abstract rationalism for the fullness of factors that make up life and development.

Men were aware that in transforming nature they were also transforming themselves, that the processes of their crafts were somehow one with the processes of creation in Nature. The Egyptians depicted the making of man by the image of the ram-headed god Khnum building up figurines on the potter's wheel.

It is not a little interesting to note the point where the word 'character' itself first occurs in human speech. It began to appear in the Pyramid Age. . . The word itself is very interesting. Its original meaning is to shape, to form, to build, and it was early employed especially to designate the work of the potter in shaping clay vessels on the wheel. (BREASTED)

Neolithic Mother-goddess. In the crucial area of south-west Asia we find a clear transition from the earlier mothercult, exemplified by the figurines from Tell Arpachiyah. The features are seldom shown, and most are in a squatting position that suggests childbirth. Stylisation at times reduces the body to a cone or peg; perforations suggest an amulet-use. The figurines are associated with dove and double-axe, bull-head and serpent, as were the later mother-images of Crete and the Aegean. So, they serve as link between the Paleolithic and the Bronze Age in the East Mediterranean and in Iran, Baluchistan, the Indus Valley. The stress on the maternal organs proves their nature as fertility-charms. In West Asia such objects are not common till the Halaf period; then they show up all along the Syrian coast to the Zagros Mountains. Male forms appear on seals and pottery, but the figurines are normally female. They squat or hold their breasts; eyes are put in with black paint; and horizontal lines on shoulders, arms and feet may represent clothing or ornamentation. At some sites the figurines thus wear clothes or are tattooed, but they also sit on stools as if giving birth, and wear turbans.

At one of these sites, Arpachiyah, we meet a series of ten domed buildings with a circular plan. The earlier, made of clay, is some 12 feet across. They then grow larger. The biggest is 31 feet and is approached by a long ante-room or dromos. The structures were sacred, as they held many clay mothers and two important burials were made right against one outer wall. (Later builders did not disturb the foundations in at least seven cases, thus showing a taboo that was still active in Sumeria some 2,000 years afterwards.) A network of cobbled roads led into the buildings or radiated from them. The date is the 6th-5th millenia. Even earlier circular buildings occur at Jericho. The tradition of round buildings has carried on in north Iraq, north Syria and south-east Asia Minor till today, though such forms are rare on early Mesopotamian sites. At Tepe Gawrah, around 3400 B.C., occurs a large circular house. The plan seems to have influenced Mediterranean builders in Cyprus and Crete, with later effects at Byblos, Jericho and central Anatolia.*

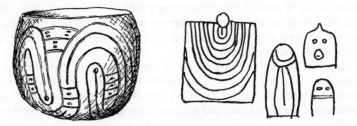

Neolithic bowl probably imitating gourd-vessel, with spiral and meander patterns: Flambon, Alzey, Germany (Danubian I). Mother figures on French megalithic tombs.

---

* One odd connection with the circular corbelled tombs at Amizaraque in South Spain are the models in stone of human fingerbones (connected with some ritual mutilation?) which occur both there and at Arpachiyah.

We need not analyse the types of the figurines in detail. They include fiddle-shapes, torsos with prominent breasts, elongated reptilian heads (among the first settlers in the marshes of the Euphrates delta) with bitumen wigs, cylindrical bodies, bodies with slender waists, large hips and almond-eyed rounded faces, monstrously-snouted heads, hair hanging to shoulders or coiled round the head, beaked noses, pellet-breasts. Oddities are the eye-goddesses of Brak; on front of one is represented a stag surmounted by a bird—an image later associated with the goddess Ninharsag. Naked mother-figures are further found in early Iran and Turkestan.

The fertility-function is clear, and the proliferation of the forms has its link with the advent of agriculture. The identification of Mother and Earth must have become stronger, with a need to placate the latter for systematically tearing at her flesh, the soil. At the same time, the division of the sexes is intensified, whether or not agriculture was at first a woman's mystery. (It is with the plough that men definitely take over the fields—the coulter being conceived as a rigid penis in coitional movement over and into the earth.)

The opposition and the union of the sexes in producing children and food become more deeply felt. There is both a heightened antagonism and a new possiblity of love and co-operation.

Marriage is a union of two like and merging units. It joins two different types of individuals, belonging to different groups of kinspeople, and it is a relationship marked by many tensions. Some Wiko describe coitus itself as 'fighting', and see the comparison. It is 'fighting with joy', and in the circumcision ceremonies men and women 'struggle with joy'. Marriage which gives birth to children, and the bringing up of those children to be full and fertile members of the tribe are seen as the unending struggle in which unity has to be established by ritual which comes from the ancestors. This unity is based on the complementary differences between the sexes. The ceremonial of the lodge dramatises the struggle and the union. . . The transvestism of the initial and final dances symbolises this ultimate unity of purpose. . . The appeals for unity at the dances, and the taboos on quarrelling show that their co-operation is of hostile partners. The social positions of men and women, like their respective contributions to procreation, and their tasks in social life, are not inevitable, but are ordained by the ancestors, for the great song of the lodge speaks of the temporary reversal of their roles, reflected in a reversal of nature, which had to be set right. The struggle is unceasing, but it works through the ritual in the interests of society; it creates power and makes the new generation fertile. (GLUCKMAN)

We may apply this analysis of the sex-roles among the Wiko to the phase we are considering. In China, as we shall see later, there is clear evidence for this new stress on the division of the sexes and their parts in work and festival as well as in marriage.

Music. We may pause here to consider the nature of primitive music in general. Like art, it is a magical power linked with dance-ritual and ecstatic liberations; it is mainly choral even when dealing with love or mourning, but the distinction of chorus and soloist is clear and never confused. There is a close relation to speech, the meaning of words and their structure; the slightest change in the words involves a modification of melody. Sound is considered a substance, a concrete and living part of the universe, playing a constructive function and echoing from the spirit-cavern. The musician's task is to localise the object (which the sound represents and is), to unite himself with it, by hitting the right note. He tries to gain this relationship by means of a sympathetic vibration, such as a rattle-shake or the singing of a short motive. If he succeeds, the spirit enters into him and sings through his voice. A mask may be useful in making a spirit recognise its tune. Every disease has its countersong which heals and restores harmony with nature. Every person has his song, which he must hold fast to as part of his magic, but which he can bequeath. From another angle the song is the ancestral home and the ancestor himself come to inhabit the singer.

African pygmies start with a wild howl from which some sort of consonance grows, melody and rhythm come together, and an ordered community-chant is achieved.

Primitive melody, which is scarcely more than continually repeated and varied motive, is regulated essentially by the tension between the beginning of the motive and its final note. All the notes between are determined by the conscious striving towards the last note. But the motive and the series of its repetitions *grow* according to definite patterns which can assume the most varied forms according to the particular culture of the ideas and feeling expressed. (SCHNEIDER)

Development seems to come about roughly as follows. The continuation of a theme is by varied repetition, with the determination of ambit aided by the attack of the first note and the form of cadence. Simple transpositions of motive are made (e.g. by the Australians). The tonal ambit is extended by more stress on the lower notes of the motive in the second exposition or by stretching the material so that in repetition the closing note is lower than in the first statement; or the voice, repeating motives of narrow compass, takes an abrupt up or down leap. Most ambit-patterns appear in early cultures, but the application is at first restricted and only slowly develops, with variations according to the culture concerned. 'Thus, according to the culture in which it occurs, a pattern which circles round a central note may become a recitative when it is interrupted, now by a high note, now by a low one, or it may develop into a gently oscillatory song.'

The repetitive system of variation and circling (or spiralling) form is common to tales, to songs (in their words), and to music—one medium reacting on the other: for all elements in primitive culture closely affect one another, just as all persons play their part in the total effect.

There is no artistic native (in the New Hebrides) or great artist or respect for art: because all are artists and their art is an essential part of their green uniform tree. Naturally some will be finer carvers, more exquisite dancers, or especial story tellers. They may be paid for their services. No man is unable to carve, dance and tell stories.

The impulse to artform is tradition, via ritual (and religion). The object of artform is the satisfaction of function or of ritual; and the intensification of life beyond mere necessity into beauty, fury and ecstasy. It plays its part in a whole cycle of prebirth to afterdeath, in sacrifice and resurrection especially—into this pattern all things fall.

The art of dancing is, in their own view, their highest art. . . The Na-leng dances include dramatic performances and improvised pantomime, sometimes exceedingly funny. Dancing is not done independent of ritual. Music is used almost exclusively with dancing, not as a thing in itself. . . Songs are a form of story-telling. Words are a native art with an intricate circular pattern. (T. HARRISON)

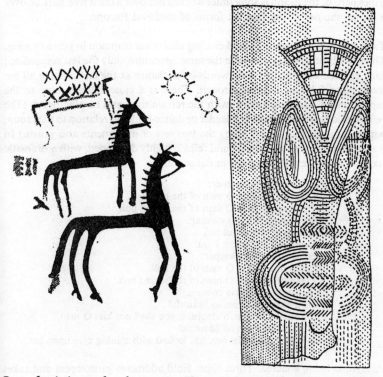

Part of painting, red and green, on Shaman's Drum, from Siberia, probably Ostiak. Geometrised female figure, engraved on mammoth tusk, Piedmost, Moravia (late paleolithic).

Work-process and dance are the great begetters of rhythm, as we have seen, and the relation is close. 'The movements of the dance are quite homologous to those of work'. But this does not mean a simple reflection of one in the other:

Some tribes innervate so that the innervation for the articulation and for the movement of hands coincide. This habit has the effect of letting the clapping, drumming, or stamping follow the accent of the song. It is also not a rare occurrence that the rhythmic pattern of body-movement and of song are not homologous but that they are interrelated in different ways or sometimes even seem to be quite independent. Negro music as well as that of North-west America offers many examples of this kind. (BOAS)

Dance and work however have provided the basis on which the elaborated patterns of song develop with rhythmical subtleties.

Polyphony has an early origin, e.g. in the more or less free imitation of the African pygmies or in the strict form found amoung the Kenta pygmies and Sakai of the Malay Peninsula. On Flores, where remnants of ancient Papuan tribes persist, the canon is sometimes worked out over a third free part or over a drone, the *pes* of the canonic forms of medieval Europe.

Tales and Songs. Repetitive and circling effects are common in prose or song. Thus, five brothers may carry out the same adventure, only the last succeeding; each episode will use the same words—the change at the end coming all the more powerfully as a break-through. There is a close relation here to the repetitions of dance and work, with the refrain used as a turning-point. (The refrain also represents the work-leader or dance-leader in relation to the group, with a dynamic tension set up by the two sets of movements and words.) In Sumerian poetry we find stanza and refrain highly developed, with a dramatic method which reveals the basis in dance-mime:

> Enlil calls to the Gatekeeper:
> O man of the gate O man of the bolts
> O man of the lock O man of the sacred bolt
> Your queen Ninlil is coming.
> If she asks you about me,
> Do not tell her where I am.
> Enlil called to the Gatekeeper:
> O man of the gate O man of the bolt
> O man of the lock O man of the sacred bolt
> Your queen Ninlil is coming.
> The maiden so sweet so beautiful
> You shall not O man embrace, you shall not kiss O man.
> To Ninlil so sweet so beautiful
> Has Enlil shown favour, has looked with shining eyes upon her.

A myth is being enacted. Three times Enlil addresses gatekeepers and takes their place, mating with Ninlil.

A fragment from Mitylene on Lesbos, dated the 6th century B.C.—about the time of Sappho and Alkaios—shows us how rhythm in the labour-song is controlled by the movements of work: 'O grind/quernmill O/grind/for/hard/ Pit-/takos he/grinds/all of our/great Mity-/le-/ne,/overlord/he'. A Kwakiutl canoe-song with each syllable sung to a paddle stroke helps us to see how such definite rhythms help to organise form: *Aw ha ya ha ya hā| ha ya he ya ā| he ya ha ya ā| A ha ya ha ya hā| aw ha ya he ya hā| he ya ha ya hei| ya hā| hā hā wo wo wo*. Sometimes a tune carried thus on vocables serves as introduction to the words of a song, or an exhortative speech may develop a rhythmic form by adding to each word a strongly-accented syllable, e.g., *ai* among the Kwakiutl. (The time for each word-group ending in *-ai* will be approximately equal, or will be pronounced with great rapidity if a longer phrase is to be covered.)

In myth-recitals also, rhythmic structure may be gained by adding such a chant-syllable, e.g., *notchee notchee* in the tales of the culture-heroes of the Fox Indians. In Paiute myths each animal speaks with its own rhythm and tune. Eskimo tales of the wandering hero are interspersed with melodic phrases. In wails a formal moaning-cry at short intervals, plus the quick even tone of recitation, brings about rhythmic structure. On the North-west Coast the songs refer to different spirits, each with his own vocable: the bear, *hei hei*; the cannibal spirit, *ham ham*.

Ham ham hamaya he who travels from one end of the world to the other *ham ham*
Ham ham hamaya the great cannibal of the north and of the world *ham ham*
Ham ham hamaya he who carries corpses to be his food *ham ham.*

Haida painting: sea monster in wolf-form.

Choric interjections in prose tales have much the same effect. Thus, when in Africa the narrator says, 'The turtle killed the leopard', the audience clap hands and repeat, 'The leopard, the leopard'.

Another form of repetition lies in the heaping up of synonyms and metaphors, periphrasis. The application of the principle of dual segmentation leads to the form of parallel statements, which provides the main basis of Sumerian, Egyptian, Hebrew poetry. Finally out of this trend to symmetry comes the rhyming couplet or quatrain. Here is a stanza from an American song of the North-west which shows the impulse to use synonym and repetition for an effect of total balance:

> *Hana hana hana* it broke down, the post of the world,
> It fell down to the ground, the post of the world,
> Our great chief has taken a rest,
> Now our great chief has fallen down.

Such a form is very close to Sumerian verse:

> Even if birdlike I had stretched out my wings,
> And like a bird flown to my city,
> Yet my city would have perished on its foundations,
> Yet Ur would have perished where it lay.

The following Cherokee formula for hunt-success shows the way in which metaphor is developed:

Give me the wind. Give me the breeze. Yu, O Great Earthly Hunter, I come to the edge of your spittle where you repose. Let your stomach cover itself, let it be covered with leaves. Let it cover itself at a single bend, and may you never be satisfied.

And you O Ancient Red may you hover above my breast while I sleep. Now let good develop, let my expressions be propitious. Ha. Now let my little trails be directed, as they lie down in various directions. Let the leaves be covered with clotted blood and may it never cease to be so. You too shall bury it in your stomachs. Yu.

The Hunter is the river with spittle-foam; the Red is the fire with whose ashes the man rubs his breast. He throws bloodstained leaves into the fire and into the water. Thus the magical action creates the sense of oneness with the river and the fire, humanising them and making the forces of nature allies in the hunt. The aesthetic sense is throughout bound up with the magical; and the sense of active unity with nature begets a conviction of abounding and triumphant life. This conviction is the basis of aesthetic judgment, and art is an expression which strengthens the feeling of harmonious relationship with the life-process, with the sources of fecundity.

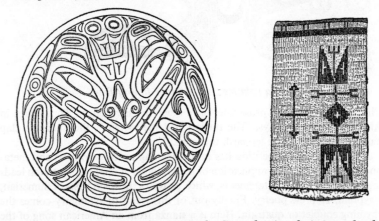

Slate dish with sea monster design, Haida. Sioux legging depicting a battle: the diamond is a man's body; triangles, village-tents; prongs, wounds or blood; lines, arrow-flights; crossed lines, arrows, lances.

The following songs have a deep delight in nature, an appreciation of beauty, but we must beware of detaching this aspect from the magical sense of power, of advancing life. The first is Apache, the second Navaho.

At the east wind where the black water lies,
    Stands the large corn, with staying roots, its large stalks, its red silk,
    Its long leaves, its tassels dark and spreading, on which there is dew.
At the sunset where the yellow water lies,
    Stands the large pumpkin with its tendrils, its long stem,
    Its wide leaves, its yellow top, on which there is pollen.

    On the trail marked with pollen may I walk
    With grasshoppers about my feet may I walk
    With dew about my feet may I walk
    With beauty before me may I walk
    With beauty behind me may I walk
    With beauty above me may I walk
    With beauty under me may I walk
    With beauty all around me may I walk
    In my old age wandering on a trail of beauty, lively, may I walk,
    In old age wandering on a trail of beauty, living again, may I walk.
    It is finished in beauty.

We may note the similarity to the Celtic *Lorica* (Breastplate), a verse-spell to keep travellers safe; and the connection is not superficial. Beauty is here a force that saves and renews, not something that is enjoyed for its own sake.

Survivals. The trails of survivals in art, poetry, folklore from the phases under consideration are endless. Here I shall merely indicate a few typical examples. Thus, we noted the turn-in-a-circle as a movement of ritual rebirth. In Cornwall the children sing:

            Turn, ladies, turn,
            The more we turn the more we may.
            Queen Anne was born on Midsummer Day.

There the birth-turn is linked with the summer solstice and the game has roots going back to the great Celtic fire-festivals. In Alsace is sung:

            Little Mary Rose, turn round three times.
            Let us look at you, round and round.
            Rose of the May come to the greenwood away.

Here the releasing turn expresses the new birth of the green year and of the initiate renewed with nature.

Or take the theme of the identity of man and animal, and the guilt of killing the latter. Here is a song of the Papago Indians of North America:

            Early I rose
            In the blue morning.
            My love was up before me.
            It came running to me from the doorways of the Dawn.
            On Papago Mountains
            The dying quarry
            Looks at me with my love's eyes.

This theme is often rationalised, e.g. in many ancient Greek legends, rationalising some sacrificial rite, where a lover kills his girl accidentally on a hunt. Thus, Cichyros thinks the beloved a leopard and kills her. In folksongs the dramatic form leaves an effect halfway between the rationalisation and the Papago guilt-pang. Thus in the Savoy the lover goes to shoot partridges, but

> O it was my darling's heart that I cleft in two.
> Sweet my darling tell me, have I done hurt to you ?
> A little bit, hardly at all. If I die in pain,
> One kiss of yours will bring me back to life again.

The last line aims only at pathos, but suggests a dim memory of a resurrection. A Devon folksong opens:

> In the night the fair maid as a white swan appears,
> She says, O my true love, quick, dry up your tears,
> I freely forgive you, I have paradise won,
> I was shot by my true love at the setting of the sun.

In other versions the girl hides under a bush from the rain and is shot. 'With her head in her apron I thought her a swan'. The lover is arrested and tried for murder, but the swan maiden appears in court to vindicate him. Here the rationalisation falls away and the girl appears as the spirit-bird, akin to spirit-bride who is won by having her plumage stolen while she bathes.

An example of the rationalising of the belief that one of a pair of twins is spirit-begotten appears in Marie de France's medieval *Lay of the Ash*. Two families live near one another; one wife produces twins and is maligned as necessarily an adultress by the other, who shortly after herself brings twins forth. In horror at the *grant deshonur* she has one of the girls exposed in a hollow ash. A further primitive motive appears in the mode of exposure; for ash is the tree specially favoured for use in a curative rebirth-rite carried on in our own days, particularly in the Celtic parts of England: the tree is split and the sick child passed through, thus being reborn of the mother-tree, purified.

Art. There are a few points that may be added to what has been already said of art at this phase. Thus, an account by a Winnebago brings out the magical nature of cave-paintings. His father took him to a sacred cave in Wisconsin and looked there 'for a stone pillar, and upon it, at about arm's length, he drew the pictures of a number of different animals. My father possessed only one arrow, but that was a holy one. Then dancing around the stone pillar and singing some songs, he finished by breathing upon the pillar. Finally he walked around and shot at it and when he looked at the stone it had turned into a deer with large horns which fell dead at his feet'.

Secondly, we may note at this phase of what we may call generally fetishistic art, the stress put on the head as the life-source. We see this stress in Oceanic, African and Celtic art; and a close analysis of Homer shows that in primitive Greek thinking: 'The head is the life or the seat of life. The head is in some sense the persons. A man is referred to as a "head".' 'The dead are particularly thought of as "heads".*

There is the complete parallelism of the lines 'sent many mighty *psychai* to Hades' and 'sent many mighty heads to Hades' and the parallelism of the descriptions of people who follow dangerous courses 'staking their *psychai*' or 'staking their heads'. Finally, the *psychai* themselves in Hades are four times spoken of as 'passionless heads of the dead'. That the *psyche* was the head or in the head will help us to understand why the distinctive appurtenance of Hades was a *kynee*, a helmet enclosing the head, i.e. enclosing the *psyche*, and rendering invisible. (ONIANS)*

It seems clear then that the fetishistic emphasis of the head comes from the fact that a spirit, not a living man, is represented.* The use of the ritual mask, which transforms the dancer into a spirit, thus becomes easier to comprehend; and the distortions of mask or fetish fall into their proper perspective. What we have is not an art that distorts human forms, but one that renders spirits. The particular tensions, emphasises, geometrisations, or rhythmic reconstructions in the forms are not made at random, but have their specific meaning in connection with the spirit depicted, even if the meaning has been wholly or partly forgotten in a long tradition.

In the Tassili rock-paintings of North Africa is a figure with bandy legs, brick-red ochre, the body covered with white chequerwork pattern and wearing only a loincloth. The elongated and horned mask of this figure strongly suggests masks still used in West Africa, e.g. initiation-masks of the Sienuf of the Ivory Coast—though there the horns are turned outwards. Plants (? flowers) issue from the man's arms and thighs. (He has been painted over a round-headed woman, another of whom still stands facing him.) From this work it would seem that the negroid mask goes back into the prehistoric period of Africa.

If the fetishistic figure, as we suggested, has an integral relation to the symbolically decorated *churinga* as a spirit-home, then we would expect it to

---

* Note the 'ransom for Hector's head', etc. Head-hunting has its roots in this outlook whether in Borneo or Celtic Gaul. The Persians dedicated the top of the head to Haoma that at death he might receive this immortal part. Heads were preserved, e.g. by the Germanic tribes, who fastened them on trees; to put a stop to a ghost's mischief, they cut the head off the corpse and burned it. It is the head that goes to *Hel*. The Celts fixed heads from the slain on their houses to gain the protection of their spirits, as Herodotus tells us the Tauri did. (We find in Greek legend the separate burial of heads, e.g. Eurystheus, the sons of Aigyptos, one of the Korybantes. Oinomaos wanted to build a shrine of the heads of his daughter's suitors.) Kleomenes of Sparta kept the head of a friend in honey, so that it might serve as an oracle. (Orpheus' head, after his body was torn to bits, went on prophesying.) Jews and other Semites kept human heads to get prophecies from them. The Celts had a bodiless head-god—as also the N. American Indians. (Note Greene's play, *Friar Bacon*, for the prophetic head.) Othin's main mantic instrument is a human head kept for consultation as an oracle; the norse sagas of *Odainsakr* tell of prophetic heads stuck on end of drinking-horns (? reminiscent of the prophetic mead of Norse myth). Oracular heads appear in the Irish saga of the Battle of Allen (given as 722 A.D.).

derive, at least in part, from a block, trunk, pole, or stick; and certainly such materials have at times determined the particular kind of distortion that the spirit-representation was to take in Oceania, America, and Africa. If we look

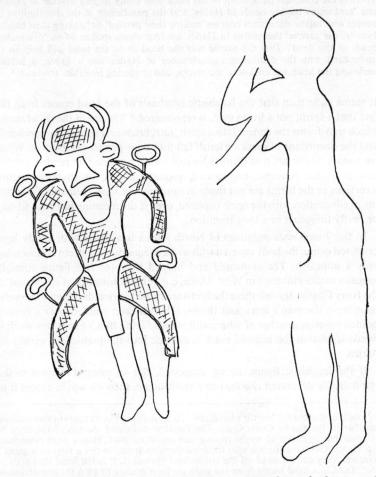

Rock-painting, Aouanrhet, showing what seems ancient form of African mask; the figure is painted over another.

closely at the head of a Quainault Indian shaman's figure, we see that,

it was his problem to reduce a post into a few finely related shapes in which surfaces and contours retain a primary attraction. The major task fell to carving, colour was used for contrast and accents were added. Eyes, using shells, were placed beside the nose, the mouth between nose and chin. The effect of the finished head is a direct result of tools, materials, and a simple technique. From forehead to chin the face is expressed by a series of subtly curved surfaces in which tool marks and wood grain add to the effect. (CHRISTENSEN)

The tool we must recall had its own magical power. Its particular facilities would thus have their sanction, their compelling power. The tool cutting or carving the wood was in some degree felt as an autonomous force working on a material with its own demands, its own ways of wanting to be treated. The Sumerian poem, *The Creation of the Pickaxe*, brings out clearly this inherent energy felt to reside in the tool. It opens with an account of Enlil separating heaven and earth. Then—

> He brought the Pickaxe into being, the Day came forth,
> He introduced labour, decreed the fate,
> Upon the Pickaxe and Basket he directs the Power,
> Enlil made his Pickaxe exalted. . .
> Whose tooth is a one-horned ox ascending a large Wall.

He sets the holy crown on it. 'The head of man he placed in the mould'. He hands the tool to the gods, who hand it to the Blackheaded People (the Sumerians). Various deities add to its powers and usefulness. A long panegyric ends:

> The Pickaxe and the Basket build cities,
> The steadfast house the Pickaxe builds.
> The steadfast house the Pickaxe establishes,
> The steadfast house it causes to prosper.
> The house which rebels against the king,
> The house which is not submissive to its king,
> The Pickaxe makes it submissive to the king.
> Of the bad . . . plants it crushes the head,
> Plucks at the roots, tears at the crown.
> The Pickaxe spares the . . . plants,
> The Pickaxe, its fate decreed by Father Enlil,
> The Pickaxe is exalted.

Finally, by considering the profound changes that occur in the change from hunting to agriculture, we can grasp why a realistic art gives way to an abstract art, or at least to one in which the decorative distortions are extreme. In matching himself against a wild animal, man is relating himself to a creature which he feels his kin; it is natural to express it in its own clear image, seen from the angle of the hunt. But what men do in growing crops is to change a seed into a plant. How is this process to be artistically expressed ?

. . . in the dance of hunting primitives, the natural object—the animal—is mimicked unaltered because it is only sought by man, not changed. The object draws the ego out of man in accurate perception. . . In neolithic art, when hunting or food-gathering man becomes a crop-raising or cattle-raising tribe, the object is not merely sought by society but changed by it. The man realises himself in the percept as social man, as the tribe changing the object according to conventions and forms rooted in the means of communication. (CAUDWELL)

Gradually art becomes humanised again by the needs of depicting the god or the chief (in funeral rites). The social essence, drawn out into the conventionalised forms that express the new disciplines and techniques, is returned to the

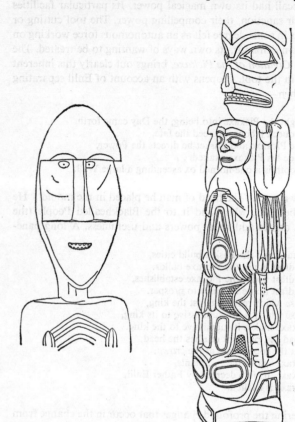

Shaman's figure in wood: Quinault Indians (Salish). Totem pole model with killer-whale design, Haida.

group in directly human forms; but now a different kind of alienation operates, and only the privileged beings (gods, chiefs, kings) have the right of realistic representation. How that right is widened is part of our story to come.

5: Bronze Age

History. In Mesopotamia city-states grew up out of the neolithic villages. By 2500 B.C. there were a score of them, each independent, with the economic surplus concentrated in the temple. Priests in hierarchical corporations administered the god's estate. But kings too rose, as the god's tenant-farmers, war-leaders and sometimes high-priests, perhaps acting the god's part in fertility-rites. The status of the small farmer steadily sank under the exactions and forced labours. In the Nile valley, however, we seem to distinguish at the outset a number of totemic clans, each with its emblem and its tract of land. Ivory knife-handles and slate palettes record what happened: the triumph of the Falcon clan. The war-chief becomes supreme ruler and takes into himself the whole totemic force, completing the process we have seen at work in pot-lach and cannibal-spirit fraternity. One totem has eaten up all the others; the king consumes it and so consumes the whole universe. Narmer becomes Horus, the divine Falcon. His successor Aha (Menes) unifies the country and begins a new sort of burial which we see at Abydos and Saqqara on the desert-edge overlooking Memphis. The graveshaft is surmounted by a monumental structure, the mastaba, in a walled enclosure, a storehouse for death-provisions and a chapel for the cult of the divine dead. Round the king's tomb are rows of graves for the slaughtered servants, who will tend him in the after-life. (Under the 11th dynasty they found magical ways of animating statues and pictures of tools.) The king grants privileges of immortality to his high officials; and a deep class-division rules, with only clerks and priests between the great lords and the depressed peasants or craftsmen. The mastaba begets the pyramid.

The developments in Sumeria and Egypt are thus radically different. In Egypt a highly centralised kingship grows up out of tribal conflicts. The long strung-out cultivated land bordering the Nile, narrow between deserts, is kept under a single control—isolated except in the Delta from all foreign contacts. In Sumeria there is a steady growth from village to town, with a close relationship of peasant and burgess. The kingship here grows up slowly from the wars of cities and the growing need for a legal system to supplant tribal custom in dissolution; but it is long before anything like an over-all imperial power is built up. The priestly corporations, born doubtless from fraternities, keep a tenacious role as the masters of industry and trade, banking and usury, whereas in Egypt the priests are the mere servants of the absolute ruler's cult of unending sun-life, and the fraternity fades out except perhaps in lowly occupational forms or in connection with village-rites. In both areas however,

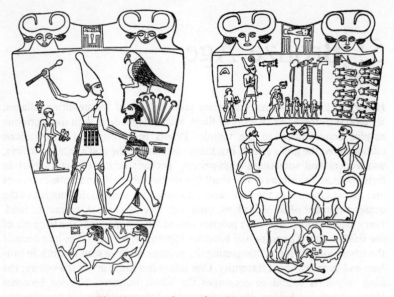

The Narmer palette of prehistoric Egypt.

some authority is needed to take charge of the water-supply and extend or keep up irrigation-systems.

In Sumeria we find the lead taken in industry and trade.

Seals, such as we met already in Halafian villages, no doubt start as amulets that confer mana on their lucky wearers. But as well as, or instead of, being carved into the shape of a totem or a 'thing of power', they are engraved with magic patterns or representations of the totem. This pattern with its magic could be transferred to a lump of clay. By pressing his seal-amulet on such a lump affixed to the stopper of a jar, an individual could put a 'tabu' on it, transfer part of his personality to it, and mark it as his property. Even Halafians used amulet-seals in this way, presumably indicating a recognition of proprietary rights. Incidentally, the standardised symbols engraved on the seal for this purpose will help to provide the characters for a conventional script when the urban revolution has made writing necessary. (CHILDE)

We must understand the term totem there as referring to the phases of tribal disintegration represented by the American potlach-groups or the Polynesians with their taboo-complexities. In the Uruk period at Erech we find accounts on clay tablets, scratched shorthand pictures and numerals, which in due time beget the pictographic script of Sumer. In the Uruk period some 2,000 signs seem used; after 2500 B.C. the number is cut down to about 800, and by 2350 B.C. to some 600, and the characters are being used phonetically. A numeral notation is also being worked out, and value-systems for the exchange of goods: fixed quantities of silver and copper, guaranteed by the State.

The full imperial form began about 2350 B.C. under Sargon of Agade (Akkad); and the link of the political unification with the trading network was shown by the way he drove his armies to the Mediterranean coast and the Taurus Mountains, seeking timber and lodes of ore. His empire did not last long in restless Sumer with its many points of thriving burgess-energy; but the pattern he had set up was permanent. A long series of empires rose and fell, leading on to the Persian State which confronted the ancient Greeks. The pattern is simple. A vigorous city-state, which still has free peasantry to draw on, becomes dominant; in its rise it forces the peasants down to a serf-status by debts, by the aggressive expansion of large estates, by all the pressures of a market-economy. It then falls to barbarian tribesmen from the periphery who have tasted the sweets of civilisation and probably served as mercenaries. The tribesmen settle down into the same system of inequalities; the peasants are broken down; and the whole process starts all over again. However, each time the new start tends to be made on a wider basis—a larger territory and an expanded productivity.* Sumeria, surrounded by tribes of the mountain or desert, was in a very different situation from Egypt.

In Egypt too there was change, slow, but moving according to the same general law. The growth of baronial estates in the Old Kingdom led to a centrifugal set of strains, to which was added the growing dicontent of the peasantry. The State broke down; and when political controls were re-established, it was from a more southern point down the Nile, where presumably the folk were closer to the old tribal forms than in the Delta, which was in contact with the rest of the Near East. Under the Middle Kingdom there was an increase of the trading and bureaucratic middle class. But again the inner strains led to collapse, invasion, confusion, from which emerged the New Kingdom. The State was now much more influenced by the trading network and was drawn into imperial expansion, into conflict with the other powers of the Eastern Mediterranean; it weakened again and finally fell before the Assyrians.

Meanwhile, in the areas round Mesopotamia a number of kingdoms had arisen, e.g. in the enclaves on the Syrian and Palestinian coast, in Anatolia, and south of the Caucasus. Into these areas, and beyond them, traders and craftsmen steadily carried the new techniques. The first farmers in Europe were peaceful folk, hoe-cultivators who kept on the move. But near the end of the neolithic period warrior-groups appeared, e.g. the pastoralists who

---

* The great Arabic thinker of the 14th century, Ibn Khaldun, expounded a thesis very close to this, showing the five stages during which the *asabiya* (ties of kin, the tribal element carried over into the first phase of the State) is gradually dissipated, with the final breakdown of the system before the attack of new people with *asabiya* intact. Ibn thus secularises the thesis of Averrhoes attributing the fall of the Almoravid and Almohad dynasties to a religious weakening.

brought the Battleaxe culture into West Europe. In China, a literate civilisation had grown up in the valley of the Yellow River by the middle of the 2nd millenium. Anyang, capital of the Shang dynasty, appears soon after 1400 B.C. Here, too, a settled State-form arose in the flood-plain of a great river, with a divine kingship and a bronze metallurgy. There certainly seems connections with central and south-west Asia, but the archaeological picture is still to be filled in. And before the end of the 3rd millennium another Bronze Age civilis-ation with skilled industries and wide trade had developed on the flood-plains of the Indus and its five tributaries; the cities here were islands of high culture in a desert jungle. They seem ruled by a divine king or a small priestly caste. In the middle of Harappa stood a strong citadel with granary close by; at Mohenjo-daro the citadel actually enclosed the granary. Fine two-storeyed houses with porters' lodges and bathrooms, of baked brick, and tenements of two rooms and a court, of mud brick, seem to show a division of merchants and labourers or artisans. The layout of the towns, with drains kept in good order, prove some strong authority, as also do the pictographic script, numeral notation (decimal), and standards of weights and measures.

The 4th millennium had been the great creative age in south-west Asia, founding civilisation. Then came the Bronze Age, lasting about 1500 years. It saw much consolidation, but few innovations. To its credit stand the inven-tion of glass, the Babylonian use of place-value in mathematics, the Phoeni-cian discovery of a phonetic alphabet, and the devising of economic ways of working iron by some tribe in Armenia.

The Concept of the Circle. The pattern of culture inevitably grows more complex and difficult to unravel with the advent of settled life, towns, in-creasing division of labour, social inequalities. Above all, the division between mental and physical labour—the priest and the scribe against the peasant and the artisan—has disastrous effects and disrupts the direct relations of ritual and dance with the productive sphere. The kings and nobles take over and

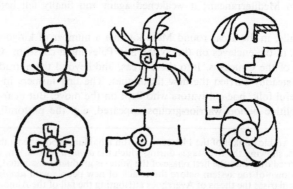

Aztec designs showing the circling swastika element.

monopolise many rites and myths, re-fashioning them to suit their purpose; the priestly corporation and the craft-fraternities keep knowledge the preserve of small groups. Creation-myths are adapted to provide coronation-myths, making the king the primordial man and the demiurge on whom the conservation of the universe depends. Fertility-myths are invaded by a new tension, an inner conflict, derived from the fate of the now divided group. Yet deep down, among the peasantry, the old forms and ideas are clung to, above all the concept of life as something perpetually dying and reborn, something made up of conflicting and united opposites. And each renewal of culture is, in fact, reducible to an uprush of the ideas, images, and life-patterns from the peasantry, at favourable moments, into the upper levels which, left to themselves, tend to become static, mechanically elaborating on given bases.

Our concern in this book is to grasp the ways in which this uprush has come about at different stages and the modified forms taken by the ancient patterns as they are applied to express the human condition at those stages.

The oval and the ellipse, which had been foreshadowed in the riverbank stage of paleolithic life, are now perfected. But, so far, they were the only geometrical shapes known. Neither the circle, nor the square, nor the sphere, nor the cube, had been conceived; and the triangle and pyramid were totally unknown. But with the neolithic and agricultural age more and more shapes emerged. The circle automatically appeared in the rims of pots as well as the roofs and foundations of huts, whose plans must have been laid down by the aid of a rough rope-compass. The circular burial mounds that were made at the dawn of the Bronze Age give us precise and accurate circles perfectly delineated by such means. The bole of the tree which held up his roof-hut gave him, all unknown, the cylinder.

These generalised shapes were not consciously thought out, but came into the mind of man only as they generated under his hand. First the ellipse, from his early cutting instruments; then the circle and the hemisphere, for the earliest neolithic pots resemble the half of a coconut; his roof-tree necessitated radial poles, and so made a cut circle and produced a cylinder. Here, in brief, was the first group of abstract shapes. There were destined to affect the whole material course of civilisation; for the basis of all mechanical invention and all solid geometry upon which applied science rests, consists of the circle, the sphere, the cylinder, and the ellipse. Rectangular shapes came much later, and are by no means so vital to the growth of mechanical ideas and inventions. (CASSON)

All no doubt true; but it does not at all explain the process of discovery. Why did the advance occur now and at no earlier phase? Not that the action of tools did not affect the development; we have already stressed the exalted pickaxe. But men did not proceed, then or at any time, by simple rational observation isolated from their total outlook and its mental forms and processes. The conscious discovery of the circle, sphere, cylinder, ellipse, not to mention the straight line, would need a powerful compulsion, a movement of the whole man. Behind them lie the patterns of the dance, in which circling and filing systems had an immemorial tradition. As men try to grasp the universe, they draw on their deepest social and organic experiences—the experiences where the greatest amount of their social energy is concentrated and where at the same time they are most fully stirred as organisms with a complex rhythmic system.

So it is from the dance they they draw such concepts as the circle, which we must realise as dynamic, entangled with a vast series of emotions and sensations. This series converges on the circle-image as holding the clue to some great mystery of life. Not that the concept could be born fullgrown in any simple leap of intuition; it is bound up with technological trial and error—and from this aspect the quotation above has considerable truth. But it is a truth that must not be divorced from the fuller context of experience. And it is not correct to say that there are no rectangular shapes. The straight line, on which such shapes are based, appears in spear, pole, needle; and we saw the meander arrive in the mesolithic period while pebbles from the Mas d'Azil have zigzags and lines, some crossing at right angles. But it is true that the momentous discovery is that of the circle.

There is no need to trace the history of the circle in architecture. We have noted the early round shrines at Arpachiyah; and the developments include Stonehenge, the endless stone rings all over the world, beehive-huts and tholos-tombs. We cannot isolate the circle in building from the circle in pottery and the cart-wheel, the potters-wheel. The two latter forms give us the dynamic circle, the circle in movement.

We see the advent of the potters-wheel in the last stage of barbarism, in what may be called the Copper Age. Thus at Sialk in west Iran, an early village of houses of packed clay gives way to one of moulded-brick houses; food-gathering is less dominant in the economy; horses are added to the stock; shells are fetched across the mountains from the Persian Gulf; copper, growing more abundant, is worked by cold hammering, though stone and bone are still the main materials for tools. However, kilns for firing pots appear. Then the village moves, though still attached to the same spring. Copper is cast for axes and a few implements without much effect on the economy; gold, silver and lapis lazuli, magical materials, are imported. Seals are used as property-marks. And a fast spinning-wheel is devised for making pots.

Early pottery from Samarra on the Tigris with circling dynamic designs inside.

We can trace the form-concepts bringing about the wheel in the decorations of the pots at Samarra on the Tigris and other sites where northern immigrants from Iran had entered early Sumeria. Outside are narrow zones packed with geometrical designs, but inside the plates and bowls are whirling compositions. The abstract patterns are animated and linked with human or animal forms, women with streaming hair together with scorpions, fishes and birds with fishes in their beaks, swastika-formations, the maltese-cross breaking into a wheel of goats. The abstract scrawls and repetitive designs of the mesolithic and early neolithic are vivified, linked with a central concept of circular movement. The productive advance suddenly begets a new quality in life.*

We find the same straining of the decorative whirl-forms in some late American pottery, e.g. the hand-made Mimbres ware of New Mexico. The designs have a circling movement; the broken-up forms are carried into a coherent whirl, as if a swastika-force was churning through them. (A Zuni potter said, 'I do not look at anything but just think what I shall draw. I always know just how it will look before I start to paint'.) But here the impact of the designs on the coiled clay did not beget the decisive technical advance of the wheel.

The Egyptian Khnum-designs of the creation of man on the wheel express the new sense of power, and also show the correlation of the turning wheel with the whole cosmic circle, the primeval waters.

Homer links dance-movement and the pottery-wheel—the dance seems the maze-dance which with an initiation-mime underlies the myth of Theseus, Ariadne, and the Minotaur inside the labyrinth.

There the famed god of the two strong arms craftily wrought a dancefloor like that which Daidalos in broad Knossos fashioned of old for lovely-haired Ariadne.
Lads were dancing and girls worth many cattle, holding their hands on the wrists of one another.
The girls were dressed in fine linen and the lads in wellwoven tunics glistening faintly with oil; and the girls had beautiful garlands, the lads had daggers made of gold and hanging from silver baldrics.
Now lightly they ran around on cunning feet as when a potter by a wheel fitted between his hands sits and makes trial whether it will spin; and now again they ran in rows towards each other.
And a great company stood round the lovely dance, rejoicing; and two tumblers whirled up and down through the midst of them as leaders of the dance.

(ILIAD XVIII)

The cart-wheel appears about the same time as the potters-wheel, e.g. at Tepe Gawra in Syria, among copper objects and poor bronze ones, with stone still

---

* These designs have affinity with the swastika, which, Bronze Age in origin, has a wide circulation in the Iron Age. It represents the turn through the four directions of the world-circle and takes on a strong solar colouration. We may further compare the discs from a first dynasty tomb at Hemaka which when rotated make the dogs represented on them chase and bite their prey or the birds fly into a trap (a band with lozenge round the disc). Compare the circle enclosing animals in a lively pre-dynastic painting from Hieraconopolis. There is also a bowl with three in-turns and open inlets, which has an odd propellor-like look and must have been concerned with some circular magic. (Compare, e.g., the wheel-magic in Theocritos, ii.)

the main tool-material, there are clay models of carts and covered wagons. By the 3rd millenium in Sumer the cart was familiar, with wheels made of three pieces of wood mortised together and bound with leather tyres. The wheels turned in one piece with the axle, which was attached to wagon only by leather thongs. (The spoked wheel appears under the Aryan dynasty of the Mitanni, e.g. a clay model at Chagar Bazar.)

The centre of the dance-circle could be a tree, stone, or fire (later altar). For the fire as centre of group-life we have the word *focus*, which in Latin means hearth. The hearthfire was attached to the mother-goddess Vesta at Rome, as the perpetual fire among the Celts was attached to Minerva Sulis in Britain and to Brigit in Ireland.* (The twirling fire-stick inserted in another piece of wood must have aided the birth of the form-concept of the dynamic circle.) The neolithic system is well brought out by finds in Cyprus. A circular enclosure at Khirokitia has an altar at centre and an outer horseshoe of massive stone; a clay model from a tomb reveals the sanctuary in action. A priest with folded arms stands before the altar, another priest is at his side, and on their right a small circle of dancers perform; the congregation are seated facing the altar. (The rite has been interpreted as a ritual ploughing.)

In ancient India the altar was directly conceived in cosmic terms: 'As to why he encloses the household altar with enclosing stones, that household altar is the world, the enclosing stones are the waters; he extends the waters round the world. It is the ocean that he extends round it; on all sides, therefore the ocean flows round the world on all sides'.

The Maze. A dynamic concept, born from the dance, which plays a considerable part in building the new sense of constructive form, is that of the

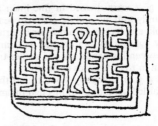

Egyptian schist seal with maze-pattern. Another with king-god in centre. 6th and following dynasties.

---

* Cf. the Chinese home-centre: 'At the foot of the hierarchy of terrestrial divinities, on the lowest rung of the ladder, stands the god of the plot of land owned by a single family. The seat of this deity used to be a place called *chong lieou*, situated under an opening in the roof of the family dwelling. The characters of which his name is composed imply that he was at the centre, that is, that he concentrated in himself all the energies inherent in the landed property of the family, and further that he was exposed to the rain, in other words, that he was under the open sky, to allow the earth of ground, which he personified, to participate in that general movement of exchange which constitutes universal life.' (CHAVANNES)

Maze or Labyrinth. Its origins lie in the meandering or spiralling movement of the ancestral wanderings, expressed both in dance and ritual-designs. The maze-movement is thus an *alcheringa*-movement. By a natural process of thought it becomes the dance-pattern or spirit-space which cuts normal life off from the ancestral land, the land of the dead, while at the same time it represents the death-rebirth passage of the initiate from one level of life to another.

Both these aspects are clearly shown in the maze-dance on Malekula. In the final movement of the initiation dance-rite of the Maki-men:

the Maki-men form a solid body arranged in rows and members of the introducing 'line' thread their way through them. Members of the introducing 'line' occupy in the Maki the position of those already fully initiated, and comparison with the version of the Journey of the Dead as recorded from Seniang shows that this progression of initiates between the ranks formed by the Maki-men corresponds with the path followed by the dead man through a maze-like design drawn in the sand by the Guardian Ghost, a figure that the dead man must know how to complete before entering into the land of the dead through the cave by which she sits. If he does not know how to do this, the Guardian Ghost devours him. (LAYARD)

This Guardian is in the position of the Minotaur in the Cretan labyrinth; and Ariadne's Thread, which has been rationalised as a clue of return, is in fact the ritual-knowledge of how to complete the maze and come through into safety on the other side. (The Malekula dances belong 'to the older matrilineal rite in which the main sacrificial monument is the dolmen'.) Sand-tracings represent the various maze-designs and are closely connected with the journey of the dead and with a mother-figure. They fall into two main types: those that depict the track followed by the initiate, and those that depict the body of the Guardian Ghost or Mother. The maze-movement is thus a passage through the mother's body.

The maze-meander form was prominent in Egypt in the early Old Kingdom, both in simple and elaborated forms; and is specially developed on coin-types of Knossos, where the Minotaur-maze was situated. Here we find it in both square, circular and swastika-forms; and the magical significance of the meander or key-pattern, as an enclosure, is brought out. What we may call the tactical maze-entry was applied to Egyptian tombs; and both Cretans and Etruscans constructed labyrinths. But the essential point still lay in the mystery-dance before tomb or cave-mouth or altar. The Malekulan type of belief appears in Virgil's *Aeneid* where the hero, seeking to enter the underworld, has to visit the female sibyl at the entry, near which is a painted representation of the Cretan labyrinth.

A very large series of maze-customs could be cited; but the following must serve. First, we have maze-constructions. Among the Tamils of south India the women draw maze-patterns, very similar to the Malekulan, before the thresholds of their houses on the month when the sun dies and is reborn, and their husbands at once walk over them. In parts of Scotland and north England women draw 'tangled thried' designs on thresholds and hearthstones to ward off witch-influences. Turf-mazes and stone-mazes, often connected with dancing, are widespread; there seems a stone series spreading up the Atlantic

Etruscan oinochoe from Tragliatella. Two horsemen emerge from the maze (one with protective beast or spirit).

coast as far as Finland, which goes back to the Bronze Age. (In historical times the Scandinavian ones were used as places of assembly.) Maze-designs were executed on the nave-floor or over the west door of many Gothic churches.

Secondly, there is the dance-relation. The maze-dance is still performed on Crete, before a marriage. An observer, seeing it in Albania, was reminded of having last seen it in the Malekulan Islands:

The significance of the particular figure of dancing known as the maze-formula is obvious when one considers that many primitive races believe that the soul on leaving the body is required to find its way through a labyrinth. . . These Albanians were treading the serpent maze that winds itself into a seemingly insoluble state of confusion and then calmly unwinds itself back to the centre—a solution that you least expect. (THORNTON)

And here is an example from Cornwall, where it was called the Snail's Creep (with apparent reference to the spiral-pattern on a snailshell). It was danced in June.

The head or band of the serpent keeps marching in an ever-narrowing circle, while its train of dancing followers becomes coiled round it in circle after circle. It is now that the most interesting part of the dance commences, for the band, taking a sharp turn about, begins to retrace the circle, still followed as before, and a large number of young men with long leafy branches in their hands as standards, direct this counter-movement with almost military precision. (COURTENEY)

Thirdly, we see the maze in initiation-relations. Japanese drama was said to be born from dances at a cave-mouth in honour of the hidden mother-goddess. And Plutarch thus describes the Greek initiation-experience:

Thus death and initiation closely correspond, word to word, and thing to thing. At first there are wanderings and laborious circuits, and journeyings through the dark, full of misgivings when there is no consummation; then before the very end come terrors of every kind, shivers and tremblings, and sweat and amazement. After this a wonderful light meets the wanderer; he is admitted into pure meadowlands, where there are voices and dances...

Lucian makes a man, who has visited the underworld, ask his companion if what was shown at Eleusis was not the same, and elsewhere speaks of the dances and rhythmic movements. The 'wanderings and laborious circuits' of the initiate are the movement through the darkness of cavernous mother-earth.

One important ritual-dance of the Graeco-Roman world, the Dance of Troy, the *Truia*, shows the maze-movement related to the initiation of the young men. And the connection with Troy brings out that that town, according to tradition, had been magically protected—made 'impregnable' like a virgin who could not be violated.* This imagery of the maze-secured town has a long history, and is linked with enfilading systems of complicated and winding approach which provide both a military and a magical defence. It has a continuous history from Sumeria down to medieval Europe with its constructions of the

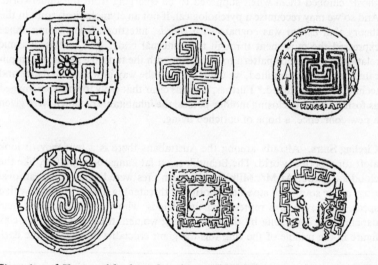

Six coins of Knossos (the legendary home of the Minotaur) with maze variations. Note crescent at the heart of one, and the heads of king and bull maze-framed—showing magical origins and meanings of the meander pattern.

* Circuiting rites play an important part in preserving the magical zone of the town's virginity. At Methana in Greece, when the winds threatened the vines, a cock was cut in two, and two men carried the halves round the vineyard in opposite directions. When they met, they joined the parts and buried the cock at the spot. Thus the space was made again a secure 'body'. The myths of Creation by separation of the cosmic parents again show the imagery of mankind embowelled inside a world which they feel as a mother-body.

Virgin Mary as a *Castellum*; and it appears in names like Maiden Castle.

The word *labyrinth* is pre-Greek and seems connected with the double-axe, *labrys*, which in Minoan Crete was important in the cave-cult of the Mother. We have seen in the last section how Ariadne in the *Iliad* is said to watch the maze-dance in Crete. Further, 'on the older works of art, e.g. the chest of Cypselus, of which Pausanias gives a detailed description, and on the François vase, Ariadne stands at the side of Theseus or her nurse, and looks at the dance, which is taken for the famous *geranos* performed by Theseus on Delos, when returning from Crete'. Plutarch says that this dance, the Crane, mimed the passage through the labyrinth, being full of 'measured turnings and returnings, imitative of the winding and twistings', and that it was danced before a horned altar.

There is a sense then in which the circular dance-floor is the site of the labyrinth, rather than any actual buildings derived from the image. At Athens, on the floor of the later orchestra, was a labyrinth of Roman pattern; and on a vase representing the Minotaur fight we see the labyrinth in Greek theatral form. The steps from the orchestra to the stage were called Charon's Steps; ghosts climbed them when supposed to be emerging from the underworld. And so we may recognise a pyschological, if not an etymological, truth in the theory that *choros* was cognate with *chorde*, intestines. The twining dance expressed the movement through the maternal body. And in this dynamic relation of the dance-pattern to the earth, with the multiple series of complicated designs that resulted, we come close to the way in which the dance and technology were linked.* Further, it seems clear that early towns were imaged as fostering and enclosing mother-bodies, the inhabitants of which were given a new coherence, a hope of enriched living.

Circling Stars. Already among the Australians there is a tendency to look aloft for a perfect world. The Buandik say a fat kangaroo is perfect, like the cloud-kangaroo. At Mt. Milbirriman seven fires were lighted round an oval ring; at the south end stood an aboriginal threatening a clay crocodile with a spear. The seven fires represented the Pleiads, who were seven young man dancing to a song sung by the three young women in Orion's belt; the clay figure in the middle of the ring was the giant crocodile frequenting the dark

---

* *Truia* seems cognate with Celtic *tro*, meaning the same as *Ilion*, a winding and turning motion; cf. Welsh for maze, *Caer Droia*. Homer often mentions the Sacred Veil of a city, which had to be rent or undone ere the place would fall. The *Hymn to Demeter* says that kings maintain the Sacred Veils of cities by right judgment. At Thebes in Egypt, the Eye of Horus, aided by the Four Montus, kept the city safe; the buildings were planned to follow the Eye's lines, with the temple of Montu corresponding to the appendage *menti* in the eye-amulet. In Babylonia the storm-demon Humwawa was represented by a labyrinthine (continuous) line that was also entrails. The stone-mazes of the west often have traditional names like Trogin, Trogeburg, Trogenburg, Tröburg, Troytown—also Babylon (Lapland), Weyland's House, (Iceland,) Ruins of Jerusalem, City of Nineveh, Walls of Jericho (Finland), Nun's Fence, Maiden's Dance, Round Castle (Scandinavia).

river in the Milky Way; the initiation-monster with whom the boys were threatened if they showed weakness in the ordeal-tests. The ancient world throughout interpreted the movements of the stars as a sort of dance-round.

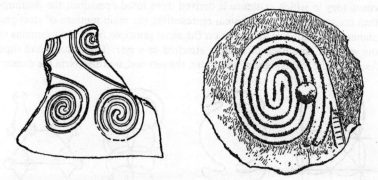

Fragment of neolithic pottery from Butmir, Bosnia. Babylonian tablet with spiral maze, connected with entrail divination.

In the Sumerian creation-myth the primal movement is that of the heavenly circle:

> The divine companions thronged together
> and restlessly surging back and forth
> they disturbed Ti'amat,
> disturbed Ti'amat's belly,
> dancing within (her depth) where heaven is founded.

Plato saw the stars as moving in the rhythms of dance, and Lucian appealed to the stars in defence of the earthly dance, which

was not invented yesterday nor the other day, but derived from our furthest ancestors; and they that have given the best reason when it began, affirm that it had its rise with the immemorial creation of all things and is equal even with Love, one of the most ancient of gods. For the frequent conjunctions of the fixed stars with the planets, their close communion and constant harmony, are indisputable indications of this divine and ancient art.

A dithyramb says that 'all the stars danced for joy and mirth of mortals hailed you (Dionysos) at your birth'. A widespread folk-belief declares that the sun dances as it rises on Easter Monday; in Norfolk they said, 'He dances as if in agony'. (Here the sky-dance is linked with the crisis-moment of change, birth-death.) The Roman spring-festival had a goddess, Anna Perenna, the Circling Ring. Cleanthes, about 300 B.C., saw the universe as a mystery-pageant with stars as dancers and sun as priestly torch-bearer. Marcus Argentarius, about A.D. 60, sang:

> My revelry is this, to scan the eve-sky overhead,
> the golden dance of starry choirs, no human dance I tread.

To perform the Mysteries was 'to dance them out'. In Egypt the gods dwelt 'in their circles'. Ra is hymned: 'You go in and you come out, you come out and you go in to your Hidden Circle'. In the *Timaios* Plato developed a cosmology in which existence is derived from fused opposites; the demiurge thus constructs a circular system representing the main motions of stars and planets; human souls are made on the same principle from what remains of the material, and each of them is attached to a star. The Indians had their festival of the revolving sun, and Indra, the sun-god, was also Nrta the dancer;

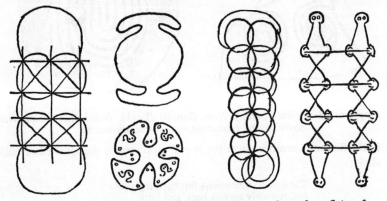

Malekulan maze-patterns. The path; the female guardian; four flying foxes hanging on breadfruit tree; the stone guardian spirit; the path of battle.

Lucian knew of Indian sun-dances 'supplying the place of prayer, hymn and sacrifice'. In Scotland there was a belief that on the morning of Mayday the sun revolved three times.

The movements of the sky-bodies thus become the ideal form of the dance as the dance was the ideal form of labour-process and coition. But whereas there was a close dynamic relation between the dance and its material, now a deep division split culture; and the spirit-world tended to become another world, not a vital complementary of everyday life. This break was linked at all points with the social divisions and the divisions of labour we have discussed. In so far as the study of the sky-bodies stimulated mathematics, it strengthened men's grip on reality; but against this gain there was the infinite loss expressed by the conviction that the real world was the sky-world and that contemplation of the stars was the only worthwhile activity, the only method of keeping in contact with 'reality', now an hypostasised term, not the essence of living in its social and organic aspects. The Babylonians cried:

> You brilliant stars, you bright ones,
>   to destroy evil did Anu create you.
> At your command mankind was named.
> Give the word and with you let the great gods stand,
>   give my judgment, make my decision.

Now there were two worlds quite distinct from one another. It was argued that as the god inhabited his earth-temple, the building was a replica of his heavenly home, a reflection of the other world prototype. Instead of a spirit-world based on the earthly life with which it is in cyclic contact (especially through the great rituals that bring all things together in unity), we have an otherworld of which earthly forms are a mere imitation, reflection, imperfect copy. Duality has become static. The temple-archetype was to be seen in the constellations, e.g. Nippur was the Great Bear; Babylon or its land was Cestus-Aries.

The earliest document stating the relation of temple and star-original is an inscription of Gudea about his temple at Lagash. In a dream he sees the goddess holding a tablet of good stars (also called 'the holy stars of the building of the temple') and a god whose tablet sets out the temple plan. The language is not decisive; but in view of later ideas, about which there is no doubt, we may assume that Gudea was being given, not an astrological relation, but a heavenly archetype. (Not that there is a lack of astrological elements, e.g. in the principle of analogy between stars and earthly life. Thus Vela was a constellation in the extreme south of the sky, so it was linked with Eridu in the extreme south of the land.) Chaldean maps show sky-regions corresponding to earth-regions. The plan of the Assyrian kings' capital was supposed to have been traced since the beginning of time in the sky, so that the heavenly Akkad, before the earthly Akkad, had been watered by two streams.

The momentous effects of these concepts may be summed up:

The East let itself be dominated by a cosmological and metaphysical type of idea which has found its repercussion in western lands much later on, it is true, like a wave that breaks into foam along the shores of a lake, long after the ship that started it off has gone from view. We are concerned with a conception of the nature of things and the world which appears to be Sumerian, unless it was born among a yet more ancient people.

The universe is considered as a synthetic unity, of such a sort that there is a harmony and reciprocal conjunction between all that is seen in the firmament and all that exists on earth. The world where men live is in all its parts the weakened pendant of a celestial land above us. The sky has springs and rivers, to which the waters here below correspond: there is a Euphrates and a Tigris aloft as down here. It's the same for the cities, and, in a general sense, for the inhabitants and the constructions of men. The holy books of the Israelites evoke a heavenly Jerusalem; Babylon in the same way is the image of another Babylon in the sky. There are marvellous towns aloft with the names of Assur, Nippur, and Susa. Each temple is the mirage of a celestial prototype, each throne reflects a divine throne. The ceremonies of the royal court are regulated according to the movement of the stars. The king himself in his kingdom, which one can conceive as itself a microcosm, is an incarnation of divinity.

It is superfluous to descend into more details. Such a conception removes from human life a large part of its reality. It penetrates its exponents with the principle that nothing happens by chance, but that all things are necessarily controlled by a universal law, since the celestial bodies move according to fixed rules. It engenders the feeling of submission to destiny and teaches the individual to resign himself to the vicissitudes of chance. Such is the base on which astrology was able to arise. An expert can determine in advance the movement of the stars. The course of earthly events depend on celestial phenomena. It is enough then to know the key of their correlation to be able to predict the future. (VOLLGRAFF)

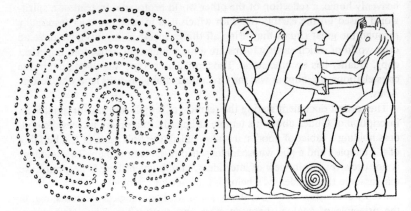

Plan of stone maze at Wisby, island of Gothland. Theseus killing the Minotaur, Ariadne with spiral thread: on a bowl from Corneto.

But astrology is only one of the by-products. The concept of two worlds enters deep into human thinking: Plato and Augustine are outstanding examples. And its effects spread very much wider than the direct application of the idea that reality lies in an otherworld; they appear in all metaphysical forms of thought—that is, in all thought which sets hypostases or absolutes of any kind over against the actual world. They turn the concepts of man as a dual being, which under totemism had their social resolution in the *churinga* and the fertility-rite, into a dualism of mind and body, which reflects the cosmic dualism. They intensify all that side of human thinking which tends to abstract, to make rigid and dead, to turn processes into things.

On the other hand it may be argued that, given the various dualistic attitudes inherited from the totemic tribe and carried into a society of class-division, there was no other way forward except this excessive stress on abstraction and division, which survives as the dominant thought-process of our own day. Science to a considerable effect, especially mathematics, owed much to the process of rigid abstraction that saw ideas, life-objects or moments as 'things'; and the metaphysical systems that have grown up between the Babylonians and our own times, whatever their shortcomings, their inversion or topsyturvying of reality, may well have been the only large-scale pictures or models of the universe and of human reality which was possible in societies of deep exacerbated division and imperfect control of natural process. (The question how far these shortcomings can now be overcome in a fuller comprehension of reality, without metaphysical abstraction and inversion, is not a theme of this book.)

Further, we must not get an impression that this inversion of reality is all that goes on in human thinking after the Sumerians: that is, after the advent of civilisation. All the while there is the counter-process, born from the fact that, however wildly men distort reality in their mental systems, they are all the while dealing with real things and processes, and that in artistic expression a profound need to grasp the concrete is present. And science is not at any point merely an abstraction; to the extent that it grapples with real problems, it has its concrete bearings. And so on. But what has certainly happened is the birth of an intense struggle in culture between the passive or abstracting elements and the vital or concreting elements. These latter derive from the intuition of life in its totality, from the productive sphere of concrete labour, and from the tradition of the fertility-rite obstinately carried on by the common folk, the peasants and the craftsmen.

More, the universe of correspondences, which develops from the Sumerian concepts of the temple as a reflection of the god's eternal home, has itself a richly positive role in the millenia to follow. For, from one angle, it embodies the totemic idea of man and nature united in a cyclic series of fertilising relations; and so there is a sense in which all that it is vital in art and science henceforth is an expression of this totemic sense of the concrete unity of opposites, however much the thought-processes on the upper levels of society are based in efforts to define a metaphysical 'higher reality' and to find in the universe a hierarchical system that reflects and justifies social division.

Spinning and Weaving. The crisscrossing patterns of the dance, the tribal concept of two opposed lines of force making up a single whole, appear in the processes of spinning and weaving. Again, many empirical observations and technological experiments—here, plaiting, basketwork and the like—played their part in the detachment of the concepts developing the loom with weft and warp. Spinning, like the twirling of the fire-stick, was a direct application of the circling turn to technical problems. (The Romans called a professional woman-dancer, *circulatrix*.) And the image of the dance as 'interweaving' still survives. 'Weave the dance about the temple, about the altar of Artemis', says Euripides. The idea of cosmic weaving is old. In the Greek epic, *Cypria*, the Graces and dancing Hours weave Aphrodite's clothes; and the imagery shows that the work is the work of nature, producing the bright robe of the spring. Circe, whose name means Circler, is another of the cosmic weavers, 'singing

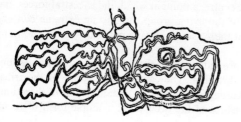

Maze-design on stone found lying flat in the chambered cairn of Bryn Celli Ddu, Anglesey.

in a sweet voice as she fared to and from before her great imperishable web, such as is the handiwork of goddesses'. (Her myth is based on beast-masking.) Claudian in his *Rape of Persephone*, which he tells us is based on the Eleusinian Mysteries, describes the earth-maid whose rape into the underworld represents the death of the wintry earth:

> Her needle pricks the elemental chain,
> the source, the laws of nature that restrain
> the ancient strifes and guide the seeds of power aright. . .
> She mingles hues. The stars with gold she dowers,
> purples the sea and gems the earth with flowers,
> like crested waves the inwrought threads go curling:
> you'd swear the seaweed round the rocks was swirling.
> Then round the edge she winds the ocean-swell
> with shadows bright as glass.

A few lines before he has said that the meaning of the Mysteries is to be found in the creation of agriculture and civilisation. The idea of productive process (weaving, sewing) as being somehow identical with the life of nature which it uses and expresses, is the exact opposite of the Babylonian abstraction. In the folktale of the Sleeping Beauty the princess falls asleep after pricking her finger at a spinning-frame; the cessation of spinning and weaving is felt as a halt to the processes of natural growth, as in the myth of Persephone. The antiquity of the imagery is vouched for, not only by the *Cypria*, but also by the cosmogony of Pherekydes of Syros in the 6th century B.C., in which Zeus weaves a cloak for Chthonie and embroiders on it Earth and Ocean and the Houses of Ocean.

The life-thread is one of the many forms of external-soul going back to the totemic level. Now the Mother is imagined as spinning the thread on terms which incorporate the conviction of pre-ordained fate. Hence the Spinning Fates or Norns, found among the Greeks, the Norsemen, the Slavs, the ancient Hindus and the Gypsies. Plato extends the image to the heavens, seeing the stars as set in the whorls of the spindles of *Anangke*, Necessity.

World-image. We can get yet further inside the world-image which we have found the Sumerians constructing. There the temple plays the part that the spirit-centre played among the Australians. The character of the latter largely lay in a depression or mound with tree or stone at the middle. This totemic centre was in effect a cosmic centre, a point at which the ancestral forces, the forces of nature and those of the living group came to an extreme concentration, a fusion in ritual. But the Australians were not asking large questions like the Sumerians.

Orientations at their level are rudimentary, though the ancestral wanderings at times have an east-west direction. The camp is a diagram of the tribal system. For instance, the Kurnai set the huts at distances and in directions which indicated the relationships of the occupants: a simple form of social geography. Among the Wotjubaluk efforts were made to orientate the dead in relation to the totemic centre.

With the crisis in tribal life there came the quest for the lost centre, the mother-navel, as expressed in the myth of the Zuni, a people who in ritual matters were very much concerned with orientations. The four quarters or winds grew important, as in the Omaha rite cited for the birth-turn. Camps and burials were more carefully oriented. Consider the Zuni system of seven village-wards or phratries, each with three clans—except the seventh which had one clan. The correlations were as follows:

1. North: Crane, Grouse, Yellow-wood (Wind, Winter, War).
2. South: Tobacco, Maize, Badger (Fire, Summer, Tillage).
3. East: Deer, Antelope, Turkey (Frost, Autumn, Magic).
4. West: Bear, Coyote, Spring-herb (Water, Spring, Peace).
5. Zenith: Sun, Sky, Eagle.
6. Nadir: Water, Rattlesnake, Frog.
7. Centre: Macaw.

The four quarters had the colours yellow, red, white, blue respectively. (Earlier there seem to have been six phratries; and before that, four. Zenith-nadir-centre, with their social correlates, would have been added as inequality in the group worsens.) Among the Ponkas of Missouri we find two moieties, four phratries, eight clans; the camp is a circle with entry generally on the west; the first quarter, left of the entry, is of fire—the others run round as wind, earth, water. In Mexico we find systems like that of the Zuni: four wards corresponding to four phratries, each with twenty clans. The four officers of the phratry are in charge of the contingents to the army; there are four signs with emblems—the rabbit with the north (black, winter, air), the flint with the south (blue, summer, fire); the house with the east (white, autumn, earth), the cane with the west (red, spring, water). Zenith, nadir and centre were also added. There had been, it was declared, four cosmic epochs.

The creation-myth of the Skidi Pawnees is of interest, linking the earth-quarters with both the life-bundles and the stars. Tirawa gave the four stars of the four quarters the power to uphold the heavens and create people. 'You shall give them the different bundles, which shall be holy bundles'. He starts on his creation-labours, aided by the four stars, who beat down the clouds with clubs and form the earth. The sky-beings then send down the Son of the Sun and the Moon to people the earth with the Daughter of the Evening and Morning Stars; the male was the first Pawnee chief, the woman his wife. Next, the lore of ceremonials is sent down. Then comes the first four-pole ritual. Evening Star transmits by a vision the knowledge of how to make the Yellow-calf Bundle. A man, instructed by Bright-Star in a vision, tells the chief the rites and songs. Yellowcalf Bundle is to be hung on a tree, and a ceremony is to imitate Tirawa. The gods who had sat in council with Tirawa had been given certain stations in the heavens and each bundle was dedicated to one of these star-gods; so, in the ceremony, each bundle was to be set in the same relative positions as the gods above. The people therefore made their camp around the ritual circle, taking up positions in accordance with the star-bundle relationships. On an appointed day the people of the four world-quarter gods

The Minoan mountain-mother with sceptre or lance, between lions; behind, a shrine with horns and columns; a rapt worshipper facing.

went into the forest to get their poles, which were fetched and set up with much rejoicing, noise and song on a cleared space: the north-east pole painted black, the north-west yellow, the south-west white, the south-east red. Each pole had its rites. Water from a running stream was put north of the lodge, and the priest made movements over it to represent the division of the land from the waters.

Here we have, in more naive terms, but in precise ritual, the ideas set out in Plato's *Timaios* as to soul and star.

The four-pole rites are carried out in an enclosure ringed with green boughs and open to the east. In the centre of the circle is a fireplace, surrounded by the four poles in their compass-positions, at the west end; inside the enclosure is an altar of earth; outside, at the east end, is a mound made of earth from the fireplace. The enclosure is divided into north and south halves, and priests and chiefs sit on the side which corresponds to their village-location, north or south of the river. The fireplace and the four poles have each a priest, the fireplace-priest being the ceremonial head of the tribe. It seems then that the centre-place was first taken over by the priest, afterwards being identified with the chief. Certainly we find at later phases that the ruler has taken over the centre. Among the Aztecs were three vertical levels, underworld, earth, and upper-world.

A large set of fourfold systems could be enumerated. The temple-palace of Quetzalcoatl has its four main sides facing the cardinal points, with colour-symbolism and feather-tapestry. The Incas told of a flood followed by a fourfold division of the world, leading to the four provinces of the empire, with Cuzco (Navel) at the centre and four roads running out from it—north, east, south and west. Cuzco like all the towns of the empire was divided into halves, north and south, upper and lower. China had the four quarters strongly imprinted; the capital had four suburbs and the central position or earth-navel was supposed to be determined by astronomical observations. In Java settlements were arranged in groups of five, one at the centre and four at the cardinal points; each chief ruler was surrounded at the points by four lesser rulers, the group making up the Holy Five. The same outlook appears in Burma: Mandalay is a walled square, with the palace in the middle, and in the exact centre of palace and city rises the seven-roofed spire considered the centre of creation. In ancient India, Burma, Siam, Cambodia, Java, we find systems with the king-centre and the four quarters, with the capital usually surrounded by a rectangular wall, one gate in each side. (At times there is a correlation of the five notes of scales with the five directions, e.g. in Bali where the centre is the realm of Batara Siva, with the colour white and the first note of a series. In China the centre is yellow.)

A long set of earth-navels could also be compiled: Cuzco for the Incans, Delphi for the Greeks. The Celtic place-names beginning *Medio-* seem cult-centres, world-navels for the worshippers. The Chinese name for China, *Chung Kuo*, means the Middle Kingdom or world-centre. On Easter Island 'in its most ancient legends the natives always call the island *Te Pito o te Henua*, or Navel of the World, but even that may be an old poetical description rather than the island's real name, for later the natives called it also the Eye which sees Heaven or the Frontier of Heaven'. But all three names have much the same ritual significance. The Egyptians saw the world as a flat platter with a corrugated rim: Egypt at the centre with the abysmal waters resting below and also flowing round the outer circle. The first known world-map, from Mesopotamia, shows a similar conception, with a symmetrical relation of the main features inside the circling waters. The Greeks with their Okeanos took the image over. Herodotos thought the Nile and the Danube to be exact geographical anthitheses.

The world-image was thus of a quartered circle with a centre rising up, stone or mound.

Pyramid and Ziqqurat. The Egyptians and the Sumerians each made characteristic use of this world-image. The Pharaoh, taking over the totemic essence, had to take over the spirit-centre; and because his absolute power cut him off from the fertility-rite of renewal, he had to make the centre the whole thing and discard the surrounding dance-arena. He wanted to own the unchanging life of the sun, not the dying-reborn life of the earth. Hence his pyramid, a world-mountain which is his exclusive property. He ascends the mountain and on its peak he enters the sky-world. 'I have trodden your rays as a ramp under my feet whereon I have mounted up to my Mother, the living Uraeus on the

brow of Ra. . . Heaven has strengthened for you the rays of the sun in order
that you may lift yourself up to heaven as the eye of Ra'. The pyramids are
oriented to the four points. 'I take the level and grasp the handle of the mallet
with Seshat [goddess of calculation]. I have turned my gaze in accord with the
movement of the stars and directed it towards the constellation of the Great
Bear. . . I have established the four corners of your temple'.

The Egyptian myth stated that the creator emerged from the waters of chaos
and made a mound of land to stand on: the primeval hill traditionally
located in the sun-temple of Heliopolis, the sun-god having been identified
with the creator. But the primitive basis of the idea appears in the fact that
the holy of holies of each temple was similarly sacred. The system lasted till
the end. The temple of Philai, founded in the 4th century B.C., was declared
to have been created 'when nothing at all had yet come into being and earth
was still lying in darkness and obscurity'.

The equation with the primeval hill received architectural expression also. One
mounted a few steps or followed a ramp at every entrance from court or hall to
the holy of holies, which was thus situated at a level noticeably higher than the
entrance. (WILSON)

As the earth floated on the waters of chaos and the subsoil waters were part
of this ocean. 'In the cenotaph of Seti I at Abydos the coffin was placed upon
an island with a double stair imitating the hieroglyph for the primeval hill;
this island was surrounded by a channel always filled with subsoil water. Thus
the dead king was buried and thought to rise again in the locality of creation'.
The yearly overflow of the Nile was a threat from the ocean to the earth; but
as the earth could not do without it, the pharaoh's business was to control the
dangerous situation.

The Sumerians, using the same idea and image, produced a structure
analogous to the pyramid but given a very different social purpose. This was
the ziqqurat; again a world-mountain, but set at the heart of the city and
expressing the concentration of burgess-energies, even if in the long run taken
over by city-king. The name simply means high or pointed; but the aim was
to raise a great world-centre inside the city where the high gods might commune with their representatives below and where the great city-rituals might
be carried out. We can see the grandiloquent idea grow, as the platform at
Eridu gives way to the artificial mountain at Warka, with the corners oriented
to the cardinal points. The ziqqurat of Enlil was the House of the Mountain,
Mountain of the Storm, Bond between Heaven and Earth. The shrine on top
was the *shakhuri* or waiting-room: a term used in ground-temples for the ante-
room before the holy of holies where the faithful awaited the opening of the
cella and the epiphany of the god. (The gods are closely linked with the
mountain-image. Thus the Great Mother is Ninhursag, Lady of the Mountain;
and indeed a god is actually a mountain: 'Enlil the Great Mountain the
Father of the gods'.)

The huge man-made mountain was the town-centre, turning the town itself into the centre of the world. At Ur the base was 65 by 43 metres, with four stages in the upper structure. Each stage had a different colour. The image seems of black earth floating on a white ocean with red (sun-fiery) air between it and the shrine of sky-blue enamelled bricks on top. Herodotos tells us that a priestess occupied the top-room and the god was said to spend his nights with her. In the eleven-day festival of the New Year the ziqqurat was the centre of an elaborate sacred drama which re-enacted creation and showed the god's triumph, his death and resurrection.

The Sumerian form was taken over by the various later lords of the Mesopotamian land. At Borsippa the ziqqurat appears to have been seven-staged to express the seven planetary heavens.

Mount Gerisim in mid-Palestine seems the navel for the northern Israelites and later the Samaritans. 'Behold men descend by the navel of the land', says *Judges* (ix 37). A *Genesis midrash* (commentary) alludes to a Samaritan belief that this mountain was never covered by the Flood, and the midsummer sun was said to cast no shadow into Jacob's well beneath it. Phoenicia too had its sacred centre. Philo of Byblos locates the mutilation of El by his father at a site 'in the middle of the land' near fountains and waters into which the mutilated parts fell—perhaps a reference to Aphaca at the source of the Adonis river that ran blood-red in the spring.

That the Hebrews were familiar with the ziqqurat is shown by the hostile account of it as the Tower of Babel. Jacob's dream of angels going up and down the stairs of heaven, on his way to Harran in Mesopotamia, uses the ziqqurat-image; and the symbolism of Jerusalem takes over the whole Babylonian apparatus. Yahweh's original habit was Sinai Mountain, but after the conquest of Jerusalem he moved to Sion, which, though not in the north, was identified with Mount Safon in *Psalms* (xlviii, 3). There the mountain of the gods was situated, and the place was an earthly paradise, surrounded by the paradise-rivers that flowed below, and including the Garden where the Primordial Man was ruler, with God enthroned on the mountain-top. In Ugaritic lore Safon played a key-part in the cosmogonic scheme: here was the site of the divine assembly where Baal was enthroned. The scheme is Mesopotamian and the Israelites must have taken it over from the Canaanites.

In the early form of the story Primordial Man is a divine or semi-divine being, the snake or demon, and paradise the abode of God himself but in *Genesis*, while the special properties of the two trees in paradise are retained, that of its water has disappeared, and even the expression 'the Garden of God' is no longer used.

(WIDENGREN)

A key-passage is *Ezekiel* (xxviii). Here in God's Garden is a divine being, the Shadower—the reference being either to God's wings or to the deity as a Tree. He is a cherub as garden-guard and is anointed by God, like his prototype in Sumeria, Adapa. The Primordial Man wears the same twelve-jewelled pectoral as the Israelite high-priest—and also the Mesopotamian and Phoenician rulers. (Such a pectoral has been found at Byblos.) The Hebrew Urim and Thummim are the same as the Mesopotamian Tablets of Destiny. The Primordial Man, like Marduk, wears the Tablets in a breast-pouch and decides the fates of the world; the Tablets are in fact those of the Law delivered to Moses.

The slaying of Ti'amat (*seal-design*).

In Jerusalem we find the Babylonian system. The Temple is the summit of the earth, and prophecies by Isaiah, Micah, Ezekiel, Zachariah, exalt the temple-mountain that is to soar above all other spirit-points. In *Revelation* the New Jerusalem is a mountain, cubical or pyramidal, of 1,500 miles height.

According to a Talmud text Palestine is higher than all lands. The culminating point, according to a midrash, is the sacred rock, which is assimilated to the stone of Bethel (gate of heaven); or it is the altar, which Ezekiel had perhaps called the Mountain of God (xliii 15), which is a tower in the Talmud, assimilated to the stair of Jacob in one midrash, and called the navel of the world in another. Similar ideas are found in Christian and Moslem writings: e.g. an Arabic writer calls the holy rock 'the highest point in the world'. (BURROWS)

This claim could be defended through a scheme in which the earth was considered a rounded mound or dome rising from the sea; the centre would then be the highest point. So a *midrash* describes the stone of foundation as the keystone of an arch; the same idea underlies the repeated statement, 'From Sion was the world founded'. (The main temple of Babylon was named the Foundation of Heaven and Earth.) In the same way as the Mesopotamian temple stood over the abyss, 'the gate of the *apsu*', sealing it for the salvation of men, so Jerusalem stood over the *tehom*, the Hebrew abyss. God was said to have cast a stone into the *tehom* and made it the earth's keystone, the temple's foundation; the *Mishna* states that the Temple stood over against the *tehom*.

A *targum* (paraphrase) says the temple-rock closes 'the mouth of the *tehom*'. The sacred rock thus has the dual relation to the underwaters we noted in Egypt. The *tehom* is both the source of freshwaters and the hole of the malignant abyss, from which bursts the great flood. When Psalm (lxxiv) speaks of working salvation in the midst of the earth, the context refers to God's battle with the primeval dragon of the waters; a central Sumerian myth. Ezekiel speaks of the 'inhabitants of the navel of the earth' (xxxviii 12); and a *midrash* declares that 'as the embryo grows from the navel, so God began to create the world from the Navel'. In an Assur document man is said to be created at a place called Bond of Heaven and Earth and possibly Navel of the Earth; in Jewish apocalypse and *midrash* Adam was created at the earth-centre (Jerusalem).

Christianity carried on the tradition. The Church of the Sepulchre has an *omphalos*, a rock-chasm, a grave of Adam; and Peter (*petros, petra*, rock) is the Rock that prevails against Hades, the *apsu-tehom*.

Isaiah addresses persons who are said to have made a compact with sheol, Hades, and who claimed thus to have secured themselves against a coming flood. . . The oracle follows: Behold I lay in Sion a Stone. . . a corner stone of sure foundation; he who believes shall not give way (or similar). Then a figure of building (line and plummet), and finally mysterious words about a flood, overflowing from its secret place and sweeping away the wicked. All is explained if the allusion is to the Stone of Foundation firmly established over sheol and the *tehom*. The same is true of the passage in *Matthew* where the figures are the same. (BURROWS)

Mother-goddess. We saw the neolithic carrying-on of both single and dual forms of the Mother. The dual aspect was strong, though one of the two figures tended to overshadow the other. The spell against physical decomposition for the pharoah Pepi brings in the two Sisters, still united, and the Brothers, violently opposed:

Isis comes and Nephthys: the one from the right and the other from the left. . . . They find Osiris, as his brother Set laid him low. . . Isis brings a libation to you, Nephthys cleanses you; your two great sisters restore your flesh, they reunite your members; they cause your two eyes to appear in your face.

Forms of the dual Mother survive in Sumeria and Greece, we noted; but in a father-dominated society the goddesses tend to be displaced from the centre of things in the hierarchical god-systems. Still, they keep a primary role in the fertility cults and in many of the mystery-forms derived from them: as shown by Inanna-Ishtar-Astarte with her son or young lover Tammuz, Aphrodite as yet another form of the same mother with Adonis, Demeter with Triptolemos at Eleusis, though her deepest link is with her daughter or younger-self Persephone; Cybele and Attis, and various others who show the same pattern. Here the initiation-imagery of death-rebirth has been fully adapted to the fertility-rite; and the pangs of a hopelessly-divided society colour the wails and lamentations uttered round the slain young god, even though the ritual finally brings him a secure resurrection. (With Isis it is the dead brother who is reborn and there seems a direct movement from initiation-forms to the matured mystery-form without passing through the phase of a fertility-cult.) It is only after the long anguish of the suppressed masses has bred a total lack of earthly hope that a purely male trinity can usurp the place of the family (father-mother-son) or of dual forms (mother and daughter, mother and son-lover). And even then the Great Mother forces her way in, as the Virgin Mary, who was aptly first voted into her high place by the Council of Ephesos, the great cult-centre of the Many-breasted Artemis.

By the time that the full light of history breaks in on the ancient scene, society has reached a stage where we would not expect to find direct totemic survivals, though we do find abundant signs of the shamanist level. The association of *glaukopis* (fierce-bright-eyed) Athene with the Owl may ultimately derive from a totemic cult, but there is no proof of it. The association may come from all sorts of post-totemic forms, such as the animal-soul or familiar. Even in Egypt, where there seem to have been prehistoric totemic clans, we cannot be sure what is the relation between totemic survivals and the many animal gods. Thus, we there meet Taurt, the Great One, the hippopotamus standing upright as the protecting Mother; she seems to go back to pre-agricultural days when the hippopotamus was a striking but harmless beast—whereas, once crops were grown, she was a trampling raider, linked with the enemy Set. Hathor as birth-goddess had a cow-head; the goddess who gave life to the foetus was shown as a frog-headed woman holding out a life-sign to animate the child. For cows produced milk and the frog came up from the watery marsh. There is an obviously magical nexus; yet the impulse that made the Egyptians feel such a need to merge the human and the animal form in their deities may well go back to a totemic feeling that the life-source lay in the animal. And Juvenal adds plant-taboos:

> All know the mad religions that defile the Egyptians.
> They adore the crocodile, the ibis gorged with snakes.
> In awe they gape before the golden image of an ape. . .
> For fishes here the clamorous rites are done,
> or dogs divine; but for Diana, none.
> The leek's taboo. Don't give the onion scorn.
> O holy race, whose gods are garden-born.
> They spare the woolly lamb and won't permit
> the throat of any goat-bitch to be slit,
> but unrebuked at meals of human flesh they sit.

It would indeed fit in with the peculiar situation in Egypt for totemic elements to survive on the lower level and fuse with more advanced religious elements; but we can only surmise.

Figurines show the importance of the Mother in the urban civilisation of Sind and Punjab. They are mostly nude save for a small skirt, sometimes decorated with medallions, secured by a girdle round the waist. Many have fan-shaped headgear and pannier-like side-projections; perhaps they were used as lamps. Some seem engaged in a ritual dance. (Horned masks are also found.) Often the figures are painted over with red slip, as was also done in early Egypt, Mesopotamia, Malta. The type in general seems of household-deities. There are males too, often horned, who do not seem in any definite iconographical relation with the females. A Mohenjo-daro seal seems to show a prototype of Shiva in a three-headed horned god seated in what has been taken for the yoga-posture; on either side are four animals, and below are two deers. A similar nude figure is associated with a pipal tree (still the sacred fig-tree) and cult animals; another seal shows a horned goddess in the midst of a pipal-tree before which a horned figure kneels, with a human-faced goat behind and a row of seven females.

There is no need here to carry on a detailed consideration of the Mother-goddess of the Bronze Age in Asia, Europe or elsewhere; but we may note the Cycladic figurines of the Aegean and the rich variety of mother-forms in Minoan Crete: Earth-mother, Mountain-mother, Mistress of the Tree, and Lady of the Wild beasts, crowned in her flounced skirts and bare breasts, some-times twined with snakes. There is also a lesser figure who may be her priestess or her *kore*-self; and the double axe and the horns of consecration accompany her. She appears as huntress, with lions and spear, or can be replaced by pillar or mountain between rampant lions. Her worship is largely associated with hills or caves. There is only the faintest hint of a son-cult attached to her.

In Egypt with the kingly cult cut sharply off from the mass-basis, even the earth is male, Geb or Ptah, though a fertility cow-form is projected on to the sky as Nut who daily at dusk and dawn bears the sun and stars, and who is entered by the dead in their quest for endless life. In any event the problem of disentangling the early levels from the later is particularly difficult here; yet the failure to do so, or at least to recognise the difficulties, often leads to false evocations of the Egyptian viewpoint. Thus, Osiris is not to be equated with the young-lover of the mother-goddess, who is slain and reborn; he is always shown as a mature man. His myth belongs to the initiation-type; but, to judge from his name, he seems to have emerged from, or been early adapted to, a cult of the Throne. Isis is then the Throne, and he is the Occupier, *Us-yri*. Behind this relationship lies the fact of matrilinear descent in Egypt, with land-inheritance by the woman, so that a man became king by marrying the queen. Osiris occupies the throne and proves his title to the land, the earth.

But deeper than this system of ideas seems the conception of Isis as the Enclosing Earth of death (Calypso, the Hider); for we find Osiris at the outset the lord of the underworld in the Delta; his realm is the Tuat, the place of the dead, airless, waterless and lightless (according to the papyrus of Ani), and set in the west.

In the Late Bronze Age, Isis appears as the great Protectress, keeping guard together with her Sister or other-self, till the resurrected god, enthroned, pre-sides at the weighing of the heart in the after-life judgment. Only in the Iron

Age does she become the lamenting questing fertility-goddess and Osiris in his dismemberment approximates to the Tammuz-type. (A memory of contact with the cults of the Near East seems to appear in the detail that she is now said to visit Byblos.)

Much Egyptian myth or ritual is deceptive; for it often embodies primitive elements with sophisticated ones. The rationalisations induced early by the kingly cult may be mixed up with long-surviving primitive myth-forms at the popular level. Sumerian religion is fundamentally simpler; for the burgess-life ensured a lively link of town and countryside, of the fertility-cults of the peasantry and the high cults of the town. Also, the give-and-take of social life, despite the semi-divine kingship and the priestly corporations, meant that something like a coherent picture of life among the gods could be developed, while in Egypt there is an uneasy confusion of popular spell-magic and priestly abstraction. Egyptian theology tends to a henotheism reflecting the pharaoh's sole power; the Mesopotamians projected the image of their State into the heavens. On earth, slaves, children and probably women had no share in the government; only the adult freemen were citizens. In the spirit-world only the natural forces that struck men with awe as specially concentrating *mana* were thought of as citizens of the universe, having a voice in heaven's affairs. The tribal assembly, adapted to urban needs, became in the spirit-world the assembly of the gods. Sumerian myth is thus an important witness to the fact that in the early days of the cities, when the myths took definite form, there was still much vitality in the assembly of freemen. In the gods' gathering:

Here the momentous decisions were made and were confirmed by the members of the assembly. Before that stage was reached, however, proposals were discussed, perhaps even heatedly, by gods who were for or against them. The leader of the assembly was the god of heaven, Anu. At his side stood his son Enlil, god of the storm. One of these usually broached the matters to be considered, and the gods would then discuss them. Through such discussions (the Mesopotamians called it 'asking one another') the issues were clarified, and the consensus would begin to stand out.

Of special weight in the discussion were the voices of a small group of the most prominent gods, 'the seven gods who determine destinies'. In this way, full agreement was finally reached, all the gods assenting with a firm 'Let it be', and the decision was announced by Anu and Enlil. It was now 'the verdict, the word of the assembly of the gods, the command of Anu and Enlil'. The executive duties (the task of carrying out the decisions) seem to have rested with Enlil. (JACOBSEN)

The seven gods suggest the rise of prominent families as well as chieftains, who could sway the verdict. The Mother, outside the assembly, remains a powerful figure, whether as the ancient Ki, Earth, Nin-tu, the Birthgiver, Nig-zi-gal-dim-me, Fashioner of All with the Life-breath (shown as a woman suckling a babe), or Nin-mah, Exalted Queen. She is even the Lady 'who determines fates' or 'who makes decisions concerning heaven and earth'. There is however also En-ki, Lord of the Earth, who is a *nun* (a great noble or councillor), a craftsman, and lord of sweet waters.

O Lord, who with your wizard's eyes, even when wrapt in thought,
    motionless, yet penetrate all things.
O Enki, with your limitless awareness, exalted counsel of the Anunnaki.

We may add that man's relation to the gods who rule the universe is stressed
as similar to that of the slave to the freemen who rule the earthly city-state.

The Epic of Gilgamesh.   The Sumerians developed the first great epic poem,
a work in which myth and legend are triumphantly carried to a new level and

*Babylonian stele of dead man on his bed, between hell and heaven. Bronze
statuette of southwest wind.*

something wholly original created. *Gilgamesh* stands at the head of all the later
literature we shall discuss here, and is already in its own way a perfected form,
a broad and subtle poem able to hold its own against the greatest compositions
of world-literature. In its earliest known text, it is dated around the start of the
2nd millennium B.C.; but it was alive and studied in later versions right into
the Babylonian world.

    Gilgamesh rules Uruk in southern Mesopotamia. He drives his people too hard with forced levies and they appeal to the gods to make a counterpart of him, so that the pair may compete against one another and give the people peace. So Enkidu is created as Gilgamesh's companion or double; and the pair set out on a conscious quest of heroic adventures.

> In my city man dies, the heart is oppressed.
> Man perishes and the spirit is heavy.
> I looked over the wall and I saw corpses floating in the river.
> I too will end like that. That is certain.
> No man however tall, can reach to heaven.
> No man, however broad, can cover the earth.
> But not yet has the fated end come on me
> and I would enter the Land
> and set up my name there
> in the places where names have been
> raised up, raise up my own.

They travel into the Cedar Forest in the west and slay the monster Huwawa who guards it for Enlil. On their return, Inanna falls in love with Gilgamesh, is repelled, and sends the Bull of Heaven against him. The pair once again triumph. Arrogantly they scorn the goddess. And so Enlil decides to kill Enkidu in requital for Huwawa. Enkidu falls ill and dies. So far Gilgamesh, secure like a Norse hero in his strong hand, has brushed aside the thought of death and the pretence that immortality is possible. When Enkidu was scared a moment in the attack on Humwawa, Gilgamesh remarked, 'Who, my friend, was ever so exalted that he could rise up to heaven and dwell forever with Shamash [the sungod]?. . . If I fall, I shall have founded fame'. But now he is deeply touched and laments, 'My friend, my younger brother, who with me in the foothills hunted the wild ass and the panther in the plains. . . now what sleep is this that seizes you? You have grown dark and cannot hear me'. Raging with grief, he refuses to accept death; all his reckless courage and his quest for fame are turned to an agonised need to search for the secret of life. At the end of the world, beyond the waters of death, lives an ancestor who has gained eternal life. Gilgamesh will seek him out.

Alone he makes his way to the mountain where the sun sets, goes through the dark passage of the night-sun, and at long last emerges on the shores of a wide area. Whomever he meets, he questions about the way to Utnapishtim and eternal life. Everyone replies that his aim is hopeless.

> Gilgamesh, where are you wandering?
> Life, which you seek for, you'll never find.
> For when the gods created man, they gave him death as his share,
> and life they kept in their own hands.

So fill your belly and make merry. But Gilgamesh refuses the easy advice; he refuses to submit to the common lot. On the seashore he meets the ancestor's boatman, Urshanapi, and gains passage over the death-waters. He finds

Utnapishtim, but gains no aid. (Utnapishtim has won his eternity by luck, rescued alone from the Flood sent to destroy mankind. Forewarned, he built his ark and brought in the pairs of living animals. Then Enlil repented about the Flood and gave Utnapishtim immortality as a reward for having preserved earthly life.)

The only way for Gilgamesh is to fight Death. Utnapishtim suggests that he tackle Sleep, who is only another form of Death. Gilgamesh decides to try. But he would have succumbed if Utnapishtim's wife in pity had not woken him in time. Despairing, he decides to return to Uruk. And then, at the wife's suggestion, Utnapishtim tells him of a life-plant which grows at the bottom of the sea. Accompanied by Urshanapi, Gilgamesh finds the spot, dives into the depths, and comes up with the plant. Sailing home, he reaches the shores of the Persian Gulf. But the day is weary and tiring. As he walks, Gilgamesh sees a cool pool, strips and swims. A snake smells the plant on the bank, slips from his hole and steals the plant. (So snakes do not die; they merely slough their skins and are reborn.) In ironic bitterness the hero considers his arduous quest, his labours:

> For whose sake, Urshanapi, have I strained my muscles ?
> For whose sake have I spent my heart's blood ?
> I brought no blessing at all on myself,
> I merely did good service to the snake beneath the earth.

And yet the last word is with the stubborn stoical note, which, repudiating all illusions, accepts a life of struggle:

> O Lord Gilgamesh, this is the meaning of the dream:
> Enlil the great mountain the father of the gods
> has destined your fate for kingship, not for eternal life.
> Do not be aggrieved, do not be downcast. . .
> The light and darkness of mankind he has granted you,
> supremacy over mankind he has granted you. . .
> battle from which none may retreat he has granted you,
> onsets unrivalled he has granted you,
> attacks where none may escape he has granted you.

Finally, Gilgamesh himself dies. 'He lies and does not rise.'*

---

* The problem of distinguishing the phases and relations of the poems in the Gilgamesh Cycle is difficult. Five G. poems survive in Sumerian; one seems to provide an alternative for the Dream and Death-of-Enkidu which are central in the Assyrian version. *G. and Agga* deals with a debate and vague war between Kish and Uruk. The Flood tale seems an independent poem in Sumer. There are also Sumerian poems about Enmerkar who reigned in Uruk before G. and Lugulbanda whom G. mentions as his semi-divine Father. The Enmerkar poem deals with disputes between Uruk and Aratta in the Persian highlands on a matter of bartering corn for metals; the two Lugulbanda poems shows a character rather like G.—a wanderer who crosses high mountains and the underworld river; left for dead on another mountain journey (to Aratta) he gains the aid of the Sungod and appears like G. as a poor hunter. (In the king-lists G. is fifth in the Uruk dynasty, after the Flood.)

The ancients described the Cycle as in 12 songs or books, each about 300 lines. The Ninevite version is composed in loose rhythmic lines, four beats to a verse; the Old Babylonian has a shorter line with two beats. Stock epithets are rare in the style. Repetitions are used dramatically and to convey a sense of time.

This great poem looks both back and forwards; it transforms myth to poetic symbolism (for it is clearly not written to serve the cult of any god); and while using the imagery of myth, it sets out in true epic fashion to present a full picture of heroic society in crisis. In a sense it is pointedly aimed at any claims to divine kingship, and it expresses a popular viewpoint in its criticism of the initial Gilgamesh as a levier of forced labour. It takes up typical themes of the shamanist level, but within a new critical focus. Thus, it expresses regret that the dual heroes have given way to the oppressive kingship: that is, in

Birdman in judgment; Akkadian seal.

symbolic terms it laments the passing of tribal equality. The gods allow an apparent return to the old days by giving Gilgamesh his twin; but the expedient does not work. The heroic exploit of bringing aid to men (by killing the destructive storm-demon) is followed by the clash with the fertility-goddess, who is treated as a temple prostitute. The heroes of clan-brotherhood do not fit in with the world of settled agriculture; their pride brings disaster; and the shamanist quest for the source of life is fruitless.

Enkidu is depicted as a rough satyr-like creature, the other-self which once ensured a harmonious union with nature. We are reminded of the Gilyaks of Saghalien, who think that one of twins is a sort of forest-deity whom they call Mountain-man. (Believing that the divine child should be returned as soon as possible to the father, and not knowing which is which, they treat both alike—presumably expose them. And they hold a sacramental meal in which the Bear is the messenger to the Mountain-man.) The importance of the symbolism of Enkidu could not be more stressed in the poem. Reared with wild creatures, as swift as a gazelle, he lost his innocence after being seduced by a city-whore; the animals rejected him and he was forced to accomodate himself to civilised ways—to wear clothes, eat human food, herd sheep and fight the wolf and lion. At last he comes to Uruk. No word of regret escapes him till his deathbed; then he cries out on what has been done to him.

Further, the bond between him and Gilgamesh is given a spirit-basis by the fact that the latter has been drawn to him in a dream as by 'the love of woman', before they meet. Together, Enkidu is the hero's younger brother—though in the Sumerian version there is a touch of master and servant.

In the aspect that looks to the future, we have the sturdy critical and realistic attitude, and the deep tragic irony. 'I brought no blessing on myself.' Something has happened to men which twists intentions into their opposites. *Gilgamesh* looks not only to the *Odyssey*, but also to Attic tragedy.

The Mesopotamians were continually exercised and tormented by the moral problem which thus pervades their epic. What force has intervened between the labour-process with its fertility-ritual and the enjoyment of the products by the group? Why is the just man not the happy man? Why is the righteous rewarded by tribulations and anxieties, as if he were the guilty?

> The lash laid upon me holds terror.
> I have been goaded, piercing is the sting.
> All day a persecutor chases me.
> At night he gives me no respite at all.

So complains the poet of *I will praise the Lord of Wisdom*. But, unable to sustain epical stoicism, he falls back on the consolation; 'The thoughts of a god are like deep waters: who can fathom them?' Men are creatures of the moment. 'Between morning and nightfall their moods may change. . . When things go well, they talk of rising up to heaven; and when in trouble, rant about falling down into Hades.' Further, no one knows when deliverance is at hand. At the last moment the situation is reversed and all is well.

This sort of poem leads on to the matured dramatisation of the theme in the Hebrew *Job*. More sceptical conclusions are drawn in a dialogue between a man and his slave.

> Servant, agree with me.
> 'Yes, my lord, yes'.
> I will love a woman.
> 'Then love, my lord, love;
> the man who loves a woman forgets hardship and misery'.
> No, slave, I will not love a woman.
> 'Do not love, my lord, do not love.
> Woman is a snare, a trap, a pitfall.
> Woman is a sharpened sword of iron
> that will cut a young man's throat'.

Another stanza rejects piety: ('Teach the god to run after you like a dog.') another, charity. The poem ends with no solution. Suicide? The slave sees no reason why not. 'No, slave, I shall kill only you, and let you go ahead'. The slave answers, 'And would my lord want to live on three days after me?'

Duality. In *Gilgamesh* the death of the other-self is taken as emblem of the new division that has come over men. The system of tribal moieties has given way to class-division: the king, nobles and priestly corporation against the peasants and the artisans. The remarkable thing about *Gilgamesh* is that its scale of values is that of the latter group, who provide the labour-levies and look back to a lost unity, who see no way of getting rid of the king but want him to be responsible and helpful. There is no clear belief about an after-life. The poems discredit it or see no moral judgment to come in death. That people in general clung to some vague notion of a continued existence on the model of earthly life is shown by the prevalence of grave-goods; but there was no real place for a human heaven or hell in the theological scheme.

In Egypt things were different. Yet another instance of the closeness of its religious thought to the totemic level appeared in a definite set of beliefs about the other-self. The *ka* was a double of oneself. When one died, one went to one's *ka*, which, like the *churinga*, was both the link with the spirit-world and an inhabitant of it. It thus had also a sustaining and a fertilising force. (In this it is like the Roman *genius*, which however lacks a full primitive scheme of relationships.) Pyramid texts address Atum and recall that when the god was high on the primeval mount, 'You spat out what was Shu, you sputtered out what was Tefnut. You put your arms around them as the arms of a *ka*, for your *ka* was in them'. And so later, 'The king is the *ka* and his mouth is abundance'. He is 'the goodly *ka* that makes the Two Lands festive and meets the needs of the entire land'. Under the Old Kingdom efforts were made to identify one's *ka* with a patron or guardian god, in personal names like Re-is-my-ka. By joining one's *ka*, one became *akh*, an effective being: the unity of the self was established. In the Osirian judgment the *ka* stood with the self in the moment of trial.

There was also the *bai*, another form of the soul, depicted as a human-headed hawk—at times fluttering down the tombshaft to visit the mummy. It is tempting to see the *bai* as the annunciatory moment of union between self and *ka*, which produces the *akh*. In the pyramid resurrection-ritual *ka* and *bai* both have important roles. The *bai* left the body, crossed the underworld (the burial chamber), gained form in the statue of the dead man, crossed the night-sky, reached the horizon and was united with the Lord of All. (We here meet yet another external-soul, the statue.)

The dual idea appeared strongly in the king, who wore a double crown and was always King of the Two Lands, north and south. He was also the Two Ladies, the two goddesses of the regions; and as the Two Lords he reconciled inside himself the battling gods of upper and lower Egypt, Horus and Seth. 'I cause them to behold your majesty as your Twain Brethren. . . and your Two Sisters I have put behind you as a protection'. The two sing of the Hor-Falcon spread on either side of his head to guard him. In the pyramid texts, he 'is come to his two Mothers, the two Vultures. . . and nevermore do they wean him'. In the representations of the birth of Queen Hateshepsut, she is shown as two babes. Another duality appears in the fact the king is simul-taneously god and man. '(Amon) took his form (as) the majesty (of) this her husband the king (Thutmose I). . . Then he at once went to her; then he had intercourse with her. . . The majesty of this god did all he desired with her'.

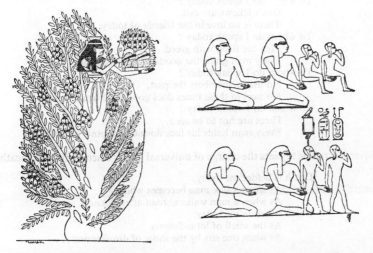

The Sycamore World-tree of Nut. Amenophis III and his double.

And at death, 'Sehetenpibre went up to heaven and was united with the sun-disc, so that the divine body was merged with him who made him.'*

Unity. These ideas did not arise all at once; but they all stem from the same primitive basis. Whereas the Sumerians were impressed by the blank gap between the god-world and the earthly fact, even though the latter reflected the first, the Egyptians, again showing how they held fast to what are at root attitudes of the totemic level, laid the stress on what we may call the consubstantiality of the universe. Spirit-force, which is the life of men, nature, and the gods, is more or less the same in all of them, even if some things have more of it than others.

Therefore, in the long lyric poem which records the debate of a would-be suicide with his *ka*, the ultimate consolation lies in the assurance that after death the man will be a sort of god, able at last to assert himself against the evil of the world. First, however, the *ka* suggests a surrender to the life of pleasure. The man replies that then his name will stink:

> Behold, you will cause my name to reek
> more than the stench of fishermen
> more than the stagnant swamps where they have fished.

---

* In the Book of the Dead, Osiris is the Lord of the Two Justices, in the Hall of the Two Justices. The mummy of the body (the sahu) represents another self. An abstract term, *sekhem*, power, also defines the life-essence, perhaps late; *ab* is the heart or will.

After eight stanzas, he bursts out in indignation:

> To whom do I speak today ?
> One's fellows are evil.
> There is no love in the friends of today.
> To whom do I speak today ?
> Men are filled with greed.
> Every man grabs the goods of his neighbour.
> To whom do I speak today ?
> No man remembers the past.
> No man in these times does good in return for good.
> To whom do I speak today ?
> Faces are not to be seen.
> Every man holds his face downcast against his fellows.

Several times he repeats the charge of universal greed. Then he turns to death:

> Death is before me today.
> As when a sick man becomes whole.
> As when a man walks abroad after sickness.
> Death is before me today.
> As the smell of lotus-flowers.
> As when one sits by the shore of drunkenness. . .

And finally he has the vision of after-death power:

> Nay, but he who is yonder
> will be as the living god
> and will inflict punishment on the workers of evil. . .

It is characteristic of the Egyptian situation that in the debate on the world's woe the man addresses his soul, whereas in the Sumerian debate the man addresses another man, his slave. It is also characteristic that the Egyptians devised an abstract theology while the Sumerians devised great myths which lead into epic, and turned their abstracting faculty to mathematics. The highest Egyptian achievement in theology was made at Memphis, giving the old creation-tales a new depth of meaning. Atum still arises out of Nun, the primeval waters, and brings his ennead of gods into existence; but his method of procedure is fundamentally changed. In place of an act of production (the making of the universe of gods and men) he uses a mental act by means of *Hu* (power-utterance) and *Sia* (perception). The dead king, in pyramid texts, supplants the ruling god by siezing his *Hu* and *Sia*. Here in the Memphis text Nun is equated with Ptah, who thus gains a precedence over the sungod. Ptah's thought-of-his-heart comes into being on his tongue in the form of Atum, the creator-god. (The word is taken as the materialisation of the thought, an active power. From this basis comes all the later theology and metaphysic of the Logos, the Word of God.)

The text goes on to say that the act of creation was not a single act; it goes on all the while. The universe is sustained by the perpetual Word (command) issuing from the thought. As the text brings together with this conception the earlier tale that Atum produced the world by masturbation, since he existed alone, the Word is thus at the same time the Emitted Semen, and the act of the hand is equated with the act of the mind (heart). The word is thus a seminal or fertilising force, and the idea is not severed from the world of production. These full relationships however remain latent, giving strength to the Thought-Word process, but not begetting a dialectic that adds that of the Production-Product.

Still the text does try to develop the materialist psychology implicit in the system. It declares that the function of the senses—sight in the eyes, hearing in the ears, and so on—is to report to the heart. On the basis of these sensory impressions, the heart arrives at its decisions; it releases 'everything which is completed', so that the tongue may 'announce what the heart thinks'. (Behind the great power attributed to the Word is the fact of incontestible authority in the word or command of the pharaoh, even if he comes to his decisions on the basis of reports from his functionaries. And it is this identity of the god-word and the pharoah-command which throws the system of thought out of balance and diverts the tribal dialectic of fused opposites into a metaphysic of the absolute Word.) Out of Ptah's thought-word has come the whole cosmos, society, the State: the controlled systems that have produced food, brought about all arts, crafts, and human activities, established moral distinctions built cities and governmental districts, and set the gods in their places of power. 'Thus it was discovered and understood that Ptah's power is greater than (that of the other) gods. And so Ptah rested (or was content) after he had made everything, as well as the divine order'. The divine order is the god-word, which begets by its command a system already thought-out.

The text comes from a stone dateable round 700 B.C., but the language and arrangement bears out the claim that the pharaoh of the time was copying out an inscription of his ancestors. The theology seems to go back, at least in its first forms, to the days when the first dynasty made their new capital at Memphis, stirring that town into an assertion against the older religious capital, the sun-centre of Re, some 25 miles off.

Western Europe. We may turn aside here to glance at what has been happening in Europe. In the Aegean we find a culture with some five or six subdivisions: one of which included the bridgehead-town between Asia and Europe, Troy, where five superimposed settlements belong to this culture. The hoe was giving way to the ox-plough, and vineyards and orchards added to crops. A few professionals roved about, potters, smiths, stone-cutters of vases, ship-builders. Probably the smiths and potters were the sons or apprentices of Mesopotamian craftsmen who moved out as the home-markers grew crowded. At Troy, goldsmiths made the same types as on the Anatolian plateau, Egypt, Mesopotamia, and even along the Indus—though with local touches. Emery, apparently from Naxos, reached the predynastic Nile, and in Troy II were beads made of what seems Baltic amber and lapis lazuli from Afghanistan.

Many sites show fortifications; but in most there is no sign of a chief. There are no artisan's quarters; the burials suggest a simple social system. There are no temples, though the Cretans have cave-shrines; plain female figurines or clay vases are used as offerings. A stele with the owlface of a goddess has been found outside Troy I's walls, and a few Cycladic marble goddesses are large enough for cult-statues—but the statuettes include musicians. There are a few phalli. Finally, after warrior-bands come in from the north, we meet rulers and subjects at last; the mainland towns of Greece are destroyed and a new culture appears. In Crete too with the 2nd millennium we find rich princes arising out of trade and doubtless piracy.

Only a slight scatter of objects proves an expansion westward from the Aegean; but the intrusive collective burials of men with steep heads are what we should expect. On Malta a megalithic culture arose in the early Bronze Age, in the second half of the 3rd millennium, flourished till the first two or three centuries of the next, and perhaps served as the launching-point for the megalithic movement in the Western Mediterranean and along the Atlantic. From rock-cut tombs, it seems, there grew up architectural systems ranging from simple trefoil plans to complex forms with five or even seven apsidal or transeptal rooms, while the temples themselves are enriched with various internal structures and relief-decorated. The religion seems based on an ancestor cult as well on that of the Mother of fertility.

Signs of trade in copper and tin are lacking. But tin was commoner in the Aegean than in south-west Asia or Egypt, and central and west Europe had rich ores. On general grounds it seems likely that the quest for bronze-materials was behind the western expansion of megalith-builders in the Mediterranean; but we cannot yet prove it. There are, however, a number of signs in Malta and elsewhere of Aegean and other connections: e.g. the Maltese reliefs seem connected with the style of pyxides from Melos and Naxos, and the statuettes derive ultimately from the Cycladic figures, while in Almeria and Portugal is callais (from Brittany?), jet (from England?) and amber (from the Baltic?). A series of stelai from South France, only once found in association with a collective burial, depict a goddess who resembles one on a stele from Troy I. In Almerian and Portuguese tombs we meet stylised figurines painted on horse-bones or engraved on limestone cylinders or slate plaques. It seems

Sacred bull-games: Knossos. Octopus design: Tiryns.

likely that the cults of the dead and of the fertility-mother had come together.

The bringers of megalithic buildings and collective burials may have been the evangelists of a new form of the mother-cult. Expanding it seems by sea as north as Sweden, they sometimes reproduced plans based on the Mediterranean corbelled vaults or rock-cut rooms, but mostly built with big stones above ground, covering their structures with cairns or mounds. The grave-goods show no single culture concerned in the movement, and links with a missionary teaching of agriculture or metallurgy are hard to forge. The megalithic idea or faith seems borne by small groups, who settled among the local neolithic folk. The evidence from the Orkneys suggests each stone tomb was made for a noble, or leader, with his family.

Martial touches, such as an axe, appear in connection with the goddess. A secondary conquering expansion seems to go on from round the Paris basin: to Brittany, Hesse and the upper Rhine, South Sweden, the Cevennes (if not to the Mediterranean). In Sweden and Denmark battleaxe herdsmen-warriors had already arrived; in Brittany and Jersey, megalithic missionaries of the seaboard; and in South France, more missionaries with varying versions of the faith. There must have been fighting, subjections, mergings. Neolithic surgical practices (trephining) seem used by the megalith-folk, especially in the Marne Area: apparently representing some ritual attempt to extract the source of illness or to confer some new head-power.

Warrior-pastoral groups indeed had been coming from the Caspian to the North Sea in late neolithic times. Stockbreeding and the hunt were probably the most effective ways of exploiting the European situation at this phase. We find the Ochre-graves cultures in South Russia, the men of the Battleaxe in Central and North Europe, the makers of globular-amphoras in Central Europe and Podolia. Into this scene burst the Beaker-folk, small groups travelling fast and far, generally roundheaded bowmen with flat-tanged knife daggers, who used flat graves, sometimes in small cemeteries. They are met from the extreme west to the Danube, the upper Vistula and Oder, and in North Italy; and their origin has been attributed both to Central Europe and to the Tagus estuary in Portugal—or even to Africa. A group with a Rhenish style entered Britain, bringing the Bronze Age, and were followed by groups with mixed cultures. Other prospectors may have come along the megalithic sea-routes. They seem also to have crossed the Brenner Pass and opened up the trade-route between the Mediterranean and Central Europe. Smiths accompanied the bands, with techniques that seem of the east Mediterranean; sometimes their daggers were mounted in Egyptian style. They replaced the aristocracies of the megaliths or absorbed them. Now the rule was individual burial, normally under a round barrow. Sacred enclosures were built, encircled by big stone uprights or by bank and ditch—incorporating older local plans, e.g. the neolithic circular henge monuments. The bands finally absorbed the neolithics, but not till they had transformed the farming situation. They preferred barley to wheat; and their beakers may have been used for drinking beer, which played a part in ecstatic dance-rites. But they themselves liked stockbreeding, and fostered the extraction of Cornish tin, Irish gold, and the coppers of highland Britain and Ireland. They kept up trade-relations with their continental starting-points. Under their controls the flat axe-head quickly gave way to a socketed type, which was as efficient as a shaft-hole axe and more economical of metal.

The mixture of Beakerfolk and secondary neolithics in Wessex led to a strong overlordship, straddling the trade-routes to Ireland and owning close connections with the Aegean about 1500 B.C. All along the trade-routes across Europe, Bronze-Age cultures had grown up; but in Wessex the richest point of concentration occurred, expressed by Stonehenge III. (Stonehenge I, with ditch, bank and ritual pits, was some sort of neolithic temple. The Beaker-folk built stone circles, e.g. the Avebury group, where probably both Bell-beakerfolk and those with Nicked Beakers were at work; and Stonehenge II with its double circle of 82 bluestones and its avenue seems clearly a Beaker-folk product: the bluestones being brought afar from the holy mountain of Priscelly which overlooked the trade-route in Pembrokeshire, near the Irish Sea.) The warrior-chiefs of Wessex, whose graves show a wealth of bronze tools and weapons, called in an Aegean engineer or architect to construct the final Stonehenge with its horseshoe of trilithons and its sarsen circle equipped with tenoned stone-lintels that suggest Mycenai.

6: Breaks and New Starts

Revolt in Egypt. The growth of baronial powers sapped the centralised State of the Old Kingdom; and the collapse was accompanied by an outburst from the peasantry and artisans. Indeed, this outburst may well have been what finally crashed the State down. The people seized power; but as usual in all such situations, they had no clear cut political programme. To return to tribal brotherhood was impossible; and so in the end the old controls reappeared. But the world had been changed in the process of throwing off the previous system, and things were never quite the same again.

Our authority for what happened is a poem, *The Admonitions of a Prophet*, which laments the situation:

Behold. A thing has been done, which never happened before. It has now come to this, that the King has been taken away by Poor Men.

Behold. The land is full of confederates. The Wretched now rob the Mighty of their
    goods.
Behold. Ladies lie on cushions and magistrates in the storehouse. He that had no
    wall on which to sleep now sleeps upon a bed.
Behold. The rich man sleeps thirsty. He that once begged him for dregs now possesses
    strong beer.
Behold. They that possessed clothes are now in rags. He that wove not for himself
    now possesses fine linen.
Behold. He that had no shade has shade now. They that had shade are now in the
    full blast of the storm.
Behold. He that had no knowledge of harp-playing now possesses a harp. He to
    whom never a man sang, now praises the goddess of music.
Behold. She that had no box now possesses a coffer. She that looked at her face in
    the water now possesses a mirror. . . .

One lasting effect of the revolt was a change in the Osirian cult. The cult of
solar immortality, developed under the Old Kingdom, had been a monopoly
of the pharaoh and the privileged members of his court to whose immortality
apparatus he wished to contribute. Now the people decided that they too
wanted to partake of eternal life. They were putting into political action what
Gilgamesh had attempted as a single-handed deed.

The judgment of the soul at the tribunal of Osiris.

They expressed their claims through the Osirian cult, which, centred in the
Delta, may well have taken in elements from Syria. During the Old Kingdom,
when the court adopted the sun-cult, there was a violent clash between the
followers of the Lord of the underworld or Tuat and those of Re, the sun-god,
with his heaven of light. By the 4th dynasty the priests of Osiris were themselves claiming that the Tuat was in the sky. The pyramid texts show the fear
and hatred of the Re-followers, with their exclusive heaven, for the multi-
tudinous dead of Osiris. Magical formulas were devised to stop him from
appropriating the royal pyramids. 'Do not allow Osiris to come here, for his
coming will be an evil thing'. It seems that already in the 3rd dynasty his
followers had taken over a derelict royal tomb at Abydos, where his passion-
play of death and resurrection was yearly represented, and where his holy
sepulchre was a place of devoted pilgrimage. In any event his cult had come

to express the need of the people for a religion of hope, of the renewal of life, as against the pharaonic lust for an existence of 'millions and millions' of years in the unchanging patterns of the sky. At root it was an assertion of the underworld of the masses against the skyworld of the lords. The poem cited above cries out indignantly, 'The poor man has achieved the state of the Ennead', that is, of the high gods; he has broken into the most precious preserve of the mighty.

The 'imperishable stars of Re' had become 'the followers of Osiris', and Osiris himself had seized the ferryboat of Re, commanding its steersman, Herf Haf, to fetch king Pepi. He also seized the Ladder that Re had made for the use of his followers, and ascended to heaven by it. Finally he became the Ladder itself and souls climbed up through him to heavens. Under the 7th-11th dynasties his cult went steadily southwards, and by the 12th it was as firmly established at Abydos as at Busiris. For many centuries the Egyptians held he was buried at Abydos, which lay in a district with the old name Ta-ur, the Great Land; as supreme death-god he usurped the powers of the ancient Jackal-god Anpu. Under the 12th dynasty his role was at its height and he became a sort of great ancestor of the whole land.

In the struggle for power that came with the disintegration of the Old Kingdom, the new masters appeared far to the south, where presumably there were more remnants of tribal organisation among the villagers. Theban supremacy began with the 10th dynasty. A town middle class had come into being, and a more complicated State-system, a bureaucracy involving town-mayors. But in due time the centrifugal forces reasserted themselves; disorder broke out, and invasions of the Delta from the Near East. Again a fresh start was won by forces in the south, and the New Kingdom arose, showing increased mercantile elements. The pharaoh assumed complete ownership of the land; and for the first time Egypt became a warlike power, seeking to expand in competition with the other States of the Eastern Mediterranean.

But the new form of the Osirian cult had come to stay. Its essence lay in the idea of an afterdeath judgment, when each man had to account for his earthly deeds, and was weighed in the divine scales. Lords and ladies had to submit to the inquisition as well as any commoner; and a profoundly moral element thus entered Egyptian religion. Commentators make much of the fact that all sorts of magical formulas were worked out for the enrichment of the priest-hood, whereby a man might hope to outwit the god by knowing all the right answers. And the rich put statuettes in mummy-form in their tombs, with tools, so that if Osiris called them up for labour in the heavenly fields, the statuettes would do the work for them. But such devices merely underline the real fear of the Osirian confrontation. An elaborate ritual was built up to enable the spirit of the dead man to pass through the many dangers and difficulties of the death-journey—a sort of stereotyped shamanist procedure, codified and sold for set sums. And the night-journey of the sun was visualised in the same terms of serried danger-points that had to be overcome if light was to return to the world. The pharaoh ended by accompanying Re in his travels through the night and by joining the other gods in protecting him from

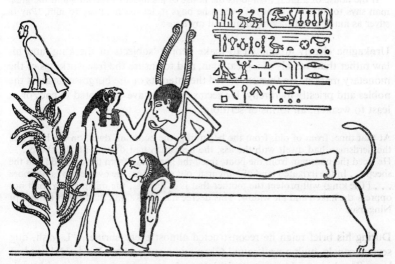

The resurrection of Osiris as shown at Abydos.

the attacks of the lurking monster Apophis.

Revolt in Sumeria. We do not know the circumstances in which Urukagina rose to the government of the city of Lagash. But he soon showed himself a stern reformer. 'It is very likely that he was set up (perhaps after a civil war) by a popular party who were weary of the corrupt rule of the ancient and once magnificent house of Ur-Nina'. Clearly he had the support of the trading class and of the small farmers. 'The liberty of the Akkadians and of their sons likewise', he declares, 'have I established'. He drastically cut the fees charged by the priests for funeral rites and reduced the amount of food and property buried with the dead. He went on to challenge the grip of priestly officialdom on all aspects of life, and attacked the many forms of bribery, corruption, and rake-off. Thus, the soothsayer foretelling the future from the shapes taken by oildrops in water, though he had a temple-salary, charged a shekel of silver; the chief minister and the governor had been asking fees of one and five shekels respectively on every occasion. Divorce was taxed; commoners had their irrigation-wells seized without payment; the fish were taken from the fish-garth; freemen had to toil in forced-labour levies, and the masters 'did not give them drinking-water; an ass (to carry) the water was not provided'. Now the high priest was prevented from 'coming into the garden of a poor woman' to take its wood and to gather from it a tax in fruit; the executives of the temple-estates, from taxing widows and orphans. An effort was made to free business and trade from the burden of irregular depredations:

If a fair ass is born to the king's subject and his overlord says, 'I will buy it', when he buys it, let the man say to him, 'Pay in silver as much as satisfies my heart'.

If the house of a great man joins the house of a subject of the king and the great man says to him, 'I will buy it', when he buys it, let the man say to him, 'Pay in silver as much as satisfies my heart and my house'.

Urnkagina clearly attempted to make people 'subjects of the king' and his law rather than vassals of a great man, and to ensure the free workings of the monetary market. He thus expressed the interests of the burgesses against the nobles and priestly hierarchy. He seems even to have attempted to end, or at least to weaken, all forms of serfdom.

At that time, from of old, from the beginning, the boatman dwelt on the boat and the herdsman had dwelt with the ass, the herdsman had dwelt with the sheep . . . He freed the boatman from the boat; freed the herdsman from the ass and from the sheep . . . In the irrigated land of Ningursu, out to the sea, the overseer was no more . . . (The king) will protect the mother that is in distress, the mighty man shall not oppress the naked and the widow. This decree has Urukagina made with the aid of Ningursu.

During his brief reign he reconstructed almost every shrine in Lagash, dug several canals, built a wall round Girsu and a strong fort. But he did not last long. The king of Umma attacked Lagash, probably in concert with malcontent nobles and other neighbouring kings. And a lamenting hymn expressed the misery of the men of Lagash:

The men of Umma have set fire to the Eri-kala, they have set fire to the Antasurra. They have carried away the silver and the precious stones.

They have shed blood in the palace of Tirash, they have shed blood in the Azubanda. They have shed blood in the shrine of Enlil and in the shrine of the Sungod, they have shed blood in the Akush. They have carried away the silver and the precious stones.

They have shed blood in Abzu-ega, they have set fire to the temple of Gatum-dug. They have carried away the silver and the precious stones.

And they have destroyed the statue. . . They have removed the grain from Ginabaniru, from the field of Ningursu, and that of it that was under cultivation. The men of Umma by the despoiling of Lagash have committed a sin against the god Ningursu. The power that has come upon them shall be taken away. Of sin on the part of Urukagina, king of Girsu, there was none. But as for Lugal-zaggisi, prince of Umma, may his goddess Ninaba bear this sin upon her head.

A fierce cry of rage, anguish and hope rings through the Mesopotamian liturgies, a memory of the city of hope that has fallen, and the first notes of messianic aspiration:

For the city Girsu alas the treasure my soul is sighing
In holy Girsu the children are all distressed.
Into the heart of the Splendid Shrine he pressed.
O Lady of my desolate city, when will you come home again ?
O Shepherd, may my prayers appease you.

O afflicting Shepherd, I would that I might appease you.
O afflicting Shepherd, be appeased.
O Lord of Lamentations, by the woes of my city, by the woes
of my temple, be appeased.

Lugalzaggisi in turn did not last long; but in his counterclaim we see the other side of the mercantile advance which had found utterance through Urukagina: the drive to imperial expansion, which was to lead to Sargon:

When Enlil king of countries had given to Lugalzaggisi the kingship of the land, when he had established full justice before the land, when he had subjugated the countries from the sunrise to the sunset, he imposed tribute upon them. At that time from the lower sea, the Tigris and Euphrates to the upper sea Enlil took for him as a possession. The lands reposed in safety, the country was irrigated with the waters of joy. . . May he be for ever the shepherd who lifts up the head of the ox

Ea, watergod of Eridu. Gistubar strangling a lion (a Babylonian form of Gilgamesh)—in symmetrical form this design lead on to Daniel with his lions.

The last Sumerian moment of prosperity, we may note, appeared at Lagash revived under Gudea, who, building a temple for Ningursu, claims that 'the lash did not strike and no one was oppressed with its blows. . . To Ningursu their king they have joyfully offered their labour as a gift'. No doubt he exaggerates; but we see that the protest organised under Urukagina was not without its effect. For even if rulers do not keep up to their professions, the professions may still set a moral standard by which the facts can be judged and the demand for justice be kept alive among the people, who note the discrepancies. Besides, there was a genuine communal element in the Meso-potamian temple, as well as an exploiting hierarchy; and Gudea's words remind us of the burgess-enthusiasm generated by the building of the Gothic cathedrals in medieval France.

After Lagash, Ur rose, with kings 'of the four quarters of the earth', representing a fusion of Sumerian and Semitic; the king founding the third Ur dynasty, Ur-Nammu composed the oldest legal code that we know. Urukagina's idiom is revived in less vehement terms. Ur-Nammu says that he has got rid of dishonest officials, the men who profited through the citizens' oxen, sheep, asses; he has established just and fixed weights and measures; he has taken care that widows and orphans shall not be oppressed by the great ones, and that the man with one small coin shall not be victimised by the man with coin of greater value. We are on the way to the full-length code of Hammurabi, in which however the humanitarian spirit weakens before the increasing demands of property.

Thus, in Mesopotamia the movement of revolt from below ended in liturgies with a deep sense of guilt and in the creation of legal codes that guaranteed the traders their property-rights. In Egypt, the people gained the comfort of a place in the afterworld where they could accuse the unrighteous mighty of this world; but these religious gains were also accompanied by the growth of a mercantile middle class. The high god revalues the fourfold world:

I relate to you the four good deeds which my own heart did for me. . . to silence evil. I did four good deeds within the portal of the universe.

I made the four winds that every man might breathe them like his fellow in his time. That is the first deed.

I made the great flood that the poor man might have rights in them like the great man. That is the second deed.

I made every man like his fellow. I did not command that they should do evil; it was their hearts that violated what I had said. That is the third deed.

I made their hearts to keep ceaseless remembrance of the West, so that divine offerings might be made to the gods of the provinces. That is the fourth deed.

That is, the god has made all nature equally accessible to all men, equally their right, and this includes the invaluable irrigation-waters. He has made all men equal in brotherhood, but men themselves have violated his law and instituted inequalities. Finally, he keeps alive in them the memory of the afterworld (where the inequalities will be wiped out). A vast distance has been traversed from the early days when the king was supreme cannibal of the universe, eating up the gods, and the rest of mankind were of no importance.

Rites of Renewal. In a way we may describe the history of Egyptian religion as a slow regurgitation by the monarchy of the rites it has swallowed in its first great gulp. In actual process, the details are obscure. All sorts of local fertility-cults continued under the State-rites, and from time to time one or other of them rose into importance. By the end we get great rites of renewal associated with Osiris, in the daily rebirth of the endangered sun and in the yearly festivals of the dying-reborn earth.

The king's death broke the Two Lands, which had to be re-united in the coronation of the new king. In a baptism the latter was purified by the gods of the four cardinal points, then led into the Dual Shrines (Per-wer and Per-

The scribe Ani, advised by his wife Tutu, moves a piece on the draughtboard: their souls are seated on their tomb facing a libation vessel of water and flowers.

neser) and crowned by the gods. A coronation-drama (preserved in a 12th dynasty text, which has a much older original) shows 46 scenes, each made up of four elements: description of the action, the mythological meaning, conversation between gods (using words, and puns on them, which the gods utter in the situation described), and stage-directions. The action covers the coronation, the burial of the dead king, and a feast (which may be concerned with the transfiguration of the dead). In another rite connected with the kingship, the *sed*-festival, which has many problems still obscure, we find strong orientation-motives. The king sits on four thrones facing the cardinal points, is proclaimed from each point of the compass, and an arrow is shot at each point. In the Min festival in the first summer-month, the rites in the harvest-field, to which king, queen and sacred white bull have gone in processional, include the despatch of geese to the four points of the compass to announce that both Horus and the king have assumed the crown. (In the Edfu rites in Ptolemaic time there are again geese and arrows sent to the four quarters, to announce that Horus the Behdetite has assumed the White and the Red Crowns.)

At the popular level there were Osirian pageants which enacted the death-birth of the god. Herodotos saw one in the Papremis district. One group rallied to the defence of the god's statue, while another group attacked them with maces; heads were broken, though the Egyptians insisted that nobody was killed. The faithful were enacting myth-episodes, in particular the fight between Osiris and Set: Osiris' murder, Isis' lamentations, Osiris' resurrection. At Abydos the same mystery was performed yearly. A procession was headed by Upuatu, a jackal-god who had become the son of Osiris; he was the Opener of the Ways. Next came Osiris in his boat, with priests, and the people behind. A mob attacked the boat with sticks; Upuatu repulsed them. Then came a yet larger mob and the defenders fought back. Then it was found that Osiris was missing. For three days a search went on, with women loud in lamentation and the fight continuing. At last came a proclamation that the god's footsteps has been found. The god was tracked down by Anubis. He lay dead on a dyke, cast there by the murdering brother. (In one myth the Two Sisters found him, flying about as swallows, They were also present at the dyke-discovery.) A boat was fetched to take the dead god back to town. Scenes of mummification were acted while Isis recited the spells. The god was arrayed in splendour and set in another boat to be borne to the tomb. Again during the march occurred a fight between the dual forces. This time it was won by Horus, the avenging and justifying Son. After that came the return of the Living God to his temple-home.

Here are some of the words from scenes of mummification. In the first hour comes a fertility-marriage of heaven and earth:

Master of Ceremonies.   Heaven and Earth join.

Woman (four times).   Rejoicing of heaven on earth.

Master.   The god comes. Down on your knees.

Woman (four times).   Rejoicing of heaven on earth.
(*She strikes her tambourine.*)

The Two Women (four times).   Heaven and earth rejoice and are glad.

Master.   Earth brings your Sisters to your side. . . . You shall be justified.

Woman.   I weep for the god whom I love. Rest in your house and remain in your tomb. Fall down, O evildoer—but you, beloved come in peace.

The Bai of Ani hovers over his mummy in the tomb. The sun rises over the tomb of Nefer-uben-f; closeby stands his shadow with the bird-soul above.

Some of the cries are rich with pathos: 'I weep because he was forsaken. I invoke heaven and I cry to the underworld. I clothed the naked and dressed the divine body. I travelled through the land and traversed the abyss and searched the stream. I lament with tears because you were forsaken. The two mourning women, the two sisters, lament for you. Their wings are over you'.

In Egypt, as in Greece or Polynesia, there were groups of actors who performed the mystery-plays. We have an inscription that one of them left in Edfu. 'I accompanied my Lord in his journeyings and did not fail to recite. I gave the responses to my Lord in all his recitals. If he was the god, I was the king; if he slew, I restored life'.

New Year. A mock-battle also took place on New Year's Eve at the erection of the *djed*-pillar. In Mesopotamia the New Year was carried out with a great ritual re-establishing the universe and the city-state. For twelve days there were purifications of sanctuaries, sacrifices and prayers. The main features were the death-resurrection ritual accompanied by mimic battles and the settling of the destinies of the coming year. The gods were thought to arrange those destinies at this moment, and the ritual was the earthly reflection of the crucial events in heaven. The fertility-aspect of the cyclic life of the earth was present, but dominated by the idea of fixed laws, the star-cycle. An important part was played by the myth of creation, in which Marduk was chosen by the gods in assembly to achieve what others had failed to do—the destruction of the monster of the abyss, Ti'amat. (Marduk is the young hero of the Babylonian version, but it is clear that earlier Enlil of Nippur played the main role.)

The opening days were taken up with lamentation. The priests carried out rites of expiation and the people mourned, crying that Marduk was imprisoned in the mountain, which was certainly represented in ritual by the ziqqurat. On the evening of the fourth day the priests chanted the *Enuma elish,* the creation hymn. On the fifth, the king entered Marduk's sanctuary; and there the high priest divested him of his regalia, slapped his face and pulled his ears. The king on his knees protested innocence. The priest reinvested him with the assurance that Marduk would increase his dominion. Meanwhile the people hurrying the streets went on asking where was the god held captive. A goddess went forth wailing from the city. She too seems to have been considered a prisoner in the underworld, into which she had gone down. (The underworld was presumably represented by the basement of the ziqqurat.) On the sixth day, state-barges arrived from the main cities of the empire, each with the statue of its patron deity. The people engaged in mock-battles in the streets. On the seventh the god was liberated by his son Nabur, god of Nippur. On the eighth the statues were arranged in order of precedence, under the king's direction, in a part of the temple called the Meeting-place of the Gods. (They thus enacted the assembly of the gods going on above.) The gods, in the ritual, appointed Marduk as their champion; and another ritual expressed the combat with Ti'amat—the king miming Marduk. On the next day came the march, with the statues, to the Festival Hall outside the walls, where Marduk's victory was proclaimed. Next day, after a banquet, the procession returned into the city; and that night the god was united in marriage with the goddess— most likely, at the ziqqurat-top. (At Isin and elsewhere, and also it would seem at Babylon, the god was again mimed by the king.) On the last day there was another god-assembly of statues, when the fates for the year were fixed. Next morning normal life began afresh, and the work of ploughing and sowing was taken in hand.*

In the myth Marduk builds the universe out of the body of Ti'amat, whom he has killed with an arrow through her gaping jaw. He smashes her skull and splits her body in half, raising one half to form the sky. Then he creates man. 'Ea then imposed toil on man and set the gods free'.

In the ritual we see the descent of the god and of the succouring goddess in a hell-harrowing, followed by a justification and rescue, then a resurrection-ascent that concludes in a sacred marriage. This ritual-pattern sank deep into men's minds, providing for them the signs by which they might recognise significant events, and the system according to which they might interpret history. Thus, we find in the themes of the Hebrew prophets a set of key-ideas or images drawn from the New Year Festival: 1. The State of Chaos: The victory of the god's foes in temple and city, drought and famine, desertion of temple and city by the god, the people's dispersion, the god's imprisonment and sleep, drunkenness; 2. The Return: The messenger with glad tidings, the awakening of god and people, their return, the battle with evil, the defeat of death, the liberation and gathering of the people; 3. Victory: the sacrifice, the communion meal of victory, the enthronement of the manifest god.

In the myth of Inanna's descent to the underworld we meet the direct fertility-expression of the death-rebirth theme, with the Mother at the centre. Gathering the appropriate divine decrees, and decorated in queenly robes and jewels, she sets out for the Land of No Return (certainly, to rescue her lover Tammuz). Below, the queen is her sister and enemy, Ereshkigal. Inanna takes the precaution of bidding her messenger set up hue and cry for her in the hall of the gods, if she is not back in three days. At the worst, Enki, 'who knows the food of life, who knows the water of life', will restore her. At the underworld gates she gives a false reason for her visit, and is led through the seven gates, at each of which, despite her protests, part of her garments are removed. Finally, naked, she is brought before Ereshkigal and the Seven Judges, who give her the look-of-death. Dead, she is hung from a stake for three days and nights. Then she is revived with Enki's aid, but is accompanied out of death with a horde of bogies, harpies and shades, and cannot shake them off as she wanders through Sumeria. (Here the text breaks off.)

---

* The idea of a 'new start', deep in New Year rituals, leads to festivals of the Saturn-alian type, which temporarily bring about a return to the equalitarianism of the Golden Age (under Saturn), with the slaves free and sometimes the masters waiting on them. (Today in the British Army the sergeants wait on the other ranks at the Christmas dinner.) The roots go back to the alcheringa-moment in totemic-rite, but the colouration now comes from the social division and the guilt-sense it gener-ates. The Hebrews had their Jubilee as a new start, and the weekly sabbath had the same meaning in a lesser way: hence its importance to the Puritans obsessed with money-making. By total abstinence on the Sabbath they purged themselves of guilt and got a 'new start'.

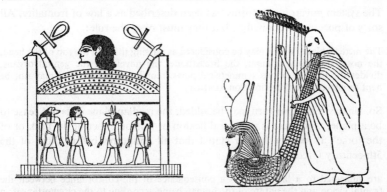

Osiris, grasping life with both hands, emerges from the coffer which his four sons have protected. An Egyptian harpist.

The poem has the slow liturgical sweep of Sumerian compositions, the long repetitions, together with a sharp ballad-like dramatisation of event.

My lady abandoned heaven, abandoned earth, to the netherworld she descended.
Inanna abandoned heaven, abandoned earth, to the netherworld she descended.
Abandoned lordship, abandoned ladyship, to the netherworld she descended.

At the gates, with only a variation in the items that she discards, she speaks with the gate-keepers:

'What pray is this ?'
'Extraordinary, O Inanna, have the decrees of the netherworld been perfected,
O Inanna, do not question the rites of the netherworld'.

Egyptian Art. The great impulse had come from the need to provide grave-scenes for the *ka* in his eternal abode, and images of the dead which the spirit would recognise and inhabit. Thus was reborn the impulsion to achieve realism. The artist was *sankh*, life-giver. Art, *hemwt*, has as determinative sign the mason's drill, and the sculptors, indeed artists in general, worked under the supervision of the high priest of Ptah in Memphis, who had the title Supreme Master of the Artists. The period of great creative achievement was the Old Kingdom, with the climax in the 4th-5th dynasties. Then were laid the bases which the later periods elaborated in various ways, with added charm and virtuosity of textures, but with a steady loss of the profound organising power of the first realism. The same poses were repeated for thousands of years: and though now and then some artist invented a new model, his invention was superimposed on accepted themes and soon stereotyped.

The canon had appeared already, in fact, in pre-dynastic times, on King Narmer's palette, with schemes based on geometrical calculations. 'Exact calculation is the gateway leading to all things', declares the Rhind papyrus.

The system governing artforms has been described as a law of frontality. All sorts of poses are permissible, but they must obey the rule:

The median plane, which may be considered as passing through the top of the head, the nose, the spinal column, the breastbone, the navel and the genital organs, divides the body into two symmetrical parts, remains invariable and may not be bent or curved in either direction. (LANGE)

So, whatever bend or turn may be added, the median plane does not cease to be a plane, 'and there is no lateral flexion or torsion either of the neck or of the torso'. It may be further stated that all sculptures before those of the 5th-century Greeks,

are subjected to a law which is a consequence of the concordance between the frontal vision and the nature of the human being according to the circumstances; a primary plane is conceived as being seen frontally, and all the other main vertical planes of the trunk and limbs form with it an intersection of, or perpendicular, contiguous or parallel planes. This rule is applied both to single figures and to groups considered as a sculptural unity. The figures are in harmonious juxtaposition, whether they are on the same plane or at right angles to one another. (SCHAFER)

These principles applied both to sculpture and to relief. They enabled a view to be made of the figure from several aspects, while a convincing unity was maintained on a flat surface despite the distortions. As though the person represented were present and active, however approached.

This realism is very different from that of the paleolithic artists, who worked by an intuitional grasp of wholes, which were sub-divided, given modelling and texture, only as a secondary act, as a modulation of the dominant whole. The Egyptian artist was analytic, drawing on the long period of abstract reductions and geometrical designs. And his essential organising idea was one of a symmetrical duality: the form divided into halves which obey a single law and yet oppose one another according to laws of movement.

The frontal basis helped to bring about a fundamentally cubic concept of form, as also did the method of working from a squared block on which outlines had been traced in ink. The outline on each of the four sides was cut until the points of contact were reached; then the details were elaborated. This approach by means of vertical and horizontal planes produced the cubic effect. The four sides do not overlap, with one plane merging into another. In one type—that of a man seated on the ground with his arms on his knees—a directly cubic mass is gained: the head grows out of the massive cube, but in an organic way. A certain relation may be noted to the hard flat lines of Egyptian scenery, the flat low horizons against which any upright forms stood sharply out.

The artist could break the canon if he chose, e.g. where sculptors at work are shown, the men are depicted in terms of the canon, but the sculptures in correct profile. But such divergencies were rare and peripheral. Inside the cubic frame and the frontal canon a remarkable fullness of realistic form was achieved; and at times an almost perfect coincidence of realism, canon and cubic form came about, as in the Louvre scribe. Naturalistic details were sometimes added, e.g. crystal inlaid for the eyes, and physical deformities might be portrayed. The artist's pride in a sense of proportion and poise, in an ability to grasp the momentary effect in terms of the essential balances of the canon, can be read in the inscription of a 'chief craftsman, painter, and sculptor', who says of his modelling, 'I know how to work up clay, how to proportion it according to rule, how to mould and introduce it by taking away or adding, so that (each) member comes to its (appropriate) place'. Of his drawing, 'I know (how to depict) the movement of a figure, the carriage of a woman, the pose of a single moment, the cowering of an isolated captive, or how one eye looks on another'.

The need implicit in the canon, to produce a realistic representation controlled by an inner system of balances, fitted in with the idea that the statue was to be the residence of the *ka* and thus in a sense a portrait of it. The dead man was shown in perfect calm, yet with a profound concentration of vital force in a dynamic balance of his members. What we see is not relaxation, but the body felt as a whole in terms of the geometrical equipoise through which it is apprehended. The man is gathered to a single point of energy, which is total character. (This point is a shamanist moment of possession, but in perfect inturned tranquillity and acceptance.) The natural asymmetry of the two sides of the face is disregarded.

The reliefs or paintings provide a series of typical acts into which the dead man will enter and which he will magically animate. The Middle Kingdom shows the dead man participating in the scenes, and the New intensifies this form. Besides the funerary pictures there is a tradition of narrative art glorifying the king.

The Old Kingdom saw the maturing of great form, noble and intense, human and yet rapt in apotheosis, individual and yet defined with a simple breadth. In the Middle Kingdom the breakdown of the mortuary systems begot a feeling of scepticism. The poet who disputed with his *ka* explained:

Then my *ka* opened its mouth to me, to answer what I had said: If you call burial to mind, it is sadness, it is the bringing of tears, it is the making of a man sorrowful, it is the hauling of a man from his house and the casting of him upon a hill. Never will you go forth again to behold the sun. They who builded in granite and fashioned a hall in the pyramid, who achieved what is goodly in the goodly work—when the builders are become gods, then their offering-tables are empty (and they themselves are) even as the weary ones who die upon the dyke without a survivor. The flood has taken its end (of them) and likewise the heat of the sun, and the fish of the riverbank hold converse with them.

Hedonism is preached, and a split occurs in the art-concept. One trend stresses the human aspect, but with an abandonment of intensity and singleness of vision, with a reliance on charm. The gesture of the husband embracing his wife's waist becomes formal, lacks warmth. The other trend seeks to maintain the effect of power, but with a realism that loses its massiveness and grows more meagre: the idea of authority is imposed on the form, not educed by the revelation of a majestic balance. Under Akhenaton, whose religious reforms we shall consider later, a new sort of realism is added, an effort to abandon all stereotypes and to depict the intimately particular, the momentarily actual. There seems an exodus of Cretan craftsmen to Egypt, bringing their light lively sense of plant and animal forms. The new aesthetic which rejects the time-honoured formulas is linked with the ethic of Ma'at or Truth at all costs, and faded out with Akhenaton's religion.

Ramessid statuary after him lacks any tension. The state of beatification thins down to a set smile; and the colossal or the charming, with textural virtuosity, prevails, The New Kingdom attempts scenes of action, to match its imperial expansion, and shows with vigour the horse in battle. But as political energy wanes, there is a return to a smooth empty archaism.

Painting had reached its height under the 4th dynasty, as shown in the finely-realised geese at Medum; by the 6th it was going downhill. In the New Kingdom it dominated over the reliefs, and we meet Aegean influences, e.g. the rushing hounds (shown as if flying through the air) in hunt scenes, which suggest a Tiryns wall-painting.

In architecture, the great geometrical form of the pyramid, worked out with a fine precision, was part of a group that included funerary temple and covered arcade ending in a vestibule. The temples show rectangular plans, as we would expect from the cubic outlook shown in the sculptures. But the pillars were based on plant forms, the stems and flowers, e.g. the lotus-bud column, the bundle-of-papyrus, the palmtree. The New Kingdom developed composite floral columns with buds open or closed as well as an hexagonal column called proto-Doric; the capitals of Hathor-columns had two goddess-masks. But there were also granite columns with square or rectangular shape, against which at times a statue of the king or of Osiris was set. Egyptian tombs show the first large-scale use of stone in building: by means of columns an effect of lightness and variety was gained—whereas in Mesopotamia the need to use bricks led to heavy unbroken walls.

The funerary temple of the Old Kingdom, with its rectangular plan, consisted of a sacred and arcane part, and a part open to the public. In the sacred way or approach an attempt was made to bring out the cosmic nature of the temple. Where the way was covered, the ceiling was painted with yellow stars on a blue ground, while floral columns stressed the nature-scene. The temple-forms tended to grow more rambling, e.g. under the 18th-21st dynasties. The pylon with its pair of obelisks, a monumental doorway surmounted by heavy cornice and enclosed within two rectangular towers with sloping walls, went on multiplying. At Karnak there were six from west to east, and four from north to south. A hypostyle court generally intervened between the rest of the temple and the god's own dwelling. It consisted of a central nave upheld by two rows of columns, and two side-aisles: the number of rows in which was variable. The columns of the central chamber were often higher than those of the laterals, and the architect used the difference in roof-levels to light the interior with a stone clerestory. The side-aisles were lit by narrow ceiling-slits, and even at noon a semi-dark reigned against the lateral walls. Often a single structure was not enough and the architect set two or even three in a line, and then also doubled the sanctuary—composed, say, of a hypostyle hall with four columns for the sacred boat, and beyond, one or several rooms where the god received his daily toilet and worship.

In the magniloquent New Kingdom great complexes grew up, like that at Deir el-Bahri, where two arcaded terraces gave access to sanctuary chapels cut in the rockface, the whole series of forms included in a great rugged amphitheatre. Megalomania goes hand in hand with decline.

There were also simpler temple-forms. We meet two main types under the 18th dynasty: a single chamber with or without columns in the interior, and a peripteral structure, e.g. the chapel of Khnum at Elephantine, a work of precision and elegance, which brings out the debt of the Greeks to the Egyptians. The halls with naves and aisles look also to the Roman and the medieval worlds. But the Egyptians did not evolve clear and disciplined systems on the Greek or Gothic bases. They were mainly concerned, apart from monumental entries, with the interiors, with an impressive movement through cavernous spaces mysteriously glowing with reliefs, into the sanctuary or primeval hill where the god was made manifest. They were seeking to translate a mystery-experience into stone.

Literature and Music. We have only a fragmentary part of the literature, but there is no sign of epic. We meet however the lovesong, the banquet-song,

Egyptian battle of the cats and rats.

romance and fantasy in tales (folktales), spell-myths, hymns, a didactic and wisdom literature, and we may safely deduce the animal fable. The poets were early aware of the deep pangs of frustration they felt in trying to express the new and the true. Khekheperre Sonbu, under Sesostris II, whose work was copied out by a schoolboy of the 18th dynasty as a classic, complains:

I wring out my body because of that which is therein, as one that separates himself

from everyone that has spoken previously. . . What is said is said. A man cannot
pride himself on the speech of men of former days. In this matter there is not
speaking one who has spoken; there speaks one who will speak.

And he declares that this impulse comes to him as a man labouring under a
weight of oppression. 'The heart accepts not the truth.' While the early
Instructions of Ptahhotep has already discovered:

Take counsel with the ignorant as with the wise, for the limits of art cannot be
reached and no artist fully possesses his skill. A good discourse is more hidden than
the precious greenstone, and yet it is found with slavegirls over millstones.

The tales can be outspoken as in *The Peasant's Complaints*, which tells of
Khunanup's troubles with an official and his appearance in the high steward's
court. The moral is that 'he who should lead according to law, commands to
rob. . . The magistrates do evil. The eloquently ordered speech is partial. They
that give hearing are thieves. The arbitrator is a spoiler'. Khunanup chatters
in a mixture of rhetoric and proverbs; he ends with a threat to appeal to the
dead, to the judgment-to-come—'I have made my petition to you and you do
not listen to it; now I'll go off and make my petition on your behalf to Anubis'.
He runs out, is caught and brought back, quaking at the courage he has
shown, then finds that he is to be pardoned. As an example of the rhetoric
which is both parodied and gleefully elaborated, we may take this working-
out of a metaphor:

If you go down to the lake of truth, sail over it with a fair wind. The canvas of your
sail shall not be stripped off, the boat shall not lag, misfortune shall not befall the
mast, your legs shall not be cut through, the current shall not carry you off, you shall
not taste the evils of the river or see the face of fear. The timid fish shall come to
you, and you shall capture the fat fowl. Forasmuch as you are the father of the
orphan, the brother of her that is put away, and the apron of him that is motherless.

We have here the beginning of low-life realism, which continues in the Graeco-
Roman mimes and in the *Satiricon*, and issues finally in the picaresque tales
of Spain.

Another genre is the Letter to the Dead. An official writes to his wife's
pestering spirit, 'What wrong have I done you ? . . . No, you cannot tell good
from evil'. From the older period we have the narrative of Sinuhe, who,
exiled, took refuge with the Beduwin and became a chieftain, had to prove
himself in a fierce duel, and at long last regained his home. And the tale of
the Shipwrecked Sailor, who was cast on an island with a huge bearded serpent. From the New Kingdom comes the amusing record by the ambassador
Wenamen about his mishaps in trying to get timber from Lebanon in the days
of Egypt's decline; a ghost story; and the myth broken down into folktale and
fairystory—*The Tale of the Two Brothers* and *The Enchanted Prince*. Thus, in
the *Two Brothers* we find the theme of the quarrelling brothers, whose names
betray a divine origin (Anubis and Bata, both of whom were worshipped at

Saka); Anubis' wife tries to seduce Bata, fails, and falsely accuses him; Anubis means to kill Bata, who is however warned by the cows. A flight with various magical motives makes up the latter part of the tale.

A fragment shows another debate-theme: an argument among the various parts of the body about their precedence. A series of letter-compositions exalt the lot of the scribe as against all other professions, which are pilloried with realistic detail. The division of manual and mental labour is proclaimed. 'The man of no sense stands there and toils, and his eye looks enviously at them' (the schoolboys who will become scribes).

The hymns often have powerful imagery, *e.g.* these words addressed to Ptah: 'You are the Babe born daily, the Aged One on the limits of eternity, Aged One traversing eternity, Lord of the Hidden Throne, himself being hidden, Hidden One whose form is unknown, Lord of Years, giver of life at will'. And the love-poems have much grace and sweetness:

My brother, it is pleasant to go to the pond and bathe while you look on, so I may let you see my beauty in my tunic of the finest linen, when it is clinging-wet. . . I go down with you into the water and come out again to you with a red fish beautiful on my fingers. . .

My young wolf is your drunkenness. I will not let go of your love, even if I am beaten . . . as far as the land of Palestine with stick and clubs, and to the land of Ethiopia with palm-ribs. . .

Egyptian dancers in Psarou's tomb.

We meet lyric formulas with a long life ahead of them:

I would I were the negress waiting on my love, for if I were then I'd see her body's colour, every bit of her. I would I were the signet-ring in which she thrusts her finger.

Here to follow are some Greek couplets, the first from the 6th century B.C.,

the second from a thousand years later:
> I would I were a lovely lyre that's made of ivory,
>> and lovely lads would carry me to the Bacchic revelry.
> I would I were the salt seawind, as you walk on the beach apart
>> and bare your breast and let me blow right up against your heart.

Music, religious or secular, was *hy*, primarily joy, at times a glyph representing a lotus in bloom. One part of the temple liturgy was known as the Going-forth of the Voice. We hear of the songs of Isis and Nephthys lasting five days with the lamentations taking up one day. Except for an Osiris-hymn by the lector-priest, the songs consisted of alternate duets by two priestesses and solos by the one miming Isis. In the Old and Middle Kingdoms the court-musicians held high rank, and under the New we meet female temple-musicians, who were often the wife or daughter of priests, looked on as the god's harem. Highborn ladies took part, and a powerful corporation developed; in the Saite period the lady-superior shared sovereignty with the kings. In the New Kingdom, under Syrian influence, the early slow dances had become fast and furious.

Here as in Mesopotamia it was recognised that the length of string, other things being equal, determined the pitch; and there seems in theory a stress on the planetary number seven, as shown in the seven-stringed harp and the occasional occurrence of bands of seven harpists and seven flautists. There certainly was some magical concept of music, which gave each note a cosmic value; and we may therefore deduce that there were modal formulas.

Sumerian Art. In Sumeria all statuary was for the temples, and the stress was not on funerals but on appeals to the gods. The statue for the Egyptian was primarily a link between the dead man, still on earth in the statue and the mummy, and the spirit dwelling in bliss; for the Sumerian it was a link with the gods, a magical means of affecting earthly life. Gudea thus instructs, 'Statue, say to my king (the city-god) . . .' He calls his statues names like *It-offers-prayers* or *To-my-king-whose-temple-I-built-let-life-be-my-reward*. Some two thousand years later an Assyrian says that he has set up a statue to appeal for life before the gods in whom he has faith.

Few cult statues have come down, as they were valuable loot with their gold and precious decorations. But we have two examples from the second early dynastic period, which were buried with other articles from a sanctuary at Tell Asmar when some danger threatened. They differ from the images of worshippers by their size and the huge diameter of their eyes. Gods and worshippers alike carry cups, and some of the latter also hold branches or flowers, perhaps to state that they had taken part in the New Year festival.

As the cube was the basic form in Egypt, here the cone and cylinder dominate. The effect is of rotundity. Instead of the right angles of the Egyptian seated figure, there is a tendency to reduce or to exaggerate the stretch from hip to knee, to get rid of the angles. The artists are most at ease with standing figures whose hanging clothes or kilts fit in with the wish to round forms off. Disliking all separate articulation of forms, they try to minimise the gap between two legs by simply leaving the stone there uncut or by stumpily thickening the ankles.

There is much disparity in value among the works—whereas in Egypt works may be mediocre but are rarely tasteless or lacking in certain traditional qualities. And after the first high achievement of rounded form, the artists turned often to bronze, which in many ways suited better their aims—whereas in Egypt stone always remained the great material. In the earlier stages the stone-cutters modified particular forms in terms of the general effect. Thus, a skull might be foreshortened to provide a better setting for the piercing eyes and to fit into the system of cylindrical curves. Now the artists sought to maintain natural proportions and to achieve fluid modulations of surface, with concern for individual details of character. As a result Mesopotamian sculpture hovered between the secure Egyptian fusion of realism and geo-metry, and the later Greek reliance on organic form, without being able to come to rest and find a decisive basis for its development. The restless burgess-element disrupting the systems of the divine kingship is to be seen here, as in the refusal, despite the astrological ideas, to pin all hopes on an afterworld of light and of belated justice.

That something more like the Egyptian attitudes could have developed is suggested by the finds in early Jericho of clay-covered skulls with shell-inlaid

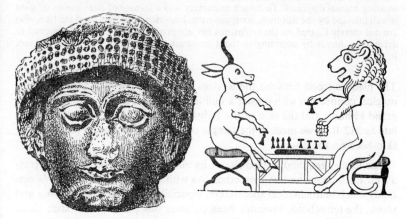

Gudea. Lion and unicorn playing a draught-game (Egyptian).

eyes as well as flattish modelled heads with similarly inlaid eyes. One complete head, spade-shaped and featureless, had shoulders and bust rendered with a considerable degree of realism. It seems efforts were made to represent a dead man as closely as possible.

Music and Literature. Music must have been highly developed in the intoned liturgies. Guilds of precentors seem housed in the temple-college like vicars-choral in medieval Europe. Sumerian remained the liturgical language long after it had ceased to be spoken, like Latin in Europe. Later, however, an interlinear version in Akkadian was added. In Sumerian days a single psalm, *ersemma*, generally a lamentation, was given; but by the time of the first Babylonian dynasty a complete service, *kisub*, had grown up—a succession of melodies with changing refrains and musical motives. In time the *ersemma* was set at the end as an intercessional hymn. As in medieval Europe, liturgies came to be called by their opening words. The *kisub* had processional movements and interludes; the antiphon and the refrain were common. A lamentation of the time of Naram-Sin had women of various towns participating, it seems, in two groups; each half-chorus sang in turn the relevant lines about the destruction of the towns by the Guti.

Animal-maskings seem prominent. On four engraved plaques of shell from a king's grave at Ur:

there are a hound and a lion bringing in food and drink, an ass plays the harp, while a bear dances before him and a small creature shakes a sistrum with one hand, resting the other upon a flat instrument on its knees. Lowest of all is seen a strange scorpion-man. . . He is followed by a gazelle which brings two tumblers of drink freshly drawn from a great jar. . . (One lion's) hand appears from under a skin, which can be plainly descried hanging down the forearm and over the hand. . . The conclusion is very strongly suggested that all these 'animals' are in reality men wearing animal disguises. That such mummery was a feature of Babylonian religion is well attested by the fish-men, scorpion-men, lion-men, bull-men, and the like, who are not merely figured on the sculptures but are prominent in the ritual designed to drive away fiends by opposing to them monsters of an animal and fabulous kind. (GADD)

The plaques stood between the forelegs of a bull-statue. The bull had some magical connection with music; a bull-image was set on the soundchest of a grand kithara; and the skin of the Babylonian drum was from bull-hide. As late as 312 B.C. we meet in the temple of Ea an elaborate rite for fixing the skin-head on the drum.

The liturgy required a fixed chant; its virtue depended on exact interpretation. Each chant had its own ethos. As with the Egyptians, there was certainly much mathematical speculation, especially about the numbers four and seven, the tetrachord. Probably Mesopotamia was the source of such ideas. Much of the lore later expounded by Pythagoras came beyond doubt from Egypt and Babylonia. He was said to have been initiated into the mysteries of Tyre and Byblos, to have resided twenty-one years in Egypt, then to have been carried off by Cambyses to Babylon, where he stayed twelve years, acquiring the lore of the gods, arithmetic, music; finally he went to Samos. We cannot trust such tales, but their tradition may well point to fundamental connections.

We have already noted the great elements in the literature, *Gilgamesh* and what we may call the myth-ballads, the hymns and lamentations. There were fables, often in the form of a debate about the merits or demerits of creatures or objects: bird and fish, tree and reed, pick and plough, iron and bronze, shepherd and farmer. Also, a wisdom literature with proverbs like, 'When you see a quarrel, go away without noticing it. Unto your opponent do no evil; your evildoer recompense with good'. A didactic genre, which included school compositions: one tells of a schoolboy who is late and is caned; he asks his father to invite the teacher home to dinner and give him gifts; the master, won over, praises the boy and hopes that he'll be head of the school. A large number of spells against waylaying demons, especially those of the sudden storms that burst furiously over Mesopotamia:

> They are the widespreading clouds which darken the day,
>   with the stormwind they blow and cannot be withstood.
> Haloed with awful brilliance like a demon they carry terror far and wide,
>   they make the secrets of the couch as clear as day, spreading terror afar,
>   they stand in the broad places and circle round the highways of the land.

The fear is deep. All round are the spirits. 'Through the door like a snake they glide. Through the hinge like the wind they blow, estranging the wife from the husband's embraces, snatching the child from the loins of a man'. The evil demon 'like a cloak enshrouds the man'. At times the imagery is striking.

> Headache lies like the stars of heaven in the desert and has no praise,
> Pain in the head and shivering like a scudding cloud torn from the form of man.

The Sumerians had early found a sign for ten. A decimal and a sexagesimal system were used concurrently; but from late in 3rd millenium B.C. the latter alone was kept. Fractions other than two-thirds were expressed as aliquot parts. Measures based on the cubit (forearm) were turned into conventional lengths.

The unit for area was a measure of grain, the word for 'volume' means literally 'mass of earth'. The chequer patterns so easily made on mats of coloured reeds and particularly popular on painted vases of the Jemdet Nasr phase, gave visual demonstrations of our rule that the area of a rectangle can be obtained by multiplying length by breadth. A brickyard gave the corresponding 'formula' for volume. (CHILDE)

By 1500 B.C. there were multiplication tables. Even back in the 4th millennium field areas were calculated as length by breadth; soon the ratio of the circumference of a circle to the diameter was approximately worked out. Scholars were getting at the first generalised laws of mathematics and were developing astronomy. Under the dynasty of Hammurabi, with its rise of the middle class, the higher mathematics seem fully grounded. A conventionalised system of signs with place-value was evolved and applied to fractions as well as whole numbers. Not till late in the last millennium B.C. did signs for zero and the decimal point remove ambiguities which had not however been serious in practice. Tables of reciprocals (expressed as sexagesimal fractions) were compiled for use in division.

Some properties of numbers which we should express by algebraic formulas were discovered empirically. But the general principles could not be worked out; and the scribes had to base themselves on examples devised so as not to raise problems which the available methods were unable to solve. (Lacking algebraic notation, they solved 'equations' by a procedure like the 'false position' of medieval arithmetic.)

Similarly, they experimented with geometric figures, inscribing squares in circles, and so on. By 1800, as well as the rules for area and volume, they had discovered certain geometrical relations. Thus, they knew for nineteen different instances the result of what is now termed the Theorem of Pythagoras. 'None of the tablets that survive suggests an interest in numbers as such or any conception of abstract empty space'. (CHILDE)

7: More Breaks and New Starts

Hittite History-writing. Round about 1500 B.C. various invading peoples set up new and strong states in the Near East: the Kassites in south Mesopotamia, the Hurrians in the north, and the Hittites in Anatolia. The latter had an Indo-European element and a strong remnant of tribal democracy; and one of the results was a new sort of narrative prose. For the king had to treat his fellow-warriors with respect as a kind of equals: he had to explain himself, not take refuge in lordly announcements with a divine backing. Thus king Hattusilis speaks to his assembly:

Lo, I feel sick. I had presented to you the young Labarnas as him who should sit upon the throne: I, the king, called him my son, I embraced him, I exalted him, I cared for him without a break. But he proved himself a young man not worth looking upon. He did not shed tears, he did not sympathise, he is cold and heartless. Then I, the king, called him and made him come to my bedside. No longer could I go on treating a nephew as a son. . .

And so on, with a logical explanation of motives. That the method was a genuine Hittite development is shown by the way in which Myrsilis and others use the same style. Myrsilis, dealing with his expedition against Carchemish, begins with a detailed account of his motives. The Assyrians have attacked the town, and the king has to choose whether to proceed against them or Hasaya. He would prefer to tackle Hasaya first; but he ponders on the effect such a tactic would have on the Assyrians, who'd assume he had left Carchemish to its fate. So he decides to launch his expedition against them.

In this passage the Annals of Mursilis once more rise to the height of a truly historiographical work. We can see into the king's very mind and follow his thoughts and reflections on the events which were taking place before his eyes, and whose course he himself, at least in part, directed and determined. The king further tells us the motives which led his adversaries to act in this way or that... This is, perhaps, the first true historiographical work of the ancient civilisations which preceded that of Greece. (FURLANI)

Akhenaton. Under Amenophis IV, in the earlier half of the 14th century B.C., a strange revolt was made against the ruling systems of the Theban priesthood and their god Amon. The king restored the ancient cult on the sun in the form of a worship of the heat (later, fire) of the solar disc. He changed his name to Akhenaton, Pleasing to Aton, and founded a new capital, Horizon of Aton. Under the New Kingdom the previously modest temples had grown in size and pomp, and had come to own a third of the land and one out of every five inhabitants; by the end of the period political power had fallen wholly into the priesthood's hands. Akhenaton's reform was thus in part aimed at asserting the kingship against priestly encroachments; but in his mind it went much further than any economic or political measure. There was present in his position a revulsion against the aggressive wars of his predecessors, a sort of quietist monotheism; but he rejected the funerary cults and thus infuriated the priesthoods whose power and wealth had thriven on them; he rejected the Osirian mysteries and thus alienated the masses who found their one comfort in the idea of an after-life judgment. A materialist warmth and tenderness attended his conception of the sole god, the vivifying sun-disc; but he narrowed his creed by an emphasis on himself as the single mediator between mankind and the god.

Your dawning is beautiful in the horizon of the sky, O living Aton, beginning of life... All cattle rest upon their pasturage, the trees and the plants flourish, the birds flutter in the marshes, their wings uplifted to you in adoration. All the sheep dance upon their feet, all winged things fly. They live when you have shone upon them... Creator of the germ in woman, maker of seed in man... When the fledgling in the egg chirps in the shell, you give him breath there to preserve him alive; when you have brought him together to the point of bursting in the egg, he comes forth from the egg to chirp with all his might... How manifold are all your works... You make millions of forms through yourself alone: cities, towns and tribes, highways and rivers...

You are in my heart. There is no other that knows you save your son Akhenaton. You have made him wise in your designs and in your might.

Despite the lack of any popular basis for the Aton-cult, we need not look to influences of the Aryan Mitanni, with whom the royal family had inter-married, and need not attempt an equation of *aton* with *adon*, Syrian for Lord. Akhenaton, who seems to have been an epileptic with physical abnormalities,

Akhenaton and family worshipping the Aton and receiving blessings. Note the rays ending in hands.

was carrying to an extreme certain strong elements in Egyptian religious thought. The earliest known hymn to the sun-god opens, 'Hail to thee, Aton', and not long before Akhenaton the sungod Re was being hymned as 'Sole likeness, maker of what is, sole and only one, maker of what exists. Hail to you, say all cattle; Jubilation to you, says every country, to the height of heaven, to the breadth of earth, to the depth of the sea. Save me, shine upon me, for you make my sustenance. You are the sole god, there is no other'. And not long afterwards Amon of Thebes was hymned as both the One and the head of a trinity. 'One of Amon, hiding himself from them, concealing himself from the (other) gods, so that his (very) colour is unknown. . . No gods know his true form; his image is not displayed in writings. . . All gods are three: Amon, Re, and Ptah, and there is no second to them. Hidden is his name as Amon, he is Re in face, and his body is Ptah'.

Whereas the early concept of sun-unity has been one embracing Egypt alone, now in a world of imperial states which clash in their claims to universal

Akhenaton and family throwing golden collars to the people.

power, the sun-power spreads over the whole earth. The conception of a single god, rather than of a god who is more powerful than the others, steadily emerges. Akhenaton prematurely expresses the creed that the one god of power, even when that power is seen as a fostering fertility, requires a living mediator on the earth, not merely a mystery-god of death-rebirth who brings the righteous, when dead, into the land of light. And he puts far too great demands on the suffering masses in hoping to eliminate the idea of the other-world altogether. He failed, and at his death the enraged priests tried to obliterate his name and his work from the memory of man. The following pharoahs attempted to resume a strong military policy in Asia.

The fierce self-assured vigour of the men of the Old Kingdom was however now far behind the Egyptians.

The key word for the developed spirit of this period was 'silence', which we may render also with 'calm, passivity, tranquillity, submission, humility, meekness'. This 'silence' is linked with weakness and poverty in such contexts as 'Thou art Amon, the lord of the silent, who comes at the voice of the poor', and 'Amon, the protector of the silent, the rescuer of the poor'. (WILSON)

The silence advocated is not the opportunist silence of the earlier injunctions, which bade men hold their tongue if they wanted to keep out of trouble. It is opposed to loudness of tongue and uncontrol of passion; it is born from a quietist resolve to withdraw into oneself from an irrational and unjust world. At the same time the fostering *ka* is no longer looked on as the guiding spirit of one's fate. Fate and Fortune stand over each man, callous and impersonal. 'Do not (try to) find for yourself the powers of the god himself, (as if) there were no Fate and Fortune.'

Indo-Europeans. We have noticed the Hittite State, formed by a fusion of Indo-European immigrants and native Hattians in Anatolia about 1700 B.C. and lasting till about 1200. The idiom from which the known Hittite tongue grew had arrived about 1900 or earlier; and kindred-idioms had been carried into Iran and Greece by 1500 at latest. The Indo-European language embraces (Vedic) Sanscrit in India, Persian, Greek, Latin, the Celtic and Slavonic tongues; and it is deduced that some group or groups of people, before dispersing, spoke the parent-tongue. The term Aryan is applied to sections within the Indo-European groups who spoke closely related dialects and even worshipped common deities: the Hindus, Iranians, and the Mitanni warrior-nobles.

The original group or groups seem to have been stockbreeders with the ox and probably the sheep and pig, who knew one metal (copper or bronze). They were familiar with the horse and probably tamed it, since early they used wheeled vehicles; the chariot they probably developed in Iran. A patriarchal tribal society, they practised at least a primitive agriculture with temporary settlements. The monarchy of early Rome, Macedon, and the Germany of Tacitus may be an inheritance from early times; among the Hittites there was both a council of elders or senate and a larger assembly (*pankus*, apparently a 'full' gathering), possibly of all free warriors, which had the power to put on trial before another body a king who persisted in a feud. There seems a division of functions between king and war-chief at Pylos and among the Germans, but not among the Hittites, who were a minority in Anatolia.

The homeland may have been central or northern Europe. The most likely area is that which extends from the Danube to the Black Sea. Linguistic similarities suggest contacts with the Finno-Ugric peoples of the north. The Germans seem to have moved into western Europe rather late, driving the Celts from the middle Rhineland about B.C. 500; and there seem close pre-historic contacts of the Germanic and Italic peoples in a European environment. The Celts moved further out from the homeland than the *Italici*, but kept in touch with them, as later still with the Germans. The proto-Latins and some Celts moved out first, with other Celts and the Osco-Umbrians still awhile close together; then migrated into Italy before the Celts started for the west. Celts still occupied Bohemia and Pannonia in the last century B.C. In the first millennium Iranian groups were still living north of the Caucasus and the Black Sea; and as the Indo-Iranian emigration seems relatively late, it may have come about from a secondary centre. The Greeks entered Greece, presumably from the north, in the first half of the 2nd millennium; and the Phyrgian invasion of Anatolia occurred about 1300-1200, apparently via Thrace.

Probably any signs we find of matrilinear descent in the Greek area, *e.g.* among the Lycians, represents an inheritance from the pre-Greek period. Similarly the Hittite queen's right to continue office as widow doubtless derives from a compromise with Anatolian mother-power.

An important Indo-European contribution lay in the field of language. Sumerian was an agglutinative language, in which meaning was achieved by a complex clustering of units rather than by any clarity of logical structure. The Indo-Europeans

were almost unique, for instance, in possessing a substantive verb and at least a rudimentary machinery for building subordinate clauses that might express conceptual relations in a chain of ratiocination. It follows then that the Aryans must have been gifted with exceptional mental endowments, if not in enjoyment of a high material culture. (CHILDE)

It follows rather that the Indo-Europeans were on the periphery of the old civilisations, but still possessive of a strong basis of tribal equality, so that they were able to add to the ancient inheritance a verve of initiative and independent outlook which we have noted in Hittite history-narrative. A sense of time was one of the slowest things to develop in human thought and language. In a world of collective thought-clusters the present was the sole point of cohesion, the sole point to which the various ideas or emotions converged. The future tense did not exist in any language; and was still immature even by the time of Homeric Greek. In Hebrew we note:

A characteristic feature is the ease with which the individual passes from one standpoint or picture to another. Thus, the conditional proposition may consist of two distinct mental pictures, the juxtaposition of which causes them mutually to determine each other. Again, impending or future events can be regarded as actually present; conditions and results can be associated, and what was once future (from some past standpoint) can be regarded as still unaccomplished. The tenses in Hebrew hardly express time from our point of view, but rather states of development, and the language is dominated by the action and reaction of living ideas and the judgment of the speaker. The Indo-European scheme of three distinct time-periods (past, present and future) is not expressed, although even in the old Babylonian the Semitic 'imperfect' was slightly differentiated in order to distinguish what we may call present and preterite. (COOK)

It will be seen how such a language as the Hebrew helped to concentrate past, present, and future in a fierce heaving sense of potentiality, and so was appropriate for prophetic ecstasies. On the other hand, without the new kind of constructions made possible by the Indo-Europeans, it is hard to see how the stage represented by Greek art, science and philosophy could ever have come about.*

Iron. Iron had been known for some time, but an effective process of iron-making seems first devised by barbarian tribesmen in the Armenian moun-

Egyptian carpenters making chairs. Goldsmith at his crucible.

tains. The Aryan invaders of Mitanni incorporated the iron-workers in their military rule and guarded their secret; and the Hittites after them carried on the same policy. Mercenaries in their armies however came to learn the process and divulged it. Cheap iron, by spreading implements on a very much larger scale than bronze could, 'democratised agriculture and industry and warfare too'. Infantry grew important, recruited from yeomen farmers; and there was a waning of the heroic single-handed exploits of nobles in chariots. The Bronze Age of the Near East went out about 1200 in a fresh burst of barbarian invasions, which almost plunged the civilised areas into chaos. Assyria however continued to flourish. About the same time the Shang capital was sacked in China, and the Chous began their empire.

---

* The Chinese ideogrammic script is the same sort of thing as the Sumerian, though subjected to continual refinement. The Chinese never reached the phonetic stage. Thus, in Pekingese *i* has 69 meanings; and though the use of 4 tones reduces the number of exact homophones, there are still 38 meanings of *i* with a falling tone. There were no common, i.e. future forms; and before dialect differentiation, tense forms seem to have expressed aspect rather than time.

As a result of iron, in some 500 years, a zone of literate and more or less urbanised communities grew up from the Atlantic coasts of Spain to the Jaxartes in Central Asia and the Ganges in India, from south Arabia to the north coasts of the Mediterranean and the Black Sea. (China was rather slow in developing iron-techniques.) There were corresponding advances in mercantile and cultural contacts. Even barbarian groups like the Celts in the west and the Scyths on the steppes were much affected. And in the civilised centres a series of empires rose and fell—those of the Assyrians, the neo-Babylonians, the Aryan Medes and Persians. By 500 B.C. the empire of the Persian Darius extended from the Nile and the Aegean to the Indus and the Jaxartes.

Assyrians. The Assyrians were marked by their ruthless organising powers, and in some respects they foreshadowed the Romans. Their art showed some independence from about 1350 B.C. and revealed an anecdotal interest in secular events; on the religious side it remained stiff and cold. Inheriting many elements from the Mitanni, it was at root as dependent on the Babylonians as Roman art was on the Greeks. A basic motive was the stylised sacred tree, as also the crested griffin: common Mitannian motives, which are sometimes combined. The tree-cult was one of the oldest elements in Mesopotamian religion; trees and plants appeared on the earliest monuments, but only in unequivocal contexts can we be sure they were sacred. In Assyrian art ritual-acts prove that the artificial tree was holy; and at the New Year festival a bare trunk, with metal bands (called yokes) attached, as well as fillets, played an important part. In Syria too a bedecked maypole was an object of worship;

Assyrian relief; lion leaving cage.

on one cylinder seal the head of the inhabiting deity appears at the top.

The prominence of the sacred tree was not the only example of the Assyrian tendency to represent the gods by emblems. In sculpture, relief dominated— though the bull-guards are halfway between statues and reliefs as they detach themselves in part from the slab to watch the oncomer and cast their spell over him. The architectural situation kept them squared in an impressive way. (They expressed the heavy power-world as well as mounted guard on it.) The rulers, responsible for the acts of the whole people, scapegoats as well as absolute monarchs, spent much of their time in penitential rites and averting magics; but the art ignored this side of their life. (In one ceremonial scene, however, a procession is followed by a man in a lion-mask, with cloak falling over back and sides; he holds a whip and seems to impersonate a disease-demon.) The art concentrated on war and hunting, The Egyptian stereotype was avoided, and the artists managed to combine a decorative sense with a keen interest in particular event. Spatial depth was not attempted, though there were now and then some plastic hints; details were generally added by engraving. Under Senaccherib the reliefs showed three registers, with the middle one kept for the scenic setting.

The art gained its character from its brutal secularisation. Symbolism retreated to the emblems of the gods, as if to leave the life which these heavily built men most honoured, that of the hunt and the battle, to reveal itself without making the gods responsible. Man was cruelly the builder of his own world and stood on his own feet. From Assyria the Greeks and Etruscans, via the Phoenicians, gained models in their orientalising phase; and there was a broad link between the reliefs and Roman narrative art, such as that of Trajan's Column.

Converging Influences. Gradually through the latter half of the 2nd millennium the trading contacts, especially in the Phoenician area, were bringing about a confused meeting-point of cultural elements from far and wide, and sharpening the need for simplified forms of accountancy and writing. A great step was the alphabet of 29 cuneiform signs worked out at Ras Shamra. As an example of the merging art-influences we may take the round lid of an ivory box from the port of Minet-el-Beida, dated in the first half of the 13th century. The chief figure is certainly meant to be the great mother of the Aegean. She has that goddess's bare bosom, flounced skirt, coiffure and cap; but her heavy breasts are Asian in style and derive from the Mesopotamian tradition going back to protoliterate times, which stresses them for their fertility-force. She is seated on an hourglass-stool on a mountain; her goats too are on a mountain. But the artist could not achieve the clear articulation of limbs shown in an Aegean seated figure. In Asia, further, the mountain is the field of action of fertility-gods; in the Aegean it is a setting for the goddess in her manifestation—she would not sit there. And in the Aegean the hourglass-form is used for altars. The ivory then as a whole shows a mixture of Aegean and Asian elements. We

may note in addition the corbel-vaulted roofs of tombs at Ras Shamra with
an Aegean look, and the medley of misunderstood Egyptian themes that
largely composes Phoenician art.

Phoenician bowl found at Praeneste, Italy.

The Persians had their own styles from prehistoric days; but by the 7th
century in west Persia we can see a merging of Assyrian and Scythic influences.
Imperial Achaemenian art brought together elements from all over the empire.
The architects liked square rooms and used capitals lavishly—with styles
drawn from Egypt (the capital rising from a ring of drooping sepals) and
Ionian Greek towns (fluted shafts and torus with horizontal flutings as
capital-base). Both the Ionian and the Achaemenian columns are products of
a development centred on the east Mediterranean: though the first is a clear
logical member and the latter tended to grow bizarre, with splendid mass-
effects. In the tomb of Cyrus at Passargadai we meet the ziqqurat applied to
funeral purposes: a shrine-chamber was set on top of a small pyramid of
stone steps, surrounded by a cloister of columns.

Persian Religion. Persia thus provided a great gathering and sifting point for the multiple forms and forces growing up after the Assyrians all over the Near East. The Greeks made contributions to this growth, but also drew considerably from it. Without the imperial system of the Persians as a complement to the city-states which they spread all round the Mediterranean, the Greeks as we know them could not have evolved. In time the Persians were overtaken by the same fate as the other empire-builders. The yeomen farms were swallowed up in estates of the nobles who had given up the hard-living ways of the early clansmen. One result was the creation of Paradises, great hunting-enclaves in which the nobles could imagine themselves as living the life of their ancestors, the free and equal warriors of the clan still secure in its brotherhood. The word *paradise* was taken over by the Greeks from the Persians; and the image merged with that of the edenic garden of the Primeval Man. The 'return to nature' had already become a nostalgic idea which identified nature with the lost tribal life of equality.

Another result was the creation from below of a mass-religion of protest, which was not satisfied, as had been the Osirians, with getting a share in an afterworld of light and of social reversal. A reformer Zarathustra rose up— at a time, it seems, when the Iranian herdsmen were in conflict with nomadic raiders from Central Asia. He appealed to his fellows to cleave to the one great and good god Ahuramazda, who would deliver them. (The god's name is known from an earlier Assyrian inscription.) Ahuramazda was invested with the guardianship of the cosmic order, *Asa* or *Rita:* we may compare Akhenaton with his *Ma'at*. And Zarathustra launched an attack on the many nature-deities, who became *daevas* or demons.

The Gathas include sayings attributed to him among their hymns, prayers and instructions; with later accretions they make up the *Zendavesta* which has likenesses to the *Upanishads* of India. The life revealed is a simple and heroic one, in which the ideal is independence with 'ten mares and a camel in peace'. The ethical rules are 'to make him who is an enemy a friend, to make him who is wicked righteous, and to make him who is ignorant learned'. Further, 'that nature alone is good which will not do unto another whatever is not good unto its own self'. And the call goes forth to ceaseless struggle for the good life. 'Give us a world that is free again. Now it is the prey of raving fiends. Life is constricted by nobles and priests. But if we live, victory is ours'. The faithful 'they who are the day's enlighteners, to hold the Righteous Order of the world upright, and forward pressing... When will the dawn of that day be seen when humanity turns its gaze to Truth? When the voice of the helpers at last is heard and men do their bidding? Let it be when it will. I shall labour as if it were now'.

Though later the element of duality hardened, in the early phase the vision of dual struggle is contained within the sense of the resolving unity of Ahuramazda. *Yasna* 30 from the *Gathas* makes the most coherent statement:

Open your ears to what is the sovereign good; contemplate with clear mind the two ways between which every man must choose for himself; being aware in advance of that which the great ordeal (day of judgment) shall decide in our favour.

Now in the beginning the two spirits which are as it were twins are the one good, the other evil, in thought, word and deed. And between these two the wise make a good choice but not the foolish.

And when the two spirits encounter one another they establish the origin of life and not-life, and in the end the worst state is for the wicked, but for the just, Good Thought.

Of these two spirits, the evil choose to make evil things. But the Most Holy Spirit, clothed with the everlasting heavens, is on the side of Justice; and thus do all those whose pleasure it is to satisfy the Wise Lord (Ahuramazda) through good deeds.

The climax of the struggle is then the great ordeal or judgment. What among the Egyptians had appeared as an individual event, repeated with every death, becomes among the Persians a collective one, a final test towards which all history is moving. Without this development of religious thought, we cannot imagine Judaism or Christianity.

Legends grew up round Zarathustra. He was miraculously conceived; all nature rejoiced at his birth; attempts were made to murder him by a prince; he retired into the mountainous wilderness to meditate; was led into the presence of God and given a revelation; then was tempted by the Lord of Evil. About 520, Darius recognised the Zarathustrian monotheism and tried to suppress the old nature-worship. In 485 the followers of the latter rebelled and were put down by Xerxes, who did his best to enforce Ahuramazda's cult. But the attempt had little hope, and by 404 a compromise was effected. The reformed religion was swamped by the old worships, though the prophet's name was kept in the liturgies.

In the *Zendavesta* appeared Mithras, champion of Ahuramazda, a young god of light and truth. Among the Parsis of Bombay, the main surviving followers of the Zarathustrian creed, he is only one of the powers attending the high god; but in the form in which we know his cult in the Roman world, he has become a saviour-god with his own rites of death-rebirth. He mediates between eternity and man; the sun does homage to him; he is born from a rock (the primeval mount); he tames a bull and drags him to a cave to be killed. The bull-sacrifice, expressive of the god's and the initiate's mystery-death, is based on a creation-myth. All plants, wheat, and the vine spring from the flesh, marrow, blood, despite the efforts of serpent and scorpion to defile the life-giving flow. From the semen, gathered by the moon, come all useful animals. Mithras goes on to preserve mankind from the powers of darkness; he is received into heaven and there holds a banquet with the sun—expressed ritually by a communion meal among the faithful. His initiates had grades with names like lion or raven—the raven advised Mithras at a crucial moment and ministered food at the sacred meal.

Yahweh. One of the small kingdoms that sprang up in the lull and confusion near the end of the 2nd millenium was that of Israel; for a while there were no large scale empires looming up and the small kingdoms could imagine that they were of stable importance. Hence the way in which the Hebrews looked back to the 'great days' of David and Solomon. They had a high god Yahweh, who at first was one of many. In the account of his triumphal procession in ancient times from Sinai, he comes from Myriads of Holy Ones. A *psalm*, lxxxix, says, 'El is a terrible master in the great council of Holy Ones'. In Daniel the seer listens to a conversation between two of these Holy Ones. *Exodus* cries, 'Who is like thee among the gods, Yahweh, who is like thee, glorious among the Holy Ones'. In the cited *psalm* we hear of his faithfulness in 'the assembly of the Holy Ones. For who in the clouds is equal to Yahweh, can be like Yahweh among the sons of gods?'—in Semitic idiom the sons-of-gods mean gods. In *psalm* lxii, El stands in the assembly of the gods, judging them.

Yahweh is accordingly the highest god in a council or assembly of gods, called the Holy Ones of God, or simply the gods (the sons of gods). (WIDENGREN)

All this is in accord with Canaanite theology, behind which stands the Mesopotamian picture of the god-assembly.*

In his epiphany Yahweh appears as a god of storm, thunder and lightning —'the rider on the clouds', 'the rider of the heavens'. He rides horses as well as a cherub. Again the trail leads back to Mesopotamia and its stormgod. *Habakuk* says of Yahweh, 'before his Pestilence, *Rašaf*, marched, and Plague, *Dabar*, went forth at his feet'. *Rašaf* was a west-semitic deity and Dabar we may assume to have been something of the same sort. *Psalm* lxxiv shows that Yahweh was also associated with the dragon-fight. 'Thou didst split in twain the Sea in thy strength, thou didst break in pieces the heads of the dragon in the waters. Thou didst smash the heads of Leviathan, thou wilt give him for food. . . ' And we saw that he had his primeval mountain. There were horses of the Sun with their chariots in the Temple, and a Brazen Sea, representing

---

* The Ugaritic texts from Ras Shamra, in Canaanite akin to ancient Hebrew and Phoenician. Leading roles are played by Aleyan-Balla and Anat, his wife-sister the Lady of the Mountain. The god pushes the remote El out of the picture; established as god of wind-clouds, rain and crop-growth, he becomes a sort of Thammuz, going down to the underworld; he seems installed in a heavenly palace after beating the dragon Yam or Nahar. At first he won't have any windows lest Yam of the sea or Mot of the underworld get in; then, his fears ended, orders a lattice to be made. (Probably temple-windows were opened in the autumnal rainmaking festival; and rain let through skylight on to the god's image.) We find Anat in quest of her dead lover, whom Mot has killed. Anat cleaves Mot with a ritual sickle, winnows him, scorches him, grinds him in mill, scatters his flesh over the fields, gives him to the birds to eat. There is also a battle of Baal and Mot, and we seem to have a libretto of sacred fertility-drama in which El, after drawing water for cooking and getting a bird for the pot, mates with his two daughter-wives, who bear Dawn and Sunset. In the cosmogony given by Philon of Byblos, El (Kronos) rescues Mother-earth whom Heaven is raping, and castrates the latter. (Compare the epic of Kumarbi.)

the world-ocean and copied from Marduk's temple in Babylon. The *Song of Songs* is based on the fertility-ritual of the booths of greenery at the Feast of Tabernacles; and we know that in the 5th century Yahweh was worshipped at Elephantine in Egypt together with a goddess Anat; the cult had been carried there by Jewish immigrants who were in correct relations with the temple at Jerusalem. Solomon had had Aštart officially worshipped as the deity of the Sidonians, and later we meet a Queen of Heaven to whom official sacrifices were offered by the kings and priests in Jerusalem and the other cities of Judah; she must be the Astart who as late as about 610 was given official worship. Sacred prostitution was carried on in the Jerusalem temple till the Deuteronomic reform.

In Semitic tribal ritual a key-part was played by the worship of the divine ancestor, *'amm*. Names in the Old Testament are often compounded with *'amm*, e.g. Ammiel (My *'amm* is El). The tribe was considered to come from the mating of the ancestor with his wife; and in *Hosea* this idea was connected at length with the idea of a covenant entered into by Yahweh the lover, who seeks his bride. Israel has commited the sin of adultery in leaving Yahweh. Further the Wisdom of God described in the *Book of Proverbs* is identical with the concept of Ma'at among the Egyptians. The origins of this Wisdom-thought lie in Persia, where they can be traced further back to Babylonian accounts of the House of Wisdom. The Hebrew version also draws on the Egyptian *Wisdom of Amen-em-ope* and has affinities with other such Egyptian works. We find a certain humanism mixed with individualism, e.g. the contempt for the manual worker and the elevation of contemplation. At the same time there is a quest for social justice tempered by ideals of prudence and worldly success. Already we see many signs of what were to be the worse aspects of Graeco-Roman culture: the cult of rhetoric divorced from life and become a game of formulas.

The Prophets. In their first appearance the prophets are not distinguishable from those of Baal; they are shamanist groups of ecstatic dervishes. The moral preacher appears only with the break up of the Solomonic kingdom. That kingdom had in fact destroyed tribal unity and brought about a cleavage of rich and poor—with forced labour for building, a court and harem, and hordes of military and priestly officials: a provincial effort to imitate the great imperial powers. In the early 9th century the kingdom was carried on in the north by Omry, whose son Ahab legitimised the worship of the Tyrian Baal. Elijah in his nomad's garb denounced the court, and Ahab's infringement of Naboth's vineyard was the emblem of the new oppressions. Elisha, working with the professional guild of prophets, brought the dynasty down and acted as adviser for Jehu and his son. Elijah and Elisha thus represent a popular movement which hopes to end inequalities and exploitations, and to restore something of the simplicity and brotherhood of old tribal days.

To understand why in Palestine prophets were able to come up, one after

Assyrian cavalry charging.

the other, passionately proclaiming the need to return to uncorrupted ways, we must look at the geographical situation:

The original basis of land tenure in Palestine, in ancient and modern times, was unquestionably communal. The same may be said of many primitive communities, *but the principle was likely to be particularly tenacious in Palestine owing to the proximity of the Arabian deserts from which the population has been continually refreshed.* Among the Bedouin, boundaries are unknown and each man has an equal claim upon the pasturage and water within the area commanded by his tribe. The idea of keeping a cow tied by the leg while eating its daily ration, familiar enough in intensively cultivated lands like Egypt or France, is entirely foreign to Bedouin conditions, with whom the pasturage is wide and free.

In practice the grazing is organised by clans and their sub-divisions, and each member contributes some service in person or by proxy to the common tasks. Among the semi-nomads, who sow and reap, the same principle is observed. So in Palestine, among the settled population of today [1934] all the members of a small village, or a family group from the larger towns, work their land in common, though each owns his portion and receives his due proportion of the yield. Division of the land, with the setting up of fences, arises, under such conditions, not so much for the purpose of establishing an individual claim to ownership as for protection, against goats and robbers, of the fruits of more intensive cultivation, such as young forests, vineyards, and orchards.

Such allusions as throw light on this matter in the ancient records suggest that the same communal system prevailed in Canaan before the coming of Israel, and it was at once and unquestionably adopted by the Israelites. With them it involved obviously a vital principle, affecting the unity of the people, as well as the liberties of the individual. It was only in the later history of land tenure, when the development of agriculture and the monarchial system with its social changes had led to the sub-dividing of the soil, that the inalienable right of each citizen to the ownership of his parcel of ground was recognised, as is attested by numerous biblical stories.

(GARSTANG)

And those stories make clear to us what horror the prophets felt at the division of the land, which was to them the division of the people, the rending of the flesh of unity.

The earliest recorded prophecy is that of Amos, made in the north under Jeroboam in the 8th century. Assyria was menacing the kingdom and the free peasantry was going down. So Amos, a shepherd and dresser of sycamores, came to denounce and warn. He saw no hope. He mocked at those who looked to Day of Yahweh: the battle-triumph of Israel's god. He had no illusions about what was happening to society. 'It is darkness and not light'. Disaster would come because 'they have sold the righteous for silver and the needy for a pair of shoes'. Hosea continued this position. These prophets insisted on direct inspiration like a shaman. 'I was no prophet, neither was I a prophet's son', says Amos, rejecting any institutional form but insisting that the god of his people has spoken through him. 'The lion has roared, who will not fear? The Lord God has spoken, who can but prophesy?' The words are clear:

They pant after the dust of the earth on the head of the poor and turn aside the way of the meek. . . and they lay themselves down upon clothes laid to pledge by every altar . . . As your treading is upon the poor, and you take from him burdens of wheat; you have built houses of hewn stone, but you shall not dwell in them; you have planted pleasant vineyards, but you shall not drink wine of them. . . Hear this, O you that swallow up the needy, even to make the poor of the land to fail, saying, When will the new moon be gone, that we may sell corn? and the sabbath, that we may set forth wheat, making the ephah small, and the shekel great, and falsifying the balances by deceit?

A money-economy cannot but have this effect on a free tribal society. The integrity of a man like Amos is shown by his refusal to accept the Osirian way out and to seek a redemption and a reversal of things in another world. Sheol remains a primitive limbo; there is no hint of personal immortality or of a desire for it. The fertility-rite remains the marriage of the tribal god and the earth, even in these moral judgments, and is not abstracted; fulfilment must be on earth or not at all. And there is a sharp repudiation of the idea of con-ciliation, of a restored balance, by the act of sacrifice.

The small Kingdom, with its prophets who want a return to tribal brother-hood, is environed by world-empires. There is irony in the fact that the new universality which was slowly invading the idea of the tribal god is born from the imperial State and its extending yet tightening network of relationships, productive and mercantile as well as political. Willynilly the people think more and more in world-terms, not merely in terms of lost Bedouin simplici-ties. Yahweh, repudiating in the mouths of his prophets a political system based on inequality and oppression, is changed from a tribal god to a god of national and then human unity. The fertility-rite is revalued in terms of both the broken group-bond and the desire for a yet-higher harmony. As first necessity, however, Israel must be denounced for whoring after strange gods. 'And now will I discover her lewdness in the sight of her lovers'.

The northern kingdom fell in 721 and all hope was centred on Judah under the kings of David's line. Samaria was conquered and the southern kingdom seemed likely to fall. Micah, a peasant from the Philistine borderlands and Isaiah of Jerusalem rose to the occasion. Isaiah's work covered the last forty years of the 8th century and came to its head under Hezekiah in 701 when the Assyrians reached the walls of Jerusalem. Now the social passion of Amos with its clear grasp was fading out; no demand was made for a return to nomadic brotherhood. Though there was still a call for justice to the peasantry, an attack on injustice and the greeds born of luxury, a wish to keep clear of international commitments, the stress had shifted to the concept of holiness. The Assyrians met a check and Isaiah's prestige was ensured. Yahweh's worship might have been obliterated in the north; Judah was saved for a century. A faithful remnant gathered round Isaiah and he saw in this small community the promise of ultimate restoration.

If chapter ix (1-7) is by Isaiah, we meet there the nearest he ever came to a hope of restoration. Chapter xi holds the great vision of a return to the golden age of simplicity when 'a little child shall lead them'—an *alcheringa*-vision of accord among the animals. 'They shall not hurt nor destroy in all my holy mountain.'

His influence led to the reforms under Josiah (639-608). The Deuteronomic Code issued in 621 was the product of his school; it forbade idolatry and image-worship and other aspects of the Canaanite cults. The houses of the sodomites and the sacred prostitutes were destroyed. Judah was separated as thoroughly as possible from the surrounding systems; local sanctuaries were ruthlessly put down; and Yahweh's worship was wholly located in Jerusalem. But the failure to have much effect on the mass of the people led to Jeremiah's pessimism on the eve of Jerusalem's fall to the Babylonians. The reformation seemed a mockery; Yahweh's temple, a mere shibboleth. 'The prophets prophesy falsely, and the priests bear rule by their name; and my people love to have it so'. He meets children gathering wood in the streets so that their fathers may kindle fires, while their mothers knead cakes in which the image of Yahweh's wife will be inscribed.

The political aims seemed to have quite miscarried. Jeremiah staked everything on purity of heart as opposed to the formality of temple-ritual. He felt himself the victim offered up: 'like a lamb or an ox that is brought to the slaughter'. He yearned to escape. 'O that I had in the wilderness a lodging-place for wayfaring men: that I might leave my people and go from them; for they are all adulterers, an assembly of treacherous men.' The covenant of Yahweh and the people had broken down; the covenant of Yahweh and the faithful individual remained.

Judah passed into captivity; the leading men were deported; Jerusalem lay in ruins. But the message of Isaiah and Jeremiah was remembered. The doctrine of the covenant had been changed in time, so as to weather disaster. In the earlier years of the captivity, Ezekiel, a deported priest, took up the cause (692-70); he asserted individual responsibility for what had happened. But there was still no thought of a future life which would lift the problem of justice right off the earth.

Prophecy became a written thing, and apocalyptic texts grew up. The sense of good and evil deepened, so that the old idea of suffering as the penalty of sin was questioned. At the same time the notion of the restoration of brotherhood and unity was still narrow; non-Jews were to survive Israel's triumph only to acknowledge Yahweh's power. Also, the formalism rejected at one level entered at another: as we see in Ezekiel's idea of what constituted purity, and his scheme for the new world's government by a priestly hierarchy upheld by Messianic princes of David's house, which strictly controlled the people's life from the restored Temple. Circumcision became a divine order; legalist theocracy ruled.

At the same time the baffled aspirations led to lyrical outbursts in psalms. Then Cyrus the Persian conquered Babylon and let the Jews go home. About 458 the restored community was joined by a priestly group under Ezra, who brought the new law, the work of Babylonian Jews. This law was promulgated in 397 and served henceforth as the basis for Jewish society; the Deuteronomic Law was changed into the priestly code and all records of the past were carefully edited and censored. The Pentateuch assumed more or less the form in which it now appears in the Bible; and the separation of the Jews from all other peoples was given its final rigidity.

The local synagogues throve, with meetings for public prayer, for the reading and interpretation of scripture; they took on a life of their own, which made possible the later organisation of Christian groups. Psalms continued to be composed; and the moral questioning went on. Men felt that the individual's fate was bound up with that of his fellows, and that it was hard to see a clear system of rewards and penalties; yet they could not quite reject the deep-ingrained idea of suffering as the retribution for sin. In *Job* a grandly dramatised attempt to grapple with the issue was made; in *Ecclesiastes* a cynical and sceptical answer was returned—probably not without Greek influence. The chastened mood appeared in the Second Isaiah. 'Comfort ye, comfort ye, my people'. The stress was on mercy; and the four songs of the Servant of Yahweh came as close to Christianity as was possible without breaking the mould of Jewish separatism.

At last under the stress of defeat and humiliation, in the last two centuries B.C., the idea of bodily resurrection of the dead took hold. During the exile, Zoroastrian ideas had permeated the Jews with the concept of world-end, of general resurrection and judgment, of the advent of a purified world, and this concept underlay the apocalypses with their millenarian views. The Jews were drawn into the world of the Hellenistic kingdoms; they made their Maccabean revolt and set up a theocratic State. But the Romans were looming near; they swallowed Judea without effort. More revolts merely brought about the destruction of the Temple and the Jewish dispersion under Hadrian. Jewish lore, embodied in the *Torah*, was worked on by scribes and expositors, whose work appears in the *Mishnah* and later in the *Talmud* compiled in Galilee and

Babylonia, in the 4th-5th centuries A.D. But meanwhile Christianity had been born of Judaism under the early Roman empire.

The prophets, turning a high god into an only god, had cut him off from all relationships except to his people; the result was the unconditioned nature of the Hebrew god, whose will assumed a peculiar quality quite unlike the will or pleasure of gods expressed in polytheist oracle or ritual. It becomes indivisible from his people's history, and then from all history; and history itself becomes not 'whatever happens as God's will', but a logical sequence of events with a beginning and an end, a pervading purpose: the realisation of God's will in and through his chosen people. It ceases to be a blind cyclic process and moves by a dialectical principle of development.

The Animal-nurtured Hero. We may pause here to add, as a commentary on Isaiah's *alcheringa*-vision, some instances of the little child 'who will lead them' among the friendly animals. The hero who founds a city or seems to give his people a new chance is often threatened by some sort of Herod, cast forth from the world of men into that of nature, and then returned to society as a redeemer. Moses is an example. He is hidden among rushes in a basket as a result of a scared tyrant ordering all male babes to be cast into the water; he is found by the king's daughter. He gains a name only when, grown up, he is taken to the princess. 'And she called his name Moses: and she said, Because I drew him out of the water'. Cyrus, the creator of the Persian empire, was taken from his mother as a babe; her jealous father, king of the Medes, had been warned in a dream that her son would rule Asia. But the herdsman who

Winged Assyrian gate-bull.

was told to expose the child took pity on him and reared him. Here too the name is given late: a clear sign of a myth-formula drawn from initiation-ritual. (Strabo says the name came from a river; and a variant, recorded by Justin, has the babe suckled by a dogbitch.) Sargon, the first Mesopotamian empire-builder, thus declares in an inscription:

> Sargon the mighty king the king of Akkad am I.
> My mother was poor, my father I did not know.
> My father's brother lived in the mountain.
> My poor mother conceived me, in secret bore me,
> she placed me in a chest of reeds, fastened my door with pitch
> and gave me to the river which was not running strong.
> Then the river bore me along, to Akki the sprinkler it brought me,
> Akki the sprinkler took me out with a grappling iron.
> Akki the sprinkler took me for his son and reared me.
> Akki the sprinkler made me into his gardener.
> While I was the gardener, Ishtar loved me.

Here we see how the rejected babe is identified with the fertility-god (Tammuz) who dies and is reborn. Aelian tells of Gilgamos, Babylonian king, who was informed by the Chaldeans that his grandson would take the kingdom. He confined his daughter; but she mysteriously bore a child, whom the guards threw out of the citadel. An eagle caught the boy on his back and carried him down to the garden, where the gardener adopted him. Aelian adds, 'If anyone considers this a fable, I confess that I don't credit it myself; yet I am informed that Perses the Achaemenid, from whom the noble stock of the Persians is derived, was an eagle's nursling'. And the gardener appears in *Gilgamesh* as a stockfigure of the fertility-goddess's ruined lovers:

You loved Ishullanu, your father's gardener, who constantly brought you dates and daily made your table luxurious, but you raised your eyes on him and said, 'My Ishullanu, let us eat of my pomegranates, put forth your hand and take our bread of fine meal'. Ishunallu spoke to you, 'As for me, what do you want of me? Hasn't my mother baked and I eaten? That I should eat breads of shame and cursings. . .' When you heard this speech of his, you smote him, you turned him into a hog and caused him to dwell on . . . nor does he ascend . . . nor does he descend. . .

The fertility-mother here appears as both the fruit-tempting Eve and the Circe-metamorphoser—the earth-goddess whose magics have gone wrong, slaying instead of enlivening, and fastening-on the beast-mask of the ritual-dance so that it will not come off.

Chingis Khan, who welded a number of tribes into the vast Mongol empire, was born of a girl who had been put by her father in an underground chamber and who managed to get one glimpse of the bright world. The Eye of God at once impregnated her. She was then locked in a gold chest and set afloat on the sea; but two heroes, hunting, saw the chest and opened it. Her child was Chingis; but he was envied by the three sons she bore one of the heroes, and he fled into the wilds, where he lived in a skin-house. Finally the people deposed their useless ruler and called Chingis back. His half-brothers disputed with him for their father's place. At their mother's advice they tried the test of seeing who could hang his bow on a sunbeam. Chingis won.

The variants of this sort of tale in myth, legend, hagiography, and folktale are very large: e.g. Semiramis, Romulus and Remus, Shakuntala, the hero Karna of the *Mahabharata*, Scyld Scefing of *Beowulf*, Habis of the Cunetes (see Trogus for this interesting forest-creature), many characters of Celtic legends. The Greeks were specially prolific in such tales. Apart from gods reared by nymphs or heroes reared by the centaur Cheiron, there are Paris, Oedipus, Perseus, Erectheus, Cypselus, Comatas, Daphnis and Chloe, and others. Deep went the belief that any hero who played a significant part in the foundation or reorganisation of group-life must return to nature, to the *alcheringa* of the totemic ancestors, in order to gain the spirit-force of the act of renewal. Elements from initiation-ritual and shamanist experience play their part in keeping alive the pattern of such legends. A passage through water, for instance, is a very common ingredient. Jesus himself, who was threatened by Herod, and rejected by the chaffering world, was born amid the beasts of the stalls and hailed by the shepherds.

India. We may now resume our survey of the great series of religious and philosophical outbursts that occurred all over the civilised world roughly between 800-400 B.C. In India the Aryans, appearing from the north about 1700, broke up what remained of the Indus civilisation; they called the Dravidian folk Squat-creatures and did much to formulate the system of castes. But before long the two religions and cultures were intermingled. The Vedic period of this Aryan-Dravidian union lasted on till about 800; the next three hundred years saw a period of Brahmanism with the institutions of priestly Hinduism; then came the period of philosophical reforms, carrying to about 100 B.C.—and indeed persisting another six hundred years or so with deep changes in the original forms, to which Nestorian Christianity contributed. After that the Moslem invasions culminated in the Moghul empire of the 16th century: while from the 13th there was the rise of the Bhakti saints and their cults.

The *Rigveda* consists of hymns said to belong to the earlier period; later *vedas* added hymns for sacrifice, liturgical compositions, charms and incantations. (*Veda* is cognate with the Greek *oida*, 'I know', and means knowledge.) The *vedas* show tendency towards henotheism, but also a stress on possession and ecstasy through a drug or drink: we may compare the *haoma* of the Persians.

> By means of the unfailing fleece the daughter of the sun
> cleanses your Soma which is streaming forth.
> Him seize and hold fast in the fight ten slender maidens,
> sisters all, in the decisive day of war.
> Him forth they send, the virgin band, they blow the bagpipe
> musical; threefold protection is the juice.

Milch-kine inviolable anoint the infant Soma with their milk,
    Soma for Indra as his drink.
In the wild raptures of this draught, Indra slays all his enemies;
    the mighty one bestows wealth.

About 700 B.C. the belief grew up that the *vedas* were a direct revelation,
received intuitively by the *rishis* or seers in a series of cosmic vibrations. The
Upanishads set out various teachings, and in turn were commented on.
Brahma becomes the high god—in the *Rigveda* the name means a spell or
sacred formula—and embraces all things; the Atman is the invisible part of a
person, breath, spirit, self; in time there emerges the concept of one Atman
differentiated into the many selves; finally Brahma is made the one Atman
or Great Self. There is a strong inturned element, defining blessedness as a
dreamless sleep or state of being beyond the ordinary states of consciousness
Duality is overcome by negation. In the *Katha Upanishad*, Yama the god of
the underworld expounds the way-out through Yoga:

When cease the five (sense) knowledges, together with the mind (*manas*), and the
intellect (*buddhi*) stirs not—that, they say, is the highest course. This they consider
as *Yoga*—the firm holding back of the senses. Then one becomes undistracted. Yoga,
truly, is the origin and the end. . . When are cut all the knots of the heart here on
earth, then a mortal becomes immortal.

The hypnotic techniques of Yoga are a sort of systemised shamanism severed
from social function and made a personal satisfaction alone. Men seek to
escape from the chain of births, and from *karma*, the chain of retributive
justice. Thus the idea of reincarnation comes powerfully to buttress the caste-
system, linking it with punishment for sins committed in previous lives.

There is endless elaboration of the given premises, but also some wider
speculative thinking, especially in connection with *prakrti* or matter—though
the trend always is to develop any system of relationships so as to help the
thinker towards an absolute of independence: freedom deprived of attributes
and projected on the blank screen of death.

Unsafe boats however are these sacrificial forms,
    the eighteen, in which is expressed the lower work.
The fools who approve that as the better
    go again to old age and death. . .
They who practise austerity and faith in faith in the forest,
    the peaceful knowers who live on alms, depart passionless
through the door of the sun, to where is that immortal Person,
    even the imperishable Atman. (*Mundaka Upanishad*)

The use of ascetic techniques to gain control of the body is central; and the
three main expressions come in Jainism, Buddhism and Bakhti.

Jainism accepted nothing less than total escape from the chain, and vener-
ated a small group of noble selves who had escaped into perfection, while
while Bakhti represented the groups who personified nature as a sort of over-

soul or universal lord and expressed a passionate yearning for personal union with him, Isvara. (The overstrained sexual ecstasy of Bakhti recalls the swooning joys of many Christian saints in their mystical marriage with Christ.)

Jainism was said to be founded by Vardhamana, born about 569 B.C., an ascetic who gathered the usual marvellous tales of birth, childhood and initiation. The Jains have carried *ahimsa* or non-violence towards all creatures to an extreme, e.g. they filter their breath with respirators so as not to swallow living organisms. They have survived as a minority-sect; like the Quakers in 18th century England they have played a leading part in banking, and in parts, Bengal and Assam, hold almost a monopoly of retail trade. There is a certain bitter irony in the way in which quietist sects, especially when persecuted, seek to heap up treasure in heaven, and by their extremely abstinent lives end by heaping up treasure on earth and playing a leading role in money-accumulation. We may compare the historical functions of Monophysites, Jews, and Nestorians.

Siddharta Gotama, born about 560, was the son of a nobleman, around whom also the usual mythical formulas gathered. There was an angelic annunciation and virgin birth, with *devas* singing and a prediction of future greatness, a fast of 49 days, a temptation by the spirit of evil (to turn the Himalayas into gold), 32 healing miracles, a transfiguration, a band of twelve disciples. The master fed 500 people on a small cake, had a disciple who walked on water, and, when taken to a temple ceremony, conformed but said it was unnecessary. An effort was made to kill him, but the hired bowmen fell to the ground at the sight of his face; he made a triumphal entry into his home-town; and there was an earthquake on the day of his death.

His teaching was handed on orally. The age was one of intense inquiry and argument, of experiments with the disciplines of *tapa* and *yoga*. Up to the age of 35 the Buddha indulged in extreme asceticism, then decided that he was on the wrong track. Meditating under the mother-peepul tree, he reached the stage of enlightenment, and after some days he preached in a grove near Benares, gained his first disciples, and set off on his wanderings for forty-five years, teaching and founding groups. He insisted on the law of cause and effect, but wanted to get outside it, preaching a technique of detachment, the noble ninefold way, which lay as a middle path between the ascetic *tapas* and self-indulgence, in a quest for the Great Self. There was no appeal to any god. The way was simply one of personal purification, a search for Nirvana, the waning-out of the little-self and of suffering. (There are faint signs of a postmortem tribunal by the Lord of the Way.)

Asoka, a king of the Mauryan empire, about 270-40 B.C., turned from war to pacifism and set up rock-inscriptions praising the new faith. During his reign the inner conflict in Buddhism, between those who clung to the original simplicities of the creed, and those who wanted to ritualise it, came to a head. At a council of Buddhists held at Patna, the majority expelled the minority. The former group wanted to carry detachment to the point of ego-extinction;

the latter argued that the man-in-the-man should grow steadily enriched. The expellers became in time the southern Buddhists, called the sect of the *Himayana*, the Little System, by the northerners, who developed theories of a buddha-spirit incarnate in a series of Buddhas or Bodhisattvas, saints who from love of man refrain from Nirvana—with a series of heavens and hells that they must pass through in seeking beatitude. In the *Lotus Sutra* the glorified Buddha preaches from a mountain-peak to his disciples and is transfigured before their eyes; the doctrine he sets out is that of the cosmic Buddha 'in whom all things consist', the repeated rebirth of Gotama in Bodhisattvas, and the need of every man to be buddhified. Nirvana becomes a pleasurable heaven. This adapted creed, the *Mahayana* or Great System, conquered from Tibet to Japan.

The precise message of the original Gotama is hard to decipher, but seems to lie in such utterances as the following:

Nowhere can any cover up his sin. The Self in you, man, knows what is true or false. Indeed, my friend, you scorn the noble Self, thinking to hide the evil self in yourself from Self who has witnessed it. Thus he who has the Self as master, let him walk with heed. (*The 4th Anguttara Nikaya*)

I lay no wood, brahman, for fires on altars. Only within burns the fire I kindle. Ever my fire burns, ever tense and ardent. I, as an arahant, work out the life that is holy. . . the heart's an altar, the fire on it is man's self, well-tamed. (*The Samyutta Nikaya*)

By the time of the *Diamond-cutter Sutra* the mood is opposed even to recognition of the reality which causes suffering 'Belief in the unity or eternity of matter', says Buddha, 'is incomprehensible; and only common worldly-minded people, for purely materialistic reasons, covet this hypothesis'. While in the *Lotus* the mood is exalted and authoritative: 'I shall refresh all beings whose bodies are withered, who are clogged to the triple world. I shall bring to felicity those that are pining away with toils, give them pleasure and final rest. Hearken to me, ye hosts of gods and men; approach to behold me: I am the Tathagata, the Lord, who has no superior, who appears in this world to save'.

Whereas then among the Persians and Jews the sense of conflict in the world-system led to religions of struggle and to a belief that a deep purpose was expressed in human history, the Indians turned aside in a despair from a world of inequality and injustice, and sought for personal solutions. The lost relationship between man and society, man and nature, was expressed in the relationship between him and his own body—in the techniques of *tapa* and *yoga*, which sought to overcome duality by losing the everyday consciousness of the little-self in the hypnotically-induced sense of a perfect equipoise, the Great Self. From these practices came the elaborated metaphysics. But the displaced collective element reasserted itself in the *Mahayana*, developing a church of the faithful, a theory of history with periodic redemptions, and monastic forms for those who wanted to keep closer to the original impulses of rejection without disturbing the compromise with the world.

China. China has had a development so unlike that of any other large centre of civilisation that we cannot even use the same terms in describing it. We see a Bronze Age emerging late in the 2nd millenium B.C., though its roots are not yet clear. The urban growth was connected with the two great river-systems, where there appeared many communities or tribal states, with a highly-organised ruling-class built up from the tribal chiefs. The Chou State overthrew that of the Shang about 1050, and established *Feng-chien*, a system of parcelling out blocks of conquered land to relations of the ruling families and to allies. Thus the rulers everywhere belonged to the same kin-groups. All land was the property of the tribal states, to whom slaves also belonged. In the period of the West Chou and the Warring States, which ended in 256 B.C. the nobility handed over the details of government to a clerk-class, the *shih*, who were paid by the tribute they collected. Irrigation works were maintained, but only, it seems, on any substantial scale from the time of the Warring States.

In the last centuries of the Chou dynasty iron came into use. (The centre of China was then in the north.) The area of tillage was extended. Currency of small coppers was minted from about 524 B.C. and the class of merchants and usurers grew. About 350 the king of Ch'in took the decisive step of abolishing the village-commune, and in 221 the first emperor of Ch'in abolished *Feng-chien*, dividing the empire into areas under appointed officials—the *huan-liao*, developed out of the *shih*. Entry into the *huan-liao* was by literacy; the exam-ination-system, started under the Hans, was in full growth under the T'ang. Most landowners' sons, and a few peasants', went to school. Till the T'ang period the hereditary nobility had much weight; then the dominant class were the scholars and the gentry who included examination-candidates and retired officials as well as scholars who never entered the service. The officials drew their income from land, with no tax or only a small one.

The Great Wall built against the nomads was completed in the late 3rd century B.C. Like the palaces and mausoleums, it was the work of forced levies. There were many revolts of the discontented peasantry, which shook but could not transform the State. The Ch'in empire had been helped in its unifying controls by the backing of the rich merchants, who became landlords. But iron as well as bronze and salt was a state-monopoly, and this fact checked the growth of the middle class. Land, however, was alienable, and ownership tended to concentrate in a few hands.

There were thus two main classes. The landowners, merchants and usurers, linked with the bureaucracy, on the one hand; and on the other, the small farmers, artisans and landless peasants. Serfs and slaves existed, but not in enough numbers to determine the system; the main producers were the free peasants who could move about and buy or sell land, but who were subject to a heavy tax and to forced labour. Of the main peasant groups—the small independent farmers and the tenants—the former was the backbone of the country, though they were continually harassed by debt, corruption, foreclosures—a mounting condition of misery that in time led to another revolt and a new start on the old bases. A fresh dynasty arose or the nomads broke in. Only one ruler at the end of the Han dynasty tried and failed to return to the village-commune. Other rulers made efforts to curb merchant-capital, but with no permanent effects. So the State continued with unchanged basis for over two thousands years, with slow changes going on inside the given frame. A special crisis came on after the Han monetary economy; there was a considerable return to a natural economy, with the arable of north China falling back to pasture. The government had to come to rest on the newly-developed region of the Lower Yangtse, conveying grain thence to the northern capital; an imperial canal united the Yangtse and the Yellow River. A revival came under the T'ang and the Sung; but the T'ang dynasty was overthrown by the peasants and the Sung by the Mongol nomads.

China thus developed its odd bureaucratic empire directly out of the Bronze Age; it did not develop a slave-owning economy and could not produce the kind of feudalism that emerges from the breakdown of such an economy, let alone the capitalism that emerges out of feudalism. First the village-community, based on tribal kinship, was the basis; then the free farmer, caught in a free money-market of land, yet subject to a feudal type of labour-levy.

Chinese society has long been modelled on a basis not of slavery but of free farmers, and that has very important bearing on the humanitarian character of Chinese philosophy in all forms, whether Confucian or Taoist. It is not at all obvious at first sight what was the reason for this, because there would have been nothing to prevent the ancient Chinese from having a large slave population from captives taken in war, people of the Mongol or Hunnish tribes to the north or the Tibetans and Tanguts in the west. (NEEDHAM)

The cross-bow was early invented in China and the peasant levies of the early armies (800-300 B.C.) were armed with it, while the knightly armour was of bamboo and wood. So the *Tso Chuan* is full of tales about lords killed by arrow-shots and the country lacked the sharp differentiation in war-equipment which makes possible the rise of a powerful nobility backed by heavily-armed retainers. Nor could there be anything like the Macedonian hoplites or the Roman legionaries for overawing a slave-population.

In the fourth century B.C., in a State such as Sung or Wu or Ch'u, the people on whom the lord depended might well desert to his opponent suddenly on the field of battle. They had to be convinced of the justice of their cause. To effect that it was necessary to have a class of 'sophists' which afterwards became the Confucians, to commend to the mass of the people the activities and virtues of the feudal lord, and gather them round him.

Bronze-casters. The origins of Chinese culture are still obscure but it is fairly certain that the links were with Siberia and south-west Asia: thus, the neolithic pots are very like the painted wares of the latter area. An important part was played by jade as a magical life-giving material worked for ritual objects, some of which are miniatures of tools. The squared spiral and the lozenge seem motives borrowed by the bronze-casters from the jades.

The cult of the ancestors was very early. Oracle-bones, found in north Honan, are dated about 1300 B.C. These *shangyin* consist of questions put to the ancestors who operated as oracles for the ruling-house and who were addressed through priest-diviners. The latter wrote the questions down on the bones. A favourite bone was the ox-scapula. 'Every important principle of the formation of modern Chinese characters was already in use, in a greater or less degree, in the China of the oracle-bones, more than three thousand years ago'. That is, there has been no fundamental change in thought-forms and methods of communication over that period; there has been only refinement and elaboration. A more remarkable example of the failure of a culture to develop it would be impossible to find. The only parallel lies in the way in which the Australian aboriginals have clung to their paleolithic bases despite the impact of new methods through New Guinea.

At the same time as the oracle-bones there was in action a bronze-metallurgy of a high craft-level; we have no clue yet as to the stages leading to the fine products of the period. The towns grew up on the basis of the bronze-workers; and the earliest myths and rituals that can be made out from the old records suggest that the kingship grew up out of magical craft-fraternities, perhaps out of conflicts inside them. (We may compare the role of the iron-smith in Africa. When the Portuguese first reached the mouth of the Congo, they found that *mani* or king of the Congo was a member of the blacksmith's guild; and all over the south Sahara the smiths had large fraternities, which provided the prime-ministers for every chief.) The Chinese myths in question are largely concerned with transformation-magics in which shamanist dances play a large part.

The bronzes had a ritual purpose and each was made in honour of some particular ancestor.

In the Shang-Yin vessels a few graphs record the ancestor's name and perhaps add that of the person responsible. By the early Chou period the inscriptions increase in length; they name the ancestor or ancestors, the donor, and the circumstances that led to the casting—the gift of a fief or clothing, or some such act of recognition, by the man's overlord. The final words express a hope for long life on the part of the donor—may he enjoy 'a myriad years and the bushy eyebrows of old age!'—and for the continued use of the sacred vessel by his posterity.

Most of the bronzes seem to have had pottery-prototypes. An important decorative motive is that which I have called the dual or symmetrical form, and which is found in the early Aegean and south-west Asia as well as in America. Here it is called the *t'ao-t'ieh* and is based on an animal mask set fullface between two confronting zoomorphs in profile. Chinese explanations conflict and are good examples of the rationalising tendencies which moralised away primitive elements. We are told of harmful spirits of the hills and wastes, which the great founding king-caster Yu had represented on his Nine Cauldrons to enable people to learn what they looked like; and by the 3rd century A.D. the *t'ao-t'ieh* was declared to be one of these. An earlier passage, attributed to the 3rd century B.C., declared that the Chou form had a head but no

Chinese t'ao-t'ieh *mask, early phase; crest, mid-top, flanked by horn, tail, quill either side; lower centre, fang, snout, upper jaw or trunk; circular eye either side, with lower jaw under; leg at outsides.*

body. 'He is eating a man and is going to swallow him, but already his own body is destroyed. The object was to warn people that the hour of disaster was at hand'—that the State was swallowing up the people, the land, but in the process had lost its 'body' or digestive organs. The Sung moralisers therefore explained the *t'ao-t'ieh* as a warning against greed and gluttony. Such analyses however bear no relation to the original conception, which we have found to lie in the effort to reassert totemic duality-and-unity in a breaking-down tribal system. The Chinese forms, which progressively disintegrate the organic aspect of the design, are close in feeling and method to those of the north-west Indians of America.

The squared spiral, which is the next most important design on the bronzes, has close affinities with the art of Central America. We may call it a maze-pattern—though the Sung cataloguers related it to thunder, apparently from its likeness to the archaic character for thunder, *lei.*

What is beyond doubt is the great magical force of these motives. The bronzes are covered all over with them or with allied designs, to charge them with power, especially with dragon-force. In the second phase, however, the decorations grow less fervently rich and the zoomorphs practically disappear, except for handles in animal form; in the third phase the designs are treated almost wholly as decorations. There is a simultaneous weakening of magical and artistic energy.

Yang and Yin. For the moment we shall leave the later developments of Chinese art and literature and consider the great period of philosophy, from the 8th to the 2nd centuries B.C. For the background we must turn to the ancient book of odes, where we find the songs of the youths and girls at the spring festivals and in autumn after the mating. The dance-places were also spirit-centres, ancestor-centres, from which the community had originated, like the Australian totem-centres; but with the advent of the towns, the lords captured the holiness of the dance-sites and transferred it to the sacred mound or temple of their town. This early loss of the peoples' dance-sites to the town-lords perhaps explains why there was no large scale growth of popular festivals such as we find in Egypt or Sumer, no transformation of primitive ritual-elements into epic or drama. The folksongs however begot the Chinese lyrical poem and played their part in forming the Chinese vocabulary.

The Chinese song, most simple in form, consists of a series of slightly modified couplets; each couplet consists of the juxtaposition of two strictly correspondent phrases. The earliest poems are nothing but a sequence of dictichs. . . In order to express their sentiments, the actors who face each other gradually outline with the help of such vocal gestures as accompany a figure in a ballet: thus they work out two symmetrical designs. . . The yoked phrases are composed of words musically corres-ponding, the musical correspondence being more strongly emphasised in the rhyming words ending each phrase. (GRANET)

The sentences pair by parallelism or antithesis; and the ideas or emotions are expressed in the movements of the alternating choirs.

These movements are of two kinds. Sometimes elementary, they are simple gestures, utterances and body-movements so closely connected that *the vocal gesture* retained for ever, in its short characteristic music, all the concrete flavour, all the summoning force of a whole representation. Doubtless the chief effort of original invention for these poetical contests was directed towards finding descriptive auxiliaries; the search for them has been of first importance in the formation of the Chinese vocabulary, which is very rich in concrete expressions; it has also been of first importance in the creation and history of ideographic writing in which the ideogram comes in to restore to the word, always associated with the thing seen, the help of a sketch and of gestures which depict it.

Sometimes the image, more complex, appears from the organisation of rhythmical movements. . . Usually one of the two juxtaposed sentences describes a phenomenon relative to persons, and is more directly intelligible; the other, describing the circum-stances of that phenomenon, or if one prefers it, the natural phenomenon in sym-metry with it, seems to refer less directly to the act illustrated by the whole.

As a result of the rhythm, or if one prefers it, as a result of a figure of speech, one of the two formulas placed in apposition appears as *symbolic double* of the other: *a natural image seems to express indirectly and as allegory the human fact with which traditional experience associates it*. By what seems very like artifice, the natural correspondences seem to become something like images as we conceive them. How-ever, far from their invention depending upon a play of fantasy aided by a developed system of syntax, the rhythmic effect from which they proceed, which is the first principle of poetry, does nothing but show, under various aspects which tradition has consecrated, the mysterious bond between men and things.

This analysis, though directed towards early Chinese poetry, brings out the way in which the dual or symmetrical principle, expressed in alternating choirs, plays a key-part in developing the disciplines and form-balances of poetry (or music), and in which the opposed symmetrical parts develop poetic symbolism or imaginative imagery. Thus we may take the first song of the *Shih Ching*:

> The peachtree young and beautiful
>> how profuse its flowers.
> The girl is about to be married:
>> it is right that they should be husband and wife.
> The peachtree young and beautiful
>> abundant are its fruits.
> The girl is about to be married:
>> it is right that they should be husband and wife.
> The peachtree young and beautiful
>> luxuriant are its leaves.
> The girl is about to be married:
>> it is right that they should wed.

The peachtree shows that mating-time has been reached, and at the same time represents the girl with her descriptive auxiliaries: her beauty, nubility and perfect physical condition. But beyond these analogical points there grows up a fusion of girl and tree which expresses 'the mysterious bond between men and things', the living place of men in the universe.* The ritual-double or *churinga* has come to lovely life in the vivifying and resolving rhythms of song and dance; and the principle is capable of an endlessly enriched application.

These wooing and mating spring-tourneys of the sexes united the young couple by the spell of the traditional analogies which were evoked as they faced one another. Any improvisations came directly from the dance-rhythms. The grouping by the sexes was according to labour-division; and the songs brought about the union of those destined by the community's traditional rules to marry.

From these festivals then was born the idea of two alternating principles *Yin* and *Yang*, which make up a system of universal classification and are also two concrete categories, two cosmogonic principles, female and male. Space was seen as an organised whole made up of two different kinds of extension, *Yin* and *Yang*, confronting one another. Thus, in labouring, the men worked in the sunlight of the fields, the women in the shade of the orchard or the house; and each corporation had a definite place on the dance-ground—the male position being *yang*, the female *yin*. Time, too, was not a matter of a mechanically divisible duration, but was composed of a regular alternation of two different kinds of time. The sex-corporations cut the year into sections,

---

* The pedantic type of analysis developed is shown by the *Imperial Commentary of the Ch'ing Dynasty* on this poem: 'The good government of the State is reflected in the proper ordering of the family ... also (the government of K. Wen being good) it was inevitable that in all the States the women should be capable of ordering their households aright'. The proverb-competitions, found in the *Shih Ching*, involve an effort to prove a proposition by 'analogic rhythm' and a host of traditional formulas which seek to establish an effective correspondence; there is a link with the chain-syllogism important in Chinese philosophy.

one season for men in the fields, one for women at home, and so on. Hence the principles of alternative correspondences and of symmetry of position, which are the basis of time and space: *Yang* of the south, summer, sun, and *Yin* of the wintry slopes, north.

But the town-lord took over the regulative power and holiness of the festival play. The division of the sexes assumed a new and deepened form—women, save in rare instances, being excluded from public life and worship. The chief's marriage abrogated to itself the importance once held by the spring-festival; the primitive rites broke up and were distributed about the calendar; natural features were feudalised, and mountains and rivers took on the appearance of dukes and counts. The legends of miraculous birth, drawn from the festivals, were handed over to the lord's genealogies. The rain-season festivals, when the groups of men and women enacted a tourney of courtesy that ended in mating, expired in myths of the battling and coupling of dragons that controlled the rains, or grew even more remote in star-myths.

Thus, the dual conception, which the Persians and Hebrews translated into terms of a moral conflict conditioning history, was expressed by the Chinese in terms of a harmonious flow of alternating opposites—a cyclic movement that suited their undeveloping society. Their position, under its refinements and abstractions, was close to that of tribal society.

Philosophy. *Yang-Vin* concepts underlie all Chinese thinking, but are used in diverse ways. And the two main schools, Confucian and Taoist, take very different attitudes to the State and to the purpose of life. The Confucians were the counsellors of the lords, aiming at a rationalist ethical approach, and seeking as much social justice as the system could afford. A parable tells of the master finding a woman in tears by a grave; a tiger had killed her husband's father, her father and her son. Asked why she still stayed in the place, she answered, 'There is no oppressive government here'. The master commented to his disciples, 'My children, remember this: oppressive government is fiercer than a tiger'. There was a utopian attitude in his thinking, that men only needed to be intelligent and all problems would be solved.

The centralisation of wealth is the way to scatter the people, and letting it be scattered among them is the way to collect the people... Among the truly educated there will be no distinction of classes...

When the Great Principle [of Similarity] prevails, the whole world becomes a republic: they elect men of talents, virtue and ability; they talk about sincere agreement and cultivate universal peace... They do not regard as their parents only their own parents, nor treat as their children only their own children.

In such a world, men will produce in brotherhood, 'not wishing to keep for their own gratification'. The golden rule, of not doing unto others what you would not wish done unto yourself, is stated; and an agnostic attitude is turned towards death. When asked, 'Do the dead have knowledge or are they without it', Confucius merely changed the subject. Asked about serving the dead, he replied, 'While you are not able to serve men, how can you serve your spirits?' Asked about death, he replied, 'While you do not know about life, how can you know about death?' The emphasis is on impartial inquiry. 'The Higher Man is anxious lest he should not gain truth; he is not anxious lest poverty should come upon him.'

Here are a few more of the aphorisms attributed to him in the *Analects,* which show both his boldness and his conformity, his rationalist sense of superiority, his wish above to preserve traditional pieties:

The commander of a great army may be carried off into captivity, but the humblest man of his people has a will which need never be surrendered.

The gentleman (princely man), contemplating the world, is free from unreasonable likes and dislikes. He stands for what is right. The man of honour makes demands upon himself: the man without a sense of honour makes demands on others.

Tzu Kung asked whether men of honour also hate, and the Master said: They do. They hate those who proclaim abroad other men's evil. They hate those vulgar fellows who slander those above them. They hate those who are bold in action but have no idea of good form. They hate those who are presumptuous and obstructive.

The Master said: Be trustworthy in every respect, be devoted to the acquisition of learning, steadfast unto death for the Good. Do not enter any area which is running dangerous risks, nor live in one where the people are in rebellion. . .

And lastly the Master said: Men of true breeding are in harmony with people, although they do not agree with them; but men of no breeding agree with people, and yet are not in harmony with them.*

Mo (Mo-ti) preached universal benevolence, not Confucius' 'graded-love' with its preference for one's own relatives.

Heaven wants men to love and be profitable to each other, and does not want men to hate and maltreat each other. How do we know this? Because Heaven embraces all in its love of them, and embraces all in its benefits to them. How do we know that Heaven embraces all? Because it does so in its gifts of food. Take then the Great Society. . .

Mencius (Meng Ko) disliked war. 'There has never been a good war.' He wanted general education and saw poverty as causing crime and discord. A king who failed to prevent famine should abdicate. 'The people are the most important element . . . the sovereign is the lightest'. The people had the right to depose, even kill, their rulers.

There is nothing that is not destiny. Therefore accept obediently your true destiny. Thus a man who comprehends destiny does not stand under an overhanging wall. To die because of complete fidelity to one's principles is a true destiny. To die because one is a criminal in chains is not a true destiny.

---

* The Legalists were anti-mercantile; they developed paradoxical ideas. Yang Chu wanted men to make the best of the world as it is, in their brief lives. Mencius worked out a fourfold system: of compassion (individual morality), shame at wickedness (public morality), reverence (ritual propriety), and a sense of truth and error (wisdom). These senses are intrinsic in men and 'it is possible for all men to be good'.

That is, a man's true destiny is to follow scientific principles and the sense of right and wrong.

Hsun-tze, while denouncing the unrighteous world, stressed the need for scientific understanding:

> You glorify nature and meditate on her.
> Why not domesticate her and regulate her ?
> You obey nature and sing her praises.
> Why not control her course and use it ?
> You look upon the seasons with reverence, and await them.
> Why not respond to them with seasonal activities ?
> You depend on things and marvel at them.
> Why not unfold your ability and transform them?

The Confucians wanted conformity with the *yang-yin* principle, and sought to distinguish where the world around them truly expressed that principle and where it failed to do so.   But they did not want to make any fundamental changes. The notion of the Confucian middle way was set out in a later classic, *The Doctrine of the Mean:*

At the point where the feelings of pleasure and displeasure, of sadness and joy, have not yet made their appearance, at that point is the germ of our spiritual being. Where these feelings express themselves and all strike the correct rhythm, at that point is the state of harmonious motion. That spiritual germ is the great root of all being. This harmonious motion is the only path in the world which leads to the goal. If the spiritual germ and the harmonious motion are realised, heaven and earth are in order, and all beings are developed.

The mean is the line of *yang-yin*, identified with the will of God. The follower of the Way must stick to the line, not falling astray on either side of it.

The Taoists also sought to follow the Way (*Tao*), which they identified with the Order of Nature. But they did not believe that the life of society any longer truly incorporated the *yang-yin* principle; corruption and inequality had gone too deep. So they preached withdrawal and the studious contemplation of nature. They would not have echoed Confucius' advice to live where the government is not a tiger; they would have replied that all governments by their very nature are tigers. But in declaring for inaction they were in fact declaring for a total opposition to a divided world. The wisdom, knowledge and morality they wanted to banish were those of the Confucian compromise.

Heaven and Earth [guided by the Tao] unite together and send down the sweet dew, which, without the directions of men, reaches equally everywhere of its own accord.
  As soon as it proceeds to action, it has a name. When it once has that name, men can know to rest in it. When they know to rest in it, they can be free from all risk of failure and error. . .
  The Tao of Heaven is not to contend and yet be able to conquer.
  Not to declare its will and yet to get a response,
  not to summon but to have things come spontaneously,
  to work very slowly with well-laid plans.
  Heaven's net is vast, with wide meshes: yet nothing is lost. . .

Let me do nothing and the people will transform themselves.

Let me love quiescence and the people will put themselves right (*Tao-tê-Ching*)

Banish 'wisdom', discard 'knowledge', and the people will be benefited a hundred-fold. Banish 'benevolence', discard morality, and the people will be dutiful and compassionate. Banish 'skill', discard 'profit', and thieves and robbers will disappear. If when these three things are gone, they find life too plain and unadorned, then let them have accessories. Give them Simplicity to look at, the Uncarved Block to hold. Give them Selflessness and Fewness of Desires.*

Inaction is the real part of fame, the storehouse of all plans, the responsible head of all business, the master of all knowledge. Identify yourself completely with infinity-eternity and wander in the non-self. Carry to the highest what you have received from heaven, but do not reveal your success in this. Be empty, that is all. The perfect man's use of his mind is like a mirror. He does not anticipate events, nor does he run counter to them. Thus it is that he is able to master things and not be injured by them.

Chuang-chu, it is said, was once asked by a duke to take office; he replied that he'd rather amuse himself in a filthy ditch than live in a palace. He equated kings and governors with brigands. He had the *alcheringa*-vision:

In the age of perfect virtue men lived in common with birds and beasts, and were on terms of perfect equality with all creatures, as forming one family: how would they know among themselves the distinctions of superior man and small men?

Taoism was closely connected, in its views of nature, with the metallurgical fraternities and the alchemists. Its followers felt that the problems of transforming matter and of transforming men were intimately related. Chuang-chu announced:

Let us now regard heaven and earth as a great melting pot, and the author of transformation as a great founder, and wherever we go, shall we not be at home? Quiet is our sleep, and calm is our awakening.

The Mother-cult survives in them in symbolic form:

The Valley Spirit never dies.
It is named the Mysterious Feminine.
And the doorway of the Mysterious Feminine
is the base from which Heaven and Earth sprang.
It is the thread for ever woven
and those who use it can accomplish all things. . .
He who knows the male, yet cleaves to what is female,
becomes like a ravine, receiving all things under Heaven. . .

The concise style of ancient Chinese makes it capable of many interpretations.

---

* *Cf.* Blake's lines, 'Pity would be no more, if we did not make somebody poor,' etc. The close Taoist version runs: 'It was when the Great Tao declined that benevolence and righteousness arose; it was when knowledge and wisdom appeared that the Great Lie began. Not till the six near ones had lost their harmony, was there talk of filial piety. Not till countries and families were dark with strife did we hear of loyal ministers.'

Thus, it has been pointed out, a poem from the *Tao tê Ching* can be translated in different ways, mystically and socially:

(a) Thirty spokes together make one wheel
and they fit into nothing at the centre:
herein lies the usefulness of a carriage.
Clay is moulded to make a pot
and the clay fits round nothing:
herein lies the usefulness of the pot.
Doors and windows are pierces in the walls of a house
and they fit round nothing:
herein lies the usefulness of a house.
Thus while it must be taken as advantageous to have something there,
it must also be taken as useful to have nothing there.

(b) Thirty spokes combine to make a wheel:
when there was no private property
carts were made for use.
Clay is formed to make vessels:
when there was no private property
pots were made for use.
Windows and doors go to make houses:
when there was no private property
houses were made for use.
Thus having private property may lead to profit,
but not having it leads to use.

At first glance the Taoists seem negative. They find nothing good at all in class-society and want a return to primitive tribalism. But if we go deeper, we see that willynilly they are only using the perspective of tribal equality for the critical insight it gives them into a divided world. They despise the Confucian compromisers with their efforts to whitewash and moralise away the actual social situation. They have a series of emblems for the united world they want —the Uncarved Block, the Log, the Post, the Bag, the Bellows, and a word that is translated Chaos. Some of these names suggest the craft-world, *e.g.* Bellows. Others however may relate to early clan-groups or clan-heroes who resisted the advent of the kings. For the legendary kings like Yao and Shun fight monsters with names like the Empty Bag, the Uncarved-up Stake; and these monsters may be the victors' version of their foes. Also, names like the Three Miao and the Nine Lei suggest craft-fraternities.

It looks as if the earliest kings or princes recognised bronze metallurgy to be the basis of feudal power over the neolithic peasantry. . . It looks as if the pre-feudal collectivist society, which developed metal-working, resisted the transformation into class-differentiated society, and under the legendary labels we should perhaps see the leaders of that society which resisted the change. There is another phrase to be found alongside these curious phrases—'returning to the root'. That has been translated in a religious sense, but I am not sure that it has not a double political meaning, because in the *Shu Ching* (the Book of History) you find a phrase, 'the root was kept in check and could not put forth shoots' side by side with a remark about the hosts of Kun flying away. Kun was one of the most prominent of these early rebels. (NEEDHAM)

The Taoists then used the idea of a subtle harmony with nature and its rhythms, but did not seek a conforming mean, which enabled a man to consider himself on the *yang-yin* line without rejecting the class-world. They sought for a point of resolution or transformation, which would overcome the conflicts; and by merging the backward-looking *alcheringa*-dream with the alchemist struggle to grasp the clue of material transformation, they faced to the future.

8 : The Greeks

The Greeks. We have seen how a great wave of thought, seeking afresh to grapple with the nature of life and man, swept over the civilised world as the Iron Age's effects matured. We have yet to consider the Greek contribution, which was by far the greatest. All ancient city-states began with an adaptation of tribal forms to the new situation; the Greeks alone managed to find ways of continuing to develop those forms inside the city so as to eliminate the kingship and to reconstitute tribal democracy—to devise methods of preserving its essence in systems appropriate to city-needs.

We know now that the Minoan script Linear B expressed a form of early Greek. The tablets from Pylos and Mycenai show that an Arkadian dialect was spoken in the south-west and north-east Peloponnese (though by the 7th century, when the relevant inscriptions begin, such dialects were restricted to the mountainous interior and to Cyprus). Mycenean or early Greek society is revealed as akin to that of the Hittites or any other of the kingdoms of the East Mediterranean: a centralised autocracy with efficient priestly accountants. Its farflung trade had close connections, not only with the Near East, but with the bronze-working groups of the West, including the Wessex of Stonehenge III. The Mycenean period of the Greeks went out under the barbarian surges drawn in all over the Near East at the advent of the Iron Age. New groups such as the Dorians from the north-west broke down the Myceneans and helped to create a dark-age; but they are archaeologically hard to trace: perhaps they were pastoralists, travelling light, and taking over crafts from the conquered areas. Linear B tablets show that Zeus and other members of the Olympian highgods were already established in the Mycenaian world, though small female figurines were very widespread and presumably point to the continuing mother-cult below the Olympians. And it is certain that much of the epical tradition of the Near East—*Gilgamesh*, the Creation myth, Keret's Siege of Udum, and other such works—had been absorbed.

In the dark-age the overlordships such as those of Mycenai were broken down; power passed to the tribal nobles. Thus, at Athens, which survived unsacked, the divine king faded out and his palace was taken over by the city-goddess Athena. The king, *basileus* now instead of *wanax* as in his proud days, steadily lost his powers as against other members of the aristocracy. Gradually, however, the level of prosperity rose. Athens had served as a rallying-point for refugees, who sailed across the sea and founded cities on the western coast of Asia Minor. These towns grew into thriving mercantile centres, seaports and entrepots linked with the Asianic inland—Smyrna, Miletos, Ephesos, and so on. A dark-age, which from one angle seems a collapse of civilisation, may at the same time represent considerable gains for the common man, the peasant, who is perhaps relieved of much oppression and tribute-exaction, and who develops new or expanded forms of production. And so, when town-life revives, it does so on a much higher level than before. Thus, the techniques of viticulture and olive-growing recounted by the poet Hesiod may be taken as inheritances from the Helladic pioneers in the Aegean, which the peasants of

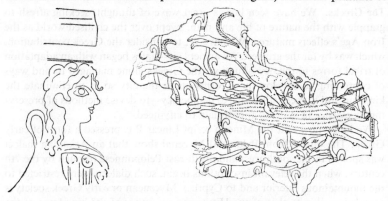

Knossos figure. Boar hunt with 'flying' hounds, from Tiryns.

the dark-age further developed; his farming calendar includes the lore that had been heaped up throughout the periods in question. Pottery went on all the while being turned out on the wheel: form and decoration change, but not technique. Myths suggest that the smith-fraternities had never ceased to function; and Homer shows that the bards kept alive the memories and traditions of the Bronze Age.

A crucial innovation was that of the stamped coin, supplementing weighed-out and probably debased silver. Soon after 800, Assyrian and Syrian kings stamped bars with their guarantees. Coins proper, the Greeks said, were first coined by Croisos of Lydia, a kingdom based on transit trade. These early coins were of high value; but soon after 600 the Greek city-states of Aigina,

Athens, Corinth issued small change, copper or silver, with enormous effects
on trade. Coins were made accessible to the small producer and craftsman on
an increasing scale; the manufacture of cheap goods was rendered profitable;
small farmers could turn from crops to olive-oil crushed for the market. At
the same time the coin brought a new threat. The main previous danger for
the peasant, apart from capture leading to slavery, had been reduction by a
noble or big landlord to some sort of serfdom; now money-debt and usury
gained a new strength, involving loss of the land and various forms of enslavement. The impact of the new money-power must be taken into consideration
in gauging the protest-movements such as those of the Hebrew prophets or of
the Taoists against the forces that have broken up tribal unity.

The expansion of Greek trade can be measured by the sherds of pottery
from sites like Corinth, Athens, Rhodes, found all round the Mediterranean
and Black Sea as well as far into the hinterland. By the 6th century even small
peasants in Attica could turn to specialised work on vines and olives. A clash
with the Persian empire, which had absorbed the Ionian towns of the Asian

*Priestess, Tiryns wall-painting. Dolphin vase (Middle Minoan III-Late
Minoan I).*

coast, was inevitable. That empire, as we have noted, was an important part
of the total situation, and the Greeks could not have grown as they did without
it. With its high level of organisation and its vast inner exchange of ideas and
methods, it had brought about a great increase of wealth. Real wages were
doubled in Babylonia—though a large proportion of the surplus was taken by
the exchequer. It was no accident that coins appeared first in Lydia, at the

point connecting the Aegean with the Persian system; and the part played by Greek artists inside the empire, where they took their craft and learned things from others, is exemplified by two drawings lightly scratched on a Persepolis relief—heads of bearded men so like the heads in Greek vase-paintings of the date 510-500, that the authorship is obvious: the artists had expected the drawings to be obliterated by red paint.

As part of the mercantile expansion, colonisation went on busily in the West Mediterranean, by Phoenicians and Etruscans as well as Greeks. The new towns were collecting-stations for a surplus to be applied partly as tribute to the parental city—though the tie was traditional and commercial, not enforced. The new level of literacy made possible by the phonetic alphabet—taken over by the Greeks from the Phoenecians via Cyprus—further helped the trade-expansion. Indeed, in estimating the Greek achievement, there are four fundamental factors: the potential virtues of the language for logical structure and exposition, the increase of literacy through a phonetic alphabet, the fluidity of an exchange-system based on coined money, and the adaptation of tribal democracy to the city-state. By the 6th century mercenary soldiers, Greek and Phoenician, could scratch their names on Egyptian statues. From the Greek colonists on Italy the Etruscans and Romans learned to read and write.

The clash of the Persian empire and the city-states of the Greek mainland came; and despite the heavy odds the Greeks beat back their huge foe. The superior initiative and mobility of peoples still close to tribal life defeated the cumbrous levies and mercenaries of an empire. The Greek mainland and the western colonies were now the centres of industrial and trading activity. Athens rose to a key-place, carrying the democracy of the city-state to its highest-level; but she tried to consolidate her position by building an Aegean empire and by considering democracy not for export. In the war she fought with the champion of the oligarchic forces, Sparta, not only she was exhausted, but the whole Greek system of independent city-states. The scene was set for the rise of semi-barbarian Macedonia, where the kingship was effectively developed on the tribal basis. Macedonia dominated Greece, then under Alexander the Great led the Greeks in a conquering expansion eastward, taking over the Persian empire. The new Greek empire almost at once broke up into several kingdoms; but its effects were lasting. The Celts in the west based their coinage on its staters and in north India the impact created the Mauryan empire. In general it brought about the situation where the next step could only be something like the imperial system of the Romans.

Religion. We can trace exogamous systems among the Indo-Europeans, but any signs of totemism are slight, if they exist at all. Among the Greeks there are abundant myths, rites, and customs that show the importance of initiation-ceremonies and shamanist practices; but when we come down to detail, the problem of distinguishing what is originally Greek (Indo-European) from

Aegean or Anatolian elements, taken over from earlier peoples, is extremely difficult. To all intents and purposes, when we speak of the ancient Greeks we mean the people of the Aegean area who emerged from the dark-age speaking one variety or other of Greek. They appear in tribal form. Thus, the Ionians had four tribes, each divided into four phratries, with each phratry divided into four clans; the Dorians had three tribes. The word *phrater*, which in other Indo-European tongues is cognate with the word used for brother, in Greek means the fellow-member of a phratry.

The religion was again a welter of original-Greek and Aegean or Anatolian elements. In Homer we meet a deceptively worked-out hierarchy of high gods, largely inherited from the Mycenean kingly world, which through his poems had much effect on Greek thought; but any analysis of the gods of a city or district shows a very much more complicated situation, the high gods only in part corresponding to the Homeric gods of the same name, and an accompanying crowd of fertility-deities and local spirits, with no clear-cut system. The patriarchal household of Zeus on Olympus we may take as a generally idealised version of the early Greek social system. But the gods of the peasantry and artisans were of a very different type: gods of death-rebirth, of dance-ecstasy, of the hungry spirit-world, and so on. At the crises of democracy in the city-state these gods of suffering, death and resurrection, gain a new life, transformed into mystery-gods along the lines of the crisis in the Old Kingdom of Egypt that made the Osirian cult a mass-possession, imposing a creed of afterworld-judgment on society as a whole.

The cult of Dionysos was the main form through which the ecstatic trance-possessed dances broke through into the upper levels of religion and culture; that of Orpheus showed the same elements with a more specific mystery-colouration, an interpretation of life as a thing of injustice and misery which the initiate, sharing the god's death and rebirth, could overcome by turning

Hero-mound (note snake) from a black-figured lekythos.

all his thought and hopes to another world. Local mystery-cults, like that of Eleusis, concerned originally with fertility-magic, gave their initiation-ritual the wider colouration of the great missionary mass-religions, which had broken through the old bounds of territory or clan in claiming a universal congregation. These religions, again like the Osirian, lifted the humble dead of the mirky underworld into a space of solar or stellar light.

The Orphics, having first segregated in the underworld the regions of the blessed Elysium, from that of the damned, Tartarus, the next step was taken by their followers, the Pythagoreans, in removing Elysium from the underworld to the region of the moon and in identifying the Blessed Islands with the Sun and Moon. The Pythagoreans were therefore the first to preach celestial immortality to Greece and south Italy, and were dogmatic on the stars and planets, especially Sun and Moon, as the abodes of the elect souls. (ANGUS)

Even the Orphic purgatory went aloft; and the earth itself, the sublunar world, received the position previously held by the under-earth, becoming a dark cave of imprisoned souls yearning for the upper light.

The City-state. By the end of the dark-age, many Greek cities, as well as Etruscan or Phoenician, had become republican; the stage of the divine king was over. Magistrates were elected yearly as the executive while a council of elders and an assembly of leading clans or families decided general policy. Under the growing money-economy the clan-chief became the big landlord and the tribal forms more and more lost any democratic element, serving merely as the masks for the assumption of power by rich oligarchies, in which the merchant families bought land and the landlords shared in trading profits. This was the sort of system growing up among the early Ionian cities, which were captured by the Persians before they developed serious internal crises. But the mainland, which inherited their mantle of trade, also inherited their social contradictions. The aristocracy supported creditor and landlord against debtor and tenant or share-farmer. The fusion of landed nobles and wealthy traders had not gone on more or less equably over a long early period, as in Ionia. The mercantile middleclass found themselves opposed to the clan-nobles and called on the poor for aid, not only on small farmers in debt but even on landless artisans and labourers. At this phase the violent inner cleavages of the city-state led to the rise of powerful individuals, who raised the standard against the nobles and fostered the new class grown rich on trade, manufacture, usury or control of mines. Their system was called a Tyranny, and its programme included the defence of the poor against the mighty, the diversion of wealth into valuable public works, such as harbours, into industry, or into city-beautification. The tyrants did not have a long run. The nobles mustered forces and regained power, or the lower and middle classes, chafing in time against the barriers of the new power, carried the revolution further into democracy.

In Athen the most complete forward-movement was made. The old clans, controlled by the nobles, were deprived of political power; property-qualifications for magistrates were ended; most offices were filled by lot, not by election; all citizens were expected to attend assemblies and sit on juries, so they were paid for such attendances. To achieve this result the two great reforms of Cleisthenes and Solon had to be achieved by much class-conflict. As a result the 5th century saw the great maturing burst of Athenian culture. Public works, as also the navy, were paid for by rich citizens—not on compulsion, but as an honour in which general opinion exerted its pressure. Contracts for works were cut up into small items so that any competent citizen or resident-alien might compete.

The defects of the system included the secluded condition of women and the jealous limitations of citizenship: the aliens, perhaps a tenth of the population, played an important part in manufacture and craftwork, but were denied full rights. And industry had come to be based on slavery; it is estimated that at least a third, and perhaps more, of the whole population was servile. (There were however many free citizens or aliens who worked with their hands, e.g. on piecework contracts for fluting temple-columns for the State. And the Laurion silver mines had been developed by free labourers who played a large part in putting the tyrant Peisistratos in power; though by the 5th century most miners there were slaves.) Even small farmers had one or two slaves each; most employees in factories and mines, even in the Athenian police-force, were slaves. As a result the free citizens mostly had abundant leisure to attend to politics, art and intellectual matters—but at the cost of a rapidly widening gap between the upper levels of culture and the productive sphere. Thus, the social division which had been overcome at one point reasserted itself at another. The prized leisure of the free men degenerated into parasitism, and democracy became a mask for empire-building. To maintain the privileged positions of the citizens, Athens turned the Aegean league against the Persian menace into a system of dependents dominated by herself. When she lost her small empire, her worm-eaten democracy collapsed.

Though some genuine efforts were made to develop federal forms and friendly groupings of city-states, the Greeks were unable to think outside the categories of free city and empire. The violent class-conflicts inside the city were linked with the violent wars between cities. The idea of the nation, and the political forms capable of actualising it, did not evolve till the later medieval period of Europe.

Philosophy. We find in the Greeks a power of detachment, of generalised logical thought, which has no previous parallel. They had nimble quicksilver minds, and the capacity to abstract a general idea or law from particular instances, which we cannot separate from the democratic energies we have discussed, or from the effects of a monetary economy which breaks up the old concrete equations of bartering (or of bartering accompanied by crude metallic values) and puts in their place a set of abstract values which reduce everything and anything to the same set of numerical correspondences or formalised quantities.

They were thus able to take the intuitional accounts by the Egyptians or Mesopotamians of the origin of the universe, and turn them into speculative theories. They turned myth into science, symbol into experimental inquiry.*

Diodoros, in a summary obviously drawn from the Ionian philosophers, remarks: 'In the original composition of the universe, heaven and earth had one form, their natures being confounded. Later, with the separation of these bodies from one another, it comprised the whole of the visible order. The air acquired the property of continual motion'. Sun and stars were caught up in its whirl; the wet parts condensed into mud and living creatures were generated by the heat, and so on.

We see there the rationalisation of a creation-myth, with the elements replacing the god-names. The first known philosopher Thales, said to have been concerned with trade and engineering, astronomy and geometry, argued that all things evolved from a condition of water and that the earth floated on water. The picture is precisely that of the priests of Egypt and Sumer, but the erms are wholly untheological. Anaximander, who composed a world-map and wrote a cosmology, saw that one must go further than merely choosing one element as the source of all things; he called his *arche* the *apeiron* or boundless, which he saw as a substance. He held to the common origin of all things, perpetual motion, and the conflict of opposites: all ideas that we have found as central in primitive thinking, but here abstracted as general principles. In explaining how things come into being and pass away according to necessity, he comments that 'they give satisfaction to one another for their wrongdoing according to the order of time'. His terms are those normally used for the settlement of disputes between rival clans. We see once again how concepts of measure and relationship are derived from social forms, social activities. 'According to the order of time' seems to involve a rhythmic image similar to that of the *yang-yin* principle.

In the thinking of Thales and Anaximander we see the seeds of a scientific approach; but we must beware of misreading the idiom and seeing it simply as a crude embryo of later scientific formulations. The materialism here is that of totemic thought, which sees all things as full of spirit and spirit as inherent in things. Thales, who defined water as the *arche* (origin or principle), also declared, 'All things are full of gods; the magnet is alive, for it has the power

---

* The Creation Myth is assumed in Homer with his Ocean the origin of all things. (Thales turns the mythical figure Okeanos into mere Water; and Anaximander takes Homer's 'boundless Ocean' and abstracts the boundless.) Hesiod reveals the full-blown Asianic myth. Alkman says that Thetis made out of matter Poros (contriving) and Tekmar (end) as well as Skotos (darkness), then Day and Moon. (As he interprets Thetis as the Arranger, he probably made her use Mud, pelos, as a pun on her husband Peleus.) A symmetrical system appears in Homer, Tartaros being as deep as Heaven (Olympos) is high.

of moving iron'. And Ionian thinking was able to develop in due time an atomic theory—not because the thinkers saw matter as made up of dead units in mechanical motion as the post-Newtonians did, but because they saw it as alive, moving because it was alive. Thus, while in one sense they still incorporate the wholeness of primitive thinking with its unrealised inner-conflicts, they also, by reason of their tremendous effort to banish theology and to build a logical structure which experience can test, look forward to the most advanced aspects of modern science, where once again an effort to advance to unified conception of the wholeness of things is being tentatively attempted—e.g. when Anaximander sees motion as the mode of existence of matter. (In turn he and his fellows were able to make the effort to break through the religiously crusted formulations because they belonged to a society moving in a new way, gaining a new fluidity and feeling that it was discovering the laws of its own motion through the freedom of its citizens.) Even Hesiod, when in his poem about 700 B.C. expounding a theology, shows the new spirit by speaking in his own voice, his own right, and not acting as the mouthpiece of some god or temple-system. (The inspiration he claims is that of a prophet, a shaman.)*

The climax of the first phase of Greek thought comes in Heracleitos, a noble of Ephesos, who despised the worship of Dionysos but based himself on an interpretation of the mysteries in their clan-forms. Because he does not want any reconciliation with the democrats, he draws on the old idea of a ceaseless tension: 'they do not understand how it agrees by differing, a concord of contrary tensions as in bow and lyre'. He sees unity as gained by this inner conflict but as unstable by its nature, for the tensions must at once reassert themselves. 'Strife is justice'. And so he prefers the image of consuming fire to express innermost reality. 'This universe, which is the same for all, no one of the god's or men has made; but it was ever, is now, and ever will be an everlasting fire, with measures of it kindling and measures going out!'

At the same time he feels the impact of Pythagoras and uses the term *logos* or word to express the mystery-statement which is apprehended only by the initiated. He divides men into three groups: those who have heard and under-stood, those who have heard and not yet understood, those who have not heard. (His book seems to have been presented in the manner of the holy words of the Orphics and the *legomena*, ritual utterances, in the Eleusinian mysteries.) By *logos* he means reason, discourse, ratio: the law that governs all things, including men and gods. He denies the rules of formal logic can grasp a universe which consists of a perpetual cycle of fire, air, water, earth, air, fire, and is an organic unity of mind and matter.

---

* Circular images appear in Anaximander: the earth is in the middle like the drum of a column, surrounded by air, outside which is fire like a tree's bark. The fire is shut in rings of air like chariot-wheels with hollow rims pierced to let the fire flow out. Anaximenes says the stars revolve round the earth like felt wound round our heads (? as in a turban)—compare the later image of the Phrygian cap of Attis as a sky-dome.

In one aphorism he shows his awareness of the relation between his cosmic
fire and the new monetary medium of exchange which is breaking up old
forms in society and which disruptively equates in value the most unlikely
things. 'All things are an exchange for fire and fire for all things, even as wares
for gold and gold for wares'. We may compare the passage in *Antigone* where
Sophocles, the poet most acutely aware of the dilemmas now snaring men,
sets out his view of money as the displacer and transformer:

> Money wins friendship, honour, place and power,
> and sets man next to the proud tyrant's throne.
> All trodden paths and paths untrod before
> are scaled by nimble riches, where the poor
> can never hope to win the heart's desire.
> A man illformed by nature and ill-spoken,
> Money shall make him fair to eye and ear.
> Money earns man his health and happiness
> and only money cloaks iniquity.*

In Heracleitos, then, we see the Ionian method of speculative thought carried
to its limits. The formulation of general ideas from the modes of tribal thought
and from the intuitional myth-forms of previous societies is no longer enough.
Thinkers must proceed to grasp the nature of mental processes and their
relation to reality, 'the thought by which all things are steered through all
things'. Otherwise the Ionian speculative methods would be bogged down in
the intuitional symbols they attempted to master and relate rationally to the
world of experience; it would founder on an unrealised subject-object
relationship.

Pythagoras and Plato. Pythagoras was already at work on the necessary new
lines—though with the loss of the wholeness of Ionian thought; the analytic
instrument is developed, at the cost of dynamic fullness. We have already seen
how he draws for his material on the musical ideas of the Egyptians and
Babylonians; what he adds is the new clarity of abstraction, which constructs
a complete and logical system out of mystical intuitions. Number is seen, not
only as a method of analysing the multiplicity of the universe and reducing its
forms and forces to quantitative formulas or patterns, but also as itself con-
stituting the structure and interrelationship of things—a substance as well as
an abstraction. It is thus taken as a superior reality; and the opposition of
number's rational and law-abiding systems to the untidy flux of earthly facts
is equated with the Orphic opposition of the light-born soul to the dark sphere
of its fall. Not that at the outset the Pythagoreans were pessimistic; their
fraternity worked to gain political control of important mercantile towns such
as Kroton or Sybaris, in south Italy. But their initial successes were followed

---

* 'Man is money' was proverbially current from the 7th century. *Cf.* the proverb,
'Riches have no limit' and Anaximander's *apeiron*. 'Money is the *psyche*', says Hesiod.

by defeat about 450 B.C. The fraternity was broken up and its members
violently expelled.

The Pythagoreans recognised ten pairs of opposites—the limited and the
unlimited, the odd and the even, the hot and the cold, etc. The number could
have been extended, but ten was a perfect number, the sum of the first four
integers. In any event the idea of the unity of opposites loses its force; the
universe is seen as a continual oscillation between the opposites, and the mean
is the point of rest sought by the wise men. Solon had had the idea of the
mean as an imposed point between two extremes—his reform sought to hold
society together despite the violences of nobles and commoners. The Pythagoreans saw the mean as a harmony brought into being by the conflict it
negated. The universe had an underlying system of numbers or harmonies,
from which men had wandered; the problem was simply to get back to a
predetermined order. Herein lay the metaphysical effort to arrest or deny the
real world with its endless variety and contradiction; but a contrary impulse
was set into action by the need to investigate the mathematical properties of
harmonic progressions, which led to much fruitful work.

The Ionians had thrown off myth and theology; but their naive unitary
concepts could not in the end distinguish man from nature, spirit from matter.
After Heracleitos it was clear that the abstracting method would have to
jettison the unitary grasp and concentrate on the *logos*. Thus the movement
from Pythagoras to Plato was in essence a counter-movement to the Ionians
—though in Plato an effort is made, despite everything, to regain a unitary
outlook, an effort which, however, nobly fails.*

The 5th century saw the rise of the sophists, professional teachers and
thinkers, who attempted to deal with the multiple problems of knowledge and
ethics which arose in the post-Pythagorean world; in particular they dealt one
way or another with the nature of words, with the question of the relativity of
our ideas and our moral principles. Generally their approach seems to have
been humanist, though at times individualistic and entangled with sophistries
which reflected the moral dilemmas of democratic Athens turned imperial and
gave solipsistic or expedient justifications for betraying the ideals of equality

---

* Parmenides was active in politics, drew up law-code for his hometown in S. Italy;
seems originally Pythagorean; his poem opens with a mystery-vision; he sees divisions and contraries as illusions; light is being and is One. He seems to divide the
intelligible from the sensible world. Empedocles of Akragas, Sicily democrat and
shamanist prophet, was close to Orphism, studied medicine and declared men thought
with blood. (Alkmaion had distinguished thought and sensation, and made brain the
organ of thinking.) Empedocles saw Four Elements (roots) endlessly changing into
one another and affecting structures, through Love and Strife: he is close to Ionian
unitary thinking. Anaxagoras, accused of impiety at Athens for saying the sun was a
molten mass of metal, saw infinite seeds (elements), each holding in itself more or
less all the opposites, so that even snow is black and anything has a portion of everything, but the unmixed seed Mind penetrates into the others, combines, separates.
He thus sticks to the unity of opposites, with one element superior to the rest and
with a postulated source of motion.

or brotherhood. We know about them largely from Plato, who saw them merely as symptoms of unscrupulous democracy and moral collapse; but his judgments were certainly in part unjust. In his blind reaction against what had gone wrong in the social situation he identified democracy with mob-instability and so with a submission to dark irrationalities.

In this aspect of his thought he seems to have followed Socrates, who left no writings of his own and who appears in idealised form in the works of his admirers, Plato or Xenophon. We may surmise that Socrates was skilled in tearing to shreds the assumptions of thought on which the 'commonsense' of the ordinary citizen was based, and that he was oligarchic in sympathies. But almost anything said about him is guesswork; and we are driven back to Plato's dialogues in which he plays so large a part as the author's mouthpiece.

We have seen how Plato's notion of a world of Ideas, *eide*, or seminal forms, superior to the earthly world which reflects it, derived directly from the Babylonian world-view. But his philosophy cannot be reduced to these metaphysical abstractions. Above all, his method is concretely concerned with the working of people's minds and the dialectical process of arriving at knowledge, which is ultimately one with the processes of development and movement in nature. Thus, in the *Meno* he ostensibly sets out to show that all true knowledge is the discovery of the *eide* in the mind, which are derived from the heavenly world, but what he actually demonstrates, with remarkable skill and fullness, is the fact that the mind works on a dialectical principle, accumulating details and proceeding by a leap into a new whole, which is not deducible mechanically from the details taken one by one. The principle of the unity of opposites thus operates throughout his work, despite his metaphysical dogmas and the otherworldly location of the *eide*. It appears alike in the psychology of the *Phaidon* or the cosmogony of the *Timaios*; and he sees its application in society. 'In the seasons, in plants, in an organism, and above all in civil society, excessive action results in a violent transformation into its opposite'. Life exists on a precarious balance, brotherhood and justice clashing all the while with greed, egoism and injustice, and men's aims are in action turned into the opposite of what was intended. Plato is here close to the tragedians, though in his anguished reaction against a democracy that has betrayed all its principles he desperately seeks to draw up watertight schemes of society, in which the existing forms are abstracted into fixed categories and an authoritative rule prevents any change. As in the Spartan constitution, elements from the tribal system with its set of balances are drawn on, but in order to perpetuate in a rigid form a society of divisions and inequalities, with the tribal communal element reserved solely for the rulers.

In Plato's work there is then the most acute set of inner contradictions. He brings together the Ionian unitary outlook, its concept of the unity of opposites, and all the post-Pythagorean subtleties of analysis and abstracted notions of unity, adding his own profound psychological grasp. He thus represents incomparably the highest level of thought in the ancient world; and though in the late medieval period, with Nicholas of Cusa and Bruno, the attempt to regain his fullness of vision reappears, the subsequent working-out of philosophy in its vital aspects is in a sense largely the rediscovery of his positions and his conflicts—a voyage of thought in which we are still far from the end.

In the ancient world, it was to a considerable extent the metaphysical and pessimistic side of Plato that had an effect, his Orphic rejection of earthly life. But the positive side also helped to keep alive aspects of the Ionian dialectic.

The tone of Plato's dialogues is itself dramatic, and though borrowed not from tragedy but from the more realistic mime, preserves the organic form and high social purpose of tragedy. Indeed Plato's own thought remains still a compound of the mythological and the logical. (LITTLE)

And the mythological element goes deeper than the direct use of myth-narratives; it resides in whole conception of the concrete unity of opposites which goes back to tribal ritual and belief.*

After Plato much of the time of the philosophers was taken up in the unprofitable question of the relation of the One and the Many, in which the Ionian concept of the One as the result of fused opposites was dropped and a formal issue, drawn from logical classification, put in its place. In the same way, paradoxes of the relation of movement and rest were developed: insoluble because of the form of presentation in metaphysical terms. However there developed the atomic hypothesis of infinitely divisible space, which came to a head in the thought of Democritos of Abdera, Thrace. He formulated the idea of an endless number of atoms, falling in a void, colliding, combining, according to the fixed laws of *ananke*. Epicuros of Athens added the idea of the atoms having weight and so causing their own motion along oblique as well as vertical lines. Now the city-state was no longer the centre of political and social life. Epicuros, deprecating any ideas of deities who interfered in the affairs of men, encouraged the growth of scientifically-minded but quietest groups who, no longer able to play a part in politics, turned their backs on the power-world and made their retreat into a 'garden' of peace and inner balance. The Phoenician Zeno proclaimed a new universality, the Stoic conception of Nature in which men were in harmony with the universe and realising their common brotherhood. But after such ideas played their part in uprisings of the slaves and rebellious efforts to actualise social justice in Sparta and Pergamon, the Stoics grew less forthright; their stress became subjective and they ended by being interested only in the individual who 'freed' himself from

---

* Adjectives are used for things in Mycenean Greek; we meet neuters 'of the people' and 'of roses' for public land and rose-oil; and long the neuter use keeps a material basis. Indeed it carries on into Plato, i.e. 'the good' is material for him, so that he can proceed to hypostasise it, a thing-in-the-sky, and Idea. The first forms of syllogistic logic derive from Pythagorean ideas as to proportional relationships, and proportional arguments survive into the early Hippocratic treatises and Plato. (WEBSTER)

a corrupted world by achieving alone the necessary harmonies and with-
drawals.

Science. The abstracting, rationalising side of Greek thought which we have
noted, could not but give a powerful stimulus to science. But the theoretical
stimulus was quickly frustrated by the difficulties of applying scientific conclusions in a slave-economy—in a world where the cleavage of manual and
intellectual work had received a deep new ratification. In Aristotle all the
scientific trends from Thales up to Plato's day culminated; but his classifica-
tory work represented rather an end than a fresh start. In his philosophy the
formal and scholastic trends, not the dialectical, predominated—questions of
the relation of form and matter, of categories and formal logical relationships,
and so on. In ethics the idea of the mean is mechanically applied; and the
rationalisation of the *status quo* leads to a defence of slavery as based in
nature.

After Alexander's imperial expansion, especially at the university-centre of
Alexandria, there was much brilliant theorising in science, but scarcely any
effort to apply the discoveries, except in the milling industry. Babylonian
mathematics had not yet died and Greeks still liked to attend the Mesopotamian seats of learning, to acquire the title of Chaldean. 'It is an open question
whether the Babylonian Kidannu or the Greek Hipparchus first recognised
the phenomenon termed the procession of the equinoxes'. And the Alexandrians took over many mathematical ideas and notations from the Babylonians. They used O (*ouden*, nothing) for zero, but only in connection with
sexagesimal fractions; through the Arabs the system came back into Europe
and led to our decimal notation in A.D. 1583. But the Greek with their use
of letters for numbers had lost Babylonian place-value.*

Their greatest gains were in geometry; and such studies as those of conic
sections were not made without stimulus from the ballistics of artillery and
the shadow-movements on sundials. Archimedes of Syracuse laid the basis of
mechanics, and showed how to use the principle of specific gravity. Astro-
nomers set out to measure the earth, not to mention the sun and moon.
Aristarchos rejected the old schemes of concentric spheres composing the
universe in terms of the hypothesis that made the earth revolve round the sun.
In geography, parallels of latitude were devised; longitude was more difficult
through the lack of accurate clocks, so that eclipses had to be used; but by

---

* India made important contributions to mathematics and algebra; but I shall not
here attempt the arduous task of disentangling the relationships with Babylonians,
Greeks and Arabs. There is also the difficult field of the relation of Chinese scientific
and technological developments to the Near East and the West, not to mention the
part played by the steppe nomads. If the ancient world was held back by slave-
systems from large-scale industrial developments, the Chinese were held back by
their rigid bureaucratic system. It is enough to note here the close interconnections
as well as differences between the Graeco-Romans, the Indians, the Chinese (and
later the Arabs).

1 Australian rock painting: dancing women from Obiri, Arnhem Land (copy James Cant, photo Berkeley Gallery)

2 Bushman dance, Jamestown, C.P. (copy Walter Batiss)

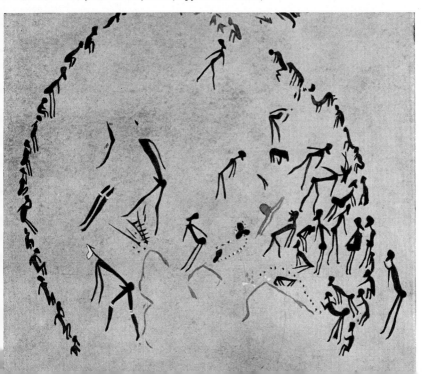

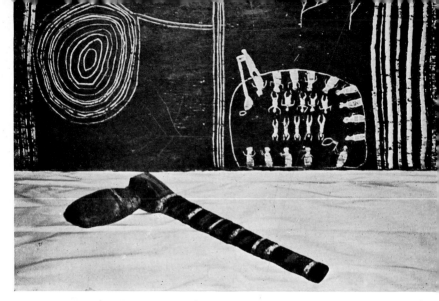

3 Bark painting from Melville Island recording a dance in honour of the discovery of an ancient stone axe (photo Australia House)

4 Cedarwood mask of cannibal spirit from British Columbia (British Museum)

6 Ancestral figure from West New Guinea

5 Clay figurine, formative culture, Mexico (photo Berkeley Gallery)

7 Ancestral figure from Easter Island (British Museum)

8 Ancestral figure from New Zealand, Maori (British Museum)

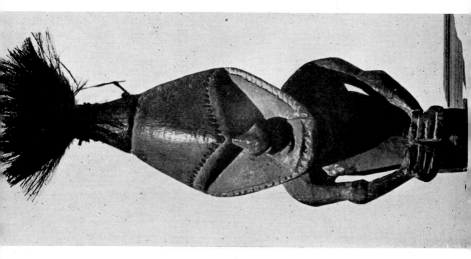

9 Ancestral figure from Sepik River, New Guinea (photo Berkeley Gallery)

10 Aztec figure, Mexico (Museo Nacional, Mexico)

11 Figurine from Guanajato, Mexico, before 1000 B.C. (photo Berkeley Gallery)

12 Stone figure from the caves of Lung Men, China (photo Berkeley Gallery)

13 Sumerian statue of early dynastic times, from Tell Asmar, Mesopotamia (Oriental Institute, Chicago)

14 Mask from a Tlingit headdress, British Columbia (photo Berkeley Gallery)

15 Statue of King Chephren, in diorite, Gizeh, fourth dynasty, Egypt. Note protecting falcon behind his head

16 Egyptian wall-painting of a feast, with blind harper, Thebes, Tomb of Nekht

17 Egyptian statue of a scribe (Louvre)

18 Wolf-mask of Haida, British Columbia, about 1800 or earlier (photo Berkeley Gallery)

19 Figurine of light grey burnished clay, young girl resting, back view showing plaited hair, from Hacilar, Southwest Anatolia, *c.* 5400 B.C. (photo James Mellaart)

20 Yakshi in sandstone, from Sanchi, Central India, first century A.D. (British Museum)

21 Minoan ivory figure, a boy toreador with golden loincloth. Crete, about 1550 B.C. (Ashmolean Museum, Oxford)

22 Parian marble-harper, Keros, Athens, third millennium B.C., Aegean (Athens Museum)

23 Cretan bronze of group of a bull-leaper, *c.* 1600 B.C. (Coll. Capt. Spencer-Churchill)

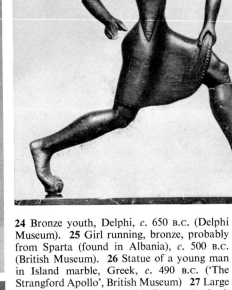

24 Bronze youth, Delphi, *c.* 650 B.C. (Delphi Museum). 25 Girl running, bronze, probably from Sparta (found in Albania), *c.* 500 B.C. (British Museum). 26 Statue of a young man in Island marble, Greek, *c.* 490 B.C. ('The Strangford Apollo', British Museum) 27 Large agate intaglio engraved with lion on the back of a plunging bull, from the Royal Tomb at Dendra, *c.* 1500 B.C. (Athens Museum)

28 Greek bronze of Apollo, lips and nipples of copper; he perhaps held a bow in his left hand, *c.* 490 B.C. (photo Giraudon)

29 Silver ten-drachma coin of Athens, minted 486 B.C. Head of Athena, with owl on reverse with olive-twig (Berlin Museum)

30 Bronze charioteer, dedicated 476 B.C. at Delphi. Originally there was a chariot with four horses. The eyes are onyx and enamel, lips inlaid with copper, silver damascening on the diadem (Delphi Museum)

31 Apollo from the temple of Zeus at Olympia, *c.* 460 B.C.

32 Roman emperor, probably Valentinian I, a gigantic statue looted by the Crusaders from Byzantium (photo Bruckmann)

33 Head of Christ, mosaic from the narthex of St Sophia, 886–912 A.D. (showing the humanism resulting from the Iconoclasts)

34 Back of ivory casket made in Byzantium (Constantinople) 850–950, showing Aphrodite, Ares, Europa on Bull, Children with a Mare (Victoria and Albert Museum)

35 Bronze head from Ife, Nigeria (British Museum)

36 Theseus after slaying the Minotaur, wall-painting from Pompeii

37 Dance of women to the lyre, from a fresco in a Greek tomb, *c.* 400 B.C., Ruvo di Puglia, Apulia

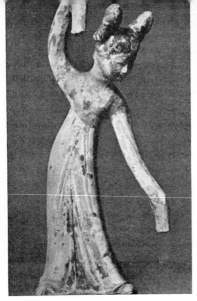

38 Chinese terracotta of T'ang period, *c.* 700 A.D. (Guimet Museum, Paris)

39 Dancer from Borobodhur, Java. Note the hand-play to the tune of two transverse flutes, tambour and tambourines. From a Buddhist stupa, *c.* 750 A.D.

40 Flemish miniature, The Dance in the Garden of Pleasure, from a MS of the *Roman de la Rose*, *c.* 1480 (British Museum)

41 Dormition of the Virgin, fresco from the Monastery of Sopotchani, Serbia, *c.* 1255–65

42 From a Bogomil Tomb: scenes of the hunt and dance, from Brotnyitse (Yugoslavia)

43 Garden-scene from a French tapestry, *La Vie Seigneuriale*, c. 1500 (Cluny Museum)

44 Wooden pillar from Salerno; Romanesque (Victoria and Albert Museum)

45 Giotto, *Mourning over the Dead Christ*, fresco from Arena Chapel, Padua, *c.* 1305

46 Piero della Francesca, *The Dying Adam with Eve, Seth and Others*, detail from the Legend of the Cross, fresco at Arezzo, *c.* 1551

47 Bosch, *The Ship of Fools* (Louvre, Paris)

48 Grünewald, *The Temptation of St Anthony*, from *Isenheim Altar*

49 Bellini, *Allegorical Sacred Subject* (Uffizi, Florence, photo Mansell Collection)

50 Giorgione, *Fête Champêtre* (Louvre, Paris, photo Mansell Collection)

51 Breughel, *Carnival and Lent* (Kunsth i s t o r i s c h e s Museum, Vienna)

52 C a r a v a g g i o, *Resurrection of Lazarus* (National Museum, Messina, photo Mansell Collection)

the 2nd century A.D. Ptolemy had made a map of the globe with a frame of astronomically-determined latitudes and longitudes. Realistic drawings of plants were achieved and dissection led to discoveries in physiology. The mechanical inventions were not to be equalled in number and variety till A.D. 1600. Artillery was worked by torsion; the screw was applied to water-raising; a pump was made with valves, cylinders and pistons (though probably never used); pneumatic and hydraulic devices were worked out. Watermills with gears to convert horizontal into rotary motion and increase power by reducing speed, were invented—and in this case actually used. Metal gear-wheels, employed in the water-clock, started off the trails that lead to all later clockwork mechanisms. Hydrostatics were applied also, for supplying water on aqueducts—the siphon was known, but seems not used, perhaps because lead pipes would not stand much strain. Glass-blowing was invented, probably in Syria.

Generally then little use was made of the magnificent series of devices and constructions, except as toys and dinner-spectacles or as temple-mechanisms to astound the credulous. The great period of proliferating ideas was the 4th-2nd centuries B.C. when the expansion initiated by Alexander was going on both east and west. After that came the political consolidation of the Romans, but all essential springs of inner movement had dried up. Many factors no doubt played their part in the failure of Greek science to transform society. All the ideas and mechanisms for the transformation were there; but nothing happened. Certainly the slave-economy was a major factor in arresting development. Roman writers recount two parables, which help to explain the outlook. Petronius tells how a man invented an unbreakable glass and was put to death by the emperor, who had found out that no one else knew the recipe: otherwise 'we should treat gold like dirt'. And Suetonius says that Vespasian rejected the invention of a crane for building operations: 'Suffer me to find employment for my poor'. Further, the author of the treatise *De rebus Bellicis* in the 4th century A.D. is the only one known to discuss the need of labour-saving devices; and he does so in view of the acute need of man-power that had then developed in the army. He notes that 'the barbarian nations are by no means considered strangers to mechanical inventiveness, where nature comes to their assistance', although they 'derive no power from eloquence and no illustrious rank from office'.* It is clear then that though slavery was the main social obstruction to scientific applications, we must see it within the general focus of a culture which for multiple reasons had cut a

---

* The list of Roman borrowings from the barbarians includes 'not only such valuable contrivances as trousers and fur coats, but also "cloisonné jewellery, felt-making, the ski, the use of soap for cleansing and of butter in place of olive-oil, the making of barrels, and tubs, the cultivation of rye, oats, spelt, and hops", to say nothing of the heavy plough. References to falconry in Roman literature become frequent soon after the Huns first made their appearance on the northern frontier ... The stirrup and the horse-shoe are said to have been introduced from the wide steppe-lands' after the western empire collapsed. (THOMPSON)

deep line between manual and intellectual activity in the division of labour. There is however present in the poets a tradition of the Golden Age when men, through their accord with nature, had lived without labour; and at least in a poem by Antipater of Thessalonica, perhaps 1st century B.C., the machine is seen as the means whereby this Golden Age can be actualised:

> Cease from grinding, O you toilers. Women, slumber still,
>   even if the crowing rooster calls the morning star.
> For Demeter has appointed Nymphs to turn your mill
>   and upon the waterwheel alighting here they are.
> See how quick they twirl the axle whose revolving rays
>   spin the heavy roller quarried overseas.
> So again we savour the delights of ancient days,
>   taught to eat the fruits of Mother Earth in ease.

He is writing about the water-mill. The feelings of the manual worker have for once slipped through into the upper levels of culture; and we may note how the circling movement of the machine is connected with the dance of the Nymphs.

Art. The way in which the Greeks were able to throw off all the stylistic fixations which had previously governed was foreshadowed in Minoan Crete. There the designs from octopus or dolphin on the vases preserve an immediate sense of the movement of living forms. The bulls on the Vaphio cup swing their heads towards the spectator; the peasants on a steatite cup, led by an Egyptian-looking priest with sistrum, have a jovial actuality. There is a secular and lively feeling that goes far beyond even the devices of Assyrian narrative reliefs.

Mycenean designs tended to barbarise Minoan methods, partly because of the growth of large-scale markets for pots; but the artists still used figure scenes and animal or plant forms. With the dark-age came a fall into geometrical abstraction. Horses now and then appeared on protogeometric vases, and figures returned before the mid-8th century, but in a very formalised fashion. The growth of mercantile energies and the expansion of epic poetry brought about a wide range of themes. With the 7th century the artists were able to regain realistic form, while using the geometric tradition to maintain standards of clarity and precision. The geometric silhouette was filled in with shadings. The black-figure style arrived with the late 7th century and led on to masters of dramatic action like Exekias.

The increase in wealth had made sculpture possible, both in mythological scenes for buildings and in portrait statue or relief. Efforts were now made to represent the dead person for a grave; and though the result was far from portraiture, there was an advance in realism—with varying approaches in different regions. The Peloponnese concentrated on the structure of the body, Attica on the pattern and the decorative aspect, Ionia on volume and texture. The Greeks were struggling to break away from abstract frameworks and base their work purely on natural proportion and balance. They had to struggle for centuries. Thus, at one time they seemed ready to accept the principle of depicting each form in its broadest aspect. They had to experiment long with wooden cult-statue or *xoana*, to humanise the post or tree-trunk. (Pausanias describes the Aphrodite of Delos, 'a small statue with right hand damaged by time, it goes down into a square block instead of feet'.) *Kouros* or *Kore* stood upright in stiff dignity, staring with a faint archaic smile as if they were welcoming the new life that welled up into them from the earth—but which may be a piece of court-etiquette. The cylindrical framework compelled a simple structure; but within the given form something new was happening— not merely an adaptation of human proportions to unyielding geometric pressures, but rather an absorption of the geometry into the organic structure. The artist grew aware of the muscular details, the limits of each plane, the modelling of the surfaces. A conflict emerged between the realism of sections and the over-all stylisation; for the artist was unwilling either to break form into its components or to unify by identifying the body with a given non-human framework.

With the 6th century the struggle reached a new level. The realism grew more assured, the strain between the parts was being overcome, and in the last decades came a fine fusion of idea and expression, an intensity of feeling that heightened the definition and subdued the formal system, e.g. the marble horseman or the girl with ringlets falling over her shoulders, made in Athens by the so-called Rampin Master; or the bearded man carrying a calf dedicated by Rhombos c. 575 and found on the Acropolis. In such works a deep inner breath seems filling out the form organically without disturbing the old disciplines. Then about 480 the frame falls wholly away, one section flows imperceptibly into another, the body no longer needs to be supported on abstract structure. It moves, it swings off the symmetrical axis and finds a balance completely derived from its own organic system. The disciplines exist now only as an unseizable canon of beauty, an image of the body flowering in perfect growth, strength, grace. Nothing like this had ever been dreamed of before. The marvellous quality carries on through the masterpieces of the 5th century, in such varied examples as the bronze charioteer at Delphi, dedicated in 476, the statuary decorating the temple of Zeus at Olympia (c. 460), or the Three Fates or the Theseus or the Ilyssos of the Parthenon pediment—as well as irradiating many another large or small work.

In the Parthenon of Pheidias however we also see a weakening, an ideal-ising element already tending to turn the splendid inner balance and tension into harmonious formulas. With the 4th century the idealising tendencies are in full charge. Already in the late 5th, Polycleitos had produced his canon of proportions; his own work still owned a powerful tension of weight and grace, repose and movement; but his strongly intellectualist position heralded the break-up of the great creative synthesis. The last phase of that synthesis appeared in Praxiteles with his capacity to combine breadth of form with the utmost sensuous delicacy of surfaces, his sense of individual character held within a general harmony and movement of one part into another. With the work of Lysippos the old balances are broken in order to gain an enhanced effect of emergent action and of varied points of view. Such a divergence might have meant a leap into a new dimension without loss of the previous high quality; in fact it heralded the exploitation of virtuosities in the post-Alexander world, the attempt to build large-scale compositions of action, as in the Pergamene school. Though works of much power were produced by the Hellenistics, there was a lack of vital cohesion. The harmonies lost inner tension and the dramatic structure revealed an imposed rhythm. We feel that the men did not know what to do with the astonishing sensibilities and craft-skills that have been accumulated; they could not find the point at which to relate design and life, the tension inside art and the tension inside themselves and society. Yet in the countless representations of battle, conflict, ecstasy, dance, there were many richly evocative moments; and the lunge of the diagonal appeared to control the world of baroque exuberance and violence. Important new compositional systems were liberated. Thus, the Pompeian mosaic of the battle of Alexander and Darius, a faithful copy of a late 4th-century work, shows an advanced use of perspective and of light-and-shadow modelling in a

Darius and Alexander: version of a Pompeian mosaic.

large entangled movement of forms, which would hold its own among any group of Renascence paintings. The new skills and insights are linked with the first burst of scientific inquiry after Alexander; and like the Alexandrian inventions cannot find their place in the world. Despite the immense new potentialities that have been born, our final impression is of a confused explosion, a rapid depletion of creative energy, a growing vulgarisation and emptiness.

The discarding of the abstract framework in art was the exact counterpart of the discarding of priestly myth in philosophic speculation. Greek art, in freeing itself from hieratic controls, freed itself also from the patronage of kings and priests during its great days; it was not tied to any set tradition that required an undeviating style. (Greek priests were normally ordinary citizens.) The gymnastic contest supplied both models and a new feeling for the body. Both Plato and Thucydides show the Hellenic pride in having risen above the barbarians by reason of the acceptance of nakedness. With the fall of the free city-state the peculiar conditions that had given vitality to Greek art were ended, though the skills survived.

Finally, there is a striking continuity from the first stiff *kouroi* down to the athletes and Apollos of the 4th century. This shared element comes from the strong semi-magical viewpoint, stressed by Plato, that art powerfully affects life with its transformative virtues, its compelling energies of form. The Greeks sought to define the young, the graceful, the healthy, because they felt sure that thereby they were deepening the quality of youth, grace, and strength in their people. And it was this implicit faith in the dynamic influences of art, sustained by the democratic spirit and drawing on the new sense of proportion, geometry, logic, which brought about the steady and consistent definition of organic balance.

The 5th century had seen the first traces of interest in individual features, but the tendency was to idealise, to work from the particular to the typical. The kingly patrons of the 4th century however wanted to see their own faces, and the portrait proper devloped in the 3rd. There was, however, no magical overstress of head or face; the head was still seen as only one of many members making up the total character. Two trends had grown up: one more impressionistic, studying facial play and gesture, the other refusing to consider passing effects. (Lysippos used life-casts, moulded in wax and retouched before casting in bronze.) From the mid-2nd century, the severe and the impressionistic trends combined.

Greek architecture developed essentially along the same lines as art and thought. The architects took over the elements of the previous societies and reorganised them on logical clear-cut lines. The *megaron* or hall of the Aegean Bronze Age played a key-part. (At Mycenai it shows axial planning and symmetry, but it may be of Anatolian origin.) Out of a welter of forms the rectangular hall emerged dominant, gabled at either end of a roof that needed tiling; save for the pediment the whole form seems derived from a wooden prototype. In the change to stone, at first, more solid proportions were needed; but with increased skill and experience, and especially after marble was used, the members could be refined afresh and better proportions established. Perspective and foreshortening were handled by scarcely noticeable distortions.

The Greek temple was a deity's house, not a place for congregations. There was no need for a large interior; and the architects concentrated on the external volume considered geometrically as a series of proportions united in a single harmonious pattern: a Pythagorean set of resolved tensions. Unnecessary decorations or elaborations were excluded, and all organic forms that would suggest plant or animal. (The Corinthian capital alone gave a chance to introduce foliage; but it was never an order like Doric or the more slender Ionic. Its effect was too ornate for repetition on a large scale outside a religious building.) Though abstract, the forms were related to human proportions, with a clear demarcation of parts aimed at keeping the eye in movement. Each member was subordinate to the total effect; each line led on to another at a different angle; the total network of relations and proportions was worked out on precise mathematical schemes.

But by its nature it was not a form capable of development in new ways. The application of the principles could be varied; but the building as a unit was too complete as a system, too unrelated to landscape or to other buildings to undergo any deep changes or to modify its nature by connections, mergings with other forms. It simply stood there perfect of its kind like the sculpture of the 6th-5th centuries.

Behind the Greek forms seems to lie a cosmic symbolism, e.g. the tomb at Mycenai called the Treasury of Atreus was domed, with rivets that seem to have held bronze stars; the megaron of Crete or the mainland, square or rectangular, with a large circular hearth at the centre and four surrounding columns, seems a world-structure. The rounded form seems to have persisted in the Prytaneum at Athens where the sacred fire was always kept burning. In the east pediment of the Parthenon are sculptures of the rising sun and setting moon; and it was usual to paint stars in the coffers of the ceilings.

In Asia Minor we find direct expressions of the world-mount, e.g. by Alyattes, father of Kroisos in Lydia. Many large burial mounds have been found in the area, one nearly half a mile round. A massive masonry-cone was built on Mount Sipylus. Antiochus I of Commagene (who died c. 38 B.C.) was buried on the highest peak in his dominions, a spur of the Taurus mountains, where a huge cone-mass was piled up, with colossal statues nearby of gods and himself; he declared his aim to have 'a sacred monument hard by the heavenly throne' whence his soul might go forth to the throne of Zeus. And in Italy, the Etruscans, who seem in part from Asia Minor, had built great conical mounds in stone, e.g. at Cervetri.

The hellenistic kingdoms tried to merge Greek classical architecture with that Asianic mound. The mausoleum at Halicarnassos used the world-mound to express the god-king's apotheosis: a pyramid of steps high above a columnar structure set on a tall basement; and the so-called Nereid monument at Xanthos had a temple on a high basement—the 'nereids' probably representing Winds. The great altars of the gods, especially those of Zeus, were mounds often of a terraced form, e.g. the vast altar of Pergamon (Satan's Seat), which seems to have taken the place of a holy site on a mountain crest. In such structures we see the break with the classical Greek outlook, the first step towards the new outlook of the later Roman and the Byzantines.

9: Greek Literature and Music

Poetry. Greek literature also liberated itself from old types of control and became secular, completing the trends that we have seen in *Gilgamesh* and in the non-religious poems of Sumer and Egypt. In liberating itself from restrictive traditions, it achieved an inner discipline of form that lifted it on to a wholly new level in comparison with previous literatures. The logical structuration of Indo-European speech helped in this development, but the creation of the free city-state without kings or priestly controllers was also essential, together with all the social forces we have analysed in relation to philosophy. The forms of tribal poetry were developed into a number of genres in which the emancipated poet might express himself.

On the one hand the personal lyric grew out of the folksong, and out of tribal choral singing emerged a series of forms which in turn contributed to the drama. In Homer we find accounts of the dirge, the hymn, the processional marriage-song, the song accompanying a dance-mime, and songs sung by choirs of girls; we may add the processional hymn as certainly old. In the 7th century the Dionysiac cult produced the dithyramb, and the next century the victory-songs for the games, while the age of the tyrants brought in the *enkomia*. The choral song, *molpe*, has a leader, *exarchos*, and there is usually dancing of some kind. The music was of the lyre; flutes were sometimes also used, but they were in general the instrument for the elegiac couplets. The great exponents of the choral song were the Dorians, the latest comers of the Greeks, who were nearest to the old forms of tribal life, so that the great choral poets, even when not themselves Dorians, went to Dorian lands. On the other hand the monodic poem reached its height on the coastlands and islands of Asia Minor, where tribal life had been sapped by the trading cities.

A crucial point was the establishment of a musical scale, which Terpander of Lesbos is said to have fitted to the lyre. What had happened was that the poet-musicians had taken over the musical lore of Egypt and Babylonia, and given it a new precise significance and reference, which, linked with the movements of the dance, brought about the birth of exact metrical forms—forms as varied as the dances which they accompanied. The metrical form was made possible by the convention that a long syllable took twice as long to pronounce as a short one, so that the verse, in its alternation of long and short syllables, had in itself a definite rhythmic shape; the music and the words were born indivisibly and one could not be thought of in separation.

But before we consider the development of ode and lyric, we must glance at the Homeric epics, the *Iliad*, which deals with a crucial episode in the Siege of Troy, and the *Odyssey*, which tells of its hero's return from the Trojan War. The material is often that of the dark-age, with elements intruding in the similes and elsewhere from the poet's own period, though the themes are legends that derive from the Mycenean world or from even earlier levels. The *Odyssey*, for instance, has *Gilgamesh* behind it as well as age-old sailors' tales of dangerous passages. The epical world centres on the *oikos*, the nobleman's hall-home, and the background is that of the tribe in violent disintegration under war-pressures, with the *thes*, the masterless free-labourer, in the most wretched state of all. But the audience whom the poet addresses is that of the *panegyreis*, the great tribal gatherings or fairs. The prospering 8th century has leisure to look back into history, to wish to dignify itself with ancient titles; even a new city like Corinth lays claim to a Mycenean hero Bellerophon and the Dorian nobles of Sikyon listened to choruses singing of the sufferings of the Mycenean Adrastos. An epic which told of the great wars and disasters in the proud Bronze Age was sure of an audience; and it seems clear that Homer composed the *Iliad* for the All-Ionian *Panegyris* of Poseidon on the promontory between Ephesos and Miletos, and the *Odyssey* for the festival of Apollo on Delos.*

The moment was ripe for gathering the old lays into a new and comprehensive form; for the traditional bards had now come into a world rapidly becoming literate. Epic could still base itself on the traditions and yet hope for a fixed literary form. Homer siezed the opportunity and his work quickly spread over the Greek world. True epic is an end-product, emerging after a period of extreme dislocation, which it seeks to explain; it deals with a period that has passed away, normally a dark-age of some sort; but though it uses the traditions and even the artforms of this age, its perspective is that of the age which has followed. Looking back, men want to know and understand what happened in the stormy age that brought their own to birth, what was the cause of all the violence and how was it overcome. At the same time they expect, and will give most response to, an answer which has relevance to their own day. Virgil tried to interpret the legendary days of Rome's origins, but in a perspective which explained the revolutionary struggles through which Rome had recently passed, and which sanctified the new State of Augustus, making it seem closely linked with the faraway days of the first Rome. Dante built a huge panorama of the medieval world, in terms of a timeless vision

---

* The epic dialect was never spoken; it consisted of Ionian with an admixture of new and old elements of Aiolic, and with a substratum of Mycenean Greek. The vernacular however began to intrude in other forms, e.g. short elegiac poems for inscriptions.

that justified the long labours of history between Virgil's Rome and his own Florence, but his stimulus comes from the violent struggles in which he has been an actor, and he depicts his eternal world-image at the moment its basis

Agamemnon carrying off Briseis.

is being rent by the opposed claims of pope and emperor. *Beowulf* looks back on the dark world of the bloodfeud from a Northumberland of king's law. Milton uses the accepted myth about the origin of evil to explain to himself and mankind what had really happened in the revolutionary struggles in which he had participated and which seemed to have been wholly defeated— paradise lost. In the same way Homer explains the dark-age to the folk of the Ionian towns, who have reached a stage of law that banishes that age's insecurity, its ethic of vendetta and honour, but who have developed their own divisions of mercantile and landlord oligarchies against peasant and artisan.

The *Iliad* deals with the inner dissentions of what was meant to be a united effort of the Achaians against a common enemy, Troy. The cause of the war is the carrying-off of a woman, Helen, and the cause of the troubles inside the Achaians is a dispute over a woman, Briseis, between the leader Agamemnon and the outstanding hero Achilles. Unity is re-established through Achilles' love for his comrade Patroklos, who has been killed. The theme is thus the disunity within barbarian society and the way in which this inner conflict is resolved. The accord which brawling over loot (woman) has broken is re-knitted by an impulse of the love of man for man. But the full poetic focus far transcends the actual social framework that holds the picture together; it involves a critical and humanist outlook which is in no way that of the dark-ages. And this it is that brings the work home to the clansmen listening to the bard at a *panegyris;* it is this that enables the bard to fill out the barbaric picture and present an image of life in its fullness. With its emotional depth, its breadth of view and its realistically-defined variety of action and character, the *Iliad* reveals a leap forward so enormous that its originality as a work of art cannot be overstressed, nor the debt that all succeeding literature owes to it. Such a work can only be the product of a single poet, however much traditional material he employs. Whether or nor the same poet wrote the Odyssey is a more difficult matter,

The *Odyssey* is a *Gilgamesh* tale much secularised but at almost every point revealing its mythic substratum.* It has a direct underworld journey and many images of the spirit-world, shading from Isles of the Mother such as Calypso's —she is the Hidden One, the Earth as Death—to utopian dreams such as Phaiacia (which doubtless also holds memories of Minoan Crete). The passage through a dangerous point—the cave of the Cyclops or the Isle of the Sirens —is also an important motive: shamanist fantasies based on the initiation-test—though such crisis-points have no doubt also gone through a process of re-interpretation in terms of Minoan and Greek sea-tales and sailing-manuals. Finally, Odysseus passes back to his home out of a magical sleep or trance, to undergo one of the tests that we noted at the end of Tatar shamanist tales. Again the theme is filled out with rich and vivid detail achieving a full picture of human life within the subtle critical values of the poet.

The rhapsodists who recited epic did so in a declamatory chant intoned to a simple accompaniment on the lyre. (Other poets used Homer's technique to cover the whole tale of the Trojan War, but without his power and insight —without the typicality of character which comes from the coincidence of old material with a new need, the sudden emergence of a new perspective which vivifies the material and gives it a profound significance to the audience. We have only to try to think of a poet of the Latin Silver Age trying to compose an *Aeneid*, a Dante of the 15th or 16th centuries fabricating *Divine Comedy*, or a Milton of the 18th century attempting a *Paradise Lost*, to see how important for the epic poet is the right moment of transition between two epochs.)

Hesiod of Boiotia in the 8th century used two oriental forms—the theogony and the didactic counsel addressed to a member of the family—but gave them a new individuality. He argues with his brother Perses, who has gained more than his fair share of the family property through bribing the kings or nobles, and who now wants yet more; and advocates a world of justice and hard work. He tells the tale of Pandora and of the Five Ages—gold, silver, bronze, heroic,

---

* Mythic elements underlie the Trojan War, but they are negligible in the *Iliad*. Helen was a goddess at Sparta, worshipped jointly with Menelaos; her cult was specially that of unwed girls, who paid rites to her yearly. She was worshipped as a tree, *Dendrites*, on Rhodes, and Theocritos mentions that the plane was sacred to her in Sparta. She was said to have been carried off by Theseus, but rescued by her twin brothers when that hero was in the underworld. Her carrying-off by Paris thus seems to have behind it some legend of a spirit-bride; Troy the magical town would easily fit into a spirit-world setting. But the mythic elements are securely rationalised in Homer.

iron—a first attempt to define history in terms of stages, with the paradisiac phase at the outset.

We may now return to the world of song. Monody, the work of a single singer, was closely derived from folksong. It found its first great outburst on Lesbos in the age of the tyrants, though its best exponents, Alkaios and Sappho, were aristocrats. There was still here something of a unity of culture; for the diction of both poets is essentially popular:

The strength of folksong is that occasionally it can state truths of great moment in simple passionate words, and this same strength belongs in an unprecedented degree to Sappho... The sense of her poems goes naturally with the metre and seems to fall into it, so that it looks like ordinary speech raised to the highest level of melody and expressiveness. (BOWRA)

Her repetitions and her circular form (her liking to end a poem with a word or idea used in the opening line) are instances of her closeness to folksong. And it happens that we have a Lesbian quatrain that shows how close was Sappho's method to that of the anonymous singers:

> Now the moon has gone down
> and the Pleiads, and in the sky
> is midnight. Time slips past
> and alone I lie.

But though there was still on Lesbos a cultural harmony between the clan-noble and the folk, it is wrong to see in the self-assertion of Alkaios or the immediacy of emotion in Sappho the old type of dark-age individualism.* The poets live in a mercantile world where the dissident and ironic character, mockingly aware of the break-up of the clan-controls and loyalties, has already found lively expression in the iambics and trochees of Archilochos of Paros, the bastard of a noble and a slave girl, who lived a life of violent ups-and-downs, dreaming of a farm on the rich plain of the Siris and saying just what he thinks of anyone or anything:

> Not for me the general renowned or the well groomed dandy,
> nor he who is proud of his curls and is shaven in part;
> but give me a man who is small and whose legs are bandy,
> provided he's firm on his feet and is valiant of heart.

(Such a character indeed is already present in Homer's world, where he is

---

* Alkaios' lament in exile belongs to the new world: 'I live in my misery like a peasant, though I long to hear the Assembly called and the Council. What my father and my grandfather had in this city of mutual wrongs, I am driven away from, exiled on the outermost edges . . . I live, keeping my feet clear of troubles, where the Lesbian girls trail their skirts in the beauty-contest and around me rings the wonderful sound of the holy cry of women every year.'

satirised as Thersites; and we cannot understand the Homeric detachment unless we see that it involves a Thersites-Archilochos element, kept under control. Break the bonds that unite the Ionian clansmen a little more, and Thersites emerges as the new man of the people, accepting nothing at its face-value.)

A type of monody sung to the flute, in which the unit was the couplet, begot the elegiac poems that date from the 7th century; the flowing restless epic line, the hexameter with its quick dactyls ($- \smile \smile$) and stabilising spondees ($- -$) had attached to it a second line in which a check in the middle gave an effect of a suddenly asserted balance. The metre was first used for marching or love songs, then extended its use, and created the elegiac epigram, which later among the Alexandrians was used, among other things, for the personal love-lyric.*

Tragedy. The Athenian tyrant Peisistratos played an important cultural role. He introduced recitations of Homer at the Panathenaia, which helped to stabilise the text, and he founded the City Dionysia, a spring-rite of five, or six, days. This rite began with a procession of the image of Dionysos Eleutheros or Liberator, with a bull sacrifice, then turned to contests of drama and dithyramb. Under the Democracy, the dithyramb was a hymn in the god's honour, not necessarily about him, sung to the flute by a choir of fifty men or boys in a ring round the altar. Various tales were told of the song's origin. Herodotos says the poet Arion first 'produced' a dithyramb at Corinth —which apparently means that he first gave the song a definite theme and grouped the dancers round an altar. We also hear of early dithyrambs by Bacchiadas of Sicyon, where a tyrant had encouraged the Dionysiac cult, and by Archilochos, who sang: 'I know how, thunderstruck with wine, to lead the dithyramb, the fair strain of Dionysos'. As leader, he seems to have improvised stanzas to each of which the group sang a refrain. Aischylos further tells us, 'It is fitting that the mingled notes of the dithyramb should accompany Dionysos in his *komos* (revel'). The dithyramb thus seems to have arisen as a processional song in connection with rites such as those of the City Dionysia.

Further, it is possible that the singers were once women. An epigram on a winning poet speaks of the *Horai*—the Hours, who are further here called the *Dionysiades*, the name of a real *thiasos* at Sparta—as crying glory at the ivy-bearing dithyrambs and 'shading the hair of skilful poets with headbands of blossoming roses'. We may also note the legend of Eleutheria (whence the cult image of Dionysos had come to Athens). It tells of Eleuther's

---

* The following version of an epigram of two couplets by the astronomer Ptolemy gives as good an idea of the metrical form as can be given in English: 'Mortal though I be, yea ephemeral, if but a moment—I gaze up to the night's starry domain of heaven,—Then no longer on earth I stand; I touch the Creator,—And my lively spirit drinketh immortality'. (R. BRIDGES)

daughters going mad after a vision of goatskin-clad Dionysos and being cured when their father, obeying an oracle, instituted the worship of Dionysos of the Black Goatskin. (A goat was the prize in the tragic contests.) *Eleutherai* is equivalent of *aphetai*, the women freed or loosened by the god possessing them. We may then suggest that the dithyramb was once sung by *thiasoi* of women in processional, then taken over by the men and sung at a stand, *stasimon.*

The original theme must have been the Passion of Dionysos, with the leader impersonating the god. (Aristotle says that tragedy evolved from the

Dionysos as a draped tree-stock with mask.

leader of the dithyramb.) But after the form had given birth to tragedy, it itself, denuded of its motive force, became a song in which music played the main part. On the other hand, in the drama the words took charge; the single masked actor turned into two, then three. No more were ever added.

The pre-Aischylean form thus appears as follows. The chorus enter with a song, take their stand round the altar and sing, the hero appears, explains his identity and situation in a dialogue with the chorus, he then goes out and there is another stasimon, a messenger announces his death, the chorus laments, the messenger goes and the chorus leaves with a song. (Aristotle says the first plots were brief and ridiculous; Thespis, the traditional founder of tragedy, is said to have written a play on Pentheus, who was torn to pieces by his daughters, Bacchanals.) The original measure would have been the marching trochaic tetrameter, which the iambic superseded as closer to ordinary speech.*

We find in the tragedies the same structure as in initiation-ritual with its departure of the initiate as a child, his death and resurrection, the revelation of sacred objects, a catechism or lesson, and the initiate's return as adult. In Greek mysteries these stages appear as the procession, the representation of the god's passion (*agon* and *sparagmos*, the conflict and the rending of the god), the showing of sacred objects (*anakalypsis*), the teaching of hidden truths (*ainigmata* and *dokismasia*), and the joyful ending (*komos*). In tragedy the corresponding stages appear in the choric entry or *parodos*, the action of disaster and reversal (*peripetia*, *kommos*), the moment of recognition of the truth (*anagnorisis*, often brought about by the production of birth-tokens or the like), a dispute which is usually carried out in strict line-for-line question and answer (*stichomythia*), and finally, the exit of the chorus, *exodos*.

Aristotle distinguishes the complex from the simple plot as one in which the change of fortune coincides with the *peripeteia* (reversal) or the *anagnorisis* (recognition), or with both. *Anagnorisis* is 'a change from ignorance to knowledge, resulting in friendship or hatred on the part of characters marked out for good or ill fortune'. We may say that we have here the structure of all significant works in literature. An inner conflict brings about a change in relationships, which issues in a widening or a deepening of consciousness; a new sort of union and disunion is brought about. What has happened is not just a quarrel or dispute; the clash precipitates a leap in consciousness, a qualitative change in the understanding of life. The person who undergoes the experience of the artform is no longer the same person; he has 'died and been reborn'. Without the structure born of *agon*, *peripeteia* and *anagnorisis* no work of art can cut deep into life or express development. And this compelling structure was achieved for the first time in Attic drama, where through the reassertion of popular rights under the tyranny the farmers and craftsmen,

---

* The forms that contributed to Dionysiac drama are numerous. At Lenaia or Anthesteria the Dionysos mask was nailed on a tree or pillar; women mixed wine underneath and seem to have danced as maenads; at the Anthesteria, if that was the festival, the mask was doubtless worn by the man acting as Dionysos when the god came in the ship and later when he married the King Archon's wife. Both festivals probably go back at least to the 11th century. From vases and other sources we see multiple sets of phallic and satyr dances, e.g. phallic songs at the Return of Dionysos (in connection with which Heracleitos adds that Dionysos is one with Hades). The fat (padded) man was an important fertility-dancer, linked with the satyr; and fat men were specially associated with the Return of Hephaistos to Olympos (after he had 'bound' Hera); Dionysos played a part in the motive (getting H. drunk). In one version Daidalos, the craft-god of Mycenean Crete, takes the place of H. Ugly women danced round the dread Ortheia, enacted by a masked priestess, at Sparta, and so on. One day of the Dionysiac Anthesteria was connected with ritual of the dead.

the producing class, bring their mystery-rituals right into the midst of the cultural situation.*

Aischylos, who fought at Marathon and was perhaps a Pythagorean, died in 456. He made the decisive contribution, expanding the simple mystery-play into the full grown tragedy. His concern was to show how it was that men courted self-destruction, what irresistible impulses drove them from the line of safety into the abyss on either side. The doomed man is driven by a *daimon*; he is controlled by the family-curse of discord, of *hybris* (the pride or passion that blinds a man to the correctly human course), but he is also exercising his free choice. Aischylos' characters are thus simultaneously masked *daimons*, ritual-personifications, compelled images, and living people caught in a network of complex emotions, impulses, motives. The *Oresteia* has both an hieratic stiffness and majesty, and a seething human vitality.

The formal links are provided by what is called 'tragic irony'. The dialogue is so contrived that, instructed by the lyric, we can catch in it allusions to grander themes than any of which the speakers are conscious, and follow the action with eyes opened to a universal significance, hidden from the agents themselves. Tragic irony, however, is not a deliberately invented artifice; it arises of itself from the purely symbolic stage of drama. In that earliest stage the whole dialogue might be called 'ironical', in the sense that it is the poet's message to the audience, not the expression of the persons' characters, for they have none. But it becomes ironical in the strict sense only when the persons began to have elementary characters and minds, and so to be conscious of one meaning of their words, which is not the whole meaning nor the most important. The effect is now no longer merely symbolic, but *hypnotic*; the speaker on the stage is like somnambulist. . . (CORNFORD)

A somnambulist struggling to awaken; a *daimon*-possessed person struggling to regain normality. And at the same time a normal person seeking to understand an inherited situation, to arrest the accumulative forces of hate and corruption, and gain a new start.

Sophocles, working as the contradictions of Athenian democracy were wearing through, carried tragic irony to its limit; for he was aware that men had delivered themselves up to a situation, of their own making, where every aim was twisted into its opposite. Elektra, in achieving her deepest hope, her freedom, is made finally 'desolate, stripped of all I loved'. Oedipus is caught in a dilemma where every effort of extrication can only plunge him deeper in sin. Euripides wrote as the democracy was nearing shipwreck; he was well acquainted with all the humanist and rational endeavours of the sophists; and he showed men in a focus of everyday realism, unlike the symbolic

---

* The dithyramb had a triadic arrangement of stanzas; the choral odes of drama were composed of strophe and antistrophe, both alike in form, though the latter might have a refrain. In drama then the chorus kept a symmetrical dual form, while the tragic scenes unfolded the conflict of opposed sides and the resolution, a triadic movement. By creating the trilogy Aischylos used three small dialectical units to build a larger one; each play had its own conflict and resolution, yet existed as a phase of the total conflict and resolution of the three plays taken as a single statement.

realism of the preceding masters. They seem much more aware of their relations to one another and of the tasks to which they set their hands; but

Dionysos rapt: Athenian vase.

the uncontrolled element is not thereby dissipated. It has been merely pushed for the moment out of sight. Men think to escape it by pretending that it isn't there. Suddenly it sweeps up and engulfs them. In his last play, *Iphigeneia in Aulis*, most of the scenes are taken up with a ruthless exposure of the power-lust and vanity that drives the war-leaders; the psychology could not be more rational and realistic in its bitterness. Then the girl, realising that she cannot escape, accepts her murder at her father's hand; ecstatically accepts it and goes singing to the altar. The hypnotised element in people which makes them accept the claims of the lords of war and murder is expressed in her submission —but more than that: a sense of the total human condition, beyond all irony. And somehow the girl's acceptance becomes a defeat of the murderers, a pledge of the love and understanding that will some day carry mankind to a redemption beyond the utter contradiction of the scheming egoisms and the victimised renunciation.

From the most primitive level we have treated, that of the Australians, onwards, we have seen a continual remoulding and revaluing of myth in order to express the changing fates of the group. This process is inevitable, since in myth is expressed the deepest thought and emotion about life. Thus, in the fertility-rite the Young Year kills off the Old Year and wins the Earth-bride. No moral problems arise while the figures are kept at the simple seasonal level. But when a group feels that something has gone wrong, they are liable to reconsider the myth. The hero is seen as contaminated; for whom has he killed but his father, and whom has he mated but his mother? So an Oedipus is created. The tragic themes are at root the fertility-myths given this sort of twist.

An interesting example is the Judgment of Paris. The triad of Mothers, Nymphs, Hours, Graces and so on, is one of the commonest forms in the mother-cult. But in a society where division of labour has taken large strides, how can the three goddesses remain anonymous and like-faced? So Paris, one of the children brought up in a shepherd-world of 'nature', has to choose between Aphrodite, Hera, Athene—who in sophisticated terms represent the lover, the wife, the craftswoman; and the golden apple he gets is no longer a mere fertility-symbol—it is the emblem of strife and violence. (Aphrodite, the apple-offerer, becomes Nemesis—the tempting Eve.) And Paris' choice in turn leads to the rape of Helen and the Trojan War, the great themes of dark-age disaster and conflict.

Another interesting way in which an old theme is refashioned appears in the resistance-motive of tragedy. In ritual the young god of the reborn earth has to fight the old year; in tragedy he is shown as being resisted by authority, whom he defeats. The theme thus expresses the mass-cult's struggle to emerge into the world of the nobles, and at the same time embodies a deeper hope of social reversal. (Legend brings out the fertility-aspect of the resisted Dionysos. Pegasos of Eleutherai was said to have tried to introduce the god into Athens; the Athenians, refusing, found themselves impotent and were bidden by the Delphic oracle to accept the cult, in which phalloi were offered to Dionysos, Archilochos was opposed in trying to introduce the god into Paros; and again the resisters became impotent and an appeal had to be made to Delphi.)

Comedy. Comedy was based on the village-*komos*, with an underlying death-rebirth rite; and as it remained a more primitive form than tragedy, at times the direct transformation-rite intruded into its action, as in Aristophanes' *Knights* where at the end Demos is regenerated from imperial corruption by being cooked:

Let the Theatre sing for the news I bring, and welcome a wondrous tale.
O star in the night to Athens the blest, O help of the Islands, hail !
Say what glad thing is this you bring, and our altars shall smoke in the street.
I have boiled your Demos in magical herbs and turned him from rotten to sweet.
O worker of wonders! where standeth he now, or where hath he laid him down ?
He dwells in Athens of ancient days, or Her of the violet Crown.
How can we look for him? how is he changed? what like in carriage or dress ?
As he was when he sat at Miltiades' side or with great Aristides at mess.
But soon ye shall see him. There, hearken, above us the Gates of the Rock unfold.
Uplift your voices, and open your eyes on Athens, our Athens of old.
The wonderful city, the City of Song, true home of our Demos, behold!

And the chorus often used animal-guisings. In the cult of Artemis Orthia at Sparta there was an early ritual drama with a quack doctor and an old woman; at Sicyon a band of mummers entered the orchestra with an improvised hymn to Dionysos, the leader's face was smeared with soot and he carried a phallus, and after the hymn the band ran among the audience, mocking them. The debate and the flyting contest of fertility-ritual also played a part in building the full comoedic genre, which developed among the Megareans under a democracy established about 580 B.C. Attic comedy grew up at the Dionysiac festival, the Lenaia, held in December and probably identical with the Country Dionysia; official prizes were given from 487-6. The Lenaia was originally the feast of the *Lenai* or Madwomen (i.e. a *thiasos* of possessed women), and like the City Dionysia had the elements of procession, *agon*, and *komos*. In Aristophanes we find a structure made up of chorus-entry, *agon* (a debate at times preceded by a fight), an address by the poet to the audience, and an exodus generally in some revel-form. Interspersed are scenes in iambic dialogue.

The only complete Old Comedies we have are those of Aristophanes, a marvellous mixture of lyrical fantasy and realism, relentless satire and joyous acceptance of life, bitter mockery and deep political seriousness. He courageously in the midst of war championed peace and attacked the demagogues. He continually used women as his mouthpieces and made them the champions of life and plenty against the world of greed, war and egoism which the men had built up. In *Lysistrata* they bring peace about; in *Ecclesiazusai* they put beards on and vote in a form of communistic living, a fantasy-return to communal ways. Fragments from other playwrights show that the theme of a return to the Golden Age was common. The following passages run the same sort of imagery as medieval fantasies about the Land of Cockaygne. The first is by Crates:

'Then no one shall possess a slave at all, female or male.
He'll do his own work now however old he is'.
'No, not at all, I have a capital solution. Listen'.
'And what will all your notions do for us ?'
'Why, everything you summon will come forth
and no more effort needed than a word.
Say, "Table, lay yourself", and look, it's laid.
"You kneading-trough, prepare your dough, and you,
cyathos, pour out wine, and where's the cup ?
Come here, you cup empty and wash yourself.
Trot up, you cake, and you, you loafing dish,
get busy, sir, and bring along some beetroot.
Slidder this way now, fish". "O, but I can't,
I'm only one side fried yet".
"Then, you fool,
flop round here in the oil and fry both sides".'

We see that the question of slavery and labour-saving devices did agitate the ordinary citizen, at least under the democracy. (Recall also the viewless attendants who provide for the needs of Psyche in *The Golden Ass*.) Telecleides summons up an *alcheringa*-picture:

> I'll tell you of the life I gave the dead
> in the first days when there was peace for all
> easy as scooping water with the hand.
> Earth brought forth then no fear and no disease
> but everything desired broke blossoming.
> The mountain-sides were cleft with hurrying wine
> and barley-cakes were quarrelling with loaves
> which got the first bite from the mouths they wooed. . .
> The fishes, gliding houseward, then would leap
> fried from the water, flapping on the tables.
> A stream of soup, with joints and chops still warm
> and bobbing amid its savours, wreathed along
> past the couched diners, while from pipes there dribbled
> perpetual fronds of mincemeat richly spiced
> for all to lick the luscious stalactites. . .
> Those were the days when men were properly nourished
> and thewed like giants.

In tragedy the contradictions whelming the individual triumph and he is rent like the saviour-god; the resurrection is expressed in the moment of deepening consciousness, the recognition of the rending forces. In Comedy the pattern is the same, but the renewal of life is directly expressed in the concluding *komos*, which ratifies the triumph of the hero.

In the prologue the revolutionary demands of the hero are explained, and he is about to materialise them, when the chorus enters and opposition develops. The feelings of the group are expressed in a short sequence (or *syzygy*) on their entrance; a second sequence contains their murderous threats against the hero, his pleas that they listen to reason and the final acquiescence of the chorus or the character who pleads their cause. Then comes a debate—the *agon* or conflict—in which the opposed elements are rationally tested and the revolutionary one is found to be the better. The opposition is now over and the new order becomes a *fait accompli*. (ZIELINSKI)

That is the Aristophanic system; but we must remember that the revolutionary view looks backward—to a sort of primitive democracy before the money-corruptions began, or to an *alcheringa*-fantasy.

With the end of the democracy the old uproarious comedy, with its sharp criticism of the world around it, flagged and died out. The hellenistic world saw the birth of the New Comedy of manners, refined and humane, but lacking the large dynamic of the Old. The city-gods are gone; men look to Tyche, Fortune, or to personal saviour-gods. The tragic and comoedic patterns are supplanted by romanticised myth-motives. The rejected hero reared in the bosom of nature becomes the foundling exposed by parents in distress, who is ultimately found and recognised, with a sudden rise in fortune.

Thus the romantic formulas are born as a vulgarisation of fertility-myth, the collective element minimised and the *komos* reduced to the marriage of middle-class characters who rise in the world. Only in the romance of *Daphnis and Chloe*, written under the Roman Empire, an effort is made to use the formulas for a lyrical return to the original bases, with a delightful picture of young love in a 'natural world' as the result.

Katharsis. The idea of life as a fusion of opposites in harmonious balance appeared in the medical theory that illness was a failure of that balance. If harmony could not be restored, the sufferer died; but at the crisis it was possible to expel the morbid matter and restore the equipoise of the bodily humours or elements. (The idea goes back to the shamanist practices of extracting the stone or other matter which had disturbed the system.) Off-scourings were buried, thrown into the sea, or carried to mountainous wilds. In particular, epilepsy, the sacred disease, required purifications to end the state of possession it was considered to represent; and the Korybantes, who seem a magico-medical fraternity and who induced trance-states by their dances, were held to have the power of curing madness by incantations. The ecstatic release of the dance was thus itself an emotional purgation. Alcibiades in Plato's *Symposium* says, 'Whenever I listen to Socrates, my heart throbs harder than in those who participate in the rites of the Korybantes, and his words evoke in me floods of tears'. When, then, Aristotle saw a kathartic function in tragedy, a purgation by pity and fear, he meant that the experience of the tragic work brought to a head the unsettled and unbalanced emotions in the spectator and at the same time expelled them, restoring an inner harmony. His explanation draws its terms from shamanist experience, but at the same time begins a profound analysis of the conflict and resolution inside a work of art.

History-writing. All literary forms are developed under the Greeks except the novel. After Alexander there are romances, however, often with a utopian quality, especially when the Stoics stimulate the idea of a way-of-nature opposed to existing society and even look to tribal systems for lost virtues of equality and brotherhood. Works like Iambulos' *City of the Sun* played their part in the uprising at Pergamon which seems to have attempted to found an egalitarian society and which was quickly put down by the Romans in 130 B.C. The idyll or little picture was worked out in verse as well as the realistic prose-mime; Theocritos perfected the idyll in its pastoral form, mixing realism and overtones of the Golden Age, and thus linking the genre with the complex of emotions we noted gathering round the image of Paradise among the Persians. Ode, satire, elegy, letters, dialogues, essays and other forms were exploited. The Cynics carried the creed of a return-to-nature to its extreme, attacked and discarded all conventions, and introduced into literature a contempt for the class-world with an exaltation of the poor and oppressed;

from their impact came forms like the Cynic tragedies, satiric elegies and the satire mixing prose and verse, epic parodies, and various moralising genres; the street-corner speech led to the Diatribe, generally in prose, which foreshadowed the Christian homily or sermon. Thus Cercidas of the 3rd century asks in a verse diatribe:

why doesn't heaven empty these men of their swinish wealth and distribute it among the poor so that they might meet their bits of expense? Can it be that Justice is moleblind, the Sun sees crookedly with his single eyeball, and the lustre of Themis has been dimmed?

He ends with a warning that 'should the wind change, the rich will be compelled to disgorge their possessions'.

In the writing of history too the Greeks made a decisive step forward, on the basis of realistic narrative such as we saw beginning among the Hittites. Herodotos uses the epical method in organising his material—a method that suits his main theme, the defeat of the Persian colossus by the Greeks, who unite before the common danger. At the same time his busy and interested eye notes the differences of the Greeks and the people of the older civilisations or the outlying barbarians. In Thucydides, who deals with the war between Sparta and Athens that wrecked the Greece of the independent city-state, a more concentrated method is employed, akin to that of tragedy. The writer is keen to discard all superstitions and legends; but otherwise he seems at first glance to have no comprehensive method. His analysis of the causes of the war lacks even the faintest understanding of the economic, social and political forces at work; and yet in his total presentation he achieves for the first time a powerful insight into historical reality. How is this insight achieved? By his tragic vision, which, ignoring the real forces at the analytic level, grasps them at the level of dramatic representation, in which the systems of tragic irony we noted in Aischylos are powerfully used. The imperial corruption of the democracy is defined in Cleon, who, possessed by ruthless 'insolence', is unable to control his greed and covetousness. The final moment of fall or degradation comes in regard to Melos, where the Athenians decide to make an exemplary massacre of the citizens to frighten the other allies against revolting.

The Melian Dialogue presents with tragic irony the impasse to which Athens has been brought by attempting to base democracy on imperial exploitation and oppression. 'And Fortune contributes to intoxication; for sometimes she presents herself unexpectedly at a man's side and leads him forward to face danger at a disadvantage; and cities even greater than individuals, in proportion as their stake is the greatest of all—freedom or empire'. Thus through the symbolic psychology of tragedy Thucydides penetrates his picture at all points with a profound dramatic tension and significance. His objective manner is throughout at odds with the passionate vision of betrayal; Athens herself is the tragic figure, caught in a network of relations defined by Cleon, Alcibiades, Nikias and others. His outlook has aspects of kinship with that of

the Hebrew prophets; otherwise he stands unique in the ancient world as able
to present the conflicts of history with depth, concretely grasping the structure
of hidden movement.

Music. Greek was a language with a pitch-accent, though we are unable to
calculate its effect; stress-accent no doubt also existed; but today we can
only analyse the verse-structure in terms of vowel-length, which gives us
some idea of the musical rhythms that up till the 5th century were coincident
with the metrical form—apart from the metres like the iambic related to the
speaking voice. The one thing we are sure about is that the music must have
been as precisely organised as the verse. Verse and music could not be separated, but the music had a meaning in its own right, a representational power,
a direct grasp of objects formed by the ethos and pathos of performer and
listener. It was a kind of possession, which was why the philosophers took it
so seriously as a formative force. To invoke the wrong sort of music was to
hand oneself over to an evil daimon. The bard Phemios in the *Odyssey* cries,
'I am self-taught and the god has planted in me all sorts of song'. Even the
downright farmer Hesiod calls on the Muses who dance 'round a spring dark
as violets, round the altar of mighty Zeus' on Helikon. They give him a
shamanist wand:

> and they plucked from the sturdy baytree a wonderful rod for me,
> and they breathed in my frame a voice divine,
> and the power to tell of the past or future was mine,
> and they bade me sing of the gods who never may die,
> and ever, the first and the last on themselves to cry.

The secular tradition split off from ritual and magical song.

The Greeks knew the octave interval (diapason), but their unit was the
interval of the perfect fourth (ratio 4:3), which is the natural leap of the human
voice: the tetrachord, comprehended by the four lyre-strings. The four notes
were defined as two limiting notes with two moveable ones in between, which
changed according to three genera (diatonic, chromatic, enharmonic) as well
as varying within the genera. In the enharmonic genus we meet the ditone (a
little larger than our major third) and quartertone—though the major third
may have been known from the last century B.C. The tetrachord was also
classified according to the order of its three intervals. Two tetrachords, joined,
made up an octave-scale, and various modal forms were derived from each
note taken as a starting-point.

The most important note was called *mese* (middle), which was the centre of the
Greek scale-system. . . The sequence of notes in the octave-scales are sometimes
referred to as modes. . . But the Greek word for mode (*tropos*) referred to something
of which such a scale was only the bare bones: it connoted a melodic style or idiom
having a particular ethos. (CROSSLEY-HOLLAND)

The conception of musical movement was circular, revolving round the *mese* or taking positions between the two limiting notes. The philosophic basis remained always that laid down by Pythagoras, who had divided the mono-chord by ratios, seeking to reach a satisfying scale (conceived as a structural and substantial element of the universe). The heavenly world was considered to emit the music of the spheres, which in turn held it together; the spheres in their circlings gave out a series of tetrachords.

With the collapse of the city-states the whole basis of united music and words broke down. The Pythagorean theory carried on; but the music of the spheres was now a wholly theoretical one—indeed, unheard music came to be held superior to music heard. Philosophy and the science of harmonics took over the term *mousike* that had once meant music and words (with dance). In the last days of Athenian democracy the divorce of words and music was beginning, watched angrily by Plato and Aristophanes from their differing viewpoints. Pratinas depicts the situation:

What is this uproar? what these dancings? what outrage has attacked the trampled altar of Dionysos? . . . It is the Voice that is Queen, by order of the Muses. The *aulos* (pipe) must dance behind, being indeed a servant. Only in the rout and fisticuffs of young mummers banging on the door, let him act the General and be thankful. Beat that bad breath of a coloratura-mottled toad. Burn that varlet of a low crooning babbling reed that wastes spittle and spoils time and tune as he steps along, with his body all gimlet-holes. Now look at me, O god of the ivied hair, Dionysos triumphant in dithyrambs: this is the right fling of hand and foot. Hear my own performance, the Dorian.

The death of democracy was the death of the choric drama. In the *Frogs* Aristophanes cries, 'The City must be saved and have her Chorus still'. She was not saved and the Chorus faded out. The dithyramb survived through its appeal to the rich as a virtuoso artform; in the last quarter of the 5th century it had taken to stressing a quivering intonation suggested by the *aulos* and copied in the kitharist nomes. The tautness of the old style gave way to *kampai* (bends—modulations or decorative shakes) and a varied but formless melodic line. After the war the modernists gave up being aesthetes and turned tough. The bombastic libretto of Timotheus' *Persai* was illustrated by naturalistic noises; the music had a definite programme of imitative effects. 'I do not sing the old things, because the new are now the winners. Zeus the young is lord today, once on a time Kronos held sway, Old Lady Music, get away!' But the chromatic music rapidly exhausted itself and gave way to the common diatonic of all the later pieces.

The ancient world had no idea of a composer who was not poet or performer. After the 5th century the serious composer thus ceased to exist and 'here began a divorce between the citizen and the professional, between theory and prac-tice, from which Europe still suffers'. Popular music continued to flourish and theory ascended to the spheres; the two did come together again in the ancient world.

In hellenistic times the pantomime became a highly enjoyed form; and mummers, called often by some local name, gave mixed shows—acrobatics, lewd jokes, comic scenes of drunks and foreign quacks, with romantic touches, success-stories, parodies of myth, runaway endings. On a more pretentious level, there were myth-episodes as a sort of sung ballet. A chorus of Euripides might be given as a concert-piece, though not with the original music. But that was all.

Speech and Song. Greek in the 5th century had been spoken with a predominantly pitch accent. It is clear that in linking the voice with a musical instrument the natural pitch of each syllable must have been respected. Otherwise chaos would have set in. If then the music was in accord with the vocal pitch and at the same time rhythmically followed the length of the syllables (long or short), we can see that the relation of spoken and sung words would be very close. Aristoxenos, pupil of Aristotle and the only Greek writer who discusses musical practice instead of being content with Pythagorean abstractions, remarks that there are two movements of the voice: continuous or speaking, and discrete or musical, proceeding by intervals. In discrete movement the voice stays for a certain time on each note, then passes by a definite interval to another. 'In the former [speech] it is continually gliding by imperceptible degrees from higher to lower, or the reverse'. And Nicomachos, 1st century A.D., says that 'if the notes and intervals of the speaking voice are allowed to be separate and distinct, the form of utterance becomes singing'.

But if the pitch-accent fades out and the stress-accent takes control, this closeness of speech and song is ended. And so Aristides Quintilianus (sometime between 2nd and 4th centuries A.D.) recognises a third or intermediate movement of the voice: that which is employed 'in the recitation of poetry'.

Why did the original unity of speech and song break up? We can only surmise that under the change lie the increasing division of labour and the break-up of the unity of culture itself and production. The vocal change must also, in turn, involve physiological changes in men. (The survival of pitch-accent in China must be connected with the remarkable failure to develop fundamental changes in methods of communication since 1300 B.C.)

10: The Romans and Christianity

Rome. The same process that had made the Greeks the centre of things in the last millennium B.C. ensured that the next point at which political power and cultural energy were to find their highest concentration would be further west in the Mediterranean. There were three competitors: the Phoenicians, Etruscans, and Romans. The hellenistic kingdoms had spread Greek city-life far to the east; specialised farms producing for the market were developed by Greek colonists in Russian Turkestan and India. But the political storm-centre steadily swung westward, among peoples drawn into the world-market but still preserving many elements of tribal organisation. The city-state of Roma in Latium threw off Etruscan domination, after learning many lessons from its masters, and steadily dominated an ever-larger area in Italy, then in Sicily and the nearer parts of Greece.

The Romans did not attempt a reconstruction of tribal equality in a city-state like the Athenians. From the outset we find them divided into patricians and plebeians; but they maintained voting-systems based on tribal forms and they detested the name of kings after the Etruscan expulsion. There was thus a basis on which the small farmer or town-artisan might continue to struggle against the patricians and their privileges. In that struggle they used the strike-weapon, threatening an exodus from Rome; and there were many points when it seemed that the balances, weighted on the patrician side, would break down. Finally the later 2nd century B.C. and a large part of the 1st were taken up in bloody social conflicts: between the Romans and the other Italic peoples, who wanted to share in Roman citizenship, and between the nobles and the commoners. The details do not concern us here. The main thing is the prolonged and stubborn struggle which went on, using the elective system based on tribal divisions (long after any reality of tribal life had gone). In this sense, despite the dominance of the patricians, there was a genuine democracy, which was able to carry on through many changing phases, unlike the Greek form. This inner struggle went on at the same time as the external expansion. Because of the continuing imperial triumph, the ruling class were able to buy off the commoners in various ways, by doles or by land-gifts; but in the end they had to face a powerful challenge, which issued at last in the civil war between Caesar and the Senate, and which was settled only under Augustus, who sought to reconstitute the rule of the big landlords with various concessions to the trading and industrial middleclass all over the empire.

We noted the system of dual magistracies under the Republic, which persisted after the principate, but with less and less significance. The tenacity that had shown itself in the political struggle had appeared also in the slow creation of a system of law adapted to a world of private property, with considerable flexibility within that framework; and this continued to extend. Under Stoic influences, and expressing the positive aspect of the Roman development, the idea of a law of nature, concerned with human and not with property rights, also played its part in the evolution of the highly complex legal instrument which Rome bequeathed to medieval and later Europe.

The Romans continued the Greek work of spreading the city-state, though steadily under the empire the amount of self-government dwindled. To urbanise barbarian areas, however, remained always the great aim of the Romans, and the extent to which they succeeded was their pride. The rule of law and the growth of urbanisation were the tests of Romanisation. Property-law tends to equalise or level in one aspect; for it is no respecter of persons, it respects only money. And so by the early 3rd century A.D. equality of civil status was extended to all the free men of the empire. But the system which such a law guards is far from bringing a material equality about; it tends to deepen the divisions of class and of property-ownership. So the 3rd century saw also an increased split of the empire's inhabitants into rich and poor, into *potentiores* and *humiliores*, which already foreshadowed a sort of baronial system. It saw the outbreak of continual civil war in which the peasant armies expressed their discontent and brought down the Augustan system in its last stages of decay. Constantine stabilised the situation and carried out the preliminaries that ensured Christianity its position as the sole State-religion. The farmer, the *colonus*, was tied to the land, and the worker was tied to his guild.

The Romans had kept on sending out their trade-tentacles into the surrounding barbarian areas, thus unsettling tribal systems and precipitating the invasions that grew ever more dangerous and in the 4th-5th centuries swamped the western half of the empire.

In Gaul and Britain, as well as in North Italy and parts of Spain, the Romans had subdued many Celtic peoples, who had moved west as well as into the Balkans and Asia Minor after the upheavals brought about in Central Europe by the advent of iron. Further north, the Germans though gaining from the Celts the secrets of iron-making, had remained in barbarism, inventing it seems the heavy plough which made possible the cultivation of the heavy clay lands of the northern forests. Celtic art had developed, fed by Etruscan contacts, its rich decorative forms, which had links also with the animal-art of the nomads. Here, however, the essential shape was human: a wild scurry of curvilinear forms with strange organic hints leading to a human head in clear or disarticulated form, to haunting eyes laired in plant-scrolls. This role of the head in Celtic art was certainly connected with the practice of head-hunting and with beliefs that the head was the centre of life and power. After the Roman Conquest, the progress of Celtic art was checked; but elements remained, now and then asserting themselves, though mainly out of sight. With the break-up of the Roman State in the west, Celtic art revived and found new forms.

Literature. Though the literature of republican Rome, apart from Catullus and Lucretius, is now known only in fragments, we can see that it had considerable vitality and range. The native Saturnian metre was early displaced by Greek forms, and metres based on the Greek system of long and short syllables were imposed on the language. As we have seen, the Greek forms had grown up in close connection with music and the dance; and their drastic imposition on a tongue without the same sort of development cannot but have maimed and limited its natural qualities—even if forcing it ahead to new sophistications and endowing it with a new set of possibilities. However that may be, poetry between Ennius (239-169 B.C.) and Lucretius (born about 98) went through a varied development of epic, drama, chronicle-poem, satire, lyric, and expository poem. Ennius, who introduced the hexameter in his *Annals*, has a clear strong character 'I only write my verses when I've gout', he says, and takes an Epicurean standpoint: 'I've said the gods exist, and still I say it's true; but I don't believe they care at all what mortals chance to do'. Thus he describes a Roman general and his friend (behind the picture was said to lie his own relations to M. Fulvius Nibilior, who subdued Aitolia):

> He called his friend, with whom he loved at ease
> to share his board, his talk and his affairs,
> companionably, when tired with lengthy hours
> he left the imperious councils of the State
> in holy Senate of broad Marketplace.
> Boldly, small things and great, or little jokes,
> he told, his bitterness, his hidden hopes,
> he showed without reserve at whim, in trust.
> They often laughed, alone or with the world.
> No thought could sway his mind to evil ends,
> malice or guile; for he was cultured, staunch,
> gentle, contented, fortunate, speaking well
> and seldom: rich with buried treasure dug
> from ancient ways, the lore of past and present,
> manifold ways of time, of gods and men:
> which taught him wisdom in his speech and silence.

---

* The Saturnian seems accented, and runs something like, 'The queen was in the parlour, eating bread and honey'. Naevius (c. 270-199) who wrote plays on Roman subjects and an epic on the Punic war, in which he had served, used it—as had Livius Andronicus, who translated the *Odyssey*. Naevius clashed with the nobility, and fragments such as the lines from *The Girl from Tarentum* are very lively.

And thus he sums up the trends of his world:

> Wisdom's pushed out, force wins the day. They scorn
> the worthy orator, not the brutal soldier.
> Contending not with learning nor clashed words,
> they mix and hustle in unending strife.
> These are not hands of law they stretch, but swords
> that aim at wealth and power with clanging frenzy.

Lucilius (180-102 B.C.) shows a torrential energy in his satires, which he directs at incapacity and corruption in high places as well as at greed and cruelty:

> Hack, servant, comrade—no one's at his heels.
> Alone with the cash in his money-bag he reels.
> He dines, sleeps, bathes with the bag, and keeps it tied
> to his shoulder; for he's got his soul inside.
>
> From dawn to dusk, workday or holiday,
> plebs and patricians act the selfsame way.
> Mad to be in the swim, from home they go
> and haunt the streets, with crafty passion stirred;
> vying with courtesies and moral show,
> they scheme, each man his fellow's deadly foe.

Like many of these early poets, he experiments boldly with language:

> No wife for me, to do me out of my cash !
> a silverplate-mantilla lavish spender,
> an ivory-mounted handglass cutter-of-dashes.

while he parodies the poet Pacuvius' tragic compounds by depicting a heroine:

> Tormented with hunger, cold, unwashedness,
> unbathedness, undouchedness, unkemptness.

The lyric poet Laevius likes diminutives, jingles, and adjectives such as *gracilenticolorem*, beauty-coloured.* Catullus created a new kind of lyric altogether, combining the lucid simplicity of Sappho with an immediate impact from the corrupted hurly-burly of the everyday world; the pang of a hopeless inner conflict ('I love and hate: you ask how this may be? I do not know: I know my agony') with a delighted surrender to the variety of life. Lucretius set out the Epicurean materialist philosophy in a long poem of

---

* Varro in his *Menippean Satires* (prose and verse mixed) complains of the end of the old plain farming days; in *The 60-year Old* he has the Rip-Van-Winkle motive to bring out the shock of an Old Roman arriving in a world where all is for sale. *Marcipor* (? dialogue of master and slave) seems to have the flight to another sphere: Midnight with its fires 'displayed the dance of starry choirs', when a wind-storm tears off 'tiles, branches, brooms', and 'we, in wreckage fallen, like storks whose balanced plumes the lightning-forks have scorched with flame: we from on high crashed down to earth most wretchedly'. Aulus Gellius cites some early poets whose love-epigrams have just the conceits of fire-and-ice that Renascence sonneteers indulged in.

powerful intellectual compression, made passionate by his horror of the way in which religion worked on the fears and divisions of men, alienating them from nature.

The drama was also alive through the later Republican years, often dealing with national themes. Naevius boasted, 'I have always prized freedom far above wealth', and 'We shall speak with the tongue of freedom at the feast of freedom's god', and made his boast good by enduring jail. Praetextatus dealt with Roman legend and contemporary history, though after Naevius the rule seems to have been that no living person should be mentioned. In comedy, despite the imitation of Greeks like Menander, the native bases asserted themselves. We know of fescennine jestings at harvest-home, rival clowns in cork masks, all sorts of local farces and mimes, which from the titles and fragments appear strongly rooted in daily life. *Fabula togata* was the native comedy; *trabeata* dealt with the middleclass; *attelana* and Oscan farces had traditional characters which in due time led on to the Commedia dell'Arte— Bucco, Pappus, Dossenus, who indulged in rustic horseplay, drunks and gluttons, obscene laughters, fools. Manducus champed with the jaws of his ogre-mask and scared the children—from the slang *manducare* comes the French *manger*, to eat. Short pieces with intrigue-plots, these plays developed into a literary form with strong popular elements, *e.g. Bucco the Gladiator*, from which survives the line, 'He killed the bull so bloodily, he gored me with his love'. The diction was sharp and succinct as proverbs: 'A shortlived blessing like Sardinian cheese'. There were mimes with jugglers and acrobats: there were turns, and plots with abrupt changes of fortune. Probably from the outset women took part in them in Italy. Mountebanks ranted and were in

Scene from a phylax *comedy: note the plain wooden stage.*

turn parodied. In South Italy the *phylakes* played lowlife scenes and burlesques.

Terence and Plautus show how the Greek New Comedy was taken over and considerably changed. In Plautus, whose very name (Flatfoot) suggests the barefoot mime, there was an enormous gusto; and music still played a strong part, as all but the iambics were accompanied—though song and recitative are very difficult to distinguish. The irreverent guileful slave is often the character who guides the action.

Laberius, a man of the middleclass who wrote mimes in the late republic, dealt with political themes; for we find references to a looting governor of a province, to Caesar's appointment of market-overseers and his supposed plan to legalise bigamy. Laberius had a popular humour, *e.g.* 'I fell in love like a cockroach into a basin', and some fragments show inner rhymes and puns. His *Paupertas* may be a Debate between Wealth and Poverty. (Novius wrote a *Mortis et Vitae Iudicium*.) Caesar forced him to declass himself by appearing on the stage with the ex-slave Publilius Syrus, who also wrote mimes. In his prologue Laberius expressed himself with much dignity. 'Romans, we are losing our liberties . . .' And he referred to Caesar: 'He must fear many whom so many fear'. Never again was such an outspoken voice to be heard on the Roman stage.

Under the Empire. The lively onward movement of Latin literature was rudely checked by the advent of the empire. At first the poets carried over technical and emotional elements from the late Republic. The elegists, Tibullus, Propertius and Ovid, expanded the themes of Catullus and Calvus, with much charm and wit—and in the case of Propertius with felicitous moments of genuine passion. With a brilliant tour-de-force Horace transplanted the Greek lyric metres into Latin; but as they had no roots there in song, they put forth no shoots or further flowers. Virgil made a great effort to encompass in Latin something equal to the major Greek achievements; he did all that could be done by a first-rate power over the ordinance of words, an extreme metrical finesse, a delicate eye for nature, and a profound sense of the pathos of the human condition. His *Aeneid* seeks to combine the *Iliad* and the *Odyssey* in a tale of the wanderings of Aeneas, which lead to the foundation of Rome. But for his fundamental method he draws, not so much on the Homeric poems, as on the literary and romantic epic of the hellenistic Apollonius of Rhodes: the *Argonautica* which, dealing with the quest of the Golden Fleece, managed to achieve something of a symbolic relation to the post-Alexander world, its eastward expansion, its search for a new fullness of life, its inner betrayal. In choosing the Venus-born hero who was claimed a Caesar's ancestor, Virgil sought to propagandise on behalf of the ruling house and to prove that its ascent to power was in accord with the fate of Rome; but it is the tension between this purpose, with its effort to create a model hero, *pius Aeneas*, and the poet's deeper sense of the tears of things, *lachrymae rerum*, his personal love of country-life, which lifts the epic above the level of a pastiche. The wanderings of Aeneas become the wanderings of men lost in a broken world, their effort to regain roots, their need somehow to harmonise their distracted personal existences with a larger purpose or destiny. Aeneas remains a weak priggish character; but the wider emotional references of the poem as a whole save him from becoming intolerable. And so Virgil's work, with its fine and inexhaustible summary of the ancient rhetorical devices, continued to be of supreme importance to men in a world where the grass-roots of life had been cut and where culture had become a withered thing, a game of given counters; that is, wherever the deadened form of Graeco-Roman culture which the empire brought about remained the key to intellectual life. (Where there was a deep-rooted vernacular literature, as in Elizabethan England, the *Aeneid* could not become important.)

During the 1st century A.D., while the memory of republican days persisted and there was still a measure of resistance to absolutism—even if *libertas* had generally narrowed to the rights of the nobles to have a share in the control of things—some vitality remained. Satire was alive in Horace, Persius, Martial, Juvenal, even if it feared the political field. The epic of senatorial *libertas*, Lucan's *Pharsalia*, had force and dignity, but was essentially a work of undisguised rhetoric; Tacitus, also the exponent of that *libertas*, achieved a certain depth by willy-nilly responding to the law of nature, so that he simultaneously expounded the Roman theme, which Livy had set out in uncritical enthusiasm, and the case for barbarian freedom, in his harshly astringent style. After him the inner life of the Roman intellectual is flattened, impoverished, submitting to the rigid system of rhetoric as to the absolutist rule.

Andromeda in tragic costume. Comic actor: terracotta.

Only two works in prose show full creativeness after the Virgilian synthesis: the *Satiricon* of Petronius and the *Metamorphoses* of Apuleius. In the first the picaresque novel is born, with a massive power of characterisation in the dinner-scene at Trimalchio's house (the only part come down in complete form) which looks to Shakespeare on his comoedic side, to Dickens, even to Gogol. Such an achievement could not have come about without an all-round critique of Roman society, and we have enough passages from the novel to show that Petronius had thought deeply on his world; indeed he makes what is by far the fullest analysis of what had gone wrong with ancient society. He condemns the deepening gap between life and education; he insists that the cash-nexus, the rule of money and its values, has destroyed art and science; he rejects the idealistic analyses of history, which see the Caesarian revolution as a conflict between 'ambition' and abstract 'nobility'.*

> The nation's blotch, the moral fall, was this:
> What met defeat was not a single hero,
> the Roman Glory fell. And broken Rome
> was price and prize, despoiled with no avenger.

Apuleius, writing in the 2nd century, cannot take so explicit an approach as Petronius. He writes when the empire seems settled and prosperous, but is already rotten at the core. He is deeply aware of a contradiction between reality and men's thoughts of it; and he expresses his intuitional sense of this situation in the allegory of the rashly curious Lucius who is turned into an Ass, a beast-of-burden, and who is finally redeemed into human stature by the roses of Isis. His tale is thus of the 'fall of man', and he subtly uses his symbolism to bring out his conviction that nothing short of a total transformation and conversion can affect the situation. (He uses the tale of Cupid and Psyche as a doublet of the main theme.) The central point of the fall is the bakery-episode, where the Ass Lucius finds himself in the plight of the driven slave-workers. Here we meet the only passage in the whole of ancient creative writing where the reality of the slave-economy is faced and realised. (Diodoros has an honest account of the condition of miners; but his matter-of-fact picture lacks any element of imaginative grasp or understanding of the relation to his society and its nature.)

Both these great works were connected rather with the lively current of popular expression, of which we gain only momentary glimpses in our sources, than with the dominant traditions of rhetoric that made up the accepted culture. Their roots lay in the mime, the farce, the bawdy tale, the fable, the

---

* The serious thinkers of the first century were aware of the crucial issues raised by the educational system of Rhetoric, which had lost contact with life, e.g. Votienus Montanus, Cassius Severus, Velleius Paterculus, Tacitus, Longinus. But Tacitus tries to define great oratory (i.e. vital and free expression) as 'the fosterchild of the licence that fools call liberty', and Longinus evades the problem that a despotism kills free expressions by saying that the problem is purely ethical (love of money and pleasure).

folk-tale, the parable. Under the empire, serious drama had died out or become a closet-matter, as in the Senecan plays, though there were rare revivals of an old work. Pantomime was the typically Roman form now on the stage; the Greeks called it the Italian dance. A masked dancer performed in dumbshow, with words sung by a chorus; the theme was mythological and the libretto was specially written. We also find an actor singing a personal interpretation of some tragic role, e.g. Nero in the role of Orestes, Oedipus, Canace. Here other figures seem present solely to supply parts of the action.

Comedy was in as bad a way as tragedy. *Comoedus* was used for the slave who read extracts of comedies at rich men's dinners—though there are also purely literary efforts, and an occasional revival. (A 2nd-century epitaph, of M. Pomponius Bassus, says: 'Lest I should live a life of bestial sloth, I translated some dainty plays of Menander and composed some new plays of my own'.) Atellene farces, still rustic in flavour, were being played in the 1st century A.D., and literary mimes were written. The mime that held the stage was largely improvised, working on stock-forms and figures, and might be anything from a bit of mimicry to a playlet with several scenes. Adultery was the main subject, and Heliogabalus ordered the copulation to be enacted on the stage. In the 6th century the church excommunicated all mime-actors, but could not kill the shows. The strip-tease actress Theodora married Justinian. All through the dark-ages, which were in no way dark in the east, the mimes continued.

But all forms of popular literature were scorned by the men of the upper-levels, and we only have scraps and anecdotes.*

Art. The unbalance we noted coming over hellenistic art was not unconnected with the new attention paid to ideas of personal immortality, with consequent concentration on the face that mirrors the soul. The bust-form discarded the rest of the body. At Rome the patrician *gentes* had sole right to keep at home the masks, *imagines*, of ancestors, which were brought out and paraded at funerals. Probably, if we may judge from the anthropoid death-jars, the masks were generalised, though certainly in late republican times deathmasks proper were used and Polybius shows that in the mid-2nd century the images were made as like as possible. (The Etruscans also had a tradition of realistic portraiture; and hellenistic influences may now have come in. The

---

* In music the situation was rather like that in the drama: popular vitality and no advance in the higher levels—though the grandiose effects begun in the hellenistic age (large bands and massed choirs) were exploited; also the growing complexity of instruments. The organ became important. (Two portables have been found at Pompeii; at Aquincum the remains of one, in a cellar among fire-debris—it had fallen from a clubhouse above: the organ was inscribed 226 A.D.) There were four ranks of pipes, 13 pipes in each, levers, sliders, sounding board: action by water-pressures though later by pneumatic force. There were street musicians and many combinations on the popular stage. 'The colourful popular music of the empire with its emphasis on rhythm and percussion, was probably, in the main, an Italian growth separable from Greek traditions', SCOTT. But there were also all sorts of local trends.

Italic style was sharp, concerned to draw out salient points in an expressive way.) Further, in the late republic, all magistrates gained the right to put up statues of themselves. After 100 B.C. the Roman art of portraiture flowered, a mixture of the homely Italic outlook and hellenistic verism. Hence the many portraits on tombs of hard-faced citizens and their uncomely wives, under the republic—a series that came back under the thrifty Vespasian. Under Hadrian there was a classicist revival.

The Roman attitude transformed the allegorical style of Hellenistic artists by imparting to it a sense of actual history. The more majestic aspect of this new style appears on the Altar of Peace reared by Augustus; its simpler

Scene from Trajan's column: disembarcation, with emperor offering sacrifice.

realisms in the narrative of Trajan's Column. Versions of it are to be found on many panels of arches or other reliefs, where the grouping has the casual truth of everyday life and at the same time the dignity of the historic moment. If we compare the *Ara Pacis* with its nearest Hellenistic analogy, the Altar of Pity in Athens, we note that

all the reliefs of the *Ara Pacis* can be directly linked with a single, definite occasion: there we have a concrete moment of present history stated realistically, legend viewed as past history foreshadowing and, in a sense, participating in, the present happening, and personifications summing up present and future historical situations realised and guaranteed by that specific event. On the Greek altar contemporary, but loosely-connected, events are veiled beneath a series of myths unanchored in time and history. (J. C. M. TOYNBEE)

The link with the attitudes of the *Aeneid* are clear. The Romans, no doubt using Greek artists, brought coherence and balance into the heaving forms and forces of the Hellenistic epoch; and in doing so they opened the way to medieval art. Already in works like the Trajanic Column and panels of the time of Marcus Aurelius we see a particularity of character, together with forms of grouping that break away from classical rhythms. By the 4th century, with the collapse of the Augustan world, there is a stress on frontality and on the face, which becomes an emblem of power and exaltation, the eyes especially enlarged and made the emotional centre.*

Painting had made considerable strides in the Hellenistic epoch; we see the fruits of this development at Pompeii and Herculaneum. The painters had a skilled control of impressionistic effects and atmospheric suggestion, of romantic landscape or seascape, and could handle groups on a large scale. At times there is a subtle penetration into the essence of the scene, which goes far beyond anything in sculpture, e.g. in the Pompeian painting of Theseus after the slaying of the Minotaur. The hero, with an awed crowd on one side and a boy clasping his hand on the other, stands in a rapt state, exalted by his deed and yet still enclosed in the moment of danger. It would be hard to find any later painting which more deeply grasps the spiritual essence of struggle.

The efforts which we find to transform the walls of a room with an illusion of garden-spaces all round, have more than a decorative value. Here is the domestic version of the paradise-theme. A house, a town, is in a sense a

Bacchus and Ariadne: Pompeii and Herculaneum.

blasphemous thing, a desecration of mother-earth; the garden is the token of earth redeemed, paradise regained. Every garden is a holy garden, a pledge of communion with nature, a hope and a safeguard.

---

* From early times, Italic art shows a stress on action, on colour, on particularity, and on expression, transforming Greek influences even in the Greek colonies of the south. Note of the Ruvo dancers: 'plasticity of form has no importance, but colours are sufficiently nuanced and the heads do not lack a certain individuality' (VAN ESSEN). Action is the main thing.

Architecture. The Romans under the empire brought important changes into the Greek architectural schemes; they did not do this merely by their enhanced engineering powers, for the Hellenistic builders already knew how to be magniloquent and pompous. True, the Romans had their engineering triumphs in bridges, aqueducts, drainage and central heating. Their great contribution came through the use of concrete; but as they faced their structures with brick, it looked as if the bricks held the forms together and took the strains. The bricks did so in fact only until the concrete hardened.

The use of brick in this way however mainly appeared in the transitional period when the Romans were learning to do without stone, discarding stone arches or flat timber roofs in favour of concrete barrel vaults. What they liked was the speed and cheapness of the new material; only slowly did the architects grasp that new possibilities had opened up. Doubtless many of the stages in the changed outlook occurred in lost Julio-Claudian mansions, especially in their pavilions and baths; we see the first definite break under Nero (60-70 A.D.) and the completion of the new trends by about 130.

In Nero's Golden House a long oblong block faces on to a lake below a terrace; into the facade's middle was set a half-hexagonal courtyard. Previously we meet such forms only on their own, flanked by free-standing porticos. Further, an octagonal room intruded mid-wing on the west, with central dome and vaulted chambers radiating out (fitted in by means of passages and small service-rooms). If we look at the Palatine palace some 25 years later, we still find nothing unusual in the main plan; but rooms are often circular or oval, with windows set obliquely and doors opening off axis. And square recesses alternate with round ones.

The final steps were taken under Hadrian. In the baths of his Tivoli villa the interior comes right into view.

A building like the vestibule to the Piazzo d'Oro, with its ring of projecting lobes marking the apsed recesses within, would have looked as startling to Vitruvius as it would have looked familiar to the builder of one of our medieval cathedrals. And rightly so; for it stands at the head of a long series of buildings—that calidaria of the great bath-buildings, the temple of Minerva Medica, Santo Stefano Rotondo, San Lorenzo at Milan, san Vitale in Ravenna (to name only a few of the best known examples on Italian soil)—a long series of buildings which are the direct ancestors of much that was most vital in the architecture of the middle ages. (WARD PERKINS)

Hadrian's Pantheon was the first great building of the Graeco-Roman systems that was planned essentially as an interior. The porch lessens the shock by being planned along old lines; but, once inside, a new conception of architectural space bursts on the observer. The brickfaced rotunda takes a secondary place; what matters is the great coffered dome with a single oculus at the top to let a broad gush of light in on to the marble and porphyry of the floor. To prevent the encrusted walls from intruding with any effect of weight pressing on the round that bears the dome with its width of 140 feet, they are broken with square and apsidal recesses. The dome floats.*

The Greeks had sought to control space, so that one was aware of it only in terms of the geometrical canon, the strict and yet easily harmonious sequence of forms. Now space has its own rights and plays a dynamic role, liberating the forms so that they can flow in all sorts of rhythmic combinations. The architects were free to take as their bases squares, oblongs, crosses, circles, ellipses, polygons, sigmas, hemicycles and foiled forms; and to modify these by annexes, recesses, niches, apses. Then these elements were co-ordinated axially, bilaterally, and radiating from a centre.

Bacchus and Ariadne: Pompeian wall-paintings.

All kinds of expedients were adopted for continuing vistas, suggesting symmetry and masking irregularities, both in single buildings and in the laying out of cities. An admirable example of this power is shown in the laying out of the great colonnaded street of the city of Gerash. The conditions of the problem necessitated a decided change of angle in its course. At the elbow a vast circular place was constructed around which the colonnade was continued in a circle, thus gaining an additional beauty while veiling the deflection. (LETHABY)

The Roman contribution to art and architecture was thus essential. Under the Romans the impasse into which Greek art had led was broken down and multiple possibilities of development were brought out. The actual products

---

* Van Essen stresses the Italic temple, or house, as a composition in depth, drawing the eye to follow the axis and enjoy spatial effects, while Greek forms invited the spectator to put himself at their heart and enjoy the totality: the principle of sub-ordinated as opposed to co-ordinated composition. He notes the early use of central court, the Etruscan arcades on pillars; the basis of the new Roman architecture in the Temple of Fortune at Praeneste descending the hill in terraces; in terraced houses and the sanctuary of Gabii; the Tabularium on the steep Capitol with its adapted facade and inner stairs; central markets; the cupola on the terrace of the Temple of Venus at Rome; the Forum of Caesar.

were not at all the work of the men of Rome; they came from Greeks, Syrians, Egyptians, and who knows what. But it was the Roman empire which created the conditions making the new break-through possible. And we may note that it was by introducing the circle into the Greek rectangular constructions that the great change was initiated. As the ancient Chinese said, 'Heaven is round, Earth square'.

The world-mount image was not lacking. We have seen it in the rounded and raised temple of Vesta. The Etruscan mound-form appeared in the tomb on the Appian Way known as that of Aruns. Pliny, following Varro, describes the tomb of Porsenna as consisting of five pyramids set on a base 300 feet each way; and the pyramid of Cestius at Rome seems to have had a column near each of its angles. Roman pyres were erected, it seems, in stepped form, doubtless to suggest the sky-mountain as the place of apotheosis. But the great impact of cosmic imagery on Roman forms came from the east, not from a rediscovery of Etruscan meanings. However the mausoleum of Augustus was certainly of the world-mount type, possibly with a hellenistic background, but not without local inspiration, e.g. the tomb of Lucilius Poetus had a huge drum of stone blocks, 114 feet in diameter, and a cone of brickfaced concrete on top. In the provinces great trophies of the world-mount type were erected, e.g. at La Turbie near Monaco and at Adamklissi in Rumania. The Augustan mausoleum in turn influenced the Celts and led to the barrows of the Belgic area and south-west Britain.

Aesthetics. Plato had both provided the basis for a true evaluation of the creative act, and cancelled out his aid. The inner conflict of his thought here was worked out by the neoplatonists, especially Plotinus, who remarks:

If any think meanly of the Arts, on this ground, that when they create they do no more than mimic nature, we have a threefold answer. First, we shall remark that all nature is in its place an imitation of some other thing. In the second place, we are not to conceive that the Arts imitate merely the thing seen; they go back to the principle of Form out of which Nature is generated. Thirdly, in many of their creations they go beyond imitation: because they possess beauty, they supply from themselves whatever is lacking in the sensible object.

Though using metaphysical terms, this definition goes deep into the nature of art-process and marks the highest point of ancient art-criticism. Indeed, there is nothing to compare with it till near the end of the 18th century. Plotinos discards Plato's rigid opposition of Heavenly Form and Earthly Reflection, in which art appears as either a mere copier of the latter or a blasphemous rival of the first; he approaches an understanding of the dynamic and formative nature of the creative act. Stoicism with its elevation of Nature and its processes has contributed to this position; for it implies that if artistic process is in key with natural process, it must be organic and not an 'imitation'.

A cluster of grapes hanging, the brow of a lion, and the foam that curls from the jaws of a wild boar, and other similar things, are far from beauty if they are considered separately, yet, because they happen in the course of nature, they are comely and delightful. (MARCUS AURELIUS)

Note that all his examples are spiral or curvilinear, as if he were speaking of Celtic art.

Plotinos goes even further than his above statement. He realises in beauty a reassertion of symmetry over asymmetry, i.e. a unity which emerges from fused opposites.

We have to recognise that beauty is that which irradiates symmetry rather than symmetry itself, and this it is that truly calls out love. Why else is there more of the glory of beauty upon the living, and only faint traces of it upon the dead, even though the face still retains its fullness and symmetry? Why are the most living portraits the most beautiful, even though others seem to be more symmetrical?

Beauty does not lie in an abstract symmetry, but in the living unity that overcomes discords and asymmetries without discarding them. Plotinus thus for the first time in history relates aesthetics to the life-process.

He also used the Pythagorean arguments to reinforce a deep pantheist feeling for the interrelation of all living things.* A prayer 'is answered by the very fact that different parts of the universe are wrought to one tone like a musical string which plucked at one end vibrates at the other as well'. And so, the incantatory tune and 'a significant cry . . ., have power over the soul, drawing it with the force of . . . tragic sounds'.

Plotinus and the Alexandrian scholars, repelled by Aristotelian formalism, tried to grasp the flow of life, its passion and the source of its passion, by insight rather than by discursive thought; and, what they achieved, they strove to express in allegory or metaphor; for they felt the impossibility of putting ultimate reality into logical form.
BOULTING

At the same time the neoplatonists were acutely aware of the logical problems. In Porphyry's *Isagoge* (the work that the Monophysites and Nestorians handed on to the Arabs) is a passage that sums up in a few words the issues that were to obsess Alfarabi and Avicenna, and then the western scholastics:

Concerning genera or species, the question indeed whether they have substantial existence, or whether they consist in bare intellectual concepts only, or whether, if they have a substantial existence, they are corporeal or incorporeal, and whether they are separable from the sensible properties of the things (or particulars of sense) or are only in those properties and subsisting about them, I shall forbear to determine.

---

* Educational theory was not unconnected with Pythagorean doctrine, e.g. the Quadrivium of basic study, a fourfold system. (Porphyry refers to Archytas' *On Maths* for the classification of astronomy, music, geometry, and arithmetic.) Nichomachus of Gerasa (2nd c. A.D.) associates music with maths and astronomy with magnitudes: the first pair dealing with multitudes, the second pair with magnitudes. It was through him that this classification became the basis of medieval musical aesthetics. (He discusses the divine nature of the numbers 1-10, each a symbol of a deity.)

We see in that sentence how far the neoplatonists have progressed from Plato's dogmatism about the ideas; they feel that it is necessary to clarify what is logically at stake—and for the rest to grasp at an intuitive logic which penetrates the dynamic transformative process of life.

The horse being taken into Troy: Pompeian painting with night-effect.

Their world is one in which the classical balances have broken down; all sorts of popular and provincial elements are pressing in; and pagan types, given a new symbolic value, change into Christian images. Thus, the Philosopher and his Disciples foreshadow a Byzantine Christ and his Apostles as well as a Byzantine priest-portrait, the individual bishop represented as the Eternal Priesthood. Spatial depth tends to give way to a pattern of figures set in a single plane, with the main figure frontally presented and staring straight out at the spectator and dominating him. At the same time narrative art, defining the movement of history in accord with prophetic systems of purpose, takes on a new life. And deep-rooted images are revived. At San Apollinare, Ravenna, as the spectator ends he is drawn onto the movement of the martyrs, women on the left, men on the right, towards the apse, towards Mary and Christ throned among the angels; the eye moves along a series of varying accents to the point of rest, Christ on the completed curve of space. And one is reminded of the onward swing of the interlaced dancers painted in the ancient Campanian tomb at Ruvo.

Thought. Except in neoplatonist aesthetics, the Roman world saw no advances of thought such as had characterised the Greek. Certain philosophic trends which the Greeks had started off continued to develop, but not by coming down to earth afresh and gaining a new start by grappling with the needs of men. The developments were all in an idealistic direction, either laying stress on the inner world of the isolated individual or heaping up fancy on fancy in the Platonic spiritworld. Stoic thought ceased to deal with social injustice and inequality as it had attempted at the outset; now the foe was the tyrannical thought inside the man who wanted to withdraw into an *apatheia* that nothing from outside could disturb. At its worst this sort of thinking could lead to the pretences of the usurious millionaire Seneca to live a life of philosophic calm—even if he managed to die at Nero's hands with a certain dignity. At its best it led to the genuine nobility of Marcus Aurelius, torn between his imperial duties and his sense of human unity:

Whatever you are, you are cast forth from the unity of nature. You were born a part, and now you have cut yourself off. Here then is a matter of rejoicing that you can once more join the living whole. The god has granted it to no other part that, once separated and cut off, it may come together again. But behold the goodness which is revealed through man. He was first made so that he need not separate from the whole except by his own act, and yet after separation he can come together again and join the life of the world.

Villa and park: mosaic on the Isle of Tabarea, Tunisia.

As it were from a high place to look down upon myriads of flocks, and myriads of sacrifices, and ships of all kinds, some caught in storms and others in placid seas, and the vicissitudes of things coming into birth, mingling with one another, and departing from one another.

Bear in mind also the completed life of all the men of past times, and the life of all those to come after you, and the life shared by the numberless men of barbarian races breathing at this moment, and the host of men who have never even heard your name, and the host of men who will presently forget it, the men who are now evaluating you justly and who will yet presently calumniate you. So fame is worth nothing, and honours nothing, and nothing all else that the world offers.

There remains peace of mind towards all things coming upon you from an external cause, and justice in all the acts of which you are yourself the cause. In a word, impulse and act co-ordinated in the effort to realise a common good.

Which is to act according to your nature as a man.

The same note, in a milder and more long-suffering way, speaks in the words of the slave Epictetus.

Children put their hand in a narrow clay-vessel to take out figs and nuts, and this is what happens. If they fill the hand, they cannot take it out. Then they cry.

If you desire to be good, first believe that you are wicked.

Let them look to it who pity me. But I am neither hungry nor thirsty nor cold. But because they are hungry and thirsty, they think that I am.

How should a man take revenge on his enemy? By determining to live the best life in his power.

Do you not care? I do not care. I will show you that I am master. You cannot do that. The Lord God has set me free. Do you think he meant to allow the slavery of his Son ?

But out of the stoic network of ideas there were also servile developments, which sought to glorify the absolute monarch as the sun of the human universe and to draw arguments from man's unity with nature to justify despotism. The cult of the divine king, taken over in its weakened form from Egypt, had been used to gild the post-Alexander ruler, drawing strength also from the Greek hero-cults and the saviour-religions of the people. Ptolemy Epiphanes was the Living Image of God, the Son of the Sun; Seleukos was God the Conqueror, and his son, Antiochos, Apollo the Saviour. After the murder of Julius Caesar at Rome there was a spontaneous movement of the masses to deify him. Soon Athens called him Saviour and Benefactor, and Ephesus hailed him God Manifest and Universal Saviour of Human Life. Augustus was flattered by the poets: 'a god who has given us this peace', said Virgil, and Propertius named him *mundi salvator*. The Greek cities vied in repeating these sentiments. Thus, a decree of the cities of the province of Asia in 9 B.C. declared of the emperor's birthday that men might

rightly regard it like the first beginning of all things. . . He gave a different aspect to the whole world that would otherwise have readily fallen a prey to ruin. . . The birthday of the God was the beginning for the world of good tidings (*evangelia*) which he brought.

Augustus, without overdoing things, carefully organised the imperial cult to cement the industrious freedmen into the system; and it steadily grew till it became the central sanction of the State. That was why Christianity had to clash with it.*

---

* Note the centrifugal and asymmetrical element in late Hellenistic art; under the Severans and Gordians asymmetry again asserts itself, and the term flamboyant has been used for the style of many sarcophagi.

Behind the early inscriptions to Caesar and Augustus there was an element of genuine hope; but as the empire failed to actualise a rule of justice and plenty for all, the emotion fell away. Now the great tide of human hope and disillusion flowed to the mystery-cults with their healers and saviours. Petronius, under Nero, could make a direct criticism of Roman society and its culture; the only way that a man in Apuleius's period could grapple with the core of things was by allegory and symbolism revolving round the mystery-cults of rebirth. The religions of the Great Mother and Attis, of Mithras, of Isis and Serapis, of Asklepios the healer and other lesser figures received an ever-increasing worship. The last book of Apuleius' *Golden Ass* shows how deep the fervour and how rich its implications. Cult-sites became the goal of endless pilgrimages. Neoplatonism and Gnostic creeds with elaborate systems of purification and redemption attracted ever more thinkers.

One reason for the failure of drama lay in the fact that the mystery-cults ministered to the deepest needs for symbolic representations and ritual-plays. Tertullian could deride the pagan spectacles by comparing them with the magnificent show that the faithful were going to enjoy with the Second Advent and the Last Judgment. 'Then what immensity of spectacle!' The murderous gladiatorial shows which had been introduced from Etruria under the strain

Seascapes: Pompeii.

of the first Punic War had their roots in funerary ritual; and their dominant position under the empire expressed both the demoralisation of a people deprived of all active controls of their own lives, a desperate need for redemptory or vicarious sacrifices which could not be satisfied by the imperial cult. The empire, depriving the masses of all political and cultural initiative, condemned them to the bloody Circus, just as the fertility-magics of the war-maddened Aztecs could find no outlet save in the frenetic offering of still-pulsating hearts to the Sun. Any need for dramatic representations that would express the essential patterns of what was happening to people was quenched at the source. Tertullian says:

You have lately yourselves seen Attis mutilated, that famous god of Pessinos, and another man playing Hercules burned alive. We have laughed also in the cruel noon-intermission at Mercury testing the dead with a red iron. We have seen again Jove's brother, armed with a hammer, carry off the corpses of gladiators.

Martial tells of an Orpheus in the circus, who charmed wild creatures, only to be eaten alive by a bear; of the play of Laureolus, a renowned brigand, whose crucifixion was actually performed; of a man on a cross torn by a bear.

> This criminal beats the crimes of ancient tales,
> for here the Myth becomes True Suffering.

How could tragedy exist in such a world? The only possible rival of the circus was a mystery-religion—and not one which indulged in blood-baths of bull or ram. What was needed was a mystery-religion which forbade sacrifice altogether. Only Christianity could end the slaughters of the Circus.

Christianity. Once again a political revolutionary movement was defeated in its dream-objectives of a return to an *alcheringa*-world or in even its more modest hopes of a world of small farmers united in tribal brotherhood, and found its outlet in religious protest. Caesar's murder, after his war against the senatorial big-landlords, made him seem to the masses a saviour-god; and a star rose over his sacrificial death. Antony became for the soldiers the Avenging Mars. Then, throwing his lot in with Cleopatra, he tried to mime the god-part in earnest. He played the Dionysiac role to her Isis. Sibylline verses show us how this god-masking seemed to the eastern masses. They proclaim the nearing world-end.

> The wrath of the Latin men will blaze with a quenchless hate,
> three men shall hold Rome broken and doomed to piteous fate.
> All men shall perish then as they crouch down in their homes
> and the cataract of fire from the heavens pours and foams.

Cleopatra is the Widow; the widow of Caesar, also the lorn Isis or Demeter.

> And when the Widow shall queen the whole wide world
> and in the sea divine have the gold and silver hurled
> and into the waters have hurled the bronze swords of men
> those creatures of a day, all the world's elements then
> shall be widowed lorn and God who aloft in aether is found
> around shall roll the heavens, as a book turns around.

A reference to Isaiah's words: 'The heavens shall be rolled together as a scroll'. All things will become One and there will be no more night or dawn, no more seasons or anxieties. 'Then the Judgment of Mighty God shall come in the midst of it all'. A fierce hatred of Rome burns the words:

> The wealth that Rome as tribute from Asia has taken away
> Asia shall thrice as much get back from Rome on a future day.
> Insolent Rome shall be judged, Rome to the full shall pay.
> How many Asian folk as slaves in Italy stay !

There is a threat to do to Rome what Rome had done to Asia; but in the complete picture the whole world shares in the coming regeneration:

> O Rome, luxurious Rome of gold, you Latin child,
> Virgin drunken with lust in many beds you've run wild,
> but you'll be married without due rites, a slave-slut of despair
> while still the Queen crops off your delicate head of hair
> and uttering judgments hurls you down to earth from out the sky,
> then takes you up from earth and sets you up again on high:
> O serene Peace shall journey to all the Asian land
> and Europe too shall be blessed, prosperous on every hand,
> flourishing strong. Of cold and hail alone shall there be a dearth.
> O rich in cattle and all the beasts that move on the face of the earth,
> O blessed shall be the man that lives in that wonderful time,
>   blessed the women shall be. . .
> True Order shall come for all from the starry heavens to men
> and Justice shall be ours, and with Justice there must come then
> Sane solidarity of men, the best thing life can give,
> love and faith and friendship for strangers, all that live.
> And all disorder and envy, all blame and wrath shall flee,
> no man shall then be poor, for gone is necessity,
> gone is the murder-lust, mad hatred and bitter strife,
> and the thieves that come in the night, and all the old evil of life.*

So great was the hope of renewal that we find Virgil in his 6th eclogue echoing the imagery of the nameless poets of the people and using it to sanctify the imperial rule. And if further we set the Sibylline verses by the *Book of Revelation*, a work older than the synoptic gospels, we see how deeply the hatred of Rome and the hope of a world-judgment had sunk into the labouring masses of the East.

The ordinary mystery-cults could not contain this passion for a reversal of the existing situation. Only among the Jews had there been built up a tradition of obdurate resistance to the empires of the corrupted world; only from the Jews could come a mass-religion which linked the rage and hope represented by the Sibylline verses with a mystery-form of initiation into the worship of a

---

* Solidarity is *homonoia*, the word used by Alexander the Great in announcing (from the imperial level) the new dispensation of unity. Here the people take it over. Cleopatra-Isis suckling Horus (her child by Caesar) contributes to the image of Mary with her baby Jesus. (*Homonoia* had also a political sense, 'an entente, something less than summachia'; it was used for a Koinon of villages: Tarn (c).)

murdered and resurrected god. But Judaic religion itself could not renounce its national exclusiveness, and so the new mass-religion could only emerge from Judaism by a process of union and schism.

The Jews had persisted in rebellion. About 88 B.C. in the repression of the Pharisees, 800 rebels were crucified, with their wives and children killed before their eyes; thousands fled to Egypt and the *Wisdom of Solomon* was composed, speaking of ungodly rulers that tortured the righteous. But though the latter seemed to die, they would triumph in the end:

> They shall judge nations and have dominion over peoples;
> and the Lord shall reign over them for evermore.

A Sibylline oracle, dated about 80 A.D., declared:

> Then shall one come again from heaven, an excellent hero,
> he who spread his hands on a tree of beautiful fruitage,
> best of all Hebrews, who stayed the sun in his course once.

The redeemer was there identified with the legendary Joshua who made the sun stand still. (Messiah Joshua in Greek runs Christ Jesus.) Dissident sects had broken off into communal ways of life. Thus a minority-group of the Maccabean rebels, dissatisfied with anything but a complete rejection of the world's ways, formed the Essenes and tried to set up a utopian system, practising community of goods, condemning slavery, and living in small self-governing societies of workers and peasants, with common meals; some members renounced sexual intercourses altogether. They refused all oaths except their initiation-pledge of obedience, after a novitiate and baptism, and they rejected animal sacrifice. From the Persians they took over the doctrine of a judgment awarding eternal bliss or torment, and probably their prayers before dawn, 'as if beseeching the sun to rise.'

It it likely that the community represented by the Dead Sea scrolls was Essene. We learn of a Wicked Priest and a Teacher of Righteousness who was put to death; and there was a vision of a last judgment when Israel would be justified. The sect called itself the New Covenant, Congregation, Assembly and so on. 'Everything shall be held in common, truth and fair humility and faithful love and just consideration for one's fellows in the holy council'. Women and children had some place in the community; and there was a strict system of order at the meetings, with a hierarchy of priests, elders and people. The initiation had three stages; and the image of the totemic soul-bundle persisted.

> I thank thee O Lord
> that you have tied my soul in the bundle of life
> and fenced me around from all the snares of the pit.
> Ruthless men have sought my life
> because I hold fast to the Covenant.

The core was the sacramental or messianic banquet, in which the chief officiants were the two messiahs, the high priest and the davidic or lay messiah.

The sect saw life as a ceaseless battle of the Sons of Light with the Sons of Darkness, for which they had to be in a state of general mobilisation: the young men as the foot-army, the men from 30 to 45 years as the cavalry, the next age-group as officers, and those over 50 as commanders. Each man had two spirits, Truth and Perversity, assigned at birth, who clung to him till the day of visitation, the world-end.

Such withdrawing groups were not unique to the Hebrews; they were liable to arise wherever a tribal group was rent by class-forms. Thus, among the Dacians were the Polistai, whom Josephus equated with the Essenes; and among the Moesians of the Danube, the Ktistai, also known as the God-fearers, ate no meat, lived on milk, cheese and honey, forbade marriage and kept to community of goods.

What happened then to bring about the proto-Christian movement? It is hard to be sure. Apparently under Tiberius there was a revolt in which the leader was crucified.* Some uncensored references to the insurrection seem to survive in the Gospels. Thus *Mark* tells us, 'There was one called Barabbas lying bound witht the insurgents, men who in the insurrection had committed murder'. Yet the narrative has no previous reference to a revolt. *Matthew* gives no explanation of Barabbas' imprisonment; *Luke* says that he was in jail 'for a certain insurrection made in the city, and for murder;' *John* merely calls him a bandit. A curious passage in *Luke* makes Jesus bid his disciples on the eve of the disaster sell their cloaks and buy swords. We may add that all the Gospels make him ride into Jerusalem as a messianic king a few days before his death, and that in three he is hailed by the seditious cry of *Hosanna* (Deliver us); while all four agree in making the cross bear the superscription, 'King of the Jews'. Finally we may note that in *Matthew* and *Luke* there is the practically identical passage:

Woe to thee, Chorazin! Woe to thee, Bethsaida! For if in Tyre and Sidon had been done the mighty works which were done in you, long ago in sackcloth and ashes they would have sat and repented. Howbeit I say to you, it shall be more tolerable for Tyre and Sidon on the day of judgment than for you. And thou, Capernaum, shalt thou be exalted to heaven? Thou shalt be brought down to Hades.

The fates called-down on the three sites may be interpreted as the penalty for rejecting the Messiah; but it can hardly be accident that all three localities were along the shores of the lake of Gennesareth, the scene of bitter fighting between Jews and Romans in A.D. 67.† Certainly in the early document,

---

* Cleomenes, king of Sparta, who had tried to bring about a return to communal ways, was driven out by the Macedonians and took refuge in Alexandria. He tried to raise a revolt, but failed and took his life. In Plutarch, he has a last supper the night before with his twelve comrades; after his death he was crucified; a prodigy occurred; the Alexandrians called him Hero and Son of the Gods.

† Matthew (xxiii) in a strong passage on the slaying of the prophets cites only Abel and Zachariah son of Barachiah, presumably Zacharias son of Baruch, a rich man lynched in 68 as a suspected traitor 'in the middle of the temple' (Josephus): *cf.* Luke xi, xiii. Matt. xxiv and Mark xiii (Luke xxi) have passionate 'prophesies' which seem accounts of the Roman destruction of the Temple by Titus and Hadrian.

Revelation, there is a passionate rage against Rome and all who accept the imperial cult, the mark of the beast:

And there followed another angel, saying, Babylon is fallen, is fallen, that great city, because she made all nations drink of the wine of the wrath of her fornication. And the third angel followed them, saying with a loud voice, If any man worship the beast and his image, and receive his mark in his forehead, or in his hand, the same shall drink of the wine of the wrath of God, which is poured out without mixture into the cup of his indignation; and he shall be tormented with fire and brimstone in the presence of the holy angels, and in the presence of the Lamb: And the smoke of their torment ascendeth up for ever and they have no rest day and night, who worship the beast and his image, and whosoever receiveth the mark of his name. (xiv)

Chapters xvii and xviii have the vision of Rome as the Great Whore, drunken with the blood of the saints: a tremendous outcry of sustained hate that is without parallel in all literature:

. . . And every shipmaster, and all the company in ships, and sailors, and as many as trade by sea, stood afar off, and cried when they saw the smoke of her burning, saying, What city is like unto this great city! And they cast dust on their heads, and cried, weeping and wailing, Alas, alas, that great city, wherein were made rich all that had ships in the sea by reason of her costliness! For in one hour she is made desolate. Rejoice over her, thou heaven, and ye holy apostles and prophets, for Goth hath avenged you on her. And a mighty angel took up a stone like a great millstone, and cast it into the sea, saying, Thus with violence shall that great city Babylon be thrown down and shall be found no more at all.

And the voice of harpers, and musicians, and of pipers, and trumpeters, shall be heard no more at all in thee; and no craftsmen, of whatsoever craft he be, shall be found any more in thee: and the sound of a millstone shall be heard no more at all in thee. And the light of a candle shall shine no more at all in thee, and the voice of the bridegroom and of the bride shall be heard no more at all in thee: for thy merchants were the great men of the earth, for by thy sorceries were all nations deceived. And in her was found the blood of prophets, and of saints, and of all that were slain upon the earth.

Unfortunately, whatever happened in Judea was too small a matter for the Roman chroniclers to bother about. Tacitus in describing the persecutions under Nero mentions Christ as suffering under Pontius Pilate; Suetonius confusedly tells us of one Chrestus who caused trouble at Rome under Nero; and Celsus in the 2nd century called Jesus a 'ringleader of sedition'. Josephus referred to him as organising a revolt against the Romans. The interpolated passage in his *Jewish War* comes straight after an account of demonstrations and fighting against Pontius Pilate, and perhaps supplants the one authentic story of Jesus written by a non-Christian historian.

Many efforts have been made to prove Jesus a mythical character; and it is true that a large number of details in the gospels can be plausibly explained away as derived from myth and ritual. Sometimes, however, one rationalising argument cancels out another. Thus, Philo describes a mummery which he had seen at Alexandria. A madman was dressed up as a king in robe and crown, and then led in a procession, carrying a sceptre. The man's name, says Philo, was Karabbas. There is probably a link between this Karabbas and the Barabbas who was crucified. But we can hardly have things both ways; Barabbas cannot be both a mock-king in a scapegoat ritual and an actual rebel who had killed someone. There seems no doubt that there was a real person, Jesus, and that he became the centre of a religion which looked on him as the saviour of the world, crucified and rejected, and arising on the third day.* It was this existence of the saviour as an historical individual which sharply differentiated Christianity from the pagan mystery-cults of Attis, Mithras, Isis, Dionysos, and which gave the new religion its strength, its total opposition to the Roman State. There was no reason for the worshippers of Attis or Mithras to challenge the State's sanctions; the worshippers of Christ had no choice but to do so. This basis in history was linked with the whole Judaic attitude, its tenacious belief in a definite divine purpose expressed in all events, large and small, and shaping life at every moment to a universal pattern. The Christian expectation of the last judgment had an urgency and comprehensive clarity that outwent the Zarathustrian hope.

Matthew (xvi), *Mark* (ix) and *Luke* (ix) all have the plain prophecy, 'There are some of them that stand here, who shall in no wise taste of death, till they see the Son of Man coming in his kingdom'. The words must have had a great emotional significance; for even when facts had disproved them, they were retained. The belief that the end of the world was at most only a few days off was central in early Christianity. But we can trace in the Gospels the gradual acceptance of a widening time-gap.

In describing the Roman invasion of Judaea Mark preserves an older wording than Matthew. The 'abomination of desolation' stands 'where he ought not'; the Roman eagles are around Jerusalem. In Matthew the 'abomination' stands 'in the holy place'; the city has already fallen. Or the more precise wording may have been substituted in the second century after Hadrian had rebuilt Jerusalem as Aelia Capitolina and erected a temple of Jupiter on the site of the demolished temple of Jahweh.

In the original source the fall of Jerusalem is to be followed 'immediately' by the signs which portend the coming of the Son of Man. A very few years were enough to falsify this prediction; and that fact helps to date it. Matthew nevertheless lets it pass. Mark deletes 'immediately'; but retains the vaguer phrase 'in those days'. Luke rewrites the whole passage and says that Jerusalem will be 'trodden down by the Gentiles, until the times of the Gentiles are fulfilled'—implying a much longer interval. (ROBERTSON)

---

* In *Revelation* however the saviour is only a ritual Lamb. The popularity of this book is shown by the issue of two editions by the author himself, and its early acceptance as a canonical work. Papias cites it as authoritative in the first half of the and century. However, as the church sought accommodation with the State, it proved embarrassing; Eusebius in the 4th century hesitated how to class it. But it echoed too powerfully the mass-feeling for the Church to drop it; and right up to the 16th century it provided effective ammunition for the extreme dissenters who wanted to overthrow the existing frame of things.

With each new social crisis in the empire, the sense of urgency awoke again, and the Church had to deal with a multitude of malcontents. At first Christianity was contained inside Judaism; but the fall of the Temple gave the final rupture and the creed was free to develop without the impediments of Jewish exclusiveness. For centuries it remained however essentially eastern; the Church at Rome spoke Greek till well into the 4th century.

Since the world had not ended, the Church had to face the task of organising itself inside the empire which it could not accept. Again the adaptation was slow and painful. Paul's epistles give no hint of a local clergy and lay all stress on the shamanist types: apostles, prophets, teachers, those with the powers, those with healing gifts; presbyters and deacons concerned with organisational work trail in at the rear. The *Didache* shows that late in the first century many groups depended on wandering apostles, allowed to stay only three days, or prophets, who might settle down; deacons and bishops were not highly esteemed; priests were not mentioned. But by the 2nd century the overseer or bishop was gaining a strong position, and by the 4th century a graded hierarchy had arrived, with the election of the bishop growing less and less democratic. The parochial system was slow in developing, as the higher clergy feared the common priests who might express the dissident views of their congregation. Indeed, the first great schism was launched by a parish priest, Arius, of Alexandria. (The parochial system grew up in the more democratic east; in the 5th century it was still held down at Rome.)

Slowly the Church adapted itself to the empire by territorial systems. The first stage was based on the single town and its municipal forms; the *curia* (councillors) and *populus* appeared in the Church as *ordo* and *plebs*. The ecclesiastical officers and overseers were based on those of the *municipium*, dealing like them with legal disputes and doles. (As late as Origen the Christians were aware of the likeness.) Next came the linking of one group with another, with the provincial capital taking precedence over the surrounding areas. By the 3rd century provincial councils were being regularly held and had taken the place of underground revolutionary correspondence-society, the 'laired and light-fleeing nation' that Minucius Felix had described, Thus the bishop of a provincial capital rose in power and had much influence on the election of bishops in his area. Constantine called the first General Council.

Changes in the imperial governmental forms had immediate effect on the Church's system. And the bishops of the great imperial towns, like Alexandria, Antioch, and Ephesos, gained a prestige over other metropolitans; they came to be called patriarchs and claimed the right to exercise control over the Church as a whole. With the foundation of Constantinople (Byzantium) as the new imperial capital a new claimant to the highest rank in the Church appeared in its patriarch; and for long a complex fight went on between Byzantium, Alexandria, Antioch, and Rome. The ecclesiastical competition of the various regions often masked the growth of separatist proto-national aspirations, e.g. when James of Sarug sang of Edessa as alone faithful and called Christ the fellow of the Syrian poor.

Each step in the Church's compromise with the world saw fresh heresies, in which a renewed effort of ascetic world-rejection was made. Part of the compromise was the need to draw on Greek philosophy for terms and modes of exposition, without which the educated classes could not be expected to listen. Yet the accepted culture was a part of the detested State; and there was a continual struggle between the claims of direct inspiration and the psalms of common life, and those of the rhetorical and philosophical levels. Major steps to the inclusion of Greek philosophy were made by Clement of Alexandria, who at the same time made the Church safe for bankers, and by Origen.

The great crisis which would probably have wrecked the Church if it had lacked the support of the State came in the 4th century: expressed by direct rebels such as the Donatists of north Africa, in whom theology and social objectives were closely fused, and by the indirect rebels, the secessionists or monks.* With the aid of the State, the Church put down the Donatists; and by patient work was able to tame monarchism into becoming a support. The greatest intellectual threat came in the work of Pelagius, a Briton, in the early 5th century, in which a monachal position was allied to an intense humanism. But the Augustinean attitudes, insisting on original sin and grace, won the day. Both sides of the controversy had their inner contradictions. Pelagius was moved by a belief in men and their powers, which had its roots in a sense of the unity of human and natural process; but he did not see how men could remain human in a corrupted and divided society, and he therefore supported the monachal ideal of withdrawal into systems unimplicated in any way with the State. The stumbling-block for all such systems was sex and marriage; for as soon as a man accepted family-emotion he began to compromise with the world. Yet without sex the life of a man came to a halt. The monachal position thus harmonised with the conviction of world-end and last-judgment; for if the world was going to end tomorrow, what did it matter if one brought the wheel of generation to a stop? On the other hand, the Augustinian attitudes insisted on the omnipresence of original sin in order to put all power of grace in the hands of the Church, where alone men were safe, and thus paradoxically acclimatised men to accept the world with all its corruptions as something that could not fundamentally be changed. There were two worlds, one of earth and one of heaven, one of men and one of God. For Pelagius there was only one

---

* An important heretic was Mani, who began preaching about 242 and met Magians; he travelled widely, may even have reached India and China. His disciples in S. Babylonia were related to the Mandaeans and the early Christian elements associated with John the Baptist. His system was sharply and darkly dualistic, and his church had two levels, the elect and the listeners. His faith burst out in two big waves:3-7th and 9-14th cs. Aspects of it appeared in the great peasant heresies, Paulician, etc. Mani himself was a skilled painter and enjoined painting as part of his ritual. Through the destructionof Manichaean works it is hard to be sure, but their influence may well have underlain the rise of illumination at Bagdad, 9th c. and later Persian art.

world in the sense that men must give up a divided existence and take wholly the way of salvation; to accept a Church which was 'in the world' was to accept the world and casuistically to fritter away all the reality of the Christian message of brotherhood in a series of deadening compromises.

Baptism and Martyrdom. The inner crisis of the Church, we have seen, all revolved round the failure of the second coming to appear in quick succession after the crucifixion. Once it was felt that the pattern of death and renewal, collapse and last judgment, was not going to actualise itself at once in history, the devotee had to adapt himself one way or another to society. He had either to compromise and take thought for the morrow, or to withdraw into a lonely cell or a group united in labour and the rejection of generation. The problem of the relation of the Son to the Father then cropped up in ways which could not be solved by the terms used in the Gospels. It was no longer possible to imagine the son of mercy fully and immediately united with the father of justice in a stable world-judgment. The agony went on, the crucifixion never ended, the ritual pattern coincided with life only in its first half, the half defining pain and death. And so a complex set of tensions was born round the Father-Son relationship, which issued in the dogma of the Trinity and the endless theological arguments to which it gave rise.

The problem became finally mysterious when the Church accepted the State and provided its sanction. The early Christians could not have conceived this situation; for they were not in a position to distinguish the State as a political category from the actual state, the Roman State with its imperial cult, which had riveted division and oppression on men. Thus it was possible for the compromising hierarchial Church to slide imperceptibly into the position where it could accept the State as long as the pagan cult was dropped. But in doing so, it struck a blow at the heart of the original impulse, the conviction of the State by its very nature as evil.

In the early Church the baptismal rite was the moment of profound choice when, as in all initiation-ritual, the devotee consciously left one level of life behind and entered into another. It was prepared for by fasting and vigils, and the whole body was immersed—'so that each of the saints by sharing in Christ may be born a Christ', as Methodios says. 'We give thanks for being made not only Christians but Christ', adds Augustine. Christ's own birthday was thus, not the day of his birth from Mary, but the day of his baptism in the Jordan. Not till the 4th century, after the Church's establishment, did the festival of the Virgin Birth come into being to displace the Baptismal Birth. In Egypt, Armenia and Mesopotamia, the new festival was merely added to the other, and both were held on January 6th, the Jordan date. When the State-Church had a more thorough control of things, the Virgin Birth was moved to December 25th, the day of pagan festival of the Birth of the Sun.

A crucial break was thus made with apostolic traditions. The practice had also crept in of baptising babies. Tertullian knew it as commonly done, though he thought it a bad thing. In early days, further, the practice had been to combine baptisms with the festivals of Easter or Pentacost, so as to stress the initiation-experience and the collective hope.

Christ was the supreme martyr, whose cult unified the Church. But each local group also needed its own martyr, its own testimony to the need of the new life. He was their hero, and his death-day was the birthday of both himself and his followers into a life which was not that of the corrupted world. The community assembled at his tomb for a yearly sacramental meal, which was their renewed pledge of union and resistance. The ritual was substantially that of the pagan Hero, with a new orientation. The anti-Christian sophist, Eunapios, says in the 4th century, 'Pickled heads and mouldy bones have

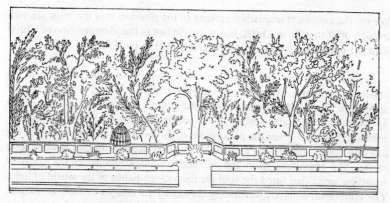

Garden scene: Rome, villa ad Gallinas.

become the new gods of the Roman people'. The martyrs were felt to have the right to a direct hearing by God, so that they might 'call on him to bring all things to an end'. This position was set out in *Revelation* as well as works like *Enoch*, where the martyrs demand immediate vengeance and are to get it as soon as their number is complete. Thus, for the delayed second coming, there was substituted the idea of the fulfilment of the list of the martyrs.

A community that lacked a martyr and his relics was no true community; it lacked its essential witness to catch God's ear and hasten the end of the world. And inevitably magical ideas gathered round the relics, which were used in divination. Trafficking in bones began, forbidden already in 381 and 386. With the Church's triumph, the great cities vied in collecting relics, and Rome's special sanctity lay in its possession of a large amount of the Blood of the Martyrs. But Christianity had been the creation of the eastern section of the empire, and there it was, apart from Rome, that the martyrs had been massed.

Asceticism. *Askesis* drew much of its strength from a horror of sex as the force compelling compromise with the world. The family was considered the arch-enemy of holiness and the Christian virtues. But there were other elements present. The ascetic felt himself perpetually representing and miming the passion of Christ, which in turn expressed the unrelieved suffering of the labouring masses. Cyprian declares:

The body is not cherished in the mines with couch and cushions, but with the refreshment and solace of Christ. The frame wearied out with labours lies prostrate on the ground, but it is no penalty to lie down with Christ. Your limbs unbathed are foul and filth-disfigured, but within spiritually cleansed though the flesh is defiled. There is lack of bread, but man lives not on bread alone but on the word of God. Shivering, you lack clothes, but he who puts Christ on is abundantly clothed and adorned.

We see the argument insensibly moving to the position that the poor are well enough off if they have Christ, but its origin lies in the identification of Christ with the oppressed who have no part or parcel in the State.

Askesis is the normal Greek term for exercise, training practise as an athlete or craftsman. An ascetic was anyone trained to an art or trade; but the term came more and more to refer to the athlete. *Askesis* was the way of life by which a man trained himself for victory in one of the great festival-contests. The ascetic was the popular hero, the winner at games. But when the free city failed, *askesis* was applied to spiritual matters. In the Mithraic cult we see the transition from the athletic training-grounds to the spiritual wrestling arena that fitted the soul for the victory-palms of the world of light. The symbolism entered Christianity through Paul and was widely employed. Tertullian explained how the *askesis* of the faithful was a form of preparation for the cruelties that the State would inflict:

That is how one is hardened against prison, hunger, thirst, privations and agonies. The martyr's dried-up skin will serve as a cuirass, the iron claws will slide over it as over thick horn. Such a man will he be who by fasting has often come close to death and discharged himself of his blood, that heavy and importunate burden for a soul impatient to be free.

But after the establishment *askesis* became an end in itself, the only way in which the faithful could prove their devotion. Christ's Athlete is a basic phrase in the *Lives of Saints* to express the nature of the striving for perfection, the unceasing repudiation of the world's ways.*

---

* The idea of intercession was pagan. Tomb-inscriptions show people praying to their dead for aid; early Christians likewise invoked their family-dead. The martyrs gathered such attitudes to themselves with a great new force.

11 : Byzantium

Byzantium. Constantine gave the empire a new start, tying the peasant to the land and backing the baronial landlords, stabilising the currency on a gold standard, creating mobile armies added to defences-in-depth, and attempting to arrest town-life on a fixed guild-system with hereditary trades. He chose a strategically strong site for his new capital and recognised the need for the State to take over the Christian Church in order to gain a new powerful cementing force. So far from the emperor losing stature, he Our Lord, had important new sanctions added to his semi-divine role. In the west the State went to pieces under the constant pressure of barbarian invasion, and the dark-ages began in the fusion of the local Roman landlords with tribal nobles. In Britain, where alone the natives fought back against the invaders, the Anglo-Saxons, who were at a much lower level of development than the Franks, did not amalgamate with Romano-Celtic landlords; and the Celts were driven into the western regions.

In the East, despite moments of great strain, the Roman State survived till the treacherous attack of the Crusaders in 1204. And so there survived also the *collegia* of artisans, the slave-economy (for a while), and town-life. We may distinguish four main stages: the dynasties of Constantine, Theodosios, Justinian and Heraklios (306-717); the Isaurians and Amorians (716-867), the Iconoclasts; the Macedonians (867-1057), the Doukases and Comnenoi (1057-1185), with the Angeli as the final tailing-off (1185-1204). In the first stage there are setbacks after the Constantinean stabilisation; under Justinian the empire expands again; then come heavy losses and threats on the eastern frontiers from Persians and Arabs, and on the northern from Slavs. In the second stage, the State has to be reorganised to meet the challenge of Islam and drastic changes are made. In the third, there is a fresh stabilisation on the landed magnates, with a reassertion of absolutism by the emperor. In the fourth, the empire loses much of its splendour and power, and settles down towards the position of being merely one more among the many European feudal States. So far from staying in one fixed condition, politically and culturally, the Roman Empire as it survived in the East went through a continual change, with many brilliant readaptations of its forms, and on the whole gave the lead and acted as the pace-maker for the rest of Europe.

We can note here only a few points from Byzantine history. First, in the early phases there grew up political parties organised as circus-factions or clubs which were linked with the territorial demes, the leading citizens of which provided the money for various liturgies or state-works. (In the late 6th or early 7th century the demes were officially organised for city-defence.) The clubs controlled the games and had their colours; they existed in all the main towns. There were four colours, Blues and Greens, Reds and Whites; but the first pair were the main adversaries, the Reds being linked with the Greens and the Whites with the Blues. The Blue bosses were the landed nobility of old Byzantium; the Green bosses, the rich merchants and employers of the new city, who had close connections with their fellows in the other eastern cities.

The bosses of one party wanted to grab the power and property of the bosses of the other; one of the main fields of conflict was the distribution of taxes. At the court the eunuchs, who often gained posts of high importance, were mostly easterners, with the outlook of the trade-towns and connected with the finance-bureaucracy; they were thus able to exert influence on behalf of the Greens. Also, most of the economic experts that the State needed came from the ranks of the Greens. Even Justinian, a Blue, had to use for the control of his finances John of Cappadocia, who had risen as a Green.

At moments of political crisis, especially at an emperor's death, the factions were liable to clash. And political and economic differences were exacerbated by religious ones; thus the Blues were orthodox, but the Greens were often Monophysite, especially at Antioch. The climax of the faction-struggles was the Nika (Conquer) riots under Justinian.

One interesting point is that the fourfold division with its colours had a cosmic significance. At Antioch the factions stood for the four city-quarters; and Syria may well be the source of the whole Byzantine faction-organisation. John Malalas, an historian with many popular elements, links the factions with the origins of Rome and considers the four colours to represent the four elements. When Domitian had earlier tried to bring in the imperial colours, gold and purple, the people objected so strongly that the emperor dropped the idea. A Jewish *midrash* testifies to the political significance of the colours. (Constantine VI noted the hair-colours in the names of Pecheneg tribes, corresponding to the sky-region towards which the tribe in question was oriented; and Wallachian towns in the 19th century still had quarters marked by colours.)

Secondly, we may note the comparative strength of the village-commune in the east, and the way in which the Slav invasions in the 7th century gave a new life to the free peasantry. Thus the empire had a source of peasant soldiers which made possible the great second phase of its history. When the Arabs first attacked Byzantium, the peasants of Asia took a hand; they shared out the land of runaway landlords and had something to fight for. They carried on the war as guerillas in the hills, and from Taurus to the Lebanons they kept on launching attacks on the Moslems. They were described as a 'Wall of steel'. The Greeks called them *apelatai*, Clubmen; the Moslems, *mardaites*, Rebels. Nothing at all similar occurred in the West.

Thirdly, there is the magnificent period of the Iconoclastic emperors, especially Constantine V, in which drastic reforms were carried out. Monasticism was attacked, as well as the cults of the saints and the Virgin; and religious art was banned. A great stimulus to secular and humanist art and thought was given; but the inability of the emperors to rely in the last resort on the peasants rather than on the landlords weakened and then destroyed the Iconoclast State; orthodoxy triumphed in the end and the magnates came fully into their own under the Macedonians.

Fourthly, the persistence of the village-commune and the free peasants, while making possible the Iconoclast State and its reforms, also led to a great new wave of heresies, when the political situation hardened afresh. The Paulician heresy expressed the rebellious emotions of the Asian peasants; the Bogomile, that of the peasants of the Balkans. The creeds were generally dualistic. The Paulicians had two absolute principles; the Bogomiles tried to avoid such a definite dichotomy, but they took the universe to be wholly the devil's work. The attitudes were ascetic. The Paulicians had held a series of fortified towns on the Armenian border and hoped to conquer all Asia Minor; they sought to maintain the apostolic bases, with a system of initiation leading to an equalitarian brotherhood. Their towns had *isopoliteia*, equal rights among themselves. The first work that the Macedonian reaction set itself was to destroy and massacre them. The Bogomiles lacked the resilient hopeful element of the free Paulician village-communes; but they rejected churches as the abodes of devils and respected the memory of the Iconoclast emperors; they accepted no distinction of lay and clerical, and women had the same status as men.

Finally, in the revived Byzantine State of the 14th century, the Zealots made an effort to take power in the cities. The poor folk rose in 1342, threw out the nobles, and took over the administration; but after a hard fight they were betrayed and defeated. (The artisans had doubtless been affected by news of the rising at Genoa, which in 1339 had overthrown the oligarchy there; but the Zealot movement went back at least as far as the 12th century.)

The New Centre in Art. Into the entangled mixture of forms arising over the empire from the 3rd century on, as local and provincial types emerged out of the breaking-up classical idiom, there came with Christianity a new unifying force. This took two aspects. One we may call the symbolising or illustrative aspect, which was largely taken over from Judaism, as has been proved by the discoveries at Dura-Europos, a frontier-town on the middle Euphrates. The synagogue there shows a grandiose effort to express the messianic hope in a series of paintings with interrelated motives or themes: the whole setting out the history and significance of Judaism. Here is the same system as we find put to Christian uses in the later Byzantine or medieval church, where the mosaics, carvings and paintings all come together to express a philosophy of life, a vision of history, a ratification of the cosmic nature of the church-form.

The second aspect lies in that form itself. And here the impulse comes from the cult of the martyr. The church is the place of initiation, daily worship or ritual repetition of Christ's death-rebirth, and communion with the god. But for each local group, as we saw, the general Christian idea is given cohesive force and point of contact through the local martyr and his cult. The martyr's tomb, the site of the yearly deathbirth-day and its meal, is one with the altar of Christ which commemorates his last-supper, crucifixion and resurrection. The martyr-cult had its own suitable form of architecture, developed from the pagan *heroon*. Originally the *mensa* or tomb lay open to the sky, though enclosed with walls and owning a sort of grotto or apse as a funerary *cubiculum*. Add a roofing (to take the place of the sky) and you naturally select a rounded or polygonal form.*

The great *martyria* were those connected most directly with Christ, but the form was everywhere in the east needed to express the new force of upheaving life. Already under Constantine the impact is clear and strong: in the Octagon of Antioch, which succeeded a Heröon of the Sacred Palace, in the Holy Apostles at Byzantium, which constituted the collective *heroon* of the new religion, in the great Palestinian foundations of the Holy Sepulchre, Golgotha, the Nativity, which merged the central plan with the basilican, and in the Roman monuments, which showed the *basilica* transformed to *martyrion*, with the sacred corpse under the apse and as the altar's foot. With the 4th century relics came into the churches, and soon a relic under the altar was a necessity; otherwise the building was felt to lack the sanctifying witness against iniquity.

The result was a great new dynamic force brought into the achitectural sphere, working on the new possibilities which we have noted the Romans developing out of concrete. At first the *martyrion* had been independent of the church, though set close-by or even against it. The dynamic change occurred when it moved inside. The cupola'd basilica represented the effort 'to assure to the aspect of cultural edifices a likeness to the *martyria* made fashionable by the fervour of the masses'. (The Baptistery, as the place of entry into the new life, had close affinities with the *martyrion*; it tended therefore to be circular or polygonal.)

In the west, despite the intrusion of Byzantine forms in Italy, the situation was not the same, because of the lack of martyrs. The main form is basilican: that is, based on the Roman secular hall, a rectangle. Not an exact copy; for the typical town hall was an oblong with inner colonnades facing all four sides,

---

* The origins go far back in tomb-forms, e.g. effort to put a round cover over a rectangular plan, transform a square into an octagon, by corbels astride one another: Vetulonia (van Essen, pl IV, 2). The Greeks in Mycenean days triumphantly grappled with the cupola, then avoided it.

a complete ambulatory—and sometimes with apse, or even two apses, cut off from the main body by the colonnades. The church-form was based rather on the type of hall devised for mystery-cults, such as Mithras, where the pillars

Funerary paintings from the Fayum.

inside are parallel with the long sides, allowing a free movement from the entry to the further (and often apsed) end. The result then is a nave down the middle, with an aisle on either side. Into the oblong church a crypt may be inserted as a *martyrion*, without effect on the general structure, though with a slow attraction of burials towards the altar. In the east no burials inside the church were allowed and the relics had a dynamic effect on the structure, without relation to the altar. (The western inhumation *ad sanctos* ended by modifying the eastern apse with radiating chancels, deambulatories, and so on, increasing the difference from the eastern church-types.)

The climax of the Byzantine experiments came under Justinian. We may briefly consider three of his churches. Holy Apostles at Byzantium was a detached Greek cross vaulted with five domes. Here we see the domes erected on square walls, using pendentives (spheric triangles) to connect curve and straight line. S. Vitale at Ravenna was an octagon with inner ambulatory and gallery, and with a dome raised over the central space on squinches (small arches across the corners, set on top of each other). There was also a *narthex* or porch, with apses at either end and a projecting altar flanked by two circular forms. The domed centre was upheld and separated from the ambulatory, not by mere arches, but by seven apsed shapes (the eighth is the chancel) each cut through by three small arches. The effect is to break the separating forms with a flood of light and shadow that lifts the whole inner structure into a dimension of changing floating space. Finally, St. Sophia at Byzantium, built on the space cleared after the damage of the Nika riots, was planned by

Anthemios of Tralles, with Isidore of Miletos as assistant. Here the most dramatic and powerful union of the basilican and the central plan was devised and triumphantly carried out in less than five years.

Inside, the longitudinal constructions passed fluidly into the great central-ising dome which pulled everything radially up into itself and swam aloft like a winged crown. The pillar has become, not a structural unit, but a decorative and dynamic adjunct. Those below, set in curves, lift the eye to their gilt capitals; those above, upholding galleries, run into the bright upper walls of porphyry-plaques. The four triangular pendentives, each with its mosaic of winged cherubim, move out to sustain the dome's cornice where Christ Pantokrator looms up to judge the world. Over it all, high in curved mosaic, broods the Mother with Child, blue, white and gold, on a red throne with green footstall; and at dome-summit swims Christ on the starry heavens. The roof, covered with pure gold, mixes its lights with the many hues of the marbles, green, white, serpentine, crocusgold, red-and-white, whitemisted rose, porphyry: a blending of fires of stone, night-lighted with gold.

The great effect is of space and light—the aerial depths aided by the half-domes, the forty windows. The enormous centrality of light is saved from bareness by the aisles with galleries, screened from the dome by five arches on the ground floor and seven on the upper. The light-burst is balanced by mysterious distances and rhythmical recessions.

We know what effect was intended, and what the men of the 6th century felt at the spectacle, from the prose account by Prokopios and the long verse-panegyric by Paul the Silentiary. Prokopios discusses the 'mass and harmon-ious proportions', the simultaneous effect of breadth and length, the light-burst seeming to explode from within. 'It appears somehow to float in air on no solid base; it seems poised on high to the peril of those within; yet in fact it is braced with exceptional strength and stability.' The dome 'less reposes on the masonry than is hung by a golden chain from the highest heaven'—a neoplatonic metaphor that correctly states the symbolism. The massing colours concentrate on the walls all the essences of blossoming growth: 'a meadow with flowers in fullest bloom. . . the purple, the green tint, the stones of glowing crimson, and those with the flash of white, and again those which Nature, like a painter, varies with the richest of colour-contrasts'. Paul com-posed his poem for the completion of the building: a paean to the colour and light concentrated in the building, both by day and during the evening-services with the myriad lamps. He sees the gleaming as a Round Dance of Lights. (Diogenes, bishop of Amisos, describes a church as a *chorostasia* in his line: 'Rest by the dancing-circuit of the blest'.) The church is simultaneously the universe, the heavenly mount, with the circling lights of the stars, and the paradisiac garden, the abode of the blest.

The unity of conception and form, derived from these images given dyn-amic life by the idea of the *martyrion*, is in turn linked with the dramatic function of the church. The ceaseless drama is expressed in the liturgy, with its suggestions and proliferations of dramatic moments, scenes and symbols. The churches are

doing the work of theatre-halls, divided into two sections, one reserved for the immaterial, spiritual, symbolic, spectacle, and the other surrounding the first in the form of the two-storeyed galleries for the audience. Hence the symmetry of plan and the close link between the different compartments of the interior, the partitions of which are pierced by a multitude of large openings. (BRUNOV)

Christian painting in the Cemetery of SS. Marcellus and Peter, Rome: Vibia entering the Garden of Paradise.

We may add that, in the moment of liturgic participation, the two sections become one.

The poets of this period, to express the life they feel in a work of art, do not use terms to suggest that it is a deceptive likeness—i.e. painted flowers that attract bees—as the Greeks used to do. Their image is of a dynamic fusion. Thus, Agathias, describing a picture that one Thomas painted of a harlot in Byzantium, ends:

> To show his soul's desire, he used his art;
> for, even as melts the wax, so melts his heart.

And here are two epigrams by Paul the Silentiary:

> Art and not nature gave this Bacchant gladness;
> for with the stone it fused the burst of madness.

> He's caught her eyes, just caught them, but O her hair!
> O the supreme lustre of her skin is gone.
> Paint first the dazzle-sheen of the gold sun,
> then Theodora's flesh will glisten there.

And the painter feels himself a part of the world he depicts. Eulalios, creator of the mosaics in the Holy Apostles, depicted himself in the scene of the holy women at the tomb, 'in his usual dress and looking exactly as he appeared when he was at work' on the mosaics.

Mosaics were the natural artform for such a world. They represented forms on the walls and yet set them in a space which was neither on the walls, behind them or in front; the rich broken colours, in the varied sweep of light and shadow, gave the walls an insubstantial weight, a flickering surface, an unanalysable depth. The forms were heavily present and yet rapt into a spirit-world which surrounded the earth and gave it density, mystery, an ever present force of hope and fear.

Iconoclasts. After its great period, Byzantine architecture settled down to a ground plan of the equal-armed cross inscribed in a square—with central dome and four smaller domes at the corners. The high vaulted transepts terminating in curved or triangular façades clarified the lines of construction and gave architects a chance to consider the outside as well as the inside of a building. The growing stress on height sends the dome soaring. Forms tend to move upwards, a series of lessening vaults ascending to the main dome; and slender columns replace the weighty piers. A work like St. Sophia needed a certain solid cubical mass, to control the variety and splendour of light. Now such forms might grow dull; the builders seek a fluidity of relieving curves in a triple eastern apse or in hemicycles at the ends of the narthex.

But the new impulse which arrived in art came from the break caused by the Iconoclast reforms, not from any gradual development of 6th-7th century forms. The hieratic was thrown overboard. Hellenistic and classical attitudes were revived, and all sorts of secular and genre themes as well as portrait-sculpture were encouraged. Constantine V encouraged historical paintings; nature-motives filled the churches; even humour and satire appeared. The bitter caricatures that George Asbestos made of the orthodox were later burned at the Eighth Council; a mixture of elegant fantasy and humorous realism appears in the Khlidor psalter, where the proud who 'set their mouth against the heavens and their tongue walketh through the earth' are represented by two bearded men with long tongues on the ground and upper lips beaked to the sky (which is a cross-surmounted bowl). Fantasy was let loose in works like the *Physiologus* with its sirens, nymphs, centaurs. At the same time decorative elements flowed in from the Bagdad caliphate's art—itself a synthesis of Greek, Mesopotamian and Persian elements.

All the major art of the Iconoclasts was destroyed. But we can piece together the evidence which demonstrates that the late 7th and early 8th century was:

a period of intense creative activity in the Empire, when new plastic conceptions were appearing in one technique after another, and the forms were being worked out which were to be exploited to the full after the close of the iconoclast controversy. (PIERCE and TYLER)

When in such artworks as the head of Christ from the *narthex* of St. Sophia, dated 886-912, we see an altogether new depth of human realisation and concreteness of form, we understand how the artists who took up the orthodox orders could not help but bring to their definitions the humanity which they had learned in the Iconoclast period, which, with varying degree of harshness towards the orthodox, had lasted over 150 years. A quatrain gives us the feeling of the new union with his material that the artist felt as a result of the long struggle:

> I, also Peter, who have not been granted
> sight of the Lord's livegiving Tomb,
> carved it here on this disk, where, bending
> low, I see Christ's body clear.

The artists were aware in a new way of classical balance, and sought to work out rhythms based on the human body, as well as deepening the human content of Christ, Mary, the Saints, and achieving something of spatial depth. In the 9th-10th centuries we meet a large number of single figures treated with a new realism and arranged according to a set of rules, mainly in niches or the vaulted parts, contrasting with the quieter tones of the marble-lined walls. A consistent scale of sizes, optical devices to control distortions, and differentiated keys of modelling to stand up against the lighting conditions, all combined to bring about a unified effect. Hellenistic elements strongly affected book-illustration, but also influenced wall-decoration, to which scenic aspects were added. The culmination came in the lovely meditative grace of the Daphni mosaics, with their gently flowing rhythms and calm but intense relationships.

The Macedonian period is usually taken by historians as the great period of Byzantium, because of the new start that the feudal system was able to get after the work of the Iconoclasts, with expansions based on exploiting the social and economic capital that had been heaped-up. From the 9th to the 12th centuries, however, there was marked dwarfing of the church's proportions and a weakening of the functional elements in the structure. Dogmatic and liturgic schemes tended in the 10th-11th centuries to control the schemes of decoration once dominated by a concept of history; then came a slow revival of narrative. The increasing poverty of the Byzantine world from the 11th century led to a greater use of fresco painting, which in whole or part drove out mosaic and broke down balance-systems based on mosaic and marble; at the same time the change of medium intensified, if indeed it was not also initiated by, a desire for more mobility and interrelation of forms with environment, an extension of sympathies.

The 12th century saw a great outflow of Byzantine influences to the east, north and west. But this we shall consider later.

Literature. Byzantine literature cannot be compared with the art for greatness and scope; but it played an important function in keeping various elements of the Graeco-Roman heritage alive over the difficult centuries. In the first stage there was much valuable historical writing, which ranged from Prokopios with his keen sardonic mind and his study of the classics such as

Thucydides, to popular chroniclers like John Malalas who saw only an odd hurlyburly. One sentence will give the flavour of Prokopios' astringency:

Anxious to unite all men in the same opinion about Christ, he indiscriminately destroyed dissidents, and that under the pretext of piety; for he did not think the killing of men was murder unless they happened to hold his own religious views.

The popular elements in Malalas also appeared in legendary histories of the Trojan War or Alexander, compilations or proverbs, animal fantasies. Theology was developed by the three great Cappadocian Fathers of the 4th century; John of the Golden Mouth added a more strongly social note. Byzantine mysticism developed its stress on 'becoming God' in the initiation-experience, on the organic unity of man and nature, and, at the same time, on God-Nature as composed of a series of hierarchical levels. Many Lives of Saints were genuine and vivid biographies. Poetry gained a new life in Egypt from the 4th century, in Claudian who wrote in Latin, and Nonnos who wrote in Greek. Nonnos' vast *Dionysiaca* was a romantic epic of transformations, which linked with alchemic ideas. (Accentual rhythms are appearing, and the main aspects of Nonnos' versification are an elegant lightness and supple speed.) George of Pisidia in *Hexameron* sought to give symbolic depth to the Persian Wars by seeing Heraklios as a demiurge recreating the world. A strong Aristotelian element appeared among heretics like the Nestorians and Mono-physites, with a keen interest in medicine. John of Nikiou depicted in clear popular style the tumults or heretical mass-resistance to the empire in his native land, Egypt.

Out of the conflicts of the Iconoclast epoch came the need for the orthodox to put their case with a new fullness. John of Damaskos, who grew up under Islam, composed the *Fountain of Knowledge*, the first comprehensive exposition of Christian dogma which underlay all similar works later done in the east or the west, and which Aquinas took as his model. John sees all human development as a series of phases, each essential in its time and place, with Christ's revelation cleaving history but not ending it; more important even than the sacred texts are the ceaseless labours of men to grow along the new way.

The classical revival initiated by the Iconoclasts saw men turning back to Homer and Plato, with large-scale work of encyclopaedic compilation and codification. Important influences were flowing in from the east, from Persia whence Indian tales were handed on. Satire in prose and verse revived; and out of the sagas of the marchlands, where Paulicians and Clubmen and frontier-guards were to be found, came the rousing popular epic of *Digenis Akritas*, with its theme that peace must be won by a union of Christian and Arab, its mixture of chivalric and popular elements, its dream of the edenic garden. Lyrical forms were developing among the people. When the Byzantines rose up against Michael V, 'the folk of city and marketplace', says Psellos, 'made up dance-groups and composed *tragoudai* on these events, improvising the songs on the spot'.

These trends were strengthened from the 11th century onward. In that century the scholar Michael Psellos, with his omnivorous interests, brilliantly anticipated the men of the Italian Renascence and in his *Chronographia* wrote a court-history of remarkable psychological insight: something quite new with its pictorial clarity, its dramatic verve, its sustained characterisation. It is biography with a new depth, and at the same time an imaginative creation akin to the novel.

But when I came near the altar that Michael was gripping, and when I saw the two fugitives—the Emperor clinging to the holy table of the Word itself and the Nobilis-simos standing up on the right of the altar, both of them changed in clothes and spirit, both utterly shamed—then I felt the last trace of resentment ebb from my heart . . .
The crowd that had burst into the church gathered in a circle and stood round the two men like a pack of wild beasts wanting to devour them; and I, standing against the rail on the right of the altar went on grieving . . .

Psellos, the detached observer, who yet feels himself humanly part of all that happens, has brought something new into literature.

Dramatic Forms. Byzantine culture was warmly alive with popular forms, even though these generally failed to break through into decisively new expression. One source of drama came from Syria in the homily, a rhetorical form of bringing biblical history to life. Some homilies have long dialogues which paraphrase a brief exchange in the sacred texts; others are new creations, though generally linked with the texts, and may give an episode in several scenes; a third group consist of fully dramatised episodes in the life of Jesus and Mary, followed by oratorical bursts in a strongly rhythmical style close to that of the hymn-writers. The homily-drama developed its own systems, which are shown at length in the *Enkomion* attributed to Proklos of Byzan-tium; but it remained tethered to the sermon. We may assume that it was rendered by various voices in the church, and with the aid of the choir; probably gesture and movement were used. The *enkomion*-drama seems further a part of the *panegyris* reserved for great liturgical commemorations. There appear to have been two cycles, each a triology: Annunciation, Nativity, Flight to Egypt, and Baptism of Jesus, Passion, Hell-harrowing. The icono-clast period ended the development.

Behind the homily-drama lay the Syrian *sogitha* or homily-canticle. An extended use of *sogitha* themes appears in the twelve Nativity hymns of Sophronios, patriarch of Jerusalem from 534-8, with Joseph, Mary, Narrator as characters. The mime also impacted on the homily-drama and brought about a humorously realistic treatment of the themes of Jesus' conception and birth. Thus, Mary mistakes the Angel Gabriel for a young man trying to seduce her and warns him of Joseph's jealousy; when Joseph is upset at finding Mary with child and upbraids her, she teases him.

After the iconoclasts there was a development of mystery-plays. Further, the secular drama had never ceased in Byzantium. Some verse-plays were written for recitation. The long *Christos Paschon* (in part a *cento* from Euripedes) shows what is no doubt an unconsciously cinematic technique of action emerging direct from narrative. All sorts of guisings went on, even inside the churches, sometimes in animal-forms; the guilds too carried out maskings. But

we must resign ourselves to saying that of the Byzantine stage we know only one thing certainly: that it existed under the form of a Revue and Variety Theatre, farce-comedy and political satire. (VOGT)

That it strongly affected the more barbarous west there is no doubt. Thus, the *Bombinaria* or *Bomaria* was the festival of the Castanets or Rattles, instruments favoured by comedians; from Justinian's time derivations of the word were used to define activities that mocked at Church or State; and the same name was given to pieces of the popular Venetian theatre played during

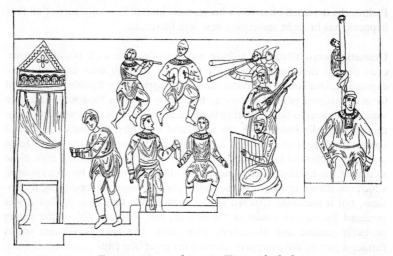

Eastern mimes: fresco in Kiev cathedral.

wedding-banquets. There seems no doubt Venice had borrowed from Byzantium; and Byzantine mimes most probably did much to provide the basis of the *Comedia dell'Arte* as well as various Indian and especially Chinese shows. As to the liturgic drama the western forms show every sign of having been offshoots of the Syriac-Byzantine creations—partly through translation and adaptation, and partly through the introduction of the homily-drama into regions of the west, in particular Italy, where the empire still ruled.

The Byzantine Nativity cycle were dramatic in the same sense as the Italian oratorio at the beginning of the seventeenth century. . . The same Syriac patterns, we may assume, influenced hymn-writers in Western Europe, where from the sixth century onwards the Syrians had colonies in Italy, France and Spain. It is an established fact that Syrian iconography influenced French art from the fifth to the twelfth centuries. The representation of the Nativity and the Adoration of the Magi in western sculpture, ivory and miniatures can be traced back to Syro-Hellenistic formulas. The mystery play of the Magi, which appears for the first time in an eleventh century MS. of St. Martial of Limoges, may be derived from the same Syrian source which inspired Sophronios. The great achievement of the West consisted in carrying the semi-dramatic form of the East on to the stage of the mystery-play. (WELLESZ)

Music. In music again it was Syria that provided the essential method which was to take the place of the dead classical one. The oldest versions of both Byzantine and Gregorian melodies go back to a common source, the churches of Antioch and Jerusalem, with the Synagogue behind them. Both western plainsong and Byzantine liturgical music represent new elements among the Greek or Latin-speaking peoples of the empire. The new music was characterised by the recurrence of certain formulas, not by a basis in any particular mode, and many formulas in both Byzantine and Ambrosian (pre-Gregorian) chant are identically or closely related, with their roots in the Syrian-Palestinian region.

This church music was wholly vocal. At first readers and precentors converted from the Synagogue were used, who brought over the Jewish methods of antiphonal singing and solo psalms. From early days the Church was fiercely opposed to instrumental music as a blind form of spirit-possession, dedicated to carnality; but singing could not be barred out. The established Church however did its best to control even that, and to reduce the popular improvised element which had been the keynote of religious feeling in apostolic days.

The main popular methods were based on cantillation or *ekphronesis* (elevated recitation). In Byzantine music the *enechemata*, the cue words and closing formulas of psalm-tones, were the essential elements, and to the end the psalmodic method dominated. Syrian psalmody had been strongly affected both by Greek and Semitic forms. The modification it introduced consisted of merging broken-down hellenistic elements with elements making for accentual forms from the Jews. The Syrians thus devised metres and stanzas with one note for each syllable of the words: a transitional form between the strict quantitative metres of the ancient Greeks and the strict accentual ones of later Europe. (In psalmody the unit is the whole sentence; and the parallelism of the scriptural phrases brought about the dichotomic structure of the music.)

The function of psalmody was to draw the congregation into the worship, to weld the mass into a single body of praise. And the psalm itself was opposed to the more sophisticated literary forms which expressed the attitudes of the upper classes; it was held to be the utterance of the workers. Thus, John of the Golden Mouth says that while the High Powers (angels) prefer hymns, the common folk should chant psalms all day, on journeys, in the workshop, at home: 'no artificial accompaniment or musical study is necessary'. The monastic trends exalted the psalm as the one non-corruptive form of expression.

However, an important new impetus was given to the hymn and its musical form by heretics such as the Gnostic Bardasanes, who knew classical Greek poetry and worked by modifying the older patterns. His biographer says of his son, Harmonios, that he was 'well instructed in Greek literature and the first to subject his native language to metres and musical laws; he adapted it to choirs of singers, the way the Syrians now commonly chant, using indeed not the words of Harmonios but his tunes'. The orthodox like the Syrian Ephraem had to reply and use the same methods, which were closely linked with the dance.

Ephraem rose up against the games and dances of the young folk, and he gathered the Daughters of the Covenant and taught them songs, both refrain songs (?) and alternating songs . . . and each time the Daughters of the Covenant gathered in the churches on the festivals and Sundays . . . and he like a father, teaching them various kinds of song and the change (? modulation) of songs, until the whole city gathered about him. (YAQUB OF SERUG)

Many other heretical groups, being close to the people, were distinguished for their hymns—the Markionites, Paul of Samosata, and the Arians. John of the Golden Mouth thus denounces the period of Arian supremacy: 'Psalmody is silenced, blasphemous tongues babble from the sacred thrones. Add to this, dancing and screaming. Our holy mysteries are blasphemed'. That is, there was an influx of popular forms, connected with dancing. Again the orthodox had to retort and use the reprobated form. The *Life of St. Auxentios* tells us how that saint, who came from Syria, taught hymns to the pilgrims frequenting his hermitage. Using plain tunes from a psalm or paraphrase, which would be remembered and disseminated, he sang the first hemistich of a line; the pilgrims answered with the second.

The main forms in Byzantine liturgy were the *troparion*, which by the 5th century evolved out of free interpolated refrains into a strophic structure and which was later enlarged into a hymn dealing with the event or saint commemorated in the day's office; the *kontakion*, a homily in verse of 18 or more similar stanzas; the *kanon*, introduced into the Morning Office, late in the 7th century, and made up of nine Odes (modelled on the nine Canticles from the scriptures). The *troparion* had been a big step forward, but the form was still unstable, based on the turning-points (beginning, middle and end) of the psalmodic chant in typical melisms: short melodic formulas. Certain melisms were playing a key-part, e.g. the jubilant rendering of the *Allelujah*, highly popular in Christian-Judaic circles. Even when anti-Jewish feeling was at its height, no one thought of throwing out this melism, which Jewish tradition and Christian exegesis agreed in considering a song of both man and angel, and which in fact derived from magical incantations such as the pre-Islamic Arabic trill *il ilil*. About the mid-4th century it was made a general mode of jubilation, a controlled musical version of the wild babbling esteemed in apostolic days.

The *kontakion* came from Syrian church-songs and was used at Byzantium to give a description of the festival's object; its greatest exponent was Romanos, the religious poet of the Justinianic age, who developed the form with much grace and strength. But though the *kontakion* represented musically a considerable advance on the *troparion*, it failed to break through into definitive new structures. Allied to the Hebrew *keroba*, it was based on a system of limited improvisations, on the prevalence of standing or wandering melisms. Byzantium thus, despite much refinement of the given bases, failed to achieve the integrations which the cruder west in time achieved; its music remained essentially melismatic. By the 11th century there were so many hymns that the Church gave orders for their composition to stop. But musical elaboration went on, with sterile embellishments and extended coloratura.

Its theory declared that the hymn was the Echo of Heavenly Harmony which the musician had managed to catch. When performed, it was a mystery-act turning the singers into angels and the church, the ritual-space, into heaven itself.*

Organ. The organ was common at Byzantium, used for circus-processions, weddings, receptions. At times the emperor had two of his gold organs at an entertainment; each faction had a silver one. The organ played as singers ended the acclamations, though at times it also accompanied singers. There were no harmonies, but some concords may have been used. The players employed both hands and in octaves, while other instruments brought in a sort of heterophony.

Organs were sent as gifts to the Frankish rulers in Gaul, with technicians to teach their use. Frankish craftsmen learned how to make the instrument, which was used to help the monkish teachers of plain-chant. The organ thus crept into the churches, growing in size, and the secular Byzantine instrument became ecclesiastical. But conservative Rome refused to use it, and even today the Sistine Chapel permits no organ. Thomas Aquinas disliked the instrument as a 'Judaising' thing. (Hymns too were suspected at Rome; the year 1000 had gone before the office-books there mentioned them, though they had long been popular in Gaul and Ireland.)

---

* Psellos attempted to state in pantheist terms the relation of music to the rhythms of life. 'We finally discover the movements of created beings follow a rhythmical, their voices an harmonic order, and that dances composed from both are well constructed . . . and then we observe that the power emanating from music is extended to everything'. He makes the Pythagorean connection with astronomy and finds 'connections between the order in our chants, rhythms or dances, and divine music'. 'The ancient Greeks had music for all social occasions', but 'the kind of music that occupies our minds today is only a faint echo' of what has been.

12: Asia and Africa

Mohammed. Around 600 A.D. there were many hermit ascetics called *hanifs* wandering in Arabia. Mohammed of the Quraish tribe, which had charge of the sacred megaliths at the national sanctuary of Mecca, was brought up by his uncle, with whom he made journeys into Syria. Till the age of forty he carried on trade at Mecca, married to a rich widow. Then he turned *hanif* and roamed in the desert; he began to hear voices and had a seizure in a cave, where he saw fiery letters on a cloth. He set about forming a group of followers, denounced the Mecca idols, and after many troubles established himself at Medina, carried out raids, and proclaimed the Holy War. Conquering Mecca, he overthrew the idols but kept the place as a pilgrim-centre. He announced the equality and brotherhood of all Moslems, finally 'One Prophet, one faith, for all the world'.

His messages were set down in the *Qu'ran*. The main point is that deity is One—Allah is simply *Al Ilah*, the Mighty. And the ideal believer is the *'abd* or slave, who submits absolutely to the absolute will. Religion is essentially a matter of revelation; revealed, it must be strictly obeyed. The *Qu'ran* accepted Moses and Jesus as important prophets, but saw the culmination in Moham-med. The five compulsory practices were recital of the creed, recital of the five daily prayers with ablutions, fasting (especially in the moon-month of Ramadan), almsgiving, and pilgrimage to Mecca. Usury, games of chance, pork, and alcohol were denounced; polygamy allowed. Sacerdotalism is at a minimum; any Moslem of good character may lead at prayers in the mosque, though there is usually an *imam*, known for piety and learning, attached.

Mohammed gave a dynamic unity to the Arabian tribes, who then burst outwards in an irresistible onslaught. In 634 they irrupted into Syria and defeated the Byzantine troops. The long struggle of Moslem and Christian had opened, which led to the fall of the Near East, North Africa and Spain to the Moslems. The Byzantine empire, with various ups and downs, held them out of the rest of Europe till the Crusaders, on the pretence of attacking the infidels, sacked the great city and destroyed vast quantities of works of art and manuscripts; and though the Greek forces were able to drive out the Latins and reconstitute the Byzantine State, their powers had been weakened, and in mid-15th century the Turks broke through into the Balkans.

The Arabs developed a rich culture, which achieved fine things of its own and did much to hand on elements of the Graeco-Roman civilisation to the west, especially through the Jews of Spain. In this respect its main achievements lay in carrying on the work of the Nestorian and other heretics, who had based their outlook on Aristotle and who were much interested in medicine and alchemy.

Alchemy. Alchemy was the key-science of the medieval world, representing the first stages of the effort to bring dynamic concepts into the essentially geometric world of the Greeks. It appeared as a mixture of Egyptian metallurgy and other crafts with gnostic and neoplatonist philosophy; it carried on the primitive idea of Gold as a lifegiving substance and tried to develop the spells of the metallurgical crafts into scientific method. The Egyptians, concerned with alloys that looked like gold, had experimented with ways of obtaining golden or yellow colours—here the industrial quest for fabric-dyes also helped. Indeed, many alchemical processes, such as dipping into mordanting baths, show the link with dyeing. Gradually the idea of changing the colours of a metal gave rise to the idea of transforming a base metal into a more precious one; and systems of change were devised, in mystical terminology, which drew in the prevalent notions about the elements. Four basic substances were sought—often lead, tin, copper, iron. This basic function (which produced a black hue) was whitened by heating first with silver, then with mercury of tin; then yellowed with gold and sulphur waters as reagents; finally turned violet, probably by alloys with a small amount of gold in them.

The *kerotakis* (a closed vessel where a continuous reflux-effect was gained by a condensing cover) and other forms of the circulatory still gave a revolving space-movement, things above and things below interchanging. Cleopatra's *Making of Gold*, of which we have a single sheet, shows a still with two condensing arms, a *kerotakis* used for fixing metals, and the serpent Ouroboros with the words 'All is One'. In a circle is written, 'One is All and through it is All and into it goes All and if it lacks Nothing is All', and 'One is the Snake that has Venom after two Matings, *synthemata*. The snake-of-unity with its tail in its mouth is born from the fusion-of-opposites—or rather unity gains life-and-death power, venom, out of the fusion. Mercury and sulphur were no doubt the metals most used in the *kerotakis*; they provided the basis for the later mercury-sulphur theory of metals: fire and water, the opposites, begetting the gold of irreducible substance or unity.

The alchemists were fascinated by bright red sulphides of mercury made by fusing mercury and sublimed sulphur in the kerotakis; the colour shifted from black to white to yellow to violet. Their theory involved the cosmic symbolism we have seen in tribal orientations, the ziqqurat, the planets, the circus-factions. Sound-harmonies were linked with colour-progressions, the seven vowels with the seven planets: the Pythagorean system which had been highly elaborated as the years went on. Zosimos discusses the Egg of the

Four Elements, the Four Musical Elements, and so on. The problem of chemically colouring the Egg is dealt with—a process of transformation equated with initiation into the mystery of Egg, the Whole, which with its four elements is the embryonic stone-of-perfection. Alchemic process is one with the Mithraic mystery of baptism and death-rebirth. 'Everything caused by nature', Zosimos adds, 'is one, not in form, but in system' (*techne*, craft or industrial process). At Dura, we may note, letters (*stoicheia*, also meaning elements) in the Zeus temple were given a symbolic connection with the heavenly bodies and related to the paintings; *stoicheion* also meant the soul-object, which at Byzantium was lodged in a statue or work-of-art. The mosaic or ikon was thus a soul-object linked with the alchemic concepts of trans-formation and a cosmic symbolism of colour.

At Byzantium there was considerable alchemic activity, as also in Syria. One practical result was the invention of Greekfire by Kallinikos, an architect from Heliopolis in Syria, who had fled to the capital from the Arabs. A liquid fire was squirted through metal tubes. At least in one form the material was sent through a copper tube, and the account of its explosive propulsion implies a transformation of matter into gas and the use of the gas's force.

The constant perfecting of which Greekfire was the object, gradually led to the discovery of fire-arms with tubes, rifles and cannon. It was then used in solid state, in powder form, to cast projectiles which were first of stone, then of metal. (LENGHELIS)

Greekfire saved Byzantium at several crucial moments of attack.

The Arabs made important advances in alchemy, working on the Syrian bases. Geber's two principles, sulphur and mercury, based on Aristotle's two exhalations, held the ground till the 18th century. But we must understand that alchemic ideas were fundamental in all medieval thinking, and were con-tinually reborn in craft-process. The high craft-skill in all Byzantine areas in work that needed chemical knowledge—dyeing, glasswork, pottery, jewellery, etc.—implied a vital carrying-on of alchemic ideas. Thus, recipe-books of workshops like *Compositione de Tingenda* and *Mappus Clavicula* (the first known in an 8th-century MS., the other in a 10th-century one), the *De Artibus Romanorum* by Eraclius and *Schedula Diversarium Artium* (11th-12th century) all show traces of what we may call craft-alchemy.

Music and Alchemy. We can trace the idea of an eightfold modality far back in the Mesopotamian area. A Hittite text says that hymns to the gods are best done eightfold (eight ways or with eight hymns). There are calendar connec-tions, e.g. with the Pentacontade (seven weeks of seven days plus one day) linked with a unit of seven seasons and seven winds, over each of which a god reigns. This calendar affected Christian and Jewish computations and survives in the forty-days between Easter and Pentecost. The Monophysites had a liturgical *oktoechos*, a hymnbook for the eight Sundays of the seven weeks after Pentecost. This calendaric system brought about in turn the idea of musical correspondences to time-changes, and by the end of the 7th century the *oktoechos* was a system whereby each hymn of the pentacondal Sundays was sung to a different mode.

The Pythagorean idea of the octave as made up of two tetrachords (manifestation of the cosmic *tetraktys* of the four elements) shows a further relation of the eightfold system. In magical and gnostic texts the Omnipotent Name is Ogdoas. The *Acts of John* describe Jesus as making the disciples hold hands and dance a round-dance, and ending his song:

> The Eight (*Ogdoas*) sings praise with us. Amen.
> The Twelve (*Dodekas*) dances on high. Amen.
> The Whole on high has part in our dancing. Amen.
> He who does not dance knows not what comes to pass. Amen.

The Valentinian and other heretics further elaborated the relations of vowels, qualities, heavens, and elements along similar lines; and we meet the Ogdoas as the supercelestial *topos* or world-mountain.

A craft-relation is again brought out by the statement of Gaudentius that Pythagoras realised the correlation of number and tone, cosmos and music, when he heard the different tones of smiths hammering on anvils. Porphyrios says he was told the secret by the Daktyls (Fingers), the gnome-miners, the dwarf-craftsmen of the Idaian Mother; and elsewhere we are told that it was these dwarfs who discovered in hammer-rhythm, in anvil-tones, the clues to the nature and form of music. That is, the transformative activity of the smithy revealed the system of dynamic harmonies making up both human and natural process. The *oktoechos* thus introduced ideas of changing yet interrelated forms in music as in alchemy. Bar Hebraios puts the Arab-Syriac position:

The inventors of the *Oktoechos* constructed it on four fundamentals, following the number of physical qualities. We cannot find a mode in pure condition without it entering into combinations with another, so it happens also with the elements; whatever is warm is also wet, as the air and the blood, or dry, as fire and the yellow bile . . .

And he follows with the Christological application of the *tetraktys*. The Cross is taken as the four quarters of the world, embodying the principles of orientation and world-centre; and Christ is crucified on the universe.

The Arabs richly worked out the musical-alchemical principles. Al-kindi shows that they were well aware of the Byzantine *oktoechos* by the 9th century; and in the same period Ikhvan es-Safa makes such typical statements as the following:

The musicians restrict the number of the strings of their lute to four, no more nor less, that their work may resemble the things of sublunar nature in imitation of God's wisdom. The treble string is the element of fire, its tone dry, hot and violent. The second string is like the element of air, its tone corresponds to the dampness of air and its softness. The third string is like the element of water, its tone suggests water-like moisture and coolness. The bass string is like the earth, dry, thick and heavy.

It was in the west however that the full systematisation was made. The Gregorian chants show a certain congruence of scalar mode and melodic pattern; but what defines the mode is the *finalis* and its relation to the dominant tone of the psalmody. *Octava* as the term for the eighth day of the week had been familiar since Augustine, but with Guido of Arezzo in the 11th century the octave was plainly conceived as the eighth tone of the scale; the modes of the oktoechos could be set out in a diatonic scale.

In Arabian music there was a strong shamanist element. Some composers took a wand to beat out the rhythm, then uttered an improvised song. Ma'bad leaped into his saddle and beat on the pommel with his wand till the melody took shape. Ibn Suraij put on a robe with jingling bells, swaying till he had a new melody. Ibrahim-al-Mausili worked himself into a trance, then visualised the rhythm, inside the frame of which his tonal images took shape. He, his son, and Ziryab claimed to be taught melodies by the devil and by genii. Ziryab, after being inspired by jinn in sleep, jumped from his bed, called singing-girls and made them memorise the music while it was still fresh in his mind.

Architecture. The Arabs at first occupied churches for their mosques, then used Syrians, Persians, Copts as architects, so that diverse elements were combined. The minarets were tall square towers. The Ummayyad dynasty of Syria later used brick walls and vaults derived from Iraq, and had a variety of arches, including the semi-circular, the rounded horseshoe, the pointed—as well as arches braced with tie-beams or flat lintels with semi-circular relieving arches above. They built desert places where larger surfaces were covered with glass mosaic than ever before and the frescoes included human figures. In Persia the mosque had a square plan and flat timber roofs without intervening arches. Bull-headed capitals from Persepolis were re-used.

With the end of the Ummayyads the purely Arab period was over. The Khalifate removed from Damascus to Bagdad. Hellenistic influences gave way to Sasanian-Persian and produced the art of Samarra, which sent out influences to Egypt, to Samarkand, and to Bahrain. The square minaret was carried as far west as Cordova and became the standard type for western Islam. Bedouin ideas of tribal equality were now finally jettisoned and the Khalifs took over the semi-divine role expressed in Persian ceremonial. Mausoleums were unusual as the Moslems at this time did not want their graves marked. (When Al-Mansur died, a hundred graves were dug, to confuse the trail.) Geometrical ornament was still rare, chiefly used for window-grilles. Lustre-tiles came in from Persia; and the four-centred arch, which was not Persian. (Ummayyad art had gained a new life in Spain, whither many Syrians had emigrated.)

At Samarra, the 9th-century Great Mosque, covering some 45,500 square yards, was the largest in the world. Its minaret, Malwiya (Spiral), stood free from the north wall on the central axis. It consisted of a tall tower, with winding ramp. (The same principle appeared at Abu Dulaf.) The system was derived directly from the ziqqurat. As late as the second half of the 12th century Benjamin of Tudela saw the ziqqurat of Babylon standing with its spiral-stairway.

Indian Art. Buddhism, if not actually generating Indian sculpture, was the force which developed it. Asoka set up many monuments at places sanctified by Buddha, or where relics were buried; and his own secular palace at Patna is described by Arrian as splendid. The dynasty of Sungas who followed the Mauryas were probably not Buddhists, but they patronised Indian art, as did the Greek and Parthian rulers after them. Zoroastrian, Greek, Mithraic and other iconographies intruded and were assimilated. In the 1st century A.D. there rose in the north the empire of the Kushans, a branch of the Tueh chi nomads; and the two great art schools of Gandhara and Mathura flourished, the latter more purely Indian in style. In the south the dynasty of the Andhras in the Deccan for five centuries built such magnificent works as the gateways at Sanchi and the monuments at Amaravati. The 3rd century A.D. was a

Buddhist carving, Yusafzai valley. The Great Renunciation: prince rests with wife on couch, with female musicians; below he steals off while she sleeps.

period of violence and disorder, ending when Chandgupta brought a large part of the north under his sway. As a result we find the fully-matured Indian art of the Gupta sculptors.

But Buddhism was not the only force at work. In the Mauryan epoch the pre-Vedic mother-goddess (the Brahmanical Lakshmi or Sri, the Buddhist Sirima Devata) reasserted herself. And with her came the earth-spirits, Yakshas and Yakshinis; the Nagas, snake-people, water-spirits; Apsaras, nymphs, born of Ocean when it was churned by the gods in their quest for *amrita*, nectar; and Lokapalas, guardians of the four world-quarters.

As artforms we meet the great monolithic pillars of Asoka, with lotus-capitals (from Persepolis) surmounted by four lions supporting a wheel or other such symbols, as well as large sandstone statues of Yakshas and Yak-shinis, powerful in their sensuous simplification. With the Sungas, or earlier, comes the Buddhist stupa, a cosmic mountain, set up at sites sanctified by the Buddha's movements or at the burial-places of him or other saints. (The Jains also erected stupas over their saints' relics.) From bas-reliefs on the railing of the Bharut remains we see that the original form was a solid hemispherical dome on a cylindrical base. The dome was topped by a flat platform enclosed with a stone rail and a stone umbrella (a sky-emblem). There was a processional path round the stupa, fenced by an encircling massive balustrade. The railing had openings at the four cardinal points, decorated with pillared gateways.

Bharut, like later stupas, was sculptured with reliefs depicting the Buddha's life-history and showing a tradition of wood-carving.

These sculptures tell a story, describing scenes from Jakatas [stories of the Buddha's previous lives], and historical events relating to Buddhism. These are portrayals in a simple folk-art. The landscapes show trees and forests, lakes and rivers, and various aquatic animals, elephants, deer, monkeys, and birds. There are human figures in a palace, a procession, domestic and monastic scenes. But there is no suggestion of perspective or horizon. All the objects are shown successively in semi-bird's-eye-view. There is no battle-theme or picture of conflict such as appear in later stupas. The friezes of these sculptures reveal only festival events and peaceful serenity. (KAR)

Buddha is represented at first by emblems only: umbrella, wheel, throne, tree, stupa, lotus. The importance of relics in Buddhism as in Christianity, is shown by the tradition of a War of the Relics, waged for the Buddha's remains, which is represented at Sanchi, where are the most magnificent stupas; and by the story of Asoka having divided the dead Buddha into 84,000 bits for distribution under stupas. With Gandhara art, with its strong Graeco-Roman influences, the Buddha is shown with a softened Apollo-head, in ascetic robes, and the Bodhisattvas in princely dress. Also appear the host of Brahmanical deities already present at Bharut. Gandhara and Mathura both contributed to the image of the meditating Buddha seated in a yogic attitude on a lotus (of birth) with halfclosed eyes and haunting smile. In Mathura art we meet the fullblown sensuous types, the lascivious Yakshinis leaning on a tree with one hand raised to a bough. Sanchi shows such figures in further development.

The stupa went south as well. At Amaravati we see both Kushan and West-Asian influences: perhaps the apex of Indian classical art—together with Gupta sculpture, which carries on till the 6th century. Then comes a gradual change to medieval forms with a tendency to lose plasticity in linear design, with a primarily architectural value. Even so, Indian art long maintains a high level, which we cannot, here, examine further. Many influences had contributed but an essentially Indian approach dominated throughout, even when the Graeco-Roman impact was strongest. The Indian quality lies in a concept of form as an harmonious flow of interrelated lines and surfaces. Plasticity is strongly present, but is not achieved, as in Greek art, through a final domination of the analysed parts by a grasp of the whole organism in movement. Rather, it develops from the strong sensuous feeling which operates within the over-all flow of modulated harmonies.*

Music. Intoned formula was the basis of the elaborate structure of Vedic verse at offerings and sacrifices. Three accents were used in the line-units of the hymns, showing a difference of pitch and set against the multitude, the unaccented syllables. In the classical system, the octave was recognised in theory as the complete cycle of sounds and was divided into two disjunct tetrachords as among the Greeks. The mathematical proportions of this analysis were closely linked with the architectural designs of the medieval period. The usual cosmic relations were discussed, but here they were related to the idea of liberation from the cycles of birth.

Complex and delicate systems were devised. The octave had its seven main notes, but was also divided into 22 *srutis* or microtonal steps; there were two basis seven-note scales, with six-note and five-note forms as well, and with 14 extensions, *murcchanas*—though only half of them were in fact used as foundations for yet more complex structures, *jatis* (seven principal and eleven mixed), which by further elaboration became the *ragas*. The *raga*, the true basis of the classical system, was a melody-type with various rules:

It must, for instance, use both tetrachords . . . and any given raga is defined, inter alia, by its particular scale (whose descent may be different from its ascent); by the emphasis given to a particular note (*vadi*) and to its fourth or fifth, as a contrast with the tonic; by the frequency of certain notes and intervals; by a characteristic melodic pattern; by pitch-range (*tessitura*) in which the melody mainly lies; and by the particular types of movement between notes. (CROSSLEY-HOLLAND)

Each *raga* had its own particular ethos or emotional nexus; and *raga*-music was thus calculated to define the utmost nicety and nuance of thought and feeling within a given traditional frame. The *raga* had its skeletal system in the

---

* It would be of interest to explore Indian medieval architecture—both because of its intrinsic quality and because of the light it would shed on our theses. We must note in particular the considerable development of cave-shrines (at times with important art-effects, *e.g.* the Ajanta paintings; and the many soaring tower or dome forms both in classical and medieval buildings, *e.g.* the domed and pillared Buddhist temples with three storeys (shown at Jappayyapeta and Amaravati); the sikhara temples of Gupta, *e.g.* the great brick temple over 300 feet high at Nalanda monastic university or the Hindu temple at Konch with curvilinear spire; the towers of the Nagara style; the Towers of Gloty in Gujerat; the domed Jaina temples of white marble on hilltops as pilgrim-centres; the towers of the Cola period, etc. We see the stupa or world-mountain image leading to a large number of powerful forms, with effects on the sculptural art that decorated them.

starting-note, the centre-note which occurred most often, and the ending note. After the influx of Moslem culture, the north and south styles differentiated, the north carrying specialisation so far that the musical shape was felt to give rise to a physical shape, *e.g.* the *Raga Megha* is the Youth with a body like a blue lotus and garments like the moon, who, dressed in yellow, is implored by thirsty cataja birds (who drink only raindrops), and who, smiling sweetly as nectar, is resplendent among the heroes, in the midst of clouds. The north, too, classified the *ragas* according to their genders; the males with their wives even had children-*ragas*. The composition generally has four divisions: theme, second subject, development, coda (which may be replaced by a return to the theme).

Rhythm is subtly developed in the interplay of drum and solo instrument, each making its own variations on the underlying structure and both coming together on the first beat of the next period. Cross-rhythm is richly worked out, but the simple movement from stressed beat to stressed beat is not easily managed. The time-unit is the *laghu*, of which three make a *pluta*; and the *pluta* is said to embody the Hindu Trinity with Brahma presiding—just as triple measures were preferred by the medieval west for their trinitarian basis.

Drama. India had many ritual playforms from Vedic times, e.g. the rite of buying *soma* for the *soma*-sacrifice when the seller was pelted with clods and beaten, to represent the wresting of *soma* from its guardians. The Mahavrata was a summer-winter struggle between a White and a Black man for a round white skin, the former winning; and the rite included a dance of maidens about a fire, to bring rain and aid the herds. (We may compare the Boiotian fight of the Blond and the Black man, the former aided by Dionysos of the Black Goatskin). In a flyting between a Brahman student and a hetaira, the debate originally ended with coitus. We hear, too, of epic recited in temples. In the early 7th century a Brahman gave a temple in Cambodia a copy of the *Bharata* so that regular recitations might take place even in an outpost of Indian civilisation. A rich man might pay reciters, *kathakas*, to come to a village and spend three months declaiming, while the *dharakas* expounded the poem. A Sanchi relief proves that dance and music played their part in the recitals.

The name *Bharata*, later used for comedian, seems to show a link of the rhapsodes with drama; for the Bharats must be the rhapsodes of the Bharata tribe, whose special fire is known in the *Rigveda* and who have an offering of their own. The *Mahabharata* is the great epic of the family, preserved by their care. What seems to have happened is that the rhapsodes in time took on the art of drama.

Indeed there is abundant evidence to show ritual growing into dramatic dramatic forms, e.g. in the cult of Krishna, his feat of slaying Kansa was performed in an amphitheatre before spectators, who were shown his defeat of the court-wrestlers and his killing of the tyrant. The festival of his nativity was a popular spectacle; and the *yatras*, songs which survived the breakdown of Sanscrit drama proper, told of his love of Radha in a paradisiac pastoral world. The drama itself perhaps came into being in the 2nd century B.C., combining the epic recitations with the dramatic moments of the Krishna cult. The words *nata, natya, nataka* (drama) are derived from *nat, nrit*, to dance. Patenjali, about 150 B.C., writes of actors as singing; people go 'to hear the actor'. And he mentions two themes from the Vishnu cycle: the Kansaslaying by Krishna and the binding of Bali by Vishnu. Using mimic action and declamation, the shows must have been rather like the western medieval mystery-play.

The first complete play that we possess seems *The Little Clay Cart*, perhaps of the 6th century A.D., which, though crude, has more social vitality than the later plays. It deals with the love of a Brahman merchant, who has fallen into poverty, and a courtesan. The king's brother chases the girl, and a cowherd rebel takes refuge in the hero's house. The king's brother thinks he has killed the girl and accuses the hero of murder; but the girl turns up at the trial and the rebel overthrows the king.

The Sanscrit drama has no care whatever for unity of time and space, and permits no death or indecorum; the ending must be a happy one. The dialogue is in prose interspersed with lyrical passages of verse; the hero and leading males talk Sanscrit, the women and inferior males talk various Prakrit dialects, which in turn become fixed literary dictions. The higher levels of culture were reserved for the ruling class, the Brahman and the Ksatriya castes; and the idealist outlook of the Brahman dominated the drama, weakening or driving out the popular elements. The aim, as generally in Indian poetry, was to suggest feeling rather than to attempt precise definitions; the dramatist takes a familiar theme and treats it so as to arouse the appropriate emotions. Thus, Kalidasa in his *Shakuntala* alters the tale, not for dramatic force or for revelation of character, but for opposite reasons, to idealise the events.

The crudities of the epic tale left Shakuntala a businesslike young woman and Duhsanta a selfish and calculating lover; both blemishes had to be removed in order that the spectator might realise within himself, in ideal form, the tenderness of a girl's first affection, and the honourable devotion of the king, clouded only by a curse against which he has no power. (KEITH)

The emotions to be aroused were strictly limited by Brahmanic theory. All actions, all status, depend on the deed done in a previous life, and these again are explained by earlier actions from time without beginning. There can thus be no real conflict; all obstacles are external. No tragic struggle; all conclusions must be concord. The sentiments allowed are the heroic and the erotic, with wonder as the cause of the deepest excitement.

So with the Nataka, or heroic play. The lesser form, the Natika, deals with a romantic stereotype of love, jealousy, parting, reunion. On similar lines the Prakarana are taken up with erotic sentiment and the Vyayoga with heroic.

Realism is excluded by all the varieties. No questions can be raised as to the structure of society, the meaning of life, the workings of the world. Kalidasa, greatest of the dramatic poets, accepts without the faintest doubt the given fabric of Indian society. The Brahmanic ideal had no interest in individuality and permitted no deviation from type; the caste system was reflected in art. The positive results were a lyrical sweetness and romantic charm, a capacity to suggest moods and feelings within the boundaries of the accepted systems. But by the 10th century the aloofness from life had devitalised the drama; the dramatist's aim was merely a king's favour. A logical result was *The Moonrise of Intelligence* by Krishnamisra, about the 12th century, where the characters are all abstract ideas and symbols divided into two conflicting hosts in the struggle between King Error and King Reason. Given an upsurge from below, such a play could have provided a new start; as things were, it represented the end.

As an example of how playful and delightful the fancies could be, how warm the feeling of harmonious union with nature, here are four lines attributed to the pre-Kalidasa Bhasa:

When moonrays fall on the cat's cheeks, he licks them, thinking them milk.
The elephant thinks them a lotus, caught in a cleft of the tree.
When they rest on the love-bed, a girl catches them, 'Look, my robe of silk'.
Yes, the moon cheats the whole of the world, proudly and brilliantly.

Graeco-Roman influences have been denied in the Indian drama because no direct imitations are traceable. But there can be no doubt on general grounds that Greek actors and mimes would have carried their plays into the Indian world for many centuries; and it seems highly probable that their impact helped in transforming the ritual into the secular drama. There are many elements in Greek New Comedy and in the Roman mime that have close affinities with the romantic formulas of the Indian plays, e.g. the recognition through marks. We may note that the early *Little Clay Cart* in particular suggests the Graeco-Roman mime in its sudden change of fortunes. Similarly in art, India was for millenia in contact with West Asia and its developments, and after Alexander was powerfully influenced by Graeco-Roman sculpture. The plan of Asoka's palace is thought to be identical with that of the Achaemenid palace at Persepolis. Architecture in Central India (e.g. Kasmir, 8th-13th centuries) shows Graeco-Roman elements such as fluted columns with Ionic or Dorian capitals. That such adventurous characters as the mime-actors would not have journeyed into north India is impossible; an inscription in Central India, at the ancient city of Vidisa, records the appearance of a Greek ambassador. But both in art and in drama the Indians quickly absorbed influences and used them for their own purposes.

Epic. In epic the roots must go far back, but the two great examples are well past the Vedic era. The *Mahabharata* in its present form cannot be earlier than the Greek invasion, about 300 B.C. and seems to have been completed by 200

A.D. The prominence of Krishna shows the influence of the Bhagavata sect. The author is called Vyasa (the Arranger or Compiler). In the mass of legendary and didactic matter, the core seems an historical feud of two peoples in the middle-land between Ganges, which ended with the fall of the Kuri dynasty. There are episodes of forest-withdrawal and a spiritworld-journey, to Mount Meru, with various tests for the right of entry to heaven. Some events outrage Brahmanic morality, such as the marriage of the princess won by Arjuna to all five brothers; they must have been too deeply imbedded in tradition for censorship.

The *Ramayana* is later, shows even more folk-elements, and is a little less than halfsize the Mahabharata with its 100,000 couplets. Ascribed to the poet Valmiki, it tells of the carrying-off of Rama's wife, Sita, by the monkey-king of Ceylon and the resulting wars. Again there are episodes of forest-withdrawal; and the monkeys aid Rama in the crossing to Ceylon. The ultimate basis in myth is clear. Rama is the god Indra, the rain-bringer, and Sita is the Furrow, the goddess of the tilled earth; the ravisher corresponds to Vritra of the *Rigveda*. The *Ramayana* shows the beginning of literary stereotypes that lead to a large number of further epics.

In these two works we meet all the elements that are present in Homer, plus a tumult of other motives from folklore, didactic moralisings, legends of all sorts. The fundamental themes, rankly overgrown by the other elements, are of the true epic kind, at least in the *Mahabharata*, where the interjected *Bhagavat-Gita* has the effect of a religious-philosophic effort to overcome the confusions by dwelling at length on the real inner conflict of the feud-theme. What Homer does by sheer objective artistry is here done by a long rhapsodic exegesis. Arjuna is uncertain whether or not to fight: he thus represents the Achilles-motive and indeed is brought up more sharply against the essential issue than Achilles was. Is he to fight and slay his own kinsmen? Krishna, in the form of his charioteer, addresses him at length and finally appears in a terrific theophany. Karma must be accepted. 'Cast off all your works upon me, put away your fever and fight.

> Who sees inaction in action, and action in inaction,
>> he is enlightened among men; he does all actions, disciplined.
> All whose undertakings are free from desire and purpose,
>> his actions burnt up in the fire of knowledge, him the wise men call
>> the man of learning.

But this abstract acceptance of life, by which all actions can be justified if the doer is 'free from desire and purpose', is very different from the Homeric acceptance, which arises from the depiction of life in its fullness, with all its inner conflicts and resolutions. The comrade-love that draws Achilles out into acting with his fellows is very narrow when set beside Krishna's generalisations, but it leads on into a truly widening love-of-man-for-man; Krishna's course leads to a barren self-perfection, a hope of personal escape from the cycle of births.

The Indian caste-system and the Brahmanic ideals thus end by arresting the development of Indian poetry and forcing it up blind-alleys. But though, in consequence, we need not look for tragic masterpieces or for clear-bodied epics, there is a seething vitality underlying the products. And this too appears in the endless number of folktales, fables, legends, which overflowed into Persia, the Arab lands, the West, through devious channels, e.g. when a romance-version of the Buddha's life, *Baarlam and Ioseph*, was done into Georgian, and thence into Greek. The Arabs played an important part in passing on all sorts of Indian tales to medieval Europe, and themselves created vivid collections of romances, fantastic and chivalric.

Chinese Art. With the intrusion of Buddhism in China there came figure sculpture based on Indian models. More truly Chinese were the graceful T'ang terracotta figures used as grave-goods. Under the T'angs (A.D. 678-906) also came the great flowering of Chinese pottery. Many of the forms seem derived from the Persian and Greek world, but the Chinese used them with a perfect elegance and developed rich harmonious glazes. The same system of refining any given basis produced the fine calligraphy for the ideograms. Paper was invented, first as a substitute for silk, in the early 2nd century A.D. (The technical idea presumably came from the felting processes devised by the nomads of the steppe-lands.) From the Sung period painting showed its lyrical control of landscape. In the early phases it seems that a larger scope was attempted; for Kuo Jo-hsu remarks under the Sungs:

In comparison with the past, modern times have fallen back in several respects, but have also made further progress in others. If one is speaking of Buddhist and Taoist subjects, secular figures, gentlewomen, or cattle and horses, then the modern do not come up to the ancient. If one is speaking of landscapes, woods and rocks, flowers and bamboos, or birds and fishes, then the ancient does not come up to the modern.

Certainly by the Sung period the masters were concentrating on the latter themes; and in their work something of the Taoist position is beautifully expressed. The attitude is contemplative, completely accepting the natural scene or detail, yet the selective process is central in the vision. It is almost as though the Taoist passivity was in fact before our eyes producing the desired transformation. And yet the effect is not wholly Taoist; there is also a Confucion element of rationalism, which uses the stylisation to ensure that nature remains under control, subtly revalued and enjoyed, and yet held at arms-length.

. . . in the Neo-Confucianist cosmogony of the school of Chu Hsi (A.D. 1130-1200) was the motion that to all sentient lives, and indeed to all things, events, and relationships, attached a governing principle, *li*, which was distinctive of the class to which each belonged. Though there might be more classes of *li* than classes of things, the number was yet fixed and irreducible and amounted to the *T'ai Chi*, or 'Supreme Point of Perfection', often equated with the *Tao* of the Taoists. Corresponding to this formal cause of each existence was its material cause, *ch'i*, which seems to have been envisaged as a highly tenuous substance or vital gas, that by cohesion and compaction in various patterns produced the events and things of each distinct category; if *li* gave them inherent natures, *ch'i* invested them with their material forms.

According to the Neo-Confucianists, perfecting one's knowledge (*chih chih*) meant awakening to the fact that one had *T'ai Chi* within oneself, that one existed in each and every object, event, and relationship in the external world and that each was part of oneself. It meant reaching out to all the *li* in the universe from the foothold of the *li* one knew; and to know *li* one had to 'investigate things'. (WILLETTS)

In fact there is a conflict in such statements, between the intuitional sense of the *li* and the investigation-of-things. And this conflict is present in Chinese art, resolved momently in a successful grasp of pattern and atmospheric effect, but determining the narrow limits of the art-tradition and the mode of apprehension. The positive side appears in what has been called the 'balanced asymmetry' of the compositions, which enable the artists to escape from stereotypes, the main danger of such a calligraphic art, and to impart a simultaneous effect of the casual angle, the casual vision, and the *ch'i yun* of the object, its essential nature and vital rhythm. It also enabled the artist to assume that the eye-position of his vision was not fixed. Three types of angle-view were accepted: those of deep, high and level distance (or looking up, down, or along). And various devices in the treatment of planes were used to harmonise pattern, aerial perspective, and emotional intention. (In the middle of the 11th century the combination of ink-outline and graded washes had brought to a head the problems we are discussing.)

Chinese lyric poetry is close in its qualities to the landscape paintings; it shares the same mixture of realism and symbolism gained by a concentration on essentials, and the same limitations, the same intense development within a narrow round of possibilities. Epic and drama failed to emerge. The T'ang period saw the growth of imaginative literature, built up out of earlier legends and folktales. Peasant revolt stirred a series of tales, set in 'an imaginary world where success was not denied to worth'. But with the Sungs there was a return to formalist values. In the later periods there was much refinement of techniques in all forms of art-expression, but a loss of vitality and depth.

Chinese patrician art in these centuries was a sterile dessicated affair; but it was not the only art that existed in China, as witness the popular coloured woodcuts of the seventeenth century, certain wall-paintings, and many minor applied arts and handicrafts. (WALEY)

Also, there were many important discoveries in applied science. Chinese alchemy had been specially concerned with the gold of eternal life; but as off-shoots there was valuable work done in the fields of metallurgy and chemistry. The invention of the astrolabe and the compass made possible the European sea-expansion of the 15th-16th centuries.

Music. Musically a uniform culture exists all over the Far East, ranging from Korea and Japan down to Malaya and Java. Despite contacts with more western areas via Turkestan, China held fast to the minor-third pentatonic genus, with the fourth as the dominant unit. The usual cosmic ideas were present. Music was considered not a matter of sounds but a transcendent power; by the 3rd century B.C. a system relating notes to the order of the universe was worked out. The orderly generation of sounds from a pitchpipe was equated with other types of order: with the four directions, the sequence of seasons and the categories of substance—F equalling autumn, C spring, G winter, D summer. 'Music expresses the accord of Heaven and Earth', declares *The Memorial of Music; The Record of Rites* explains that 'since 3 is the numeral of Heaven and 2 that of Earth, sounds in the ratio of 3:2 harmonise Heaven and Earth'. As the fundamental note had to move in accord with the 12 months, and with the 12 hours, it had to be transposed, with its scale, in each period. Twelve-note series, generated by a method of ascending fifths and descending fourths, were thus needed, with each of the twelve notes becoming the starting-point of the scale.

Since music was a spirit-power able to sustain or destroy the universal harmony, a single note could influence men for good and evil, and a ruler's first duty was to keep intact the traditional ways of performing music and the State-ritual. The zither has the name *ch'in*, which means 'to prohibit', i.e. 'to check the evil passions, rectify the heart, and guide the bodily actions'. The instruments provided the accompaniment of the meditating philosopher.

The tones of Chinese speech, with its limited number of monosyllables, were classified by Shen Yueh (441-513). As the meanings depended on inflection and pitch, the heightening of the tonal accents stimulated the growth of melodic song. In 485 dancing was officially accepted as part of Confucian ceremonies. The dancers, we learn from a hymn, took up 32 positions per stanza, holding flute or wand in the left hand and pheasant's feather in the right. The dance-positions were based on the poem's calligraphy; for the ideograms were also the neumes (directions as to pitch) repeating the melodic shape inherent in the words. Similarly, words, movement and music were integrated in the marionette-plays.

There were also exorcisms, dance-songs performed by a troop of beast-makers and led by a shaman at the yearly rite of driving disease out or at funerals where spirits had to be frightened away. In Han texts we meet the term *koeileei*, which survived as a term for marionettes. The puppet-play may well have served as an intermediary from between ritual and entertainment. Under the Sung 'flesh puppets' began to appear in the streets, singing and dancing. The words were derived from banquet-music both in the north and south, in a verse-form with lines or irregular length and with syllables following one another in an ordered pattern of tones. Thus new types of varied melodic structure were made possible, leading into music-drama. The first complete dramas arrived under the Mongol dynasty (13th-14th centuries), with four scenes of mime and pantomime, declamation, and metrical songs (each of which had its form marked by a song-label).

At first the north dominated, but in the later Ming period the southern plays were revised and operas lasting several hours with anything up to thirty acts were produced. As men and women actors were not allowed to act together till 1911, men sang the women's parts in falsetto. The Ming melodies were not always syllabic, as had been the case with Chinese song since ancient times, but were at times melismatic—possibly as a result of popular intrusion. An act opened with the entry of a leading character, who declaimed a prose prologue setting out the situation, then came a song, then a prose monologue, and so on. Generally there were ten tunes in an act, all in the same mode and key. The song-labels tended to reinforce the associations of a mode with a particular verse-form and emotional situation; and as the number of melodies was smaller than the number of lyrics, a given melody suggested at once the dramatic situation. We may compare the associations attached to the moods of the Indian *raga*. The themes of the plays were often lively, popular, and embodying elements of social criticism.

Zen Buddhism and No Drama. The Japanese term *Zen* is the same as the Chinese *Ch'an* and the Pali *Dhyana*, and means a technique of meditation. Ch'an Buddhism was closely related to Taoism; indeed, we may define Ch'an or Zen as a Taoist critique, from inside Buddhism, of the intellectualist attitudes grown up in *Mahayana* in relation to the Great Self. It sets out the way of intuition and of the dialectical leap, and seeks by means of a sudden jolt, *satori*, or meditation on a paradox, *koan*, to see directly into the nature or structure of reality. Taoist passivity here appears as *wu-wei*, inaction—in effect a union of attack and defence, of subjective and objective, of inaction and action. One should not resist intellectual difficulties; one should let them pile up till they destroy or cancel themselves out. Zen is linked with the sport of Judo.

The disciple must not separate himself from life or detach himself: that is the way that leads to the intellectualist illusions and abstractions. One must be vitally a part of life. (Zen here comes close to the idea of the unity of theory and practice. The idealist lesson of the *Gita* as to acceptance becomes many-sided and integrative, involving conflict as well as harmony.) As examples of Zen question and answer, we may take the following. What is the Tao? Just ordinary life. What is the Buddha? Three pounds of flax. When a Zen follower lit a fire with wooden images of the Buddha, he explained, 'There are no holy images'. The *koans* had a mixture of Greek Cynic vindications of the way of nature, and of the paradoxes about movement and rest, freedom and determinism.

The negative side of Zen appears in the way in which it appealed to the military caste of Japan; the positive side in No dramas where symbolism is used in the way of *koan*, to rend apart the normal acceptances of things, and in the way of *satori*, to throw a flash of intense insight upon the reality under the surfaces.

Architecture. China, we have seen, had the ritual mound and the heavenly-mountain image, which appear in such structure as Temple of Heaven in Peking, which had the central circular mound, the celestial symbolism elaborately worked-out, the enclosure entered by four ceremonial gates, the larger park or paradise. (Relic chambers were at times built of stone slabs disposed in swastika form, with entries also on a swastika plan.) But on account of making wood its main building-material, China did not develop large mountain-structures in its architecture. Under the pagoda lies a Chinese tradition of towers, but in effect the form is the Chinese version of the Indian stupa. In north-west India the stupa-dome was raised on a cylindrical podium with image-niches, which stood on a high square platform used for walking round. The *harmika*, which at Sanchi is a square coffer above the brick dome, had several courses of corbelled masonry set on top, and the spire was thickened and elongated. Thus the stupa grew more tower-like approaching the *sikharas*.

The northwest-Indian stupa was known to the Chinese, e.g. one is shown in a Tun-huang fresco. But the Buddhists in China may have taken a native storeyed tower (perhaps representing the sky-ascent) and converted it into the pagoda, carrying over the stupa-spire and reducing the main body of the stupa itself to a vestige at the spire-base. It is also possible that storeyed stupa-towers in India had provided a much more direct basis for the pagoda. In any event the latter is a world-mount—with names like Moon-girdle-hill or Thunder-peak (holding down the flood-demons) near Hangchow.

India also spread the architecture of the heavenly-mountain to the south-east. In the 8th century a young Ganga prince with a few retainers founded an empire in Java; and the dynasty took the title King-of-the-Mountain from the Kailasa or Mountain of the Gods. The Kailasa was expressed by the monument of Borodur in the 9th century, a great circular mass of riotously exuberant carvings tapering upwards.

In Java, but more especially in Cambodia after the coming of Jayararman from the Sailendra Court, this Symbolical mountain, the speciality of the Sailendra kings, who no doubt brought it with them from India, gained an ever-increasing importance in connection with the Royal God, a kind of divine essence presiding over the destiny of the kings and resident in a linga (phallus) or emblem of Siva, which was enshrined in the sacred mountain . . . This artificial mountain, or *phnom*, was built at the centre of the capital, and its evolution . . . led to the development of some of the classical Kmer temples. (WALES)

Angkor Wat shows the mountain in a version of graceful proportions. And we may here add that the great cultures of pre-Columban America also knew the sky-mountain. The *teocallis* of the Mexicans was yet another version, and in Peru the pyramid, stepped or terraced, with a temple on top, was known in the highlands and on the coast in the early periods. Huge adobe pyramids were constructed, topped with a temple, such as the so-called temple of the Sun at Moche or the great sun-pyramid at the ritual site of Pachacamac, which covered twelve acres and rose some 75 feet. The Incas however did not use this form in their megalithic works.

Africa. Twelve to fourteen thousand years ago Africa was inhabited by pale-olithic folk, perhaps linked in ethnic type with the Bushmen and Pygmies, or what are called Boskopoids. When the Negroes first came in, is not yet clear; but 5,000 B.C. may be taken as a fair guess. Negroid types were certainly

Benin bronze. Wooden mask, Urua, Congo.

common among the early Egyptians, and some rock-painting of north Africa may have been done by negroes about 4000. Another intrusive type was the Hamitic, of so-called Caucasian stock. The mingling of Boskopoid, Negroid, and Hamitic seem to have produced the ancestors of the present Africans.

Some time before the 4th millenium the Sahara began drying up, cutting off central and south Africa from the Mediterranean world, though trading and raiding groups managed to get across. We know much from Egyptian records of contact to the south and south-east, Kush and the Land of Punt. The Kushites asserted themselves strongly in the 8th century B.C., but after the Assyrian attack on Egypt their centre moved more south, to Meroe (in the Sudan), where they carried on a great iron-working culture till the 3rd century

A.D., after which they fell to the Ethiopian power of Axum. Here seems the centre from which iron-working groups spread over large parts of Africa. These groups however had been preceded often by neolithic agriculturists. Thus, in the Nigerian area the iron-working kingdoms followed the farmers who made the Nok figurines. Four important States built on urban trade and a pastoral-and-agricultural economy emerged. Ghana, already a centralised State when the Arabs first mention it in A.D. 800, was weakened by Arab devastations and brought down by the 13th century. Mali, flourishing in the 13th to 17th centuries, had great centres of trade and learning like Timbuktu and Djenneas. Kanem, later Bornu, also rose to a high level, as did Songhay of the Middle Niger, with its big city of Gao, which was ravaged by Almoravid hosts of north Africa, then by desert Tuaregs and Mossi of the Sudan. Even so, its power increased till the attack by Moroccans with firearms in 1591. Other states of west Sudan met similar fates, including Christian Nubia submerged by Islam in the 14th-15th centuries. All these regions could more than hold their own in civilisation with west Europe of their periods.

Down the eastern coast the iron-workers had built many fine towns, and there were inland towns only now being explored. Old roads and terraces reveal the movement of the colonising groups, as well as stone-built settlements and deep wells. Zimbabwe, Mapungubwe, and many other sites in Rhodesia seem linked with the iron-workings, while the coastal towns had a thriving trade with Arabs, Indians, Chinese. At their height in the 12th-15th centuries, they supplied much of the iron made into swords at Damascus. Hilltop forts and walled cattle-pens reveal that the groups were often at war with one another; they had also to meet the threat of less-developed nomads moving down from the north.

What such dangers failed to achieve, the Portuguese managed in the 16th century; and the havoc of the English slave-trade in the following centres completed the work of breaking down the civilisations of Africa.

These facts must be born in mind when considering African art; for the art-objects labelled African are very largely of recent fabrication and represent a tribal folk-art. We cannot define African art simply in their terms, as we are reminded by the Nok terracottas, the stone figures of Esie, the bronzes of Ife and early Benin. In these latter works we see the great tradition of African art.

The Nok figurines which certainly go back to the 1st millenium B.C. have strong expressive simplifications; a complete kneeling figure from Abuja shows a large head and a rhythmically organised whole. The Ife bronzes are entirely realistic, but with a massive and subtle unity of form, which surpasses anything in ancient art except the best Greek work. They seem the creation of priests, intended for a second funeral; the buried body of a chief or family-head was dug up and reburied ceremonially, with a puppet to represent the dead man—the head being made as like as possible. From Ife the art of bronze-making was introduced about 1400 to Benin, where the realistic tradition was carried on, with more varied applications and with certain stylisations. The finest work is the earliest; by the Middle Period (probably 17th and early 18th centuries) the forms show stereotyping, and then comes a decorative flamboyance in detail that upsets sculptural unity; by the 19th century the tradition is in decay. The downward movement of Benin art cannot but be connected with the demoralisations of the slave-trade, which also had brutalising effects in religion.

Against the background of the Nok-Ife-Benin tradition of plasticity and realism, we can proceed to appreciate the remarkable qualities of rhythmic expressiveness in the tribal arts. Ancestor-worship plays a key-part; often ancestral figures, fetishes and masks are more important than god-statues. The Dan make only masks. (Some tribes however like the Dogons and the Yoruba have an elaborate hierarchy of gods, looked after by a small priest-group. Among the Dogons the high priests had their own ritual, with an art-expression attached to it.) Ancestral figures are often the home of the ancestors; they attract the spirits, who settle down in them instead of wandering round. Generally the representation does not have to be a likeness; the spirit can recognise its own figure, which is addressed as if alive.

The skull plays an important part in African beliefs as in Oceania; and it has been suggested that ancestor-figures derive from the skull-cult and the pole set over a grave. The skull was first put on the pole and then a carving replaced it. Some Fang figures, the skin-covered Ekoi masks, and the Bakota figures fit in with this theory, as also the many pole-like carvings, e.g. the doorposts of Cameroon chief's with their superimposed heads or the long cylindrical torsos of the Dogon ancestors. In Dogon grave-statuettes the figure is a pole in three parallel sections. We find also masks based on the skull, with high brows, closed eyes, fallen cheek, bared teeth, and with white paint, to represent the spirits of the dead. Through these the ancestors speak in funeral rites. Ekoi masks use human hair and teeth, eyes of metal or wood, and the skin of men or animals; they seem carved after the skull. Masks in general however are made out of all sorts of things; as well as the materials mentioned we meet beads, shells, mirrors, string, textiles, sheets or strips of copper, plant-materials, and so on.

Next in importance to the ancestral carvings are the fetishes, to which a magical substance is added, to provide spirit and power. The fetish can then be appealed-to, to mediate with spirits from whom the man wants something; it also cures ailments. Special fertility-fetishes exist, but mostly the figure is not tied to a single purpose. The nail-fetish, especially in the lower Congo, is a rough wooden carving, one hand on hip, the other hand raised with a dagger. To drive home a request and to confirm contact, a nail is hammered into the wood. Some fetishes of Mendi in Sierra Leone serves as oracle to deal with sickness; they are kept in the house of a female society, the Yassi. Anointed, they are set by the medicine, to take in its diagnostic powers; then the second-in-rank of the Yassi goes into a trance; when she awakes, the figure is once more rubbed with oil. The head of the Yassi takes it up, presents it twice to the Yassi fetish, turns it to herself, and swings it, holding its hips. An answer is deduced from its motions.

Ivory statuettes, generally of mother and child, are found in the central Congo. In Togoland clay is used for ancestral figures and animals.

Mostly woodworkers carry on agricultural work as well; but there is a tendency for specialisation, the men carving and the women doing other handicrafts. In the Sudan the smith was a full-time worker, and also a wood-carver; at times his rank in the secret society was second only to that of the chief. In an enquiry among the Yoruba

stylisation was found to be less rigid than it may appear to be; the artist would take liberties within the framework of his style, and the Yoruba carvers had no words to differentiate naturalistic and stylised. The same Yoruba carvers were at times to be found equally competent in stylised and naturalistic carving. Yoruba carving differed in one respect from other West African carving; the shape of the block exercised less influence on the final form. The 'treetrunk' theory seemed to apply less, at least in the Yoruba style. (CHRISTENSEN)

Where, as among the Cameroons there is vigorous realism, there is also stress on movement.

Negro music has the complex rhythmic quality that we would expect from a people with such tribal arts. Now that we are beginning to see the contemporary Africans against the background of their rich medieval and earlier civilisations, with periods such as that of the Mali kingdom developing centres of high culture and far-spread trade, we cannot think of African art or music as primitive in the sense that Australian or Oceanic art is; the large iron-working states or towns belonged to a higher level of social development than the Amerindians ever reached; and we must expect to find Arabian and Indian influences in the music. At the same time we must not forget the way in which, first the Arabs, then the Portuguese and English, systematically wrecked the higher developments of African culture, so that the tribesmen of 1900 must not be equated with those of 1500 or earlier, however much continuity there may be in certain craft-skills.

13: Medieval Art and Drama

Western Europe. We noted that in Britain the Celts fought back against the Anglo-Saxon invaders. Driven back into the west of England, there and in Ireland they developed their own form of Christianity, which had Egyptian connections but which was at root a direct growth from tribal society—a monastic form with the abbot taking the place of clan-chief. Thus among the Celts various elements of late Roman culture survived, fed by refugees from Gaul. The result was the relatively high level of scholarship they maintained, which they later passed on to the Anglians of Northumberland through their missionaries and monasteries. At the same time the suppressed remnants of Celtic art-tradition reasserted themselves. From the resulting fusions of Celtic and Germanic elements, and the rapid raising of the cultural level, in Northumbria emerged the stone crosses, Bede and *Beowulf*. Anglo-Saxon scholarship in turn flowered, and England was enabled to supply teachers for Charlemagne's illiterate Frankish kingdom and missionaries for converting the Saxons on the Continent—a task for which Italy and France lacked the initiative and piety.

Gradually the barbarian kingdoms knitted together, till the Frankish empire appeared. The Papacy, daring at last to draw away from the Roman Empire surviving in the east, which was hard-beset by the Moslems, took the step of throwing in its lot with the Franks and thus achieving a position of ecclesiastical supremacy in the west, unhampered by the claims of the Byzantine patriarch. In the process it created a secular power which was to challenge its own position, the German empire. The violent clash of papal and imperial claims which distinguished Dante's world then gave way to the struggle between the papacy and the emerging national states, which ended with the breakaway of the northern nations in the Reformation.

A key-problem is to explain why the west of Europe developed differently from the east, and why the national states displaced the imperial forms, did not redevelop slave-economies, and ultimately created a middleclass at long last able to break through the barriers always previously set up by baronial landlords and beget an industrial system based on the free market and wage-labour.

Why did the feudalism of western Europe develop in a new direction? It was not through intention on the part of the feudal nobles, who would have liked to destroy all the towns of insubordinate burgesses, all the free communes. Nor was it through any ruling ideology that deprecated slavery. The Christian ethic, born in large part from the suffering slaves and town-workers of the Roman empire, certainly held an element which in the long run helped to accustom men to the idea of doing without slavery; but the Church throughout took the line of moralising and humanising slavery, not of abolishing it.

The Church held many slaves, and while their treatment was in general sufficiently humane to cause the number to grow by voluntary accretions, yet it had no scruple to assert vigorously their claim to ownership. When the papal church granted a slave to monastery, the dread anathema, involving eternal perdition, was pronounced against anyone daring to interfere with the gift; and those who were appointed to take charge of the lands and farms of the Church, were specially instructed that it was part of their duty to pursue and recapture fugitive bondsmen. (LEA)

There seem about 25,000 slaves in Domesday England. In the medieval period as in the dark-ages ecclesiastics took part in the slave-trade. A large-scale exportation of slaves from Bristol went on, and slaves were bred for the market like cattle. On the manor a slave was classed with the lord's cattle and chattels. In the case of theft:

If the thief was a man and a slave, he was to be stoned to death by 80 slaves, and if one missed his mark 3 times that one was to be whipped 3 times. If the thief was a female slave, and had stolen from any but her own lord, 80 female slaves were to attend, each bearing a log of wood to pile the fire and burn the offender to death.
(PIKE)

In the Elizabethan age vagabonds could be sentenced to enslavement; in the 17th century many thousands of Irish, men, women and children, were sold under Government licence for slaves in the West Indies; and England's 18th-century advance cannot be understood if we ignore the huge monetary gains through the African slave-trade.

Such facts, which could be much multiplied, suffice to prove that it was no moral consideration which led the towns of western Europe away from a slave-economy. We can only infer that the general economic level had this time reached such a high level of potential development that the townsfolk could now challenge the feudal lords, with the aid of peasants and farmers drawn into the market-exchange, and at the same time could think in terms of labour-saving devices rather than the exploitation of slaves.

The expression of the new power existent and potential in the burgesses appears in the important aid they gave to the king in his effort to impose a centralised government on feudal anarchic tendencies. The guild organisations at certain decisive points in Italy, Flanders, France and England were strong enough to hold their own against all disruptive pressures and ensure the birth of a new sort of town. The commune at first seems, at least in Italy, to resemble the self-governing city of the ancient world. But if it had been no more than that, there would have been no essential changes. In the last resort it was the relation of the free or chartered town to the new national state which constitutes the great difference. What happens is not a series of separate communes that go down in the end before some imperial overlordship. It is the nation that emerges, given colour and direction through the new towns sharing the king's-law. (In both Lombardy and Flanders we can see the development of tribal kinship into guild-solidarity.)

The way was opened to the application of science to the productive machine, the labour-saving device, and thus science itself was given a great new impetus, which began to operate in the 16th century and was in full swing by the next. By the 18th century the theoretical developments and the practical needs could come together with dynamic effects unparalleled in world-history. The result is the world in which we live today.

The dark-ages had laid the basis for this whole advance. Then it was that the decisive bases were laid for the medieval struggles. Because men were released from crippling lordships, a series of important technical advances were made or older methods were extensively applied—the heavy plough, the watermill, the bridle and horsecollar, the rudder, the lateen sail and fore-and-aft rig, and many other lesser inventions of this sort. Mostly the place of origin is extremely obscure, though sometimes we can guess. Thus, the windmill, with horizontal sweeps, seems a Persian invention; carried across Russia, it was brought down the Atlantic coast; taken over by men who knew the watermill, it achieved vertical sweeps.

The revolving mill, apart from the potters-wheel, was the first machine to replace to-and-fro movement by a continuous rotary one. The principle of most modern machinery was born. But how the spinning-wheel, for instance, was created we have no clue. Perhaps the first impetus to the idea was given in India, when the rotation of a spindle by means of a wheel had been long known. By 1298 the guild at Speyer permitted its use for the wool, though not for the warp, of cloth. In 1533 a citizen of Brunswick was said to have cranked the axis of a large wheel and added a treadle, so that spinner could rotate the wheel by his foot and keep his hands free. Drawings by Leonardo show a flyer, twisting yarn before winding it on a bobbin, and a device to move the bobbin up and down the spindle. In the 16th century a machine of this type, called the Saxony wheel, which made spinning a continuous operation, was spreading. No further important advances occurred till the 18th century.

Again, an essential activity that made possible the new level of productivity was the slow steady clearing of forests, which had speeded up during the dark-ages and went on all through the medieval years. Thus the Germans, who had swept all over western Europe, were able to begin their return movement eastward, pushing back the Slavs who had pressed in to fill the empty spaces left by the migrations.

Art. Early Christian art took over many pagan elements, in particular the the cupids, seasons, tritons, nereids: neutral emblems of immortality and the passage through the elements. Apollo, the Good Shepherd (Hermes carrying a ram), and Orpheus, were used as models for Christ. The 4th century dropped the idyllic character and wanted a figure of bearded majesty. That is, with the establishment of the Church, Christ became, not the welcomer into a state of blessedness, but a stern admonitory power, using the faces of Zeus, Asklepios and grave philosophers, and taking over the nimbus of Children of the Sun such as Circe. The Church assumed the apparatus of imperial Triumph; the Victories became angels. On a humbler level the bridal couple changed Juno or Cupid for Christ as their blesser; and the poets in the front of MSS. abdicated for the evangelists.

We have seen how in the Dura synagogue the Jewish artists had worked out designs for the Old Testament; but now designs had to be standardised for the New. Various adaptations were made. Christ entering Jerusalem followed the pattern of the emperor's arrival at city-gates. The catacombs took over the forms from the walls of Roman houses, sketchy and weak descendants of the lively impressionist style of the early empire. Local styles flourished in the provinces, ranging from Palmyra's hard-edged manner with spiral hair and palmette eyebrows, to the coffin-portraits of Egypt with all a man's life concentrated in big eyes dilated with the blindness of vision. In Mesopotamia hieratic forms had never died; the steppes were always swarming with animal patterns. At Carthage crude shapes were set in zones divided by a line down the middle, as in early medieval work; in Palestine acanthus-designs petrified into deep V-cuts with a sharp black-white alternation.

Generally we see an effort to use schematisations and frameworks, as if going back behind the Greek achievement. The regional and plebeian styles moved into the central areas. Craftsmanship weakened, but the cause of the changed outlook went deeper than that. There was a slackening of interest in people as individuals; the pagan mysteries and Christianity alike focused on the hereafter. As the hope of a speedy second-coming went, the human form tended to stiffen into hieratic power, or took on distortions that expressed the unrelieved inner strain, the hope now wholly directed on another world. The Romans, we saw, had brought about the fusion of allegory and actual event; now the event was flattened out behind some symbolic or otherworld significance. The emperor was not a man who had won a high position; he was power itself and the aim of art was to force the spectator down on his knees. Later, when the saint was defined, the aim was to cut the earth off from under your feet into communion with a form which disregarded the complex delicately-balanced forms of real people and existed as a single upthrust, a trance-aborption in the act of hypnotic faith. Hence the frontality and staring eyes. We are on the first stages of the road that leads to the fully-developed iconography of the Byzantine church or of the Gothic porch with its packed symbolism: all history and nature gathered into key-images and raised to an abstract level of overwhelming power—with tenderness and promise for those who totally submit.

But we must not look on this transformation of the world into the other-world as something done quickly or decisively. The struggle that begins in the 3rd century goes on right through the medieval period. Then, as one kind of harmony is reached in mature Gothic, it is overthrown by the counter-harmony of the Renascence, and the field is opened for a further series of oscillations, mannerism, baroque, rococo, neoclassic, romanticism, and so on. And in speaking of a conflict between the classical inheritance and the provincial or barbaric element in the dark-age and the medieval period, we must remember that the classical aspect consists of an imitation of classical models and does not represent an effort to see nature afresh through the methods of Greek artists—though in Byzantine art there are moments when the classical revival does entail an effort to encompass nature through a classical approach (especially under the Iconoclasts and their immediate successors) and the impact of this effort merges with western elements to produce the Gothic of Chartres. Further, the barbaric elements are not themselves simple.

From the earliest times, both in Europe and in Asia, there was an interplay of influences between North and South. Northern Asia developed a very specific art of its own, not, however, independent of southern influence. The northern art system of Asia—what we call Scythic—spread west and south to Asia Minor and to southern European Russia. From these regions, as well as via Perm (described as a Finno-Scythic culture) it directly influenced Germanic art. (PICTON)

The basic elements of Germanic art were derived from forms which Iranian-Greek influences moulded on the steppes among the Sarmatians who dominated there till the Goths and Huns came. Many place-names, *Sermaise, Saumaise, Semizelles*, show the widespread Sarmatian colonisation in Gaul. Mosaics from the Great Palace prove that Byzantine artists of the 5th century had a stock of barbarian subjects of the sort supplied to the markets on the coastlands of the Black Sea. And so on. The motive of the Cross with the leaf was strongly developed in Armenia; floral crosses were favourites of the Nestorians, who carried them to China (about 981) and to St. Thomas Mount near Madras. The image 'probably travelled westwards from Mesopotamia along with numerous other eastern elements', penetrating Byzantine art in the 8th century, 'especially in the decorations of textiles, pottery and sculpture'. In Italy, where the motive became popular, it seems that Lombards and other invaders from the north brought it.

These examples give some hint as to the complexity of the mixtures going on from the 4th century, when provincial or sub-antique elements affected the official art in Italy, flattening relief-figures into linear two-dimensions and seeking hieratic symmetries or symbolic gestures. Soon after came a classical revival, linked with the movement of the noble families into the established church. Narrative and anecdotal systems replaced the symbolic event such as Jonah swallowed by the whale—emblem of resurrection (the initiate in the monster who later vomits him out). At Byzantium the court tended to support works with a classical look; yet here too were present the strongest hieratic styles, and the impulse to the expressive and the graphic. The two approaches went on side by side, not without affecting one another. The war-crises of the 7th-8th centuries, with the overrunning of rich art-areas like Syria by the Arabs, weakened Byzantine art for a while as a European force. But at no

The Mouth of Hell: Caedmon MS (Bodleian).

time did that art cease to have a strong influence in the west—not necessarily in a way connected with its own tempo of change; for portable objects like ivories could travel about and were often not the latest thing turned out in the capital's workshops. In the west, Celtic and German elements, with their spirals and zigzags, their animal interlaces and so on, were powerfully at work, yet modified by classical and Byzantine influences, not to mention Coptic and Syrian, in carvings and in illuminated books. The Carolingian effort to build an empire encouraged the classical side; the Chapel Palatine at Aachen took its plan from San Vitale of Ravenna and had in front of its colonnaded fore-court a horse-statue looted from that town. At the same time it showed some-thing of the changes that had gone on; the broad plain openings on the ground floor, flanked by short sturdy piers, had a touch of Byzantine space, despite the polished columns superimposed above. In the workshops of palace and monastery artists from many lands, and all sorts of articles serving as models, were brought together—with the resulting divergences of style, conflicts of the linear and the plastic, and new fusions of northern and southern motives. The struggle going on in the north is complicated by the struggle going on in Mediterranean lands.

The 10th century, we saw, was the golden age of Byzantine art, rejuvenated by the Iconoclasts. The classical element deepened in plasticity, while from the east came in afresh the monumental and the popularly realistic, sometimes combining. But in the west the divergences increased, helped by the political situation, the Danes invading Britain and the Huns pressing into Central Europe. The Cluny reforms of monasticism stirred new energies and in the late 10th century England revived, drawing on Carolingian art, yet merging it with Irish and Northumbrian elements. German Ottonian art was again imperial. Figures lengthened, hollow-eyed and monumental, isolated or in groups of stark vertical design; action was defined without loss of symmetry. In the 11th century forms hardened and in the scenes were more interrelated. England and Germany showed much greater vitality than Italy, which fell back on early-Christian models, plain and linear; but in the latter part of the century Byzantine influences brought a fresh life through Monte Casino. In Spain forms were flat with an angular rigidity of arrested torment, together with Islamic ornament.

Throughout the western development, at key-points, we meet direct impacts form the Byzantine area. The Palace Group of illuminators under Charlemagne, who were of primary importance during these centuries, were probably Byzantines; one of them appended a Greek signature. The Lithard group exploited Hellenistic suavities while the Adad group with their heavy outlines looked rather to Italian art. Venice was emerging as a vigorous trading-centre, which for many centuries was a steady diffuser of Byzantine objects and ideas. Again, monks and ikon-painters fled from Cappadocia and the Caucasus under the Iconoclasts to Italy as well as various parts of Asia, where they founded cave-habitations and hermitages, which they painted. Gifts by the Byzantine emperors to princes in the west, or articles that came along through trade, were often models for the local craftsmen, e.g. the *pala d'oro* at Venice, the enamelled reliquary at Limburg, the enamelled gold triptych at the Abbey of Stavelot (Belgium), and the richly designed cloth in churches all over France and Germany. Even Anglo-Saxon England shows many examples of direct imitation of Byzantine originals, e.g. a York slab of the Virgin and Child, a variant of the Hodegetria or Shower-of-the-Way, in which Mary holds the the Child in her left arm while pointing at him with her right, while he extends his hand in blessing. The York example is close in form to Our Lady of Vladimir, painted at Byzantium in the 11th century. Further Byzantine types can be found at Deerhurst, Romsey, Stepney (St. Dunstan's), Bradford on Avon. The Alfred Jewel is Byzantine in method, though local in style. Even the braided and knotted motives seem Coptic in origin; at least they were much used in Egypt. (The sons of Edmund Ironside, expelled by Canute, took refuge in Kiev.*)

We may note, too, that all over Europe the numismatic influence of Islam was felt; in Anglo-Saxon England, from the 8th century the *mancus*, the Moslem coin without an image, was the standard for payments in gold. Mercia made bad imitations of the gold dinar of the caliph al-Mansur; and in 955 Eadred of Wessex still ordered 2,000 *mancusi* to be struck.

A Germanic version of the cosmic image is worth noting. The early Germans believed in a world-tree or pillar, *Irminsul*. Under the Romans there developed the so-called Jupiter column of the Rhineland, a world-pillar resting on a block of four gods, above whom were carved the gods of the weekdays (also a cosmic seven). The image persisted in the Anglian crosses. The Gosforth cross "is carved to look like a tree; the bole is patterned as if with bark. All four sides, where the trunk has been, so to say, squared, exhibit carvings susceptible of a two-fold interpretation, either Scandinavian or Christian' (COOK). At Ruthwell and Newcastle we see the rising-up from the underworld where the old serpent writhes to the heavenly cross-head with the Lamb and the four watching creatures.

Romanesque. In architecture there grew up a new way of organising form and mass. The shapes were often heavy and rigidly monumental; but there is no mistaking the strong effort to impose on the intellectual disorder a clear dominating idea. Walls rise upwards with pilasters dividing the length into equal sections; tiers of arcades, galleries, windows give a horizontal movement. A rhythmic progression carries on along the inner space, as if the Ravenna line of martyrs had turned into architectural forms. And because of the sudden explosion of orderly motion, ornament too comes to life and bursts out of the joints; pilasters flank the porch; lintels and tympana, capitals and friezes play their part in the unified conception. A world-view is dramatised at the outset with Christ in Judgment over the door, and painting or sculpture within reinforce the message. Yet all decoration harmonises with the basic construction-forms, which it underlines and stresses.

The roots of the new style lay in the late Roman buildings, e.g. Diocletian's Spalato palace with arches rising direct from columns, entablature bent over to suggest a deeply moulded arch, arch-headed windows, roll-moulding carved round a door, a long wall-arcade on a small scale. And Byzantine influences kept coming in to drive the new systems forward.

---

* As the importance of Russian culture in the world-arena comes later, I have not traced the growth of Russian towns, and the rich variations made on Byzantine culture, which was fused with Caucasian and other influences. Russia took heavy blows from the Mongols and other invaders, but in doing so did much to save the rest of Europe. Russian art developed its fine rhythmic qualities, its decorative and emotionally evocative use of colour, in the period late 12th to 14th century. The dome became onion-shaped by the 12th c., with elongated drum turning almost into a turret. A rich heroic balladry with folk-roots also appeared.

The Byzantine genius at this time, say 500 to 800, so dominated the expression of the arts in Italy and the West that it would be well to call the style Byzanto-Romanesque or Byzantesque. (LETHABY)

In Carolingian times we see the first Romanesque signs. The choirbay intrudes between transept and apse, and another innovation is the ambulatory. (Occasionally there is a central plan, e.g. Germigny-des-Prés, inspired by Catalonia—as is also this church's dome on squinches. Ealier there was a circular church at Toulouse.) The decorations are still by painting; where we find a mosaic as at Germigny, it is Byzantine. The Romanesque church is vaulted in stone—the point of essential break from the static basilican idea, the low-pitched wooden roof. But the typical vault is the Roman barrel one. Piers gain a complex cross-section; generally there is a nave and two aisles (necessitating three vaults, which support one another).

The transept and choir developed in a way until then unknown. The most common systems were those of apses built parallel to one another, on the same axis as the nave and generally decreasing in proportion to their distance from the central apse, or that of the ambulatory with radiating chapels. (LAVEDAN)

The essential effect of Romanesque is of a building conceived as a large work of sculpture, a series of volumes controlling space and realised as simple geometrical forms—the cube, the truncated cone or pyramid, the cylinder or half-cylinder. The plan may be deduced from the outside.

A monumental sense appears even in small art-objects. In England the Norman style in effect founded medieval architecture and brought Romanesque to its climax in the cathedrals of Winchester, Ely, Durham. In Central Europe the long walls had been cut into separate units; the Normans kept bay apart from bay by tall shafts running from floor to ceiling; and at Durham the nave seems to soar with the rib-vaulting that carries on the upmovement of the shafts. The longitudinal progression, in its culmination with the opposing symmetrical units is united with a heavenward lift, given strength and stability by the curving ribs—though here at Durham the great massiveness of the forms still holds down the up-movement.

Byzantium lacked the Romanesque, since she had no need to transform the basilican structure; she had already achieved her forms of spatial movement in the 4th-6th centuries. It was the lack of martyrs in the west which made the domed *martyrion* there an intrusive form, without roots. Because Italy and the west had taken over the rectangular hall as the basic plan, the new life as it surged up had to tackle that hall-plan and transform it. (The elements of austerity and simplification in Byzantine architecture of the 10th-11th century must not be read as due to western influences; they are post-iconoclastic.) In Spain, on the other hand, in the Asturias where the liberation-struggle against Islam had begun, we meet a strange mixture of furious forms striving to find cohesion in the 9th century: tunnel or barrel vaulting, twisted-rope columns, capitals with barbaric foliage or figures, shield-like medallions from which spring the transverse vault-arches. Part of the effect comes from the proximity to highly-developed Moslem buildings such as the Cordova Mosque, 786-990, with eleven aisles, each twelve bays long, and with star-ribbed vaults and interlaced arches.

Gothic. The monks had played a central part in the creation of the new architecture; and the pilgrim-routes facilitated the exchange of ideas. With the growth of the new towns in the west came the drive that changed Romanesque into Gothic. Late Romanesque had indeed created all the forms on which Gothic based itself (the pointed arch, the flying buttress, and the rib-vault); what was needed was a new impulse quickening the sense of space in

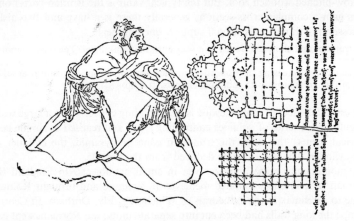

Pair of wrestlers, a Cistercian churchplan; from Villard de Honnecourt's textbook.

movement, permeating the masses and developing a system of innovated lines of action. The twofold effect—along and upwards—which we found at Durham had to be made dynamic and lightened in various ways, so that the worshipper, entering the church, felt simultaneously carried in spirit towards the altar and aloft into the heavens. A new set of tensions and of releasing rhythms were needed, and they appeared in the choir of St. Denis in the 1140's. But if the movement towards the altar was given a fresh richness of involved rhythms, the ultimate stress was on verticality. The harmonious universe of Romanesque had become the dynamic up-sweeping universe of Gothic; the image of the heavenly mountain had triumphed once more. The vertical leap took final form in the spire.

The external features were in harmony with the inner, and revealed how the structure had been put together and built up; but inside all stress was put on the emotional impact. If the outside was the holy mountain joyously achieving contact with the heavens, in the hollow interior (as in a venus-mount or a fairy-mound) was a whole world of rhythmic forms which simultaneously liberated and contained. The century that created Gothic also was the great period of scholasticism, the attempt at encyclopaedic systems of knowledge which harmonised natural and spiritual fact, history and God's purpose, reason and faith, and defined the place of man in the universe. Similarly the cathedral was a cosmic statement, allegorising and yet organic.

Aquinas recognised beauty as consisting 'of a certain consonance of diverging elements'. Out of the conflict of heaven and earth, vertical and horizontal, death and resurrection, the medieval man saw the cathedral in its totality as the image of earth transformed to paradise. Abbot Suger of St. Denis wrote of the church's doors:

> Bright is the noble work. But, being nobly bright, the work
> should brighten the minds, so that they may travel, through the true lights,
>   to the True Light, where Christ is the True Door.
> In what manner it be inherent in this world the golden door defines:
> the dull mind rises to truth through that which is material and, in seeing
>   this light, is resurrected from its former submersion.

When Canterbury was burned in 1174, Gervase lamented the church 'hitherto delightful as a paradise of pleasures'. Theophilus, an artist of north France in the later 12th century, wrote: 'Having illuminated the vaults or the walls with divers works and colours, you have shown forth a vision of God's paradise bright as spring with flowers of every hue, fresh as green grass and as mantles embroidered with spring flowers'. And in the *Life of St. Hugh*, we read of the saint's work at Lincoln:

With a wondrous art he built the fabric of the cathedral. In the structure the art equals the precious materials, for the vault may be compared with a bird stretching out its broad wings to fly; planted on its firm columns, it soars to the clouds. . . Precious columns of swarthy stone close-set in all its pores; it may suspend the mind whether it be jasper or marble. Of this kind are formed those slender shafts which surround the great pillars as a bevy of maidens assembled for the dance.

Again the church as the *chorostasia* of the blessed. (We must not forget the mosaic maze-patterns with which the architects signed their buildings.)

We have noted the cathedrals as the expression of the new energies united in the communes. And this aspect is described by Abbot Haimon of St. Pierre-sur-Dives in Normandy, writing to his brethren at Tutbury in England:

Who has ever seen? Who has ever heard tell, in times past that powerful princes of the world, that men brought up in honour and in wealth, that nobles, men and women, have bent their proud and haughty necks to the harness of carts, and that, like beasts of burden, they have dragged to the abode of Christ these waggons loaded with wines, grains, oil, stone, wood, and all that is necessary for the wants of life or for the construction of the church?

A thousand or more, he says, attached to the carts, in dead silence. At a halt they confess or pray. 'At the voice of the priests who exhort their hearts to peace, they forget all hatred, discord is thrown aside, debts are remitted, the unity of hearts is established'. Whoever refuses this concord has his offerings thrown out. The people, old and young, cry out, sob, sigh. Then trumpets sound and banners are raised, the march is resumed. Reaching the church, the folk 'arrange their waggons about it like a spiritual camp, and during the whole night they celebrate the watch by hymns and canticles. On each waggon they light tapers and lamps; they place there the infirm and sick, and bring them the precious relics of the Saints for their relief'.

No doubt such scenes of exaltation occurred; at St. Denis, Suger freed the townsfolk, and the monastics, especially the Cistercians, played an important part in the building drive. But there was also much conflict, with the bishops ferociously at loggerheads with the burgesses, as at St. Laon. And the artist himself might be opposed to the Church, more concerned with its abuses than with its promises of paradisiac union. Peter the Painter, Canon of St. Omer, in his *Why Study any more*? attacks the Church as hopelessly corrupt and corrupting:

> I'm ashamed to be honest, ashamed to go scribbling verse,
> for day and night I lead a life that's a curse.
> All night without a stop I'm versifying,
> all day I paint, my work of god-making plying,
> To hell with god-images! To hell with poetry!
> since all this prettifying brings no good to me.

Some of the carvers even seem devotees of the witch-cult in which the peasantry, using a fraternity-form of pagan origin, expressed its resistance to the Church of the State.

The Gothic style was settled at Chartres in the early 13th century, with the nave soaring 120 feet. Stress grew more on space-in-motion, by intricacies of form in England, but on open breadth on the Continent. The Friars, who wanted aisle-less halls suited for large congregations intent on hearing the sermon, had a strong effect on the 14th century. In Germany, where Gothic lagged till the mid-13th century, the hall-church went back to Romanesque days and now became the main form, with diagonal vistas all round and the Gothic dynamic missing. Such structures were also better suited for long sermons than the old type with nave and aisles.

The contrast between plain outer walls with undecorated windows and the Waldweben inside [at St. Laurence, Nuremberg] is eminently characteristic of late Gothic mentality, especially in Germany, a combination of mystical piety and sound practical sense, faith in a godly life within this world, the gathering of the ideas out of which Luther's Reformation was to grow. Luther was born before the tabernacle and the Annunciation (by Veit Stoss) were commissioned. The discrepancy between the interiors of undulating flow, in which the individual may lose himself as between the trees of a forest, and exteriors of powerful solidity with unbroken walls and two rows of windows, heralds the mood of the German Reformation, torn between mystical introspection and a hearty new thrust into this world. (PEVSNER)

It also expresses the breakdown of the medieval world-image, which has the primitive unity we discussed in relation to Ionian thinking. In France towards the 15th century the decorative exuberance of the Flamboyant and in England the vaults of the Perpendicular with their complicated patterns of ribs reveal the Gothic principles carried to an extreme and ending in an inversion of the original intention. The Perpendicular ceilings become solid tunnel-vaults covered thickly with decoration. Such a building as King's College Chapel, Cambridge, has eliminated any difference between nave and choir; we are back at a boxlike structure, which is skilfully disguised by the elaboration of repetitive ornament; a basic simplicity is masked by a fountaining luxury of forms, caught and held in the fan-vault. The great thrust of energy in early Gothic, mysterious because of its effort to compass a world-image, has become an impressive piece of rational planning.

The sort of arguments going on is illustrated by the report on building operation of Milan cathedral, Sunday, 25 January, 1400:

Concerning the claims, however, which were made by certain ignorant people, surely through passion, that pointed vaults are stronger and exert less thrust than round. . . it was objected that the science of geometry should not have place in these matters, since science is one thing and art another. Said Master Jean [Mignot] says that art without science is nothing and that whether the vaults are pointed or round, they are worthless unless they have a good foundation, and nevertheless, no matter how pointed they are, they have a very great thrust and weight.

Whereupon they [the Masters] say that the towers which they wanted are for many reasons and causes [desirable]. Namely, in the first place to integrate aforesaid church and transept so that they correspond to a rectangle according to the demands of geometry, but beyond this, for the strength and beauty of the crossing-tower. To be sure, as if a model for this, the Lord God is seated in Paradise in the centre of the throne, and around the throne are the four Evangelists according to the Apocalypse. .

Art and science have become abstract principles which can be opposed, and the cosmic image is brought in only as an afterthought to defend a constructional plan. Specialisation of functions was in fact implicit in Gothic as distinct from Romanesque, involving a co-operation of artist and engineer; but only as the system broke down did the division come sharply out.

Painting. Byzantine art had had a new birth in the 12th century, with stress on dramatic motives and genre-themes; and the outer areas into which its influence extended made important advances, combining Byzantine methods with their own folk-traditions—the Balkans, Germany, Russia, Georgia and Armenia. Late in the 12th century, the humanist note deepend in the frescoes, a note of pathos and tragic sympathy, expressed particularly in the theme of the Descent from the Cross, e.g. at Nerez, Serbia; and with the 13th century, characterisation and realism increased, especially in Serbia and Bulgaria— together with a fresh interest in landscape and architectural backgrounds. Henceforth, despite the disaster of 1204, the artists continued along the road of realism and dramatic tension, with varying rhythms and scales of colour. The struggle between tragic rhythms and patterns of deep brooding gravity went on, culminating in the work of Manuel Panselinos of Thessalonika and Theophanes of Crete (el Greco).

Gradually the Italian artists, who had before them such fine Byzantine monuments as St. Marks, Venice, or Monreale, Palermo, began to take their place in the movement by the late 13th century. One aspect of the Byzantine tradition was taken up at Siena, in the development between Duccio and Simone Martini, in which inventive suavity, elegance, and colour-charm were added to a growing sense of solidity. It was with Giotto however that a fuller grasp was made, opening the way to a whole range new of applications. His designs are less complex than those of the Balkans, heavier and at first glance more elementary; but he infused them with a deep sense of the emotions and relationships depicted. Above all there was an architectonic unity of dramatic idea, realised with a strong feeling for tactual and visual values, a solid feeling for depth. Light played its modelling part, but the essence of his approach lay in the functional unity of the design, where every line, charged with tactile

The Minstrels' Pillar, Beverley. Note the dancer standing on head.

values, is also instinct with activity. People, grasped in simple massive form, exist in relation to one another and to a world of which they are vitally a part. The emotion or state of being—tenderness, saintliness, majesty—which was concentrated in the ikon, now overflowed, broke up, is diffused and defined wholly in terms of action and interaction. The artist's position was linked with the humanising of dogma by St. Francis, his warmth and respect for all living, though he was himself still at root a provincial Byzantine artist, affected by tendencies at work all over the Byzantine area.

Still, he contains in himself all the main elements which were to be developed, with particular stresses, by the painters between him and the High Renascence, even though his direct influence waned from the later 14th century, despite its revival in Masaccio and even Michelangelo. Masaccio in his short life did much indeed to restore Giotto's qualities of dramatic economy and solid realism of form, as against painters such as Gentile da Fabriano who was carrying on at Florence what has been called International Gothic, a court-style originating in France and Burgundy, which kept a naturalistic touch for details with an overall Gothic elegance of design. Masaccio indeed may be said to make the definite break from the Byzantine tradition which still encloses Giotto and Duccio. The way was opened to the new great stride forward, in Piero della Francesca, which utilised the discoveries made in scientific perspective and described by Alberti. The method of linear perspective cannot be systematically applied; it presupposes a single standing-point, the same for all observers. But it provided new intellectual frameworks for organising material with a greater subtlety and complexity of spatial relationships than had been possible for Masaccio. Piero was a mathematician as well

as painter; late in life, too blind to paint, he published two mathematical treatises.

He paints everything in the same way so that the common laws which govern them may be more easily seen. The correspondences in Piero's work are endless. He did not have to invent them, he had only to find them. Cloth to flesh, hair to foliage, a finger to a leg, a tent to a womb, men to women, dress to architecture, folds to water —but somehow the list misses the point. Piero is not dealing in metaphors—although the poet in this respect is not so far removed from the scientist: he is dealing in common causes. He explains the world. All the past had led to this moment. And the laws of this convergence are the true content of his art. . .

Look again at Piero's faces, the ones that watch. Nothing corresponds to their eyes. Their eyes are separate and unique. It is as though everything around them, the landscape, their own faces, the nose between them, the hair above them, belonged to the explicable, indeed the already explained world; and as though these eyes were looking from the outside through two slits on to this world. . . He is the supreme painter of *knowledge*. (J. BERGER)

But all that means he is the painter of *abstracted knowledge*, announcing the end of medieval concreteness; he is the painter of the science that sets objective against subjective and exalts the laws of mathematics as supreme. In defining the split between the observer and the observed, he reveals the first full emergence of the dilemma bequeathed by Renascence science. But because he is in fact inhabitating a world that is still medievally concrete to a considerable extent, his forms have the vividness of original discoveries; there is a vital conflict between his concrete sense of things and his intellectualist concepts. At a less intense level the same sort of conflict appears in Uccello, who applies the principles of perspective to a sensibility acutely responsive to decorative pattern and Gothic detail.

Within the space thus cleared the 15th century saw diverse trends and applications. Donatello as a sculptor sought to reproduce antique forms and balances, yet, under the strain, was driven to romantic distortion in order to express strong emotion in his *Magdalen* (about 1455). Botticelli turned to an archaic approach in form to preserve elegance and arabesque movement. Pollaiuolo carried on the scientific attitude, applying it to the male nude and to a violence of action. Piero himself, we may note, in his later years shows Flemish influences, both in his portraits and his *Flagellation of Christ*.

It is of great interest also to note how extremely difficult it was for painter or sculptor to recapture the harmonious nude. We can treat this problem as a technical one, noting how the methods of Gothic design were hostile to the sensuous grace of the body conceived in terms of curve-flow and organic balance; but the root-difficulty must go deeper, to the body-spirit division which had held the world in its spell, to the sense of sin and the conviction of something inherently ugly and disgraced in the body. When we begin to grasp the deep forces of tradition that had to be defied and overcome, we can appreciate what a tremendous effort was made by Donatello and the others who once again released the sensuous harmonies from their long dogmatic night.*

In the north neither the impact of the Byzantine nor the antique was so direct; the painters were able to develop more steadily out of Gothic positions. They carried over the love of detail, of the realised small-particular, and a

---

* When Villard de Honnecourt in the 13th century tried to copy two nudes in the antique style, he uses 'Gothic loops and pot-hooks' and constructs 'according to the pointed geometrical style of which he himself gives us the key'. (CLARK) The stomachs of the early Greek *kouroi* also are inscribed within elongated ovals such as we associate with Gothic decoration. The nudes of late medieval art, dominated by the pointed arch form, do in fact display very much the same characteristics. Note how Botticelli in his Venus, using classical proportions and sensuous modelling, yet has to maintain a Gothic rhythm. The Gothic female nude with its long body, sloped shoulders, small close breasts, is centred on the slack outfalling stomach-pouch, a perverse mixture of immature child-forms and mature swollen-belly, whereas the Greek pivots on the hips.

sense both of the fantastic and of the terrible. Jan van Eyck perfected the use of an oil medium, with a varnish, which enabled him to add to the minute particulars the subtlest light-effects. At the same time he was able to control tone and colour in terms of a broad grasp of form, and to achieve spatial depth. No one before had brought together so large a number of aesthetic factors in a unified vision. His method is carried on by Rogier van der Weyden, Memlinc, Pieter Bruegel, and in the later 15th century began to affect the Italians.

The Closed Garden and Landscape. In part the richness of colour in Jan van Eyck came from the tradition of illuminated manuscripts where in works like

Rosa Rosarum, Benedictneuern MS, 13th century. Lovers and Imp in Closed Garden, Der Seelentrost 1478.

the calendar of the *Très Riches Heures* made for the Duke of Berry, we see landscapes and work scenes rendered with a mixture of realism and decorative charm, with a quality of soaked light.

In painting, the effect of a light in the dark was first successfully achieved by Geerthen of Sint Jan of Haarlem, in his Nativity, but long before this the illuminators had tried to render the light of the torches reflected on the cuirasses in the scene of the apprehension of Christ. The master who illuminated *Cuer d'Amours espris* by King René had already succeeded in painting a sunrise and the most mysterious twilights, the master of the *Heures d'Ailly* a sun breaking through the clouds after a thunderstorm. (HUIZINGA)*

In Flanders light and colour became one, and were held together with a surety of tone; and this new unity of clarity of vision and luxuriant enjoyment was the work of the burgess world. But behind the new grasp of the fullness of the earthly scene there lay the tradition of Paradise Garden, which we noted as strong among the Romans and which goes back to the Osirian Field of Reeds and the Garden of the Jun in *Gilgamesh*. The medieval artists, with the paradisiac image powerfully developed in the cathedrals, also attempted to depict the more limited version of the *Hortus Conclusus*, the enclosed flower-space, in which the Garden of Eden was given a second life as the scene of Christ's childhood.

> Wailing of the newborn child
> proclaims the spring to earth and sky.
> Now the world, reborn, has smiled,
> with ugly winter-rags laid by.
> Child, the desert wakens now
> with flowers welcoming your birth.
> Obdurate boulders learn to bow
> and grass has clad the ribs of earth.

So sang the 4th-century poet, Prudentius. Not unaided by Persian miniatures, the medieval artists loved to show the Child in his recreated Eden, walled from the rest of the unredeemed world; and the tradition carried on well into the 16th century. The ancients and the Byzantines had tended to see only a desert of Obdurate Boulders outside the garden-reclamation, though in the *Odyssey* series (in the Vatican) there is romantic delight as well as horror in the bare rock-and-seascapes. Giotto took over the Byzantine boulders, the bare symbolic mountains, though the Sienese began to look more fully at nature

---

* Froissart is stirred by ships pennon-streaming in a sparkling sea and by knights bannered and steel-glinting. Jewels were sewn thickly in garments (as, later, ribbons and rosettes); primary colours are liked in clothes, and each colour has its symbolism, e.g. Henry of Wurtemberg paraded before Philip of Burgundy with his men in yellow, to show hostility. At a 'lower level of awareness' light-movement and colour dominate over form, and the distinction of figure and background weakens. Compare the 'counterchange-pattern' common in primitive art, where one can see a black ornament on a white ground or white pattern cut in black. Much modern abstract art shows the light-colour dominance and figure-ground ambiguity. We might say that significant art arises where there is the greatest *tension* between realistic representation and these more primitive underlying elements; representation without them is thin and naturalistic, while art pitched at the 'lower awareness-level' disintegrates personality and has validity only where it is, in fact, the expression of a primitive group agreeing in its symbolism and using the patterns to focus consciousness on reality, on the world of nature and experience.

and enjoy it. And Petrarch pioneered in discovering wild nature. 'Would that you could know with what joy I wander free and alone among the mountains, forests, streams!' It was in the north however that the bold movement of adventure was made into the forest and the mountain-lands.

Perspective had helped the Italians to gain their first realistic landscapes, but they found it hard to link foreground and background. Piero used the traditional device of a high ledge. The paradise-garden tended to break up and yield to the world in all its depth and variety. Only in Flanders, as we noted, did the gradual transition from the Gothic world to the Renascence enable the Garden to hand on the fullness of its beauty, so as to encompass the whole world in integrated light and colour. *The Adoration of the Lamb*, which we may attribute to Hubert van Eyck, forms the bridge between the medieval dream and the fully achieved landscape.

From one point of view this marvellous work will be considered as the culmination of the landscape of symbols. It is still conceived in terms of a paradise garden, in the centre of which stands the fountain of life. Leaves and flowers are all rendered with a Gothic sense of their individual entity and decorative possibilities. Round the garden there are still the remains of a Gothic forest, dense thickets of trees, with their trunks very close together. But the landscape is not shut in with trees, nor even with a hedge of rises. As in a landscape by Claude, our eye floats over the flowery lawns into a distance of golden light. (K. CLARK)

In the paintings of Jan van Eyck, on the contrary, a parapet cuts the figures in the foreground from the framed and delicately-rendered distance. It is as though the painter were saying that the city-wall has somehow put a new distance between man and nature.

Music. The Gregorian chant had become the basis of church music; popes called on Frankish emperors to enforce it. Instrumental music was looked on as the dangerous work of the devil. In the 7th century Isidore of Seville was aware of elementary polyphony based in symphonies: the 5th and 4th, with the 3rd and the 6th as discords. The bagpipe, the British harp, and the organ must, however, have played their part in enabling ears to take in two simultaneous sounds. From the 10th century the use of polyphony deepened the choral interpretation of the Gospel; a contrapuntal whole was created by all the parts of the choir being brought into action. Church polyphony continued elaborating the Gregorian elements till the end of the 16th century by three to six-voice groups, each moving along its own vocal line. All groups were of equal importance like all souls before God; the result was a subtle hypnotic flow without beginning or end. The Church attempted to control carefully what sections of Mass or Office might thus be worked on with extra voice-parts; generally the degree of elaboration corresponded to the importance of the feast. And there were various other rules, e.g. in hymns and sequences only alternate verses might be set; in psalms only the antiphon was allowed a developed setting.

The harp had probably been accepted by Celtic Christianity; and instruments continued to thrive in secular entertainment. Girald of Wales mentions the popular use of churches and churchyards for songs, love-carols, quickstep dances; he also says that the Welsh sang in many parts. After 1100, some soft-toned instruments such as psaltry and dulcimer crept into church, and there was at the same time an expansion of vernacular poetry. The organ had come in from the 10th century; that at Winchester had 26 bellows and 400 pipes, and needed three players, each managing one large key, so that three-part harmony was possible. Baudri of Bourgeuil wrote of the Worcester organ:

> The organ, whence harmonious voices run,
> is joy that gives our lives their ordering.
> Driven on various ways, we draw to one:
> as one we chant the praises of our king.
> The power of unity in differing voices
> is that which spreads our energies, yet controls.
> The driven air along each reed rejoices:
> so God combines with flesh our struggling souls. . .

But there were also attackers. Ethelred, Abbot of Rivaulx, demanded, 'To what purpose, I pray you, is that terrible blowing of Belloes, expressing rather the crakes of Thunder, than the sweetness of a voyce?' Dance-music was denounced at Council after Council; and minstrels, though taking part in mystery-plays, were suspect. Indeed they sometimes stirred popular unrest. In 1402 the House of Commons decided 'that no westours and rimers, minstrels or vagabonds, be maintained in Wales, to make Kymorthas or quyllages of the common people, who by their divinations, lies, and exhortations are partly cause of the insurrection and rebellion now in Wales. *Reply: Le roy le veut*'. In 1491 a shepherd-piper, Boeheim of Niklashausen, started the revolt of the peasants in central and southern Germany.

An important development occurred in the sequences of the 11th-12th centuries: rhymed verses with words set to freely improvised melodies of the *Alleiuah*, those long jubilatory vocalisations. The words imitated the style and form of the older hymns, and controlled the music, which had long repeated periods, with energy concentrated at the ends. (In the vernacular in England, the Germanic alliterative verse was yielding to Middle English with rhyme and regular metrical beat.)

Early English popular music used the fullgrown major and minor modes, which were only much later theoretically accepted by the church as Ionian and Aeolian. Secular music liked a tonality in C, which the Church disapprovingly called the wanton mode, *lascivus tonus*. The modes of chant were based on hexachords, with no leading note to come back to the *finalis*. (The leading-note, as the tonic note of the piece by a halftone, was the shortest possible interval in the scale.) What was to become the close functional use of dominant and tonic was thus absent and alien; instead the basis was the two axis-tones of the melody, the *finalis* with which the piece starts and ends, and the *repercussio*, the note round which the melodic line mainly circled. The leading-note with its tendency to abandon was felt a special foe, and there was resistance to the melodic cadence liable to form in the major scale. All the same, church-music could not but find itself taking in elements from the thing it fought, and thus it willynilly strengthened its own thews, e.g. the stiff motet style warmed with popular ingredients in Dunstable.

A stimulating instrumental form was the *carole*, originally a round-dance, which was sung by a leader with refrains by a chorus. Dance-forms proliferated, coming ever more to the fore; hornpipe, dumps, *basses danses*, and so on. At the same time the polyphonic influence elaborated and stylised the dances. For long, instrumental music was mainly tied to the dance and had to fight hard for an independent existence.

Meanwhile the central struggle was going on in the Church. In the French school of Notre-Dame of Paris, from the mid-12th to the second half of the 14th century, we find an increasing freedom, a play of arabesques, with the use of contrary parts. Pérotin introduced chromatism and invented the fertile procedure of imitation, juggling with three or four parts. The *Ars Antiqua* spread to Italy and Spain, where popular dances with their binary time had been resisting the church dogma that music should be ternary to express the Trinity. The 12th-13th centuries saw the great burst of song through the Trobadors and Trouvères, the Minnesanger and Meistersanger in Germany, the wandering Franscisan singers in Italy, and others. Early in the 14th century a further step forward, the *Ars Nova*, was made, begun by the treatise of Philippe de Vitry. The 3rd and the 6th entered tonality; the change of tone by an accidental sign before a note prepared the way for fullblown chromaticism; and there was no escape from the leading-note whose sliding semitone was in time to impose the major and the minor scale. Despite the timeless flow in Gregorian chant there is a drive for architectural constructions; the sense of endless interlaces is replaced by awareness of the harmonies at a given point; the motet lengthens, with increased virtuosity. And secular music extends its form in complexity and unity. The polyphonic song arrives. There are *ballades* with varied rhythms, even cross-rhythms, and with syncopation; *rondeaux*, sometimes iso-rhythmic; *virelays* simpler in structure and using birdcalls. Guido, in a highly syncopated rondeaux, says, 'God save the man who can sing this'; and Dufay depicted a lover's confusion by writing each of three voice-parts in a different rhythm. The French *chase* and Italian *caccia*, from which our *catch*, is canonic throughout, a hunt-description with the hunter chasing his quarry and never losing sight—also with effects of yelping hounds and sounding horns. Naturalistic imitation becomes the fashion, leading on to Jannequin in the early 16th century, with his Paris streetcalls, birdsongs, gossip of women, battle-noises.

The French had dominated the 14th century, with music still essentially medieval, concerned with extended detail in ornamentation. But there was a break between the *Ars Nova* and the polyphony of the next century; Agincourt in 1415 installed the English as masters of France and they brought their own musicians. John Dunstable came to the fore, revealing a new suppleness, rhythmic freedom, pleasant consonances, chains of thirds and sixths. French musicians migrated to Artois, Flanders, the Netherlands, leading to the work of Ockeghem, Obrecht, des Prés, and others, in the later part of the century. The way was opened to the music of the Renascence, though none of these men trod it far. They developed the song and the instrumental ensemble to the point where they combined in new ways and began to break away from medieval bases.

Drama. We have seen how liturgic drama grew up at Byzantium and helped along similar developments in the West. A trope, or additional melody, introduced into the Mass of Easter morning, led to a little mime, three voices representing the Three Maries coming to the tomb and a fourth Angel on guard. Probably in the 11th century this small play was acted separately, growing less formal and moving from choir to nave, where some structure stood for the tomb. Actions were developed: the lifting of the pall and the finding of the open sepulchre, the display of the cast-off gravecloth; the sequence *Victimae Paschali* was added, with dialogue between the Maries and the choir (the whole body of disciples) or two singers (as the spokesmen); then the two singers were turned into Peter and John who visit the tomb, John arriving first but Peter getting first into the tomb, and these two took up the *linteum* or gravecloth. More scenes were worked-out: in the garden and at the spice-merchant's shop from whom the Maries bought unguents. So more dialogue and structures came in, as the representation was processional. Other little plays grew up at Christmas, with the Magi or the Three Shepherds visiting the Child, led by a moving star. A third embryonic drama was born from the regular sermon on the prophecies of the Messiah. The priest was aided by voices representing the prophets and citing their words; then other characters were used. Thus the material of both Testaments was made available for the sacred drama.

The French and Anglo-Normans seem to have led the way, but the development was widespread, linked with the broad movement that created the cathedrals. With the 12th-century *Adam*, in Anglo-Norman and Latin, the presentation is on a platform set up outside the western door for the Garden, and on another for Hell, the audience filling the square before the church. Already there is much sophistication of form. God, the *Figura*, retires into the church after giving commands to Adam and Eve, who are hidden in their nakedness by curtains from the shoulders down. The Devil efficiently tempts Eve; God appears again; the sinning pair are expelled; Abel is murdered; the prophets arrive in procession; and a vision of the Redeemer concludes. Already the townsfolk were taking over in England, merchant guilds, in France local brotherhoods or confrèries, in Italy companies of youths dedicated to various saints.

Through the 13th century the scope widened, with miracle plays and saints' lives, on their festivals, e.g. *The Miracle of Theophilus* by Ruteboeuf about 1284 on a man who sold his soul to the Devil, or the play of *St. Nicholas*, about 1200, by Jeal Bodel, set in the Crusades. The Easter play expanded and was cut into acts, each needing a separate stage; then became a number of different plays, acted on different platforms. The performances came to be spread over several days. In France and south Europe the platform stayed in the main square, but in England and Flanders the players were mounted on waggons and moved round the town, stopping at certain places. Corpus Christi, established in 1311, had no direct connection with scripture or the lives of saints, and so offered a good chance for expansion in new directions. Great cycles of plays, giving the whole range of biblical history, from the Fall to the Harrowing of Hell, were created, in which craftsman-groups forged an instrument for expressing their view of the world; even in the smaller towns and villages many minor plays were produced by the parochial organisation.

To the world-vision in all its epical sweep and homely simplification were added rich folk-elements that promised a high future for drama when their fecundating qualities were fully absorbed into the schematic structure. Pathos of Abraham winding his kerchief round Isaac's eyes and kissing his 'fair sweet mouth', episodes in which craft-details could be exploited, such as that of Noah's ship, with drollery of Noah and his wife (which Chaucer tells us was much enjoyed), realistic humour in the beadle of Pilate, the Roman soldiers, the shepherds looking for a stolen sheep, the midwives at the holy birth, mime-themes like Joseph's suspicion over Mary's pregnancy. Balaam had been brought in, and a bit of business with the ever-popular Ass. (We must not forget *The Prose of the Ass*, e.g. at Beauvais on 14 January, where an ass was introduced into church in the representation of the Flight into Egypt, and brays were introduced into the mass; instead of saying *Ite missa est*, the celebrant brayed three times and the people brayed back; the *Prose* hailed the Lord Ass.) Connections came about between the Christmas Play and the Feast of Fools; possibly Herod was acted by the mock-king. Leaders of the fool-rites bore his name; and buffoonery centred round Herod as a roarer and ranter, in fact, a fool-figure.

The plays indeed often became strongly anti-clerical, as in the *Antichrist* done at Advent at Tegernsee. The blackened devils suggested fertility-figures as well as frightening demons; and the dialogue might hold ironies and double-meanings:

> Sire, hear what tricks this mad priest sets
> Water out of a ladle he gets,
> throws it on people's heads, and says that they
> are all of them Saved when they go away. . .
> Roman Lords, I am informed that their plan
> is to set a crucified gallowsman
> over our empire as a god reigning
> without even deigning to ask our permission—

the laugh that Domitian got in the French play about St. Denis had treason in it.

In the original core of the sacred drama we see very much the same elements as in the Greek. The *pathos* of the crucifixion, the messenger (angel), the discovery and theophany; the *planctus* of the Maries, the *agon* of the nativity, with Herod as the villain trying to kill the baby culture-hero. The elements did not cohere in the Greek way to develop directly into tragedy; but their presence was none the less significant. Three centuries were needed before the potentialities of the new form could be brought to a head; and during that period new genres added their quota to the fullgrown Renascence drama. Farces, linked in their material with the *fabliaux*, led into the interlude; and the morality-play appeared as a new effort to schematise and work out the dramatic structure in relation to contemporary life. In Holland the Rederijker, burgess guilds of verse-lovers, produced Moralities and organised literary competitions and pageants. In England and France there were companies of interlude-players. Satirical elements grew stronger, e.g. in the anonymous *Maitre Pierre Pathelin*, dealing with a rascally lawyer. And at times this side of the interlude linked with the *sottie*, the small play for a company of fools.

Now we touch the aspect that shades off into the countless festival-forms of broken-down fertility-ritual—the May-games and spring-rites; the fire-festivals; the rites of the dead at Halloween; the midwinter feast, with Christmas mock-mayors, Yule and Yule's wife, the German Night of the Mothers (on 24 December); the games of the opposed sides, often given a dramatised form with some pseudo-historical reference, e.g. at Coventry in 1575, depicting the Danish defeat in 1002 'in actions and rhymes'; the mimes of the mock-king, harvest-lord, Abbot of Bon Accord, any title that would express the reversal of things, with the productive group supplanting the lords of power; the changing of clothes between the sexes; trails of the saturnalia as when the shoemakers chose their mock-king Crispin on 25 October; Epiphany kings and kings of the Bean; beast-guisings and the use of animals even in ecclesiastical processions; heads and hides of cattle worn in dance and song-perambulation; the hobby-horse; the fool with his cow-tail, hare-tail, or fox-brush; the maskings and face-blackings; dances like that surviving at Abbot's Bromley at Christmas with its horned dancers and hobby-horse, clown, woman and archer; mumming-plays of death and resurrection; morris-dances and sword-dances, fertility-leaps and the mimings of the struggle between summer and winter for the earth-bride; dressing of wells; driving-out of winter or dearth—and so on in an endless catalogue.

The fifteenth century saw the full efflorescence of the medieval drama-elements. In such a world the ritual forms could not freely develop into tragedy and comedy on the Greek lines. For one thing, the Church was radically opposed to the fertility-aspects, even if it could not stop a continual infiltration of folk-forms into its festivals. The inner conflicts in the scholastic world from the 14th century on, which could only issue in Reformation and

Renascence, prevented any point of intellectual rest. It was necessary therefore for the medieval drama to break down and new forms to arise out of its wreck. By 1500 the cycles had been completed and decay was setting in.

One further point needs to be made. The morality-play was in many respects, together with the interlude, the link between the medieval drama and the drama of the 16th century. It was directly allegorical, with virtues and vices for its characters; but the particularising element in medieval thought, which accompanied its generalising and symbolising tendencies, inevitably kept on turning the abstract idea into social type, and the social type into something of an individual. Behind it lay the Debate-form and the Dance of Death. Thus the English *Pride of Life* showed Death and Life contending for the soul of Rex Vivus, Man; and the Dutch *Everyman*, which was done into English, showed God sending Death to Everyman, who then sought round for friends to go with him on his spirit-journey. The earliest reference to the Death-dance seems by Jean Le Fèvre, '*Je fis de Macabre la dance*', about 1376. But from the 13th century French literature knew the motive of three living men who meet three dead men; the latter recount their own past grandeur and give warnings of the near end for the living. Art took the theme over, e.g. in the frescoes of Pisa's Campo Santo, the sculptures of the portals of the Innocents at Paris, 1408. Miniatures and woodcuts broadcast the imagery, and the death-dance was enacted; in 1449 the duke of Burgundy had it done at Bruges. The Innocents, since 1424, had elaborated the popular theme in paintings on its cloister-walls, which were used for the cuts of the *Danse Macabre* issued in 1485. The dancer however is not Death; he is the living man as a dead man, and so he is called in the stanzas of the book, which copy the lines from the Innocents. The origin of the fantasy seems to lie in the roundabout dance of the dead folk emerging from their graves—a theme later used by Goethe in his *Totentanz*. The dancer is thus the deathly-double of the person approached; and only near the century's end does the corpse become skeleton, as in Holbein's cuts. The terror-of-death seems to have grown acuter as the medieval epoch drew near its end, expressed in countless poems (with two main forms: the *Ars moriendi* and the *Four Last Things*, of which Death was the first) and in such gruesome use of the cloisters and charnel-houses of the Innocents as a promenade and rendezvous in 15th-century Paris.

There were circular stages, as in Cornwall. It has been suggested that these derived from the use in some places of surviving Roman theatres. But the round theatre was a world-image. We have the plan for the *Castle of Perseverence*, in Henry VI's reign. A large circle is enclosed with 'watyr a bowte the place if any dyche may be mad there [where] it schal be pleyed; or ellys that it be stronglye barryd al a bowte'. In the middle was a *castellum* and below it a bed for Mankind; mansions at the four cardinal points: God had his in the east, Belial in the north, World in the west, and Caro in the south—Covetousness being slipped in in the north-east. (At Lucerne and Donaueschingen we also meet the north as the site of evil.)

15th-century Architecture. In Italy there were early signs of the failure of Gothic to take root. Thus, at Florence, even when there were aisles, as at S. Maria Movella or S. Croce, they were so shallow and the arcades were so wide that there is no feeling of Gothic movement. A different spirit from that of France or England also showed up in the way in which artists were called in to take charge, e.g. Florence electing Giotto as master-mason—a tradition carried right on into the 16th century. Already by 1419 the Renascence had taken charge of architecture. Brunelleschi, a goldsmith, then began the Foundling Hospital, using fine Corinthian columns and wide semi-circular arches, and, above them, rectangular windows under shallow pediments that corresponded to the arches below. An architrave divided the two floors, and medallions by Della Robbia filled the spandrels in the arcades. The same architect designed the first wholly centralised church of the Renascence.

In the north of Italy the attitudes were different. Gothic lingered in the flamboyant cathedral and Venice did not admit Renascence-styles till after 1455.

Alberti was the theorist of the new style, studying ruins at Rome as well as the recently-found text of Vitruvius; at Rimini he adapted the Roman triumphal arch to church-forms. The approach was static, conceiving form as made up of separately added spatial units. In a sense, by dropping the Gothic dynamic movement of light, mass and design, it went back to Romanesque, where also the wall was solid; but it quite lacked any organic feeling. At its best, all it could do was to attempt to revive the Greek tradition that the form, both in its general system and in its decorations, should obey the laws of reason, in geometrical ratios and in relation to human uses and proportions. Linear perspective and a sense of order were its controlling factors.

14: Medieval Literature

Breakdown and Renewal. The literature of the dark-ages and medieval period came about through a steady fusion of remnants of the ancient tradition and the new elements brought by the barbarians. Inevitably there was a rebirth of epic, which we may divide into two sections: that which is still close to the tribal world and its bases of ritual-myth, and that which is a feudal recreation. Elements of both types carry over into romance.

First, however, let us glance at the trends during the empire's breakdown in the West. As in art, provincial and local trends asserted themselves, with a romantic stress on colour, as in *The Vigil of Venus*, which has been claimed for both north Africa and Gaul. (The only area with an intellectual development able to stand up against the East was north Africa, with Tertullian, Cyprian, Augustine; but after the Vandal invasion this centre of Roman culture was extinguished. The Papacy was deprived of the one highly-cultured Latin area, but at the same time no longer had to fear its objection to a centralised control.) In Gaul in the 4th-5th centuries we see the imperial culture breaking down and taking in all sorts of new elements. Quantitative verse is already shaken; strange groups pedantically argue on grammar and at the same time make extreme experiments with language as in the *ars scissendi*, where words are cut up and put together again, sometimes in sheer gibberish. These groups were not without effect in Ireland and south-west England, where we find such contorted works as *Hisperica Famina* composed. Rhyme, which the ancients used as a rhetorical ornament for ornate prose, comes in as part of the stress-system; for now the rhyme is connected with the desire for clash and emphasis in stress-accents, it picks out the line-end and pinpoints the turns, giving a new force to the symmetries of couplet or quatrain. Germanic alliterative verse complicates the situation; but it is a mixture of learned and folk-elements, not unconnected with the dance, which ultimately creates the new stress-metrics triumphant with the 13th century. Wandering scholars, many of them Irish in the early phases, played their part in this obscure phase; for they alone were familiar alike with the learned Latin world and the folksongs and dances. Thus we find in Latin a lament on the Death of Charlemagne, which seems by an Irishman (as he addresses one Columban) and which has a strong folk-element. It opens:

> Now from the Sunrise-lands to Seas that bound the West
> let songs of grieving beat the world's afflicted breast.
> *O but my heart is sad.*
> Grief is a shadow now that reaches to the Sea,
> too great for us to reckon, hovering hopelessly.
> *O but my heart is sad.*

And while the Germanic singers were carrying on their own epical tradition, there were bards in Gaul, like the Angilbert, who sang in Latin the Battle of Fonteney:

> I, Angilbert, beheld it all, this crime of which I tell,
> and I make a song upon it, for I fought where others fell.
> Alone I'm left of that front-line that fought and perished well. . .

We may compare the early Welsh *Gododdin* with its tragic note and its bard's escape. 'There escaped but three . . . and myself out of the slaughter, because of my fine songs'.

Finally in the 11th and 12th century we see these scholar-poets writing vividly in the folk-tradition, with considerable stanzaic and rhyming dexterity; they clearly gave as well as took. By that time also poets of strong character like Hugo of Orléans and the Archpoet were foreshadowing Villon in their Latin.

Germanic Epic. One great work was created by the Germans, *Beowulf*, the fruit of the high development occurring in Northumberland. The theme is the hero who clears the land of monsters. Multiple elements are compressed— history, folktale (especially the tale-type, *The Bear's Son*, which we have discussed in connection with Siberian shamanism), and myth. The problem it deals with is essentially that of the blood-feud, which is the curse of a breaking-up tribal system and which continues till king's law can be imposed. The action is set in Heorot, the mighty meed-dwelling hall which the poet environs with a sense of doom. It is fated to perish by the bloodfeud—in a story that was among the most famous of the day. And echoes of the bloodfeud of which Ingeld was the centre are woven into the epic. (The Northumbrian Alcuin, writing to the bishop of Lindisfarne, reproved the monks. 'In your houses the voices of those who read should be heard, not a rabble of those who make merry in the streets. In the refectory the Bible should be read, the lector heard, not the harper, patristic sermons rather than pagan songs. For what has Ingeld to do with Christ?') Further the harper at Heorot sings the fate of Hengest and Finn, 'the legacy of mourning and vengeance', while the monster Grendel is the ever-looming shape of the feud in darkness:

Thus the noble warriors lived in pleasure and plenty, until a fiend in hell began to contrive malice. The grim spirit was called Grendel, a famous march-stepper, who held the moors, the fens and the fastnesses. The hapless creature sojourned for a space in the sea monster's home after the Creator had condemned him. The eternal Lord avenged the murder on the race of Cain, because he slew Abel. He did not rejoice in that feud. He the Lord drove him far from mankind for that crime. Thence sprang all that evil spawn, ogres and elves and sea monsters, giants too, who struggled long against God. He paid them for that.

In repeated ominous phrases the poet builds the image of Grendel and his mother, and the dark desolation they inhabit, and throughout the image is of the man exiled for the blood-feud.

For years he bore bitter hatred, violence and malice, an unflagging feud; peace he would not have with any man of Danish race, nor lay aside murderous death, nor consent to be bought off... Two great march-steppers, alien spirits, hold the moors. One of them, as far as they could certainly know, was the likeness of a woman. The other wretched creature trod the oath of exile in man's shape, except that he was greater in build than any other man...

Beowulf's desperate chase after Grendel is a spirit-journey into the under-world; in the tale-type this is quite clear and the enemy he there must tackle is the earthmother in her horrible form. Though the poet of *Beowulf* keeps this female foe, his need to make the monster symbolise the bloodfeud compels him to add her son as the main enemy. The story of the feud that brought Heorot down is told in the *Bjarkamal*. Bjarki is the hero of loyalty there, and is a figure closely related to Beowulf. We may then say that Beowulf is the myth-form of the loyalty that carries on despite the bloodfeud, and expresses the emotion of human solidarity which will one day eliminate the feud; Bjarki is the direct embodiment of this loyalty. (Hrothgar, the ruler of Heorot in both epic and saga, symbolised in legend the kingship at its most beneficent.)

Heorot seems Leire, which with Upsala was a Norse royal centre where a ritual drama involving sacrifice was enacted, perhaps at Yule. The roots of *Beowulf* may well go back to this drama. According to Saxon Grammaticus, the legendary king Hadingus killed a sea-monster at Upsala and instituted the festival of Frey, apparently the great fertility-rite; also we hear that Frey brought in human sacrifice there. Leire played for the Danish kings the part which Upsala did for the Swedish, and we may infer similar rites. Tales ultimately derived from ritual-myth tell of fights with water-monsters in many areas of England, Scotland, Normandy, Scandinavia.*

The *Nibelungenlied*, medieval in form, has elements going back into the Germanic past. It shows all the typical epic material of feud and violence in breaking-down tribal society, generalised in terms of the world-end familiar to Norse mythology; but it lacks the cohesive power of *Beowulf*. A more important development of epic method appears in the sagas. Here indeed epic merges with history and has gone through many changes; but the method, as in *Beowulf*, seems to go back to ritual drama, the disciplines that we see in the Eddic poems. The peculiar objectivity is derived, not from a lack of feeling but from a vision that concentrates on action and the revelation of character by word and act; the tensity is that of a drama which the spectators are observing with the utmost concentration of attention, so as to miss no clue, no significant gesture or tone. The earliest and best sagas, *Grettir the Strong* and *Burnt Njal*, tell of the feuds arising in the early days of settlement. The men of Iceland, torn from the homeland and its traditional pieties, were dominated by the question as to what constituted personal integrity, loyalty, manhood. The individual was starkly isolated, with only his right hand as sure ally; but honour was a need deeper than self-preservation, and the pang of desperate loneliness and self-reliance becomes the pledge of a new compact. The same atmosphere and the same technique appear in the best of our Border Ballads.

Chansons de Geste. In the early medieval world the same problem as to what constituted loyalty persisted; but the savage forms of the bloodfeud were gone,

---

* The ancestral dead were placated with blood at the Alfblot. The word *alf*, elf, is linked with the spirits of the dead, both in early Scandinavian and N. German beliefs. In one district till recently there were yearly ritual-plays. Youths with blackened faces took the roles; one played the victim, slain to music and song. A woman with blackened face and hideous get-up officiated, then partnered the victim in a dance (of resurrection), which ended with a mime of coitus. Note the dramatic tone in general of Anglo-Saxon narrative verse. The poet of *Beowulf* has difficulty in rapid movement; his method suggests the declamatory actor rather than the story-teller. Note also the restricted number of speakers and compare what is said of the *Edda*.

though feuds long continued. The centralising kingship was present, however insecurely, and the towns were taking on their new life. But in the feudal world of service, with the continually broken oaths of fealty, there was no

Court Mummers: Harleian MS 4379

easy answer to the question of loyalty and order. The *Chanson de Roland*, written perhaps by a cleric Théroulde in the early 12th century, tells how Roland, Charlemagne's nephew, made an heroic defence againts the Moslems at Roncesvalles. In fact, Charlemagne was little concerned to fight the Saracens; he did not take the Moslem Saragossa, but sacked the Christian Pamplona; and the Roncesvalles rearguard-action was fought by the Count of the Breton Marches against the Basques. But the facts of feudal disorder and treachery are ignored, so that the poet (or his folk-sources) may treat the theme of honour and loyalty, and relate the events to the Crusades for Jerusalem. Théroulde may even have had mainly in mind a desire to stir up the nobles of France and England into doing something.

Roland, with his friend Oliver and a fighting archbishop, takes over the the weak rear of the army at the instigation of a malicious stepfather; he is moved by his high sense of honour and refuses reinforcements. In the doomed battle he refuses also to blow his marvellous horn and summon Charlemagne. His devotion is swallowed up by his pride and he must atone with his death.

At this point, says the poet, in effect, the selflessness of a true vassal passes over into the headstrong worship of his own image. That is the poem's central theme. Its ethics, in fact, are based in the idea of disinterested action, as exemplified by Achilles in the *Ilias* or by Krishna's counsel to Arjuna in the *Bhagavagita*. (COHEN)

But it is disinterested action in terms of the poet's world; the poem is concerned with the conflict of the heroic ideal of individual battle-devotion with group-unity. The feudal obligation is finally lost in the overriding need of all Christians to unite against the infidel. 'Will the true God in the end be vanquished by Mahomet?' The style is direct and bare; the work as a whole is rather the sketch of an epic than the thing itself, unlike *Beowulf*, which, though weak in some structural points, is magnificently full. In *Roland* the myth-element has faded out.

Roland is by far the best of the *chansons de geste*, some of which are meandering legends with folk-elements of the marvellous. Many are oriented towards the Crusades, *e.g.* the series dealing with Count William of Orange, where, as in *Roland*, the perspective is that of the vassal rather than that of the lord. It is possible that initial impulse towards the *chansons* was given by the Viking invaders who became the Normans; the Germans are less likely candidates.

The Spanish *cantar de gesta* belongs to the same complex. One of the first dealt with a man who fought on the side of the Moslems and defied the French. *The Cid* (Arabic, *Sidi*, My Lord) told the life of a man who had died only forty years earlier: his adventures, wars and rehabilitation, his feud with the princes who marry his daughters. The moral impulse of epic is lacking, but the realistic elements look forward to the great prose works of Spain in the 16th century.

This is the period, roughly, of the epical outburst in the Byzantine world—of poems like *Digenis Akritas*, the Armenian *David of Sasun* with its strong folk-elements, and Rust'haveli's accomplished *Knight of the Tiger Skin* in Georgian—as well as of prose works like the Georgian cycle, *Amiran-Darejaninai*, ascribed to Mose Khoneli, or the Arabic chivalric romances, not to mention Firdousi's *Shahnemah* and the other Persian works that followed. To analyse these would bring richly out the entanglement of epic and romance, myth and folklore, in the large-scale poems and tales of this epoch.

Trobador. Before we glance at the romances, it would be best to consider Provençal verse, the first considerable body of lyrical poetry in a western vernacular. Here it seems that Arabian influences were important, fusing with popular elements. The first known *trobador*, William, Count of Poitou (1071-1126), crusaded in Syria and Aragon; and his father had brought dancing-girls captive from Spain. The earliest poems have a form like that of the Moorish *zajal*; they suggest eastern imagery with their nightingales and their flowers scented for love; and William has a coda with four lines of undiluted Arabic. The *zajal* may well be the parent of the *virelai* and *ballade*, even of the *rondeau*; in any event we may be sure it played a part in the new formations.* A long series of poetic genres rapidly evolved: *aubade, sestina, pastourelle, chanson* or *canzine*, and (in Spain) *copla*, as well as those just mentioned.

The *trobadors* wandered round with a *joglar* who played the music. Much of the love-treatment in the songs was related to the system of *courtoisie* or fashionable gallantry; but it would be a great error to reduce the *trobadors* to the position of mere exponents of courtly love. Their region of south-west

Festival Mummers; Bodleian MS.

France was making a prosperous burgess-advance and was thick with heresies and anti-clerical emotions. Some *trobadors* like Bernard de Born took a firm stand on their noble status; but many belonged to the world of the commoners. Marcabrun had been an exposed child; Bernard de Ventadour was the son of an oven-heater; G. de Borneil was 'without fortune'; A. de Mareuil was a 'clerk of poor birth'; G. Faidit was son of burgess in a small Limousin township and 'took for wife a *fille-de-joie*'; R. de Vaquyras was son of a 'poor knight' considered 'out of his head'; P. Vidal was son of a furrier; P. d'Auvergne, J. Estève, F. de Marseille, G. Riquier were of burgess origin. Others came from the minor impoverished nobility; and a few, like the Monk of Montaudon or P. Cardenal, who were of higher birth, were the very singers with nothing courtly about them, who took the strongest satirical positions.

One form, the *Sirventes* or Service-song, quickly lost its feudal implications and became the form for attacking privilege, especially in the Church. Cardenal was never tired of mocking at priestly greed and cruelty, but he also widened his satire in a general defence of the poor:

---

* *Aucussin and Nicolette* (from Arras) with its mixed prose and verse is close to Arabic method; it is surprising, too, in its bravado about hell, its mock-battle, its account of *couvade*. For the form, compare the *Gulistan* of S'adi in Persia—and pieces from the MSS found near Tun-Huang in China, dated 5th-11th centuries. Perhaps the genre spread east and west from Persia.

> If a poor man has snitched a piece of rag,
> he goes with dowcast head and frightened eye.
> But when a rich man fills his greedy bag,
> he marches on with head still held as high.
> The poor man's hanged that stole a rotten bridle.
> The man who hanged had stolen the horse, O fie. . .

And he used the imagery of the Land of Cockaygne in his denunciation of the rich:

> With loving kindness how they quicken,
> what boards of charity abound.
> If stones were bread upon the ground,
> and if the streams with wine should thicken,
> the hills turn bacon and boiled chicken,
> they'd still grudge crumbs. Such folk are found.

Some forms of song derive directly from the spring-rites, e.g. the *pastorela*, which tells of a love-encounter between poet or cavalier and peasant maiden. A *trobador pastorela* ends:

> He kissed her thrice, but still
> she closed her mouth, until
> he kissed her for the fourth time, and
> 'Take me, sir', she said.

We may compare for the formula the song sung at Helston in Cornwall in May for the Furry Dance, a serpentine maze-dance which winds in and out the houses throughout the town:

> John the bone [beau] was walking home
> when he met Sally Drover.
> He kissed her once and he kissed her twice
> and he kissed her three times over.

There were elementary dramatic forms: *Jocs partitz*, where the challenger postulated a subject of amorous casuistry and had to give the other man the choice of which side to take up; *tençons* or debates. (The debate-form, having deep roots in the fertility-rite, always crops up. Alcuin had a *Contest of Spring and Winter*; and medieval verse was thick with such arguments, e.g. *The Violet and the Rose*, ending with the moral: 'And do not call your associates slaves; call them sister-friends'. Or the 15th-century English *The Flower and the Leaf*, where worker-leaf is set against flower-of-display.) The *aubade* or dawn-song was again an old form. Here is the short anonymous one that seems the oldest Provencal example:

> O while the nightingale, early and late,
> sings away at the side of his mate,
> warmly I clasp my darling and wait
> under the flower,
> while the watchman, high in his tower,
> sings: Arise, you lovers, arise,
> the dawn is up in the brightening skies.

Shakespeare dramatised the *aubade* in *Romeo and Juliet;* but the genre was familiar in ancient Egypt:

> I hear your voice, O turtledove,
> the dawn has spread its glow.
> Weary am I with love, with love,
> O whither shall I go ?

In China about 700 B.C. they sang:

(*Woman*) I hear the crowing of the cock, the sun is in the skies.
(*Lover*) It wasn't the cock that you heard crow, but the buzz of those
green flies.

And about the same time in Greece, there was heard:

> What's wrong? Don't spoil it all for us, I pray.
> Before he finds us here, be up and well away.
> Don't get yourself into a mess, and wretched me—
> Already, through the window breaks the dawn, O see.

But we come closer to the *trobador* love-ethic in one of the May-songs sung as part of a round-dance. The girls circle round their leader, while a man acts the part of a jealous old husband and tries to break through. The girls taunt him, praise their leader and sing of the young lover who will carry her off. Here we have in a simply rationalised form the conflict of the young and the old year; and the *trobadors* took the theme up in its courtly form. The poet-lover adores a beautiful woman from afar, unable to approach her because of the Jealous. The latter figure is never precisely defined, but is abominated as the denier of life, the obstructive power that spoils what otherwise would be a blissful union. The theme of the unapproachable beloved thus serves to express on the one hand a feeling that there is some force or gap in the present which makes it impossible to actualise the image of beauty, of plenty and joy, and on the other hand to build a powerful dammed-up reservoir of desire, of all that is potential in the image. In the system of paradoxes that result, dearth and loss become the sole pledge of joy and plenty; and because the poet is so sure that he has rejected the existent bond that corrupts, he is equally sure that he looks forward to the moment when a different sort of bond, without corruption, will be possible. In the intensity of his rejection and hope, he indeed feels the future in the present; he realises love in the only form that is pure from egoism, greed, possessive lust. Thus Bernard de Ventadour utters the paradox:

> My heart's so filled with deep delight
> it changes all I see.
> The frost appears a blossom of white,
> yellow or green, to me.
> When the wind blows up the rain, it's right:
> my fortune sprouts with the tree,
> So thrives my worth with freshening might

and my song gains loftier glee.
Such is my love and such the power
of joy and sweetness in its dower,
each icicle seems to me a flower
and the snow seems greenery.

William of Poitou had started the theme off:

I love, but do not know her name,
together yet we never came,
and so I've naught to praise or blame,
and that's my aim.
No messages I get or claim,
it's all the same.
It's mad on such a love to stray.
She never made me sad or gay
for, missing her, I smile and say:
Here's holiday !
I find a fairer guest who'll play
a better way.

His robust touch made him jeer at the mode. And since he stood at the start of the tradition, his jeer makes all the more likely that he was aware of the eastern mystical ideas that came to a head in the Persian poet, Hafiz, of the 14th century:

Far through the world I've roamed and found a thing that I can claim
to be most sweet and ravishing, but please don't ask the name.
Her footsteps everywhere are wet with tears of my desire,
but as to how this came about, I beg you'll not enquire. . .
Sad in my cottage left alone, with you gone off afar,
I suffer endless agonies, but don't ask what they are. . .

But poets like Bernard de Ventadour, with the theme of love's constancy or Jauffre Rudel with his imagery of the 'distant love', had taken the system deep into their spirits, into their art, and had provided the terms of poetic conflict in which men of the medieval world could most deeply grapple with what they felt the innermost secrets of life, the joyous and bitter anomalies of experience.

Provençal culture and its *trobadors* was wiped out in the bloody crusade launched by the Papacy against the Albigensian heretics, who stemmed from the Bogomile east, in the late 12th century. At least hundreds of thousands of people were massacred by the looters masquerading as righteous defenders of the faith; thus, at Béziers, the first town they struck, all the men, women and children were murdered, including those taking refuge in church.

Roman de la Rose. What we may call the *trobador* theses, then, accepted the medieval split of body and mind, drove it to an extreme in the thesis of unrealistic love, and sought to find a resolution by paradox. The antithesis of body and soul, of earthly and spiritual love, at one level expressed the hope-less split in medieval society and the impossibility of actualising the hopes of a good and free life on earth while that split existed. It thus enabled men to get at grips with the reality of their situation in a way that any easy effort to bridge the gap directly could not have done. Yet it was necessary for those efforts to be made as a complement to the *trobador* position; and the work which put the counter-attitudes was the *Roman de la Rose*.

Even in the way in which it was written, the *Roman* showed the deep conflict from which it issued. For Guillaume de Lorris, the young man who about 1235 began the work, died after writing some 4,000 lines; and Jean de Meun took it up and completed it before 1280.Guillaume, it is likely, had meant to carry on the *trobador* ethic in an idealist way and deny the lover his rose of consumation; but Jean was a satirical realist, who brought the allegorical theme down mockingly and warmly to an earthly fulfilment. The dream-tale told of the attempt of the Lover to enter the Garden of Love and pluck the Rose. It thus transplanted the paradise-garden into the erotic world, and employed at vastly extended length all the allegories of courtly love for an end that turned out to be the subversion of the courtly conventions. The lover is admitted by Dame Leisure, while Gaiety leads the dance, Amor holds Beauty's hand, and so on. Guillaume's section ended with Reason's descent from its high tower and the advent of Venus. Jean carried on with a bold defence by Venus, Nature, and Genius, of sensuous enjoyment and ended with Bel-Accueil permitting the lover to pluck the Rose.

A variation of the *trobador* ethic appeared in the circle of Charles d'Orléans, where the pangs of love were compared with the sufferings of the ascetic and the martyr. The poets were *les amoureux de l'observance*, referring to the sharp reforms put into action in the Franciscan Order. 'Here are your Ten Com-mandments, True God of Love', Charles began a poem, and in another he celebrated his dead love in *le moustier amoureux*, with a service sung by dolorous Thought. This attitude culminated in *L'Amant rendu Cordelier de l'Observance d'Amour* of the late 15th century, which told of the reception of the hopeless lover in the convent of love's martyrs. At the same time bawdy tales as in *Les Cents Nouvelles Nouvelles*, as well as many songs, took over religious symbolism and applied it lewdly. The defenders of the *Roman de la Rose* used sacred terms to designate the genitals.

Romance. The courtly romance had soon succeeded the epic, largely directed to the ears of wellborn ladies. In drawing on the Matter of Britain, however, it gained a rich source of folklore and broken-down myth, which had gathered the aspirations of the Celtic peoples round the figure of the liberator, Arthur. The theme of the Arthurian court in France was fused with another important myth-theme, that of the Quest of the Holy Grail, in which the fertility-rite had been Christianly allegorised. Arthur, as the saviour of his people, like Charlemagne, took the place of Christ at the Round Table, and the Dish of the Last Supper became the grail-cup. The epical aftermath appeared in the use of the motive of betrayal and failing loyalty to explain the collapse of the world of justice and prosperity. Arthur was betrayed both by Modred and by Launcelot; and the motive of love against duty, the romance-form of the epic honour-motives, is at the heart also of the tale of Tristan and Iseult.

The folk-themes of the Pure Fool and the Forest Withdrawal, closely linked with the similar themes we noted in Indian epic, break into the Romance. We meet them in a Breton tale of the forest-babe with talismanic dish that provides a wonderful food and can be equated with the Celtic cauldron of plenty; we may also compare the Greek cornucopia. Chrétien de Troyes in the 12th century took up the theme. The child is brought up by his mother, the widow of a man treacherously slain; later he emerges as a perfect knight of chivalry, avenges his father, marries a highborn girl, and acquires the dish, the Breton Graal. This tale, *Perceval*, had many continuations and in France and Germany, and from it grew the full legend of the grail-quest. The Graal was linked with the Last Supper and Perceval joined the Round Table; the grail-cup was said to have caught Christ's blood and thus connected with the wounding Lance. The tale is rounded off by Wolfram von Eschenbach. A knight, Titurel, after fighting the Saracens, has a vision of the Graal and founds a church to guard it; he is led through lonely woods to the top of a Mountain, where he builds his church, Montsalvat, mount-of-salvation, another heavenly-mount. Perceval is his grandson. Another grandson, Amfortas, has been wounded and cannot die, having been hurt in a quarrel unconnected with the grail's defence. This lingering death of the king

Country Revel: Royal MS 2B VII.

(the fertility-hero) brings about a universal famine, the blight of the Waste Land—just as the temporary death of Tammuz or Persephone. How is plenty to be restored? The Fisher King is sick and impotent. (In one version the king has to be made young again.) Perceval decides to leave his forest-lair. His protesting mother dresses him as a Fool, so that he may be scorned and driven back; she also gives him the most impracticable advice. Thus, equipped with ideas exactly contrary to the facts of the world, he sets out. He makes many errors, but goes on wandering, considered by all a poor mad fool. At last he reaches the castle. He sees the dying-undying king, but does not ask what is wrong. The castle vanishes and he is thrown back on his wanderings. A hermit tells him that he should have asked the Question. At long last he gets his second chance and asks. Then all is well; plenty is restored; Perceval is crowned. 'Hail to you, Perceval King of the Graal, seemingly lost for ever, now are you blessed for ever'. (We are not surprised when the women he has wedded in his wanderings turns up with Twins.)

The theme of the culture-hero born and reared in nature is here closely linked with various motives from initiation-ritual, e.g. that of the question. Only the pure fool, child of nature, has the power to look at the world and see what is wrong, to ask the essential question which is impossible for those who have grown up with a distorted and corrupted world.

The Fool is a folk-version of the shaman, the individual cut off from ordinary life by his direct intercourse with the spirit-world. Madmen are taken to be possessed by a demon; the Fool is possessed too, but by a beneficient spirit that shames the listener with its inability to see the reasons and motivations that are sufficient for the men of this world, his unerring ability to grasp the pure human truth. In forms closer to tribal thought, the deranged fool appears in Celtic legend, e.g. in such characters as Mor Muman, Suibne, St. Moling, Lailoken connected with St. Kentigern. Merlin belongs to this series and shows the link of the forest-life with the rejection of blood-guilt; in him the oracular shamanist aspect comes to the fore.

The theme of the pure fool in its comic aspects extends from the ancient Greek epic-parody *Margites* to the folk-tales of the Wise Men of Gotham or other fool-villages such as Coggeshall. And we see the culture-hero breaking down into the fool or buffoon in Africa and America. Among the Algonquins, Michabo was creator and inventor of writing; yet

modern Indian tales concerning Michabo make him a mere tricksy spirit, a malicious buffoon, but in these we can see his character in process of deterioration under the stress of modern conditions impinging upon Indian life. It is in the tales of the old travellers and missionaries that we see him in his true colours as a great culture-hero, Lord of the Day and bringer of light and civilisation. (SPENCE)

We may recall also how in Attic comedy Herakles tended to appear as a rowdy boozer and butt.

The Question appears in other romances. Gawain, who is a grail-quester, is riding with a nameless knight; the knight is killed and Gawain takes his place, carrying on with a quest about which he knows nothing. Again a blight has to be overcome—it has been caused by the mysterious death—and Gawain has to face the Question. When it is asked, 'the waters flowed again through their channel and all the woods were turned to verdure'. In *Peredur* the hero's failure to ask in the Castle of Wonders ruins the world:

Had you asked, the King would have been restored to health and his dominions to peace, whereas from henceforth he will have to endure battles and conflicts and knights will perish and wives will be widowed and maidens left portionless, and all this because of you.

Gerson tells us that he met a man at Auxerre, who held stoutly that All Fools Day was as sacred as the day of the Virgin's Conception; perhaps the man was not so foolish as the theologian thought.

Gawain has many important myth-motives attached to him. In *The Wedding of Sir Gawain and Dame Ragnell* he weds a hag who turns into a lovely girl: a very common Celtic transformation attached to the earthmother. In the splendid 14th-century poem *Sir Gawain and the Green Knight* he is engaged in a magical fertility-combat.

The romance-theme of entering the Forest still relates to the underworld-journey; it occurs in the opening of Dante's *Commedia* as well. And we have seen how it goes back to *Gilgamesh*.

'Thou shalt see a vale like a great waterway and in the middle of the vale thou shalt see a great tree with the tips of its branches greener than the greenest fir-trees. And under the tree is a fountain'. So Cynon is directed by the keeper of the forest in his wanderings, 'through the world and its wilderness' as told in the late Welsh romance from the Mabinogion. There he found 'the fairest vale in the world, and trees of equal height in it, and there was a river flowing through the vale and a path alongside the river'. Although this is twelfth century Welsh it describes what Gilgamesh and Enkidu saw when they entered the cedar forest in almost the same phrases: the cedar in front of the mountain, the glade green with brushwood, and the broad way where the going was good. The guardian of the forest in the romance had power over animals, which grazed round him in the glade, and the guardian of the cedar forest in the Semitic poem could 'hear the heifer when she stirred at sixty leagues distance'. This Humbaba is the perennial Monster Hersdman, like the ugly man with a club whom Cynon met or the Green Knight of the northern romance; he is a divinity of wild nature. . . (SANDARS)

He is more importantly the guard of the underworld like Cerberus; sometimes in Celtic legend he guards the spirit-tree like the Snake-Dragon of the Hesperides. What is striking is the close resemblance of the underworld journey in Celtic legend or romance and in Mesopotamian poetry.

Chivalry. The chivalric idea, largely derived from the east, though including elements drawn from Germanic tribalism, postulated a hero who had both elements of the pure fool (as in Gawain) and of the *trobador*-lover. The medieval mind saw actuality as a confused and broken process which gained meaning only in so far as it conformed to certain archetypes; history had meaning only in so far as it expressed the chivalric idea. From one angle then the knightly hero had to merge with the saint. Relics of the heroes had their own qualities of virtue, e.g. a sword of Tristram was among King John's valuables lost in the Wash, and another was found about 1300, in an ancient tomb of Lombardy. The motive of killing a monster to rescue a virgin was both a saintly act and a typical initiation-experience. The tournament, with its erotic colourations, was in the 15th century connected with the romance-imagery of the ordeal or test; it was based on some episode of chivalric adventure and set in a scene with a name like *L'arbre Charlemagne, La fontaine des pleurs*. Yet the ascetic element was deeply implicated in the ideal and appeared in the military orders. Chrétien wrote *Erec* to show how marriage hampered a knight; and chastity-tests are common to the Gawain tales. As the reality grew ever less like the ideal, the fantasy of the knight-errant, staking all things on his devotion to some noble quest, in turn grew stronger.

The medieval mind was never upset in its theories by the failure of people to live up to ideals; the important thing was to have the ideals to set over against the failures. As long as life seemed now and then to coincide with the archetypal ideas, all was well.

Popular Outbursts. We have seen in epic, in romance, and in *trobador* song, how close the upper levels were to the folk-levels, and this closeness continued till the early 15th century. It was not then lost, though the upflow from below was no longer decisive; the medieval world was beginning to break up. Meanwhile, however, let us glance at some of the forms in which the popular impulse is clear. In north France the *trouvères* are close to the peasantry, as shown by the spring-mating *pastourelle* and by the characteristic type of the 12th century, the spinning-and-weaving songs, lyrical in form but often dramatic in treatment like our Border Ballads. There is also much satirical and homely-realistic poetry, which in Ruteboeuf, 1250-85, looks to Villon. This *jongleur* developed the *fabliaux*, often bawdy tales, as well as miracle-plays, propagandist songs for the Crusades; and joined in the battles of Paris University, attacking the friars.

By the end of the 12th century five collections of fables, *isopets*, were being read in France, the oldest one being by Marie de France and based on Latin originals. But the folk had abundant material of its own in this field. The *Roman de Renard* mixed *isopet* and *fabliau*, dealing with Renard the fox, Isengrin the wolf, Chanticleer the cock, Tibert the cat, and developing sharp satire against the feudal world. The wily Renard defeats his more powerful enemies. The suppressed peasant and burgess had to use his wits against the lords; but as the money-power rises, Renard is less of a hero. He then contributes to the satire of the picaresque world.*

The *jongleurs* travelled the pilgrim routes, especially that to St. James of

---

* The animal fable went back to Egypt. The Greeks developed it strongly, e.g. *The Battle of Frogs and Mice* parodied the war-epic, and the *kerkopes* told of monkey-men, 'liars and cheats' who wander round 'deceiving men', to be put down in the end by Herakles. The Phrygian slave Aesop perfected the animal parable. (We find it used early by poets like Archilochos in their personal conflicts.) Phaedrus, a Thracian or Macedonian who had also been a slave, wrote a Latin collection (1st c. A.D.) and stated directly the need to use the beast-fable to hide political comment. 'Why to invent these did men bend their skill? Slavery, fettered to another's will, dared not express the theme it wishes; disabled, to guise its inner meaning, thus it fabled, escaping censure by a jesting fiction'.

Compostella in Galicia; and so in Galicia, too, we find a sudden growth of varied song-forms; the *cantiga da amiga* (the girl lamenting her absent lover), the *pastorela*, the *barcarola* (the girl asking a sailor for news of her lover), and the *cosante* or round-dance. In Germany as well the outburst was brief, with less formalism of *Minne*, courtly love, than in south France, and with a feeling for natural beauty.

From Arras in the north of France came the *Jeu Adam*, with sub-title *Play of the Leaf*, a show given on platforms erected in the open and greenery-framed. The poet appears in person, and a debate is held whether he will stay in Arras with his newly-wedded wife or go to Paris to finish his studies. He brings his father (on whom he relies for funds) on to the stage, as well as neighbours and other town-burgesses, whom he subjects to raillery. A monk

Influences of the Planet Venus; German or Swiss Block-book c. 1475.

exhibits relics; a quack tells fortunes and tries to heal a babbling madman; the monk is merrily swindled in a tavern-scene. Finally the Three Fairies who preside over the fates of men, Morgue, Maglore, Arsile, appear and tell Adam to forget all his worries in his wife's arms. In his *Play of Robin and Marian*, the *carole* and the *pastorela* take dramatic form. The tale deals with the trials of two peasant lovers; a knight tries to take the girl, maltreats Robin, but is thwarted. The dialogue is entwined with dance-songs, and the piece ends with a farandole.

Robin and Marian in England became the spring-dancers of the morris. Robin from one angle seems a nature-spirit. A Yorkshire saying runs, 'The only thing that Robin could not stand was a cold spell', a ballad tells us that he was born in the greenery, like a proper culture-hero; and Little John gives his name to the sheriff, 'Men call me Reynold Greenleaf when I am at home'. He and Robin throw stone-quoits like the giants of folklore. But as Robin develops in the ballads, he is Robin Hood, the outlaw champion of the yeoman farmers, protesting against the loss of the land to the money-lords exemplified above all in the abbeys. 'For the abbot and the high justice would have had my land'. That is the call for aid to which he responds. 'Hast thou thy land again?' And he makes his position clear: 'What man that helped a good yeoman, his friend then will I be'. And 'Look ye that ye do no husband harm that tilleth with the plough. No more ye shall no good yeoman that walketh by the greenwood shaw'. The enemy are 'these bishops and these archbishops' and their ally in law, 'the high sheriff of Nottingham'. Robin mocks the churchmen, 'And ye have churches and rents both, and gold full great plenty. Give us some of your spending, for Saint Charity'. He is done to death by a prioress.* We can trace many early ingredients of the ballad-image, *e.g.* an Anglo-Norman ballad of Edward I's reign, which makes the same attack on the church-lords and the law. 'The poor man now is sold, I ween, whatever the rich may win'. And the wildwood is the free man's home.

> This rhyme was made within a wood, beneath a broad bay-tree. . .
> In honesty I speak. For me, I'd rather sleep beneath
> the canopy of a green tree, yea, on the naked heath
> than lie even in a bishop's vault for many a weary day.

About 1377 Langland (whose great poem opens as a May-dream) has a character who says, 'I can rhyme of Robin Hood and Randolf Earl of Chester', coupling two popular champions; and a Scotch chronicler of 1447 mentions that no one had such a hold over the common folk as Robin.

A ballad that holds immemorially old elements is *The Bloody Murder of John Barleycorn*, which describes the harvest-acts and the process of fermentation as a fierce attack on the corn-spirit, who is visualised as a farm-labourer. The enemy plough him up, bury him, harrow him, eat him and so on, but he always revives and arises again. Finally he triumphs as those who drink him

---

* There were many medieval plays about Robin, but they are lost save for fragments; the Elizabethan stage saw Munday's *Robert, Earl of Huntingdon*, and Chapman's *Mayday*. The minstrels, broken down into balladmongers, kept Robin's memory alive. Robin Hood's Ale was drunk; May was called Robin Hood's time. Parish records tell of Robin Hood and his Company, so strongly had playing troupes become identified with their chief character. Dunbar wrote *Cry for Maying with Robin Hood*: Henryson, a pastoral *Robin and Marion*. In 1555 the Scotch Parliament ordered that no one be chosen Robin Hood, Little John, Abbot of Unreason, Queen of May, 'neither in burgh nor to landward in any time to come'.

fall to the ground. (A Worms altarpiece shows Mary throwing Jesus into the hopper of a mill, from which he issues as bread to feed the people).

Dante. More important was the transference of Provençal forms to the German court at Palermo in Sicily, where the sonnet was born. When the court life there broke up in 1265, the poetic centre moved north. Already in Lombardy there had been such developments as the canticles of St. Francis, derived from popular poetry and aiming at a direct popular appeal; and the *laude* of Jacapone da Todi carried on the work, often using a lively dialogue-form, with a breathless immediacy of violent impact.* But now sophisticated *trobador*-poetry was appearing in Tuscany, among the communes of the north, and great new advances were made.

The Beautiful Unknown appears in the poems of the Bolognese Guinizelli, who develops an idea latent in the trobadors, which was important for Dante. Only the noble-minded can truly love, and so the lover owns nobility, *gentilezza*. But the ambiguities of the Provençal idiom, where the bar of the Jealous and the distance of the lady suggest a deferred rather than a rejected fruition, now fade out, and the lady becomes finally cut off, absorbed in the idea of love, the 'divine reality'. The split in medieval society is deepening; the emotional opposition of flesh and spirit grows ever more philosophical in its terms of definition.

Cavalcanti (*c.* 1260-1300) carried on the theme. His *ballata* from exile is to come before his lady as from one already dead. Angolieri introduced the counter-note of realism, reducing the whole business to a trivial hell of sordid money-worries. Then with Dante (1265-1321) the system was carried to a new level. In his *Vita Nuova* he developed the theme of possession-by-loss; in the *Convivio* twisted it into allegory. His impossible love was Beatrice, whom he may have seen for the first time when he was nine years old, though nine may be merely a symbolic number; she now became Truth, while remaining a particular woman. By carrying the trobador-paradox to its philosophic limit, the intangible love in effect turned into the Virgin Mary, whose cult was at its height. The only way to embrace her was to encompass the whole universe

---

* Jacopone, of noble birth, was shocked into asceticism when at a wedding the floor collapsed and killed his wife, who was found to be wearing a hair-shirt under her fine clothes; after ten years of studied contempt and himself, he was admitted with some doubts to the Franciscans. Once, to control his appetite he hung some lights in his cell till they rotted, while he sniffed them; when the friars found where the stench came from they threw J. into the privy, where he made up a jubilant *lauda*. Connected with the ejaculatory *laude*, hypnotic with repetition, was the frantic movement of the Flagellators which swept Italy, save in towns where gallows were set up to keep it out. Whole towns marched in a body to flog themselves for their neighbours' edification ... Byzantine influences were not negligible at any time. The *Ritmo cassinese*, one of the earliest Italian poetic texts, celebrates the Basilian hermits of S. Italy, especially St. Nilos the younger, who came to Monte Cassino c. 980. (GALDI). Dante seems to have based the moral order of the *Inferno* on a Byzantine treatise on Vice and Virtue, which was 'very probably one of the sources of our own *De Virtutibus et Passionibus*'. (TRYPANIS)

in a vision which amounted to a last judgment. The whole of contemporary society had to be depicted, and the poet must ascend through all the hierarchies of being.

Death and the Fool (from Brant's Ship of Fools, German edition).

The world-image is still that of the heavenly-mountain or ziqqurat; and Dante draws on a large number of sources, Virgil, Aquinas, Ibn-Arabi, Tundal the Irishman. He winds his way up the ziqqurat of timespace to the point of a final blissful vision of Mary; but in the process he has defined his whole world in the scheme of irreconcilable conflict and unbalance, repentance and purgation, liberation and fulfilment. The *Inferno*, which holds the realistic panorama of the Italy he has known, is pervaded with the lurid stormlight of a vast impending doom of change, the irruption of Henry of Luxemburg bringing political unity or Christ bringing the day of millenary wrath.

There are a few points to be noted. Dante was deeply torn by the political struggle between papacy and empire, which involved his passionate ideas about human unity and the meaning of life. He had gone beyond the position of Aquinas, who saw reason as serving faith; he denied that the two touch one other. Philosophy gives us here the beatitude of which we are capable, and the authority of the pope is eliminated from the natural life of men.

O Italy, you slave, you hostelry of woe, ship without pilot in rough tempest. . . Alas, you priests, who should be at your priests and let Caesar sit in the saddle, if well you understood the word God has written for you, see how the steed has grown vicious, for not being corrected by the spurs since you placed your hands upon the reins. (*Purgatorio*)

And in *De Monarchia* he shows how he applied the Aristotelian categories in a humanist way:

The work proper to the human race, taken as a whole, is to keep the full capacity of the potential intellect constantly actualised, primarily for speculation, and secondarily (by extension, and for the sake of the other) for action. . . The speculative intellect by extension becomes the practical intellect, the end of which is doing and making. . . There are things to be done which are regulated by political wisdom, and things to be made which are regulated by art. But they are all alike handmaids of speculation as the supreme function for which the Prime Excellence brought the human race into being.

There is still the idealist split, with its elevation of the theoretical mind, but the notion of speculation is growing less abstract; and the stress on potentiality being ceaselessly transformed into actuality by the practical intellect swings the scheme away from the cyclic universe of theology into the world of men. The aim of society is the *vita felice;* to actualise the potential intellect by bringing into play the whole capacity of the mind, the first essential is peace. Dante's political ideas all relate to this point. The way is open to the secular positions of such humanists as Marsiglio of Padua, who in his *Defensor Pacis*, shortly after Dante's death, contends that the State exists to enable men to live well: 'to have leisure for liberal tasks, such as those of the virtues of the soul as well as of thought as of action'.

Finally we may note that in the *Purgatorio* (xv) Dante sets out the principle: 'By so much more there are men who say "Ours", so much the more of good does each possess'. He does not however see any way of applying this to the things of earth.

He made his great summarising vision of the medieval world, in its thought and in its action, in its world-view and in its daily embittered existence, at the moment when the system was entering on a crisis, with much of the inner contradictions of its ideas and attitudes breaking through the scholastic frame. More, the terms of his presentation embodied the crisis; for he sought, while using the given imagery of his world, to define a condition of political and human unity which was quite inconsistent with that's world premises. Hence the profound inner tension in the great unrolling fresco of judgment and rapture.*

---

* An important date was 1176, when the free communes of Lombardy defeated the emperor Barbarossa, while the Papacy blocked the southern kingdom from spreading north. In Dante's day, feuds and feudal brawls mingle with the class-conflict, the Grandi seeking to hold down the Popolo Grasso. (The 13th century had seen the wings of the nobility clipped; then Florence had to call in mercenaries.) The *Commedia* is linked with the Jubilee of 1300, but has its roots in the following bitter years. Florence expanded to take in most of Tuscany, and a few major States arose, Venice, Milan, Florence, Papacy, Naples. In 1329 the Pope condemned *De Monarchia* to the flames; in 1555 it was put on the prohibited list.

Petrarch to Chaucer. Petrarch (1304-74) carried on the theme of the conflict of spiritual love and earthly life. But now the world-image underlying the work of the *trobadors* and Dante faded out, and the poet was simply torn by an insoluble issue. That is why Petrarch has been called the first modern man; he is no longer medieval, upheld by a comprehensive body of doctrine and symbols even in his moments of revulsion and fear; in him the contemplative life becomes secular, and he is left only with the problem of himself and his relation to things, to situations and people. He inherits the medieval split, but without its compensations, he has to go on wrestling with himself. In Dante, the aspiration towards Beatrice moved from an actual woman to philosophic truth and thence to the Virgin Mary as the Mater Ecclesia, the enwombing All—a concept close to the heretical position of the Montanists in Asia Minor in the 2nd century A.D., which had spread to Gaul and North Africa with its imagery of nuptial union. In Petrarch the individual is alone; the relationship to the adored Laura reveals simply the conflict of his own divided flesh and spirit. What matters is the psychology, the problem of the will, the question of death dissociated from the medieval myth-images. Death becomes the emblem of a personal judgment, shredding all its overtones of a world-end crisis. As befits such a man, Petrarch is a restless scholar, concerned with self-improvement, watching his reactions and his torn impulses by the small sharp light of a new self-consciousness, both as man and as artist. Solitude is his refuge, yet also the space of his self-inquisition, delivering him up, despite his romantic enjoyments, to the thing he flees.

With Boccaccio (1313-75) the secularisation continues. The rose-garden becomes an actual garden of lovers, and we see the change from the rhetoric of courtly love and the interminable meandering of etiolated romance to psychological inquiry and homespun humorous realism. The desired one is now hedged off by nothing more mysterious than the suspicious eyes of husband and censorious world; all the tricks whereby the Jealous can be defeated are aired. We are at the halfway house between the *fabliaux* or *Renard* and the picaresque tale. In Boccaccio's own development we see the burgess-world shaking off the fantasies of romance, pastoral or would-be epical, and introducing bawdiness, characterisation and settings from the actual world, and finally the transformation of the *Roman de la Rose* from allegory to a gay realism. (In the process he made the love-romance of Troy, *Il Filostrato*, which Chaucer, Henryson and Shakespeare were to develop; in *Amoroso Visione* he used the motive of the spirit-journey with no better goal than a set of trite love-tales; and in *Corbaccio* tried an extended flyting at women.) He came to rest in the villa-garden on the Fiesolan hillside; and though the tales there told were taken from all sorts of sources, he added to them at his best a lively verisimilitude and a convincing note of plain realism which had been lacking since Petronius, Lucian, and Apuleius.

He also, however, left a name as the 'doctor of patience in adversity' and the serious vein in his views appears in the way he heartens himself with the thought of the Golden Age. 'O what a world it had been!' How different from 'this present age, full of so many poisoned pleasures, unprofitable ornaments and shadowed pomp'. No men were worthy but those who found that 'all their joy and inward delight was for the avail of the common profit'. And, 'Shall I call the tyrant king or prince and obey him loyally as lord? No, for he

Devils and Fools (Brant).

is the enemy of the commonwealth. Against him I may use arms, conspiracies, spies, ambushes and fraud; to do so is a sacred and necessary work.'

In England the popular tradition in the 14th century came to a powerful head in the alliterative *Piers Plowman*. Langland marshals in his field of folk the entire common life of the medieval age, with a perspective of deep understanding and pity. He is torn by a divided impulse. As a deep-rooted medieval man, he cannot conceive a world without a hierarchy united in service to one another and to God; yet he responds so deeply to the egalitarian element in Christianity that he sees history moving to the last-judgment in which the Plowman is saviour and judge. As another work of the century, *Prayer and Complaint of the Plowman to Christ*, declares, 'Here is a great gift of the poor man, for he gives his own body.' Langland realised that despite the need he felt to moralise a situation of division by preaching a way of renunciation and selfless love, there was a sense in which the plowman was Christ and the lord was not.

> We have no need, says Conscience, I wot no better leech
> parson or parish priest, penitencer or bishop,
> than one Piers Lowman that ruleth them all. . . .

> By Christ, quoth Conscience, I will become a pilgrim
> and walk as wide as the world lasteth
> to seek Piers Plowman. . .

so ends the Vision of Antichrist. Christ in departing for Heaven has deputed his power to Piers, who thus remains as his image and champion on earth, in history, to carry on the good fight; and the *castellum* of Unity to which conscience summons men is in the last resort the peasant's cottage.*

The span covered by Boccaccio is repeated by Chaucer on a higher level of poetic comprehension. Drawing on various aspects of French and Italian culture—the *Roman de la Rose* and *Filostrato* in particular—he takes into himself the world of the romances, the love-rhetoric, and the allegories, and swings English metric definitively from alliterative forms and dipodic basis into the regular syllabic systems secured on the iamb. But like Boccaccio he moves also to a broad and realistic definition of the common life of his world, achieving characterisation on an incomparably fuller basis, both in regard to observed details and the grasp of essentials. In *The Canterbury Tales* he builds a rich and comprehensive vision of medieval life, which adds clearly-defined largescale figures to the kaleidescope of Langland or the vast heaving tragic turmoil of Dante's *Inferno*. For the first time since the days of Homer, the Attic dramatists, Petronius, fully-realised individuals, who are also social types, appear in literature.

Though Langland had had no intention of stimulating rebellion, his poem holds the essence of the Peasants Revolt of 1381, its hope of affirming human dignity and worth that went beyond any of the direct social objectives and found its highest expression in John Ball's demand for all things to be held in common, for a total rejection of privilege and division. Chaucer, though coming on Langland's heels, belongs in spirit to the post-1381 world; he can assume the worth of all men by the simple process of depicting them as individuals in their own right. There is a moment of achieved balance, which is both medieval and anti-medieval, which does not hint at any deep-going social criticism and yet looks ahead to a world where a man is judged by what he is, not by his relations inside a hierarchy.

The 15th Century. On the whole the 15th century was a period of stagnation; new elements were coming up, but they were still impotent to make any fundamental changes. The medieval bases, refined and elaborated, failed to yield any new impetus. The chivalric romances were recast from verse into a meandering prose, most importantly in the hands of Malory; and the chron-

---

* One can make these broad generalisations without entering on the vexed problem of the poem's structure and its relation to the theme of Do well, Do better, Do best (active labour in the world; withdrawal into contemplation, poverty, charity; the return to the world on a new level). This dialectical idea was widespread, e.g. in Aquinas or W. Hilton (*Book that is called Mixed Life*); but Langland attempts to give it a concrete poetic definition.

icle, in such hands as Froissart's, took on picturesque romance-qualities. The mood was that of Deschamps:

> Sad, I can't make anything nowadays, men say,
> though once came many new good things of mine.
> I've got no subject-matter to display,
> nothing from which to make good things or fine.

Reading was superseding recitation, and rhetoric was developed to make up for the lack of material and of general ideas; only where verse approached the popular levels, and especially where it showed humour, was there an escape from flatness. The one great exception, Villon (1431 - c. 1463), carried on the tradition of Ruteboeuf, Hugo of Orleans, the Archpoet, Bodel with his *Congès*, to its culmination. He mingles the popular elements with a fine lyricism, which, while at times using courtly forms, transcends them through the omnipresent irradiation of the poet's vivid personality with its unashamed implication in all aspects of common life. The Testament-form itself, in which he sums up his rowdy and driven years, has its link with the death-dance in that it assumes a glance back over the whole vista of life at the moment of death, the stark gallows-view. The *Testament* is an extended version of a popular form, ultimately going back to the dismemberment or sacrificial song of the Great Beast, which survives in broken-down form in such folksongs as those of the Cutty Wren or the Derby Ram; the satirical *Will* is usually put in the mouth of a beast-of-burden, Ass or Horse.

Jailed at Meun and racked with the terror of death as he coughs in his damp cell, Villon faced the reality of his world with the last illusion gone. Nothing remained but hunger and thirst, the unquenchable bitterness and mirth of the hopelessly dispossessed, the sense of an inconsolable sweetness. Over all was a steady consuming anger and an unavailing pity. Where Langland, with deep sympathy, gave us an imaginative vision of the poor, Villon was the poor himself, so completely a part of the lost and the oppressed that he can mock at himself, his fellows, and give away all their flaws without any loss of solidarity.

> Poor I am and poor began,
> my people poor, unknown to fame.
> My father was no wealthy man,
> nor was his sire, Erace by name.
> Poverty dogs us with her claim.
> The tombs of my ancestors (on whom
> may God have mercy all the same)
> reveal no sceptre and no crown.

In the reckless self-revelation, with its hurrying jeering note, Villon shows up as a fool-figure, shaming the world in his own shameless despite.

Dissent. Even at the height of the medieval synthesis, with scholasticism building up its systems at the young universities, dissent was strongly appearing. The Apostolic Brethren of Chalons preached against property, wine, meat, and infant baptism near the mid-12th century. Arnold of Brescia tried to revive the republican rights of the Rome against the Papacy; and from him sprang the sect of the Poor Men. In the early 12th century heretical movements began in south France against image-worship, and a leader, Pierre de Bruys, was burned; a larger movement under Henry of Lausanne arose; Peter Waldo, a rich merchant of Lyon, gave his property over to his wife and the poor, and started a Poor Men movement, which held that laymen, including women, had the right to preach, denied masses for the dead, and put all stress on individual sense of vocation. Then, spread from the east largely through trade, especially in the textile sphere, the Cathar movement took root in Italy, France and Central Europe. The Cathars considered war and legal hanging to be murder, and marriage to be the same as incest or adultery; they had initiation grades of the Perfected and the Believers. We have already noted the desperate measures of the Papacy to counter these developments by general massacre.

The Church made some efforts to contain the new spirit, e.g. in the case of the Franciscans, where a potential threat was mastered. In 1196 Celestine III allowed a new order founded by Joachim of Flora, who had been much affected by Byzantine ideas in Calabria. Joachim was a prophet recognised by Dante. *The Everlasting Gospel* appearing in 1254, seems composed of his three main works with notes and introduction; in the latter there was in effect an heretical proclamation of a new religion, that of the Holy Ghost, based on *Revelation* xiv 6. (It seems the work, not of Joachim, but a Franciscan.) Joachim foretold three cycles: the Judaic, the Christian, and that of the Holy Ghost, which was to commence in 1260. Already there were quarrels among

World-end and Fool-quest for Utopia (Brant).

the Franciscans between the Conventuals or compromisers and the Spirituals, who wanted a complete order of poverty. In the light of Joachim's thought, St. Francis appeared as the announcer of a new epoch, a new dispensation; and the struggle went sharply on. In 1323 John XXII issued a bull denying that Christ and the Apostles lacked property; in reply Lewis of Bavaria, for political reasons, denounced the pope as a heretic for denying Christ's poverty; and thus the argument broadened into a general one between papacy and empire, with men like Marsiglio of Padua and William of Ockham on the secular side.

A shamanist character, Sergarelli, had himself reborn by being circumcised, swaddled and suckled by a woman. He started a movement in Parma that reached as far afield as Germany. The Church burned him and persecuted his Apostolic Brethren. Fra Dolcino, considering himself a messenger direct from heaven, built up a community in the Alps, which it took a ferocious papal crusade to exterminate. Dolcino himself was torn to pieces by red-hot pincers. Similar movements began in Germany under the name of Begards or Beguines; one leader, Ortlieb, was so pantheistic as to include Satan in the divine essence. The mystical creed here was called Illuminism. Mendicant communities and wanderers went on increasing, with women in their ranks. The Flagellants began flogging themselves in Italy from 1259 and spread north. Great marches were held through Hungary, Germany, Flanders, Holland— the marchers bloodily slashing themselves and chanting prayers of doom. The movement lasted into the 14th century. In 1349 in Germany, after a plague, bands were organised in a fraternity under a leader to whom they swore blind obedience; they used strips of leather studded with iron nails. The papacy ordered strong counter-measures; but in 1414 we find another outbreak of Flagellants joined with Brothers of the Holy Cross, who attacked the Church and were jailed or burned. The mass-hysteria of the St. Vitus Dance had gone on in the 14th-15th centuries.

Philosophy. In these sorts of blind outbursts we see the maddened reaction of the poorer classes. But at the same time a steady revolt was going on against the scholastic positions which relegated reason to the rôle of handmaid to faith. Partly fed by Arabian thought such as that of Averroes, the demand asserted itself by a rational justification of dogma. One of the earliest voices making such a demand, that of the Irishman Eriugena, insisted on the supremacy of reason over authority, and the 11th century saw the dissident views of Berengar of Tours and Roscellinus. In the 12th century came Abaelard, who, brilliantly playing on the contradictions in the Fathers, buttressed the claims of reason. The 13th century brought an influx of new texts from antiquity, including Aristotle's, which were no longer known only from the schematic summaries of Boethius.

The first great Arabian philosopher, Alfarabi, had been neoplatonist in thought, aristotelian in method; his successor, Avicenna, was aristotelian both in content and in his logical scheme, holding that universals exist only in thought, that matter is uncreated and eternal, and that God (First Cause) is Mind or Intelligence, *Nous*, and acts by a constant process. In Bagdad such thought was denounced by Ghazali and the orthodox reaction. But in Spain, Avempace and Abubacer in the early 12th century saw life as a progress from purely animal existence into the divine essence, while the latter held that religions approximated to absolute truth, but philosophy attained it. Averrhoes saw Aristotle as the apex of wisdom and attempted to develop an undiluted aristotelian system, based on the concepts of the eternity of matter and the unity of the intellect.

Averrhoism was carried into the Christian areas and was particularly strong at the medical schools. In the mid-13th century the Dominicans set themselves the task of bringing philosophy into harmony with the church, and began a violent polemic against the Averrhoists such as Siger, whom Dante put in Paradise. Aquinas made the large-scale effort to reconcile dogma and Aristotelian thought, defeating the Augustinian version of decadent Platonism. Despite Aquinas, however, Averrhoism held its own at Paris, then found its centre at Padua. The deepening conflict brought about the Inquisition in the 13th century; and the first secular law against heretics with a death-penalty was issued by the emperor Frederick II, who in 1224 brought in death at the stake; he had strong Averrhoist sympathies, protected Jews and Moslems, but had no objections to Catholic heretics being burned. The Bull of Innocent IV, in 1252, completed the system of intolerance to new ideas; and the mendicant orders, changed into papal bulldogs, helped the introduction of the Inquisition into most of the western lands during the century.*

Later Medieval Thought. The struggle to reconcile dogma and reason, embodied in scholasticism, thus led to a deepening conflict between theology and philosophy, which in the 14th century begot confusion, scepticism and crisis. The position taken by Dante was the one necessary for a major step forward. In a world where no direct challenge of the Church was possible, since any challengers were promptly burned at the stake, the only way was to drive as deep a breach as could be between faith and reason, and to disrupt the Aquinas system. God therefore had to be defined as unknowable. Duns Scotus took this step, and William of Ockham went further, seeking in effect to restrict knowledge to experience and practice. By his idea of God's absolute power he upset the use of the idea of his ordained power in decrees drawn from the Bible and the Church; anything was possible and reason could not be used to support faith. His followers stressed the relation of absolute power to grace and to future free actions; both they and their opponents centred

---

* The first secular law against heresy seems English, 1166, when two Cathars were branded, whipped and exiled. Before the fear of mass-heresy arrived, the papacy was more tolerant, e.g. in 1076 Gregory VII excommunicated the folk of Cambrai for burning heretics.

their arguments on free will. Ockhamite attitudes discredited the belief of any need for grace, excluded theology from its own domain, and produced a fluid situation where good and evil were not necessarily exclusive. The only effective answer, as in Bradwardine, was to exclude everything but God.

By 1360 this stage of the clash of ideas had worked itself out. A definite break had been made. (In the field of political thought Dante, Marsiglio, had similarly banished the Church's rôle, denying any connection between theology and the State.) Though the arguments carried formally on, the decisive point had been reached and the ground cleared for the scientific and humanist thought of the Renascence. Meanwhile the rise of Lollardy in England and then the Hussite moment in Central Europe revealed the heavy threat to the Papacy in the union of dissident ideas with the emerging nationalisms.

The crisis of thought was also a crisis of the artistic image; for the medieval approach to form was determined by the idea that the universal, the true unifying image, was in another world. While there was a rich mass-quality in medieval thinking and feeling, this idea acted as a powerful organising factor, as in the Romanesque and Gothic church; but as soon as the intellectualist approach triumphed, as part of the disintegration of medieval society and its bases, there was a steady weakening of the central world-image to which to relate the individual image. The latter tended to become isolated, linked abstractly with its other-world archetype. Forms of Gothic stylisation continued, often charming and effective, but falling away from the great organic quality of the earlier work.

Casuistical systems took the place of philosophic thought. Every question was assumed to have an ideal solution, which could be found by means of formal rules. Casuistry, in morals, etiquette and ceremonial precision of detail, exact regulations for love-making, dinner-precedences, or battle-behaviour, were characteristic; an excessive formalism was the mark of the belief in set models, existing for all eternity, to cover all eventualities. And so any action was at once reduced to its place in some general system and seen as a repetition of some well-known Biblical or historical event. And because the event had meaning only in terms of its universal, it was seen and felt in terms of allegory. Lust, Sloth, Greed and so on easily displaced the human actors. Theologians loved to group and regroup, divide and subordinate and interrelate, in the most mechanical ways, all human actions, virtues and vices.

This attitude of mind had worked in two ways. It converted the complex field of real life into a limited number of set forms, emblems, allegories and abstractions; but at the same time it converted the idea, considered as the superior power, into all the objects around, which assumed an enigmatic and active life in their effects and aims. Once a set of symbols had become fixed, they exercised a magical life of their own.

Symbolism, with its servant allegory, ultimately became an intellectual pastime. The symbolic mentality was an obstacle to the development of causal thought, as causal and genetic relations must needs look insignificant by the side of symbolic connections. Thus the sacred symbolism of the two luminaries and the two swords for a long time barred the road to historic and juridical criticism of papal authority. For the symbolising of Papacy and Empire as the Sun and the Moon, or as the two swords brought by the Disciples, was to the medieval mind far more than a striking comparison; it revealed the mystic foundation of the two powers, and established directly the precedence of Saint Peter. Dante, in order to investigate the historical foundation of the pope's primacy, had first to deny the appropriateness of the symbolism. (HUIZINGA)

In the later middle ages, as the cohesive forces broke down, the most puerile forms of symbolism developed, not merely in art, but in life itself. Thus, the mystic Suso cut his apple at dinner into four, ate three parts to glorify the Trinity and the fourth to commemorate the love with which Mary gave her child an apple; and as small boys do not peel apples, this last quarter was eaten with the pared skin. After Christmas he dropped apples, as then Jesus was too young for them. In such minute ways men tried to infuse their life with significance; but the trivial dissections expressed, not the great days of all-embracing symbolism, but the days of disintegration and mechanical elaboration.

An important dissident thinker of the later 13th and early 14th century was the Spaniard, Raymond Lully, who came close to condemnation. A neo-platonist with pythagorean ideas about numbers, he was intoxicated with visions of finding some simplified clue to all the secrets of the universe, and sought to delve into the procedures by which we gain knowledge. He worked out a diagram of a circle marked with nine basic questions, and five other concentric systems, which could be made to revolve independently; by this means he held that the middle terms of any syllogism could be discovered. The thing was a first attempt at the complete symbolic logic that Leibnitz wanted, and later it affected Bruno. Lully, with his sense of the unity of process, came close to denying any difference between theology and philosophy, between the natural and the supernatural; his bias was to a sort of alchemical pantheism applied to the laws of thought and logic. His central notion was that man 'corresponded' to nature and mental processes to natural.

The next step was taken by the one great thinker of the 15th century, Nicolaus Cryfts of Cues, 1401-64, the son of a Moselle fisherman who became cardinal. He sought to break theology down into philosophy by expounding the Trinity as the dialectical principle of all life and process. He saw sense-impressions as united in the activity of thought and considered that knowledge though real could only be approximate, like a polygon trying to become a circle. Knowledge therefore had its relativity to the instrument of thought; yet by intuition men could rise above the contradictions or antinomies in experience, by holding the opposites together in a unity. Thus man repeated the divine process of three-in-one. The universe was boundless in space and time, and the centre of it was where the observer stood. Nature was animate and articulated; everything was a more or less imperfect mirror of the universe in its own place and preserving itself in relation to, and in community with, other things. Reason unfolded itself in numbers. (In things he held there was an indivisible minimum; in conscious thought an indivisible continuum.)

Cusanus made the first effort since the Greeks to explain the universe on scientific principles; he foreshadowed the law of inertia and declared that the earth was in motion, but thought that the lack of a fixed point for observation would prevent the motion from being measured.

The popular mystics who wrote in the vernacular were often linked rather with the pantheist and alchemical attitudes to be found in Lully and Cusanus, and the Church correctly suspected them. Thus Meister Eckhart was accused of heresy and called to Avignon, where he died; Luther looked back on Tauler as his spiritual ancestor; Suso met much opposition. Tauler drew on the apocalyptic tradition and used the imagery of trades and crafts. The same tendencies appeared in various groups, such as the Friends of God, with its inner section, The Secret Sons of God. Small bands of devotees sprang up in the Netherlands in particular; and from them came Thomas à Kempis. Among them were the Brethren of the Common Life and the Congregation of Windesheim. Gerson remarked of such groups, 'Spiritual love easily slips into naked carnal love'. The mystics indeed tended to revel in sensuous imagery, drinking the Virgin's milk and the blood from Christ's side, or rapt in the ecstasies of a nuptial union, as with the Breton Alain de la Roche, who founded the Universal Brotherhood of the Psalter of Our Lady. (Alain also poured out fantasies of hell, was linked with Windesheim and the Brethren of the Common Life, in whose Zwolle house he died in 1475; and was preceptor to his fellow-Dominican, Sprenger, the fierce witch-denouncer, who spread Alain's Brotherhood in Germany.)

Close to these trends again were the alchemists with their systems of correspondences and transformations who drew largely on the Arabs. Albertus Magnus, Roger Bacon, Arnold of Villanova, Lully, Petrus Bonus, John Dastin, and many others, advanced the theory and practise, mixing chemical experiment with wild concepts of spontaneous generation and hierarchies of change, and with imagery drawn from mating and initiation-ritual. Apart from a haphazard development of laboratory apparatus and chance chemical discoveries, alchemy stimulated men to seek a unitary conception of material and spiritual process and to believe that all sorts of dream-ideas could become actual, as in the passage where Roger Bacon looks into the future.

Machines for navigation can be made without rowers so that the largest ships on rivers or seas will be moved by a single man in charge with greater velocity than if they were full of men. Also cars can be made so that without animals they will move with unbelievable rapidity. . . Also flying machines can be constructed so that a man sits in the midst of the machine revolving some engine by which artificial wings are made to beat the air like a flying bird. Also a machine small in size for raising and lowering enormous weights. . . Also machines can be made for walking in the sea and rivers, even to the bottom without danger. . . Bridges across rivers without piers or other supports, and mechanisms, and unheard-of engines.

He also suggested the aid of sight by suitably shaped lenses and foresaw the circumnavigation of the globe. His independent mind and his conflicts with his Franciscan superiors seem to have earned him fourteen years of confinement at Paris.

Time. The break-up of the medieval synthesis and the in-movement of a new outlook, that of the burgesses of the free market, was expressed succinctly by the development of a new mechanism, that of the clock, which underlies alike the precise measurement-systems of modern quantitative science and the organisational forms of industrialism, of a machine-world.

The ancient Greeks had found that Man is Money, the new burgess class were learning what was later to be enunciated by Franklin, that Time is Money. In the past there had been sundials and waterclocks, clumsy mechanisms with a limited effect in the regulation of existence. But the clock proper made possible a total new system of controlling and arranging human activity; it broke men from the agricultural year with its seasonal changes as the basic measure of life, a matter of rhythms and of adjustments to the phases of nature. Now men could in many important spheres increasingly ignore the earth-rhythm and treat time as an abstract line divided into equal moments or lengths. For the idea of time as a maze, a circle, a spiral, a series of rhythmic coordinates, a unifying moment, there was substituted the idea of time as a mechanical succession of rigid units. If we look at the periods of early industrialisation we see what anguish it was for the peasant, brutally torn from the land, to accustom himself to the treadmill-cage of the relentless clock, which he felt as identical in its beats with the nagging finger of the new master, money.

Here was a new kind of power-machine, in which the course of power and the transmission were of such a nature as to ensure the even flow of energy throughout the works and to make possible regular production and a standardised product. In its relationship to determinable quantities of energy, to standardisation, to automatic action, and finally to its own special product, accurate timing, the clock has been the foremost machine in modern technics; and at each period it has remained in the lead; it marks a perfection towards which other machines aspire. The clock, moreover, served as a model for many other kinds of mechanical works, and the analysis of motion that accompanied the perfection of the clock, with the various kinds of gearing and transmission that were elaborated, contributed to the success of quite different kinds of machine. (MUMFORD)

The growth of monasteries devoted to large-scale production, for instance under the Benedictine rule, did much in driving the world economically on to the point where the clock was necessary.* By the 13th century mechanical

---

* There is irony in the fact that monastic settlements, arising from a passionate need to escape the world of the market, thus came in time to be used as centres of wealth-accumulation for the Church and as pace-setters for secular forms of exploitation. Thus, the Church helped to bring about the situation inevitably leading to its own expropriation in the 16th century in the areas of advanced production.

clocks were being made; by 1370 Heinrich von Wyck in Paris had constructed a modern type. About 1345, it seems, the division of hours into 60 minutes and minutes into 60 seconds was widespread: an abstract framework not unconnected with the circular movements of the sky. Early in the 16th century a young Nuremberger is said to have made 'many-wheeled watches out of small bits of iron', and by the century's end the domestic clock was working in Holland and England.

15: The Sixteenth Century

Architecture. The developments in art and literature in Italy of the medieval period and of the Renascence were closely linked with the fates of the town-communes and their strenuous inner struggles; but it has not been necessary for us to analyse the social situation in its details and its changing phases. The 15th century however had seen the weakening in general of the democratic elements, despite such upheavals as that under Savonarola at Florence. Everywhere was going on the movement towards the national State, the burgess struggle for free markets against feudal controls, and the steady imposition of centralised power. In England and the Netherlands at the turn of the 16th century the aristocracy long-sightedly accommodated themselves to the needs of the new age; also to some extent in France, though the wars of Catholic and Huguenot were to impede this development. Germany was hampered by its excessively feudal subdivisions grown out of the Holy Roman Empire, and Italy was badly divided through the way in which the Papacy had blocked any movement to national unity—a situation that had favoured the early rise of the free communes, but had shown its disadvantages when larger forms of political organisation were needed. Here, and in other places where the aristocracy had not been converted to some degree of cooperation with the merchants, a seignorial reaction set in. We see it for example clearly at Genoa.

This change in the social situation must be borne in mind throughout one's consideration of the High Renascence. In architecture we see the triumph of the direct imitation of ancient Roman building and the almost simultaneous advent of a new system of unbalances leading into mannerism and the baroque. The Roman imitation was exemplified by Bramante's work at Rome, with its stress on sculptural effect. The human scale tended to be forgotten, and the conflict between classic harmony and baroque plasticity emerged.

The architects went on pedantically studying the ancient forms, with ever less sense of any human or aesthetic point of reference. The equipoises of the Renascence were being lost. Michelangelo brought in gigantic energies caught at a moment of angry strain; and from 1520-30 to the turn of the century, Mannerism dominated, a discordant and distorting art, whether full of turbulent clashes or seeking a strained deliberate elegance. Michelangelo's *terribilità*, his soul torn between Christ and Beauty, belonged to the epoch of saints like Ignatius and Teresa. (In 1542 the inquisition is reintroduced, and next year the censorship.) In his dome of St. Peter's we see the battle of titanic forces against huge masses in which he delighted; but the struggle was largely in a void. We have only to think how clearly Dante visualised the conflict in which he was engaged, whether in heaven, purgatory or hell, to see how Michelangelo was dramatising a cosmic struggle inside himself, not putting himself into a cosmic struggle. Thin out his passion and you get mannerism; blow it up a little more and you get baroque.

Vignola in his *Gesu* linked the medieval stress on length with the Renascence liking for a central plan. He was probably following Michelangelo, though he employed in a more florid way Alberti's method of devising a façade to correspond with the aisles and nave behind—using a ground-floor triumphal arch and an upper floor pedimented as wide as the nave and joined to the ground floor by volutes that covered the front of the lean-to aisle-roofs. His solution was in mannerist terms, but provided the general scheme on which countless baroque churches were to be built. In a sense the reaction had combined the worst of both the Gothic and the Renascence worlds to produce a new type of building, full of excitement, luxurious decoration and moments of sensuous thrill.

Mannerism flowered however in the work of Palladio, in the style that Giulio Romano, a pupil of Raphael, used for a house which he built for himself. A certain Renascence formalism elegantly transgressed in various details begot a style capable of extension and variation in tactful and graceful ways. At last an architecture was developed for secular use; Palladio built no churches. He liked curved colonnades in his country mansions, using them to link a square main block with out-reaching wings, and he included low outbuildings in his scheme, thus embracing the landscape and showing concern for the whole setting of his buildings.

Art. In literature the 15th century, apart from Villon, was an era of tapestry flatness; the vital new impulse in Boccaccio and Chaucer were not followed up. But in art there were great new advances. Here, in a medium that was also a handicraft, the burgess-elements, linked with the scientific work done in anatomy and perspective, steadily produced great works. Especially in the period 1420-1500, art provided the means for an endless discovery of the world, its people and its objects. Enough of the medieval synthesis remained to make the forms interesting in themselves, not as abstracted formal units, but as fascinating units which without further question took their place in a world of close and integral relationships. The unity of the general and the

The Riders of the Apocalypse by Dürer: woodcut.

particular still held, though it was gradually being stretched to breaking-point since the synthesis on which it depended was not finding its renewal in life but was being broken down by the very force that was driving the artist along. Painters, in general, achieved a fullness of definition which was soon to depart from art or to be recaptured only by an extraordinary effort of vision on the artist's part.

The characteristic artists of the High Renascence were Leonardo, Raphael and Michelangelo. In Leonardo the scientific aspects came to a head, stimulating his art and creating impasses. The innocence of Piero was no longer possible. Leonardo, though opposed to neoplatonist ideas, accepted the pythagorean premises: 'proportion is not only to be found in number and measure, but also in sounds, weights, times and places, and in every power that exists'. He wanted the Renascence solution of antique forms mathematically ordered into a perfect canon; but his search for a precise order conflicted with his feeling for organic balance and movement, which, in accord with the Florentine tradition, he interpreted in terms of continuously flowing and harmonious contours. He was driven to find new systems of organisation, the pyramid and the diagonal, while, following the movement of light and shadow over curved surfaces, he discovered how to centralise by chairoscuro. He might attempt to fix scientifically, to generalise mathematically, his vision and to offset its dangerous entanglements by diagrams of light impacting on sphere or cylinder; but all the while his systems broke up into new convolutions of organic pullulation, despite his effort to devise decorative knots and plaits of grace. He could not escape the knowledge of life as a ceaseless flux, all things returning to water, symbolised in water—while water itself flowed and swirled until there seemed no barriers between men and the primeval Flood, the end of the world, the nemesis come on the artist and his fellows. Geometry broke down into the labyrinthine complexity of the inexorable whirlpool.

Look at certain walls stained with damp or at stones of uneven colour. If you have to invent some setting, you will be able to see in these the likeness of divine landscapes, adorned with mountains, ruins, rocks, woods, great plains, hills and valleys in great variety; and then again you will see there battles and strange figures in violent action. . .

The principle of reverie, anticipating Romantics like Coleridge, begot the mysterious self-absorption of the Mona Lisa, the Annes and Maries, Leda, St. John: the animal life from which the intellectualist artist had cut himself off but which returned from deep down, from darkness, to beckon him out of his mathematical certainties. The number of uncompleted projects, the growing reluctance he felt to paint, the obsession of certain forms, all revealed the intense inner strain felt by the artist who had introduced new architectonic elements and yet felt the omnipresent pull of the water-patterns, who sought a mathematical canon and yet surrendered to the darkening plasticity of light, who saw all form as sinuously moving and yet gained a dramatic centrality out of the conflict of light-shadow. The world had been suddenly changed and deepened; and though the artist attempted to build an image of dream-grace and sweetness, he was expressing all the while a rending set of contradictions in his world and himself. Though his method led directly on to Correggio and Giorgione, there was already looming up the figure of Caravaggio. In maturing the High Renascence, Leonardo had already doomed it to a speedy breakdown, so insecure was the basis on which he constructed his synthesis, so sinister was the smile of animal life which fascinated him and into which he could only enter at a dream-level, so deep was the gap between his projected imagery and the conflicts that it masked.

In Raphael the deadlock appeared in the harmonious idealisation of forms without Leonardo's deep conflicts; in Michelangelo, in the violent sense of unrelieved torments and tensions. Raphael accepted the point of arrest and proceeded to idealise the given forms, in much the same way as Pheidias had done in an analogous situation; Michelangelo refused to accept a situation of what the Romantics later were to call Fettered Energies, and, chafing against the bars, built up his anger and aspiration inside his figures, which, in painting, sculpture, or architecture, were essentially isolated in their sphere of their own furious tensions. At the same time there is deep in them a fierce impact of a new sort; for the most intense expression of Christ's sufferings in Gothic art always implied a common ground between artist and spectator, whereas Michelangelo broke this link, seeing himself as Christ rather than in him. And yet he reacted passionately against the egoism of the Renascence, while expressing it in his own rarefied form, in a ceaseless attempt to destroy it.

Other artists followed tamely in the trails of Leonardo, Raphael, Michelangelo. Fra Bartolommeo and del Sarto imitated Raphael's eclectic perfectionism without his harmonious insights and mastery of design; Leonardo's subaqueous shadows and dreamy smile led to Correggio; Michelangelo's influence underlay Mannerism, with his wide range from the elegantly-imposed patterns of Bronzino to the wind-tossed emotionalism of Tintoretto or the stormily-formalised anguish of El Greco. Only in the Venetians a broad new impulse arose, linked with their Byzantine connections Leonardo's innovations and Flemish colour. Bellini began with a liking for the metallic forms of Mantegna, who was impressed by the friezes and processional pomps of ancient Rome; but he steadily subdued such elements to the demands of light and colour, achieving a mild clear evening atmosphere. In his *Allegory* we meet the paradise-garden secularised with cupids by the tree of life and a

---

* Note the link of his reverie-method and Goya, also Daumier. The ending of the 15th century saw an outburst of apocalyptic literature, often using *Revelation:* people fled to the hills and some German villages were abandoned. Dürer records in 1525 a dream of a Deluge. He, too, was obsessed by the hope of a canon of form. It is surely significant of setback, of forces thrown back on themselves at the moment of a great new liberation, that both Leonardo and Michelangelo were homosexual. Though the two men disliked each other and had opposed outlooks, their arts both share a need to use *Contrapposto*; the twisting of the body in two directions. Leonardo controls the effect; with Michelangelo it becomes a main way of expressing unresolved tension and leads into the most extreme distortions in the hands of others.

centaur not far from the cross; here is the transition to the pastoral soon to appear at the heart of Venetian painting. With Giorgione and Titian that style reached its highest level. The sense of discovery, lost in the analytic sphere of linear perspective, returned in the sphere of form-as-colour. It is not that Venetian colour was particularly bright. Florentine could be gayer; but Venetian colour permeated and the forms were realised with a mass that was inseparable from it. Titian is fond of silvery greys and dull purples, but the hues are soaked into the forms, are an aspect of the subtle plasticity. Giorgione is a master of serene lyricism, of a meditative dreamlight; an enigmatic quality emerges from the golden light and fluid harmonies of contour. There is a pastoral and paradisiac air, and also a feeling that the meaning lies elsewhere —in the unheard music to which, as Pater noted, the people, the whole of nature, is listening. In the *Tempestà* the figures are parted by the cavernous glimpse of the natural world storm-lighted in the centre; it is only in the music, in the dream, that the unity of man and nature is precariously maintained. Titian carried the vision further; his nudes are often sleepy, lost in a reverie that is like the aroma and reflection of their rich sensuous being; but though he is seldom happy in action unless it can be caught at a moment of relaxation, of surrender, his people have come awake and his world is real. By a great effort he can compose with a massive emotional effect, as in the *Entombment*, but his method of organisation is essentially by a simple placing of forms so that a maximum effect of breathing mass is produced, a balance determined by the secret centres of organic life. And he has the power of communicating the same living solidity to his landscapes. In Tintoretto the balance goes; a cold wind of disturbing rapture blows over the forms, chafing and kindling them into dark blue flames. In Veronese the rich vision becomes a pageantry.

But a new force had entered Italian art, again in the north, reacting against the skilful and tasteful use of elements from the High Renascence by the Caracci. Caravaggio (1573-1610) revealed the emptiness of such solutions as well as the ending of the Venetian colour-trance. A man who lived in storms and collisions with authority, in 1606 he killed an opponent in a quarrel during a game of tennis at Rome; made a Knight of the Order of St. John at Naples, he assaulted a justiciary, fled to Sicily, was expelled from the Order, was wounded in a tavern-brawl, and died of fever after an outburst of rage in another tavern. His art was like his life. He worked, it is said, direct on the canvas from a model; he sought to catch common life in all its sweaty and coarse facts in a hard cold light; when he painted the Virgin dead, he is said to have used as model a drowned whore fished up swollen out of the Tiber. He rejected all idealisations, used contemporary settings and costumes (contrary to the Renascence method, which had deodorised the saints by giving them classical garb), and employed much detail, relying on his powerfully dramatic chairoscuro to achieve a radical simplification and give his message a violent impact. The new vision created by Leonardo had had a radical and angry working-out, which cut art finally from its medieval bases and opened up a new set of problems.*

Italian painting was now too deflated to absorb Caravaggio's strong lessons except in small doses, though he had some effect in Naples as well as on the Utrecht School. But through Ribera he influenced the early Velasquez; Rubens admired and studied him; he deeply affected Rembrandt; and in France his impact showed in La Tour and the Le Nain brothers. But 17th century art lies outside the scope of this book. What matters for us is the way in which Caravaggio shattered the traditions of the Renascence and posited a whole set of new issues. In him the tension-in-a-void of Michelangelo came sharply down to the common dust of earth; the fierce dramatic centralisation and the baroque swing and lunge of his compositions, with the intense local realism, looked into the modern world.

In Flanders and Holland the steady development from Gothic bases, with an increased enrichment of the sense of space and light went on, but the check was not without its effect here, too. Bosch showed the medieval mind thrown disconcertingly back on itself, sure that the wrong turning had been taken by history, and anxiously prying into all the crannies and dark holes of man's being to find the secret flaws and hidden monsters. His position was close to that of the more radical sects and fraternities rejecting the corrupted world; his wild fantasy was also a soberly calculated accumulation of medieval symbols for states of being, for vices, errors, aberrations and inhumanities. A devouring sense of imminent destruction drew his strange inventions together in a coherent moral and artistic aim; and lurid fires (both of hell and of contemporary warfare) break out in the darkness of the madly spawning images.

Bruegel took over and developed this vision of a perilous and alienated earth back to realism, without losing the moral impulsion. Also, using a long diagonal to cut across and yet connect foreground and background, he subdued to his aims the mannerist landscape with its high viewpoint, its long vista of river or coast closed by rugged mountains. He relied for his organising ideas on the proverb: a strongly medieval attitude, since the proverb was both folklore and a crystallisation of wisdom giving a meaning to particular cases. He was deeply shocked by the forces at work in people, which enabled them to turn aside from the great images of human unity to which they paid lip-service. The crowd watch John the Baptist in hypnotised awe, but they do not bother to follow his gesture and consider Christ crucified; they find it much more interesting to watch the cruel free-show of a man being pressed than to note the fall of Jesus on his way to the Cross. Bruegel began by depicting them as scurrying insect-creatures whose cruelties sully momently the vast earth. The landscape provides the moral criterion; the earth judges men in terms of

---

* The Inquisition tried Veronese for putting drunkards and Germans in his Cana painting; the chief inquisitor met his defence with, 'Do you know that in these figures by Michelangelo there is nothing which is not spiritual?'

the 'natural' processes which they both embody and transgress; the divine figures, which in true medieval art dominate, are here even more helpless than the busy obsessed insect-multitude. But Bruegel is too complex an artist to make a simple moral judgment; the peasant who keeps on ploughing while the high-aspiring hero Icarus falls to his death has his justification: 'The plough will not stop for a dead man', the Flemish proverb ran. The battle of Lent and Carnival is a conflict of lay-greed and clerical fanaticism, where both sides are linked by hypocrisy and lies, and where the triumph of either is equally anti-human; and yet the image is also one of a folk-rite of fertility, and there is a sheer delight, a comprehensive pity, as well as an uncompromising condemnation. The three orders all dream slothfully of Cockaygne, and yet there is a rich enjoyment of the folk-image of plenty as well as a satire of the way that men apply the dream. A marvellous skill in design, in the placing of the mass of casual and random figures, links with the architectonic use of great criss-crossing diagonals; and in the later work the broad vision of space gives way to a closer view of individual man, carefully scrutinised for the conflicts of a lying greed with plain workaday humanity. Bruegel has completely secularised Bosch's world. He too gains much of his dynamic from his reaction against the religious wars that torment his epoch; but where Bosch sees the world given over to the lie, Bruegel, with all his deep ironic insight into the fears and distortions that rend his people, achieves acceptance of a world where, amid all the horrors, there is still peasant solidarity and the proverb unites as well as exposes.

In Germany Renascence influences arrived strongly through Dürer. The Venetian painter-etcher J. da Barbari visited Nuremberg in 1500, and Dürer himself was in Italy in 1494 and 1505. He worked at the theory of geometry, perspective, and proportion; but his canon did not apply so easily to the world of German Gothic as Leonardo's had to that of Florentine art. His expressive draughtsmanship remained tethered to Gothic particularism; he perfected the techniques of the woodcut and the engraving, and showed a remarkable power of evoking mood and atmosphere in his watercolour and gouache landscapes. Artists like Altdorfer developed this poetic sense of nature, man being absorbed—or where he violently intrudes, as in *The Battle of Alexander*, begetting an apocalyptic anger announced in the world-end skies. In Grünewäld the horror, which Bosch controlled by the fascinated scrutiny of his designs and Bruegel by his robust ability to resolve contradictions, takes charge and vents itself in a storm of anguish and pity. Torn between the late Gothic imagery to which he responded, and his Protestant conscience, and oppressed by his insight into the brutalities of his world, he seems to have given up painting for soap-making and hydraulic engineering.

The 16th century, with its general breakdown of medieval syntheses, saw the advent of the self-conscious artist, asking questions about art's meaning and the nature of expression which had previously been answered by the tradition in which the artist worked before they could be asked. Michelangelo revealed this self-consciousness in an extreme degree, and with Leonardo he cut across art-history. Mannerism was the first general answer by artists who were working for patrons of the Counter-Reformation and the seignorial reaction. For the first time artists in general set themselves to the job of picture-making as an eclectic job of taste; they selected what they found exciting, without being bothered to understand how particular forms have evolved, what rôle they have functionally played, what their value for rendering truth and reality. By 1600 this phase was over, but in a general way its positions left an indelible mark on the way that artists henceforth approach their tasks.

Music. The struggle to develop church-music against the ideals of the Church had gone on, *e.g.* in the authorised though non-liturgical motet. Instrumentalisation of style invaded the *In Nomines*; cadences grew more definite; and in the free motet the Gregorian melodies were decomposed, with the final result in the emergence of the Fantasia. All the while dance-music was playing a key-part in compelling the growth of clearly organised form. In England an important factor was the existence of a large public able to take their part in performances; instruments hung in shops and houses for anyone who had to wait. Peacham in the *Compleat Gentleman*, 1622, remarks that one should be able to sing at sight and 'to play the same upon your viol, or the exercise of a lute, privately to yourself'. Generally the players numbered two to six, with no listeners or only a select few. In the music of Dowland, torn between Catholicism and the national Protestantism, a poignant personal note intruded; and round 1600 English chamber-music reached a high level. Variety was introduced into the fantasia form, with sections based on different types of theme; there was an increase in tension and dramatic force, with pieces ending on a climax, as well as contrast in the connecting-up of sections of varying character; there was a sense of light and shade; and sections became miniature movements. Gibbons, mixing tragic and gay elements, brought together two movements of opposed character. Two tendencies showed up. The fantasia sections became independent and were grouped to bring out their relations to one another and the whole; the number of sections dwindled, but those left grew in length. The first tendency led to the sonata, the second to the fugue in the modern sense, with the sections of the fantasia becoming the developments.

The culmination came about 1615-20 with chromatic harmonies and long chains of modulations; through harmonic expressionism the Italian influences broke through the English polyphonic style, which became a symbol of the 'good old times', elaborated in order to check the new forces.

A wider and more complex struggle went on in Italy, along quite different lines. Here, under the Counter-Reformation, medieval styles were carried to their highest point in the poliphony of Palestrina, in a reaction against a theatrical treatment of the Offices, as at Venice, and against the chromatic feats of the madrigalists. Keyboard instruments were being improved, and even experimental forms devised, e.g. a clavecin capable of expressing quarter-tones. Lutanists increased in virtuosity. Music tended to contract its range to four octaves and to become diatonic; there was loss in the range of expression, but the compactness helped a concentration on the main new possibilities opening up.

Music had for long been linked with dramatic forms—in the liturgy, the pastorals, moralities and *soties*, the court-ballets with their recitations. Now a new stage is reached in the relationship. The Hellenising poets at Florence disliked Franco-Flemish polyphony and dreamed of a theatre like the ancient Greeks. To assert their position it was necessary to insist on the primacy of words over music: in effect, of the human voice and emotion over the divine flow of polyphony. In 1580, Bardi, whose Camerata made essential experiments for the birth of opera, wrote, 'Just as the soul is nobler than the body, so the words are nobler than the counterpoint'. And two years later Gaililei, father of the astronomer, brought up the example of the Greeks to buttress the cause of monody. Rinucci and Peri, after attempting a pastoral *Dafne*, came closer to the ideal with *Euridice* in October 1600. Monteverdi (1567-1643), a chapel-master, was present. About the same time, the Oratorians were trying to apply the same principles of music-drama to the sacred oratorios at St. Philip of Neri. The biblical texts were turned into dialogue and declaimed; and Cavalieri's *Rappresentazione di anima e di corpo* was an outright sacred drama.

In 1602 Caccini wrote a new score for Rinucci's *Euridice*. Monteverdi then once again took up the Orpheus-theme, which was a favourite subject for poets with a mannerist self-consciousness and which provided a sort of pagan Christ for anticlerical Hellenists. The work was a triumph with its use of direct language, the energy of its recitations and airs. The sung declamation had a shattering effect and won the day for the position that, in Monteverdi's phrase, the words should be 'the mistress of the harmony'. Of a second opera, *Ariane*, we have only a lament said to have been composed by his wife's bed as she lay dying. Monteverdi had the genius to see clearly what the others had been aiming at in a more confused way; to bring together elements that had been seething for generations. The timid and fleeting use of the seventh of the dominant which had now and then been made inside the complex texture of polyphony was now bodly detached and given a free life:

... owning such a harmonic radio-activity that it was to allow Monteverdi and his successors to give the language of the passions an unsuspected warmth and elo-quence... In bequesting to his successors the formula of opera, a dramatic style, and the cell, so charged with the fluid of harmony, of the seventh of the dominant, the master on Mantua was transmitting to them a magnificent heritage. (VUILLERMOZ)

Thought. The discovery of the New World had a profound effect on medieval conventions. In 1492 Columbus sailed out into the ocean; six years later Vasco da Gama rounded the Cape of Good Hope; in 1516 Magellan sailed round the world. Reliance on Aquinas and Aristotle were heavily strained. Then towards the mid-century came the Copernican hypothesis that the earth moved round the sun. Columbus, we may note, had been inspired by the image of the ancient heavenly-mount, the earthly paradise.

When in July 1498 he first set foot on the American continent he . . . announced that it was an island. Since he had begun his transatlantic journeys, it had been his longing and his secret endeavour to find Paradise, the abode of the first human pair. His astrological and magical studies had convinced him that the site must be on an island in the Indian Sea. . . Scarcely had he landed on the coast of Paria than he announced that it was the Paradise of the Old Testament. . . Paradise lay on the top of a lofty mountain.

'The earth is not round', he wrote in his report. 'There is a sensible protuberance at the point where India joins the Ocean at the equator. When our Lord God created the sun, it stood ready to rise at the highest point of the earth in the furthest east. And this highest point, as being the nearest to Heaven, must also be the most excellent spot on earth. . . My view . . . is that the highest point is the Equator. This has occurred to no one before. Paradise is situated in a place where no one can reach, except by divine consent. It has the form of a mountain, or rather it lies upon a mountain top that resembles the thin end of a pear or a ball topped with the nipple of a female breast. The earth swells up to this nipple and approaches Heaven. (WASSERMAN)

His idea of his journey was substantially that of *Gilgamesh*.

One effect of the discoveries was to start off the writing of Utopias, just as Alexander's marches and an investigation of tribal societies had played their part in creating the Greek examples. Thomas More was stirred by the fate of the dispossessed peasantry in Britain to write his *Utopia*, but the imaginative stimulus towards visualising an ideal society came from travellers' tales of American tribal groups; his narrator was a 'sea-traveller met in Antwerp'. In Campanella's *City of the Sun*, a noble effort to describe a just society, a Genoese sea-captain tells the story; and Bacon's *New Atlantis* began, 'We sailed from Peru'. (Campanella fell into the hands of the Inquisition and was tortured twelve times, the last time for 40 hours.)

The old sanctions of the State had been shaken. We see this in Savonarola, who, for all his apocalyptic fury, in his *Treatise on the Government of Florence*, attacked the Medicean tyranny in the name of a republican constitution not unlike that of Venice. Machiavelli, devoting his life to the Republic, wrote *The Prince* when, after torture at Medicean hands, he was under house-arrest. Dealing frankly with power-politics and using a cool relentless realism with a consistent appeal to the facts of experience, he shocked the upholders of medieval idealism. From one angle, his book was simply a plain textbook for the ruler who was to unite Italy under secular rule; from another, it showed a deep irony, a wish to shame the devil by telling him the truth to his face. The double purpose appears when we set it by his *Discorsi* where he fervidly praises the popular state, rejects the creed of the people's fickleness, and maintains that a people bound by law is superior to any prince. In his *Song of the Blessed Spirits* he hymns the end of 'fear, hatred, rancour, greed, pride and cruelty'.—'The world returns into its primal state'. In his plays, especially in the *Mandragola*, we see his capacity for irony and satire, his closeness to the popular tradition.

A mixture of devotion to antiquity and its culture, with a deepening study of the Bible and the Jewish philosophy of the *Kabbala*, led to the growth of Humanism. Printing had begun in 1452, and there was a rapid increase in the scholarship of the ancient classics. The Humanists mostly had a contempt and fear of the unlettered mob as well as a wish to escape ecclesiastical persecution; but they did much to secularise thought. The incessant wars of religion and brutal persecution of this century also played their part in sickening many thoughtful men like Montaigne and turning them against theology. More radical Freethinkers or *Libertins* also arose, like Telesio of Cozena, who took as his motto, 'Not by Reason but by Sense', though he admitted that the mind co-operated with sensation.

Montaigne invented the term essay, *essai*, to express his experimenting tentative outlook; fixed medieval positions break up; he abandons the idea of the self as an entity and finds that it is 'no more than a tendency to act in this or that fashion; it is his knowledge of what he can and cannot do'. He uses the argument that God is inexplicable to banish him from the field of experience; and presents his Stoical picture of himself, a modest, thoughtful man to whom nothing human is alien, and who rejects all dogma, content with the *essai*, the direct trial of men and things.

The wars of religion, as we noted, as well as the peasants' insurrection, had deep effects. The Reformation, linked with the new national spirit, tore northern Europe away from the papal controls, expressing the need of the burgesses for a free market in God as in material goods. The jettisoning of the saints and the Virgin, and the insistence on the need and the right of a direct relation to God, reflected the new individualism and revealed a last echo of the shamanist claim to direct contact with the spirit-world as against institutional mediations. In 1343 a bull had given final form to the doctrine of the Treasure, the works of superrogation of Christ and the saints—a sort of steadily increasing capital confided by Christ to St. Peter. By the Reformation the Treasure-in-heaven was wrenched away from the papacy and made an individual property, just as the accumulated wealth of the church was expropriated by the State and its manipulators.

Both Boccaccio and Petrarch had been hungry for Greek literature, though they knew little of it; but from the later 14th century there were contacts between Byzantine and Italian scholars, e.g. Manuel Chrysoloras, after coming as an envoy to Venice, settled in 1397 in Florence as a teacher of Greek. His pupils carried on the work of translation; scholars eagerly collected Greek manuscripts and throughout the 15th century the knowledge of Greek authors expanded. Arguments about the merits of Plato and Aristotle broke out; and the visit of Gemisthos Plethon in 1439 to Florence brought about the Platonic Academy there, and the Florentine school radiated its influence all over Europe. Pico della Mirandola tried to unite the *Kabbala* and Plato in a universal philosophy; he was also a fervent admirer of Savonaraola, who in turn wrote that Pico 'ought to be numbered among the miracles of God and Nature'. Thus both Plato and the neoplatonists were made available to thinkers.

Alchemy had made some important strides. Paracelsus, who died in 1541, used chemical substances against disease and thus founded medical chemistry; delicate chemical balances were devised; Van Helmont made discoveries by observation and invented the term *gas*. Paracelsus saw all transformations of material objects as alchemical and called smiths and smelters alchemists. Considering the whole universe alive, he peopled it with sylphs of air, nymphs of water, salamanders of fire; and defined matter as made up of three primary bodies, salt, sulphur, mercury, or body, soul, spirit. But in his working-out the idea of a triadic movement was much confused with the idea of a proper balance of the three ingredients or principles. However, he and his disciples paved the way to a basic chemical law: that all specimens of a given chemical individual have identical compositions.

Bruno. The thinker who brought together all the elements which had emerged from the breakdown of the medieval world-view, and who opened the way broadly to the future, was Giordano Bruno, son of a poor farmer of Nola, near Naples. An unfrocked priest, he wandered through Italy, France, England, Germany, striking out his formulations in Italian dialogue and Latin prose or verse. Early he wrote a comedy with folk-elements and his philosophical dialogues showed often the same strain. Finally, driven by unresolved conflict, he returned to Italy where he knew that the Church would kill him; but he had a desperate hope that by sheer force of the truth he could convert the Church. After the Venetians handed him over to the Inquisition, he was jailed eight years and then burned at the stake in 1600.

He was intoxicated by the materialist vision of countless worlds and the Copernican theory, and poured his scorn on the Aristotelean system. There were many Platonic elements in his thought—monads and a world-soul; and idealist concepts continually controlled his argument. Yet the movement of his mind was essentially towards the concrete and the earthly. 'By induction we are made rich in spirit', he asserted, anticipating Bacon. He mocked the saints, the eucharist, asceticism, pessimism, and the Papacy; but at the core of all his satire was a hatred of hypocrisy and greed—the latter indistinguishable from power-lust. That is, he detested all that revealed a failure or refusal to follow ideas out to their logical conclusions and to struggle for a unity of theory and practice; all that revealed a heart of egoism, fear, and self-interest. His *Expulsion of the Triumphant Beast*, written in London, sounded a call for the concentration of energies towards a socially valid end.

Sofia. But the initial cause, the first germ. Where is one to find it ?
Mercury. In the extreme Greed, which, under colour of supporting religion, serves its own interests.

He defended the republican form and added, 'Let the virtues and studies that are useful or indispensable to the general good be encouraged, pushed to the van, safeguarded. Let those who contribute to progress be honoured and rewarded, and let those who do no work, and the misers enslaved to property, be despised and held as beings of no worth whatever'.

He was dominated by an intuition of the unity of all process and a delight in the multiplicity and transformations of matter, and sought to find out contraries change into one another.

Profound magic is it to know how to extract the contrary after knowing the point of union.

Necessity and liberty are one; hence what acts by the necessity of nature acts freely. . . The beginning, middle and end, the birth, growth and perfection of all earthly things are from contraries; through contraries, in contraries, and to contries; and where there is contrary, there is also action, reaction, movement, diversity, multitude, order, succession, change. . . The sense of contrariety, which is figured in the tree of knowledge of good and evil. . . All is in all! In particular it is a like point that opposites meet: the knowledge of the one comes perfectly out of knowledge of the other.

His atomism was linked, however insecurely, with a concept of development; and he was fascinated by the image of the foetus in its many phases of change and growth. His minimum was not merely an irreducible bit of matter; it was also an active force, an energy-centre, with a tendency to move in a certain direction. Many aspects of a theory of evolution were present in his thinking:

continuity of slight variations or changes, which, over a vast period of time, express themselves by a more or less marked differentiation; integration of purpose in the mechanism through the principle of the survival of the 'best adapted' beings; close link that binds all animate creatures and rests on their substantial identity; natural transition from the homogenous to the heterorgenous, from the indefinite and simple to the more or less complex compositions. (CHARBONNEL)

But, inevitably, if he looked forward to Darwin, he also looked backwards to Plotinus.

Permeating his thought with all its multiple confusions and penetrations into reality, there was a tragic note, a desperate and exalted call to struggle against the Triumphant Beast in society and in the individual.

O difficulties to be endured, cries the coward, the featherhead, the shuttlecock, the faintheart.

The task is not impossible, though hard. . . You may fail to reach your goal. Run the race, nevertheless. Put forth your strength on so high a business. Strive on with your last breath. The Nolan has given freedom to the human spirit and made its knowledge free. It was suffocating in the close air of a narrow prison-house, and only through chinks it gazed at the far-off stars. Its wings were cleft so that it was unable to cleave the veiling cloud and reach the reality beyond. . . .

To walk like Adam of a new world in a garden of his own creation.

When sentenced, he said to the inquisitorial court, 'Perhaps your fear in passing judgment on me is greater than mine in receiving it.'

The *libertins*, linked with Bruno's line of thought, developed various paradoxes which brought out the weakness of formal logic. Thus, Bruno said, 'Each man is at each moment all that he can be at that particular moment, but he is not all that he can be in himself and according to his substance'. Montaigne praised the unspoiled savage; the *libertins* developed the argument that the savage is more human than the civilised man—a line that ultimately leads to Rousseau. Donne showed the full working-out of *libertin* method. How can one love a woman since she has changed from what she was, and so on? Under the love-paradox on change and fidelity lay the philosophic problem of continuity and change, the nature of development.

Rabelais. In moving on to Bruno we have omitted a great humanist, with the popular element that men like Erasmus lacked. Rabelais was both a philosopher and satirist, a builder of folklore on a gigantic scale and a transmuter of the *fabliau* and the romance-parody into the first stages of the novel. He used his giant-figures, drawn from French folklore, to construct an enhanced image of the common processes of life and to launch a many-sided satire against scholasticism and all medieval idealisms as well as against contemporary irrationalities or inhumanities, e.g. the chapter on King Picrochole attacks the wars of aggression being carried on by the French in Italy. In Panurge he created a magnificent figure who is both the reckless fool and the crafty schemer whom nothing can deter or defeat.

He seems influenced by the folklore of Britanny as well as of Touraine and Poitou, having spent some of his early years in a convent of La Vendée; and in the long final quest for the truth (Panurge's 'Shall I marry?' with its medieval nexus of the bawdy flytings of women), he mixes the new ocean-traveller's tale with the immemorial sea-odyssey which we have seen to express at root the spirit-journey. (There are thus parody-links with the Utopia: we may compare ancient romances like Antonius Diogenes' *The wonderful things beyond Thule*, or Lucian's *Journey to the Moon*.) The Panurgean quest ends with the mystic oracle of the bottle—*trincq*. That is, experience is the only test and answer. Leave all abstractions and otherworld-fantasies, and return to life.

In the medieval sense *Gargantua and Pantagruel* is one great fooling; and though we have glanced at the importance of the fool-image, the fool-concept,

---

* In Britanny he saw a mystery-play introduce a saltwater-demon, Pantagruel, at time of a great drought; the demon plays tricks, throwing salt into people's throats. In a chapbook published at Lyon 1532, the parents of a giant Gargantua are created by the magician Merlin to aid Arthur; Gargantua is finally transported to fairyland by Morgane and Melusine.

Various reformers like Dolet were burnt at the stake in France; Rabelais escaped by the use of veiled satire and the protection of du Bellay and others.

we need further to fill out the picture. The outburst of fooling had strong
links with the saturnalia, the reversal of the prevailing rôles and ranks in
society. Thus on New Year's Day, the turn of the year, the despised sub-
deacons used to take over control of the ceremonies and the canons' stalls.
The core of the custom, which we find active by the late 12th century, was the
phrase in the *Magnificat,* sung at Vespers, 'He has thrust down the mighty
from their seat and raised on high the humble'. At that moment the staff was
probably handed from one *dominus* to another; and the irruption of the sub-
deacons was a typical piece of rebellious symbolism. There were Cockaygne

Arlecchino; Coviella; 16th century.

cries, 'On this day let the censing be done by pudding and sausage'. Asses were
introduced to bray responses in the Mass, as we noted before in connection
with the *Prose of the Ass.* (Bruno had an obsession with the symbolic image
of the Ass, both as representing the scholastic power of the Church and as
expressing possibilities of transformation.) Masks and guisings of all sorts
were brought into church; the priests dressed as women, pandars or minstrels,
sang bawdy songs, ate black puddings from the altar, censed with stinking
fire from old shoes set afire, ran and leaped about the church, drove through
the town in carts, and indulged in various mimings. We hear of the Precentor
of Fools shaved on a platform set up before the church-door, and the usual
array of mock-titles, Abbots of Fools, Kings, Dukes, Popes. Theatrical plays
were staged, and *Jeux de Personages,* often anti-clerical. The practices were
widespread in France, but common too in England, with dances, songs, processions, ball-play, ducking and roasting ceremonies, clothes worn inside out
or exchanged, garlands, masks. (We may compare the Festival of Fools in

ancient Rome, held in February with a communal meal and a saturnalian behaviour.) At Tournay the people, including the mayor, fought the church-dignitaries and assaulted the chaplain and vicars in defence of the Foolfeast. A milder rite, but with the same atmosphere was the election of a Boy Bishop at the three feasts of St. Stephen, St. John, and the Innocents.

In France, the 15th century saw guilds and companies of Fools, *Soties*, and *Societés Joyeuses*, similar to the religious fraternities and the literary soci-eties, *Puys*. (A *puy* produced Jeu Adam.) Each company had its Prince of Fools and its Mother Fool; and there were names like *Infanterie Dijonnaise*, Joyous Abbey, Abbey of Delight. Many writers were drawn in. The poet Gringoire, Mother Fool of the *Enfants Sans Souci* of Paris, wrote the *Sottie du Prince des Sots*, 1512, satirising the pope; and Marot belonged to the same group. Such societies took over the imagery of saturnalian reversal, had new-year rites, feasts of the ass, may-rites, birth-mimes (people being made to jump over broomsticks), and used hoods or fur-bonnets with ass-ears, green-and-yellow costumes, masks, bells. The form in which they expressed them-selves was the *Sotie* or Foolery and its allied *Sermon Joyeux*, which clowned and mocked everything, sometimes with political daring. In Germany the same impulse appeared in the Shrovetide plays, while in Normandy were Cornards, a buffoon fraternity, who guised and played farces in the streets on Shrove Tuesday, parodying the great of the world. An extensive fool-literature arose, of which typical items were Wireker's *Mirror of Fools*, Lydgate's *Order of Fools*, Brant's *Ship of Fools* (done into English by Barclay), Armin's *Nest of Ninnies*, and Erasmus' *Praise of Folly*. This fool-literature was used by the humanists; and in England the poems of Skelton with their japes and jingles are strongly in the spirit of the *sotie*. Traces of English fool-groups can be found, e.g. the Order of Brothelingham at Exeter; and the plays or revels of the Lord of Misrule at University or Inns of Court probably arose from the foolfeast or at least were allied with it.

The *Sotie* was so strongly a vehicle for the expressing of social unrest that Francis I suppressed it in France. Here is a summary of a play acted in 1524 by actors in eared foolscaps. First, they reel off satirical proverbs, drink, call on their grandmother, Folly, who advises a recourse to some trade. She introduces the Fools to the World, who agrees to take them into service and tries out their skill. They do everything wrong and give the World a bad time with shoes that pinch and clothes too tight or too slack. The priest gabbles off a mass or grows tediously longwinded, and so on. Finally they fetch a urine-doctor for the suffering World and the verdict of 'mad as a march-hare' is pronounced. World admits that what troubles him most is fear of the end of all things by fire. The doctor attacks this confession and derides the clergy who cheat and fake, keeping 'two sister sluts to warm their sleep; they kill the people for their pleasures, thrive as they will, but guard their treasures. . . Wars of extermination they wage: for what? A naught! In a Christian world."

So World abandons his fears and submits to the direction of the Fools—that is, accepts the reversal of all values implied in the fool-morality.

It will be clear then that Rabelais stands at the end of this tradition, summing it up and completing its anti-clerical satire. At the same time he broadens it with his humanism and develops the Joyous Abbey into the Abbey of Thelema with its utopian system of 'Do what you will' as the whole of the law.

Romance. The romance-forms had disintegrated in entering Italy. The *Morgante* of Pulci (1432-84) came near caricature and folk-attitudes: the kindly giant who lived for eating and the half-giant who lived on his wits and admitted to 77 mortal sins, with Rinaldo rating his belly higher than the Virgin. In A. da Barberino a yet more popular level was reached. With Boiardo (1441-94) the epic tale became a mere detritus of the old material. But Ariosto (1474-1533) raised the romance-form once more to dignity, expressing the backward-looking views of the seignorial reaction, the wish to idealise the medieval world and its imagery despite a reluctant decline into disillusionment. Whereas the true medieval man willynilly saw life crystallise as allegory, Ariosto was driven to allegorical devices as an effort to compel some sort of meaning into the chivalric theme; but for all the nostalgic charm there was a falsity pinpointed in the attempt to use the idealising terms to explain away the blood-guilt of his patron the Cardinal d'Este. Many lesser talents tried to carry on the revived romance-forms in verse, with the culmination in Tasso's Jerusalem epics, which sought sustained solemnity. Tasso wanted to lift romance to the level of the ancient epical poets, but with mannerist eclecticism; 'thinking that all most beautiful things are fitting for the heroic poem, but most beautiful is love'. The inner struggle was illuminated by his fears of the Inquisition which led him to allegory, and his mental disorders leading to breakdown. In England, Spenser took up the romance-tradition, more directly inheriting medieval elements, yet at the same time trying to make the themes serve the centralising kingship in an unstable balance of burgess and feudal positions.

Spenser brings out further how the new romance-epic was linked with a development of the pastoral, adding to the medieval basis various elements from the ancient poets. An important work was Sannazaro's *Arcadia*, which, though mostly composed by 1489, had an enormous vogue in the 16th century, aided by Bembo's work. The offshoots in verse, in plays, in prose-romances were countless, and the form was one of the seminal elements of the novel, ranging in its examples from Montemayor's *Diana Enamorada* to the novels of d'Urfé and Scudéry or the romance of Sidney's *Arcadia*, and affecting poets such as Tasso, Guarini, Ronsard, Belleau.

Cervantes. The next stage after Rabelais in the use of medieval material for anti-medieval purposes came with Cervantes. In Spain, well into the 16th century, before the huge influx of gold looted from America helped the seign-orial reaction to break down the industrial developments and the freedoms of the towns, there was a lively realistic position in writing, a strongly democratic attitude in political theory. Spanish authors were the chief urgers of the thesis of popular sovereignty, e.g. Suarez. In the early 16th century Fr. Alonso de Castrillo wrote in his *Tratado de Republica:*

All men are born equal and free, no one has the right to command another, all things in the world by natural right common property and the institution of private patrinomy is the origin of all evil.

Even in 1610 there were works like P. Mariana's book on kingship, which was burnt for discussing the best ways of destroying tyrannies. The strong human-ist element was exemplified by men like the educationalist Luis Vives.

The converted Jew, F. de Rojas (c. 1465-1541), inaugurated the great new prose outburst with his subtle conflict of character in *La Celestina*, and his varied style ranging from ironic bawdry to tragicomedy, from floridity to terse Latinity; all theological bases have gone and man is snared in the net of his own weaving, but he can achieve largeness of stature by his struggles. All sorts of folk-elements intruded in two works attribtuted to C. da Villalon: battles of frogs and rats, conversations between a cock and a shoemaker (with Lucianic derivations), spirit-journeys into the earth-centre or up to heaven, the tale of the Wandering Jew (in both books). Garcilaso acclimatised the pastoral.

Then shortly after the mid-century was born the Picaresque Novel. The rogue-fool theme which had been carrying on since Renard finds decisive form, which was able to express the new burgess world of the cash-nexus. The *picaro* represented both the oppressed and exploited poor, from whose level he failed to rise despite all his guile, and the manipulators of the market, the men of money, to whose ranks he aspired. The total effect was an exposure of the money-world, with the picaro in position of the naive fool who alone dared to ask the relevant question, to look through pretences at the obvious fact. 'All rob, all lie', says Guzman in Aleman's *Guzman de Alfarache*, 'you will not find a single one who is man to a man'. *Lazarillo de Tormes* anonymously launched the new form in 1554, a humanist work that purported to be the autobio-graphy of a poor boy who served in turn the three orders of society, a blind beggar, a priest, a hard-up gentleman, and ended as Toledo's town-crier. Aleman was of Jewish blood and had known jail and poverty as well as travelling in Mexico.

Cervantes created his masterpiece by fusing romance, pastoral and picar-esque tale on a new level. He satirised the seignorial idealisation of the chivalric life, contrasting it with the facts of the situation; but he was deeply sympathetic to his fool-hero's efforts to oppose a dedicated aim to the facts of moribund feudalism and villainous burgessdom. Don Quixote's dauntless refusal to see or accept the facts is a tragic expression of the fool's rôle of seeing the facts to which other people are blind. The deep truths of devotion, of the bond that humanly unites and stirs men, are all that the Don sees; and they are hidden to everyone else. Thus the fool-position is carried to its ultimate irony. Sancho Panza's attitudes complete the symbolism of the book; for while on the one hand he is as blind as the others to what the Don sees, and is a greedy peasant, yet he is fascinated by his master and his visions, and at certain points shares his hopes.

The picaresque tale contributed the realism and the theme of wandering through all levels of life; the romance contributed the major theme both in its ironic perspective and its deeper meaning; the pastoral less obviously contributed the element of poetic implication with the world of nature, the concept of the golden age which served as the final criterion of value in the judgment of the present. The Don remarks:

Happy times and fortunate ages were those on which our ancestors bestowed the style of Golden. Not because gold, so much prized in this iron age, was got in that happy time without any labours, but because those who lived in that time knew not those words Thine and Mine. In that holy age all things were common.

Thus in *Don Quixote* we see powerfully fused the three elements that bring about the novel, though it was not until Defoe that a point of stabilisation was to be reached—with the maturing of the new middleclass forces in 18th century England. The romance, denuded of chivalric illusion, provides an heroic element, a belief that life has a purpose that must be fought for; the picaresque tale gives the concrete point of reference to the real world, the world of the cash-nexus; the pastoral provides the persisting relation to nature and the ultimate criterion of union.

To follow out the complex conflicts and fusions of these three trends in creating the novel is beyond our scope; but we must grasp the deep elements of tradition, broken down and reconstructed, recombined, which went to the making of the novel as an artform—an artform only possible when society had reached a high level of complication, of multiple divisions and interconnections. In passing, however, we may note the link of the pastoral with the development of landscape painting.

The interest in the Golden Age had been sharply stimulated by the contacts with the tribal peoples of America. Lucretius was studied for his account of the origins of civilisation; and Corsali, friend of Leonardo, brought back accounts of primitive communities. Piero di Cosimo took up the theme imaginatively in a series of panels. And Venetian landscape, above all in Giorgione, had close links with the pastoral and its image of the Golden Age. Giorgione himself had had early associations with the Arcadian movement at the court in Asolo.

Finally we may note the rich labyrinthine form of *Don Quixote* as a result of the fused medieval, Renascence, and baroque elements: *una orden desordenada*. Each sally of the knight is a circular movement with tangential adventures, harmonised in number and tone, with tales and critical comments correspondingly inserted. Each part has its key-aspect in its middle, and the story is overlapped with a fourfold passional action, an organisation of four 'cascades' beyond the sallies, adventures, returns. With change in theme there is change in landscape—wild and phantasmal, melancholy, grotesque—in the atmosphere, the shifting planes of dust, light and shadow, tumults or hushes; and the words vary with these changes, which are linked with mood and character.

Drama. A very large number of dramatic forms had developed in the later medieval years, as we have seen. The two most important trails led to Italian opera and Elizabethan drama; but we can only fully appreciate those genres if we have some idea of the vast pressure of popular forces behind them. In Italy there was a deep tradition reaching back to the ancient world through mimes and *joculatores*; the *laude* of the flaggellants grew into the Umbrian monologues and dialogues with a penitential aim. In Umbria too the name *ripresentazione* first was heard, though the main body of *sacre rappresentazioni* came in Florence, reaching a high level of display but decaying by the 16th century. In that period the main work was done in the court-theatres, looking to Plautus and Terence, or to Seneca's closet-dramas for models; the result was a sharp inhibition of the creative flow. In comedy however the popular elements could not be excluded, and there was a lively development that included Machiavelli, Ariosto, Aretino, Cecchi, della Porta and others— while in the main cities arose a popular theatre, the Commedia dell'Arte, with professional companies and a stock repertory. At the court-level the most important form was that of the pastoral, Poliziano breaking from the sacred drama with his *Favola d'Orfeo*, and using Mercury instead of an Angel and Orpheus instead of Christ for the descent into the hell-hole. However, under the courtly strait-jackets, the pastoral play merely developed into artificial forms like Tasso's *Aminta* or Guarino's *Pastor Fido*. But the singing of the shepherds weighed down the musical side, and in becoming opera the pastoral found a sudden emotional expansion of great possibilities.

In France, too, the constricting political scene held up an effective development from the rich medieval bases. Francis I, we saw, forbade the companies of guildsmen to use satire, and an order of the High Court interdicted plays on sacred themes. In any event the popular plays were despised as fit only for 'servants and common mimes', including the moralites favoured by the lawyers' clerks of the legal fraternity, the Basoche. The farce, which flourished 1450-1550, was for the moment fruitless; but in the next century, with energies renewed from Italy, the form was to be taken up by Molière. The scene meanwhile was dominated by the sterile court-drama, at first partly in Latin, then largely composed of translations from Italian and of Senecan tragedy.

Only in Spain and England was there continuity between medieval or popular elements and the new dramas. In Spain, after a few pastorals and classical imitations, and many short *entremeses* or interludes of lowlife farce (perfected by Lope de Rueda, an actor-manager), there was the sudden expansion at the hands of Lope de Vega (1562-1635), a man of the people. His 1,700 plays, of which 470 survive, covered all sorts of themes, historical, religious, comedic. There were many popular elements and realistic pictures of village-

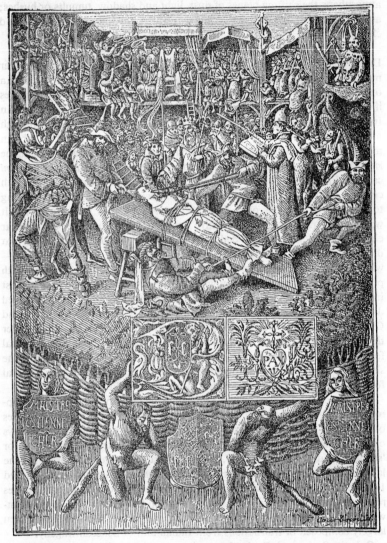

The Martyrdom of St. Apollonia: medieval stage. (*Mantzius*, History of Theatrical Art).

life, and a strong easy lyrical force pervaded the plays. Lope made much use of the *gracioso* or peasant-clown, a roguish fool-figure, who led on to Figaro and countless other characters; and he was not afraid of tackling the theme of privilege and class-distinction, as in three of his best plays, *Peribañez, Fuente Ovejuna,* and *The Fairest Judge is the King,* where peasant heroes revolt against their noble landlords—the king intervening at the end on their behalf. *Fuente Ovejuna* in particular has a remarkable picture of peasant solidarity in revolt. However, the main conflicts in Lope's plays revolved round the oppositions of love and loyalty, competition and honour. There was no deep penetration into character; conflict tends to become schematic and the aristocratic point-of-honour—morality reduced to etiquette—inhibits the growth of genuine tragedy. Lope also wrote an *Arcadia* and tried the national epic as well as a burlesque *Battle of the Cats,* sonnets and a sacred masque, *The Bethlehem Shepherds.* He fought the triumph of mannerist style in Gongora, though he ended by being affected by it. (In Italy Marino was leading the same sort of victorious mannerism in verse.)

In England then came the only full break-through; and here we find the fullest carry-over of medieval forms with new vitalities. Thus, the morality was used to express humanist ideas. *The Four Elements,* 1519, was inspired by Vespuccio's explorations and stated the need to study nature; *Wit and Science,* about 1540, carried on the same sort of theme. In Scotland, David Lindsay in his *Three Estates,* performed 1540-4, used the judgment-motive with full social reference and arraigned the estates of clergy, nobility and burgesses as led by Sensuality, Oppression and Falsehood; John the Common Weal accuses them before the King of Homanity. Lindsay polemised further with farcical interluded and a *sotie,* the *Sermon of Folly.* And folk-elements continue to fecundate non-dramatic verse, as in Dunbar's *Dance of the Seven Deadly Sins,* his use of Easter as emblem of the yearly struggle, *Done is a battle on the dragon black,* or his Flytings.

In England the out-of-work minstrels combined in companies, gained some lord's patronage, and set up as players. The Interlude took in the Fool, in a somewhat Herod-guise, as the Vice, a buffoon with long coat and lathen sword —Falstaff, in Shakespeare, is in a sense the Vice in a fully-humanised form. And many other genres added their quota to the tradition: court-guisings, students' plays, folk-farces, puppets, sets of tableaux (such as those for which Lydgate wrote verses), pageant-shows of the State-progresses (called *Mystères Mimés* at Paris), masques, ballets. In 1537 the students of Christ's College, Cambridge, were in trouble through acting the anti-papist *Pammachius;* and the government issued orders for all games and assemblies to stop in Suffolk because of a 'seditious Maygame' which was of a 'king, how he should rule his realm', and in which 'one played Husbandry and said many things against gentlemen more that was in the book of the plays'. Twelve years later the men of the Eastern Counties were up in arms and their revolt was heralded by a play about Becket at Wymondham. John Bale's Interludes were strongly anti-papist, and the chronicle play appeared in his *King John*.

Shakespeare. Thus it came about, as Defoe was to write, using the term 'art' to express the artificial stereotype accepted in the verse-drama of his own day:

> About a hundred years ago, there were five or six play-houses about the town (which was then far less populous than it is now) all frequented and full; though the stage was yet in its rude uncultivated dress, without art in the poetry or the decorations, and was only supported by the lower sort of people, yet my Lord, these LOWER SORT OF PEOPLE had souls high enough to be diverted by the Naked and Inornamental Drama,

And thus it was that Shakespeare was able to make the first fundamental advance on the Attic dramatists, creating realistic pictures with a deep symbolic content and recapturing the essential structure capable of expressing conflict and development in their fullness. The theatre into which he entered in London had a confused series of trends, including pastoral, low-life farce. Senecan drama merged with violent popular elements; but already a great poet had carried it to the high level from which Shakespeare might rapidly develop it for his purposes. Marlowe was in many ways a lyrical poet, yet he needed the dramatic form to utter his violent emotions, his challenge to the world, his Machiavellian humanism, his contempt for Christianity. His sense of topless aspiration and of 'infinite riches in a little room' outflowed in *Tamburlaine*, and contracted to a tragic point in *Faustus;* in *Edward II* he began to relate his tensions more objectively to history, to the clash of character.

In his comedies Shakespeare united courtly and popular elements, with the latter triumphing. *Love's Labours Lost* indeed directly satirised the courtly love-college and Biron made the formal rejection of aristocratic culture:

> silken terms precise,
> three-piled hyperboles, spruce affection,
> figures pedantical, these summerflies
> have blown me full of maggot ostentation.
> I do forswear them. . .
> Henceforth my wooing mind shall be expressed
> in russet yeas and honest kersey noes.

A point underlined by the peasant Fool's rout of the pedant Holofernes. *As You Like It* deepened the pastoral by means of the tormented Jacques and his clashes with the folk-fool, the apposition of real rustics to the court-dabblers, and the identification of the forest with the withdrawal from an unjust world. *A Midsummer Night's Dream* gained its weight by the addition of low-life characters to the masque-form, with Bottom transformed into the Ass-man. The problem of the cash-nexus appeared in the *Merchant of Venice,* and

Romeo and Juliet set love against the feudal bloodfeud. In the latter play, Shakespeare could not resist giving Romeo a diatribe against money—'There is thy gold. . . I sell thee poison. Thou hast sold me none—' without any reason for it in the play's action: as if at this point, where he touched on the actual agency that was to ensure the lovers' death through a trick that went wrong, he felt the need to identify it with the cash-nexus, not with the feudal conflict.

In his chronicle-plays he attempted to unfold the pattern of feudal conflict out of which his own Tudor world had evolved; but the omission of the burgess-forces left the picture incomplete—even though in *Henry IV* and *Henry V* he felt the need to introduce characters from common life. Still, he was haunted by the feeling that a clear pattern was comprehensible if one could only go deep enough:

> There is a history in all men's lives,
> figuring the nature of the times deceased,
> the which observed, a man may prophecy
> with a near aim, of the main chance of things
> as yet not come to life. (HENRY IV, ii)

> Miracles are ceased,
> and therefore we must needs admit the means
> how things are perfected. (HENRY V.)

Further, though Falstaff and his fellows may be analysed as feudal remnants and riffraff, parasites who lack privileges but will not enter the world of honest work, they also represent the dispossessed, the homeless of Shakespeare's own day; and so the break between Henry V and Falstaff, though from one angle meant to represent the advent of the responsible kingship, from another defines the cleavage of the world of power and the world of common life. What gives away this variety of levels in Shakespeare's response to the historical scene is the imagery used, of which the most striking example comes at the end of the panegyric of England in *Richard II*. 'This happy breed of men, this little world . . .' suddenly twists into the admission:

> . . . is now leased out, I die pronouncing it,
> like to a tenement or pelting farm,
> England, bound in with the triumphant sea,
> whose rocky shore beats back the envious surge
> of watery Neptune, is now bound in with shame
> with inky blots and rotten parchment bonds.

The imagery is wholly out of key with the situation in the play or with the actual England of Richard II; but it expresses the economic plight of the Tudor world. It reveals the perspective, not of king or noble, but of peasant, as in the protests cited by Robert Crowley round 1550:

In the country we cannot tarry, but we must be their slaves and labour till our hearts burst, and then they must have all. And to go to the cities we have no hope, for there we hear that these insatiable beasts have all in their hands. Some have purchased, and some take by leases, whole alleys, whole rents, whole rows, yea, whole streets and lanes, so that the rents be raised, some double, some triple, and some fourfold to that they were within these twelve years past. Yea, there is not so much as a garden ground free from them. . . What universal destruction chanceth to this noble realm by this outrageous and unsatiable desire of the surveyors of lands.

Works like *Measure for Measure* and *Troilus and Cressida* showed all the old certainties breaking down. In *Julius Caesar*, Brutus with his high aims of liberty is lost between griping Cassius and tyrannical Caesar. What is left? Shakespeare inherited the medieval concepts of world-order, of correspondences uniting all things in a hierarchial system of degrees; but he felt that something in his world, in history, was radically opposed to this order and unity. Man, in claiming to be a free agent in a world of disintegrated values, becomes either a betrayed Othello if he still trusts in love and friendship, a Hamlet broken by a burden of responsibility too great for comprehension, or a murderous accomplice like Macbeth. If he tries like Lear to treat human relationships as forms of contractual obligation, he will be abandoned to disaster.

Then at last, after the prolonged tragic tension breaks, Shakespeare lights on the innermost cause of the distortions, the levellings and twistings of things into their opposites. *Timon* reveals this sudden grasp in the denunciations of the cash-nexus; but the poet's understanding can only unpack itself in angry declamation, it cannot find dramatic form. In his final plays Shakespeare turns to something of a mannerist world, using romantic formulas of recognition—as if he contained within himself both the epochs of Attic tragedy and of the later New Comedy which reveals the breakdown of the old creative tensions. For compensation the new selfconsciousness, the use of the creative process as the actual subject-matter, enables him in the *Tempest* to achieve a new kind of symbolic depth.

These comments only touch at a few points the immense and infinitely varied life of the great plays. But the purpose of this book is not the detailed analysis of works of art; it is to bring out certain fundamental patterns and inter-relationships. The forms of *agon* and recognition, which constituted the pivotal points of Attic drama, were rediscovered by Shakespeare, as they were not by the students of antiquity, because of his personal insight, which, aided by adventurous probings of Marlowe, was able to seize the essentials of conflict in action as Bruno had seized them in the philosophic form of contraries. But we cannot abstract the creative penetration of either Marlowe or Shakespeare from the mass of popular forms which one way or another sought to use traditional patterns and imagery of death and renewal, and which lay behind and beneath the Elizabethan stage.

One such form which carried right on into that stage was dance-song-and-mime of the Jig, in which we find the theme of the (supposedly) dead man reviving. We must stress also the importance of the folkfool in Shakespeare's method and aesthetic. The fool is carried over from the comedies into the heart of the tragic situation in *Lear*, and Lear himself in his madness becomes a gigantic fool-figure, seeing with terrible innocence into the heart of things—separated from his 'sanity' which now becomes complicity with the corrupted world. Hamlet, too, is a sort of fool-figure in his distraction, his desperate oscillation between the pretence of madness and the real bursts of uncontrol —at each moment making his fool-exposure of the unshamed world. Thus *Diaphantus*, An. Sc., 1604, describes love-wildness:

> Tasso he finds, by that of Hamlet thinks,
> Terms him a madman, then of his inkhorn drinks.
> Calls players fools. The Fool he judgeth wisest. . .
> Much like mad Hamlet, thus, as Passion tears.

In the *sotie*-preface the poet remarks, 'Or to come home to the vulgar's element, like friendly Shakespeare's Tragedies, where the Comedian rides when the Tragedian stands on tiptoe. Faith, it should please all, like Prince Hamlet. . .'

In the *Tempest*, as we should expect from the play's symbolism, the theme of the Golden Age emerges. 'All things in common nature should produce,' muses Gonzalo, while the others point out with the contradictions of such a position in their world. 'No sovereignty'. 'Yet he would be king on't'. 'The latter end of his commonwealth forgets the beginning'. It is clear that the Diggers revolt of 1616 all over the Midlands had made Shakespeare aware of contradictions in his own attitudes. He owned property in his hometown's commonfields, yet in *Coriolanus* he sympathetically gives the suffering people terms of protest that echo the words of the Manifesto of the Warwickshire Diggers, with its plea against famine and against the 'encroaching tyrants' who mean 'to grind our flesh on the whetstone of poverty'. The inner conflict which cries out in the imagery cited from *Richard II* has now come into the forefront of his mind; hence the retreat into a world of symbols in the three last plays, their pastoral element (despite their moments of fierce emotion, the bitter jealousies of *Cymbeline*). The *Tempest* reveals the precise organisation of the initiation-rites of the ancient mysteries: that is, it makes explicit, lyrically clarified, the structures embodied dynamically in the great tragedies and the vivid comedies.

In *Macbeth*, *Lear* and *Hamlet*, Shakespeare defined the piling-up of anxieties and discords, contradictions and conflicts, in his world. The themes of succession derived from the contemporary problem of ensuring a successor to the barren Elizabeth without a return to feudal anarchy; but again the poet defined the feudal theme in terms of the actual tensions of his day, those of the cash-nexus. The succession-theme is also that of the inheritance of property; and what should be a moment of change inside an established world-order has become a jangling convulsion. All the claims are murderous or inhuman; the world is rent apart; and money is the canker that twists all relationships,

> Thus much of this will make black white, foul fair,
> wrong right, base noble, old young, coward valiant...
> this yellow slave
> will knit and break religions, bless the accursed,
> make the hoar leprosy adored, place thieves
> and give them titles, knee and approbation
> with senators on the bench: this is it
> that makes the wappen'd widow wed again;
> she, whom the spital-house and ulcerous sores
> would cast the gorge at, this embalms and spices
> to the April day again...

Shakespeare's structure is at root identical with that of the Attic tragedies, with its *agon* and recognition. What he has added is the surrounding density of character and historical situation, which correspondingly deepens the conflict of the protagonists. Cervantes alone has anything similar; but the differences in genre prevent any close analogy. Though Shakespeare draws in many Renascence elements, he is based most deeply in the medieval world and its folk-rituals; it is thence, and not from any learned positions, that he ultimately derives his structure. At the same time, because of the advanced stage of feudal disintegration in England, with the Cromwellian revolution looming up, both his medieval and his Renascence elements are locked in a baroque tension of convergent and divergent curves, strains and stresses, which he controls, up to the breaking-point of *Timon*, only by his sheer passionate insight, his secure grasp of the pattern of tragic conflict and resolution.

In *Antony and Cleopatra* he makes his greatest affirmation of the threatened life-process. The theme is not the world well lost for love, as Dryden coming after the flood of the Cromwellian revolution saw it; it is rather the world of love itself gone nobly down. In one sense Shakespeare is showing the death of the feudal order, which for all its brutalities and idealist falsities has the virtue of plain man-to-man relationships—its death before the cold determination of the new order expressed by Octavius. He makes us feel that the triumph of the latter is fated, yet he leaves all our sympathies with the disordered lovers. Here, as in all the great plays, we may analyse the work down to its connections with the actual tensions of a world poised on a difficult moment between two epochs, apparently stable and yet torn within by violent discords; but at the same time we recognise a grasp of the essential patterns of life and death and renewal, which lifts the definition into a humanly eternal sphere.

> The present pleasure,
> By revolution lowering, doth become
> the opposite of itself.

So he writes in *Antony*; and there, as in all his best works, we feel the naked pattern of life, beyond all the historical connections, beyond all the necessary analyses we make of the inner tensions and relationships of the poetry.

16 : Conclusions

We have now carried our survey roughly up to the year 1600—to the work of Titian and Caravaggio, Monteverde, Cervantes, Bruno and Shakespeare. Henceforth, especially after 1700, the cultural pattern becomes more complicated, as the gap between the arts and the productive sphere widens, division of labour grows, and the industrial working-class comes into existence. But in the space we have covered, from the days of the paleolithic cave-artists to Shakespeare, with all the many differences there are certain deep similarities, because the relation of men to the seasonal earth is at the heart of culture and production alike. Despite the development of various machines, generally men make whole things by handicraft processes.

Even among Australian natives the sense of the year's rhythm is powerfully present; and fertility-rites and initiation-rites alike use the imagery of birth to stimulate the life of nature or to express the movement from one phase or level of life to another. Linked closely with the dance, deep imagery-clusters grow up, above all the image of the circle with a hole or a mound at its centre. A conviction of life as a unity made up of a pair of opposites arises, connected with the relation of the group to nature and bringing about a dual form of organisation. As a sense of the part played by the sexes in procreation arrives, a new deep force is given to the idea of life as composed of united opposites. By the simple process of relating right and left to the eastern or western sun-points which one faces, a fourfold division of the circle is made, leading to all sorts of orientations and spatial divisions. The circle-and-centre is taken as a cosmic image. On this basis there grow up the architectonic ideas which we have seen express themselves in a vast series of forms culminating in the Gothic cathedral.

So much for the unity of opposites. But there is also a deep element of fear which appears as men, developing the animal consciousness into a human one, feel increasingly their kinship with one another, with all life, with all nature. The shedding of blood arouses a guilt-sense, which is expressed in the totem and the mother-taboo. Men feel cut off from nature as well as part of it; and the more they master nature, the more they realise the large odds against them. The sense of division appears in the notion of the self and the external-soul or soul-object as making up the total man, of the living tribes and the ancestors as making up the total tribe. Thus, a sense of division dogs the sense of unity; and various magical rituals are devised to overcome the resulting fear and restore the balance, the threatened security of union—the self with its external-soul, the tribe with its ancestors (who are at one point indistinguishable from the totem and the whole life of nature). Once agriculture and a settled life have been attained, the pressures of fear confuse the soul-object with personal property, and we are on the road that leads to the State.

With a settled society and a State-form, there is a great crisis in culture; for now divisions in labour are riveted on the group, with divisions in wealth and status and power. The gap between theoretical thinking and practical work which holds ancient culture in a state of arrest, except at unusual moments of deep-going social change, clamps down; and the contempt of practical work is reinforced by the social division of serfs or slaves who produce, and masters who consume. Though aspects of the opposition of thought and work still exist, it is the great achievement of the burgesses of the communes and chartered towns of the medieval world that by developing forms of manufacture without slavery they begin to close the gap and thus to make possible the union of science and production which brings about industrialism and the modern world.

These summarising comments are crude and concise; but they still serve here to remind us of some of the nodal points in our survey and to bring out the way in which till the 16th century the patterns of fertility-ritual and of initiation remain central in all the fields of culture. Shakespeare's world-image still relies on a system of correspondences between earth and sky, between all aspects of organic life, and on ideas of the unity of man and nature drawn from those correspondences. His world-image has thus a close affinity with that of the Sumerian or Egyptian, indeed with that of the Australian aboriginal, while there are profound differences between it and any post-Newtonian system. That is, the world is still essentially concrete for him, and there is no deep division between what he sees, feels, hears, tastes and touches, and what he thinks. Already things were beginning to be different with Donne, when he cried, 'The new philosophy puts all in doubt'—referring to the mechanistic world emerging from such analyses as Galileo's. After Newton we may say that science

creates an increasingly wide gulf between our perception of the phenomena and the conceptions by which we make them comprehensible. We see the sun rise and set, but we think of the earth as moving round the sun. We see colours, but we describe them as wave-lengths. We dream of a dead relative but we think of that distinct vision as a product of our own subconscious minds. Even if we individually are unable to prove these almost unbelievable scientific views to be true, we accept them, because we know that they can be proved to possess a greater degree of objectivity than our sense-impressions. In the immediacy of primitive experience, however, there is no room for such a critical resolution of experience. (FRANKFORT)

Thus we may say that in many respects Shakespeare was closer to the Australian aboriginal than to post-Newtonian man. The need of regaining a wholeness of vision, a sense of the unitary life-process, sets post-1600 culture a series of problems of a new kind. And we are still in the thick of those problems, most of which are yet unsolved—in fact, are hardly realised as problems.

This does not mean that we should shed tears over the loss of primitive immediacy and wholeness; for we have seen that it involved its own problems and contradictions, and was bound up with social conditions to which we cannot return. The analytic processes which speeded up after 1600 had been indeed in action for a long time, sapping the primitive vision; and the only way forward lay in their omnipresent emergence. Things could not have happened otherwise. Our problem is not to scrap the analytic consciousness on which the vast mechanical and scientific advances of the last three centuries have been made. It is to include it in a fuller comprehension of the life-process, where its negative aspects will be overcome.

We do not need to discuss that thorny problem here. But these few concluding remarks have been necessary to set the pre-1600 periods in their proper perspective. We cannot build satisfactory architecture now because we lack the world-image which provided all the vital and various forms from the totemic centre to the cathedral; but we cannot return to an image in which we no longer believe. We have to go on breaking down the abstract elements in post-Newtonian science till we regain concreteness in another way.

Looked at from the other side of the Newtonian Celestial Mechanism, the great organising images which this book has discussed seem reduced to mere fantasies and delusions; and there was indeed a fantastic element in them. But if we see only that, we see nothing. The images were born vitally of an organic tension between men and their work-techniques; an organic tension and release felt by men in their most intense moments of bodily expression, in mating, in work, in dancing, in all forms of rhythmic play. They had their deep enduring reality and truth, which we still experience when we look at the works that embodied them. Only, it is a reality and a truth that we cannot simply return to after the scientific mechanical abstraction splits the world of sense from the world of mind in a way as complete and as deadly as the old metaphysics of mind and body. (We must also add that it brings the possibility of overcoming in the end all such one-sidedness.)

We have seen that the great periods of expression are those in which a new organising force on the upper levels draws into itself the lively forms of expression seething at the popular level. The periods of exhaustion come when the gap reasserts itself between the two levels. In all the periods treated in this book there are vital popular forces waiting at any moment to be drawn up, because in one shape or another there are always collective forms growing up out of the fertility-rites of the seasonal earth and the allied rites of initiation. After 1600 this position rapidly fades out, the last great uprush of folk-forces occurring in the Romantic movement—though there those forces are weakening all the while and leaving in the end only the conviction of a lost earth in the lonely poet.

Though we cannot draw directly on any of the solutions of the past, it is heartening to look back over the many thousands of years between the Aurignacians and ourselves, and to trace out the wonderful variety and depth of the images and artforms which men have created as memorials of their deepmost experience of growth and of earth-rootedness, of their indomitable struggle to understand what was happening and to express in all its fullness the triadic universe of change. In seeking to compass the vast story within a single book, I have had to omit much and to select what seemed to me most validly to illustrate the most deepgoing and significant patterns. In clarifying those patterns I have sought to escape over-simplifications and to state conclusions which would stand even if one had space to bring in all the qualifications and the complicating details. And looking back, I feel that if there is much yet to explain and round off, the picture developing out of our inquiry has its own inner coherence, which emerges from the material itself and is not imposed on it.

Note on Methods

The various efforts made in the last hundred years to devise a coherent system for cultural sequences or cycles in anthropology have all more or less miscarried. Above all, the rationalist and scholastic method of relating material in Frazer has brought discredit on systematising. But his sin was not that he was an evolutionist, but that his conception of cultural evolution was so mechanically rationalist. However, in reacting against his schematisms, anthropologists threw out evolutionary ideas as well and ended with no method of interrelating the material from different cultures at all. Yet the one great value of Frazer's compilations was that they cried out for a concrete and historical scheme which would make sense of them; and the next step should have been a struggle for its working-out, so that the real questions of continuity and sequence could have been thrashed out. Things were made worse indeed by the Diffusionists, with their thesis that all civilisation derived from Egypt. Again there were interesting compilations, which did attempt to grapple with the real issues, even though in a one-sided and narrow way. Elliot Smith and the others often brought together in an illuminating way material which did have a real inner connection, though not the connection they thought. Yet again, the school that pointed to the widespread patterns of myth-ritual made important correlations, though they followed a false diffusionist clue and tended to put a dogmatic stress on the part of the divine kingship instead of seeing that the essential trail lay in the fertility-ritual which the kingship at one phase took over.

The reaction had its good points. It looked above all to fieldwork as an escape from abstract constructions. No complaint could be made about this healthy tendency if it had not been linked with a phobia as to all large scale correlations. The emphasis on each culture as a self-contained functional whole led to such impossible positions as the denial of any general meaning to the idea of Marriage and an attempt to posit a separate origin for marriage inside each society. Yet even the most rabid functionalist could not do without some general ideas or frameworks. Thus, Steiner remarks, 'The broad significance which "Totemism" had as a comparative category has evaporated. This significance was twofold: it bore the import of an assumed stage in human evolution; it also demarcated totemism as a solid block of "Otherness", which it remained even after thinking in terms of stages had been abandoned by the earnest.' (His book, excellently examining Frazer, Robertson, Smith, Marrett, Radcliffe-Brown, in fact helps towards an understanding of totemism and the taboos as a stage in human development.)

Frazer must not be left to overshadow the argument. He belonged to the scholastic wing of a splendid phase in English scholarship, to which men like Crawley, Hartland, Cook, Jane Harrison, Cornford, Chadwick and others have contributed much more important ideas and methods than he ever did. In this book I have tried to express my gratitude to them by carrying on what seems to me valid and concrete in their work. And I may point to books like L. A. White's *The Evolution of Culture*, 1959, as a sign that the functionalist disintegration of the cultural scene is itself now going out of fashion. Finally, I should like to add a tribute to the importance of the Chadwicks' *Growth of Literature* in showing the part played by the shaman in preliterate societies, and to the work of George Thomson on ancient Greece.

Notes and References

Chapter 1. Some references: Watson, Burkitt, Oakley, Zeuner, Boule, Obermeier, Le Gros Clark, J. G. D. Clark, Luquet, S. Cole, Leakey, Hawkes, Mitchell, Moir, Childe, Goury, Crawley (e), Marret, J. Huxley, T. Harrison, Bolsche, Hardy, Laming, Bataille, Lechler, Maringer, Breuil, Kuhn, Lemozi, Windels, James, Christensen, Goodall, Hallstrom, Ravdonikas, Capitan, Caudwell, Boule, J. W. Jackson, E. Smith, Coates, Daniel, Goury, Graziosi, Buecher, Kroeber, Mitchell, Moir, Passemard, Verneau, Zuckerman.

Zamiatnin has suggested that mother-figurines were used in puppet-plays to imitate (and cause) generation.

I have not dealt with folk like the Veddas of Ceylon, the Punan of Borneo, the Bushmen of Africa, who seem to represent the pre-totemic level: peaceful groups, with generally monogamous systems. 'At the lowest grades of culture, communities may be found among whom no important offence of violence has been committed within living memory.' (Diamond)

The Veddas invoke ancestral spirits famed for hunting and yam-growing: the most honoured *yaka* is Kande Yaka, a mighty hunter. Before a hunt they seek his aid by a representation of how he killed a deer. First a food-offering, then the dance, then an invocation by a shaman, into whom Kande enters and who works himself up into a possessed dramatisation of how Kande found the deer's slot, followed it up, and killed the deer with an arrow: the Seligmanns, *Veddas*, 1911 34, 131.

P. R. Leason, an Australian artist, put out theory of paleo. animal forms drawn from dead quarry (*PPS* 1939); *see* C. McBurney, *ANT* no 138, who thinks it may apply to Magdalenians. *See* Graciosi for Gravettians, not Aurignacians, as creators of the mother-figures; McBurney too.

For use of tools as shown by marks on them: S. A. Semenov, *Pervobytnaya Teknika* 1957.

For fertility-rites still linked with rock-art (Muslim Darfur), Balfour Paul, *JRAI* 1956-7.

Chapter 2. Some references. McCarthy, Birket-Smith, B. Spender, Elkin, Gregory, Kaberry, D. S. Davidson, Elkin, Van Gennap, Bettelheim, Wheeler, Roheim (valuable material if one ignores his Freudian thesis), White, Howeitt, Brough Smith, Schulze, R. H. Matthews, Berndt, Oldfield, Christensen, Radcliffe-Brown, Schmidt, Durkeim, Gregory, G. Thomson, McConnel, Brough-Smith, Cünow, Curr, Diamond, Duguid, Dunlop, Durkheim, Keane, Roth, D. F. Thompson.

Churinga=mother (Fry); part of her deathless spirit-body (Strehlow). Cosmic body: Arunta and Loritja call blue sky 'flesh', night-sky with stars 'bones', vault 'stomach' of sky beyond: behind these is the 'back' of the sky: Strehlow ii II. Natural features are continually assimilated to the broken-up animal, e.g. Dieri myth of origin of Lake Eyre: A pregnant woman sees a kangaroo, wants it for food; child in womb echoes 'H'm'. This happens thrice; child is born and at once chases the kangaroo with his mother's digging-stick, to a place where men hold a circumcision rite. The men kill the kangaroo with boomerangs, skin and share out the flesh. The boy comes up; they deny that they have seen the kangaroo, but at last give him the skin, which he pegs out; one back leg to S.E., one to S.W., tail to S., forelegs, head, neck to N.W. N. and N.W. E. Thus arises the hill Duturunna. (Siebert, *Globus* xcvii 1910 46) Note also the orientations.

In the East Pilbara tribe women and children took some share in the rite at the local totem-centres, *thalu*.

Among the Munkan of York Peninsula the myth tells of two girls finding the bullroarer in water by a rock. 'It belongs to us women. But no matter. We hide it for the men. It is they who will swing it'. The *moiya* roarer represents a girl entering puberty; it is used by initiates at the end of the first part of the first initiation-rite. Another is *pakapaka*, representing a mature girl; it is swung at the rite's end. *Moipaka*, yet larger, represents a young married man. (McConnel 119-27, and 131ff.). Here every tale describes the inauguration of a cult by some *pulwaiya*, totemic ancestor, who in the beginning sanctioned some aspect of reality and continues to uphold, create, renew, reinforce, re-sanction it. Each ground is owned by a clan, whose members take names from the characteristics of the clan *pulwaiya* over whose abode, *auwa*, they preside and perform the necessary rites. The *auwa* is marked by some hole, tree, waterhole, rock or antbed – with its ritual of approach, tale of origin, dramatic revelation. It is situated in the natural habitats and breeding places of beasts, birds, fishes, plants, etc. in which the *pulwaiya* have become incarnated.

When the Unthippa woman entered the ground, 'nothing more is known of them except that it is supposed a great womanland exists far away to the east where they finally sat down' (Spencer and Gillen 442). For figure p. 36: Roheim, frontispiece; Strehlow, i, tables i, ii; Spencer and Gillen, *N.T.* 146-9; O. Rank, *Das Trauma der Geburt* 1924 142.

Tools: JRAI 1957, Allchin; 1959 Mitchell. On segmentation M. G. Smith (lineage) *JRAI* 1956; games, F. Barth, *JRAI* 1959; theory of games, J. R. Stone, *Econ. J.* 1948 no 38; von Neumann and Morgenstern, *Theory of Games and Econ. Behaviour* 1947.

For problems of dating Australian sites: D. J. Mulvaney, *ANT* March 1961; Devon Downs is given 2890-1790 B.C. The adze, still a basic item in the aborigine kit of the 19th c., first appeared on this site in layer nine times. Cape Martin, South Australia, is given 6740 B.C. (120 either way).

Chapter 3. Childe, Davy, Perry, R. Harris, Wach, Burkit-Smith, Diamond, Finley, Firth, Swanton, Hambly, Herskovits, Mauss, Coates, W. Matthews, Onians, Lorimer, Boas, Gorer, MacGovern, Harrison, Langdon, Rose, Rivers, G. & J. M. Brown, Brunton, Butt-Thompson, Burght, Codrington, Crawley, Hartland, Forde, Fortune, Fortes, Gluckman, Frazer, Garrod, Garstang, Gortein, Haddon, Handy, Henry, Hogbin, Hollis, Hose, J. W. Jackson, Kenyon, Katz, Kern, Karsten, Merker, Mooney, Morgan, Murie, Morley, Olson, Rink, Reichard, Radcliffe-Brown, Radin, Rowe, Speck, Steinen, Swanton, Sydow, Steward, Talbot, Turner, Tylor, Thurnwald, Thomas, Worcester, Webster, Westermarck, Weyer, Opler, Schmidt, Vaillant, Soustelle, Spinden, Vega, S. E. Thompson.

Twins: Harris; Cook (a).

Geometric vases: Webster (a) 174.

Dual Pillars: of Solomon's Temple; the beams of the Dioscures (Tod; Lethaby 119; Cook); Egyptian obelisks, which were sacred and had their own offerings. For the pylons and sungates in general, Lethaby (e) 22, 112; Cook (a) ii 41; Book of Enoch. On a house-ossuary from an Azor cave (Tel-Aviv) the façade had a pair of side-columns as well as Pickaxe and Nose; they own capitals projecting above the flat roof and suggest 'the masts or columns flanking the entrance of later times Phoenician and Assyrian temple' J. Perrot, *Illus. London News*, Dec. 3 1960 (fig. 3 p. 999). The Noses and other features on the ossuaries show that the House is also a Body (clearly of a Mother.) The date is second half 4th millenium B.C.

Primitive Money: Among the Tolowa and Tututni Indians of California, dentalium shells and other 'treasures' were used in 'the purchase of social protection and prestige, in sex, and in maintaining familial status', entering 'hardly at all into the subsistence equation'. C. du Bois in *Essays . . . to A. L. Kroeber* 1936 51. For the Blankets of the N.W. Coast, F. Boas, *Social Organ. and Secret Societies of Kwakiutl* 1897 341 (cf. *N.W. Tribes of Canada* 1898 54). The prestige-objects of Melanesia (a few have commodity-value in exchange, e.g. dog's teeth of Admiralty Is.) are large in number.

14th c. dates for early neo. Malta (two megalithic tombs) 2700 ($\pm$150) B.C.; comparable ones for France and Switzerland: *ANT* no 138 143, 147.

Chapter 4. Childe, Boas, Wach, White, Schneider, Chadwicks, Coxwell, Thalbitzer, Burkit-Smith (Lapp refs. 138-40), Bancroft, Bodrigi, Bosi, Bunzel, Castage, Castren, Caudwell, Coxwell, Cushing, Czaplicka, Dähnhardt, David-Neel, Dennett, Densmore, Dixon, Dorsey, Firth, Fletcher, Folkard, Gale, Ghirshman, Goodall, Gorer, Grinnell, Linton, Sachs, M. Smith, Semper, Stephen, Winstedt, Wissler, Wundt, Sayce, Speck, F. E. Williams.

For the shaman as link between ritual-drama and drama proper: among the tribes of Upper Burma there is a sort of official shaman in the *pasan sayai;* and among the Tangkuls of Manipur the *thilapoko* for a few days represents the spirit of a dead man. Each of the 37 official Nats of the Burmese is served by a shaman or medium who acts the part of the Nat on the occasion of his or her festival. In Malaya a *pawang* or shaman is at the head of the dramatic troupe and begins the show by burning incense and praying to the local spirits.

B. Whorf showed how Hopi co-operation was aided by linguistic patterns that stress the interconnection of thought and the material universe ('Relation of Habitual Thought and Behaviour to Language' in L. Speier, *Language, Culture and Personality* 1945). The Hopi, Nitinant and Nootka tongues lack analytical elements; 'the terms verb and noun in such a language (as Nitinant) are meaningless' while in Nootka 'all words seem to be verbs . . . we have as it were a monistic view of nature that gives us only one class of words for all kinds of events. "A house occurs" or "it houses" is the way of saying "house".' (*Language, Thought and Reality* 1956). Unitary and dynamic are better terms than monistic here, understood in relation to what I have called primitive dialectics.

For the neolithic Mother of Wild Animals (with a boy god) at Hacilar, Anatolia, c. 5500 B.C.: *Illust. London News* Feb. 11 1961.

For shamanism: add N. Chadwick, *Poetry and Prophecy* 1942, and *JRAI* lxvi; J. Campbell, *Masks of God*; M. Eliade, *Le Chamanisme* 1951; G. V. Ksenofontov, *Legendy* etc. 1930, German transl. *Schamanengesch. aus Siberien* 1955. For transition from the shamanism of the hunting group to the fraternities of the agricultural group: Campbell 238. Note for fool-clowns linked with the shamans in the Tsanati dance-society of the Jicarilla Apache (a summer-winter dance). For the word shaman: Laufer, *AA* xix no 3 1917 361.

For the Tierra del Fuegans, Campbell 245; E. L. Bridges, *Uttermost Parts of the Earth* 1948 412 (women). Tatar culture shows Buddhist influences etc., but its shamanism has deep roots. Ancient Greek culture seethes in its legends with shamanism, hardly yet explored despite the Chadwicks and Dodds, etc.

Chapter 5. Langdon, Granet, G. Thomson, James, Heidel, Hooke, Jean, Jackson Knight, Casson, Lethaby, Childe, Atkinson, Blegen, Brea, Bohl, O. G. S. Crawford, Contenau, Eisler, J. D. Evans, Giot, Daniel, Hocart, Kantor, Leonard, Sandars, Segall, Widengren, Wensinck, Boyancé, Chapouthier. For maze, esp. Jackson Knight, Deedes in *Labyrinth*, Layard.

Perhaps one can see the seminal world-image in the Tuc d'Audoubert; flint-chipping floors of the Tardenoisians seem circular.

For the shield-goddess, see Lorimer 143, 446; Webster (a) 170. I think it likely that the shield came to be thought of as a mother- or world-image, thus providing a maximum of magical as well as practical protection: Note the 'omphilic' boss and compare the cosmic shield of Achilles (Iliad xviii). A Knossos tablet mentions the Lady of the Labyrinth = the goddess Ariadne (Palmer, *BICS* ii 1955 40; Webster (a) 51).

The Japanese myth tells how the Sun-goddess, quarrelling with the Impetuous Male, retired into a rock cavern and plunged the world into darkness. The gods made various efforts to draw her out, e.g. a sun (mirror) was forged on a rock-anvil, a bamboo-flute was played (with time kept by two bits of wood struck together), a harp was devised, and Uzume no mikoto danced on a circular box (thus originating the drum) and exposed herself – like Baubo in the Eleusinian myth. The gods laughed and thus was born, it was said, the pantomime dance *kagura*. The sun-goddess was lured out of her cave.

Uzume is looked on the ancestress of the Sarume, women doing comic (monkey) dances in honour of the gods. 'These dances were the origin of the *kagura* and *no* performances.' Aston, *Trans. Asiatic. S. Jap*, i suppl. i 79. Also Satow, ii 126. Compare the Miko, woman-dancer, who becomes possessed in a temple: Ridgeway (a) 330.

See Berndt (a) ch. 16 for a 'map' of the ritual centre of the Djanggawul with radiating *rangga* or umbilical-cords to the spots where people were created. Each *nara* shade which the D. built from *djuda* boughs has a clearing within and before its mouth and a symbolic mound or sandhill (Song 123).

Many more details might be added about the world-image in building. e.g. *Egypt* – domical mud structures (persisting as granaries) with a knob that seems the prototype of the dome-lantern. Early wooden coffins (e.g. Thebes) with painted stars on underside to make the box a cosmic form; late mummy-shaped covers show figures of gods of constellations and planets, signs of the Zodiac and the Decans; coffins round turn of A.D. are in the form of a rounded vault and with angle posts rising to the height of the cover; one has Nut on the full length of the inside of the curved cover, with zodiac signs either side and with the rising sun at the mummy-head, at the feet the death-door over which is the black cow of Hathor with life-symbol round her neck. Akhenaton's new town was square, with four boundary-stones. Predynastic vases show the hills either side of the Nile in pyramid-form. Phrases used for buildings are: 'It is such as the heavens in all its quarters', 'Firm as the heavens'. Later miniature pyramids (memorials) show at their apices the two Eyes of Horus (sun and moon) or the barque of Re on the heavenly waters. The sky-supports were the Four Sons of Horus at the cardinal points. The stars were hung from the sky-slab by hooks like lamps from a ceiling. (Lethaby (c) 19, 27, 33, 47, 49, 52, 58). Note also the four canopic jars with the organs of the dead.

India: Asoka was a Wheel King, i.e. ruled whole earth within the Four Seas. A Chinese Buddhist c. 400 A.D. told of a Deccan monastery hollowed in rock, shaped as an elephant on which stand one above another, lion, horse, ox, dove. Mosques and Hindu temples alike were aligned to the cardinal points; we hear of palaces with seven chambers for the seven planets (reign of Hamayun). The Delhi audience hall had the incription, 'If there is heaven on earth, it is this, it is this'. For further on the paradise-building: Lethaby, 83ff. Akbar's palace at Fatepur Sikri had a world-pillar or tree on which he sat enthroned. Indian domes commonly had the 8 ribs of the Wheel (the Law to the Buddhists, the Universe to the Hindus), related to the four quarters: Havell. For relation of Mt. Meru to the elements: Lethaby 129, Havell, E. T. C. Werner 368.

For Buddhist forms: Lethaby 33ff.; and relation of stupa to omphalos on Roman coins and idols of Artemis at Perge, Asia Minor: Roscher, Cook, Lethaby 67. Great Eyes look in the four directions on some Buddhist monuments. The Amaravati stupa was called Mount of Light.

China: the account of cosmic details in temple, pagoda, etc. could be much elaborated. For coronation-rites, Lethaby 85ff., also in Siam, 86; Cambodia, 128; Japan, 143. K'un-lun is the central mountain 3,000 miles high with the immortality-fount and the source of the Four Great Rivers, etc. For Ceylon, 143. In Java is also the 2nd c. Ananda temple, pyramidal with 7 storeys.

Assyria: Cities were founded on basis of the orientated square. And the gods received heroic souls on the summit of the Mountain of the World.

Much might be said of the *sky-pillar and soul-ladder:* see Cook (a) ii 121 etc. For ziqqurat stages: Jastrow, etc. The monumental pillars inscribed with kingly deeds e.g. by Hammurabi or Tiglath Pileser are world-pillars, cf. the plaques of a god like Jupiter Dolichenos and the whole imagery of the Mithraic cult and its monuments. Mesopotamian palaces down to the days of the Persians had cosmic aspirations: Lethaby 79ff. For sky-ceilings carrying on to Gothic days, 110ff. For planetary and cosmic colours in India and China, 125ff.

Note also the cosmic vision in *Ezekiel* and the part played by the four winds; also his four-square Holy City.

The *world-tree* is another theme about which a very great deal might be said. Like the pillar it holds up the sky and *is* the universe; it also is abstracted into a spiritworld form, e.g. the serpent-guarded tree of the Hesperides. Evans (c) for the influence of the Ash of Yggdrasil on the Cross, Evans (b) and Nilsson (b) for the Minoan tree; Cook on Diana pillars (a) ii 158 etc. The world-tree becomes the paradise-tree. Cf. the tree-pillar setting-up in Egypt and the Assyrian New-year tree. 'A carved Hittite relief from Carchemish' (a tree guarded by two bulls) shows 'clearly a palmtree and the prototype of the Ionic column. The piled-up base of the Ionic column also suggests that it was originally a single and isolated unit. The scrolled Persian capitals of Persepolis derive from the same genealogical tree. Around the throne-room of Nebuchadnezzar at Babylon was a splendid "decoration" of double-branched trees of the same type (as the Hittite) in glazed brickwork. They were doubtless sky-pillars. A cousin sacred tree to the Ionic was the Greek grave stele or pillar with its volute and palmette crown. Both were sacred evil-repelling forms. The Corinthian capital was the last efflorescence of the symbolic tree'. Lethaby (c) 107.

In India (in the *Mansara*) the coronation-rite involves a wishing-tree, 'an all-productive tree' with a seven-headed serpent coiled round. This paradise-tree reminds of the gold tree with singing birds in the palace at Byzantium by the throne. (Note *Daniel* for the interpretation of the world-tree as the king.) For the *lotus-pattern* (in Greece, the egg-and-tongue): Lethaby 135ff.; Goodyear; Havill (India); (Crete) Williams, etc.

Motive of cosmic weaving and embroidery: Russian folktale, C. F. Coxwell (Afanasiev no 158, 2nd ed.). (Anakreon, fr. 8 for weaving songs). Cosmic spindle, J. Cuillandre, *La Droite et la Gauche dans les poèmes homériques* 1944 455—a useful book for orientation in Greece. Cosmic robe, 406-11. Also Eisler (b).

For the swastika-whirl as a prelude to the concept of the circle in the Bronze Age: J. Campbell, *The Mask of God* 1959 232, with designs from shell-gorgets, Spiro Mound, Oklahoma (here the whirl of four bird-forms). For Pleiads as dancers: Callimachos, scholiast Theocritos xiii 25; Bowra (b) 51.

For the Double still believed in Egypt: *JRAI* 1926 163. The Double in Greece, G. Aigrisse, *Psychoanalyse de la Grèce antique* 1960 136ff.

Miraculous-twins cycle in folktale: R. T. Christiansen, *Studies in Irish and Scandinavian Folktales* 1959 36 etc. For Moliones in Homer, Hesiod, Pindar: Bowra 56 (as horses).

Kantor deals with relation of Minoan and Egyptian spirals and meanders: note the quadruple spiral pattern with palmette filling on roof of Senmut's tomb and the Orchomenos ceiling, *JRS* 1947 105.

Chapter 6. Edwards, Moscati, Frankfort, Lambert, Sollberger, Fairman, Moret, Gardiner, J. Spiegel, Rachwitz, Furlani (cited Moscati), Parrot, Iversen, Aldred, Allbright, Badawi, Bade, Blackman, Breasted, Budge, Capart, Cerny, Desroches, Dhorme, Donadeni, Englebach, Engnell, Erman, Greven, Falkenstein, Fisch, Galpin, Gerelli, Gilbert, Glanville, Hessan, Heidel, Hornermann, Horrath, Jastrow, Jean, Junker, Kees, Jacobsen, Kramer, Lange, King, Lauer, Lucas, Mercer, Mekhitarian, Naville, Neugebauer, Pattis, Scharff, Schädel, Schmokel, Sethe, W. S. Smith, Sollberger, Soden, Szlechter, Thausing, Vandier, Wit, Woolley, J. Wilson, Zervos, Zandee.

Also, C. Aldred, *Egyptians* 1961 (for Ma'at); *Egypt of the Pharoahs*, A. Gardiner 1961. Step pyramid out of stepped mounds of 1st Dynasty tombs at Saqqara; thence to true pyramid through Heliopolitan ideas, Edwards (2nd ed.) 24, 236. But those ideas were only a specific concentration of basic orientation and world-mount image.

Chapter 7. Gaster, Schaeffer, James, Hempel, Pritchard, Garstang, De Burgh, Boman, Bright, Buntzen, Burrow, Chwolsohn, Dentan, Driver, Eissfeldt, Garstang (b), Gordon, Gunkel, Herzfeld, Lods, Oesterley, Needham, Willetts, Anderssen, Holscher, Meyer, Nyberg, Parkes, Olmstead, Rankin, Ranston, Schaeffer, Vincent, Arnold, Crossland, Dhalla, S. Smith.

Chapters 8-9. Webster, G. Thomson, Jane Harrison, Cornford, Barnett, Berve, Onians, Chroust, Demangel, Dickins, Dodds, Finley, Foucard, Glotz, Page, Güterboch, Guthrie, Bieber, Boura, Couat, Edmonds, Farringdon, Farnell, Gaster, Haserbroek, Havelock, Heath, Henderson, Herzler, Hogarth, Jouget, Kirk, Little, Macchioro, Marinatos, Martienssen, Minns, Norwood, G. Murray, Mylonas, Penrose, Ranulf, Ridgeway, Rostovtreff, Seltman, A. N. Smith, Stocks, Stanford, Tarn, Ventris, Winnington-Ingram, Ziebarth, Zielinski, Lorimer, Wade-Gery, Fränkel, Lever, Sheppard, Stella, Germain, F. C. Grant.

Akkadian verse 'was normally a unit of two distinct halves with two beats in each half; Hittite verse according to Güterboch had a "normal" line with usually four stresses and about 12 to 17 syllables, with occasional shorter or longer verses; Ugaritic poetry according to Ginsberg falls into kola, of which there are normally two but sometimes three to a stich. There seems no reason to suppose that any of these metres had the precision of the Homeric hexameter, but neither should we expect that the Homeric hexameter had been far developed in the Mycenean age, although it is probable that Greek poetry was already composed in double short rhythm.' Webster (a) 68. 'The headings of three tablets containing orders can be scanned in double short rhythm, two as paroemiacs (a very ancient Greek metre as the fact that it was used for proverbs shows) and one as a pendant hemiepes; as more is learnt of Mycenean Greek, more examples may be found, and metrical beginnings to operation orders may prove to have been the rule. At least these certain examples show how easily Mycenean Greek with its uncontracted vowels could be adapted to double short rhythm whether anapaestic or dactylic', 92.

Greek temples: Note the apotropaic magic of the pediment sculptures, brought out strongly by the gorgon-heads, e.g. on Corfu gorgon between two lions; Selinus (c. 580 B.C.); at Olympia a golden shield with a relief and a gorgon; a gorgon on west front of Parthenon, on the aegis. Protective magic was also in 'the watching lions' heads at the four corners, the great acroteria, and the palmette (really lotus) antefixae along the eaves. . . The Hecatompedon, built in the 6th c., had a decidedly barbaric and magic character. One pediment had a great sculpture of a bull over-thrown by two lions'. Lethaby 95; Dodds, etc. Solar Discs: Cook (a); 292 – dual beasts: Lethaby, 115ff. (Hittite, India, China).

Greek art: Sculptural technique was by 'a number of different shapes of punch – a short bronze instrument with a relatively sharp but not very sharp point. He held this at right-angles to the block of marble and struck it lightly with a mallet'. Thus roughed out a figure which in its raw state looked 'rather like a honeycomb', then rubbed with pumice, sand, emery, and got the feeling of a subtly rounded whole. Did not cut into the block from one side with a predetermined form in mind, as later sculptors tended to do. (M. Ayrton, *Listener,* March 9, 1961). For proto-Doric columns in Egypt imitating a reed, *JHS.* 1949 114.

Statue and Spirit: At Orchomenos the people, to deliver the land from the wandering spirit of Actaion, had a figure of him made in bronze and fastened it to the rock. (At Byzantium later, statues were looked on as a sort of external-soul.)

Homer and Geometric Art: see Webster (a) ch. 6-7 for some suggestive comparisons, with also his ch. 3 for the relation of Mycenean and Eastern poetry; pp. 226, 296 for Homer as the precursor of Thales; 16 for specialised Mycenean workers. Myres (a) 498, 511, etc.

For Odysseus and his bow: a Hittite tale of King Gurpanzah, who with his bow kills 60 princes and 70 barons at a banquet, and regains his wife: Stella 146.

Glaukopis Athene can now be traced back to the bird-advents of Mycenean goddesses. As an example of the need to find new principles of union, we may note that the oath of Helen's Suitors has been brought in to supplant the heroic-age warrior-bond of service to the high or divine king.

For Dionysos and Ariadne in Mycenean times: Webster (a) 49-53; Glaucus 95. For the Meleager tale, told by Phoenix, as a doublet of the Achilles tale: Webster 249; Cauer, *Grundfragen* 264; Kakridis *Homeric Researches* 43. Homeric crafts: Webster 16.

Anaxagoras said, 'It is because he has hands that man is the most intelligent of the animals.' Alkaios, fr. 12: 'For as they tell that Aristodamos spoke in Sparta no foolish word: Money is the Man and no poor man is noble or honourable.' Theognis with his aristocratic hatred has an acute sense of money as the 'transformer'. For the embryonic structure of tragedy in Herodotos: J. L. Myres, *Miscellany . . . to J. M. Mackay* 1914.

Chapter 10. Barker, Beare, Bieber, R. Bloch, Boak, Cary, Delbrueck, Fowler, Highet, Homo, Lot, Grant, Angus, Bell, Cumont, Drews, Frend, Gavin, Gregoire, Liboron, Lenghelis, Nock, Strong, Ward Perkins, Rivoira, Richmond, Rostovtzeff, J. M. C. Toynbee, E. A. Thompson, Weiss, Whittaker, Wendland, Wischnitzer, Coppieters, Ginsberg, Goodenough, Cerfaux, Gustafson, J. L. (f) (h) (i) (j).

Trajanic column as world-pillar: Lethaby (e) 61. For ideas of dynamic form in Plotinos, Dodd, *JRS* 1960.

Van Essen valuably stresses the Italic elements and their persistence, but without allowance for synthesising trends. See him for early use of painted-on door; for the sense of colour (a) 66ff., 99, 118-20; proliferation of plant-forms 30ff., 40, 74; use of angle in wall-paintings, 33, 66 (the people on the walls of the Villa dei Misteri look at one another, Helbig); apse composition 47; detachment of figures 47; linear and aerial perspective, 67ff.; Italic tumuli 75 (also de Franciscis-Pane, *Mausolei Romani in Campania;* Rivoira, *Arch. Rom.* 10ff.; Messerchmidt, *Die Antike* iv 1928 27ff.); for the complex struggle of 'classical' and disarticulating-and-expressionist elements 85ff.; fear of perspective 99; Gothic anticipation 112; fear of the nude, 105, and life-size figure, 133. (Use of baked bricks in cupola tombs by Thracians, 4th c. B.C., Dimitrov, *ANT* no 138 1961) *Early Christians,* M. Gough 1960, for the new art. Apsed synagogue and basilican church: Frend, *ANT* no 138, 167.

Van Essen (a) 57 on wall-painting to give effect of escape from house; 2nd period at Pompeii, the flowering of the paradise-garden on wall (M. Schefold, *Pomp. Malerei, Sinn und Ideengesch.* 1952); with the 3rd comes the complex closing-in of architectural motives (often fantastic) with themes, using mythological figures, to express the character or 'fate' of the inhabitants, contemporary with the loss of political liberty.

Ara Pacis: see also H. Kahler, *Arch. Jahrb.* lix 1954 as well as Toynbée, *P.B.A.* 1953; T. Kraus, *Ranken der Ara Pacis* 1953; van Essen (a) 79. For verism: A. N. Zadocks-Josephus Jitta, *Ancestral Portraiture in Rome;* O. Vessberg, *Stud. zur Kunstgesch. Röm. Rep.* 98. (also G. M. A. Richter, *Greek Portraits* 1955 and 1959; Haufmann, *Obs. on Roman Portraiture* 1953.)

Chapter 11. J. L. (e), Barraclough, Brunor, Grabar, Diehl, Dyakonov, Demus, T. Rice, Obolensky and S. Runciman on the Bogomiles, Alpatov, Hitti, Hopkins, Holmyard, Lestocquoy, Magrogodato, Muratoff, Richter, E. H. Smith, Lispensky, Trypanis, L. Thorndyke, Whittimore, E. Werner, Welles, Grégoire.

Chapter 12. Buxton, Cresswell, D'Erlanger, Nehru, Havell, Burrow, Mehta, Radhakvishnar, Ghosal, Grünwedel, Le May, Majundar, Bagchi, Hogben, Datta, Lévi, Keith, McNicol, Bouquet, Shcherbatsky, A. Baker, Aufhauser, Bacot, Biot, Crooke, Cunnington, Dutt, Ghurye, Foucher, Goodyear, Growse, Davies, Marshall, Rassers, Wheeler, Creel, Willetts, Dubs, Edkins, E. D. Edwards, Waley, Fitzgerald, Granet, Giles, Grube, Barthold, Hackmann, Haloun, Holton, Lattimore, Laloy, Lachmann, Knight, Le Coq, Maspéro, Mizuno, Needham, Palliot, Rawlinson, Stein, Soothill, Werner, Watson, Wang Ya-nan, Waddell, Wu Ta-k'un, Elisofon, Davidson, Christensen, Frobenius, Leuzinger, Nassau.

For the growth of an agrarian and mercantile economy in pre-Mauryan India: Sastri's edition of Arthasatra 1924-5, Tarn (b) 211, R. Davies 103. For Asoka's effort to develop Dhamma: R. Thapar, *PP* no 18 1960; for possible Hellenistic effects, C. G. Pugliese, in *Par. Passato* (fasc. 8) xxxiii 1953 449 (*philanthropia*).

Note the Holi festival at Mathura, the great centre of Krishna worship, and the special attention to the pole, with the legend of Indra beating off the Asuras with the banner-pole when they attacked Bharata, who had been bidden to teach on earth the art invented by Brahma: a ritual combat connected once with bringing-in the maypole must lie behind the tale and the salutation of the banner. Note also the part of Shiva who with his wife was said to have invented the violent and the seductive dances prominent in drama (though this is probably later than the Krishna influence).

A remnant from early levels seems the character Vidusaka (the name denotes one given to abuse); often he exchanges sharp repartee with one of the queen's attendants, and is supposed to have a hideous appearance.

Note also the many relics of ancient dramas of contests between good and evil spirits in Tibet, played with masks; and the Buddhist monastery-plays on the Jakatas, with 'hunters' as dance chorus, in triangular masks with wildbeast hair. For the mystery-play developed in Islam: Ridgeway (a) 65ff.; L. Pelly, *The Miracle Play of Hassan and Hussein* 1879. For the closeness of the Greek concept to *yang-yin:* Cuillandre 452. Greek Fire: J. R. Partington, *A History of Greek Fire and Gunpowder* 1960. Indian thought: D. C. Lokayata, *Study in Anc. Ind. Materialism.*

African music: 'Indonesia and Africa: the Xylophone as a cultural indication', A. M. Jones, *JRAI* 1959.

Chapters 13-14. Artz, Baker, Battisti, M. Bloch, E. K. Chambers, K. Clark, Coplestone, Coulton, Coulbourn, Gaushof, Davies, Chaiffu, Focillon, Gaushof, Pirinne, Gibbs, Greene, Haskins, Hibberd, Hoyt, Hopkins, Huizinga, Hutton, Lang, La Piana, Wellesz, Kitzinger, Lévi-Provençal, Lea, Vacaudard, Leff, McIlwain, Lopez, A. Nichols, Nef, Mumford, Morey, Paetow, Rand, Swarzenka, Stewart, Turberville, L. White, Worringer, Young, Zimmer, Paynter.

Audian, Brereton, Chabaneau, Chaytor, R. M. Chambers, J. L. (g), Girvan, J. M. Clark, Cohen, Colin, Curtis, Gronbech, Hermannsson, Holmes, Koht, Owst Raby, J. Read, Whicher, Wilkins, Child.

For a 13th c. basis for Robin Hood: J. C. Holt *PP* no 18 – showing a possible origin in the knightly class, but ignoring the way in which such images arise in part from fertility-ritual and have their roots in the forest-withdrawal (fool) theme as well. Any forest-rebel becomes a popular hero; any person resisting the State attracts all sorts of dissident emotions, e.g. Thomas Becket. See Holt for more forest-outlaws in early med. lit.

Hafiz, roughly Dante's contemporary, had his poems explained away by Sufi exegesis, as St. Bernard 'with singular piety and chastity' allegorised the Song of Songs. Note *grád écmaise*, Love of the Unseen One, in Irish legend, e.g. Fann for Cuchulainn, Findabair for Fraech; cf. Shakuntala's tale with Cormac Mac Airt's: M. Dillon, *Procs. Brit. Acad.* 1947.

N. Cohn, *The Pursuit of the Millenium*, for more details of medieval underground movements. The 13th c. *Dialogue of Dives and Pauper* says, 'By the Lawe of Kinde and by Goddes Lawe all thynge is common.' The Taborites of Bohemia proclaimed the earth should be held in common and the nobles wiped out, etc. Bosch seems of the Brethren of the Free Spirit.

For Malory as a 'funeral oration' on feudal society: A. L. Morton, 'Matter of Britain', *Zeits. f. Anglistik* 8, 1960, Heft I. Malory as a possible Lollard: E. Hicks, *Sir T. Malory* 1928 40ff.; the relation of Grail elaborations and eucharistic arguments (e.g. Lateran Council 1215): C. Williams, *Arthurian Torso;* for earlier basis: A. A. Barb, *J. of Warburg & C. Insts.* 1956 xix 40ff. A. L. Morton brings out, how the hell-harrowing theme haunts the romances, e.g. Launcelot in *Eric and Enid.* cf. 'Gawain turned and looked back; and behold, across the river, all the streets of the place were filled with men and women, rejoicing and singing in carol-wise: The people that sat in darkness have beheld a great light', cited Ker, *The Dark Ages.* **Chapter 15.** It is impossible here even to begin with books on Shakespeare; here however are a few on Cervantes: Casalduero, Bataillon, Casella, Pfandl, Cassou, De Lollis, Castro, Novitsky, Mann. (Casella sees medieval allegory; Bataillon stresses Counter-Reformation; Pfandl, Humanism, etc.).

Clark, Bodmer, Berenson, Heydenreich, Popham, Valentiner, C. de Tolnay, Burckhardt, A. Rosenthal, Waetzolet, Gluck, Pevsner, Timmers, Anderson, Antal, Barone, Blunt, K. Clark, Cohen, Coles, Cummings, Dobb, Fernandez, Fioco, Fletcher, Glück, Boulting, Crombie, Gilmore, Hughes and Lynton, A. Hughes, Kiernan, Kristeller, Meyr, E. H., Robb, Rodolico, Sartor, Salis, Sellery, Tawney, Baskerville.

For the comic servant – *gracioso* or servant-fool; Pelayo the rustic clown in Lope's King is Greatest Alcade – cf. eastern drama, e.g. Bali: 'Nearly every important or dignified character is accompanied by a comic double or servant; he speaks in prose while the noble character speaks in verse, in common language instead of the literary idiom; he succumbs or tries to succumb to all the temptations the noble man must spurn. Some of the burlesque is extremely subtle; a comic houri in the story Ardjuna, for example, performed a classical dance with something slightly wrong with every movement'. Gorer.

The popularity of the Tower-of-Babel motive in the 16th c. art, linked with an apocalyptic sense of world-disaster, well expresses the end of the Gothic world-image: H. Minkowski, *Aus dem Nebel der Vergangenheit steigt der Turm zu Babel* 1960.

In medieval culture, taken as a whole, we see the influx of enormously diverse popular elements over an extended period. The process began indeed far back in the 3rd and 4th centuries A.D. as the Augustan Empire broke down; but it proceeded in no simple way. There was a strong inner conflict all the while, with resistances from the upper levels. Those levels, correctly enough, felt themselves incapable of containing the influx, and so, while continually modified and driven forward from below, they fought to arrest the situation. Still, in the Romanesque and Gothic periods, a great artistic capital was created, on which the later developments depended. Italy had a special situation, as more directly in the arts a Byzantine province. Giotto was essentially a Byzantine artist, while the Gothic sculptors of Chartres, though drawing their deepest inspiration from Byzantine movements, had more independence. Italy thus built up its art on a Byzantine basis, with changes brought about by its own revivals of the antique and its new scientific trends in anatomy and perspective. Finally in the High Renaissance, with Leonardo, Raphael, Michelangelo, the classicising trends broke as much as possible away from medieval outlooks, even though Michelangelo in his last phase strove desperately to return to the starkest Gothic. In Spain and northern Europe however the growth out of medieval bases was much more steady and organic, culminating in figures like Rabelais and Bruegel, Cervantes and Shakespeare. In Italy the two great innovating artists, Monteverdi and Caravaggio, emerged from the inner conflicts of the mannerist world, discarding the medieval basis altogether. It was only Bruno, the lowborn wandering thinker from South Italy, who showed a breadth of elements, medieval and renascence, which was comparable to the breadth of Cervantes and Shakespeare.

The 16th century saw mathematical advances by F. Viete, John Napier (who worked out logarithms), etc. Algebra had been taken over in the 13th century from the Arabs, who took it from the Hindus. Basic algebraic signs come in; 1492 Pelezzi of Nice invented the decimal point. The compass and the astrolabe of the Chinese made deep-sea voyaging possible. V. Cordus, born 1515, systematised the study of plants at Wittenberg; university botanical gardens were founded. Gilbert worked the new science of magnetism. Advances in anatomy were gathered up by Vesalius. A Dutchman invented the microscope c. 1590. Agricola founded modern metallurgy. German glass-ovens used a circular plan and dome that economised heat (medieval ovals were rectangular), probably imitating Venice.

Chapter 16. Lethaby (e) 147 sums up similarly: 'Ideas of sharing the permanence of the universe by correspondence, in form and cerem nial, by size and by accuracy of workmanship, pointed the way. The greater buildings were not only used for ritual purposes, but they themselves embodied magic. Behind all the minor categories of the "styles" there is a general unity in ancient architecture of the magic type. The passing of the old ages of magic into the ages of science has opened a widening gulf between them and us, and a great gulf is thus set between ancient magic architecture and modern scientific building. In the largest sense these are the only two architectures which man has known. . .' Broadly understood, these generalisations apply to all culture.

Abbreviations

A:	L'Anthropologie.
AA:	American Anthropologist.
AJA:	American Journal of Archaeology.
AMNH:	American Museum of Natural History and Anthropology Papers.
ANT:	Antiquity.
ARW:	Archiv fur Religions – Wissenschaft.
AS:	L'Année Sociologique.
BAE:	Annual Report Bureau of American Ethnology.
BSA:	British School of Archaeology at Athens.
JHS:	Journal of Hellenic Society.
JPS:	Journal of Polynesian Society.
JRAI:	Journal of Royal Anthropological Institute.
JRAS:	Journal of Royal Asiatic Society.
JRS:	Journal of Roman Studies.
PP:	Past and Present.
PPS:	Proceedings of Prehistoric Society.

Anc.: ancient. *Archaeol.*: archaeology. *Archit.*: architecture. *Austr.*: Australian. *Bab.*: Babylonian. *Byz.*: Byzantine. *Civil.*: Civilisation. *Cult.*: Culture. *Egypt.*: Egyptian. *Gr.*: Greek. *Hist.*: History. *Med.*: Medieval. *M.A.*: Middle Ages. *Mon.*: Monuments. *Prim.*: Primitive. *Relig.*: Religion, or religious. *Ren.*: Renascence *Soc.*: Social, or Sociology, etc.

Bibliography

The bibliography could extend more ore less indefinitely. I have had to make a select list, citing some of the works immediately used but not attempting anything like a full documentation. However, what I give should be more than enough for anyone wanting to begin on the same trails.

Aarne-Thompson, *Folktale Motives.* Aldred, C. (a) *Old, Middle and New Kingdom Art* 1949-51, (b) *Egyptians* 1960. Alfoldi, A., *Conversion of Constantine* 1949. Allbright (a) *Archaeol. of Palestine* 1932, (b) *Arch. and the Religion of Israel.* Allen, R. J., *Early Christian Symbolism* 1887. Alpatov, M., *Voprosy Istorii* vii 1949. Anderson, W. S. (and Stratton), *Archit. of Renaissance in Italy* 1927. Anderssen, J. G., *Children of the Yellow River* 1934. Angus, S. (a) *Mystery Religions and Christianity*, (2) *Religious Quests of G.-R. World* 1929, (c) *Environment of Early Christianity.* Antal, F., *Florentine Painting and its Social Background.* Arnold, *Vedic Metres.* Artz, F. B., *Mind of Middle Ages* 1954. Atkinson, R. J. C., *Stonehenge.* Audiau, J., *Nouv. Anth. des Troubadours* 1928. Aufhauser, J. B., *Buddha u. Jesus in ihren Paralleltexten* 1926. Aymard, A., *L'Orient et la Grèce ant.* 1953.

Bacot, J., *Three Tibetan Mysteries.* Badawi, *Der Gott Chnum* 1937. Bade, W. F., *Quarterly Statement Palestine Exped. Fund* lxii 1930. Bagchi, P. C., *India and China* 1944. Baker, A., *Indian Music* in Wellesz. Baker, J. N. L., *Med. Trade Routes* 1938. Bancroft, H. H., *Native Races of Pacific Coast of N.A.* 1875-6. Barker, E., *From Alex. to Constantine* 1956. Barnett, R. D. (a) *Assyrian Palace Reliefs* 1960, (b) *JHS* xlv 100 (Epic Kumarbi and Heriod). Barone, C., *Bramante.* Barraclough, G., *The Med. Empire* 1950. Barthold, *Turkestan down to the Mongol Invasions.* Baskerville, *Elizabethan Jig.* Bataille, G., *Lascaux* 1955. Bataillon, M. *Erasme et l'Espagne* 1937. Battisti, E., *Giotto*, 1960. Bazzi, C. E., *Riv. d'Ital.* 1911 971. Beare, W., *The Roman Stage* 1955. Bell, H. I., *Cults and Creeds in G.-R. Egypt* 1956. Benedict, R. (a) *Patterns of Culture* 1934, (b) 'Guardian Spirit', *Amer. Anthrop. Assn. Mem.* 29. Bentzen, A., *Messias* 1948. Berenson, B. (a) *Drawings of Florentine Painters* 1903, (b) *Study and Crit. of Ital. Art*, (c) *Ital. Painters of the Ren.* Berndt, R. M. (a) *Djanggawul*, (b) *Kunapipi*, (c) *Arnhem Land*, (d) with Elkin and C. Berndt, *Art in Arnhem Land.* Berthelot, M. D. E. (a) *La Chimie du M.A.* 1893, (b) *Coll. des Anc. Alchemistes Grecs* 1888. Berve, H., *Griech. Gesch.* 1931. Bettelheim, B., *Symbolic Wounds* 1955. Bieber, M., *Hist. of G. & R. Theatre* 1939. Biot, E., *Le Tcheou Li* 1851. Birket-Smith, K., *Prim. Man and his Ways* 1960. Blackman (with Fairman), *JEA* 1942. Blegen (a) *Troy* i 1950, (b) *AJA* xli 1937. Bloch, M., *La Soc. Féodale.*

Bloch, R. *Origins of Rome* 1960. Blunt, A., *Artistic Theory in Italy* 1940. Boak, A. E. R., *Manpower Shortage and Fall of R.E.* 1955. Boas, F. (a) ed. *Gen. Anthrop.* 1938, (b) *Prim. Art* 1927, (c) *Chinook Texts,* (d) *Kwakiutl Ethnol.,* (e) *Tmimshian Myth.,* (f) *Rep.* 68th *Meet. Br. Assn. Adv. Sc.* 1899, (g) *Race, Language and Culture* 1940. Bodmer, H., *Leonardo* 1931. Bodrigi, T., *Oceanian Art* 1960. Bohl, F. M. T., *Het Gilgamesh-Epos* 1947. Bölsche, W., *Love-life in Nature.* Boman, T., *Hebrew Thought cmp. with Gr.* 1960. Bosi, R., *Lapps* 1960. Boule, *Les Hommes Fossiles* 1923. Boulting, W., *G. Bruno* 1914. Bouquet, A. C. (a) *Comp. Religion* 1956, (b) *Sacred Books of the World* 1954. Bowra, C. M. (a) *The Greek Experience,* (b) *Gr. Lyric Poets,* (c) *Heroic Poetry* 1952, (d) *Trad. and Design in the Iliad,* (e) *Homer and his Forerunners.* Boyancé, P. 'Les deux dèmons personnels' *Rev. Philol.* 1935 189. Braidwood, L. and R., *AA* li 1949. Brandon, S. G. F., *Time and Mankind* 1951. Brea, L. B., *ANT* no 134 (Malta) 1960. Breasted, J. H. (a) *Dawn of Conscience,* (b) *Hist. of Egypt* 1910, (c) *Development of Religion and Thought in Anc. Egypt* 1914. Brereton, G., *Short Hist. Fr. Lit.* 1954. Breuil, H. (a) *4 cent siècles d'art parietal,* (b) *Anibib and Omandumba,* (c) *Cavernes de la reg. cantabrique,* (d) *La Cueva de Altamira* 1935, (e) *La Pileta à Benaojan* 1915, (f) *Font de Gaume* 1910, (g) *Les Combarelles* 1924, (h) *Caverne d'Altamira* 1906, (i) *Pinturas rup. de la Cueva Remigia* 1936. Bright, J., *Hist. of Israel* 1960. Brough-Smith, R., *Abos. of Victoria* 1878. Brown, G., *Melanesians and Polynesians* 1910. Brown, J. M., *Maori and Polynesian* 1907. Brunov, N.E., *Viz. Vremennik* II (xxvi) 1949. Brunton and Caton-Thompson, *Badarian Civil.* 1928. Budge, W. (a) *Osiris and Eg. Resurrection,* (b) *From Fetish to God* 1934, (c) *Gods of the Egs.* Buecher, *Arbeit u. Rhythms* 1924. Bunzel, R. (a) (Zuni), (b) *BAE* xlvii 467, 508, (c) *Pueblo Potter* 1929. Buntzen, *King and Messiah* 1955. Burgh, W. G. de, *Legacy of Anc. World* 1955. Burght, van der, *Dict. fr. Kirundi.* Burckhardt, J. (a) *Civil. of the Ren. in Italy* 1951, (b) *Weltgeschichtliche Betrachtungen* 1905. Burkitt, M. C. (a) *Prehistory,* (2nd ed.) 1949, (b) *Old Stone Age* 1949. Burrow, T., *Sanscrit Language* 1955. Bury, J. B. (a) *Anc. Gr. Historians* 1919, (b) *Hist. of E. Roman Emp.* 1912. Bushell, S. W., *Chinese Art* 1909. Butt-Thompson, F. W., *W. African Secret Socs.* 1929. Buxton, R. R., *Russian Med. Archit.* 1934.

Capart, J., *Egypt. Art* 1923. Capitan, *Les Combarelles* (vide Breuil). Cary, M., *Legacy of Alexander* 1932. Casalduero, J., *Rev. de Filol. Hisp.* ii 1940 323. Casella, M., *Cervantes* 1938. Cassirer, E., *Essay on Man* 1944. Casson, S., *Progress and Catastrophe.* Cassou, J., *Cervantes* 1939. Castagné, J., *Magie et exorcisme chez les Kazak-Kirghiz* 1930. Castren, M. A., *Nord. Reisen u. Forschungen* 1853-8 iv 256. Castro, A., *El Pensiamento de Cervantes* 1925. Caudwell, C., *Illusion and Reality* 1937. Cauer, *Grundfragen.* Cerfaux, L. (a) (with Tondrian) *Le Culte des Souverains* 1957, (b) *L'attente du Messie* 1954. Cerny, J., *Anc. Egypt. Religion* 1952. Chabaneau, C., *Les biographies des troubadours* 1845. Chadwick, H. M. (a) *Heroic Age,* (b) with N.C., *Growth of Lit.,* (c) *JRAI* lx 1930, (d) *Origin of Eng. Nation.* Chambers, E. K. (a) *Med. Stage* 1903, (b) *Elizabethan Stage,* (c) *Arthur,* (d) *Eng. Folkplay.* Chambers, F. K., *Cycles of Taste* 1928. Chambers, R. W. (a) *Beowulf* 1932, (b) *Man's Unconquerable Mind.* Chapouthier, F., *Dioscures au service d'une déesse* 1935. Chaney, E. F., *F. Villon* 1946. Chaytor, H. S., *Troubadours in England* 1923. Child, F. J., *English and Scottish Pop. Ballads* 1904. Childe, V. G. (a) *Dawn of Europ. Civil.* 1947, (b) *What Happened in History* 1954, (c) *Prehist. of Europ. Soc.* 1958, (d) *Man Makes Himself,* (e) *New Light on the Most Anc. East,* (f) *Magic, Craftsmanship, and Science* 1950, (g) *PP* 1952 no 2 ,(h) *PP* 1957 no 12, (i) *Skara Brae* 1931. Christensen, E. O., *Prim. Art* 1955. Chroust, A. H., *Socrates.* Chwolsohn, D., *Die Dsabier.* Clark, J. G. D. (a) *Mesolithic Settlement of N. Europe* 1936, (b) *From Savagery to Civil.* 1946, (c) *Mesolithic Age in Britain* 1932. Clark, J. M., *The Great German Mystics* 1949. Clark, K. (a) *Landscape into Art,* (b) *Leonardo,* (c) *The Nude.* Clark, W. E. Le Gros, *Hist. of Primates* 1949. Coates, A., *Prelude to Hist.* 1951.

Codrington, *Melanesians* 1891. Cohen, J. M. (a) *Hist. of Western Lit.* 1956, (b) transl. *Montaigne*, (c) *Rabelais*, (d) *Don Quixote*. Cole, S., *Prehist. of E. Africa* 1954. Coles, P., *PP* no II 1957. Colin, N., *Pursuit of the Millenium* 1957. Collingwood, R. G., *Principles of Art*. Colson, F. H., *The Week* 1926. Contenau (a) *Syria* viii 1927, (b) *La déesse nue babyl.* 1914. Cook, A. B., *Zeus*. Cook, R. M., *ANT* no 135 xxxiv. Coplestone, F. C., *Aquinas*. Coppieters de Gibson, D., *Daniel et la persécution dans le N.T.* 1956. Cornford, F. M. (a) *Plato's Theory of Knowledge*, (b) *Principium Sapientiae* 1952, (c) ed. *Plato's Republic* 1941, (d) *From Religion to Philosophy* 1912, (c) in *CAH* iv, (d) *Origin of Attic Comedy* 1914, (g) in *Studies . . . to Ridgeway* 1913, (h) on Olympic Games in *Themis*. Couat, A., *Alex. Poetry* 1931. Coulton, G. G. (a) *Inquisition and Liberty* 1938, (b) *5 cents. of Religion*, (c) *Art and the Reformation*, (d) *Life in the Middle Ages*, (e) *Chaucer*, (f) *Med. Scene*, (g) *From St. Francis to Dante*. Coulbourn, R., ed. *Feudalism in Hist.* 1957. Coxwell, *Siberian and other Folktales* 1925. Crawford, O. G. S., *Eye Goddess* 1957. Crawley, E. (a) *Mystic Rose* 1902, (b) in *Hastings Enc. Rel.* x 358, (c) *Idea of the Soul*. Creel, H. (a) *Birth of China* 1936, (b) *Studies in Early Chinese Culture* 1938. Creswell, K. A. C., *Early Muslim Architecture*. Crooke, *Pop. Religion in N. India*. Crossland, R. A. (Indo-Europ.) *PP* no 12 1957. Crum, W. E., *Procs. Brit. Acad.* 1931 235. Crombie, A. C., *Augustine to Galileo* 1952. Cummings, C. A., *Hist. of Architect. in Italy* 1901. Cumont, F. (a) *Religions Orientales*, (b) *Mystères de Mithras*, (c) *Lux perpetua*. Cünow (a) *Die Verwandschaftsorganisatioen der Australnagern* 1894, (b) *Die oekon. Grundlagen der M tterschaft* 1897-8. Cunnington, A., *Stupa at Bharut* 1879. Curr, *Aust. Race* 1886. Curtis, E. R., *Europ. Lit. and Later M.A.* 1953. Curtis, L., *Ant. Kunst*. Cushing, F. H., *ARB* xiii. Czaplicka, *Aboriginal Siberia*.

Dähnhardt, O., *Natursagen*. Daniel, G. (a) *Listener*, Sept. 8, 1960 (radio-carbon), (b) *Prehist. Chamber Tombs of France*. Datta, B. (and Singh), *Hist. of Hindu Myths*. 1935. Davy, G. (a) see Moret, (b) *La Foi Jurée* 1922. David-Neel, A. (a) *Supernat. Life of Gesar of Ling*, (b) *Initiations*, (c) *With Mystics and Magicians in Tibet*. Davies, *Origin and Develop. of Early Christian Archit.* 1952. Davies, Rhys, *Buddhist India* 1903. Delbrueck, R., *Hellenist. Bauten in Latium*. De Lollis, C., *Cervantes Reaziona ario* 1924. Demangel, R., *La Frise Ionique* 1932. Demargne, P., *Crète dèdalique* 1947. Demus, O., *Mosaics of Norman Sicily* 1950. Dennett, R. E., *At the back of the Bla k Man's Mind*. Dentan, R. O., ed. *The Idea of Hist. in Anc. Near East* 1955. Densmore (a) *Papago Music* 1929, (b) *Music of Indians of Brit. Columbia* 1943. D'Erlanger, R., *La musique arabe* 1930-59. Desroches-Noblecourt, C., *Le Style égypt.* 1946. Dhalla, *Zoroastrian Civil.* Dhorme, *Les Religions de Bab. et d'Assyrie* 1945. Diamond, A. S., *Prim. Law*. Dickins, *Hellenistic Sculpture*. Diehl, C., *Byzantium* 1957 (bibliog. Charanis). Dixon, R. B. (a) *Oceanic Myth* 1916, (b) *Building of Culture* 1928. Dobb, M. H., *Studies in Develop. of Capitalism*. Dodds, E. R., *Greeks and Irrational*. Donadoni, S., *L'arte egizia* 1955. Dorsey, G. A. (a) *Cheyenne* 1905, (b) *Myth. of the Wichita* 1904, (c) with Kroeber, *Trads. of Arapaho*, (d) *Trads. of Skidi Pawnees* 1904. Dorsey, J. O., *Siouan Sociology*. Drews, *Witnesses to Historicity of Jesus*. Drioton, E. (a) *Le théâtre egypt.* 1942, (b) *Le texte dramatique de Edfu*. Driver, *Canaanite Myths* 1956 (*O.T. Studies* 3). Du Bois, C., *in Essays . . . to A. L. Kroeber* 1936. Dubs, H. H. (a) *Isis* xxxviii 62, (b) *Amer. J. Philol.* 1941 lxii 222, (c) *Class. Philol.* 1943 13. Du Chaillu, *Viking Age*. Duguid, C., *Aborigines of Austr.* 1940. Dunlop, W. (*Austr. Folklore Stories*) *JAI* xxviii. Durkheim, (a) *La division de travail social* 1926 (5th ed.), (b) *Les règles de la méthode sociologique* 1919, (c) *Les formes élementaires de la vie réligieuse* 1912, (d) with Mauss, *De quelques formes prim. de classification*. Dussaud, R. (a) *Les relig. des Hittites* 1949, (b) *Prélydiens* 1953. Dutt, R., *Ramayana*. Dyakonov, *Viz. Sbornik* 1945 144.

Edgerton, F., *Gita* 1944. Edkins, J., *Chinese Buddhism*. Edmonds, J. M., *Lyra*

Graeca. Edwards, E. D., *Chines Prose Lit. of T'Ang period*. Edwards, E. S., *Pyramids of Egypt*. Eisler, R. (a) *Royal Art of Astrology* 1947, (b) *Weltenmantel u. Himmelszelt* 1910. Eissfeldt, *Baal Zaphon* 1932. Elisofon, E. (with Linton), *Sculpture of Africa* 1958. Elkin, A. D., *Austr. Abos*. (3rd ed.) 1954. Emmanuel, *La dance grecque* 1896. Engels, *Origin of Family*. Englebach, R., *The Problem of the Obelisks* 1923. Engnell, I., *Studies in Divine Kingship in Anc. Near East* 1943. Erman, A., *Lit. of Anc. Egyptians*. Essen, C. C. van, (a) *Précis d'hist. de l'art ant. en Italie* 1960, (b) *Med. Ned. Hist. Inst. Rome* iii, 10, 1959, (c) *RA* ii 1948. Evans, A. J. (a) *Palace of Minos*, (b) *Mycenean Tree and Pillar Cult* 1921, (c) *JHS* 1925, world-tree. Evans, H. G., *Staat aus dem Stein* 1929. Evans, J. D., *Malta* 1960.

Fairman, H. W. in Hooke (b). Falkenstein, A., *Mitt. d. Deut. Orient. Gesellschaft* lxxxv 1913, I. Farington, B., *Greek Science* 1944. Farnell, L. R. (a) *Cults of Gr. States* 1896-1909, (b) *Gr. Hero Cults* 1921, (c) *Higher Aspects of Gr. Relig*. Farmer, H. G. (a) in Wellesz (2) *Hist. Facts* 1930. Fascher, E., *Prophetes* 1927. Fernandez, R., *De la personalité* 1928. Finley, M. I., *The World of the Odyssey* 1956. Fioco, G., *Bellini* 1960. Firth, R. (a) *Elements of Social Organisation* 1951, (b) *We the Tikopia* 1936, (c) *A prim. Polynesian econ*. 1939, (d) *Work of the gods in Tipokia* 1940, (e) *Oceania* i 1931 (totemism in P.), (f) *Man and Culture* 1957, (g) *Prim. Econ. of N.Z. Maoris* 1929. Fisch, T., in *Sumer* x 1954 113. Fitzgerald, C. P., *China* 1950. Fletcher, A. C., *Omaha Tribes* 1905-6. Fletcher, J. B., *Lit. of Ital. Ren*. 1934 Focillon, H., *L'an mil* 1952. Folkard, R., *Plant Lore* 1884. Forde, C. D., *Habitat, Econ. and Soc*. 1934. Forsdyke, *Minoan Art*. Fortune, R. F., *Omaha Secret Societies* 1932. Fortes, M. (a) *Social Structure* 1949, (b) with Evans-Pritchard, *African Soc. Structures* 1940. Foucard, P. F., *Des assoc. rélig. chez les Grecs* 1873. Foucher, A. (a) *L'art gréco-boudd. du Gandjara* 1905-22, (b) *La veille route de l'Inde de Bactres à Taxila* 1940-7. Fowler, M. L., *Summ. Rep. Modoc Rock Shelter* 1959. Fowler, W. W., *Roman Festivals* 1899. Fox, C. E. (a) *JRAI* xlix 1919, (b) *Threshold of Pacific* 1924. Fränkel, H., *Dichtung u. Philos. des fruhen Griechentums*. Frazer (a) *Totemism and Exog*. 1910, (b) *Golden Bough*, (c) *Early Hist. of Kingship* 1905, (d) *Pausanias* 1898. Frankfort, H. (a) *5th prel. rep. Iraq exped*. 1936, (b) *Kingship and the Gods* 1946, (c) ed. *Before Philosophy* 1949, (d) *Anc. Egypt. Relig*. 1948, (e) *Intellectual Adventure of Anc. Man* 1943. Frend, W. H. C. (a) *Donatist Movement* 1952, (b) *PP* no 16 1959, (c) *Ant*. 1942. Frobenius, L. (a) *Die atlant. Götterlehre* 1926, (b) *Atlantis* vi 1921 261, (c) *Spielmansgesch der Sahel* 1921. Furley, D. S., *Listener*, 22 Jan. 1959. Furon, R., *Man. de Préhist. gen*. 1943.

Gadd, *Hist. and Mons. of Ur* 1929. Galdi, L., *6th Congrès* (Byz.) 1950. Gale, *Korean Folktales*. Galpin, F. W., *Music of Sumerians* 1937. Ganshof, F. S. (a) *Feudalism* 1952, (b) *Byzantion* iv 1928 659. Gardiner, A. H. (a) *JEA* xxxix 13, (b) xxxvi 3, (c) *Attitude of Anc. Egyptians to Death and Dead* 1935, (d) *K. Se* the, *Egypt. Letters to Dead* 1928, (e) *Procs. Soc. Bibl. Arch*. xviii, (f) *Egypt. Grammar* 1927. Garelli, *Gilgamesh* 1960. Garrod, D. A., *PPS* xxi 1956. Garstang (a) *Prehist. Mersin* 1953, (b) *Heritage of Solomon*. Gaster, *Thespis* 1950. Gavin, F., *Jewish Antecedents of the Sacraments* 1928. Gennep, A. van. (a) *Rites of Passage* 1960, (b) *Tabou et totémisme à Madagascar*, (c) *Formation des Légendes* 1920. Germain, G., *Genèse de l'Odysée*. Ghirshman, R. (a) *Fouille de Sialk* 1938, (b) *Tepe-Guyan* 1953. Ghosal, U. N., *Progress of Outer Indian Research* 1943. Ghurye, G. S. in Ogden (caste). Gibbs, M., *Feudal Order* 1949. Gilbert, P., *La poésie egypt*. 1949. Giles, H. A. (a) *Civil. of China* 1911, (b) *Chuang Tzu* 1960. Giles, L., *Taoist Teachings* 1947. Gilmore, M., *World of Humanism* 1952. Ginsberg, H. L., *Studies in Daniel* 1948. Giot, P. R., *Brittany*. Girvan, B., *Beowulf* 1935. Gist, N. P., *Secret Societies, Univ. Missouri Stud*. xv no 4. Glanville, S. R. K., ed. *Legacy of Egypt* 1942. Glotz, G. (a) *Anc. Greece at Work*, (b) *Aegean Civil*., (c) *Solidarité de la Famille*.

Glück, G., *Bruegels Gemälde*. Gluckman, M. (a) in *Fortes* 145, (b) *PP* no 8 1955 (peace in feud). Goddard, P. E., *AMNH* xxiv 1910 (Apache). Goldenweiser, A. A. (a) 'Totemism', *J. Amer. FL* xxiii 179, (b) *Hist.*, *Psych. and Culture* 1933. Golubev, V., *Ajanta* 1927. Gombrich, E. (a) *Art and Illusion* 1960, (b) *Story of Art* 1956. Goodall, E. (Cooke and Clark), *Prehist. Art of Fed. of Rhodesia* 1960. Goodenough, E. R. (a) *By Light, Light* 1935, (b) *Church in R.E.* 1931. Goodyear, W. H., *Grammar of Lotus* 1891. Gordon, C. H. (a) *Ugaritic Handbook* 1947, (b) *Ug. Lit.* Gorer, G. (a) *Bali and Angkor*, (b) *Africa Dances*. Gortein, H., *Prim. Ordeal and Mod. Law* 1923. Goury, G., *Origines et évol. de l'homme* i 1948 (2nd ed.) Grabar, *Martyrion* 1946. Graham, *AJSL* xlvii 1930-1 239. Granet, M. (a) *Chinese Civil.* 1930, (b) *Danses etc. de la Chine anc.* 1926, (c) *La pensée chin.* 1934, (d) *Festivals and Songs of anc. China* 1932. Grant, F. C., *Hellenistic Religions* 1953. Grant, M., *From Imp. to Auctoritas* 1946. Graziose, P., *Pales. Art* 1960. Grégoire, H. (a) *Les persécutions dans l'E. R.* 1951, (b) *O Digenis Akritas* 1942. Greene, R. L., *Early Eng. Carols.* Gregory, J. W., *Dead Heart of Austr.* 1906. Greven, L., *Der Ka in Theologie etc.* 1952. Grinnell, G. B. (a) *Pawnee Hero Stories* 1893, (b) *Cheyenne Indians* 1923. Growse, F. S., *Ramayana*. Gronbech, V., *Cult. of Teutons* 1931. Grube, W., *Relig. u. Kultus der Chinesen* 1910. Grünwedel, A., *Buddh. Art in India* 1901. Gunkel (a) *Die Psalmen* 1926, (b) *Genesis*, (c) *Schöpfung u. Chaos*. Guntert, *Calypso*. Gurney, O. R., *Hittites* 1954. Gustafson, A., *Die Katakombenkirche* 1954. Güterbock, H. G. (a) *AJA* lii 123, (b) *Kumarbi* 1946, (c) *J. Cuneiform Studies* v 1951 135; vi 8. Guthrie, W. K. C. (a) *Orpheus*, (b) *In the Beginning*.

Hackmann, *Chinese Philosophy* 1927. Haddon, A. C. (a) *Head Hunters*, (b) *Magic and Fetishism*. Hallström, G. (a) *Mon. Art of N. Europe, Ice Age* 1938, (b) *N. Sweden* ditto **1960**. Haloun, G., *Jap. Deut. Z.f.W.u. Technik* iii 1925 243. Hambly, W. D. (a) *Source Book African Anthrop.*, (b) *AA* xxxvi 1934, (c) *FMNH* no 3 1935 (cult. areas Nigeria). Handy, E. S. C., *Native Cult. in Marquesas* 1923. Hapgood, I. F., *Epic Songs of Russia* 1915. Harris, J. R. (a) *Cult Heavenly Twins*, (b) *Boanerges.* Harrison, J. (a) *Prolegomena*, (b) *Themis*, (c) *Epilogomena*, (d) *Anc. Art and Ritual.* Harrison, T., *Savage Civilisation* 1937. Hartland, S. (a) *Prim. Paternity* 1909, (b) *Prim. Soc.* 1921, (c) *Legend of Perseus*. Haserbroek, J., *Trade and Politics in Anc. Greece* 1933. Haskins, C. H. (a) *Ren. of 12th c.*, (b) *Rise of Universities* 1923. Hassan, S., *The Great Sphinx* 1953. Havell, E. B. (a) *Ideals of Indian Art* 1920, (b) *Handbook of Indian Art* 1927. Havelock, E. A., *The Liberal Temper in Gr. Politics.* Havinghurst, G., ed. *Pirenne Thesis* 1958. Hawkes, C. F. C., *Prehist. Foundations of Europe* 1940. Heath, T. L. (a) *Man. of Gr. Maths.* 1931, (b) *Aristarchus*, (c) *Archimedes* 1920. Heichelheim, *Witschaftgesch. des Altertums* 1938. Heidel, A. (a) *Bab. Genesis* 1942, (b) *Gilg. Epic and O.T. Parallels* 1946. Hempel, *Gott u. Mensch im A.T.* (2nd ed.) 1936. Henderson, I. (a) in Wellesz, (b) *Class. Q.* xxxvi 97. Henry, T., *Anc. Tahiti* 1928. Hencken, H., *AA* lvii 1955. Hermannsson, *Old Icelandic Lit.* 1937. Hershovitz, M. J. (a) *AA* xxviii 1926 (E. Africa cattle-complex), (b) *Econ. Life of Prim. Peoples* 1940, (c) *Man and His Works* 1948, (d) *Acculturation* 1938, (e) *Dahomey* 1938, (f) *Background of African Art* 1945. Herzfeld, *Iran in Anc. East* 1941. Herzler, J. B., *Social Thought of Anc. Civilisations*. Heydenreich, L. H., *Leonardo* 1954. Heyerdahl, *Aku Aku*. Hibberd, L., *Speculum* 1944 (estampie). Highbarger, *The Gates of Dreams*. Highet, G. (a) *Class. Trad.*, (b) *Poets in Landscape*. Hilton, R., *PP* no 14 1958 (Robin Hood). Hinks, R. P., *Gr. & R. Portrait-sculpture* 1935. Hitti, P. K., *Hist. of Arabs* 1949. Hocart, A. M. (a) *AA* 1916, (b) *Kingship* 1927, (c) 'The 4 quarters', *Ceylon J. Science* i 1927, (d) *Progress of Man* 1933. Hogarth, *Ionia and the East* 1909. Hogben, L., *Maths. for the Million* 1942. Hogbin, H. J., *Law and Order in Polynesia* 1934, Hollis, A. C., *Masai* 1905. Holmes, U. T., *Hist. of Old French Lit.* 1948. Holmyard, E. J. (a) *Alchemy* 1957, (b) ed. *Works Geber*. Holscher, G., *Die Profeten, Untersuch. z. Relig. Israels* x 1914.

Holscher, U., *Hermes* lxxxi 1953. Holton, D. C., *Jap. Enthronement Ceremonies.* Homo. L., *Civil rom.* 1930. Hood, M. S. F., *ANT* xxxiv no 135 (tholoi). Hooke, H. (a) *In the Beginning* 1948, (b) *Myth, Ritual and Kingship* 1958, (c) *Myth and Ritual* 1939, (d) *Origins of Early Semitic Ritual* 1938, (e) *Labyrinth* 1935, (f) *Christianity in the Making* 1926. Hoonacker, A. van., *Une Communauté Judeo-Araméenne en Egypte.* Hopkins, A. J., *Alchemy, Child of Gr. Philosophy* 1934. Hornermann, B., *Types of Anc. Egypt. Statuary* 1951-7. Horvath, T., *Art of Asia.* Hose, C. (with McDougall) *Pagan Tribes of Borneo* 1912. Howitt A. W. *Native Tribes of S.E. Austr.* (b) *Austr. Group Rels.* 1883 (c) *JAI* xvi, xiii, xviii, xx. Hoyt, R. S., *Europe in M.A.* 1957. Hubac, P., *Les Nomades* 1948. Hubert (a) *Les Celtes* 1932, (b) *Les Celtes depuis l'epoche de la Tène* 1932. Hughes and Lynton, *Renaissance Archit.* Hughes, A. (and Abraham), *New Oxford Hist. Music* iii 1960. Hughes, E. R., *Chinese Philos. in Class. Times* 1942. Huizinga, J., *Waning of M.A.* 1924. Hutton, E., *Cosmati* 1950. Hutton, J. H. (a) *Angami Nagas,* (b) *Sema Nagas* 1921. Huxley, J., *Essays of Biologist.*

Iversen, E., *Canon and Proportions in Egypt. Art* 1955.

Jackson, J. W., *Shells as Evidence of Migrations* 1917. Jacobsen, T. (a) in Frankfort, (c) (b) *J. Near Eastern Stud.* ii 159, (c) *Assyr. Stud.* ii 1939. Jacobsthal, J., *Early Celtic Art* 1944. James, E. O. (a) *Cult of Mother Goddess* 1959, (b) *Christian Myth and Ritual* 1933. Jastrow, M., *Civil. of Bab. and Assyria* 1915. Jean, C. F., *La relig. sumér.* 1931. Jeanmaire, H., *Dionysos.* Jeanroy, A., *La Poésie lyrique des Troubadours* 1934. Johnson, T., etc., *Rock Paintings of S.W. Cape,* 1959. Jouget, P., *Macedonian Imperialism* 1928. Junker, *Die Onuris Legende* 1917.

Kaberry, P., *Abo. Women* 1939. Kantor, H. J., *The Agean and Orient in 2nd mill. B.C.* Kar, C., *Class. Indian Sculpture* 1950. Karsten, R. (a) *Bull. Bur. Ethnol. Washington* lxxix 1923, (b) *Civil. of S. American Indians* 1926. Katz, F. (Aztecs) *PP* no 13 1958. Kaye, G. R., *Indian Maths.* 1915. Keane, A. H., *The Import of the Totem.* Keith, A. B. (a) *Sanskrit Drama* 1924, (b) *JRAS* 1912 411, (c) 1916 335, (d) 1917 140, (e) *Indian Mythology.* Kees, H., *Totenglauben . . . alten Agypter* 1956 (2nd ed.). Kendrick, T. (a) *Hist. of Vikings,* (b) *Druids.* Kenyon, K. M., *Excavs. at Jericho* 1960. Kern, F., *The Wildbooters.* Kiernan, V., *PP* no II 1957. King, L. W., *Bab. Magic and Sorcery.* Kirk, G. S. (with Rowen), *The Presocratic Philosophers* 1957. Kitzinger, O. E., *Early Med. Art* 1940. Klebs, L., *Die Tiefendimension in der Zeichnung des alten Reiches.* Kluckholm, C., *Harvard Theolog. Rev.* xxxv Jan. 1942. Knight, E. F., *Where Three Empires Meet* 1893. Knight, W. F. J. (a) *Cumaean Gates* 1936, (b) *Vergil's Troy.* Koehler, W., *Dumbarton Oaks Papers* i 1941. Koht, *Old Norse Sagas* 1931. König, F., *Christus u. die Relig. der Erde.* Kramer (a) *Sumerian Myth.* 1944, (b) *Israel Explor. J.* iii 1953 217, (c) *From the Tablets of Sumer* 1956. Kroeber, A. L. (a) *Source Book of Anthropology* 1931, (b) *Pima Tales AA* 1908, (c) *Configurations of Culture Growths* 1944, (d) *AA* 1940 xlii, (e) *JRAI* 1945. Kristeller, P. O., *The Classics and Ren. Thought* 1955. Kropotkin, *Mutual Aid.* Kühn, H., *Kunst u. Kultur der Vorzeit Europas* 1929.

Lachmann, R., *Musik d. Orients* 1929. Lafitau, J. F., *Moeurs des sauvages americains* 1724. Laloy, L., *Musique Chinoise.* Lambert, M. (Urukagina) *Rev. d'Assyr.* v 1956 169. Lang, A., *Myth, Ritual and Religion* 1887. Lang, P. H., *Music in West. Civil.* 1941. Lange, K. (with Hirmer), *Agypt. Architektur* etc. 1953. Langdon, S. (a) *Tammuz and Ishtar,* (b) *Bab. Wisdom* 1923, (c) *Bab. Liturgies.* La Piana, G., *La repp. nella lett. biz . . . con rapp. al teatro sacro d'occidente* 1912. Lattimore, O. (a) *PP* no 12 1957, (b) *Inner Asian Frontiers of China* 1940, (c) *Manchuria Cradle of Conflict.* Latourette, K. S. (a) *Chinese* 1934, (b) *Hist. of Expansion of Christianity* 1937. Lauer, J. E., *Le Problème des Pyramides* 1948. Laufer, B., *The Diamond* 1915.

Lea, H. C. (a) *Studies of Church Hist.*, (b) *Hist. of Inquisition.* Leakey, L. S. B. (a) *Stone Age Africa* 1936, (b) *Adam's Ancestors* (4th ed.) 1953. Lechler, G., *Man* 11 Dec. 1951. Le Coq, A. W., *Buried Treasure of Chinese Turkestan* 1928. Lees-Milne, J., *Roman Mornings* 1956. Leff, G. (a) *PP* no 13 1958, (b) *PP* no 9 1956, (c) *Med. Thought* 1958. Legge, J., *Texts of Taoism* 1927. Legge, F., *Forerunners and Rivals of Christianity* 1915. Le Gros Clarke, *Hist. of Primates* 1941. Le May, R., *Buddhist Art in Siam* 1938. Lemozi, A., *La Grotte-temple de Pech-Merle* 1929. Lenghelis, C., *Byzantion* vii 264. Lepper, J. H., *Famous Secret Societies* 1932. Leonard, W. E., *Gilgamesh* 1934. Le Rouzic, *Carnac* 1934. Lestocquoy, *Econ. Hist. Rev.* xvii (i) 1947 (guilds). Lethaby, W. R. (a) *Architecture* 1912, (b) *Architecture, Mysticism and Myth* 1892, (c) *Archit., Nature and Magic* 1956, (d) *Form in Civil.* 1922, (e) *Med. Art* 1904. Leuzinger, E., *Africa* (art) 1960. Lever, K., *Art of Gr. Comedy.* Lévi, S., *Le théâtre Indien* 1890. Lévi-Provençal, E., *L'Espagne Musulmane* 1932. Levy, R., *The Gates of Horn* 1948. Lévy-Bruhl, (a) *Les fonctions mentales dans les soc. infer.* 1910, (b) *La mentalité prim.* 1922. Lewin, L., *Phantastica, Narcotic and Stimulant Drugs* 1931. Liboron, H., *Die Karpokratian. Gnosis* 1938. Lindsay, J. (a) *Short Hist. of Culture* 1939, (b) *Anatomy of Spirit,* (c) *Song of a Falling World,* (d) *Byzantium into Europe,* (e) *Arthur and his Times,* (f) *Marc Antony,* (g) *Beowulf, Norseman* iii no 6, 1945 (h) *Petronius' Satyricon* (i) *The Writing on the Wall,* (j) *Golden Ass.* Linton, *Art of the S. Seas.* Little, A. M. G., *Myth and Society in Attic Drama* 1942. Lods, A. (a) *Israel from the Beginnings* 1932, (b) *Prophets and Rise of Judaism* 1937. Lopez, R. S. (a) *PP* no 9 1956, (b) with Raymond, *Med. Trade in Medit. World* 1955. Lorimer, H. L., *Homer and the Monuments* 1950. Lot, F., *End of Anc. World* 1931. Lowie, R. (a) *Prim. Religion* 1924, (b) *Origin of the State,* (c) *Societies of Plains Indians AMNH* no 13 xi 1916, (d) *Intro. to Cult. Anthrop.* 1940, (e) *Hist. of Ethnol. Theory* 1937. Luquet, *Art and Religion of Fossil Man* 1930. Lucas, A., *Anc. Egypt. Materials and Industries* (3rd ed.) 1948. Lycell, T., *Ins and Outs of Mespot.* 1923.

McCarthy, F. D. (a) *Stone Implements of Austr.* 1946, (b) *JPS* lxii 1953, (c) *Austr. Mus. Mem.* ix 1946 and 1947, (d) *Austr. Abo. Dec. Art* 1956, (e) with Davidson, *AA* n.s. xxx 1928, (f) *Austr. Abos* 1957, (g) *Mankind* v 1958 (culture succession). Macchioro, V. D., *Zagreus* 1930. McConnel, U., *Myths of the Munkan* 1957. McCown, D. E., *Comp. Stratig. of Early Iran* 1942. McGovern, M., *Jungle Paths and Inca Ruins.* McIlwain, *Growth of Political Thought in West* 1932. Mackay, *Further Excavs. at Mohenjo-daro* 1937. Mackenzie, D. A. (a) *Myths of pre-Col. America* 1923, (b) *Migration of Symbols* 1926. MacLeod, W. C., *Origin and Hist. of Politics* 1931. MacNicol, N., *Hindu Scriptures.* Mahoney, D. S., *Mem. Nat. Mus.* xiii 1943. Majundar, F. R. E. (a) *Anc. Indina Colonies in Far East* 1927, (b) *Svarnadvipa* 1937. Malinowski, B. (a) *Father in Prim. Psych.* 1927, (b) *Sexual Life of Savages in N.W. Melanesia* 1929, (c) *Dynamics of Cult. Change* 1945, (d) *Scient. Theory of Culture* 1944, (e) *Argonauts of W. Pacific* 1922. Mann, T., *Cervantes, Goethe, Freud* 1943. Marinatos, S., *Crete and Mycenae.* Maringer, J. (with Bandi), *Art in Ice Age* 1953. Marret, R. R. (a) *Anthropology,* (b) *Threshold of Religion* 1914, (c) *Psychology and Folklore* 1920, (d) *Sacraments of Simple Folk* 1933. Marshall (a) *Mohenjo-daro* 1931, (b) *Guide to Taxila* 1960, (c) *Oxford Hist. of India* 1920. Marti, M. P., *Les Dogon* 1957. Martienssen, R., *Idea of Space in Gr. Architecture.* Maspéro, H. (a) *Etudes hist.* iii 1950, (b) *Les rélig. chin.* 1950. Mathew, J. (a) *Eaglehawk and Crow* 1899, (b) *Two Rep. Tribes of Queensland* 1910. Matthews (a) *Navaho Legends* 1897, (b) *N. Myths, Prayers and Songs.* Mauss, M. (a) *AS* xi 296, (b) *A* 1920 396, (c) *L'Origine des pouvoirs magiques dans les soc. austr.* 1904. Mavrogordato, J., *Digenes Akrites* 1956. May, *AJSL* xlviii 1931-2 73. Mead, M. (a) *Co-op. and Competition among Prim. People,* (b) *Coming of age in Samoa,* (c) *From the S. Seas.* Meek, C. K. (a) *Tribal Studies in N. Nigeria* 1931, (b) *N. Nigeria* 1925, (c)

Sudanese Kingdom 1931. Mehta, R., *Pre-buddhist India* 1939. Meillet, A. (a) *Origines indo-europ. des mètres grecs* 1923, (b) *Etude comp. des langues indo-europ.* Mekhitarian, A., *Egypt. Painting* 1954. Mellinek, *Aegean and Near East* (Stud. H. Goldman, ed. S. Weinberg) 1956. Mercer, B. A. B., *The Pyramid Texts.* Merker, M., *Die Masai* 1910. Meyer, E. (a) *Gesch. des Altertums* (2nd ed.) 1902, (b) *Papyrus-fund v. Eleph.* 1912. Meyer, E. H., *English Chamber Music* 1946. Meyer, R. M., *Altgerman. Religionsgesch.* Miller, N., *Child in Prim. Soc.* 1928. Minns, E., *Scythians and Greeks* 1913. Mitchell, S. R., *Stone age Craftsmen* 1949. Mizuno, S., *Bronze and Stone Sculpture of China* 1960. Moir, J. R., *Antiquity of Man in England* 1927. Mooney, J., *Sacred Formulas of the Cherokees*, 7th BAE. Moorhouse, A. C., *Writing and the Alphabet* 1946. Moreau, J., *La Persécution du christ.* 1956. Moret, A. (with Davy), *From Tribe to Empire* 1926, (b) *Mysteries of Egypt* 1913, (c) *Nile and Egypt. Civil.* 1927. Morey, C. R., *Med. Art* 1942. Morgan, L. H. (a) *Anc. Society* 1877, (b) *League of Iroquois*, (c) *Systems of Consanguinity.* Morley, S. G. (a) *Anc. Maya*, (b) *Popul Vuh* 1950. Moss, R. L. B., *Life after Death in Oceania* 1925. Mowinckel, S., *He that Cometh* 1956. Mumford, L., *Techniks and Civilisation.* Muratoff, P., *La Peinture Byz.* 1935. Murie, J. R. (a) *AMNH* xi 1916 642, (b) *Pawnee Societies.* Murray, G. (a) *5 Stages Gr. Relig.* 1905, (b) in *Themis*, (c) *Rise of Gr. Epic*, (c) *Class. Trad. in Poetry*, (d) *Euripides*, (e) in *New Chapters in Gr. Lit.* 1921. Mylonas, *Mycenae* 1957. Myres (a) *Who were the Greeks?*, (b) *BSA* 1950 252, © *JHS* 1932, 1952, 1954.

Nadel, S. F., *A Black Byzantium* (Nupe) 1942. Nassau, R. H., *Fetiches in W. Africa* 1904. Naville, E., *Deir el Bahari.* Needham (a) *Science and Civil. in China*, 1954 on, (b) in *Mainstream* July 1960 7. Nef, C., *Outline of Hist of Music* 1935. Nehru, J., *Discovery of India* 1946. Neugebauer, O., *Exact Sciences in Antiquity* 1952. Newton, E., *Europ. Painting and Sculpture* 1941. Nicoll, A., *Masks, Mimes and Minstrels* 1931. Nilsson, M. (a) *Hist. Gr. Relig.* 1925. (b) *Minoan-Myc. Relig.* 1927, (c) *HTR* xxviii 1935 182, (d) *Myc. Origins of Gr. Myth.*, (e) *La relig. pop.* 1954. Nock, A. D. (a) *Conversion* 1933, (b) *Cult. Assns.* in *Class. Rev.* 1924 105. © *The Greeks and the Irrational.* Norwood, G., *Gr. Tragedy.* Nyberg, H. S. (a) *Die Relig. des alten Iran* 1938, (b) *Uppsala Univ. Arsskrift* 1941.

Oakley, K. P. (a) *Man the Toolmaker* 1956, (b) *PPS* xxi (fire). Obermeier, *Fossil Man in Spain* 1925. Oesterley, W. O. (a) *Sacred Dance* 1923, (b) with Robinson, *Hebrew Religion* 1937. Ogden, C. K., ed. *Hist. of Civil.* 1932. Oldenberg, H., *Sacred Books of the East* xxx. Oldfield, A., *Trans. Ethnol. Soc.* iii 1865 295. Olmstead, A. T. (a) *Hist. of Assyria* 1923, (b) *Hist. of Persian Emp.* 1948. Olrik, A., *Heroic Legends of Denmark.* Olson, D. L., *Clan and Moiety in Native America* 1931. Onians, R. B., *Origins of Europ. Thought* 1951. Opler, M. E. (a) *Apache Life-Way* 1941, (b) *Themes as Dynamic Forces*, *Amer. J. Sociol.* li 198. Ossenbruggen, F. D. E. van *De Oorsprong van het Javean. Begrits Montja-pat* 1917. Owst, G. R., *Preaching in Med. England* 1926.

Paetow, L. J., *Guide to Study of Med. History* 1931. Pallis, S. A., *Bab. Akitu Festival* 1926. Page, D. L. (a) *Hist. and Homeric Iliad* 1959, (b) *Homeric Odyssey.* Pagliaro, A., *Storia della Lett. Persiana* 1960. Panofsky, *Studies in Iconog.* Park, R. E., with Burgess, *Intro. to Science of Soc.* 1921, 1924. Parkes, J., *Foundations of Judaism and Christianity* 1960. Parrot, A., *Sumer* 1960. Parsons, E. W. C., *Family* 1906. Passemard, *Statuettes fém. dites Vénus stéatopyges* 1938. Paynter, J., *Hist. of M.A.* 1953. Pelliot, P., *Reflections sur l'art chin. et l'art sibérien* 1929. Pendlebury, (a) *Archaeol. of Crete*, (b) *Tell el Amarna.* Penrose, *Principles of Attic Archit.* Perkins, J. B. Ward, *Listener* Nov. 1 and 8 1956. Perry, W. (a) *Growth of Civil.* 1926, (b) *Children of Sun* 1926, (c) *Meg. Cult. of Indonesia* 1918, (d) *Primordial Ocean* 1935, (e) '*Myths of Origin' Folklore* xvi 1915, (f) 'Orientation of dead,Indonesia', *JRAI* xliv 1914, (g) *Gods and Men* 1927. Petrie, F. (a) *Prehist. Egypt* 1920, (b) *Amulets*, (c) *Tools and Weapons*, (d) *Soc. Life in Anc. Egypt*, (e) *Relig. Life*. Pevsner, N. (a) *Europ. Archit.* 1957, (b) *Listener* March 20, 1958, (c) with Meier, *Grünewald* 1958. Pfeiffer, R. H., *Intro. to Judaism* 1948. Philpotts, B. (a) *Elder Edda and Anc. Scand. Drama*, (b) *Kindred and Clan*. Pickard-Cambridge (a) *Dramatic Festivals of Attica* 1955, (b) *Dithyramb, Tragedy and Comedy*. Pickin, L., in Wellesz. Picton, H., *Early German Art*. Piddington, R., *Intro. to Soc. Anthrop.* 1950. Pierce, H., with Tyler, *Dumbarton Oaks Papers* ii 1941. Piggott, S. (a) *Prehist. India*, (b) *Neo. Cultures of Brit. Isles* 1954. Pike, L. O., *Hist. of Crime in England*. Pirenne, H., *Med. Cities* 1925. Plommer, H., *Anc. and Class. Archit*. Plose, M. (a) *Das Weib in der Natur u. Volkerkunde* (with Bartels), (b) *Das Kind*. Poland, F., *Gesch. des griech. Vereinswesens* 1909. Pope, *El in Ugaritic Texts* 1955. Popham, A. E. (a) *Drawings of Leonardo* 1946, (b) with Pouncey, *Italian Drawings* 1950. Powell, T. G. E. (a) *ANT* xxxiv no 135, (b) *Celts*. Pratt, G., 'Folksongs and myths, Samoa', *J. Roy. Soc. N.S.W.* xxv 1891. Prescott, F. C. (a) *Poetic Mind* 1922, (b) *Poetry and Myth* 1927. Pritchard, J. B. (a) *Anc. Near East Texts rel. to O.T.* 1955 (2nd ed.), (b) *Amer. Oriental Series* xxiv 1943. Puech, H. C., *Le Manichéeisme*.

Raby, F. J. E. (a) *Hist. of Christian Latin Poetry*, (b) *Secular Latin Poetry*. Rachewiltz, B. de, *Egyptian Art* 1960. Radhakrishnan, S., *Indian Philosophy* 1940. Radin, P. (a) *Social Anthrop.* 1932, (b) *The Trickster* 1956, (c) ed. *Crashing Thunder* 1926 Radcliffe-Brown, A. R. (a) *Andaman Is.* (b) *Soc. Organ. of Austr. Tribes* 1931 *Oceania* i, pt ii, (c) *Taboo* 1939. Rand, E. K., *Foundations of M.A.* 1928. Rankin, O. S., *Israel's Wisdom Lit.* 1936. Ranulf, S., *Jealousy of Gods and Crim. Law at Athens* 1933. Ranston, H., *The O.T. Wisdom Books* 1930. Rashdall, *Univs. of Europe* 1936. Rassers, W. H., *Panji, the Cult. Hero* 1959. Ravdonikas, W. J. (a) *Gravures rup. des bords du lac Onéga* 1936-8, (b) *Die Normanen des Wiking Zeit u. das Ladogagebiet* 1930. Rawlinson, H. G. (a) *Intercourse between India and W. World* (2nd ed.) 1926, (b) *Bactria* 1912. Read, J., *Prelude to Chemistry* (2nd ed.) 1939. Read, M., *The Ngomi* 1956. Redfield, R., *The Folk-Cult. of Yucaton* 1941. Reese, G., *Music in M.A.* 1941. Reichard, G. A., *Navaho Religion* 1950. Reinach, S., *Cults, Myths and Religions* 1912. Rice, D. T. (a) *Byz. elements in Late Saxon Art* 1947, (b) *English Art* 871-1100, 1952. Rice, T., *Scythians* 1957. Richmond, I. A., *Temple of Mithras at Carrawburgh*. Richter, J. P. (and Taylor), *Golden Age of Class. Christ. Art* 1904. Riegl, A., *Stilfragen* 1923. Ridgeway (a) *Dramas and Dramatic Dances* 1915, (b) *Origin of Tragedy* 1910. Ringbom, L. L., *Paradisus Terrestris* 1958. Rink, H., *Tales and Trads. of Eskimos* 1875. Rivers, W. H. R. (a) *Hist. of Melanesian Soc.* 1914, (b) *Toda* 1906, (c) (Dreams and Prim. Cult.) *Bull. Tylands Lib* 1918, (d) Totemism in Pol. and Mel. *JRAI* 1909, (e) in *Festskrift . . . Westermarck*. Rivoira, G. T., *Roman Archit.* 1925. Robb, N. A., *Neoplatonism of Ital. Ren.* 1935. Robertson, A., *Origins of Christianity* 1953. Robinson, T., in Hooke (c). Rodolico, N., *I Ciompi*. Rohde, *Psyche*. Roheim, G. (a) *Austr. Totemism* 1925, (b) *Riddle of Sphinx* 1934, (c) *JRAI* lxiii 1933, (d) *Animism, Magic and the Divine King* 1930. Roscher, W. H., *Omphalos* 1852. Rose, H. J. (a) *Prim. Cult. in Greece*, (b) *in Italy*. Rosenbaum, E., *Cyrenaican Portrait Sculpture* 1960. Rosenthal, A., *Burlington Mag.* May 1936 82. Ross, D., with Skrine, *Heart of Asia*. Rossiter, A. P., *Growth of Science* 1943. Rostovtzeff, M. I. (a) *Soc. and Econ. Hist. of Hellenistic World*, (b) *of Roman Emp.*, (c) *Dura and Parthian Art*, (d) *Dura and its Art*, (e) *Iranians and Greeks*, (f) 'C. Asia, Russia and the Animal Style', *Scythica* i 1923, (g) *L'art greco-sarmate et l'art chinois*, (h) *Rev. des Cultes Grecques* xxxii, (i) *Caravan Cities*, (j) *Hist. of Anc. World* i, *Orient and Greece*, (k) *Mystic Italy* 1927. Roth, W. E., *Ethnol. Stud. in N.W. Central Queensland*. Rowe, J. H., *Handbook S. Amer. Indians* 1946. Rowley, G., *Principles of Chinese Painting* 1960. Runciman, S., *The Med. Manichee*.

Sachs (a) *Rise of Music*, (b) *Geist u. Werden der Musik instrumente*. Salis, A. von,

Antike u. Ren. 1947. Sandars, N. K., *Epic of Gilgamesh* 1960. Sapir, E., *J. Amer. FL* xxiii 455. Sapori, A., *Le merchant ital. au M.A.* 1952. Sarton, G., *Appreciation of Anc. and Med. Science during the Ren.* 1955. Sayce, R. V., *Prim. Arts and Crafts* 1933. Schädel, *Die Listen des gros. pap. Harris.* Schaeffer, *Cuneiform Texts, Ras-Shamra* 1914. Scharff, A., *Die Ausbreitung des Osiriskultes* 1947. Schmidt, E. F. (a) *Alashar Hujuk seasons* 1928-29 (1932), (b) *Excavs. at Tepe Hissar* 1937. Schmidt, W. (a) *Origin and Growth of Religion* 1931, (b) *Cult. Hist. Method of Ethnol.* 1939. Schmokel, H., *Das Land Sumer* (2nd ed.) 1956. Schneider, M. (a) *Gesch. d. Mehrstimmigkeit,* (b) in Wellesz, (c) *La danza des espadas y la tarantela* 1948. Schott, S., *Altägypt. Liebslieder* 1950. Schroeder, von, *Mysterium u. Mimus.* Schweitzer, U., *Das Wesen des Ka* 1956. Schurz, H., *Das Afrikan. Gewerbe* 1900. Scott, J. E., in Wellesz. Segall, B., *Art Bull.* xxxviii, 2, 1956, 75 (Iconog. Cosmic Kingship). Sellery, G. C., *The Renaisance* 1950. Seltman, C., *Approach to Gr. Art* 1948. Semper, G., *Der Stil in den Technischen u. Tekton. Kunsten* 1860. Seta, A. della, *Religions and Art* 1914. Sethe, K., *Die altägypt. Pyramidtexten.* Sharf, A., *PP* no 9 1956. Shcherbatsky, T., *Conception of Budd. Nirvana* 1927. Shryock, J. K., *Origin and Develop. of State Cult. of Confucius* 1732. Sheppard, *Pattern of Iliad.* Simpson, J. Y., *Man and Attainment of Immortality* 1922. Simson, von, *Gothic Cathedral* 1956. Singer, C. (a) *From Magic to Science* 1928, (b) *Gr. Biology and Gr. Medicine* 1932. Siren, O. (a) *Hist. of Later Chinese Painting,* (b) *The Chinese on the Art of Painting.* Smith, Elliot, *Evolution of the Dragon* 1919. Smith, E. H., *Roman Sources of Christian Art* 1951. Smith, A. N., *Sculpt. of Parthenon* 1910. Smith, J. M. P., *Z. f. d. Altest. Wiss.* xxxiv. Smith, M., ed. *Artist in Tribal Soc.* 1960. Smith, R., *Develop. of Europ. Law* 1928. Smith, S., *Early Hist. of Assyria* 1928. Smith, V. A. (a) *Early Hist. India* 1924, (b) *Hist. Fine Arts in India and Ceylon* 1930. Smith, W. R., *Lectures on Religion of Semites.* Smith, W. S., *Hist. of Egypt. Sculpt. and Paint. in O. K.* (2nd ed.) 1949. Smythe, B., *Troubadour Poets* 1929. Soustelle, J., *La vie quot. des Azteques* 1956. Soden, W. von, *Sumer. u. Akkad. Hymnen* 1953. Sollberger, E., *Corpus Inscript . . . de Lagas* 1956. Soothill, *Three Religions of China.* Speck, G. (a) *Ceremonial Songs of Greek and Yuchi Indians* 1911, (b) *Double-curve,* N. Algonkian Art, *Canad. Geolog. Survey,* mem. 42, (c) *Naskapi* 1935. Spence, L., *Myths of Amer. Indians.* Spencer, B. (a) *Native tribes of N. Territ. of Austr.* 1914, (b) *Austr. Encyc.* i 1927, (c) with Gillen, *Native Tribes of Central Austr.* 1899, (d) *N. Tribes of C.A.* 1903, (e) *Arunta.* Spiegel, J., *Ann, du service des Antiqs. de l'Egypte* liii 339. Spier, L. (Sun dance) *Anthrop. Papers. Amer. Mus. of N.H.* xvi pt. 7, 451. Spinden, *Anc. Civils. of Mexico and C. Amer.* 1928. Spoehr, A. (Changing Kinship Systems) as in Speir, xxxiii, no 4, 159. Stayt, H. A., *Bavenda* 1931. Stadling, J., *Shamanism* 1912. Stanford, W. B., *Ambiguities in Gr. Lit.* 1939. Stein, A. (a) *Thousand Buddhas* 1921, (b) *On Central Asian Tracks* 1933. Steinen, K. von den, *Unter den Naturvolken zentral Brasilians* (2nd ed.) 1897. Stella, L. A., *Il poema di Ulisse.* Stevenson, M., *Rites of Twice-Born* 1920. Stevenson, R. H., *Amiran Darijaniani* 1958. Stephan, E., *Sudseekunst* 1907. Steward, J. H., *Handbook of S. American Tribes* 1945, 8. Stewart, C. (a) *Early Christian, Byz. and Romanesque Archit.,* (b) *Med. Archit.* Stocks, J. L., *Aristotelianism* 1925. Strehlow, C. with Leonhardi, *Die Aranda u. Loritjastämme* 1908 on. Strong, E. (a) *La scultura romana,* (b) *Apotheosis.* Swanton (a) *Soc. Conditions . . . Tlinkit Indians* 1908, (b) *Contribs. to Ethnol. of Haida* 1905. Sydow, E. von, *Die Kunst der Naturvölker* 1923. Szlechter, E., *Le code d' Ur-Nammu.* Swarzenska, *Mons. of Romanesque Art* 1955.

Talbot, D. A. T., *Woman's Mysteries.* Talbot, P. A. *People of S. Nigeria.* Tappoport, A. S., *Folklore of Jews* 1937. Tarn, W. W. (a) *Greeks in Bactria and India,* (b) *Hellenist. Civil.,* (c) *Alex. the Gt. and the Unity of Mankind.* Tawney, R. H., *Relig. and Rise of Capitalism.* Teggart, F. J., *Theory and Processes of Hist.* Thalbitzer, W. (a) in Kroeber, (b) *Eskimos, ARW* xxvi 1928 364. Thapar, D. R. (a) *Icons in Bronze*

1960, (b) *Asoka* 1960. Thausing, G., *Der Auferstehungsgedanke in ägypt. relig. Texten* 1943. Thomas, W. I., *Prim. Behaviour* 1937. Thomson, B., *Fijians.* Thomson, G. (a) *Aeschylus and Athens*, (b) *First Philosophers* 1955, (c) *Prehist. Aegean.* Thompson, D. F., *Econ. Structure and Ceremonial Exchange in Arnhem Land* 1944. Thompson, E., *Hist. of India.* Thompson, E. A. (a) *Roman Reformer and Inventor* 1952, (b) *Huns.* Thompson, S. (a) *Folktale* 1946, (b) *Tales of N. Amer. Indians* 1929. Thompson, S. E., *Mexico before Cortes.* Thorndyke, L., *Hist. of Magic and Exp. Science* 1923-41. Thornton, P., *Dead Puppets Dance.* Thurnwald, R., *Econs. in Prim. Communities* 1932. Timmers, J. J. M., *Hist. of Dutch Life and Art* 1960. Tobler, A. H., *Excavs. Tepe Gawra* 1950. Tolnay, C. de (a) *Michelangelo* 1945-54, (b) *Bruegel l'ancien* 1935, (c) *Die Zeichnungen P.B.* 1925. Toynbee, A. J., *Study of History.* Toynbee, J. M. C. (a) *Ara Pacis*, Brit. Acad. xxxix 1953, (b) *Roman Portrait Busts* (Arts Council) 1953, (c) *Hadrianic School* 1934. Trypanis, *Medium Aevum* xix 1950. Turberville, A. S., *Med. Heresy and Inquisition* 1920. Turner, G., *Samoa* 1884. Turner, R., *The Gt. Cult. Trads.* 1941. Tylor, E. B. (a) *Prim. Cult.* 1873, (b) *Anthropology*, (c) *JRAI* xviii 245.

Uspensky, T., *L'art byz. chez les Slaves* 1930. Unwin, J. D., *Sex and Culture* 1934.

Vacandard, E., *Inquisition* 1924. Vaillant, G. C., *Aztecs* 1950. Valentiner, W. R., *Art Bull.* (Chicago) March 1930. Vandier, J., *Man. d'archéol. egypt.* 1952-5. Vega, G. de la, *Royal Commentary of Incas* 1869. Ventris, with Chadwick, *Docs. in Myc. Greek* 1956. Verneau, *Grottes de Grimaldi* xi 1906. Vincent, *La Réligion des Judeo-Ariméens d'Elephantine* 1937.

Wach, J., *Sociology of Religion* 1947. Wade-Gery, H. T., *Poet of Iliad.* Waddell (a) *Buddhism of Tibet* 1934, (b) *Lhasa.* Waertzolot, W., *Dürer* 1955. Waley, A. (a) *The Way and its Power* 1934, (b) *New Statesman* July 23, 1938, (c) *Ballads and Stories from Tun-Huang* 1960. Wang Ya-nan, *Principles of Chinese Econ.* 1948. Wardle, H. N., *AA* ii 1900 568. Warner, W. L., *A Black Civilisation* 1937. Warren, W. F., *Paradise Found* 1885. Watmough, J. R., *Orpheus* 1934. Watson, W. (a) *Flint Implements* 1956, (b) *Archaeol. in China* 1960. Webster, H. (a) *Prim. Secret Societies* 1908, (b) *Magic* 1938. Webster, T. B. L. (a) *From Myc. to Homer*, (b) *Art and Lit. in 4th c. Athens*, (c) *Gr. Art and Lit.* 700-530, (d) *Gr. Theatre Production.* Weiss, J., *Hist. of Prim. Christianity* 1937. Wellesz, E. (a) ed. *Anc. and Oriental Music* 1957, (b) *Eastern Elements in W. Chant* 1947, (c) *Hist. of Byz. Music* 1949, (d) *J. Theolog. Studies* xliv 1943. Wendland, P., *Die hellen.-röm. Kultur* (3rd ed.) 1912. Wensinck, *Ideas of W. Semites concerning the Navel of the Earth* 1916. Werner, E. (a) *Hebrew Union College Annual* xx 1947, (d) 1948, (e) in Wellesz. Werner, E. T. C., *Myths and Legends of China* 1923. Westermarck (a) *Origin and Develop. of Moral Ideas*, (b) *Hist. of Human Marriage.* Weyer, E. M., *Eskimos* 1932. Wheeler, G. C., *Tribe . . . Australia.* Wheeler, M. (a) *Early India and Pakistan* 1959, (b) *Rome beyond Imp. Frontiers.* Whicher, *Goliardic Poets* 1949. White, L., *Speculum* xv 1940. White, L. A. (a) *Evol. of Culture* 1959, (b) *AA* xlvii 339, (c) xlviii 78, (d) *S.W. J. of Anthrop.* i 221. Whitfield, J. H. (a) *Short Hist. Ital. Lit.* 1960, (b) *Petrarch and the Ren.* 1945. Whittaker, T., *The Neo-platonists* 1901. Whittimore, T., *Mosaics of St. Sophia* 1933. Widengren, G. (a) in Hooke, (b) *Psalm* 110, (c) *The King and the Tree of Life* 1951, (d) *Ascension of the Apostle*, (e) *Religionens varld*, (f) *Mesopot. Elements.* Wilkins, E. H., *Hist. of Ital. Lit.* 1954. Williams, B. E., *Gournia* 1908. Williams, F. E. (a) *Vailala madness, Essays . . . Seligman* 369, (b) *Drama of Orokolo* 1940. Williamson, R. W. (a) *Central Polynesia*, (b) *Soc. and Polit. Systems of Polynesia.* Wilson, D. M., *Anglo-Saxons* 1960. Wilson, J. A. (a) in Frankfort (c) (b) *Burden of Egypt* 1951. Winstedt, R., *Malay Magician* 1951. Winnington-Ingram, R. P., *Mode in anc. Gr. Music.* Wischnitzer, *Messianic Theme in Paint. of Dura Synagogue* 1948. Wissler, C. (a) *AMNH* xi 1916 853 (shaman and dance socs.), (b) *Man and Culture* 1923, (c)

Rel. of Nature to Man in Abo. America 1926, (d) *Amer. Indian.* Wit, C. de, *La statuaire de Tel el Amarna* 1950. Wittkower, R., *Archit. Principles in the Age of Humanism* 1949. Woolley, L. (a) *Develop. of Sumerian Art* 1935, (b) with Hall, *Ur Excavs.* 1927 i, (c) *Sumerians*, (d) *Abraham.* Worcester, *Non-Christian Tribes of N. Luzon* 1906. Worringer, W. R., *Form in Gothic* 1927. Wortham, B. H., *Jimutavahana.* We Ta-k'un, *PP* i 1952. Wundt, W., *Volkerpsychologie*, iii *Der Kunst* (3rd ed.) 1919.

Young, K., *Drama of Med. Church* 1933.

Zandee, J., *Death as an Enemy acc. to anc. Egypt. Conceptions* 1960. Ziebarth, E., *Das griech. Vereinswesen* 1896. Zielinski, T., *Die Gliederung der altatt. Komödie* 1888. Zimmer, H., *Irish Elements in Med. Cult.* 1891. Zimmerman, R., *Gesch. d. Aesthetik* 1858. Zervos, *L'art de la Mesopot.* 1935. Zeuner, F. E., *Dating the Past* 1952. Zuckerman, S., *Social Life of Monkeys and Apes* 1932.

Index

Index

431

434